THE KNIGHTS

OF

ARISTOPHANES.

THE KNIGHTS

OF

ARISTOPHANES

EDITED BY

ROBERT ALEXANDER NEIL,

M.A., LL.D. (ABERDEEN)

LATE FELLOW AND TUTOR OF PEMBROKE COLLEGE, CAMBRIDGE,
UNIVERSITY LECTURER IN SANSKRIT.

CAMBRIDGE
AT THE UNIVERSITY PRESS
1901

CAMBRIDGE
UNIVERSITY PRESS

University Printing House, Cambridge CB2 8BS, United Kingdom

Cambridge University Press is part of the University of Cambridge.

It furthers the University's mission by disseminating knowledge in the pursuit of education, learning and research at the highest international levels of excellence.

www.cambridge.org
Information on this title: www.cambridge.org/9781107461024

© Cambridge University Press 1901

First published 1901
First paperback edition 2014

A catalogue record for this publication is available from the British Library

ISBN 978-1-107-46102-4 Paperback

PREFATORY NOTE.

THE following edition of the *Knights*, which had been in the press for some years, was almost completed at the time of the sudden death of the Editor last June. The commentary up to page 144 had been printed off: the rest of the commentary, the appendixes and the introduction were already in type. The pages which had not received final revision have been carefully read; references have been verified; and small corrections, which seemed to be beyond question, have been made. It is difficult to say how far the introduction might have been expanded: it is certain that it was not regarded as complete. In the note to ll. 1288—9, as originally printed, reference was made to the introduction concerning the supposed collaboration of Eupolis in the authorship of the *Knights*, but the introduction contains no allusion to the subject. No doubt it was intended that this and other topics bearing on the play should be discussed, and an account of the manuscripts (of which those at Ravenna and Milan at least had been collated by the Editor) and some estimate of their relative value would certainly have been included.

In other respects the book is complete, and remains the only direct memorial of Neil's work as a classical scholar, which his scanty leisure and fastidious pen permitted him to leave. The twenty-five years since he took his degree at Cambridge were devoted to College and University teaching: and however regrettable the sacrifice may seem, it is justified by the influence he exerted on the many scholars that he taught. For if Neil wrote but little, he never had a pupil whom he did not impress by the depth of his knowledge and the breadth of his interests. Greek and Latin, as he taught them, were a means of literary education: a fine sense of the humanities informed his method, and supplied a complement to the more strictly linguistic training which the conditions of the Tripos required. His mastery of the Classics was aided by a gift of simple exposition, while a wealth of illustration from the languages and records of modern times made it easy for him to show that the phenomena of language and of history never stand alone or unparalleled. Moreover he was reconciled to the drudgery inevitable in his work by a quick intellectual sympathy, which while it afforded him compensation could not but stimulate and develope the talents of his pupils.

Yet despite the many hours devoted to tuition Neil never ceased to learn. The energy of his research was unremitting: he read and re-read the Classical authors with the fullest sense of their manifold interest: he was familiar with the work accomplished by scholars, both in the present and in the past, on every side of Classical life and thought and language. The knowledge thus rapidly assimilated and ever at the command of a wonderful memory was placed fully and generously at the service of others, as is abundantly testified by the works of the many scholars who record grateful acknowledgment of his help in inspiring, suggesting and amending. His learning, moreover, unrestricted in its range, was catholic in its comprehension. Thus he escaped the possible dangers of specialism, and thus became an intellectual force of the greatest moment in the University.

The qualities of scholarship which characterised him as a teacher are manifest in his own work. A wiser commentator could not be found, for his delicate sense of language enabled him to discriminate meanings and usages, to detect the particular associations of words, to discover instances of parody and imitation, in fact, to give the fullest and the most subtle interpretation to the original text. While there is no part of Classical life or thought which he did not explain and illuminate, he sought parallels, illustration or comment from the whole range of literature. Indeed, of the many admirable qualities revealed briefly and modestly in this commentary upon a single play, none is more intimately characteristic than the universal interest in the life and literature of all ages, which marked the genius of Robert Alexander Neil.

W. S. H.
L. W.

Pembroke College, Cambridge.
October, 1901.

CONTENTS.

a 5

CODICES HUIUSCE FABULAE.

Dindorf's numbering is followed in the references to the Fragments of Aristophanes and Kock's numbering in the references to the Fragments of the other Comic Poets.

ADDENDA ET CORRIGENDA.

p. 9   At end of note on l. **19** *add* So Rousseau *Confess.* 9 speaks of 'la vapeur d'une bonne omelette au cerfeuil' as characteristic of the country)(town luxury.

p. 15   l. **61** *add* critical note εἶθ' ὁ MSS. except R.

p. 22   At end of note on l. **120** *add* In the Athenian hymn at Delphi 3 προφαίνεις λόγια is only a conjecture of Weil's: Crusius has προφαίνεις, σε καλαδήσομεν.

p. 33   Note on l. **197** (3 lines from the foot of column 1) *after* mythical serpents *add* (of real snakes in artificial poetry, e.g. *Anth. Pal.* vi 331. 1).

p. 43   Note on ll. **269—70** (last line of column 1) *for* mentioned in 255 *read* mentioned on 255.

p. 52   At end of note on l. **327** *add* Cp. fr. 514 ἡὐαινόμην θεώμενος.

p. 53   Note on ll. **333—4** (line 3 of column 1) *for* is regular *read* are regular.

p. 81   Note on l. **537** (line 10) *for* the innovation as Vahlen says, *read* the innovation. As Vahlen says,

p. 84   Note on l. **552** (line 6) *for* ὡκοπόδων *read* ὡκυπόδων.

p. 93   Note on l. **626** (line 16) for *Att. Pol.* 355—6 read *Att. Pol.* 335—6.

p. 120   Note on l. **823** (line 12) *for* Αττικίων *read* 'Αττικίων.

p. 123   Note on l. **851** *for* ἐγγένεσθαι, ἐκγένεσθαι *read* ἐγγενέσθαι, ἐκγενέσθαι.

In all cases where Demus occurs in the notes the form Demos should be substituted.

INTRODUCTION.

THE comedy of the *Knights* was produced in Athens at the Lenaea in the year when Stratocles was eponymous archon. This date[1] corresponds to the early part (probably February or March) of the year 424 B.C. Aristophanes for the first time appeared frankly as an author: the three plays he had already written had all been produced as by his friend Callistratus[2].

Aristophanes had two objects of attack throughout his plays produced in the period of the Old Comedy: these were the newer intellectual movements of the day and the politics, home and foreign, of the advanced democrats of Athens. The two were not really connected: Euripides and Socrates, with their coteries, seem to have held political opinions almost identical with Aristophanes' own. If Aristophanes had shared the views they held on subjects other than politics, he might have shared their fate. As it was, he suffered nothing worse than a prosecution by Cleon: we do not know whether he was attacked in this

---

[1] Since Böckh's treatise on the Dionysia (published in 1816) it has been generally held that the Lenaea were held in the month Gamelion (Jan.-Feb.) about a month before the Anthesteria. The old theory that the Lenaea and Anthesteria were, at least for a long time, the same festival has been revived by O. Gilbert, and is held by Dörpfeld (*Griech. Theater* 9) and Miss Harrison (*Journ. Hell. Studies* xx p. 111).

[2] We know neither the reason nor the exact effect of the poet's habitual avoidance of producing plays in his own name. He may have been under legal age when the first play was produced (as he seems to imply *Nub.* 530): but this reason would soon disappear. It is suggested by Kaibel (in Pauly-Wissowa's *Encyclop.* s.v. *Aristophanes*) and by Murray, that he was well to do, did not care for the money prize, and merely wished to save himself the trouble of training his chorus. The *Wasps* was produced under the name of Philonides, but Aristophanes speaks plainly in the parabasis of that play (1015—1050).

way as a politician directly by a charge of disloyalty to the state, or indirectly by a charge of alien birth[1].

His first play, the Δαιταλῆς B.C. 427, was directed against the first of the two movements above mentioned: the next three, *Babylonians* (426), *Acharnians* (425), *Knights*, against the second. The chorus in each play was typical: the *Babylonians* are the subject-allies of Athens, treated by her as foreigners and slaves ; the *Acharnians* are bigoted villagers, full of a narrow Attic patriotism and hate for Sparta ; the *Knights* are the young flower of Athenian life, ready for enterprise and proud of their city, but tired of the political notions and leaders that prevailed.

The Peloponnesian war was raised against Athens. Her imperialism deeply offended the Greek faith in the independence even of small states. Her allies pleaded that they had joined her in the belief that the confederacy, of which she was so much the absolute head, was against Persia and for no other purpose : they found themselves deluded and humiliated into tributaries[2]. Her democracy set an example to the commons of every state in Greece, inciting them to take power from the noble and the rich, to harass and overtax the classes, to irritate established authority by rhetoric and public discussion and litigation. She had too much commercial prosperity and wanted more : this had ruined Aegina and might ruin Corinth and other busy ports. Her amazing intellectual brilliancy had come after the fall of Miletus and the other Ionian cities which might have been as brilliant as Athens if they had remained free. Her active and successful democracy roused the slow jealousy of the great aristocracies— Thebes, Sparta, Corinth, each with its own reasons for enmity —into a readiness for war.

The war seemed to Thucydides the most important event in human history. Probably, like Plato and Aristotle, he thought that the great political question was what might be the best form for a small Greek republic, and that the contest between

---

[1] Gilbert, *Inn. Geschichte* 154. Kaibel (*Aristophanes* in Pauly-Wissowa *Encyclopädie* &c.) thinks the γραφὴ ξενίας came later than 425, if at all.

[2] This is the strong point made by the Mityleneans in their speech at Olympia (Thucyd. iii 10. 3): ξύμμαχοι ἐγενόμεθα οὐκ ἐπὶ καταδουλώσει τῶν Ἑλλήνων Ἀθηναίοις, ἀλλ' ἐπ' ἐλευθερώσει ἀπὸ τοῦ Μήδου τοῖς Ἕλλησι.

democracy and oligarchy would settle the future of humanity[1]. When the *Knights* appeared, the war had lasted for more than six years. The blows dealt had exasperated, rather than exhausted, the combatants. Athens had recovered from the plague. The conflict between states and between classes in each state was more keen and bitter than ever: Corcyra had just shown that the People and the Few could hate each other more fiercely than members of different countries; the Spartans were using their system of espionage with the result that soon afterwards they made away with many of the best Helots. The rage of class against class is nowhere more clearly expressed than in the bitter taunt addressed by an ally of Athens to a Spartiate prisoner taken at Sphacteria, "were the killed on your side gentlemen[2]?" Whatever the causes of this class-hatred, it was natural for thinking men to hope that it might be reduced to a point short of bloodshed.

Victor Cousin's brilliant theory of Nations and War teaches that every people exists in order to represent one idea, which it works out in its industry, art, government, religion and philosophy: that idea is incomplete and exclusive, but seems to its people the whole truth: this pretension brings collision with other ideas embodied in other nations: and hence "the indestructible root of war[3]." History recognises that all the ideas which nations have represented have only a partial and relative truth: the nation's great man best expresses its idea as absolute and complete[4], in its finest form and at the right time. No nation has ever had its 'idea' so splendidly expressed as Athens had in Pericles' funeral oration: enlightened democracy there finds a voice, probably for the first time, and in words that can

---

[1] It has been noted that Dionysius of Halicarnassus, from his point of view as a Greek not ill-content to be under the power of Rome, holds Thucydides profoundly unfortunate and mistaken in his subject: πόλεμον ἕνα γράφων, καὶ τοῦτον οὔτε καλόν, οὔτ' εὐτυχῆ· ὃς μάλιστα μὲν ὤφειλε μὴ γενέσθαι· εἰ δὲ μή, σιωπῇ καὶ λήθῃ παραδοθείς, ὑπὸ τῶν ἐπιγιγνομένων ἠγνοῆσθαι (*epist. ad Pomp. de praecip. histor.* 3. p. 767 Reiske).

[2] Thucyd. iv 40. 2: the translation 'brave men' for καλοὶ κάγαθοὶ quite misses the mark.

[3] *Introd. à l'histoire de la philosophie, neuvième leçon.*

[4] *Ib. dixième leçon.*

never fail to have an echo in the aspirations of freedom[1]. In the background are the subjection of women and a great population of slaves : neither of these drawbacks could rouse much indignation then ; but the assertion of Athenian Empire over other states, though not obtrusively made in the funeral speech, gave an excuse for the haters of democracy[2]. Brasidas tells the Acanthians[3] that Sparta will not interfere in party politics : she will not ignore the history of each state and enslave either the majority to the Few or the minority to the mass : he is protesting for independence merely. But when Alcibiades at Sparta speaks of democracy as essentially opposed to all sound reason, he is only giving lively expression to his hearers' opinions : and Cousin's theory finds no better instance of an inevitable conflict. When and how the conflict might have come had Athens not entered on a policy of imperialism, is hard to say.

There were men in Greece who could see no sufficient reason for the war, who hated it above everything, and who thought it might be brought to an end but for extremists. In Athens there may have been men in 424 B.C. (there certainly were later), who were much more Spartan and oligarchic at heart than Athenian. But there were also a very considerable number of moderates. Moderates in Athens were almost outlaws: the famous law of Solon, himself a moderate, forbade any citizen to abstain from party contests. Pericles and Cleon both, as Thucydides reports them, sneer at these ἀπράγμονες[4] as deserving of a harder name and as quite condemned by public

---

[1] Pericles may well have thought that before the Athenian democracy, set as an example for all men to emulate, teaching the equal opportunity of citizens, the self-respect of the poor, the mental culture of all free men as the work of the state, any political constitution depending on privilege or exclusiveness of birth or wealth would have sunk abashed. If so, he imagined as vain a thing as Napoleon did : but we cannot find in his speech that he had failed to foresee the war that came. Political and social ideas are hard to force on peoples that do not comprehend them : the force is more obvious than the ideas behind it.

[2] The Boeotians in Thucyd. iii 62. 2 actually say that Athens attacked the Greeks 'in the same way' as Persia did.

[3] Thucyd. iv 86. 4.

[4] Pericles in the funeral oration Thucyd. ii 40. 2 μόνοι γὰρ τὸν μηδὲν τῶνδε μετέχοντα οὐκ ἀπράγμονα, ἀλλ᾽ ἀχρεῖον νομίζομεν.

feeling: they may call themselves the 'gentlemen,' but their ἀνδραγαθία is inconsistent with Athenian Empire[1].

The Periclean ideal had to contend with another. This was the ideal of Panhellenism, sinking minor differences of social and political arrangements, and aiming at peace at home, war, if anywhere, abroad with the barbarian. Cimon had been the champion of this ideal: his brilliant victories on the Strymon and the Eurymedon showed that Greece might still hope for success even in aggressive war against Persia; his bringing back the bones of Theseus from Scyros to Athens had given him a hold on the peculiar religious pride of Greek cities; and his personal qualities were such as to kindle enthusiasm on his side[2]. That enthusiasm was expressed not only in battlefield and ordinary social gathering, but by two poets of distinction— Ion of Chios and Cratinus of Athens[3]. But Lacedaemonian jealousy baffled his ideal of Athens and Sparta as yoke-fellows in the procession of Hellenic glory, and his countrymen ostracised him as a philo-Laconian. After his recall in circumstances most honourable to himself, he still worked for peace with Sparta and war with Persia: and when he died besieging Citium in Cyprus, he may have believed that his policy would govern the affairs of Greece.

Soon after Cimon's death, Athens made peace with Persia on conditions which will probably never be made quite clear: but to make peace between Greek and Persian was the way to bring on war between Greek and Greek. We know too little of Thucydides, son of Melesias, to say whether he upheld

---

[1] See Appendix ii p. 202.

[2] If the head on Dexamenus' well-known gem is really a portrait of Cimon, his great inferiority in presence to Pericles must plainly be allowed.

[3] We have no proof that Ion possessed the first quality of a great poet—an original view of human life—but in charm of fancy and language his few fragments stand high in Greek literature. For his praise of Cimon cf. Plut. *Per.* 5. In Cratinus, fr. 1, the government clerk Metrobius gives fine expression to an admiration for Cimon which must have been common at the time. It is possible that Aeschylus should be added to the list: the *Eumenides* is the triumphal hymn of Athens in the Cimonian period, of the brilliant πόλις not forgetful of the rock from which she was hewn, willing to retain all that was good in the old ways, but needing to be warned against too rapid change.

Cimon's ideal; but his ostracism removed the one Athenian capable of making any head against Pericles.

Pericles made the edifice of democracy complete. No high or constructive statesmanship was shown by any Athenian after him: it is not clear that such statesmanship was possible. The one side was forced to be violent and warlike in its imperialism: the other, when not confined to a policy of clean and folded hands, was driven to a policy against which the cries of 'treasonable' and 'unpatriotic' were ready and loud.

The spirit of Attic literature is in the main that of moderate, not extreme, democracy[1]. Though Aristotle[2] pointedly omits Pericles from his list of first-rate Athenian statesmen, there is no lack of admiration for him in the great writers of earlier days. He lay exposed at several points to the shafts of Comedy: in his relations with Aspasia[3] he was a "fantastical duke of dark corners," his generalship was of doubtful merit[4], and Cratinus' frank attack[5] was no doubt thought by many to hit the mark:

Στάσις δὲ καὶ πρεσβυγενὴς Κρόνος ἀλλήλοισι μιγέντε
μέγιστον τίκτετον τύραννον,
ὃν δὴ νεφεληγερέταν Θεοὶ καλοῦσιν.

[1] It sometimes surprises us by its want of what we expect in democratic literature. For instance, it shows hardly any sign of a sympathetic and respectful attitude towards the lives and feelings of the independent poor. Such a sentiment was not characteristic of any epoch in literature before the French Revolution: Burns and Wordsworth of course asserted it, and it forms an essential element in the great and humane genius of Scott.

[2] *Pol. Ath.* 28 δοκοῦσι δὲ βέλτιστοι γεγονέναι τῶν Ἀθήνησι πολιτευσαμένων μετὰ τοὺς ἀρχαίους Νικίας καὶ Θουκυδίδης καὶ Θηραμένης.

[3] But I cannot agree with Wilamowitz (*Aristot. und Athen* ii 100) in his depreciation of that remarkable woman (see note on *Eq.* 132), or in his general judgment, finely expressed though it is, " es ist kein kleines zeichen von der würde der attischen geschichte, dass nur ein weib in ihr vorkommt, das aber beherrscht sie: die jungfrau von der burg." The absence of female influence in Attic history is of course undeniable: Plutarch *de virtute mulier.* mentions no Attic women.

[4] Hermippus 46

Βασιλεῦ Σατύρων, τί ποτ' οὐκ ἐθέλεις
δόρυ βαστάζειν, ἀλλὰ λόγους μὲν
περὶ τοῦ πολέμου δεινοὺς παρέχει
ψυχὴν δὲ Τέλητος ὑπέστης;

[5] 240.

But even that attack recognises him as the Olympian, a figure more than human. A self-contained and peaceful democracy without demagogues might have escaped censure : but a democracy of aggressive imperialism under Pericles' successors is a fair mark. And here lies the justification of the moderate party in Athens and of the literature that embodies its feelings. It was not that grumbling aristocrats might call Pericles a τύραννος at home, but that he had made Athens' rule a τυραννίς over other Greek cities. He makes no secret of this, though he adds a phrase of some regret or apology, ὡς τυραννίδα ἤδη ἔχετε αὐτὴν (τὴν ἀρχήν), ἣν λαβεῖν μὲν ἄδικον δοκεῖ εἶναι, ἀφεῖναι δὲ ἐπικίνδυνον (Thucyd. ii 63. 2). In Cleon's mouth the apology disappears and the tyranny of Athens over unwilling subjects is avowed : these subjects cannot be expected to show good-will ; they are to be kept obedient not by favours, but by force (iii 37. 2): and the commons are to be held guilty of the sin of revolt as well as the Few (39. 6).

Cleon has naturally found defenders who believe that he was carrying out Pericles' policy, home and foreign, only with an inferior air. It is the great service of Pericles to have shown that a state where equality is the corner-stone and privilege is banished may be beyond all other states humane, and splendid with all mental gifts : in such a state a political leader who lacks that humanity and culture may have less weight than if he possessed them, but he is a surer mark for censure. It is unfortunate that Thucydides probably had personal grounds for being unfair to Cleon[1]: but no reason can be drawn from ancient writers for any disbelief in Thucydides' picture[2]. It is true that they speak chiefly of Cleon's defects in style and manner, of the want of τὸ πρέπον in his oratory[3]: he was careful

---

[1] Plutarch de Herodoti malign. 3. 855 C praises Thucydides for being too much of the dignified historian to give a full account of Cleon's abounding misdeeds.

[2] I do not mean to defend, as a fair or full statement, Thucydides' black account of Cleon's motives for pressing the war (γενομένης ἡσυχίας καταφανέστερος νομίζων ἂν εἶναι κακουργῶν καὶ ἀπιστότερος διαβάλλων, v 16. 1).

[3] Aristot. Pol. Ath. 28 (Κλέων), ὃς δοκεῖ μάλιστα διαφθεῖραι τὸν δῆμον ταῖς ὁρμαῖς, καὶ πρῶτος ἐπὶ τοῦ βήματος ἀνέκραγε καὶ ἐλοιδορήσατο καὶ περιζωσάμενος ἐδημηγόρησε, τῶν ἄλλων ἐν κόσμῳ λεγόντων, Plut. de commun. notit. 13. 1065 C ἡ Κλέωνος ἀναγωγία πρὸς τὴν Περικλέους καλοκἀγαθίαν, Nicias 8, Demetrius 11, Tib. Gracch. 2 &c.

not to allow private friendships to influence his public conduct[1], and he seems to have borne himself with at least as much haughtiness as servility towards the multitude[2]. But he has been fairly placed in history as the typical demagogue, and that in the typical democracy.

The exception to the rule that Attic literature is on the side of the moderates, in favour somewhat vaguely of a restricted franchise and clearly of a Panhellenic peace, against extreme democracy, is of course found in some of the orators[3]: and almost the only reference to Cleon as a creditable figure occurs in Demosthenes[4]. But men like Cleon were condemned by a continuous literary tradition, historical, dramatic, and philosophical[5]: the Isocratean school of historical writers probably made the condemnation more definite than before[6]: and in Plutarch and Lucian Cleon is an evil genius of his country. Aristophanes' attacks on Socrates and Euripides may have been stupidly wrong: this may rouse, but it does not justify, a suspicion that he was wrong in attacking Cleon.

The Old Comedy handled subjects of public interest only: a passion for the πόλις is its inspiration. The plots would have no point but for what Mommsen calls the "republican agony," the strain of patriotism, and the hate and fear of bad citizenship. Even in the enchanted land of the *Birds*, there is no "fleeting the time carelessly, as they did in the golden

---

[1] Plut. *praec. ger. reip.* 13. 806 F.

[2] The tone of his speech in Thucydides is very masterful. Plutarch gives an anecdote (*praec. ger. reip.* 3. 799 D) that he once asked to have a meeting of the ecclesia postponed because he was going to entertain friends at a sacrificial banquet: the request was granted with hilarious acclamation. It was thought a somewhat insolent innovation on his part to begin a despatch with χαίρειν, Eupolis *fr.* 308,

πρῶτος γὰρ ἡμᾶς, ὦ Κλέων,
χαίρειν προσεῖπας πολλὰ λυπῶν τὴν πόλιν.

Cf. Lucian *pro lapsu inter salut.* 3.

[3] Wilamowitz *Arist. und Athen* i 182 calls Hermippus a radical and thinks Eupolis was clearly more democratic than Aristophanes.

[4] *Boeot. de dote* § 25.

[5] Most, if not all, the Socratics agree here: for the Cynics, ὁ πολιτικὸς αὐτοῦ ('Αντισθένους) διάλογος ἁπάντων καταδρομὴν περιέχει τῶν 'Αθήνησιν δημαγωγῶν Athen. v 220 D.

[6] Theopompus περὶ δημαγωγῶν &c.

world": the quest of a τόπος ἀπράγμων only lands the adventurers in a new sphere of civic activity.

The two essential elements of the Old Comedy are the Agon or altercation and the Chorus[1]. There can be little doubt that the former developed out of that form of entertainment, so natural, and still apparently so common, among southern nations, which consists in watching two persons improvising abuse and insults against each other.

This form of entertainment developed in Italy, as Horace's[2] admirable sketch makes so clear, into libels which the police prevented from going further: in Attica the state encouraged it in due time and the result was the Old Comedy. Dionysus was no patron of privilege or aristocratic priesthoods: freedom of speech was in his province a form of religion[3], and under his name it was raised from a coarse personal encounter[4] to a splendid picture of the contest between great principles embodied in striking, though grotesque, figures[5]. Tragedy was practically debarred from handling contemporary events; Comedy had a certain underlying seriousness naturally connected with its wide sweep of subject. Herein lies the distinctive character of the Old Comedy. The struggle depicted in it is between great tendencies or parties in a state. In later Comedy, this has been displaced by the "duel of sex": and the conclusion is not the

---

[1] Lucian *non lev. aud. calumn.* ὁ τριῶν ὄντων προσώπων, καθάπερ ἐν ταῖς κωμῳδίαις, τοῦ διαβάλλοντος καὶ τοῦ διαβαλλομένου καὶ τοῦ πρὸς ὃν ἡ διαβολὴ γίνεται.

The word ‘Agon’ was used in this technical sense by Bergk in *Philologus* xiv (1859) p. 182: it is now the recognised term, mainly owing to Zieliński's *Gliederung der Altatt. Komödie.*

[2] *Epist.* i 2. 139.

[3] Hence Cleon was shown in the *Babylonians* as harassing the god, Aristoph. *fr.* 48 Kock.

[4] The various forms of this entertainment in other literatures, Arabic, Celtic, Italian, Provençal, Scottish, do not seem to have risen above personality. It apparently died away with the Renaissance, after appearing in great men's hands with amazing vigour and coarse humour of imagination and language in such pieces as the *Flyting of Dunbar and Kennedy*, and *How a great scholar of England would have argued against Pantagruel and was overcome by Panurge.*

[5] This was probably due mainly to the genius of Cratinus: if we had some plays of his (and I would rather have the next great papyrus-find bring back him than anyone else but Sappho), we might recognise in him the Aeschylus of Comedy, the first and greatest of his kind; many of the ancients regarded him in that light.

triumph of the public weal in the victory of one side, but the happiness of two individuals by union of the two sides in marriage. It is interesting to observe that this manner of comedy owes its existence above all men to Menander—the friend and follower of Epicurus—and that the Epicurean school, bound up as it was with so much abandonment of high ideals, should be credited with this enormous contribution, through comedy and its descendant the novel, to the general feeling and conduct of society.

Yet in Menander's hands the individualising of female character and the freeing of the female will[1] have gone but a little way: women were emerging from a state hardly above slavery, and his women are mentally without distinction. His art has taken but the first step towards the charm of Rosalind or Beatrice. In a further development of that character lies the possibility of advance in comedy, as well as in other respects, in happier times to come.

In Aristophanes the very few maiden figures that appear are dumb. His women are generally types of the whole sex, banded together to use all their powers for patriotic or public ends[2]. Where public spirit gave the law for literature, its conditions would make a single love-plot appear as trivial as to us it seems essential[3].

---

[1] The importance of this for the best comedy need hardly be insisted on after Mr George Meredith's *Essay on Comedy.*

[2] In one passage of the *Lysistrata* (588—597) we are for a few lines in the grip of a powerful appeal to human sympathy for mother and maiden : the σῖγα, μὴ μνησικακήσῃς, one of the very rare touches of pathos in Aristophanes, is almost worthy of Dante ; yet even there the phrase used was mainly one of public life.

[3] Marcus Aurelius (xi 6) gives what was no doubt the accepted view, that the Old Comedy was for public edification (παιδαγωγικὴν παρρησίαν ἔχουσα, καὶ τῆς ἀτυφίας οὐκ ἀχρήσεως δι᾽ αὐτῆς τῆς εὐθυρρημοσύνης ὑπομιμνήσκουσα· πρὸς οἷόν τι καὶ Διογένης ταυτὶ παρελάμβανε), while the New tended to art for art's sake (κατ᾽ ὀλίγον ἐπὶ τὴν ἐκ μιμήσεως φιλοτεχνίαν ὑπερρύη).

ΑΡΙΣΤΟΦΑΝΟΥΣ

ΙΠΠΗΣ.

ΥΠΟΘΕΣΕΙΣ.

I.

Τὸ δρᾶμα τοῦτο ποιεῖται εἰς Κλέωνα, τὸν Ἀθηναίων δημα-
γωγόν. ὑπόκειται[1] δὲ ὡς Παφλαγὼν νεώνητος, δουλεύων τῷ
Δήμῳ, καὶ προαγόμενος παρ᾽ αὐτῷ περιττότερον. ἐπιτιθεμένων
δὲ αὐτῷ δυοῖν τοῖν ὁμοδούλοιν, καὶ κατά τινα λόγια πονηρίᾳ
διάσημον ἀλλαντοπώλην Ἀγοράκριτον ἐπαγόντοιν, ὃς ἐπιτροπεύσει
τοῦ δήμου τῶν Ἀθηναίων, αὐτοὶ οἱ Ἀθηναίων Ἱππεῖς συλλαβόντες
ἐν χοροῦ σχήματι παραφαίνονται· ὑφ᾽ ὧν προπηλακιζόμενος ὁ
Κλέων ἀγανακτεῖ, καὶ διενεχθεὶς ἱκανῶς περὶ τοῦ ἀνώτερος[2] εἶναι
τῶν ἐναντιουμένων, σφᾶς ὡς συνομωμοκότας κατὰ τῆς πόλεως
(διαβαλὼν)[3] πρὸς τὴν βουλὴν ἵεται· διώξαντος δὲ καὶ τοῦ ἀλλαντοπώλου κατὰ πόδας, οἱ Ἱππεῖς περί τε τοῦ ποιητοῦ τινα καὶ τῶν
προγόνων, ἔτι δὲ καὶ τῶν συγκινδυνευόντων σφίσιν ἐπὶ ταῖς μάχαις
ἵππων[4], πρὸς τοὺς πολίτας ἁδροτέρως διαλέγονται. ὁ δὲ ἀλλαντοπώλης περιγεγενημένος ἐν βουλῇ μάλα γελοίως τοῦ Κλέωνος,
καὶ λοιδορούμενος αὖθις αὐτῷ προσέρχεται· ἐκκαλεσαμένου δὲ
τοῦ Κλέωνος τὸν Δῆμον, προσελθὼν οὗτος διαφερομένων ἀκροᾶται.
λόγων δὲ πολλῶν γενομένων κατὰ τοῦ Κλέωνος, τοῦ Ἀγορακρίτου
μάλ᾽ ἐντέχνως τοῖς ἐπινοήμασι καὶ ταῖς θωπείαις, καὶ προσέτι
ταῖς ἐκ τῶν λογίων ὑπερβολαῖς κρατοῦντος, κατὰ μικρὸν τοῖς
λόγοις ὁ Δῆμος συνεφέλκεται. δείσαντος δὲ τοῦ Κλέωνος κἀπὶ
τὸ ψωμίζειν τὸν Δῆμον ὁρμήσαντος, ἀντιψωμίζειν ἅτερος ἐγχειρεῖ.
καὶ τέλος τοῦ Δήμου τὴν ἑκατέρου κίστην συνέντος, εἶτα τῆς μὲν
κενῆς, τῆς δὲ τοῦ Κλέωνος μεστῆς εὑρεθείσης, ἐλεγχθεὶς αὐτὸς ὡς

The arguments are not given in R. I follow the readings of V in the main.

[1] This word, so common in grammarians' Greek, correlative to ὑπόθεσις, may here
be rendered *presented* on the stage: ἐναρμόττον τῷ ὑποκειμένῳ προσώπῳ Plut. *quom.
adol.* 3. 18 B. So ὁ ὑποκείμενος καιρός, *present* time)(παρακείμενος *perfect*, as
Athen. ix 409 B.

[2] ἀλογώτερος V.   [3] Supplied by Bergk.

[4] om. V &c.

περιφανῶς τὰ τοῦ Δήμου κλέπτων, εἴκει θατέρῳ τῆς ἐπιτροπείας. μετὰ ταῦτα δὲ τοῦ ἀλλαντοπώλου τὸν Δῆμον ἀφεψήσαντος, εἶτα νεώτερον ἐξαυτῆς ἐς τοὐμφανὲς γεγονότα προάγοντος, Κλέων περικείμενος τὴν Ἀγορακρίτου σκευὴν ἐπὶ παραδειγματισμῷ διὰ μέσης πόλεως ἀλλαντοπωλῶν ἀνὰ μέρος, καὶ τῇ τέχνῃ χρησάμενος[1] πέμπεται, καὶ ἡ ἐπιτροπὴ τῷ ἀλλαντοπώλῃ παραδίδοται. τὸ δὲ δρᾶμα τῶν ἄγαν καλῶς πεποιημένων.

II.

ΑΛΛΩΣ.

Ὁ σκοπὸς αὐτῷ πρὸς τὸ καθελεῖν Κλέωνα. οὗτος γὰρ βυρσοπώλης ὢν ἐκράτει τῶν Ἀθηναίων ἐκ προφάσεως τοιαύτης. Ἀθηναῖοι πόλιν Πύλον[1], λεγομένην Σφακτηρίαν, ἐπολιόρκουν διὰ Δημοσθένους στρατηγοῦ καὶ Νικίου· ὧν στρατηγῶν χρονισάντων ἐδυσχέραινον οἱ Ἀθηναῖοι. καὶ εἰς ἐκκλησίαν συνελθόντων αὐτῶν καὶ ἀδημονούντων, Κλέων τις βυρσοπώλης ἀναστὰς ὑπέσχετο δεσμίους φέρειν τοὺς ὑπεναντίους εἴσω εἴκοσιν ἡμερῶν, εἰ στρατηγὸς αἱρεθείη· ὅπερ καὶ γέγονε. κατὰ τὰς ὑποσχέσεις οὖν ἐστρατήγει, κυκῶν τὴν πόλιν. ἐφ' οἷς μὴ ἐνεγκὼν Ἀριστοφάνης καθῆσι τὸ τῶν Ἱππέων δρᾶμα δι' αὐτοῦ, ἐπεὶ τῶν σκευοποιῶν οὐδεὶς ἐπλάσατο τὸ τοῦ Κλέωνος πρόσωπον διὰ φόβον. καὶ τὰ μὲν πρῶτα κύπτει φοβούμενος· εἶτα προφανεὶς αὐτὸς ἀνεδίδαξε τὸ δρᾶμα.

Ἔοικεν ὁ προλογίζων εἶναι Δημοσθένης, ὃς ἐκεκμήκει περὶ τὴν Πύλου πολιορκίαν, ἀφῃρέθη δὲ τὴν στρατηγίαν ὑπὸ Κλέωνος, ὑποσχομένου τότε τοῖς Ἀθηναίοις παραστήσασθαι τὴν Πύλον εἴσω εἴκοσιν ἡμερῶν· ὃ καὶ κατώρθωσε διὰ τὸ πλεῖστα τῆς ἁλώσεως προπεπονῆσθαι Δημοσθένει. ἔοικε δὲ ὡς ἐπὶ οἰκίας δεσποτικῆς ποιεῖσθαι τὸν λόγον. εἴη δ' ἂν δεσπότης ὁ Δῆμος, οἰκία ἡ πόλις. οἰκέται δὲ δύο τοῦ Δήμου προλογίζουσι, κακῶς πάσχοντες ὑπὸ Κλέωνος. ὁ δὲ χορὸς ἐκ τῶν ἱππέων ἐστίν, οἳ καὶ ἐζημίωσαν τὸν Κλέωνα πέντε ταλάντοις ἐπὶ δωροδοκίᾳ ἁλόντα. λέγουσι δὲ τῶν οἰκετῶν τὸν μὲν εἶναι Δημοσθένην, τὸν δὲ Νικίαν, ἵνα ὦσι δημηγόροι οἱ δύο.

---

[1] Sic MSS.

Ἐδιδάχθη τὸ δρᾶμα ἐπὶ Στρατοκλέους ἄρχοντος δημοσίᾳ εἰς
Λήναια, δι' αὐτοῦ τοῦ Ἀριστοφάνους. πρῶτος ἐνίκα· δεύτερος
Κρατῖνος Σατύροις[1]· τρίτος Ἀριστομένης Ὑλοφόροις[1].

Ἰστέον ὅτι εἰς τέτταρα μέρη διῄρητο ὁ δῆμος τῶν Ἀθηναίων,
εἰς πεντακοσιομεδίμνους, εἰς ἱππέας, εἰς ζευγίτας καὶ εἰς θῆτας[2].

III.

ΑΡΙΣΤΟΦΑΝΟΥΣ ΓΡΑΜΜΑΤΙΚΟΥ.

Παράγει τινὰ Κλέωνα, τὸν καλούμενον
Παφλαγόνα, κἄτι βυρσοπώλην, πικρότατα
κατεσθίοντά πως τὰ κοινὰ χρήματα·
καὶ παραλογισμῷ διαφέροντ' ἐρρωμένως
ἀλλαντοπώλην, εὐθέως τε σκατοφάγον[3],
πεισθέντα τ' ἐπιθέσθαι σὺν ἱππεῦσίν τισιν,
ἐν τῷ χορῷ παροῦσι, τῇ τῶν πραγμάτων
ἀρχῇ· Κλέωνός τ' ἐν μέσῳ κατηγορεῖ.
ἐγένετο τοῦτ'· ἐξέπεσεν ὁ Κλέων παγκάκως·
ὁ δὲ σκατοφάγος ἔτυχε προεδρίας καλῆς.

Aristophanes of Byzantium set the fashion of giving an argument (ὑπόθεσις) as
necessary in a proper edition of a play: and many of the extant arguments, especially
the metrical ones, are attributed to him; though the latter were no doubt written long
after his decease (Nauck's Aristoph. Byz. pp. 252—, Wilam. *Herakles* ed. 1, i p. 145).
We naturally find these arguments most numerous in the case of the two plays read
first—*Plutus* and *Nubes*: *Thesm.* has none. The historical style of the second
argument suggests the same hand as in the second arguments to *Nub. Pax Av.*

---

[1] No fragments of these two plays have been preserved.

[2] This remark of course has little to do with the case: the cavalry was no doubt
drawn from both the πεντακοσιομέδιμνοι and the ἱππῆς of the Solonian division: see
Martin, *Cavaliers Athéniens*, pp. 308—.

[3] "Simply a coarse buffoon": cf. κοπρίας.

ΤΑ ΤΟΥ ΔΡΑΜΑΤΟΣ ΠΡΟΣΩΠΑ.

ΟΙΚΕΤΗΣ Α΄ (ΔΗΜΟΣΘΕΝΗΣ).
ΟΙΚΕΤΗΣ Β΄ (ΝΙΚΙΑΣ).
ΑΛΛΑΝΤΟΠΩΛΗΣ
  (ΑΓΟΡΑΚΡΙΤΟΣ).
ΠΑΦΛΑΓΩΝ (ΚΛΕΩΝ).
ΧΟΡΟΣ ΙΠΠΕΩΝ.
ΔΗΜΟΣ.

The MSS. which contain this list (R omits it) give Δημοσθένης, Νικίας, Κλέων, not οἰκέτης α΄, οἰκέτης β΄, Παφλαγών. It is plain however from the second argument that these characters' names, which never occur in the play, were not given in the early copies: probably the names would have been felt as inconsistent with their stage-character as slaves, though their identity would be unmistakeable. So in the *Acharnians*, Euripides' slave was no doubt meant for Cephisophon, but he is never called by that name.

Παφλαγών, as slaves commonly had no individual name, merely the name of their race: Λυδός Θρᾷττα Σύρα Καρίων Cappadox Geta and perhaps Davus are such names and throw some light on the chief sources of the slave-supply at various periods[1]. Paphlagonian slaves would come from the Euxine pirates and the Sinope market.

A name for a Paphlagonian slave, common in later times, was Τίβιος, cf. Leuco in Kock's *Fragm. Com.* i p. 704, Strabo vii 304 c, Lucian *Timon* 22, *salt.* 29 τὸ καταγέλαστον...οἷα Δάων καὶ Τιβίων καὶ μαγείρων πρόσωπα.

Hyperbolus was presented on the stage as Λυδός by Plato, *fr.* 170.

Παφλαγών is of course intended to suggest παφλάζω, as expressly said in 919, *Pax* 314: that word is used of Hyperides' oratory by Timocles *fr.* 15, of barbarous speech by Eubulus *fr.* 109, of spluttering talk by Hippocrates *epidem.* ii 5. 2. p. 1040 Foës.

---

[1] In the list of sixteen slaves belonging to Cephisodorus, an attainted Hermocopid, at least fifteen have names of this kind Σύρος, Λυδή, Κὰρ παῖς &c. *Corp. Inscr. Att.* i 277. 16 (Hicks *Gr. Hist. Inscr.* p. 104). A slave's name was accordingly a shorter word than the compound which was the normal form of a free Greek's name: hence we find δισύλλαβοι Athen. xiv 614 Ε meaning *slaves*.

ΑΡΙΣΤΟΦΑΝΟΥΣ ΙΠΠΗΣ.

ΟΙ. Α. Ἰαττataιὰξ τῶν κακῶν, ἰαττatαί.
κακῶς Παφλαγόνα τὸν νεώνητον κακόν
αὐταῖσι βουλαῖς ἀπολέσειαν οἱ θεοί.

1. ἰαττatαί MSS. ἰαττatαῖ edd. since Dindorf, following the grammarians' rule
that τὰ σχετλιαστικὰ περισπᾶται (see Chandler *Greek Accent.* § 897). But the rule was
not always kept, τὰ σχετλιαστικὰ οὐ πεφρόντικε τῆς ἀκριβοῦς ἐξετάσεως Herodian i 507.
5 Lentz. From Arcadius 183. 18 ἡ συνήθεια ὀξύνει τὸ παπαῖ καὶ ἀταταῖ it might be
inferred that -ταῖ would appear in Tragedy (so Soph. *Phil.* 790 &c.), -ταί in Comedy,
and MSS. always give -ταί in Aristoph., except that R gives ἀτταταῖ in parody as *Ach.*
1190, *Nub.* 707.

---

1. The -άξ is comic, βαβαιάξ, παπαιάξ,
εὐάξ Plaut. *Bacch.* 247; so βομβάξ, πυππάξ,
εὐράξ πατάξ, πάξ Diphilus 96, Herondas
7. 114, Plaut. *Trin.* 889 : more serious
πόπαξ Aesch. *Eum.* 143, and perhaps
ὄμπαξ (Lobeck *Aglaoph.* 780). No doubt
the Greeks felt the ξ sound to be clumsy
as the Romans did (Cic. *orator* 153).
ἀτταταί seems to be used not only in pain,
but also in remonstrance, *tut-tut*, cf.
Ran. 57.
τῶν κακῶν 'confound it all,' as οἴμοι
τῶν κακῶν (*Plut.* 389, Luc. *pisc.* 3), an
exclamation recommended to a vulgar
orator by Lucian *rhet. praec.* 19: φοῦ
τῶν κακῶν Epicharmus (p. 251 Lor.)
ap. Athen. vii 277 F. [Such phrases
hardly occur in tragedy : Eurip. *Her.*
224 is probably spurious ; Soph. *OC*
982 has ὤμοι μοι κακῶν (the passage has
been suspected) : Eurip. *Hel.* 1223 οἷ 'γὼ
τῶν ἐμῶν τλήμων κακῶν is different : and
Lucian *fugit.* 33 calls φεῦ τῶν κακῶν,
ὀτοτοῖ, παπαιπαιάξ a quotation from
tragedy only in ridicule.] In colloquial
Greek and Latin, κακός and *malus*
were constantly used with a meaning
that would in modern times be expressed by an imprecation. 'Bad' is a
poor rendering in hundreds of such cases:
τί κακόν; *Thesm.* 1080 is *quid, malum ?* :

κακίζω is 'swear at': and the κακοδαι-
μονισταί mentioned by Lysias were an
Athenian 'Hell-fire Club.' The use is
more common in Latin: *malum* was the
common imprecation of a Roman, and
the adjective has a similar meaning in
many such cases as Horace's *mali culices*,
Catullus' *malus liber* (44. 21) and *malae
tenebrae*: *male mulcatus* (as Cicero *Brutus*
88, Phaedrus i 3. 9) is a weaker form of
Lord Wharton's '*damnably mauled*.' The
words ἀγαθὸς κακὸς *bonus malus*, so
obscure in origin, may all have had a
religious meaning once: this would suit
their social and political usage, as nobility
were διογενεῖς, and also such cases as
mala lingua, malum carmen.
2. The combination κακὸς κακῶς is of
course constant: here the order of words is
uncommon, as the κακῶς rarely comes first
(see Elmsley on Eurip. *Med.* 787) and the
κακόν after another adjective is awkward.
Possibly there is a quotation or parody
of something in tragedy: the rhythm of
2—5 suggests this. νεώνητον not so much
because his importance was recent (four
years in Attic politics gave a good standing) as because he was a *novus homo*, no
οἰκογενὴς or οἰκότριψ, as the regular stage-
slave was (Plut. *comp. Ar. et Men.* 2.
853 E).

ἐξ οὗ γὰρ εἰσήρρησεν εἰς τὴν οἰκίαν,
πληγὰς ἀεὶ προστρίβεται τοῖς οἰκέταις.   5
ΟΙ. Β. κάκιστα δῆθ' οὗτός γε πρῶτος Παφλαγόνων
αὐταῖς διαβολαῖς.   ΟΙ. Α. ὦ κακόδαιμον, πῶς
ἔχεις;
ΟΙ. Β. κακῶς καθάπερ σύ·   ΟΙ. Α. δεῦρο δὴ πρόσελθ',
ἵνα
ξυναυλίαν κλαύσωμεν Οὐλύμπου νόμον.
ΟΙ. Α καὶ Β.   μῦ μῦ μῦ μῦ μῦ μῦ μῦ μῦ μῦ μῦ μῦ μῦ.
ΟΙ. Α. τί κινυρόμεθ' ἄλλως; οὐκ ἐχρῆν ζητεῖν τινα   11
σωτηρίαν νῷν, ἀλλὰ μὴ κλάειν ἔτι;
ΟΙ. Β. τίς οὖν γένοιτ' ἄν; λέγε σύ.   ΟΙ. Α. σὺ μὲν
οὖν μοι λέγε,

5. τοὺς οἰκέτας R. **8.** δὴ R. νῦν the other MSS. **13—16.** I keep the MS. arrangement, though with hesitation. Editors generally adopt the proposals of K. F. Hermann (*Progymn.* 3. p. 21) and Beer (*Zahl d. Schausp. bei Aristoph.* p. 149), giving :—

4. In Attic ἔρρω has always a sense of contempt or misfortune: the Laconic ἔρρει τὰ κᾶλα in the famous despatch given by Xen. *Hell.* i 1. 23 might be Athenian as far as the verb is concerned. It is by no means confined to comedy: ἔρρει πᾶσ' 'Αφροδίτα Aesch. *Agam.* &c.
5. πληγὰς προστρίβεται *gets them beaten*: the nearest parallel is given by πληγὰς or κονδύλους ἐντρίβειν, ἐντρίβεσθαι Cobet *VL* p. 223: προστρίβεσθαι δόξαν, ἀδοξίαν Demosth. *Androt.* 75 (repeated *Timocr.* 183), cf. i *Aristog.* 52, Antipho *Tetral.* γ 2. 8. Cf. also the use of the compounds of ὁμόργνυμι and σμάω.
6. δῆτα is common in responses as *Pax* 978, *Ran.* 552: δῆτα . γε Soph. *OC* 537, οὐ δῆτα . γε *OC* 810 *OT* 1377, μὴ δῆτα . γε *Aj.* 111 &c. ἀπόλοιτο is easily supplied from ἀπολέσειαν. For πρῶτος Παφλ. cf. οἰμώξει μακρὰ πρῶτος μαγείρων Diphilus 43. 37.
7. κακοδαίμων '*poor devil*' was barely a serious word. It occurs only once in tragedy, in Hippolytus' cries, τὸν κακοδαίμονα καὶ κατάρατον Eurip. *Hipp.* 1362, once in the Orators Antiph. *Herod.* 43, where it is almost colloquial (*confounded fool*, cf. κακοδαιμονῶ), as it is in Plato *Rep.* iv 440 A, *Symp.* 173 C, and perhaps

Meno 78 A (the only cases in Plato). Aristotle, who has εὐδαίμων so often, avoids it altogether: so do Thucydides and Xenophon.
9. Οὐλύμπου because the rhythm and tone are tragic. To this famous Phrygian or Mysian master were attributed the development of flute music, the first composition of music without words (μουσικὴ κρουματικὴ), and the invention of the Phrygian and Lydian modes. The points here are their whining tone, like Lydian music, and the want of words, μῦ μῦ being only κρούματα or τερετίσματα (Aristot. *Problem.* xix 10). ξυναυλίαν, in apposition apparently to νόμον, implied that no articulate words were sung to the notes Semus ap. Athen. xiv 618 A. Cf. Theopompus com. 64 Τελαμῶνος οἰμώξοντες ἀλλήλοις μέλη.
11—12. 'Why this silly whimpering?' κινύρομαι may be from the same root as *whine*, or, less probably, from the Phoenician kinnōr, the κινύρα: this seems the only case of its use outside serious poetry. The rhythm changes markedly from comic to tragic as he passes from one course to another. ἀλλὰ μὴ 'and not': the Greeks emphasize the contrast, and say ἀλλ' οὐ, ἀλλὰ μή, rarely καὶ οὐ, καὶ μή.

ἵνα μὴ μάχωμαι. ΟΙ. Β. μὰ τὸν Ἀπόλλω 'γὼ
μὲν οὔ·
ἀλλ' εἰπὲ θαρρῶν, εἶτα κἀγὼ σοὶ φράσω.   15

ΟΙ. Α. πῶς ἂν σύ μοι λέξειας ἀμὲ χρὴ λέγειν;

ΟΙ. Β. ἀλλ' οὐκ ἔνι μοι τὸ θρέττε. πῶς ἂν οὖν ποτε
εἴποιμ' ἂν αὐτὸ δῆτα κομψευριπικῶς;

ΟΙ. Α. μή μοί γε, μή μοι, μὴ διασκανδικίσῃς·
ἀλλ' εὑρέ τιν' ἀπόκινον ἀπὸ τοῦ δεσπότου.   20

ΝΙΚ. τίς οὖν γένοιτ' ἄν; ΔΗΜ. λέγε σύ. ΝΙΚ. σὺ μὲν οὖν μοι λέγε
ἵνα μὴ μάχωμαι. ΔΗΜ. μὰ τὸν Ἀπόλλω 'γὼ μὲν οὔ.
Besides this, Sauppe's proposal (*ep. crit. ad Herm.* p. 111) to transpose 15 and 16
has found support from Mein. Dind. Vels. Ribb. Bergk.

---

14. ἵνα μὴ μάχωμαι has been thought
more suitable to Nicias' timid spirit, as
such phrases may have been current
about him even before Hermocrates'
jest γελοῖός ἐστιν ὁ Νικίας, ὅπως οὐ μαχεῖται
στρατηγῶν Plut. *Nic.* 16. But in argument such phrases were used to mean
'don't let us quarrel about it' as Plato
Crat. 430 D, *Rep.* i 352 B, and here the
speaker probably means only that he
will not insist on the first word, as the
Sausage-man does in 339 ἀλλ' αὐτὸ περὶ
τοῦ πρότερος εἰπεῖν πρῶτα διαμαχοῦμαι.
16. The line is Eurip. *Hipp.* 345,
where Phaedra shrinks from speaking out
to the nurse. The *Hippolytus* had appeared in its second form four years before the *Knights*, but the scandal the play
caused was not forgotten: and the φρὴν
ἀνώμοτος itself was hardly more notorious
than Phaedra's fencing in the scene quoted from here (Plato i *Alcib.* 113 C).
17—18. θρέττε· βαρβαριστὶ ἀντὶ
τοῦ θαρρεῖν schol.; and there is no other
case of it in literature : but it may be
originally the imper. of a verb surviving
in this one form [θρεσ-ιω] θρέσσω, from
the root of θρασύς.
πῶς ἂν *utinam*, as in 16. πῶς...δῆτα
as *Nub.* 1196, *Lys.* 912, *Thesm.* 211:
δῆτα giving a certain emphasis to αὐτὸ
'the right thing', '*the* point'.
κομψευριπικῶς syncopated for κομψευρι-
πιδικῶς (cf. βδελύκτροπος, *idolatry* &c.).
Adjectives in -κὸς were an affectation of
the day (1378—), and no doubt adverbs
in -κῶς came with them. It is noticeable
that Euripides first used κομψὸς in serious

literature.
19. μή μοί γε, 'O pray don't': μή
μοί γε, μὴ σύ γε are both appeals, the
former more colloquial (does it occur in
tragedy?), the latter more serious: the
pronouns may be combined in strong appeal as Eurip. *Med.* 964 μή μοι σύ.
διασκανδικίζω is given as a fair retort to
such an invention as κομψευριπικῶς. The
use of -ίζω was elastic and lent itself to
such formations. The public was already
familiar with the tale that Euripides'
mother, Clito, had plied the trade of a
greengrocer and sold bad herbs (*Ach.*
478, *Thesm.* 456). The σκάνδιξ, translated *chervil, cerfeuil* (from χαιρέφυλλον),
was not a garden-herb, *ne holus quidem
legitimum* Plin. *N. H.* xxii 80, not always
reckoned even among ἄγρια λάχανα
Theophr. *Hist. Plant.* vii 7. 1, and eaten
only by the poor (Alciphro iii 49. 1, Diog.
Laert. ii 8. 17) or in famine: Andocides
fr. 4 referring to the Archidamian war
μηδὲ ἄγρια λάχανα καὶ σκάνδικας ἔτι
φάγοιμεν: so it was familiar to the
audience. Teleclides 38 διασκανδικίσαι
seems to mean *eat coarse country food.*
"Dioscorides saith it is eaten both raw
and boyled, and that it is an wholesome pot-herbe among the Greekes: but
in these dayes it is of small estima-
tion or value, and taken but for a wilde
wort, as appeareth by Aristophanes
taunting of Euripides, as aforesaid"
Gerarde's *Herbal* (*Of shepheard's needle
or wilde chervill*).
20. ἀπόκινος, a comic dance, Athen.
xiv 629 C τὴν ἀπόκινον καλουμένην ὄρχησιν,

ΟΙ. Β. λέγε δὴ μολῶμεν ξυνεχὲς ὡδὶ ξυλλαβών.

ΟΙ. Α. καὶ δὴ λέγω· μολῶμεν. ΟΙ. Β. ἐξόπισθε νῦν

αὐτὸ φαθὶ τοῦ μολῶμεν. ΟΙ. Α. αὐτό.

ΟΙ. Β. πάνυ καλῶς.

ὥσπερ δεφόμενος νῦν ἀτρέμα πρῶτον λέγε

τὸ μολῶμεν, εἶτα δ' αὐτό, κᾆτ' ἐπάγων πυκνόν 25

ΟΙ. Α. μολῶμεν αὐτὸ μολῶμεν αὐτομολῶμεν. ΟΙ. Β. ἤν,

οὐχ ἡδύ; ΟΙ. Α. νὴ Δία· πλήν γε περὶ τῷ

δέρματι

δέδοικα τουτονὶ τὸν οἰωνόν. ΟΙ. Β. τί δαί;

ΟΙ. Α. ὁτιὴ τὸ δέρμα δεφομένων ἀπέρχεται.

ΟΙ. Β. κράτιστα τοίνυν τῶν παρόντων ἐστὶ νῶν, 30

θεῶν ἰόντε προσπεσεῖν τοῦ πρὸς βρέτας.

21. μόλωμεν vulg. and so till 26 : μολῶμεν Μ, τινες τὸ μόλωμεν προπεριπῶσιν schol. 25. Most MSS. κατεπάγων, standing to ἐπάγω as κατεπείγω to ἐπείγω: but Enger's κᾆτ' ἐπάγω is better, cf. εἶτ' ἐπάγει Athen. xi 782 D. κατεπᾴδων V Bergk. 26. ἤν R and most MSS.: see Wilam. on Eur. HF 867. 29. τῶν δεφ. MSS.

ἧς μνημονεύει Κρατῖνος ἐν Νεμέσει καὶ Κηφισόδωρος ἐν Ἀμαζόσιν Ἀριστοφάνης τ' ἐν Κενταύρῳ καὶ ἄλλοι πλείονες, ὕστερον μακτρισμὸν ὠνόμασαν: 629 F γελοῖαι εἰσὶν ὀρχήσεις ἴγδις καὶ μακτρισμὸς ἀπόκινός τε καὶ σοβάς: Pollux iv 101 ἀπόκινος καὶ ἀπόσεισις καὶ ἴγδις ἀσελγῆ εἴδη ὀρχήσεων. Such dances were probably a resource of the φορτικοί among comedians, whom Aristophanes contemns and sometimes imitates: the Ecclesiazusae ends apparently with such a dance off (ὑπαποκινεῖν is a probable conjecture of Cobet's in 1165).

21. μολεῖν was tragic: it could only be allowed in parody, and a parody of the Hippolytus is still intended: see Rutherford New Phryn. 41, Bakhuyzen Parod. 105 (the rhythm of the three fragments quoted there shows that their tone is tragic). ὡδὶ ξυλλαβών : the parallel of the Latin concipere suggests that συλλαμβάνω had the same meaning 'take part' in a form of words, and specially repeat from dictation: but I can find no instance of this use, though certain forms of incantation in which words were divided between those taking part in the spell are probably alluded to. The words mean 'taking it as I do', i. e. pronouncing,

not μόλωμεν, but μολῶμεν in anticipation of 26. (I owe this explanation to Dr Verrall.)

23. The article, as often, means the mark of quotation.

25. For ἐπάγω 'hurry', 'quicken' cf. Nub. 390, Plato Crat. 420 D.

27. Here γε might be taken as the 'yes' answering to οὐχ ἡδύ: but πλήν γε without any preceding question expressed, marking a reservation 'well—except...' occurs from Homer Od. viii 207 downwards, and in later Greek is common even at the beginning of a sentence.

30—31. Nicias' helplessness takes the form of a wish to prostrate himself before some holy image. βρέτας is a poetical word, used only of old images or ξόανα, chiefly venerated by a city: such as the old Athena of the Erechtheum (Aesch. Eum. 80 &c., Lys. 262), the Tauric Artemis, the Hera of Samos (Athen. xv 672 B). Pollux i 7 disallows βρέτας and δείκηλον, in Attic prose presumably: it is excused here by Nicias' semi-tragic tone. The distinction drawn by Hermann on Soph. Ajax 998 between θεός τις (a god, not a man) and θεῶν τις (some one god), though sometimes hard

ΟΙ. Α. ποῖον βρέτας*; ἐτεὸν ἡγεῖ γὰρ θεούς;
ΟΙ. Β. ἔγωγε. ΟΙ. Α. ποίῳ χρώμενος τεκμηρίῳ;
ΟΙ. Β. ὁτιὴ θεοῖσιν ἐχθρός εἰμ'. οὐκ εἰκότως;
ΟΙ. Α. εὖ προσβιβάζεις μ'. ἀλλ' ἐτέρᾳ πη σκεπτέον.
βούλει τὸ πρᾶγμα τοῖς θεαταῖσιν φράσω; 36
ΟΙ. Β. οὐ χεῖρον· ἐν δ' αὐτοὺς παραιτησώμεθα,

32. βρέτας R and most MSS. βρεττέτας VN βρετέττας schol. Aldus: βρέτας ὦ τᾶν
Dobr. βρέτας σύ γ' Kock βρετετέτας W. G. Clark. **35.** ἔτερά MSS. ποι MSS. vulg.

to apply, suits most of the cases collected by Elmsley and Lobeck on that passage: take as an illustration Hom. *Od.* ix 142, x 141 καὶ τις θεὸς ἡγεμόνευε compared with Aristides 27. 352 σαφὲς ἦν τὸ τοῦ Ὁμήρου ὅτι τις θεῶν ἡγεῖτο καὶ ὅστις γε ὁ θεός: it suits the rule well that Plato uses θεός τις. "To what God shall I pray?" must have been a common question with the religious, as Theophrastus' δεισιδαί-μων and several of the Dodona inscriptions tell us: so Aesch. *Sept.* 93 πότερα δῆτ' ἐγὼ πάτρια προσπέσω βρέτη δαιμόνων; It would seem that kneeling or prostration was not common in Greek worship, being thought womanish or superstitious Plut. *de superst.* 3. 166 A. **32.** The best remedy for the metre of this line, which in R is plain prose, is to read βρετέτεras, Demosthenes thus ridiculing Nicias' nervousness and chattering of teeth. It comes near the scholiast's βρετέττας: which he explains by the words ἐν παρολκῇ παίζων 'the redundant syllable is in joke': and there is a point in the extremely un-tragic rhythm. For such stammering repetition of syllables in fear, see *Av.* 310, 315, in drunkenness Plaut. *Most.* 310, 316, in cold *Rud.* 528— (Sonnenschein), in baby-speech *Truc.* 506 (Schöll).
ποῖος in this contemptuous retort of the emphatic word in the last sentence is common in Comedy and Plato: Soph. *Trach.* 427 and Eurip. *Hel.* 567 seem to be the only cases in Tragedy.
ἐτεόν is in Attic confined to Aristophanes, who uses it only in appeals for information as here.
33—34. The rhythm becomes tragic to suit the topic. Nicias' answer is 'Because I'm god-forsaken', θεοῖς ἐχθρὸς being a very familiar phrase of contemptuous dislike, so common that it was

pronounced in one word and formed the noun θεοισεχθρία. The argument was obviously good in retort either by or to one charged with atheism: Theodorus the Cyrenaic and Diogenes the Cynic both replied to such an accuser πῶς ἀγνοῶ ὅπου γε καὶ σὲ θεοῖς ἐχθρὸν εἶναι νομίζω; (Diog. Laert. ii 102, vi 42): so did Pomponius Laetus (Creighton *Papacy* iii 42): and Cicero *in Pis.* 59 "your Epicurean view of the gods will not do for Caesar: *tibi enim et esse et fuisse videbit iratos.*" Of course there is a certain pathos in the lines, and the rhythm is meant to help this; so is also the form θεοῖσιν ἐχθρὸς, as in the dying Alexander's retort to the flatterer who spoke of 'gods like you', ποῖοι θεοί; φοβοῦμαι μή τι θεοῖσιν ἐχθροί (Phylarchus ap. Athen. vi 251 C): but the main thing is the jest, and there is little of the poignancy of Job's 'As God liveth, who hath taken away my judgment'.
We need not of course look for any distinction between τεκμήριον and εἰκὸς such as we should expect to find in Aristotle.
35. προσβιβάζεις 'make me come over to your view' as *Av.* 426, where Schol. explains κατ' ὀλίγον πείθειν: so of argument or instruction μεταβιβάζω, συμβιβάζω (the regular causal of συμβαίνει in Aristotle).
36. πρᾶγμα of the *action*, *story*, of a play: this special meaning appears in 39, *Pax* 44 τῶν θεατῶν τις ἂν λέγοι, τὸ δὲ πρᾶγμα τί; *Ran.* 1122 and the Euripidean ending τοιονδ' ἀπέβη τόδε πρᾶγμα. From Aristot. *poet.* 3. 1448ᵃ 25—39 it would seem an accident that a play was called δρᾶμα and not πρᾶγμα. So πρακτικός 'suited to the drama' *ib.* 24. 1460ᵃ 1.
37. οὐ χεῖρον was a common phrase in giving a justification for going into a

ἐπίδηλον ἡμῖν τοῖς προσώποισιν ποεῖν,
ἢν τοῖς ἔπεσι χαίρωσι καὶ τοῖς πράγμασι.
ΟΙ. Α. λέγοιμ᾿ ἂν ἤδη. νῶν γάρ ἐστι δεσπότης   40
ἄγροικος ὀργήν, κυαμοτρώξ, ἀκράχολος,
Δῆμος πυκνίτης, δύσκολον γερόντιον
ὑπόκωφον. οὗτος τῇ προτέρᾳ νουμηνίᾳ

38. ποεῖν RV &c.: such seems from inscriptions to have been the common spelling of the parts of this verb where o is followed by ε or η (Meisterhans § 16 a).
41. ἀγροῖκος R: the distinction ἀγροῖκος *a rustic*, ἄγροικος *rude* was drawn by some, but was reversed by others and is denied by Thomas Magister for Attic (Chandler *Greek Acc.* § 388, Wheeler *Griech. Nominalaccent* p. 114).

---

subject at length: Plato *Phaedo* 105 A οὐ γὰρ χεῖρον πολλάκις ἀκούειν, Arist. *Eth. Nic.* iv 13. 1127ᵃ 14, Plut. *mul. virt.* 243 D, *quaest. conv.* i 5. 623 A, Athen. ix 404 E and often in Lucian (see Blaydes here).

39. Zieliński (*Gliederung*, p. 289) says ἔπη in tragedy means trimeters, in comedy tetrameters: but the distinction fails here, unless we suppose there is a parody of tragic terms.

40. The rhythm is tragicose for the first three lines: this is natural in such ῥήσεις. ἤδη 'now that the time has come' implies a satisfactory response to Nicias' appeal. γάρ has the original meaning of γ᾿ ἄρ᾿ 'well then,' and is usual in such statements: at least twenty of Demosthenes' speeches shew it, after the prelude, introducing the facts of the case.

41. ἄγροικος: Aristophanes always looks on the farmer as the backbone of the country and the proper hero for a play: he naturally attributes the temper of the farming class to Demus. The Eupatrids had all migrated to the city in early times.

The use of beans in elections was apparently specially Athenian: Soph. *fr.* 271 is attributing Attic habits to mythical Ætolians in Satyric plays; Athenians imposed the habit on some of their subjects, as Erythrae *CIA* i 9. 8— . So κυαμοτρώξ 'Αττικὸς in the comic fragment quoted by Suidas s.v.; and κυάμους τρώγειν of the dicast *Lys.* 537, 690 would lack part of its point outside Athens.

τρώγω, τράγημα, &c. are used in good Greek only of things eaten at the second course or dessert, Alexis 163. 1—2 οὐδὲ

φιλόδειπνός εἰμι, τραγήμασιν χαίρω δὲ μᾶλλον: so κυαμοτρώξ can apply only to beans *au naturel*, not to the ἔτνος made of them; cf. Herod. ii 37 κυάμους οὔτε τρώγουσι οὔτε ἔψοντες πατέονται, Agathocles ap. Athen. xiv 650 A.

ἀκράχολος was a word of the Ionic medical schools in the form ἀκρήχολος, *choleric*. In extant Attic verse it is confined to comic lines of tragic rhythm, Ar. *fr.* 535 κύων ἀκράχολος Ἑκάτης ἄγαλμα φωσφόρου γενήσομαι, Pherecrates 164 ἢ τῆς ἀχέρδου τῆς ἀκραχολωτάτης, Epinicus 1. 7 ἐσμὸν μελίσσης τῆς ἀκραχόλου γλυκύν. Arist. *Eth. Nic.* iv 5. 1126ᵃ 18 distinguishes it from πικρὸς, as 'hasty' from 'bitter.'

42. Demus is defined as Πυκνίτης: this adjective occurs again only in a comic fragment, and is probably invented in imitation of 'Αρεοπαγίτης and such words. The Pnyx was of course the regular place for the ecclesia (see on 749). Demus was known as a name, in the person of the famous beauty Demus, son of Pyrilampes (*Vesp.* 98, Eupolis 213).

δύσκολος 'hard to manage' (cf. βούκολος), 'peevish' of children or old people, Lysias i. 11, Plato *Legg.* vii 791 C, *Vesp.* 942: it is coupled with ἀκράχολος in Plato *l.c.*, *Rep.* iii 411 C, Plut. *de cohib. ira* 3. 454 B, Phryn. in Bekk. *Anecd.* p. 1. 19.

43. ὑπόκωφος: this touch is found in Plato's ναύκληρος in the ship of democracy (*Rep.* vi 488 A). Dr Jackson points out to me that Aristotle (*Rhet.* iii 4. 3. 1406ᵇ 35) took Plato's ναύκληρος to mean Aristophanes' Δῆμος, and that Cope on the passage is mistaken.

ἐπρίατο δοῦλον, βυρσοδέψην Παφλαγόνα,
πανουργότατον καὶ διαβολώτατόν τινα.　45
οὗτος καταγνοὺς τοῦ γέροντος τοὺς τρόπους,
ὁ βυρσοπαφλαγών, ὑποπεσὼν τὸν δεσπότην
ἤκαλλ᾽, ἐθώπευ᾽, ἐκολάκευ᾽, ἐξηπάτα
κοσκυλματίοις ἄκροισι, τοιαυτὶ λέγων·
ὦ Δῆμε, λοῦσαι πρῶτον ἐκδικάσας μίαν,　50
ἐνθοῦ, ῥόφησον, ἔντραγ᾽, ἔχε τριώβολον.

49. σαθροῖσι Helbig (*Neue Jahrb.* 1861 p. 535): but σαθρός is *cracked* or *leaky*
(σήθω), σαπρὸς *rotten* (σήπω) as *Vesp.* 38 ὄζει κάκιστον βύρσης σαπρᾶς. **51.** ἐνθου MSS.

The market for slaves and cattle was
held at the new moon, *Vesp.* 170, Lucian
de merc. cond. 23 τῆς νουμηνίας ἐπιστάσης...
ἡ πρᾶσίς ἐστιν, Alciphro iii 61. 2: hence the
name Νουμήνιος when applied to slaves,
id. iii 38. 1 ὡς τῇ ἕνῃ καὶ νέᾳ τοῦτον ἐπριάμην, Νουμήνιον εὐθὺς ἐθέμην καλεῖσθαι.
There is no serious reference to the date
of elections or of the Sphacterian operations.

44. Tanners in Athens might be either
free workmen as in *Plut.* 167, or slaves in
a large household as in Aeschin. *Tim.* 97.
Cleon's father had a factory of tanner-
slaves according to a scholiast here: Anytus, Socrates' accuser, had made a fortune
by this business (schol. on Plato *apol.*
18 B). The business was not in high repute: tanneries were generally forbidden
inside a town (see on 852): and Pollux
vi 128 mentions, among the livelihoods
ἐφ᾽ οἷς ἄν τις ὀνειδισθείη, πορνοβοσκὸς
κάπηλος τελώνης βυρσοδέψης ἀλλαντοπώλης. σκυλοδέψης and σκυτοδέψης are more
common synonyms.

46. καταγιγνώσκω 'see a weak point,'
the *κατα-* having the meaning 'to the disadvantage of': so Thucyd. vi 34. 8 δικαίως κατεγνωκότες ὅτι αὐτοὺς οὐκ ἐφθειρό-
μεν, Xen. *Cyrop.* viii 4. 9, Plato *Meno*
76 C, and the noun κατάγνωσις in Thucyd.
iii 16. 1 διὰ κατάγνωσιν ἀσθενείας σφῶν.

47. ὑποπίπτω 'fawn on,' like ὑπέρχομαι ὑποτρέχω ὑποκύπτω ὑποδύομαι. Demosthenes' indignation makes him heap
up the words in the next line, but the
idea of flattery is often emphasized in
Greek by the use of more than one word
to denote the art: Plato *rep.* iv 426 C ὃς
ἂν ἥδιστα θεραπεύῃ καὶ χαρίζηται ὑποτρέ-
χων, Dem. *Aristocr.* 8 ὑμᾶς ὑπέρχεσθαι

καὶ θεραπεύειν and Weber's note there.
The words here may be arranged as a
climax: ἐξηπάτα coming last, as being a
very common word in public life, *hoodwink, humbug* a jury or meeting.

49. κοσκυλμάτια 'leather-parings,' a
reduplicated form from σκῦλον, σκύλλω:
quisquiliae is from the same root.

50. "Settle one law-case first (as exercise), then your bath and your dinner."
ἐκδικάζω has the meaning of 'clearing off,'
'getting through,' a case as [Xen.] *Rep.
Ath.* 3. 2 δίκας καὶ γραφὰς καὶ εὐθύνας
ὅσας οὐδ᾽ οἱ σύμπαντες ἄνθρωποι ἐκδικά-
ζουσιν, Lucian *pisc.* 16 ἥξω ἐκδικάσασα
τὴν δίκην. For the ellipse of δίκην, cf.
Vesp. 595, Lucian *bis acc.* 7 ὡς κἂν ὀλίγαι
τήμερον ἐκδικασθῶσιν, *necyom.* 13 τῷ
Μίνωϊ μία τις καὶ πρὸς χάριν ἐδικάσθη.
Apparently it was a question whether
the dicasts should be paid except for a full
day's attendance in court: popular leaders
carried the principle that one case should
be held as a day's work, *Vesp.* 594.

51. ἐντίθημι is used of a nurse feeding
an infant, *inf.* 717, Plato *Rep.* i 345 D.
Plut. *Romulus* 2 ψωμίσματα ἐντιθέναι τοῖς
βρέφεσιν, *fort. Rom.* 8. 320 F: probably
ἐνθοῦ was a nurse's word. ἔνθεσις implies either that the eater is helped to the
morsel or that it is daintily eaten, as
Pherecrates 108. 6, Athen. iv 161 D,
Lucian *dial. meretr.* 6. 3; so ἐνθεσίδου-
λος· ψωμόδουλος Hesych.
ῥοφῶ (for σροφέω *sorbeo slobber*) is used
of thick or hot liquids, such as soup (*inf.*
360, *Pax* 716), or the lentil-porridge
called φακῆ (*Vesp.* 812, 906), or gruel (*fr.*
10 ἢ χόνδρον ἔψων...ἐδίδου ῥοφῆσαι, Strabo
xv 1. 53 ὄρυζα ῥοφητή), or thick milk
(Athen. xiii 585 C γάλα παρεκάλει ῥοφῆσαι·

βούλει παραθῶ σοι δόρπον; εἶτ᾽ ἀναρπάσας
ὅ τι ἄν τις ἡμῶν σκευάσῃ, τῷ δεσπότῃ
Παφλαγὼν κεχάρισται τοῦτο. καὶ πρώην γ᾽
ἐμοῦ
μᾶζαν μεμαχότος ἐν Πύλῳ Λακωνικήν,   55
πανουργότατά πως περιδραμὼν ὑφαρπάσας
αὐτὸς παρέθηκε τὴν ὑπ᾽ ἐμοῦ μεμαγμένην.
ἡμᾶς δ᾽ ἀπελαύνει, κοὐκ ἐᾷ τὸν δεσπότην
ἄλλον θεραπεύειν, ἀλλὰ βυρσίνην ἔχων

ὁ δ᾽ "οὐ θέλω" εἶπεν· ἦν γὰρ ἐφεστηκυῖα γραῦς αὐτῷ), or soft eggs (Athen. ii 58A, Galen de alim. facult. iii 22), or blood (Æsch. Eum. 264, and perhaps Soph. Trach. 1055). So sorbeo is always distinguished from bibo: Plaut. Mil. 834 di me perdant, si bibi...quia enim obsorbui. ῥοφῶ and its compounds may also mean sip, as of unmixed wine, Theopompus com. 76 ἀγαθοῦ δαίμονος ἐπιρροφεῖν, ἀπορροφῶ of a Persian cup-bearer Xen. Cyrop. i 3. 10 (this is the Latin sorbillo); or of iced drinks cf. ψυχορροφῶ Plato com. 259 and perhaps the French sorbet. ῥόφημα and sorbitio in medicine meant a thick or hot draught (as Persius 4. 2), or a 'slop-diet' (as Plut. de tuend. san. 3. 123 D, Senec. epist. 78. 25). See more on 700.

ἐντραγεῖν is the regular aorist of τρώγειν: though the rule as stated by Kock on Menander 146, in correction of Cobet VL 73, that the comedians never use the simple τραγεῖν is too sweeping (Pherecrates 67. 5 ἦν γὰρ τράγῃ τις). The word is of course used only of eating τραγήματα; the φακοί in Pherecrates are lentils au naturel, not made into the φακῆ, and the ἔντραγε τουτί in Vesp. 612 refers to dessert of some kind after the μᾶζα.

This is the earliest mention of the famous τριώβολον. Pay for jurymen was introduced by Pericles, but the amount in his time is never stated, and Nub. 863 is reasonably held to imply that it was originally one obol. Köhler first pointed out that the fee was probably raised to three obols when the allies' tribute was raised in 425, and this theory has been generally accepted. Arist. Pol. Ath. has not helped to settle the question.

52. δόρπον (probably connected with δρέπω, cf. snack, snatch) is almost confined to Homer and later epic (Lehrs Arist.

stud. p. 129). This is the only instance in Attic (except Aesch. fr. 181 of the heroic age), though we have δορπηστός Vesp. 103 of the evening meal, and ἐπιδορπίζομαι ἐπιδόρπισμα not uncommonly of a supper after the regular δεῖπνον and συμπόσιον (τρίτη παράθεσις Athen. xiv 664 C). δορπία was an Ionic word for the eve of a feast-day, kept in Attic for the first evening of the Apaturia. In Homer, δόρπον is always an afternoon or evening meal, later than δεῖπνον (Robert Hermes xix 469—, Ridgeway Journ. Phil. xvii 159—): when δεῖπνον was put late, δόρπον became extinct, except as an extra meal.

Cleon waits on Demus, helping him to the φακῆ and dessert of an ordinary δεῖπνον, and then asks if he may set the exceptional δόρπον as well.

54. The progress of the new-comer's influence is indicated by the tenses, imperfects 48, perfect 54, aorist 57, present 58. The passage is applied to literary plagiarism by Agathias Anth. Pal. iv 3. 21.

55. πύελος, generally a bath-tub, was suggested here by the actor's pronunciation of Πύλῳ, as a comic substitute for μάκτρα: so Pollux vii 168 says Eupolis (fr. 136) used μάκτρα for πύελος. The rare perfect of μάττω suggests μάχομαι. The distinction μᾶζαν μάττειν of barley, ἄρτον πέττειν or ὀπτᾶν of wheaten, bread is absolute: there is additional point here as the Spartans never used wheaten bread.

57. It would be interesting to know whether Aristophanes had reasons for writing ὑπ᾽ ἐμοῦ and not ἐμοῦ: it may be that ὑπ᾽ ἐμοῦ gives more emphasis (see Marchant Class. Rev. v 260).

59. θεραπεύειν of more honest service)(κολακεύειν and the other words in 48.

δειπνοῦντος ἑστὼς ἀποσοβεῖ τοὺς ῥήτορας. 60
ᾄδει δὲ χρησμούς· ὁ δὲ γέρων σιβυλλιᾷ.
ὁ δ' αὐτὸν ὡς ὁρᾷ μεμακκοακότα,
τέχνην πεπόηται. τοὺς γὰρ ἔνδον ἄντικρυς

It is the regular word of *courting* politically, Thuc. iii 11. 5 ἀπὸ θεραπείας τοῦ τε κοινοῦ αὐτῶν καὶ τῶν ἀεὶ προεστώτων.

59—60. βυρσίνην for μυρσίνην (cf. 59) a myrtle-twig used as a fly-flap or μυιοσόβη: *Vesp.* 597 Κλέων ἡμᾶς φυλάττει διὰ χειρὸς ἔχων καὶ τὰς μυίας ἀπαμύνει: cf. Menander 503 Πέρσαι δ' ἔχοντες μυιοσόβας ἑστήκεσαν, Mart. iii 82. 12 *fugatque muscas myrtea puer virga*. There is no need to see a reference to the wreath, possibly of myrtle, which Cleon wears in the play (cf. on 1227).

61. Parts of this play are a good commentary on the passages of Thucydides (ii 8. 2, 21. 2), which inform us of the extraordinary demand for oracles at the beginning of the war. The demand was still strong: and Cleon may have helped in the supply. The story that he prosecuted Anaxagoras for impiety has the respectable authority of the Alexandrian Sotion (Diog. Laert. ii 12). These oracles were no doubt sometimes forged, Ameipsias 10 ποιοῦντες χρησμοὺς αὐτοὶ διδόασ' ᾄδειν Διοπείθῃ τῷ παραμαινομένῳ. χρησμοὶ are regularly spoken of as sung or chanted metrically, ἐν ἔπεσι καὶ μέτροις ἄλλοις (Plut. *Pyth. orac.* 17. 402 B). Plutarch's tract says that even in old times the metre was sometimes the work of ποιητικοὶ ἄνδρες outside (25. 407 B); it was often bad (5. 396 C), and ultimately the priestess spoke plain prose (7. 397 D). On the distinction between χρησμοὶ and λόγια see on 120.

In the scholia and Suidas the two explanations χρησμῶν ἐρᾷ καὶ ἐπιθυμεῖ· ἢ παραληρεῖ among others are given for σιβυλλιᾷ. The terminations -άω, -ιάω, imply nearly always either a morbid state (ποδαγράω μελαγχολάω ὑοσκυαμάω &c.) or a desire, generally morbid (φονάω μαθητιάω σοφιστιάω θανατάω &c.). Rutherford *New Phryn.* 153 translates 'play the old woman': and the phrase is said to have become proverbial ἐπὶ τῶν παραγεγηρακότων (Macar. 7. 60).

The Sibyl is first mentioned by Heraclitus, *fr.* 12 Byw.: in Attic first here, then *Pax* 1095, 1116. The word is probably foreign: the old etymology σιός

βουλή (= θεοβούλη), still held by Baunack *Stud.* i 64, is nonsense; and though the Romans may have connected it with Italian cognates of σοφός (Max Müller *Lectures* i 109, Postgate *Amer. Journ. Phil.* iii 333), there is as little to be said for that explanation as for the belief that the Sibyl was indigenous at Cumae, or for the derivation of Sylla from Sibylla (Macrob. i 17. 27). Ramsay's identification with Sipylus (*Journ. Hell. Stud.* iii 59) suits the certain origin of Sibyls on the west coast of Asia Minor. Heracl. Pont. first speaks of more than one Sibyl.

Probably the Sibyl found scant honour in Athens: the misogyny of Attic feeling would dislike a female rival to poets and seers (*Pax* 1094—5, Plut. *mul. virt.* 243 B), and the termination -υλλα was barely respectable, see on 224.

62. As σιβυλλιάω from Σίβυλλα, so μακκοάω from Μακκώ, a figure of stupidity like the Maccus of Italian farces. The perfect seems to be unique in such verbs (Rutherford *New Phryn.* 154).

63. τέχνην ποιεῖσθαι might simply be a variation for τεχνάζει, by the use of ποιεῖσθαι with a noun so familiar in Thucydides: but the occurrence of the phrase with τὸ πρᾶγμα and the like (as in Demosth. *Pantaen.* 53, Hippocr. *de arte* 1 εἰσίν τινες οἳ τέχνην πεποίηνται τὸ τὰς τέχνας αἰσχροεπεῖν, Lucian *Peregr.* 18 τέχνην τὸ λοιδορεῖσθαι πεποιημένος) shows that it means "make a system," "reduce to rules," like συστήσασθαι τέχνην Plato *Rep.* vi 493 B. Probably τέχνη had already got the meaning of 'set of rules,' 'manual': Ben Jonson's 'the grammar of cheating I had made.' γὰρ is the idiomatic use 'that is,' to explain the τέχνην. As ἔνδον means οἴκοι, οἱ ἔνδον means οἰκέται, and was probably a common phrase among slaves, though it seems to be rare in literature. ἄντικρυς may be used as an adjective, ἄντικρυς δουλεία 'downright slavery,' Thucyd. i 122—4: so there is often a slight difficulty as to whether it should go with the verb or the noun, as in two cases in Thucyd. viii 92. 11.

ψευδῆ διαβάλλει· κᾆτα μαστιγούμεθα
ἡμεῖς· Παφλαγὼν δὲ περιθέων τοὺς οἰκέτας 65
αἰτεῖ, ταράττει, δωροδοκεῖ, λέγων τάδε·
ὁρᾶτε τὸν Ὕλαν δι' ἐμὲ μαστιγούμενον;
εἰ μή μ' ἀναπείσετ', ἀποθανεῖσθε τήμερον.
ἡμεῖς δὲ δίδομεν· εἰ δὲ μή, πατούμενοι
ὑπὸ τοῦ γέροντος ὀκταπλάσια χέζομεν. 70
νῦν οὖν ἀνύσαντε φροντίσωμεν, ὦγαθέ,
ποίαν ὁδὸν νὼ τρεπτέον καὶ πρὸς τίνα.
ΟΙ. Β. κράτιστ' ἐκείνην τὴν μόλωμεν, ὦγαθέ.
ΟΙ. Α. ἀλλ' οὐχ οἷόν τε τὸν Παφλαγόν' οὐδὲν λαθεῖν·
ἐφορᾷ γὰρ αὐτὸς πάντ'. ἔχει γὰρ τὸ σκέλος 75

66. τάδε MSS. ταδί edd. vulg. **68.** ἀναπείσητ' all MSS. except C (and schol.):
but this is exactly a case where εἰ with the fut. ind. is idiomatic in Gildersleeve's
"minatory and monitory" sense. For εἰ with subj. see on 698. **72.** R gives
this line to Nicias, and assigns the speakers wrongly down to 82. νὼ vulg. νῶι
R, νῷν Pierson on Moeris p. 265, "certa loquendi consuetudo requirit νῷν" Cobet
in *Mnemos.* n.s. ii 415, but see expl. note. Dual forms, extinct in spoken
Greek, were a subject of debate to grammarians, even of Alexandrine times: Cobet
Misc. Crit. 250— holds νῶϊ and νῷ (the latter Attic) as the only correct forms for
nom. dual of ἐγώ, and Dion. Thrax mentions νῶϊ only: but νὼ has the support of
critics ancient and modern (Aristarchus, Apoll. Dysc. *de pronom.* 109 B—, Herodian
ii 218 Lentz, Schanz Plato vol. vii p. xi, Kühner-Blass i § 166. 5), and of comparative
philologers (G. Meyer *Gr. Gram.* § 425, Brugmann *Vergl. Gram.* ii § 457).
73. ἦν R, but the article is idiomatic for quotation marks, as in 23, *Av.* 58. I
keep the μόλωμεν of MSS. here: though it may have been pronounced μολῶμεν as I
believe it was in 21—. **75.** οὗτος RM.

64. κᾆτα has the tone of indignation
that εἶτα and ἔπειτα very often have:
this is heightened by the emphatic ἡμεῖς
in 65: cf. the emphatic pronouns in 57,
58, 69.
66. ταράττει 'makes mischief,' a word
often used by Arist. of Cleon's conduct. On
δωροδοκεῖ a scholiast has the note δῶρα
λαμβάνει· τίθεται δὲ ἡ λέξις καὶ ἐπὶ τοῦ
διδόντος: the latter usage is of course late,
see Cobet *VL* 347.
67. Hylas, the Mysian Adonis, was
probably a name for a specially favourite
slave: Alcibiades may be meant here.
68. ἀναπείθω generally in a bad sense,
implying either hoodwinking (as *Nub.*
77, Aeschin. *Ctesiph.* 256), or bribery
(as here, *inf.* 473, *Vesp.* 101, Plat. *Rep.* ii
365 E). Innocent words were no doubt
often used with sinister meanings in such

transactions: so *appello* in such cases as
Cic. *Cluent.* 71, Liv. xxvi 38. 7.
69—70. Cf. *Lys.* 439.
72. It is well known that verbals in
-τέον can take acc. of the personal agent,
as if τρεπτέον were δεῖ τρέπεσθαι. No rule
can be laid down apparently as to when
this usage is preferred: sometimes two
datives are avoided by means of it as
Av. 1237 οἷς θυτέον αὐτούς, Xen. *Mem.*
iii 11. 2, Isocr. *Evag.* 7: but two datives
are allowed (see cases in Blaydes' note
on *Av.* l.c.), and sometimes we have two
accusatives owing to it, as here, Plato
Gorg. 507 D, Demosth. 2 *Olynth.* 13,
Plato *Rep.* iii 413 D—E, Aristot. *Oecon.*
i 6. 1344ᵃ 5. The tragic rhythm here
suggests that the usage was felt as something more serious than the dative: but
other instances hardly bear this out.

τὸ μὲν ἐν Πύλῳ, τὸ δ' ἕτερον ἐν τἠκκλησίᾳ.
τοσόνδε δ' αὐτοῦ βῆμα διαβεβηκότος
ὁ πρωκτός ἐστιν αὐτόχρημ' ἐν Χάοσι,
τὼ χεῖρ' ἐν Αἰτωλοῖς, ὁ νοῦς δ' ἐν Κλωπιδῶν.

ΟΙ. Β. κράτιστον οὖν νῷν ἀποθανεῖν. ΟΙ. Α. ἀλλὰ
σκόπει,   80
ὅπως ἂν ἀποθάνωμεν ἀνδρικώτατα.

ΟΙ. Β. πῶς δῆτα πῶς γένοιτ' ἂν ἀνδρικώτατα;
βέλτιστον ἡμῖν αἷμα ταύρειον πιεῖν.
ὁ Θεμιστοκλέους γὰρ θάνατος αἱρετώτερος.

75—76. Eupolis 290 ὦ καλλίστη
πόλι πασῶν ὅσας Κλέων ἐφορᾷ, from the
Χρυσοῦν γένος, produced probably in 423
or 422. 'He doth bestride the narrow
world like a Colossus': his foot-holds being
the ecclesia, which he controls, and the
military reputation he won at Sphacteria.

77. 'As he straddles with such a
stride'; διαβαίνω as *Vesp.* 688, Lucian
Anach. 23, εὖ διαβὰς *Il.* xii 458, διαβάσκει
of swaggering walk *Av.* 486: so διαβήτης
a compass, and διαβεβηκὼς in art criticism
of archaic statues)(συμβεβηκὼς Diod.
Sic. iv 76 (Δαίδαλος) πρῶτος ὀμματώσας
καὶ διαβεβηκότα τὰ σκέλη ποιήσας. βῆμα
in this sense is mostly poetical, of heroic
or monstrous vigour, Hom. *hymn. Herm.*
222 βήματα δ' οὔτ' ἀνδρὸς τάδε γίγνεται
οὔτε γυναικός...ὅστις τοῖα πέλωρα βιβᾷ,
Pind. *Pyth.* 3. 43, Eurip. *Tro.* 342: Plut.
de Alex. fort. 9. 331 B Alexander says
to his father πρόιθι φαιδρῶς ἵνα τῆς ἀρετῆς
κατὰ βῆμα μνημονεύῃς.

78. αὐτόχρημα, originally αὐτὸ χρῆμα
in acc. of respect, a rare word: used
specially to mark that there is a pun,
as here on Χάοσι, Alciphro iii 25. 2
on μεσοπόλιος, Lucian *Dem. enc.* 13.
ἐν Χάοσι (this seems the right accent,
Theognost. *Canon.* 167, Choerob. 289.
12): cf. *Ach.* 604, *Vesp.* 1493. This
Epirote people had joined the great
mixed force that the Ambraciots led
against Acarnania in 429. Demosthenes
had campaigned and schemed in those
parts with varying fortune: Chaonians
and Aetolians were familiar enough to
him. The Athenian public probably
knew of the Chaonians chiefly in puns:
but they had to be reckoned with in the

western policy; their land was opposite
Corcyra and the Corcyrean oligarchs got
aid from them against Attic interests.

79. For the pun on αἰτῶ cf. *Anth.
Pal.* v 63 'Αντιγόνη, Σικελὴ πάρος ἦσθά
μοι, ὡς δ' ἐγενήθης Αἰτωλή, κἀγὼ Μῆδος
(μὴ δούς) ἰδοὺ γέγονα. Eupolis 404 made
a joke against Cleon out of Γαληψὸς
(πέπαικται ἀπὸ τοῦ λαβεῖν).
Κλωπίδαι is said by a scholiast to
be a comic perversion, suggesting κλώψ,
of the deme Κρωπίδαι. The identification of this deme near Acharnae with
Κρωπεία mentioned by Thucyd. ii 19
is doubtful (Ross *Att. Demen*, Milchhöfer *Text zu Karten v. Att.* ii 39): and a
deme called Κλωπίδαι seems to be mentioned in *CIA* ii 788, iii 1111. 6, 1121. 65.

80—1. Zieliński (*Gliederung* p. 97)
sees a parody of Eurip. *Helena* 835—;
but there is no sufficient reason for
altering the traditional date of the Helena
(B.C. 412), and *Hipp.* 401 is almost as
near to our passage.
ὅπως ἂν with subj. in such clauses
occurs again 917, 925, *Ach.* 1059, *Nub.*
738: see Goodwin *Syntax* § 348, Ph.
Weber *Absichtssätze* 123, Rutherford on
Babrius 16. 2.
ἀνδρικὸς is a less serious word than
ἀνδρεῖος. It is never used in Epic,
Tragedy, Thucydides or the Orators (exc.
by Lysias in the phrase ἀνδρικὸς χορός).
Comedy and Plato used it often: Pollux
ii 20 ἀνδρείως, καὶ ἀνδρικῶς ὡς Πλάτων:
in *Polit.* 306 Ε, *Charm.* 160 D—E it is used
beside ἀνδρεῖος, and no doubt a contrast
is intended. The relation of γεννικὸς to
γενναῖος is the same, see on 457.

83—4. For the belief in the poisonous

ΟΙ. Α. μὰ Δί᾽ ἀλλ᾽ ἄκρατον οἶνον ἀγαθοῦ δαίμονος. 85
ἴσως γὰρ ἂν χρηστόν τι βουλευσαίμεθα.

ΟΙ. Β. ἰδού γ᾽ ἄκρατον. περὶ πότου γοῦν ἔστι σοι.
πῶς δ᾽ ἂν μεθύων χρηστόν τι βουλεύσαιτ᾽ ἀνήρ;

ΟΙ. Α. ἄληθες, οὗτος; κρουνοχυτρολήραιον εἶ.

87. ποτοῦ MSS. except Θ. οὖν R, γ᾽ οὖν corrected to γὰρ V.
89. -λήραιον MSS. -λήραιος Γ and Θ corr. Dindorf &c. κυνοκυθρολήρεον Suetonius in Miller's *Mélanges* p. 422.

---

nature of bull's blood see Herod. iii 15, Plin. *NH* xi 90 *taurorum sanguis celerrime coit atque durescit* (so far from Aristot. *part. anim.* ii 4. 651ᵃ4, *hist. anim.* iii 19. 520ᵇ26), *ideo pestifer potu maxime*, Nicand. *Alexiph.* 312—. An article by Roscher in *Neue Jahrb.* cxxvii 158—gives a full list of authorities: Prof. Ludwig of Leipzig suggested to him that the belief took its origin from cases of animals dying of splenic fever, when the blood would be poisonous. See also Adams on Paulus Aegineta ii p. 230, Bussemaker and Daremberg on Oribas i p. 645. Aelian *Nat. Anim.* xi 35 gives a case where it was prescribed by the god Serapis to cure haematemesis: and it was used as an ordeal for certain priestesses Pausan. vii 25. 8, Plin. *NH* xxviii 147: so the belief may have come from religious usage, "the danger lay in its sacred nature" (Robertson Smith *Rel. of Semites* i 361). Thucydides i 138 ignores the tale as regards Themistocles: and Symmachus on this passage denied it.

The line imitates Soph. *fr.* 185 ἐμοὶ δὲ λῷστον αἷμα ταύρειον πιεῖν, λῷστον being apparently avoided, though the tone here would excuse that tragic word, which in ordinary style was almost confined to the humorous ὦ λῷστε; it is doubtful in *Av.* 823, and we can feel the point it gives in Eurip. *Cycl.* 186 ἀνθρώπιον λῷστον, and Plato *Phaedo* 116 D. αἱρετώτερος is suggested by such a line as Aesch. *fr.* 395 ζόης πονηρᾶς θάνατος αἱρετώτερος. It has been altered to αἱρετώτατος by some: but the comparative is quoted by Athenaeus iii 122 A.

85. A little unmixed wine was tasted, with the words ἀγαθοῦ δαίμονος, immediately after dinner, like liqueurs now, Athen. ii 38 D. The phrase was made an excuse for drinking neat wine at other times, Theopompus com. 40—41, Xenarchus 2, though ἀγαθοδαιμονισταί Aristot.

Eth. Eud. iii 6. 1233ᵇ3 are those who do not go on with the symposium. The genitive is possessive, of the deity or hero honoured, so Pind. *Isthm.* 3. 81 αὔξομεν ἔμπυρα χαλκοαρᾶν ὀκτὼ θανόντων, Lucian *symp.* 16 προπίνω σοι Ἡρακλέους ἀρχηγέτου and Athenaeus xv ch. 47: hence came the gen. of the person whose health is drunk Antiphanes 81 τῆς σεμνῆς θεᾶς καὶ τοῦ γλυκυτάτου βασιλέως διμοιρίαν, Callim. *epigr.* 29, Theocr. 2. 151, 14. 19, *Anth. Pal.* v 136. 1, 137. 1, Athen. x 434 D, *CIG* 2448 D 22, Hor. *od.* iii 8. 13, 19. 9.

87. ἰδού *quotha* as inf. 344, 703, *Nub.* 872, *Pax* 198, ἰδού γε *Nub.* 149, 818 ἰδού γ᾽ ἰδού Δί᾽ Ὀλύμπιον, 1469, *Lys.* 441, *Thesm.* 206, *Eccl.* 93, 137. 'It's a question of drink with you, then!' περὶ τινος ἔστι τινι as Thucyd. iv 63. 2 οὐ περὶ τοῦ τιμωρήσασθαί τινα (sc. ἔσται ὑμῖν), where Shilleto quoted Lysias 12. 74 οὐ περὶ πολιτείας ὑμῖν ἔσται ἀλλὰ περὶ σωτηρίας, Demosth. *Timocr.* 5, *Androt.* 46: Madvig's MS. note here adds Plut. *adul. et amic.* 35. 73 B οὐκ ἔστι σοι περὶ παρωνυχίας ὁ λόγος. περὶ τι may also be used, as Isocr. *antid.* 2 ὡς ἔστι περὶ δικογραφίαν, *Euthym.* 13 ὥστε μὴ περὶ τοῦτ᾽ εἶναι Νικίᾳ, or πρός τι Demosth. *Cor.* 278 πρὸς τοὺς ἐναντίους ἔστι τῷ δήμῳ. γοῦν has its original meaning 'oh then,' here ironically as *Thesm.* 845, *Eccl.* 794: there is no reason *a priori* why it should not be used interrogatively, as γὰρ is so often, but that use of γοῦν is rare and doubtful, as in Eurip. *Hel.* 1227, Lucian *dial. meretr.* 5. 4.

Nicias' private life was simple and temperate, and he avoided banquets Plut. *Nic.* 5.

89. The ironical interrogative ἄληθες seems to be confined to poets, as Thomas Magister said: the cases outside Aristophanes are Soph. *OT* 350, *Antig.* 758, Eurip. *Cycl.* 241, *fr.* 878.

It is useless to alter this Rabelaisian

οἶνον σὺ τολμᾷς εἰς ἐπίνοιαν λοιδορεῖν;   90
οἴνου γὰρ εὕροις ἄν τι πρακτικώτερον;
ὁρᾷς; ὅταν πίνωσιν ἄνθρωποι, τότε
πλουτοῦσι, διαπράττουσι, νικῶσιν δίκας,
εὐδαιμονοῦσιν, ὠφελοῦσι τοὺς φίλους.
ἀλλ᾽ ἐξένεγκέ μοι ταχέως οἴνου χόα,   95
τὸν νοῦν ἵν᾽ ἄρδω καὶ λέγω τι δεξιόν.
ΟΙ. Β. οἴμοι, τί ποθ᾽ ἡμᾶς ἐργάσει τῷ σῷ πότῳ;

90. ἀπόνοιαν Sylb. on Etym. Mag. 618. 23.

invention for a 'teetotal twaddler' as given by MSS. It may have been suggested by grotesque heads at the Enneacrunos, cf. Thompson in *Journ. Phil.* v 183, Harrison and Verrall *Myth. and Mon.* 91. For κρουνὸς used of a copious style cf. *Ran.* 1005, Cratinus 186 δωδεκάκρουνον τὸ στόμα, Dion. Hal. *de adm.* vi 28, Philostr. *vit. soph.* i 24. 4.

90. After verbs of praise or blame εἴς τι is regular: Plato i *Alcib.* 111 A δικαίως ἐπαινοῦντ᾽ ἄν εἰς διδασκαλίαν, Athen. viii 343 E Δημοσθένης Φιλοκράτην εἰς ἀσέλγειαν καὶ ὀψοφαγίαν λοιδορεῖ, Plut. *Nicias* 2: πρὸς is found as a variation, Plato *Theaet.* 148 C πρὸς δρόμον ἐπαινῶν, Lucian *dial. mort.* 13. 5 ἐπαινῶν ἄρτι μὲν πρὸς τὸ κάλλος, ἄρτι δὲ ἐς τὰς πράξεις καὶ τὸν πλοῦτον. Sylburg's proposal of ἀπόνοιαν implies a misunderstanding of that word: he thought ἐπίνοιαν impossible as λοιδορεῖν εἰς is always followed by a word expressing a bad quality. This is probably true when the word expresses a quality: but ἐπίνοια does not mean 'inventiveness' in the abstract: it means 'invention,' 'a practical hit' (as also in Theophr. *de odor.* § 7 κατὰ τέχνην καὶ ἐπίνοιαν): so that the phrase is parallel to ἐς τὴν φιλίαν διαβάλλειν Thucyd. viii 88, cf. Xen. *Anab.* ii 6. 30, Eurip. *Andr.* 978. ἐπίνοια has always a practical bearing)(ἔννοια: in Lucian's *Zeuxis* ἐπίνοια is the painter's conception of the subject as he is going to paint it (so *pro imag.* 10), ἔννοιαι (ἐκεῖνα ἐνενόουν § 2) his reflections on the comparative value of conception and technique.

In literature Eubulus (Athen. ii 43 F)

and Demosthenes are among the few who took Nicias' view: cf. on 349.

91—4. The rhythm is mock-serious. διαπρακτικὸς does not occur : πρακτικὸς was used as the adjective of διαπράττω 'effective,' 'successful.' The middle διαπράττομαι is the regular form, probably owing to the well-known tendency of δια- verbs to that voice: the active is rare (*Plut.* 217, 378, Aesch. *Eum.* 953, [Xen.] *Pol. Ath.* 3. 3, *Symp.* 5. 9), never occurring in Thucyd., Plato, Aristotle, or the Orators. Amphis 33 says the wine-drinker δρᾷ τι καὶ νεανικὸν καὶ θερμὸν because he is not timid from too much thinking, but here the success throughout is apparently the imaginary triumph of vinous exaltation (the passage is so explained by Athenaeus xi 782 C, cf. Plato's etymology of οἶνος *Crat.* 406 C, and Athenaeus' quotations in ii 2), as in the fine fragment (27) of Bacchylides ap. Athen. ii 39 E. "Thus became Tom Toss-pot rich: thus went in the tailor's stitch. Thus did Bacchus conquer Inde; thus Philosophy, Melinde."

95. In liquid measure χοῦς was the *congius* of about six pints, but in common usage it does not seem to mean any exact amount (Dar. and Saglio s. v.): a σκύφος χοαῖος is emptied by one man Athen. iv 129 E, cf. x 412 E, 326 C, 437 B: Dionysus Χοοπότης was honoured by Themistocles.

96. ἄρδω of benign and genial moisture: so Xen. *Symp.* 2. 24 ὁ οἶνος ἄρδων τὰς ψυχάς, Plut. *sept. sap.* 13. 156 D οὐδὲν ἔργον ἐστὶ κύλικος, ἀλλ᾽ αἱ Μοῦσαι, ἐγείρουσι καὶ κατάρδουσι. No doubt some held a physiological theory opposite to Heraclitus' αὔη ψυχὴ σοφωτάτη *fr.* 72—4.

ΟΙ. Α. ἀγάθ'· ἀλλ' ἔνεγκ'· ἐγὼ δὲ κατακλινήσομαι.
ἢν γὰρ μεθυσθῶ, πάντα ταυτὶ καταπάσω
βουλευματίων καὶ γνωμιδίων καὶ νοιδίων.　　100
ΟΙ. Β. ὡς εὐτυχῶς ὅτι οὐκ ἐλήφθην ἔνδοθεν
κλέπτων τὸν οἶνον.　ΟΙ. Α. εἰπέ μοι, Παφλαγὼν τί δρᾷ;
ΟΙ. Β. ἐπίπαστα λείξας δημιόπραθ' ὁ βάσκανος
ῥέγκει μεθύων ἐν ταῖσι βύρσαις ὕπτιος.

101. εὐτύχησ' Cobet (after Reiske), condemning εὐτυχῶς as a solecism, and quoting Plato *Hipp. ma.* 285 E ναὶ μὰ Δία εὐτύχηκάς γε ὅτι οἱ Λακεδαιμόνιοι οὐ χαίρουσιν.

98. ἀγαθά, or the like, was a colloquial retort in such cases: it is implied in *Pax* 363, cf. Herod. iv 95.

ἔνεγκε following ἐξένεγκε: it was idiomatic in such repetitions to drop the preposition: *inf.* 366, Andoc. *myst.* 4 ἔξεστι μὲν...ἔστι δὲ..., Plato *Euthyphro* 14 A, *Phaedo* 104 D, *Theaet.* 178 A, Thucyd. iii 16. 1 διὰ κατάγνωσιν...ὅτι οὐκ ὀρθῶς ἐγνώκασιν. This usage is the Attic counterpart to the Epic epanalepsis of prepositions, where the verb is omitted.

99—100. πάντα ταυτὶ 'the whole place' on the stage, *Pax* 319, Cratinus 186 ἅπαντα ταῦτα κατακλύσει ποιήμασιν (from the Πυτίνη), Plato com. 24: πάντα ἐκεῖνα 'the whole place' off the stage, *Av.* 1158, *fr.* 460, Pherecrates 108. 1.

πάσσω and its compounds might naturally take a partitive genitive of the thing sprinkled as πάσσε δ' ἁλὸς θείοιο Hom. *Il.* ix 214: the construction here is a combination of that gen. with the acc. of the thing besprinkled: elsewhere the instrumental dat. is found instead. Words like νοίδιον lose the diaeresis entirely and are always trisyllabic, at least in Attic, as βοίδιον *Ach.* 1036: see Lobeck Phryn. p. 87. νοῦς is to νοΐδια as δᾶς to δᾴδια, cf. on 921. The want of caesura is probably intentional, to be emphasized by the delivery of the line, cf. *inf.* 165, *Ach.* 31, *Pax* 291, so in enumeration as *Vesp.* 659.

103—4. Xen. *Hell.* iii 2. 28 tells of a demagogue at Elis drunk and asleep in time of revolution. ἐπίπαστα were small salt relishes with wine Pherecrates 130, cf. Plut. *quaest. conv.* iv 3. 669 B: such

relishes were often a mixture of salt and sweet flavours Athen. ix 366 B ἅλας ἡδυσμένους ὀρῶ, Varro ap. Charisius 106. 18 Keil, Plin. *NH* xxxi 41. πάσσω is the natural word of sprinkling salt, and λείχω is idiomatic of eating it ἅλα λείχειν Diog. Laert. vi 2. 57, Arist. *Hist. anim.* vi 37. 580ᵇ31: so *salem lingo, delingo.*

Confiscation of goods followed conviction on several charges in Attic law: exile, except in case of ostracism, was regularly attended by confiscation. A tithe of the estate was due to Athena: but the bulk fell to the people and to the accuser, who got a third as his share generally. The δημιόπρατα appear with some comic emphasis in the list of state-income *Vesp.* 659. The sales were managed by the πωληταί, who rendered accounts of them, published in permanent form (*CIA* i 274—281 are parts of such an account of about 414 B.C.): these documents were collected in the book called Δημιόπρατα, so much used by Pollux in book x. Conservatives attacked the system as encouraging συκοφαντία and unjust condemnations (see on 1359): Aristot. *Pol.* vii (vi) 5. 1320ᵃ4 puts it first among the dangers of democracy.

Among the Greeks, so constantly afraid of the evil eye, βάσκανος easily became a common word of abuse: it was specially associated with the malignity of the συκοφάντης, Dem. *Cor.* 242 πονηρὸν ὁ συκοφάντης ἀεὶ καὶ πανταχόθεν βάσκανον καὶ φιλαίτιον, cf. 317, 189 ὁ δὲ (συκοφάντης)... τοῦτο βασκαίνει, Strabo xiv 22 Τίμαιον βάσκανον ὄντα καὶ συκοφάντην, schol. on

ΟΙ. Α. ἴθι νυν, ἄκρατον ἐγκάναξόν μοι πολὺν   105
σπονδήν.   ΟΙ. Β. λαβὲ δὴ καὶ σπεῖσον ἀγαθοῦ
δαίμονος.

ΟΙ. Α. ἕλχ᾽ ἕλκε τὴν τοῦ δαίμονος τοῦ Πραμνίου.
ὦ δαῖμον ἀγαθέ, σὸν τὸ βούλευμ᾽, οὐκ ἐμόν.

ΟΙ. Β. εἴπ᾽, ἀντιβολῶ, τί ἔστι;   ΟΙ. Α. τοὺς χρησμοὺς ταχὺ
κλέψας ἔνεγκε τοῦ Παφλαγόνος ἔνδοθεν,   110
ἕως καθεύδει.   ΟΙ. Β. ταῦτ᾽. ἀτὰρ τοῦ δαίμονος
δέδοιχ᾽ ὅπως μὴ τεύξομαι κακοδαίμονος.

Plato ii *Alcib.* 147 C ὁ βάσκανος ὑπὸ φθόνου συκοφαντεῖ καὶ κατηγορεῖ. In acting, the word would probably be pointed by a gesture of aversion.

105—6. ἐγκάναξον· οἱ δὲ ἐπὶ θορύβου τάττουσι τοῦτο παρὰ τὴν καναχὴν schol. : it seems to be confined to the aorist, where the ξ sound suits the sense: so ἀφύσσω is almost confined to the more onomatopoetic parts with σσ, cf. Ion ap. Athen. xi 495 B. σπονδὴν again a jocular excuse as 85 : libations were generally of unmixed wine, except to Hermes apparently, and of course always so in the case of the ἀγαθὸς δαίμων.

107. Demosthenes' reply to Nicias' hope for due piety and temperance in the libation is a call to himself to drink the cup. ἕλκω like σπάω, *duco, traho*, is used of drinking at great draughts, especially of unmixed wine, as Eur. *Cycl.* 417 ἔσπασεν ἄμυστιν ἑλκύσας, Parmeno ap. Athen. v 221 A, Alexis 5 μεστὴν ἀκράτου θηρίκλειον ἔσπασεν, Athen. xi 483 E ἀκρατοκώθωνας καλοῦσι τοὺς πλέονα ἄκρατον σπῶντας, cf. xiv 613 A, *Anth. Pal.* v 12. 2 ἄκρατον ἕλκωμεν: Eur. *Ion* 1200 of birds μέθυ εἷλκον εὐπτέρους ἐς αὐχένας. The τοῦ Πραμνίου is παρὰ προσδοκίαν: the rhythm marks this. Pramnian is the only variety of wine mentioned in Homer except Ismarian; the former is used only to mix in a κυκεών *Il.* xi 639, *Od.* x 235. It was strong and astringent (*fr.* 301, Hippocrates *gynaec.* i, ii p. 676 Kühn ἐπιπίνων οἶνον οἰνώδεα Πράμνιον): certain styles of poetry are compared to it *fr.* 563, Phrynichus 65 ἦν (Σοφοκλῆς) οὐ γλύξις, οὐδ᾽ ὑπόχυτος, ἀλλὰ Πράμνιος. The

name was a puzzle : the wine was assigned to various places along the Asiatic coasts from Lesbos to Caria, and several explanations of the word as a common noun were proposed (as from παραμόνιος, πραΰνων μένος ἐπεὶ οἱ πιόντες προσηνεῖς &c.) Athenaeus i 30 B—, Apostolius xiv 74. Hehn *Culturpflanzen*[4] 466 thinks it may be akin to the Thracian word παραβίας for a drink made from millet, Athen. x 447 D.

A daemon Acratus was worshipped in Attica Paus. i 2. 5, Harrison and Verrall *Myth. and Mon.* 12.

111—12. ταῦτα of undertaking to carry out an order or request, ἰδού of carrying it out on the spot: so ταῦτ᾽ ὦ δέσποτα *Vesp.* 142, *Pax* 275, ταῦτα δὴ *Ach.* 815, sometimes in full δράσω ταῦτα *Lys.* 1030, ταῦτα ποιήσω *Ran.* 1515: δράσω τάδε *Av.* 864, Eur. *Med.* 184, is rather more independent, 'I'll do my part.' ἀτὰρ marks a strong contrast, like the German *sondern*, which is its etymological equivalent (sn̥tár). ὅπως μὴ after verbs of fearing is probably due to a confusion between *caution* and *purpose*: see Goodwin *Syntax* § 370, Ph. Weber *Absichtssätze* 114.

κακοδαίμονος conveys a plaintive rebuke to Demosthenes for his rather daring variation in 107 of the usual phrase ἀγαθοῦ δαίμονος. κακοδαιμονισταὶ suggest a Κακοδαίμων, a profane counterpart to the Ἀγαθοδαίμων as he was called later: the club, mentioned by Lysias (see on 2), may well have been in existence at this time.

Of course Nicias *exit* here, returning almost immediately. Meanwhile

ΟΙ. Α. φέρε νυν ἐγὼ 'μαυτῷ προσαγάγω τὸν χόα,
τὸν νοῦν ἵν' ἄρδω καὶ λέγω τι δεξιόν.

ΟΙ. Β. ὡς μεγάλ' ὁ Παφλαγὼν πέρδεται καὶ ῥέγκε-
ται,   115
ὥστ' ἔλαθον αὐτὸν τὸν ἱερὸν χρησμὸν λαβών,
ὅνπερ μάλιστ' ἐφύλαττεν. ΟΙ. Α. ὦ σοφώτατε,
φέρ' αὐτόν, ἵν' ἀναγνῶ· σὺ δ' ἔγχεον πιεῖν
ἀνύσας τι. φέρ' ἴδω τί ἄρ' ἔνεστιν αὐτόθι.
ὦ λόγια. δός μοι δὸς τὸ ποτήριον ταχύ. 120

ΟΙ. Β. ἰδού· τί φησιν ὁ χρησμός; ΟΙ. Α. ἑτέραν ἔγχεον.

ΟΙ. Β. ἐν τοῖς λογίοις ἔνεστιν ἑτέραν ἔγχεον;

ΟΙ. Α. ὦ Βάκι. ΟΙ. Β. τί ἔστι; ΟΙ. Α. δὸς τὸ
ποτήριον ταχύ.

Demosthenes drinks from the pitcher,
though he more decently uses a cup
when Nicias returns.

115. ῥέγκεται· ὁμοιοκατάληκτον εἶπε·
οὐ γάρ ἐστι δόκιμον οὕτω λέγειν schol.
The middle occurs again *Anth. Pal.* xi
343. 4 in the non-Attic form ῥεγχόμενον,
but here it is merely a comic Datismus
like χαίρομαι *Pax* 291, and probably ὅταν
πεινώμεθ' ἢ διψώμεθα Hermippus 25. No
doubt the future was ῥέγξομαι by Rutherford's rule, but it is not quoted.

117. ὦ σοφώτατε, a half-burlesque
compliment, not used in Tragedy, but
common in Comedy as *Av.* 362, 1271,
ὦ σοφώτατοι *Nub.* 575, Menander 11,
Athen. viii 337 B, ix 366 B. σοφός might
be used of skill in any craft: καὶ τοὺς
κλέπτας σοφοὺς ἔλεγον schol.

120. Distinctions have been drawn
between λόγια and χρησμοί which do
not hold: Suidas and the scholiast on
Thucyd. ii 8. 2 say λόγια are in prose,
χρησμοί in verse, but this play ignores
that distinction, and Porphyry's collection
of λόγια was mainly metrical: Eustathius'
opinion that λόγια was Attic, answering
to the Ionic πρόφαντα, is adopted by
Bouché-Leclercq (*Hist. de Divination*
ii 230), but λόγια occurs often in Herodotus. Wilamowitz (*Hermes* xiii 352)
ought not to reject Eurip. *Heracl.* 405
on the ground that λόγια is not tragic.
The distinction seems to be that λόγια ap-

plies to oracular utterances of gods or seers
preserved and circulated orally, or more
commonly in writing, while χρησμὸς is
the general word. In Plut. *Theseus* 26
the λόγιον πυθόχρηστον had been given
some time previously; *Fabius* 4 and *Marcellus* 3 λόγια are the Sibylline books at
Rome; *Lysander* 22 Diopithes brings up
the λόγιον about a lame King of Sparta;
λόγια are expressly contrasted with χρησμὸς (a response just given) in *Pelop.* 20,
Nicias 13: and in *defect. orac.* 5. 412
CD a χρησμὸς becomes a λόγιον after a
time. So Herod. viii 141 οἱ Λακεδαιμόνιοι ἀναμνησθέντες τῶν λογίων, iv 178,
v 90, viii 60, Thucyd. ii 8. 2. Sometimes
the words are used as synonyms, *inf.*
194—5 &c.: but I know of no case where
λόγιον means an oracle just delivered,
except perhaps Lucian *Jup. trag.* 31.

121. ἰδού, the common phrase of immediate compliance, never takes γε as the
other usage (61) does. ἑτέραν sc. κύλικα or
φιάλην, ἃ δ' ἑτέρα τὰν ἑτέραν κύλιξ ὠθήτω
Alcaeus 41: ellipse of these nouns is
found with other adjectives, as παῖ, τὴν
μεγάλην δός Alexis 111. 1, ἄκρατον ἐβόων
τὴν μεγάλην Menander 510, πολλὰς πίνων
Theognis 492, φιλοτησία &c.

122. ἔνεστι to introduce a quotation
from an oracle as *Av.* 974, 976, or an
official document as Thucyd. viii 43. 3,
Demosth. *Timocr.* 151.

123. Bacis is often mentioned along

ΟΙ. Β. πολλῷ γ᾽ ὁ Βάκις ἐχρῆτο τῷ ποτηρίῳ.

ΟΙ. Α. ὦ μιαρὲ Παφλαγών, ταῦτ᾽ ἄρ᾽ ἐφυλάττου
πάλαι,   125

τὸν περὶ σεαυτοῦ χρησμὸν ὀρρωδῶν; ΟΙ. Β. τιή;

ΟΙ. Α. ἐνταῦθ᾽ ἔνεστιν, αὐτὸς ὡς ἀπόλλυται.

ΟΙ. Β. καὶ πῶς; ΟΙ. Α. ὅπως; ὁ χρησμὸς ἄντικρυς
λέγει

ὡς πρῶτα μὲν στυππειοπώλης γίγνεται,

with the Sibyl, as Plato *Theages* 124 D : and as with Sibyls so we hear in later times of more than one Bacis Aristot. *problem.* xxx 1. 954ᵃ36, schol. on *Pax* 1071 Βάκιδες δὲ τρεῖς, ὧν πρεσβύτατος ἐξ Ἐλεῶνος τῆς Βοιωτίας, ὁ δὲ δεύτερος Ἀττικός, τρίτος δὲ ὁ Ἀρκὰς ἐκ πόλεως Καφύης ὃς καὶ Κύδας ἐκαλεῖτο καὶ Ἀλήτης : the word being probably not a proper name. Plutarch *Pyth. orac.* 10. 398 F— says Sibyls and Bacides gave, not oracles in view of special consultations, but general prophecies οἷς πλανωμένοις ἀπήντησε πολλάκις ἢ τύχη καὶ συνέπεσεν αὐτομάτως: Cicero *Divin.* i 34 *duo genera divinationum esse dixerunt,…unum quod particeps esset artis, alterum quod arte careret,* and of the second kind prophesying *concitatione quadam animi aut soluto liberoque motu* the instances he gives are *Bacis Boeotius Epimenides Cres Sibylla Erythraea.* He is set up as a male rival to the Sibyl seriously by Plutarch, *mul. virt.* 243 B ἐὰν τὰ Σαπφοῦς μέλη τοῖς Ἀνακρέοντος ἢ τὰ Σιβύλλης λόγια τοῖς Βάκιδος ἀντιπαραβάλλωμεν, and comically by Lucian, *Peregrinus* 30. He was νυμφόληπτος *Pax* 1070, Pausan. x 12. 11, like Merlin and Thomas of Ercildoune, whom he resembles also in his importance during great national struggles. [Goethe's curious experiments, the *Weissagungen des Bakis,* are very general: but some have been interpreted as political.] His oracles attained great repute during the Persian Wars, and Herodotus quotes them with special respect viii 20, 77, ix 43. Pisistratus was nicknamed Bacis schol. on *Pax* 1071: and very possibly a collection of Bacis-oracles was made by Onomacritus at Pisistratus' command, with a view to counterbalance the aristocratic and Spartan tendency of Delphi: Pausanias iv 27. 4 quotes two such oracles of

his which encouraged Epaminondas against Sparta. Whether for this reason or not, he was evidently popular in Athens during the Peloponnesian War *inf.* 1003, *Pax* 1070, *Av.* 962.

124. The article is again for quotation-marks. There is probably no more ground for the connexion of Βάκις with Βάκχος (Bergk *Griech. Lit.* i 342) than for the oft-repeated derivation from βάζω.

125. 'This is why you were so cautious': so Herod. vii 130 Xerxes said σοφοὶ ἄνδρες οἱ Θεσσαλεῖς· ταῦτ᾽ ἄρα πρὸ πολλοῦ ἐφυλάξαντο, φυλάττομαι being absolute (Shilleto on Dem. *FL* 287). Parts of φυλάσσω were very common in oracles, see on 1039. This 'Aristophanic' use of ταῦτ᾽ ἄρα *Ach.* 90, *Nub.* 319, 335, 394, *Pax* 414, 617, *Thesm.* 168 is found also in Xenoph. *Cyrop.* i 4. 27, *Symp.* 4. 28: the less idiomatic διὰ ταῦτ᾽ ἄρα *Av.* 486, Plato *Protag.* 341 C, διὰ τοῦτ᾽ ἄρα *Thesm.* 166.

127. The tone is tragic: for the vivid present in predictions of downfall cf. Eupolis 182 (from the Maricas) ἄκουε νῦν Πείσανδρος ὡς ἀπόλλυται, Aesch. *Prom.* 171, 767, 948 αὐδᾶν πρὸς ὧν ἐκεῖνος ἐκπίπτει κράτους. There is some awe in the αὐτός, cf. *inf.* 151, as in the οὗτος ἀνὴρ of *Il.* xviii 257, the *ille* of Plaut. *Pseud.* 921, repeated with ridicule 924—5, and the *ille* (Clodius) so common in Cic. *ad Att.* ii—iv.

128. καὶ πῶς with the shade of objection or incredulity which is never absent from καὶ with an interrogative word following, except sometimes when there is no change of speakers.

129. πρῶτα μὲν: the new era dates from Pericles' death, after which the political leaders came from a lower social stratum: the well-known fragment (117)

ὃς πρῶτος ἕξει τῆς πόλεως τὰ πράγματα.   130

ΟΙ. Β. εἰς οὑτοσὶ πώλης.   τί τοὐντεῦθεν; λέγε.

ΟΙ. Α. μετὰ τοῦτον αὖθις προβατοπώλης δεύτερος.

---

of Eupolis' Δῆμος laments this falling off. Eucrates is the στυππειοπώλης, for which στύππαξ in fr. 540 is a contemptuous variation: other nicknames for him were ὀνοστύππαξ (Hesychius), Μελιτεὺς κάπρος, ἄρκτος, σῦς fr. 193. The name was a common one, and we cannot be sure that our Eucrates is the same as the Eucrates who was strategus in B.C. 432/1 (CIA iv 179 a—d, Beloch Ath. Pol. 329): nor can he be identified with the father of Diodotus (Thucyd. iii 41), or the brother of Nicias (Andoc. Myst. 47), or the general of dubious loyalty in Lys. 102, Lysias 18. 4. Gilbert Inn. Geschichte 126 thinks that our Eucrates was strategus in the plague-year 430/29, and fell into obscurity when Pericles regained popularity: but this is without proof: we know practically nothing of his short-lived influence (inf. 254). τὰ στυππεῖα, τουτέστι καννάβινα ἢ λινᾶ (schol.), must have been an important article of commerce, used not only in ship-building, but for clothes, as we see from χιτὼν στύππινος, χιτωνίον στύππινον, in the inventories CIA ii 675 &c.; Diocletian's edict (26. 1 Mommsen) fixes the price of λίνον τὸ καλούμενον στούπιον at 24, 20 or 16 denarii per pound according to quality.

130. Aristophanes always keeps the distinction between ἕξω and σχήσω, the continuous and momentary futures of ἔχω, the one verb where the Greeks developed the distinct futures (Kühner-Blass Griech. Gramm. § 229. 3). He uses σχήσω only three times, in the sense of check, Lys. 284, 380 or put in (check a ship voyage) Ran. 188, σχήσομαι only once Av. 1335 οὔ τοι μὰ τὰς κερχνῇδας ἔτι σοῦ σχήσομαι, where ἕξομαι would mean exactly the opposite. The distinction is kept in good Greek. Apparent exceptions, as far as I have noticed, are as follows: Homer has ἕξω for keep in check Il. xiii 51 (where Aristoph. Byz. read σχήσουσιν) and xx 27, using σχήσω in the same sense xi 820, xiii 151, xiv 100: Pindar has σχήσω in the proper sense fr. 256 Böckh σχήσει τὸ πεπρωμένον οὐ πῦρ, but again where ἕξω might be expected Pyth. 9. 116 διακρῖναι ἄντινα σχήσοι τις ἡρώων: Sophocles has εὖ σχήσει Aj. 684: Eurip.

Hel. 30 ὡς ἐμὸν σχήσων λέχος, Cycl. 697 τυφλὴν ὄψιν σχήσειν, Bacch. 1337 νόστον ἄθλιον σχήσουσι, and perhaps Med. 862 (but there ἄδακρυν μοῖραν σχήσεις φόνῳ seems right, end their happy life by murder): Thucydides has τὴν ἅπασαν δύναμιν τῆς Σικελίας σχήσουσι vi 6. 2, and πλέον σχήσειν iv 59. 2, vii 36. 2, viii 99, so οὐκ ἔλασσον σχήσειν vii 36. 4, πλεῖστον σχήσειν vii 36. 5. But in all these cases the writer felt a difference between σχήσω shall get, and ἕξω shall have, though the most idiomatic sense of σχήσειν is to check. The distinction is well seen in Xen. Anab. iii 5. 11 πᾶς ἀσκὸς δύο ἄνδρας ἕξει (will hold) τὸ μὴ καταδῦναι· ὥστε δὲ μὴ ὀλισθάνειν ἡ ὕλη καὶ ἡ γῆ σχήσει (will prevent). E. R. Schulze in Neue Jahrb. cxxvii 163— thinks the Orators made no distinction: he has been answered by Blass in Rhein. Mus. xlvii 285. σχήσειν Dem. FL 272 means check: ἡσυχίαν σχήσει i Olynth. 14 refers to Philip inactive even for a day, ἡσυχίαν ἕξει Euerg. 29 is of continued inaction: σχήσειν καλῶς i Olynth. 9 σχ. ἀσφαλῶς Cor. 45, mean get into a good, safe, state, for ἔσχε καλῶς can be used as well as εἶχε καλῶς. The distinction between ἕξομαι and σχήσομαι is very clear in all cases I have noticed. ἕξις and σχέσις were always recognised in medicine and philosophy as permanent and transitory states respectively. It is probable that a similar distinction was felt in the compounds also: we can see it in νομίσας αὐτὸν καθέξειν αὐτοῦ Thucyd. viii 100. 2, contrasted with νομίζοντες κατασχήσειν ῥαδίως τὰ πράγματα id. iv 2. 3. Cf. Aristot. Pol. Ath. 24. κατασχήσειν τὴν ἡγεμονίαν will gain (καθέξειν would mean retain); see on καθέξεις 838 and ἐφέξεις 915.

131. πώλης was not used separately except as comic, so monger in English (Shilleto on Thucyd. ii 60): the type of noun is really not Greek (Lobeck Paralip. 134).

132. The προβατοπώλης is Lysicles (a scholiast and Suidas give Callias as an alternative): he was strategus in 428/7, and perished that year in the Maeander valley, on a money-raising expedition, Thucyd. iii 19. Plutarch Pericles 24 quotes

ΟΙ. Β. δύο τώδε πώλα. καὶ τί τόνδε χρὴ παθεῖν;
ΟΙ. Α. κρατεῖν, ἕως ἕτερος ἀνὴρ βδελυρώτερος
αὐτοῦ γένοιτο· μετὰ δὲ ταῦτ᾽ ἀπόλλυται.   135
ἐπιγίγνεται γὰρ βυρσοπώλης ὁ Παφλαγών,
ἅρπαξ, κεκράκτης, Κυκλοβόρου φωνὴν ἔχων.
ΟΙ. Β. τὸν προβατοπώλην ἦν ἄρ᾽ ἀπολέσθαι χρεὼν

133. χρῆν Elmsley on Eurip. *Heracl.* 959 to suit γένοιτο in 135, but see expl. note on that line.

from Aeschines Socrat. the tale that after Pericles' death Aspasia lived with Lysicles and made him ἐξ ἀγεννοῦς καὶ ταπεινοῦ τὴν φύσιν ᾿Αθηναίων πρῶτον. I can see no reason to disbelieve this (see *inf.* 765), or to believe the conjectures on the subject made or adopted by E. Curtius, Müller-Strübing (*Aristoph.* 580—), Petersen (*de hist. gent. Att.* 111), Duncker (*Gesch. d. Alt.* n. f. ii 14), Beloch (*Att. Pol.* 29, *Griech. Gesch.* i 532).

133. It is very hard to say what difference an Athenian would feel between the οὑτοσί of 131 and the dual of ὅδε in 133. That ὅδε was more closely connected with the first person, οὗτος with the second, seems certain as a general rule, yet we find instances, such as *Av.* 637—8, where the case is reversed: and no doubt Latin lost ultimately by confining *iste* too closely to its connexion with the second person. Besides οὑτοσί is a step nearer ὅδε than οὗτος is, as Blass shows from the Orators in *Rhein. Mus.* xliv 2—)

134—5. The coarse word βδελυρός was used freely by Aeschines and Demosthenes: Plato has it once, in the mouth of Thrasymachus *Rep.* i 338 D. It was no doubt specially used by conservatives of the demagogues (so βδελύττομαι, Βδελυκλέων), as 193, 304 &c.: so Plutarch allows himself to use it of Cleon (*Nicias* 2, *Demetr.* 11) and of Clodius (*Pomp.* 46, *Caesar* 9).

The optative γένοιτο is excused by the fact that the oracle has fixed the man's fate in the past: so the optative is used in such clauses in citing laws *Ran.* 766 νόμος τις ἐστὶ κείμενος...αὐτὸν σίτησιν λαμβάνειν...ἕως ἀφίκοιτο τὴν τέχνην σοφώτερος, Demosth. *Androt.* 11, *Timocr.* 145: cf. Goodwin *Syntax* § 323.

137. κράζω in Attic was so much confined to the reduplicated forms that even in derivative nouns we find only κέκραγμα κεκραγμὸς κεκράκτης and the like. The words are specially applied to Cleon as an orator *inf.* 256 &c., *Vesp.* 596 κεκραξιδάμας, *Pax* 314 παφλάζων καὶ κεκραγώς: Aristot. *Pol. Ath.* 28 (Κλέων) πρῶτος ἐπὶ τοῦ βήματος ἀνέκραγε καὶ ἐλοιδορήσατο, Plut. *Nicias* 8.

Κυκλοβόρος: schol. ποταμὸς τῆς ᾿Αττικῆς χειμάρρους, ὑπὸ ᾿Αθηναίων χωσθείς. τὴν κακοφωνίαν οὖν τοῦ Κλέωνος εἴκασε τῷ ἤχῳ τοῦ ποταμοῦ. καὶ ἀλλαχοῦ

ᾤμην δ᾽ ἔγωγε τὸν Κυκλοβόρον κατιέναι
(*fr.* 539).

κυκλοβορεῖν is invented as a verb for Cleon's speaking *Ach.* 381, cf. *Vesp.* 1034. There seems to be no clue to the position of this stream except Pollux x 185, where Aristoph. *fr.* 275 is quoted showing that it was near the brick-works: it has been identified with the upper course of a stream flowing from Lycabettus to join the Cephissus under the name of Scirus (E. Curtius *Stadtgesch. von Athen* 18, 183, Milchhöfer *Text zu Karten v. Att.* ii 15): the identification is rejected by Wachsmuth *Stadt Athen* ii 274, but seems more likely than the opinion of Bursian (*Geogr. Griech.* i 257) and Wilamowitz (*Hermes* xvii 647) that the stream was near Marathon. Cf. Cratinus ᾿Ιλισὸς ἐν τῇ φάρυγι (*fr.* 186) and Pherecrates *fr.* 51 χαράδρα κατελήλυθεν.

138. 'It's fated then...' This seems to be the only case in Comedy where χρεών means *fated.* Aristoph. does not use the substantive verb with χρεών in its other sense of *right,* except perhaps in *Pax* 1029. It is not of course meant that Lysicles owed his death directly to Cleon.

ὑπὸ βυρσοπώλου; ΟΙ. Α. νὴ Δί'. ΟΙ. Β. οἴμοι
δείλαιος.
πόθεν οὖν ἂν ἔτι γένοιτο πώλης εἷς μόνος;   140
ΟΙ. Α. ἔτ' ἐστὶν εἷς, ὑπερφυᾶ τέχνην ἔχων.
ΟΙ. Β. εἴπ', ἀντιβολῶ, τίς ἐστιν; ΟΙ. Α. εἴπω;
ΟΙ. Β. νὴ Δία.
ΟΙ. Α. ἀλλαντοπώλης ἔσθ' ὁ τοῦτον ἐξελῶν.
ΟΙ. Β. ἀλλαντοπώλης; ὦ Πόσειδον τῆς τέχνης·
φέρε ποῦ τὸν ἄνδρα τοῦτον ἐξευρήσομεν;   145
ΟΙ. Α. ζητῶμεν αὐτόν. ΟΙ. Β. ἀλλ' ὁδὶ προσέρχεται
ὥσπερ κατὰ θεῖον εἰς ἀγοράν. ΟΙ. Α. ὦ μακάριε

143. ἐξολῶν all MSS. except R.
147. καταθείων R. κατὰ θεῖον other MSS. and scholia. θεόν Cobet VL 358.

---

189. Aristoph. has δειλᾶιος in the third foot *Nub.* 12, 709, 1504: in *Nub.* 552 (Eupolidean metre) the quantity is doubtful: in all other cases the word ends the line and is of course scanned δειλᾶιος, always with οἴμοι except *Plut.* 850. R here gives δείλαος: ι as the last element of a diphthong was naturally apt to be pronounced before another vowel as *y*, which was a vanishing sound in Greek. This of course explains -ᾶι -ōι in hiatus and perhaps in accentuation: it explains also the change from older forms like αἰεί 'Αθηναία &c. to the newer ἀεὶ 'Αθηνᾶ &c.: see Meisterhans § 14a for epigraphic evidence. So 'Αθήνᾶιος Pherecrates 34, Eupolis 35.
141. The rhythm is intentionally serious and without caesura for emphasis.
143. ἐξελῶν of course from ἐξελαύνω: ἐξαιρῶ=*debellare*, but ἐλῶ from αἱρῶ is fictitious. Cleon is supposed to use the word in *Vesp.* 1230.
ἀλλᾶς is a black-pudding, *Blutwurst*. It does not seem to have been a particularly poor or despised food Pherecrates 108. 8, Eubulus 15. 7, 63. 7. The father of Aeschines Socrat. was an ἀλλαντοποιός Diog. Laert. ii 7. 60.
144. I hope to show, on 551—, that there is reason to believe that Poseidon was looked on as a Tory god, in some opposition to Athena, who was certainly democratic. If this was so, it is not unreasonable to see some conservative

meaning in Nicias' selection of this appeal: so in *Ach.* 560 it is the more conservative half of the chorus who mark their feeling by νὴ τὸν Ποσειδῶ. Appeals to Athena are strangely few in Aristophanes, and those that do occur seem to have a political significance in most cases, see on 581.
145. 'Now where are we to find this hero of yours?' The future has a shade of helplessness or unwillingness: as in τί δράσομεν; Eurip. *Cycl.* 193, εἴπωμεν ἢ σιγῶμεν ἢ τί δράσομεν; *Ion* 758.
146—7. Nicias' objections are overcome by the hand of providence. Cobet's fine sense of idiom was possibly right in reading θεόν: even κατὰ τὸ θεῖον does not seem to occur: Plato *Legg.* iii 682 E ἀφίγμεθα ὥσπερ κατὰ θεόν, and cf. *ib.* 682 A, Plut. *de facie* 30. 944 F, Athen. vii 359 D, Apostolius 9. 37. κατὰ θεόν)(κατ' ἄρχοντα in dates, of the old lunar)(the later solar calendar (Reinach *épigr. grecque* 500). Dobree *Advers.* i 193 seems to hold that *to business* is always εἰς ἀγοράν, *to the agora* may be εἰς ἀγοράν or εἰς τὴν ἀγοράν: but it is hard to see what difference the article was felt to make; we have εἰς ἀγοράν of intending sellers here, *Thesm.* 457, *Ran.* 1350, Menander 962, but εἰς τὴν ἀγοράν *Ach.* 877, Lucian *Lexiph.* 22, of intending buyers εἰς τὴν ἀγοράν *Pax* 1010, Alexis 46. 6, Ephippus 21, Macho ap. Athen. 580 c, but εἰς ἀγοράν *Eccl.* 819, Strattis 44: Lysias

ἀλλαντοπῶλα, δεῦρο δεῦρ', ὦ φίλτατε,
ἀνάβαινε σωτὴρ τῇ πόλει καὶ νῷν φανείς.
ΑΛΛ. τί ἔστι; τί με καλεῖτε; ΟΙ. Α. δεῦρ' ἔλθ', ἵνα πύθῃ
ὡς εὐτυχὴς εἶ καὶ μεγάλως εὐδαιμονεῖς.   151
ΟΙ. Β. ἴθι δή, κάθελ' αὐτοῦ τοὐλεόν, καὶ τοῦ θεοῦ
τὸν χρησμὸν ἀναδίδαξον αὐτὸν ὡς ἔχει·
ἐγὼ δ' ἰὼν προσκέψομαι τὸν Παφλαγόνα.
ΟΙ. Α. ἄγε δὴ σὺ κατάθου πρῶτά τὰ σκεύη χαμαί·   155

Eratosth. 8 and 16 has εἰς ἀγοράν and εἰς
τὴν ἀγοράν in the same phrase.

151. Schol. ἵνα, φησίν, ἐκ τῆς παρόδου ἐπὶ τὸ λογεῖον ἀναβῇ. διὰ τί οὖν ἐκ
τῆς παρόδου; τοῦτο γὰρ οὐκ ἀναγκαῖον.
λεκτέον οὖν ὅτι ἀναβαίνειν ἐλέγετο τὸ ἐπὶ
τὸ λογεῖον εἰσιέναι. ὃ καὶ πρόσκειται.
λέγεται γὰρ καταβαίνειν τὸ ἀπαλλάττεσθαι
ἐντεῦθεν ἀπὸ τοῦ παλαιοῦ ἔθους...ὡς ἐν
θυμέλῃ δὲ τὸ ἀναβαίνειν. These interesting scholia are discussed by Haigh *Ath.
Theatre* 144, White *Harvard Studies* ii
165, Pickard *Amer. Journ. Phil.* xiv 289,
Capps *Trans. Amer. Phil. Ass.* xxii 65,
Christ in *Neue Jahrb.* cxlix 161: the
American scholars hold that ἀναβαίνω had
lost the sense *come up* and that therefore
no argument for a raised stage can be based
on the word. But it requires much faith
to believe that ἀναβαίνω does not mean
come up here, *Ach.* 732, *Vesp.* 1340, and
that καταβαίνω does not mean *come down*
in *Vesp.* 1514, *Eccl.* 1152. Surely the
scene represents Demos's house either as
on the Acropolis or on the Pnyx: the
agora is supposed to be in view as *Ach.*
21: and the sausage-man is seen with
his dresser and wares there below. I
cannot think that there was no means of
indicating this, that all was left to the
imagination of the audience. Dörpfeld
has shaken the old belief in a stone stage
for the actors: but I do not understand
that even he denies the existence of a
wooden one if required, Dörpfeld and
Reisch *Griech. Theater* 180, 344. See
on 169.

φανείς originally of deities, then of divine messengers or agents. In this sense
ἐπιφαίνω, ἐπιφάνεια, ἐπιφανής seem to be
Ionic and late, Timaeus Taur. ap. Athen.
ii 37 Ε Σωτῆρας ὑμᾶς ἐπιφανεῖς ἱδρυσόμεθα
ὡς αἰσίως ἡμῖν ἐπιφανέντας, Nymphodorus
ap. Athen. vi 266 D—Ε οἷς ἂν ἐπιφανῇ

οὗτοι θύουσιν αὐτῷ, Chamaeleon ap. Athen.
xi 461 B.
The new-comer is addressed in the
high style. μεγάλως is comic in rhythm,
but would be felt as a word of heroic
tone, cf. *inf.* 172, 782, 1162, *Nub.* 600.
It never occurs in good Attic prose. It is
found twice in Homer, *Il.* xvii 723, *Od.*
xvi 432, once in Hesiod, *Theog.* 429 ᾧ δ'
ἐθέλει (Ζεὺς) μεγάλως παραγίγνεται ἠδ'
ὀνίνησιν, often in Herodotus, thrice in
Tragic chorus (Aesch. *Pers.* 906, Eur.
Med. 183, *Tro.* 843). Xenophon uses it
of injuries and benefits, *Cyrop.* viii 2. 10,
Anab. iii 2. 22, *Ages.* 11. 10, *Hiero* 4. 5,
Rep. Lac. 4. 6 (Cobet *NL* 729). Lucian
quom. hist. scrib. 22 gives as a specimen
of poetic diction ἑλέλιξε μὲν ἡ μηχανή, τὸ
τεῖχος δὲ πεσὸν μεγάλως ἐδούπησε, where
the adverb as well as the verb is meant to
be inconsistent with ordinary prose style.

152—4. Nicias now shows some awe
before the new-comer: this is implied by
the αὐτοῦ...αὐτόν, cf. on 127: he confuses
the λόγια of Bacis with a Delphian
χρησμός. The word ἐλεόν for a cook's
table or rough dresser seems to have died
out by the time of the New Comedy,
Pollux vi 90: another form was ἐλεός, and
there was a doubt about the breathing.

ἀναδιδάσκω implies a conversion from
a former opinion to a new one (though
possibly a wrong one, as Herod. iv 95,
Thucyd. iii 97. 1): the meaning 'expound
oracles' seems confined to this play (*inf.*
202, 1045), but here too the idea of conversion to a new view is suggested. MSS.
give 234 to Nicias, but editors are now
mainly agreed that he does not reappear
after this *exit.*

155 = *Pax* 886. Demosthenes is more
cavalier in tone than Nicias. The active
of κατατίθημι is rare in Attic, except
when it means *pay*, or when the agent

ἔπειτα τὴν γῆν πρόσκυσον καὶ τοὺς θεούς.
ΑΛΛ. ἰδού· τί ἔστιν; ΟΙ. Α. ὦ μακάρι', ὦ πλούσιε,
ὦ νῦν μὲν οὐδείς, αὔριον δ' ὑπέρμεγας·
ὦ τῶν Ἀθηνέων ταγὲ τῶν εὐδαιμόνων.

159. Ἀθηνέων Bergk for Ἀθηναίων.

gives up connexion with what is laid down (hence καταθεῖναι ἐς μέσον and the like are common), or had no close connexion with it before, as *Lys.* 202.

156. προσκυνεῖν *adorare* means the raising of the hand to the lips, a gesture very common in Greek and Roman religion and in Eastern etiquette: it was distinct from, though often followed in the East by, kneeling or prostration. This form of salutation, still common among Turks and Arabs, was held by the Greeks to be inconsistent with freedom, μέγιστον μαρτύριον ἡ ἐλευθερία τῶν πόλεων ἐν αἷς ὑμεῖς ἐγένεσθε· οὐδένα γὰρ ἄνθρωπον δεσπότην ἀλλὰ τοὺς θεοὺς προσκυνεῖτε Xen. *Anab.* iii 2. 13: it was the mark of allegiance to a king (Plut. *Aristides* 6, *Themist.* 27, *frat. amor.* 18. 488 F) of the Eastern kind, and Alexander's introduction of it at his court was bitterly opposed (Arrian *Anab.* iv 10—11; an Athenian envoy to him was executed on his return for having stooped to it, Athen. vi 251 B). In Greek literature the salutation is mentioned (1) when paid to men, as a habit of Orientals and Egyptians (Herod. ii 80), which might spread to Greece in burlesque (Plato *Rep.* iii 398 A), or in cases of the most earnest supplication Soph. *OT* 327 πάντες σε προσκυνοῦμεν οἵδ' ἱκτήριοι : (2) when paid to divine beings, generally Earth as here (Soph. *Phil.* 1408), Earth and Sky (Aesch. *Pers.* 499, Soph. *OC* 1654), Sun (*Plut.* 771, Soph. *fr.* 771, Menander 609, Plato *Legg.* x 887 E, Lucian *salt.* 17 Ἰνδοὶ προσεύχονται τὸν Ἥλιον, οὐχ ὥσπερ ἡμεῖς τὴν χεῖρα κύσαντες ἡγούμεθα ἐντελῆ ἡμῶν εἶναι τὴν εὐχήν, Plut. *Marcell.* 6, *Pomp.* 14 τὸν ἥλιον ἀνατέλλοντα πλείονες ἢ δυόμενον προσκυνοῦσιν, cf. *Job* 31. 27), Nemesis or Adrasteia (Aesch. *Prom.* 936, Plato *Rep.* v 451 A, Demosth. i *Aristog.* 37 : so Soph. *Phil.* 776 τὸν φθόνον δὲ πρόσκυσον): rarely to other deities, as the Agathos Daemon (Theophr. *fr.* 123 ap. Athen. xv 693 D), Hermes (Hipponax

32, Lucian *Timon* 24), Apollo (Pythagoras at Delos refused the salutation to other gods, Diog. Laert. viii 1. 13), Pisistratus' pseudo-Athena (Aristot. *Pol. Ath.* 14), Zeus Basileus (Xen. *Cyrop.* ii 4. 19). [The epigraphic records called προσκυνήματα are Egyptian, Reinach 385.] Polybius xv 1. 6 implies some distinction between the salutes offered to Earth and to the other gods ὡς τοὺς θεοὺς ἀσπάσαιντο καὶ τὴν γῆν προσκυνήσαιεν, καθάπερ ἐστὶν ἔθος τοῖς ἄλλοις ἀνθρώποις. προσκύνησις was used also to things held sacred, such as relics, Lucian *Demonax* 67 τὸν θᾶκον ἐφ' οὗ εἰώθει ἀναπαύεσθαι προσεκύνουν, Heracles' bow Soph. *Phil.* 657, tombs of heroes Plato *Rep.* v 469 A, marks of divine footsteps Lucian *vera hist.* ii 7, the Tholos (sarcastically of Aeschines, Demosth. *Cor.* · 314) &c. It was often the mark of stupid superstition merely, Theophr. *char.* 16, Lucian *Alex.* 39, Plut. *quom. adol.* 8. 26 B : and it was usual on hearing a sneeze, Xen. *Anab.* iii 2. 9, Aristot. *problem.* 33. 9, Athen. ii 66 C. Here it marks recognition of good fortune as often (Soph. *Elect.* 1374 πατρῷα προσκύσανθ' ἔδη of Orestes returned, *Phil.* 533, Lucian *somn.* 9, *pisc.* 39).

157. ἰδού, see on 121. The distinction between μακάριος and εὐδαίμων implied in Aristot. *Eth. Nic.* i 10. 14—16 is not very clear, but, as Grant there says, μακάριος is the more enthusiastic and stronger word, and we do not find ὦ εὔδαιμον, while ὦ μακάριε, μακάριος ὅστις and the like are common. The wealth of men in power is a constant feature to the ancients, sometimes to our minds strangely emphasized ὦ πλοῦτε καὶ τύραννι (Soph. *OT* 380), *quo pater Aeneas, quo dives Tullus et Ancus*, Plato *Rep.* i 336 A.

158—9. The rhythm and language are of course tragic. ὑπέρμεγας would in good Greek seem almost grotesque for ὑπερμεγέθης (cf. Rutherford on Babrius 47. 1): genitives like Ἀθηνέων come in with great effect in parodies or quotations, as Σούνιον ἄκρον Ἀθηνέων *Nub.* 401 (cf.

ΑΛΛ. τί μ', ὦγάθ', οὐ πλύνειν ἐᾷς τὰς κοιλίας 160
πωλεῖν τε τοὺς ἀλλᾶντας, ἀλλὰ καταγελᾷς;
ΟΙ. Α. ὦ μῶρε, ποίας κοιλίας; δευρὶ βλέπε.
τὰς στίχας ὁρᾷς τὰς τῶνδε τῶν λαῶν; ΑΛΛ. ὁρῶ.
ΟΙ. Α. τούτων ἁπάντων αὐτὸς ἀρχέλας ἔσει,
καὶ τῆς ἀγορᾶς καὶ τῶν λιμένων καὶ τῆς πυκνός·
βουλὴν πατήσεις καὶ στρατηγοὺς κλαστάσεις, 166
δήσεις, φυλάξεις, ἐν πρυτανείῳ λαικάσει.
ΑΛΛ. ἐγώ; ΟΙ. Α. σὺ μέντοι· κοὐδέπω γε πάνθ' ὁρᾷς.
ἀλλ' ἐπανάβηθι κἀπὶ τοὐλεὸν τοδὶ
καὶ κάτιδε τὰς νήσους ἁπάσας ἐν κύκλῳ. 170

163. λεῶν Cobet, but Meineke *Vind. Aristoph.* 52 points out that there is a
reference to *Il.* iv 90 λαῶν στίχες ἀσπιστάων.
167. λαικάσεις MSS. except V corr. and B (cf. Cobet *NL* 253).

---

the accumulation of non-Attic genitives
plural in *Nub.* 335—9): and ταγὸς, known
in ordinary style only as a Thessalian
title, was a favourite Aeschylean word to
express the haughty ruler, *Prom.* 96, *Pers.*
324 &c.

160—1. The democratic spirit of
Athens levelled distinctions of class in
address, and ὦγαθέ was not specially
respectful: Socrates uses it to a eunuch
porter, Plato *Protag.* 314 D. πωλῶ *ven-
dito*, ἀποδίδομαι *vendo*, is a very clear and
constant distinction: it is of course best
seen when both words occur in the same
sentence, as Xen. *Memor.* ii 5. 5 ὅταν τις
οἰκέτην πονηρὸν πωλῇ καὶ ἀποδίδωται τοῦ
εὑρόντος: and so *Symp.* 8. 21, Demosth. i
Aphob. 32, Alexis 125. 3—4, 128. 8 ἐρῖν'
ἀπέδοτο σῦκα πωλεῖν ὀμνύων, Aristot.
Oecon. ii 1. 1346ᵇ9—20, Lys. *fr.* 7,
Athen. viii 348 B. Rutherford *NP* 48
seems to think strangely that the distinction does not hold for the future, πωλήσω
being Ionic: but though πωλήσω is not
often required, it was good Attic and had
always its proper meaning (*fr.* 460. 3,
Av. 1039, Xen. *Hell.* vi 2. 38, Aristot.
Pol. Ath. 51).

162—3. βλέπω may take acc. of
direct object in Tragedy, New Comedy
and late prose, but not in Attic prose or
Old Comedy except in parody, as *Pax* 208
(Ruth. Babrius 22. 7): here the change
to ὁρᾷς is natural, though the tone of 163

at least is tragic. στίχες and its parts
are epic and tragic, generally of serried
array: distinguish it from στοῖχοι *ranks
of a chorus*, as *fr.* 45 ἦ που κατὰ στοίχους
κεκράξονταί τι βαρβαριστί.

164—5. The word ἀρχέλαος would
be poetical (Aesch. *Pers.* 297 is a doubtful
case of it): and ἀρχέλας would be a non-
Attic contraction. Names like Λάκριτος
occur in dialects and later in Attic: Pindar
seems to have used Ἀγησίλας, and Euripides Μενέλας. The tragic tone breaks
down in 165 into a rapid colloquial
appeal: 'trade, home and foreign, and
politics will be at your mercy.'

166—7. The omission of the article
is probably intentional: 'Council! you'll
kick it. Ministers! you'll dock them!'
πατῶ as 69: κλαστάζω is the regularly
formed frequentative of κλά(σ)ω, which
is also used in this farmer's sense
pampino. δεῖν, φυλάττειν probably are
synonymous: imprisonment was rare at
Athens, and a clause in the Council-oath
was οὐ δήσω Ἀθηναίων οὐδένα (Demosth.
Timocr. 147): the new-comer is to have
in his own hands the powers of the heliastic juries. The future of λαικάζω was
used, in the southern style of coarse-
ness, to end an altercation, *Thesm.* 57,
Cephisodorus 3, Strato 1. 36, cf. Petron.
42: it is here of course a vulgar surprise
for σιτήσει.

169—70. If ἀναβαίνω in 149 implies

ΑΛΛ. καθορῶ. ΟΙ. Α. τί δαί; τἀμπόρια καὶ τὰς
ὁλκάδας;

ΑΛΛ. ἔγωγε. ΟΙ. Α. πῶς οὖν οὐ μεγάλως εὐδαιμονεῖς;
ἔτι νῦν τὸν ὀφθαλμὸν παράβαλλ' εἰς Καρίαν
τὸν δεξιόν, τὸν δ' ἕτερον εἰς Καρχηδόνα.

174. Χαλκηδόνα Palmerius *exercit.* 728, Brunck; Καλχηδόνα Dind. Mitch.
Hold. Ribb. and Boeckh *Staatsh.*³ i 361, Thirlwall *Hist. Gr.* iii 359 n. (The
spelling Χαλκ- seems to be late: Inscriptions give Καλχ- and Χαλχ- Meisterhans
§ 38. 1, coins always Καλχ-, cf. Reid on Cic. *Acad.* i 17.) In defence of Καρχηδόνα
see Müller-Strübing *Aristoph.* 9—, Freeman *Hist. of Sicily* iii 615.

---

a real ascent, ἐπανάβαινε here means 'go
up further' and the κἀπὶ favours this: that
meaning of ἐπαναβαίνω is not common,
but seems to occur Xen. *Cyrop.* ii 1. 23,
possibly *Hell.* vii 2. 8, and certainly in the
causal ἐπαναβιβάζω after. ἀνεβεβήκεσαν
Thucyd. iii 23. 1. On the statement of
Pollux iv 123 that before Thespis the
actor stood on an ἐλεός above the chorus
see A. Müller *Bühnenalt.* 2, A. B. Cook
Class. Rev. ix 271. αἱ νῆσοι often means
our allies, our empire; inf. 1319, *Pax* 760
ὑπὲρ ὑμῶν καὶ τῶν ἄλλων νήσων 'Athens
and its empire too': so Aristophanes'
comedy Νῆσοι meant 'Our Empire,' as
Eupolis' Πόλεις did. ἐν κύκλῳ may suggest the Cyclades (schol.).
171. ὁλκάδες are of course the *mer-
chant ships* in the ports: Aristophanes'
Ὁλκάδες was another of his appeals for
peace in the interests of civilisation. ἐμπόριον may be a whole town or island
(Herod. i 165 δειμαίνοντες μὴ αἱ μὲν νῆσοι
ἐμπόριον γένωνται), or a part of a town
marked off, as in the Piraeus (Wachsmuth
Stadt Athen ii 96—), Chalcis &c. (Böckh
*Staatsh.*³ i 75.) Most of the great trading
ports were Athenian allies, Corinth being
the most notable exception.
173—4. On the question between
Καρχηδόνα and Καλχηδόνα here and
inf. 1303, the only ancient authority
for Καλχηδόνα is a confused scholium
on the latter passage. Casaubon preferred Καλχηδόνα there, and the romantic
Huguenot scholar Palmerius may have
based his conjecture here on recollection
of hearing his master's note. The map
at the end of the *Corp. Inscr. Ath.* i
shows how well the extent of Athenian
rule is defined by 'from Byzantium or
Chalcedon to Caria,' where the Greek

cities, though Dorian, followed Athens
(Thucyd. ii 9. 4): the Bosporus was of
course extremely important for Attic
trade and supplies: and a line of Eupolis
279 Α. ὁρῶ. Β. θεῷ νῦν τήνδε Μαριαν-
δυνίαν (from the Χρυσοῦν γένος, which
probably appeared soon after the *Knights*)
might possibly be quoted as an imitation
of this scene and in defence of Καλχηδόνα.
But in both cases, especially in 1303,
the MS. reading is more likely to be right.
Vesp. 700 ἀπὸ τοῦ Πόντου μέχρι Σαρδοῦς
measures the Athenian empire from East
to West: Chalcedon was not so very
familiar, and Thucyd. iv 75. 2 does not
find it superfluous to tell his readers where
it lay; owing to its inferior position 'the
city of the blind' had gone down before
Byzantium, and its decay may have been
the reason for the remarkable change in
the tribute of the two cities (Byzantium
is raised from 15 talents to 18 in B.C. 438
and to 21½ in 428, while Chalcedon is
lowered from 9 talents to 6). Carthage
was within the circle of Athenian commerce: Hermippus puts its carpets and
cushions with emphasis at the end of his
trade-list (63. 23): and any spirited survey
of Attic power would take account of the
dreams men had of conquests in that
direction (Alcibiades in Thucyd. vi 90. 2,
Plut. *Pericles* 20, where the range of Attic
ambition is described as reaching from
Sinope beyond Sicily to Etruria and
Carthage). Chalcedon would hardly lie
beyond the limits of the νῆσοι of 170,
whereas ἔτι implies a new field. Though
τὸν δεξιὸν at first seems to support Καλχηδόνα, the acting would gain in farcical
absurdity, and the Sausage-man's remonstrance in point, with the MS.
reading.

ΑΛΛ. εὐδαιμονήσω δ᾽, εἰ διαστραφήσομαι;　175

ΟΙ. Α. οὔκ, ἀλλὰ διὰ σοῦ ταῦτα πάντα πέρναται.
γίγνει γάρ, ὡς ὁ χρησμὸς οὑτοσὶ λέγει,
ἀνὴρ μέγιστος.　ΑΛΛ. εἰπέ μοι, καὶ πῶς ἐγὼ
ἀλλαντοπώλης ὢν ἀνὴρ γενήσομαι;

ΟΙ. Α. δι᾽ αὐτὸ γάρ τοι τοῦτο καὶ γίγνει μέγας, 180
ὁτιὴ πονηρὸς κἀξ ἀγορᾶς εἶ καὶ θρασύς.

ΑΛΛ. οὐκ ἀξιῶ ᾽γὼ ᾽μαυτὸν ἰσχύειν μέγα.

ΟΙ. Α. οἴμοι, τί ποτ᾽ ἔσθ᾽ ὅτι σαυτὸν οὐ φὴς ἄξιον;
ξυνειδέναι τί μοι δοκεῖς σαυτῷ καλόν.　184
μῶν ἐκ καλῶν εἶ κἀγαθῶν;　ΑΛΛ. μὰ τοὺς θεούς,
εἰ μὴ ᾽κ πονηρῶν γ᾽.　ΟΙ. Α. ὦ μακάριε τῆς
τύχης,

175. R is alone in reading δ᾽ here and in the similar line _Av._ 177: the rest have γ᾽.　**177.** γίγνη γὰρ ὄντως ὡς R : ὄντως is adopted by Dindorf and Kock : if this were right, it would be the earliest case of the word, see Wilam. on Eurip. _HF_ 610, Tycho Mommsen _Präpos._ 662—.

---

175. _Av._ 177 ἀπολαύσομαί τι δ᾽, εἰ διαστραφήσομαι; so in some lost play Στρεψαῖος ὁ Ἑρμῆς παρὰ τῷ Ἀριστοφάνει παρὰ τὸ διεστράφθαι τὰς ὄψεις, Cramer _Anecd. Oxon._ ii 53. 14.

176. δέον εἰπεῖν διοικεῖται, ὁ δ᾽ εἶπε πέρναται πικρῶς schol.: so the Orators of corrupt politicians, as Demosth. i _Aristog._ 46 κάπηλός ἐστι πονηρίας καὶ παλιγκάπηλος καὶ μεταβολεύς, καὶ μόνον οὐ ζυγὰ καὶ σταθμὰ ἔχων πάνθ᾽ ὅσα πώποτ᾽ ἔπραξεν ἐπώλει. The presents are in the oracular style, as 127. There is probably a point in the πέρναται: the word was extremely rare in Attic, the only other case extant seeming to be Eurip. _Cycl._ 271: it was chiefly used of over-sea trade, Herondas 2. 18 περνὰς ἐκ Τύρου τι τῷ δήμῳ.

179. ἀνήρ, cf. 1255, _Nub._ 823, Xen. _Cyrop._ iv 2. 25 ὁ τοῦτο ποιῶν οὐκέτ᾽ ἀνήρ ἐστιν ἀλλὰ σκευοφόρος, _ib._ v 5. 33 σὺ μὲν ἀνὴρ φαίνει, ἐγὼ δ᾽ οὐκ ἄξιος ἀρχῆς. He attempts tragic rhythm, breaking down at the comic curse in 189.

180—1. After αὐτὸ τοῦτο and the like the emphasizing καί is specially common, _Nub._ 1499, _fr._ 445 a διὰ ταῦτα γάρ τοι καὶ καλοῦνται μακάριοι, _Lys._ 46, and Blaydes there.

πονηρὸς in the social and political sense which it regularly has in the 5th century B.C.: χρηστὸς or καλὸς κἀγαθὸς was the opposite: see Appendix ii.

182. ἐγὼ and ἐμαυτὸν give a strong emphasis to his unworthiness. The middle of ἀξιῶ appears to be Ionic and Tragic only.

183—4. οἴμοι, of rather sarcastic anger, as Soph. _Antig._ 86: the consciousness of anything καλὸν would be fatal.

185—6. 'You aren't come of gentlefolks surely?' The answer is given in the form εἰ μή...γε, which puzzled or baffled the copyists of several MSS. which give εἰμ᾽ ἐκ πονηρῶν γε, as well as Porson, Elmsley, Dobree. Fritzsche on _Thesm._ 898 defined it "vim habet graviter minuendi estque _tantummodo_." The other cases are _Av._ 1681, _Lys._ 942, _Thesm._ 898, probably _fr._ 19 εἰ μὴ δικῶν γε (τε vulg.) γυργάθους ψηφισμάτων τε θωμούς, and perhaps the fragment (645 Kock, not in Dindorf) εἰ μὴ Προμηθεύς γ᾽ εἰμι· τἄλλα ψεύδομαι (γ᾽ inserted by Cobet _NL_ 586). Dobree was wrong in proposing εἰ μὴ φέρεις γ᾽ in _Vesp._ 180. I can find no other instances. There is probably an ellipse

ὅσον πέπονθας ἀγαθὸν εἰς τὰ πράγματα.
ΑΛΛ. ἀλλ', ὦγάθ', οὐδὲ μουσικὴν ἐπίσταμαι,
πλὴν γραμμάτων, καὶ ταῦτα μέντοι κακὰ κακῶς.
ΟΙ. Α. τουτὶ μόνον σ' ἔβλαψεν, ὅτι καὶ κακὰ κακῶς. 190
ἡ δημαγωγία γὰρ οὐ πρὸς μουσικοῦ
ἔτ' ἐστὶν ἀνδρὸς οὐδὲ χρηστοῦ τοὺς τρόπους,
ἀλλ' εἰς ἀμαθῆ καὶ βδελυρόν. ἀλλὰ μὴ παρῆς
ἅ σοι διδόασ' ἐν τοῖς λογίοισιν οἱ θεοί.
ΑΛΛ. πῶς δῆτά φησ' ὁ χρησμός; ΟΙ. Α. εὖ νὴ τοὺς
θεοὺς 195

193. βδελυρὸν ἧκεν · ἀλλὰ μὴ παρῆς ἅ σοι διδόασιν (so R) ἐν λογίοις θεοί Mein.

---

of οὐδὲν ἄλλο, τί ἄλλο, τί δὲ or the like, after which we find εἰ μή—γε often : Xen. Cyrop. i 4. 13 τί δέ, ἔφη, εἰ μὴ μαστιγώσας γε...ἐξ ἀρχῆς χρήσομαι; Oecon. 1. 13 οὐδαμῶς εἰ μὴ πέρ γε ὑοσκύαμον χρήματα εἶναι φήσομεν, ib. 3. 12, 7. 17, 9. 1, Plato Protag. 310 B οὐδέν γ' εἰ μὴ ἀγαθά γε, Lysias 3. 33. Later we find εἰ μή—γε and πλὴν εἰ μή—γε introducing sentences, as Lucian philops. 26, vit. auct. 7, almost like the Latin nisi forte. Possibly the curious nisi quia in Plautus (Pseud. 107, 567, Rud. 1024, Trin. 936 &c.) is a translation of εἰ μή—γε in the New Comedy.
187. τὰ πράγματα, 'affairs,' 'public life': Eurip. IA 366 μυρίοι δέ τοι πεπόνθασ' αὐτὸ πρὸς τὰ πράγματα, Ion 599.
188—9. μουσικὴν τὴν ἐγκύκλιον παιδείαν · γράμματα δὲ τὰ πρῶτα στοιχεῖα schol. Education had two obvious branches, mental and physical, μουσική and γυμναστική: the former might be subdivided into elementary and more advanced, γράμματα and μουσική proper: Plato Protag. 325 D, Legg. vii 809 C τὰ περὶ τὰ γράμματα πρῶτον καὶ δεύτερον λύρας πέρι καὶ λογισμῶν, Xen. Pol. Lac. 2. 1 πέμπουσιν εἰς διδασκάλων μαθησομένους καὶ γράμματα καὶ μουσικὴν καὶ τὰ ἐν παλαίστρᾳ, Isocr. Antid. 267 οἱ περὶ τὴν γραμματικὴν καὶ τὴν μουσικὴν καὶ τὴν ἄλλην παιδείαν διαπονηθέντες. Comedy no doubt often showed an illiterate demagogue, Cratinus 122 ἀλλὰ μὰ Δι' οὐκ οἶδ' ἔγωγε γράμματ' οὐδ' ἐπίσταμαι, Vesp. 959. Quintil. i 10. 17 transeamus igitur id quoque, quod grammatice quondam ac musice iunctae fuerunt : siquidem Ar-chytas atque Aristoxenus etiam subiectam grammaticen musicae putaverunt: et eosdem utriusque rei praeceptores fuisse cum Sophron ostendit, tum Eupolis apud quem Prodamus et musicen et litteras docet, et Maricas qui est Hyperbolus nihil se ex musice scire nisi litteras confitetur. Suidas s.v. γραμματιστής quotes Procopius Bell. Pers. 70 C, who refers to our passage in his account of John the Cappadocian, οὐ γὰρ ἄλλο οὐδὲν ἐς γραμματιστοῦ φοιτῶν ἔμαθεν ὅτι μὴ γράμματα, καὶ ταῦτα κακὰ κακῶς, γράψαι. καὶ μέντοι of an emphatic reservation, as Plato Theaet. 143 B, Protag. 339 C, Xen. Anab. i 8. 20 (L and S), Riddell Digest § 145 b.
190. 'That's the only drawback in your case,' βλάπτω having its old meaning, common in Homer, hamper, obstruct.
191—3. μουσικός is of course the opposite of ἀμαθής, and χρηστός, which is used in its social sense, of βδελυρός (cf. on 134). Eurip. Hipp. 989 οἱ γὰρ ἐν σοφοῖς φαῦλοι παρ' ὄχλῳ μουσικώτεροι λέγειν (on which Aristot. Rhet. ii 22. 3 comments) may be an allusion to the new kind of popular leader after Pericles (to whom the ἔτι here points). ἀμαθία is defiantly championed by Cleon in Thucyd. iii 37. 3. To explain εἰς ἀμαθῆ most editors have supposed an ellipse of ἐλήλυθε or some such word: but the parallels quoted are not much more in point than ἐς κόρακας. It is hardly credible that the text is right, but I know of no good correction.
194. διδόασιν, offer: δίδωμι often has this inceptive or conative sense in the present as well as in the imperfect.

καὶ ποικίλως πως καὶ σοφῶς ἠνιγμένος.

'Αλλ' ὁπόταν μάρψῃ βυρσαίετος ἀγκυλοχήλης
γαμφηλῇσι δράκοντα κοάλεμον αἱματοπώτην,
δὴ τότε Παφλαγόνων μὲν ἀπόλλυται ἡ σκοροδάλμη,
κοιλιοπώλῃσιν δὲ θεὸς μέγα κῦδος ὀπάζει,   200
αἵ κα μὴ πωλεῖν ἀλλᾶντας μᾶλλον ἕλωνται.

196. σοφῶς R. σαφῶς the other MSS.   **197.** ἀγκυλοχείλης MSS., -χήλης
schol. ὁ ἐπικαμπεῖς τὰς χηλὰς ἔχων, confirmed by 205.
201. αἵ κα R, other MSS. have αἵ κε or αἵ κεν.

196. ποικίλος and σοφός are both
natural words for what would be expected in the oracle. ποικίλος is the
opposite of ἁπλοῦς (Plato *Theaet.* 146 D,
Arist. *Rhet.* iii 16. 2), applied to oracles
Herod. vii 111, cf. ἡ ποικιλῳδὸς Σφίγξ
Soph. *OT* 130. The σοφία or artistry of
an oracle would lie in its ποικίλα αἰνίγ-
ματα: Eurip. *Med.* 675 of an oracle
σοφώτερ' ἢ κατ' ἄνδρα συμβαλεῖν ἔπη,
ep. on Lycophron in Didot's *Anth. Pal.*
vol. iii, v 36 ἐνθουσιασμοὺς παρθένου φοιβα-
στρίας αἰνιγματωδῶς καὶ σοφῶς εἰρημένους.

197. The oracular style is well parodied. Many λόγια began with ἀλλ' ὅταν
and the like, the ἀλλά being of course
not adversative but injunctive, as with
imperatives: instances are the λόγια given
by Herod. i 55, iii 57, vi 77, viii 77,
Plut. *Pyth. orac.* 11. 399 C, Ammian. Marcell. xxxi 1, Pausan. ix 17. 5 (attributed
to Bacis), Suidas s.v. Ἰουλιανός: so the
parodies *Av.* 967, Lucian *Peregr.* 29—
30. Rival beasts often appeared in oracles
and parables as in portents: for the eagle
and snake see *Il.* xii 200, *Vesp.* 16,
Lucian *Jup. trag.* 31 ἀλλ' ὅταν αἰγυπιὸς
γαμψώνυχος ἀκρίδα μάρψῃ, δὴ τότε λοίσθιον
ὀμβροφόροι κλάγξουσι κορῶναι, Aristot.
Hist. Anim. x 1. 609ᵃ4 ἔστι δ' ἀετὸς καὶ
δράκων πολέμια· τροφὴν γὰρ ποιεῖται τοὺς
ὄφεις ὁ ἀετός, Thompson *Greek Birds* 7.
γαμφηλαί always of ravening animals (of
Harpies Apoll. Rhod. ii 188), except in
Il. xix 394 of Xanthus and Balius. The
real δράκων was apparently a water-snake
Aristot. *Hist. Anim.* ix 20. 602ᵇ25: but
the word is generally used of mythical
serpents, and the contrast of supernatural
dracones and everyday *anguis* gives point
to Nero's disclaimer in Tac. *Ann.* xi 11,

cf. Sueton. *Nero* 6. κοάλεμος, a quaint
word, occurring again in 221 for a
figure of Stupidity: it was a nick-name
for Cimon, father of Miltiades (Plut.
Cimon 4), for Hipponicus son of Callias
(Athen. v 220 B), and probably for
the Euthyphro of Plato's dialogue (Nu-
menius *fr.* 12 Mullach). The ancient
derivation from κοεῖν ἠλεά seems to me
unlikely: Hesychius has κόαλοι· βάρβαροι,
which connects well with the Sanskrit
çavara and çabara, *a non-Aryan, savage*:
possibly κόβαλος is akin. Several grammarians hold that -πώτης was more regular
than -πότης (see Lobeck Phryn. 456, *Paralip.* 445): but the evidence is on the
other side (Athen. xi 460 C): αἱματοπώτης
would be felt as burlesque, so ὑδατοπωτῶν
Cratinus 288.
σκοροδάλμη, a brine and garlic sauce,
may have been specially common on the
Euxine: Lucian *Alex.* 39 speaks contemptuously of Παφλαγόνες καρβατίνας
ὑποδεδεμένοι, πολλὴν τὴν σκοροδάλμην
ἐρυγγάνοντες: and the cook in Diphilus
17. 13 would please Byzantine guests
κάθαλα ποιήσας πάντα κἀσκοροδισμένα.
It is mentioned by Cratinus 143 apparently as a favourite sauce of the Cyclops,
and *inf.* 1095, *Eccl.* 292, where the point
is that its δριμύτης is like that of the
typical dicast (so ὀξάλμη *Vesp.* 331 and
ὀξύρεγμία *fr.* 398). ὀπάζω, the causal of
ἕπομαι, has a very restricted use in Attic:
Tragedians have it about 10 times, mostly
in lyrics, Aristoph. here and *Thesm.* 973
in tragicose lyric. In 201 the pathos of
the imagined situation is implied by the
spondaic rhythm and the unusual Dorism
αἵ κα (Kock).

N. A.   3

ΑΛΛ. πῶς οὖν πρὸς ἐμὲ ταῦτ' ἐστίν; ἀναδίδασκέ με.

ΟΙ. Α. βυρσαίετος μὲν ὁ Παφλαγών ἐσθ' οὑτοσί.

ΑΛΛ. τί δ' ἀγκυλοχήλης ἐστίν; ΟΙ. Α. αὐτό που
    λέγει,

ὅτι ἀγκύλαις ταῖς χερσὶν ἁρπάζων φέρει. 205

ΑΛΛ. ὁ δράκων δὲ προς τί; ΟΙ. Α. τοῦτο περιφα-
    νέστατον.

ὁ δράκων γάρ ἐστι μακρὸν ὅ τ' ἀλλᾶς αὖ μακρόν·
εἶθ' αἱματοπώτης ἔσθ' ὅ τ' ἀλλᾶς χὠ δράκων.
τὸν οὖν δράκοντά φησι τὸν βυρσαίετον
ἤδη κρατήσειν, αἵ κε μὴ θαλφθῇ λόγοις. 210

ΑΛΛ. τὰ μὲν λόγι' αἰκάλλει με· θαυμάζω δ' ὅπως
τὸν δῆμον οἷός τ' ἐπιτροπεύειν εἴμ' ἐγώ.

ΟΙ. Α. φαυλότατον ἔργον· ταῦθ' ἅπερ ποεῖς πόει·

---

207. ὅ τ' ἀλλᾶς Dawes, ἀλλᾶς τ' MSS. 210. αἵ κε MSS. αἵ κα Mein. *Vind.
Aristoph.* 53, as *Etym. Mag.* 732. 34 quotes the phrase, without giving author,
in that form: so Kock. κᾶ is very rare (Osthoff *Gesch. d. Perfects* 330). 213. ταῦθ'
Lenting, Cobet *NL* 604.

203. Compounds of ἀετός to denote
species were known—ὑπάετος, νυκτάετος,
γρυπάετος *Ran.* 929, ἁλιάετος.

οὑτοσί is rarely used of anything not
on the stage: *Vesp.* 74 and *Plut.* 800 it
means one of the audience: here it may
be supposed that Cleon is visible inside
the house from the stage.

204. αὐτό is nom., as Plato *Crat.*
402 C τοῦτο ὀλίγου αὐτὸ λέγει ὅτι πηγῆς
ὄνομα ἐπικεκρυμμένον ἐστί. The distinction φημί 'say' of the words (as 194),
λέγω 'mean,' 'imply,' of their significance,
is regular: *Vesp.* 74 'Ἀμυνίας φησ' φιλό-
κυβον εἶναι· ἀλλ' οὐδὲν λέγει, Soph. *Antig.*
403 ἦ καὶ ξυνίης καὶ λέγεις ὀρθῶς ἅ φής;
Aesch. *Eumen.* 657, Anaxandrides 6,
Athen. x 456 A, xiv 640 C: it is often
very clear in Plato, as *Phaedo* 92 B ταῦτά
σοι ξυμβαίνει λέγειν ὅταν φῇς μὲν εἶναι
τὴν ψυχήν..., *Theaet.* 166 D σοφὸν ἄνδρα
πολλοῦ δέω τὸ μὴ φάναι εἶναι, ἀλλ' αὐτὸν
τοῦτον καὶ λέγω σοφὸν ὃς ἄν..., 181 C
ποῖόν τί ποτε λέγοντες φασὶ τὰ πάντα
κινεῖσθαι; *Phileb.* 14 C—D. So ἀκούω ἅ φής,
μανθάνω ἅ λέγεις, is the proper connexion.
The Latins sometimes distinguish *loquor*
and *dico* in the same way, Cic. *Fin.* i 26.

205. 'With hands like claws,' so
ἀγκυλοῦντα δεῖ σφόδρα τὴν χεῖρα πέμπειν
τὸν κότταβον Athen. xv 667 B.

207—210. So in 1074, in a scene
of elaborate parody of interpreters, ὅτι ἡ
τριήρης ἐστὶ χὠ κύων ταχύ. φησι here, because he keeps the oracle's symbolism:
he would have said τὸν ἀλλαντοπώλην
λέγει τὸν Παφλαγόνα κρατήσειν. αἵ κε
μὴ θαλφθῇ λόγοις is an interpretation in
the oracular language: θάλπω was not
used in ordinary Attic (*Av.* 1092 is lyric),
though Xen. has it.

211. αἰκάλλω as 48: the scholiast's
explanation of this rare word as properly
applied to dogs is confirmed by Athen.
iii 99 E μὴ βαύξε, μηδὲ ἀγριαίνου τὴν
κυνικὴν προβαλλόμενος λύσσαν, δέον αἰκάλ-
λειν μᾶλλον καὶ προσσαίνειν τοῖς συνδεί-
πνοις: and so this phrase is just like οὐ
γάρ με σαίνει θέσφατα in Eurip. *Ion* 685.
ἐπιτρέπω and its derivatives are used of
political power held under responsibility
to State or Law, *inf.* 426, 929, 1098,
1259, *Pax* 686, *Eccl.* 455.

213—6. φαῦλον 'easy' was a very
common use in colloquial Attic, in Comedy
and Plato. ταράττω 'stir' may have been

τάραττε καὶ χόρδευ' ὁμοῦ τὰ πράγματα
ἅπαντα, καὶ τὸν δῆμον ἀεὶ προσποιοῦ   215
ὑπογλυκαίνων ῥηματίοις μαγειρικοῖς.
τὰ δ' ἄλλα σοι πρόσεστι δημαγωγικά,
φωνὴ μιαρά, γέγονας κακῶς, ἀγόραιος εἶ·
ἔχεις ἅπαντα πρὸς πολιτείαν ἃ δεῖ·
χρησμοί τε συμβαίνουσι καὶ τὸ Πυθικόν.   220
ἀλλὰ στεφανοῦ, καὶ σπένδε τῷ Κοαλέμῳ·
χὥπως ἀμυνεῖ τὸν ἄνδρα. ΑΛΛ. καὶ τίς ξύμ-
μαχος
γενήσεταί μοι; καὶ γὰρ οἵ τε πλούσιοι
δεδίασιν αὐτὸν ὅ τε πένης βδύλλει λεώς.

215. *om.* R (at end of a page).
218. ἀγόραιος MSS. except R. The grammarians' distinction between ἀγόραιος ἀγελαῖος ἀγροῖκος in the primary sense of the words, and ἀγόραιος ἀγέλαιος ἄγροικος in the secondary, is denied by Chandler § 380, but accepted and explained by Wheeler *Griech. Nominalaccent* 118: cf. Valckenaer on Ammon. *animadv.* 8.

---

a cook's word, like κυκάω: χορδεύω (whence χορδεύματα 'sausage-stuffs' 315, cf. ζωμεύω ζώμευμα), was of course a sausage-man's: Herodotus' καταχορδεύων τὴν γαστέρα vi 75 and κατεκρεουργήθη ἅπας vii 181 are excused by Longinus 31. 2 as too expressive to be called mere vulgarisms (οὐκ ἰδιωτεύει τῷ σημαντικῷ). ὁμοῦ implies want of order, ὁμοῦ πάντα χρήματα. The scholium on 214 παρῴδησε τὸν ἴαμβον ἐξ Ἡρακλειδῶν Εὐριπίδου can be right only on the supposition that the *Heraclidae* is now mutilated: Wilamowitz *Herm.* xvii 349 thinks the original line occurred in an altercation scene now lost. μαγειρικός 'of the trade,' used of professional dexterity, as *Ach.* 1015, *Pax* 1017: probably the μάγειρος, butcher as well as cook, had got the name of an impostor which he has throughout the New Comedy, ἀλαζονικὸν πᾶν τὸ τῶν μαγείρων φῦλον Athen. vii 290 B, and specially Posidippus 26. 3 τῶν ἡδυσμάτων πάντων κράτιστόν ἐστιν ἐν μαγειρικῇ ἀλαζονεία. ῥημάτιον only of telling catch-phrases in popular oratory, as *Vesp.* 668 τούτοις τοῖς ῥηματίοις περιπεφθείς, or of the schools, Lucian *Hermot.* 81, *bis accus.* 16.
217—18. 'You have all that has given Cleon success,' as the acting had

already made clear to the audience. The rule that γέγονα καλός, κακός, is of looks or character, γέγονα καλῶς, κακῶς, of social position, is generally borne out by some MS. authority: Cobet *VL* 157 gives cases, correcting however γεγονότας ἐπιεικεῖς in Lysias 19. 12 to ἐπιεικῶς. Other instances of the rule are Plato *Theaet.* 173 D εὖ ἢ κακῶς τις γέγονεν ἐν πόλει, Isaeus 3. 15, Lysias 19. 15, Isocr. *Paneg.* 24, Plut. *Agis* 2, C. *Gracch.* 8. 3.
219—20. πολιτεία 'statesmanship,' as Xen. *Mem.* iii 9. 15 where πολιτεία is parallel to γεωργία and ἰατρεία: in Eupolis 117. 2 οὕτω σφόδρ' ἀλγῶ τὴν πολιτείαν ὁρῶν παρ' ἡμῖν it means the *personnel* of politics. συμβαίνω, of oracles 'tallying' with the case in hand Soph. *Trach.* 173 καὶ τῶνδε ναμέρτεια συμβαίνει χρόνου τοῦ νῦν παρόντος, ὡς τελεσθῆναι χρεών, 1164 φανῶ δ' ἐγὼ τούτοισι συμβαίνοντ' ἴσα μαντεῖα καινά. τὸ Πυθικόν as all oracles were vaguely referred to Apollo, cf. on 229.
221—2. Κοάλεμος (see on 197) like Μόθων and the other demons in 634—5.
ὁ ἀνήρ, a spirited way of speaking of an enemy: so Brasidas in Thucyd. v 10. 5 οἱ ἄνδρες ἡμᾶς οὐ μένουσι.
222—4. καὶ τίς implies an objection, see on 128. The feelings of rich and poor

3—2

ΟΙ. Α. ἀλλ' εἰσὶν ἱππῆς ἄνδρες ἀγαθοὶ χίλιοι   225
    μισοῦντες αὐτόν, οἳ βοηθήσουσί σοι,
    καὶ τῶν πολιτῶν οἱ καλοί τε κἀγαθοί,
    καὶ τῶν θεατῶν ὅστις ἐστὶ δεξιός,
    κἀγὼ μετ' αὐτῶν χὠ θεὸς ξυλλήψεται.
    καὶ μὴ δέδιθ'· οὐ γάρ ἐστιν ἐξηκασμένος.   230
    ὑπὸ τοῦ δέους γὰρ αὐτὸν οὐδεὶς ἤθελε
    τῶν σκευοποιῶν εἰκάσαι. πάντως γε μὴν
    γνωσθήσεται· τὸ γὰρ θέατρον δεξιόν.

are expressed by a good and a coarse word respectively. δέδια and φοβοῦμαι are distinguished by Ammonius' rule δέος μέν ἐστι πολυχρόνιος κακοῦ ὑπόνοια, φόβος δὲ ἡ παραυτίκα πτόησις: see Shilleto on Thucyd. i 36. 1. βδύλλω 'funk' was used with accus., as *Lys.* 354 τί βδύλλεθ' ἡμᾶς; the word is formed from βδέω by the plebeian suffix -υλλω: cf. ἐξαπατύλλω 1144, στωμύλλω, ὀγκύλλομαι *Pax* 465 &c. There was always a coarse or comic meaning in words ending in -υλλος and the like, καθάρυλλος, ἠβυλλιῶ, μειρακύλλιον: and I think this can often be seen in proper names of that formation. Whether the 'Αρίστυλλος of *Eccl.* 647, *Plut.* 314, be meant for Plato or not, the name is intentionally contemptuous; Βάθυλλος is not usually a reputable person, Κρίτυλλα *Thesm.* 898 is the opposite of a heroine, Δράκυλλος *Ach.* 612 goes well with the comic patronymics Εὐφορίδης and Πρινίδης: Ξένυλλα *Thesm.* 633, Herondas' Γυλλίς, Lucian's Μίκυλλος are meant to carry something of their character in their names. Of course we find respectable men called Δίυλλος Θράσυλλος 'Αρίστυλλος in the *Corp. Inscr. Att.* i, and many more cases in later times: but I have no doubt that the formation was originally contemptuous; and a comedian would use it in inventing names for a situation. There is probably a kindly touch in the ὁ πένης λεώς for οἱ πένητες, as in ὁ θρανίτης λεὼς *Ach.* 162, οὐργάτης λεὼς *Pax* 632, τὸν γεωργικὸν λεὼν *Pax* 921.

225—9. Demosthenes' reply is mostly in tragic rhythm delivered *ore rotundo*. The number of ἱππῆς was 1000: Thucyd. ii 13. 7, Aristot. *Pol. Ath.* 24, give 1200, but that includes 200 ἱπποτοξόται. δεξιός

is often used of the capable critic, as σοφός is regularly of the original artist; *Vesp.* 65 ὑμῶν μὲν αὐτῶν οὐχὶ δεξιώτερον, κωμῳδίας δὲ φορτικῆς σοφώτερον, so 1315, *Ran.* 1370, *Nub.* 521 ὡς ὑμᾶς ἡγούμενος εἶναι θεατὰς δεξιοὺς καὶ ταύτην σοφώτατ' ἔχειν τῶν ἐμῶν κωμῳδιῶν: but in many cases δεξιὸς and σοφὸς are used indiscriminately, *Ach.* 629, *inf.* 421, 1377, *Pax* 1096, *Ran.* 1118—21: δεξιός is applied to Sophocles by Phrynichus 31. 2, to Euripides by Strattis 1. 2: and so σκαιός is the opposite of σοφός Eurip. *Med.* 190. Like so many other words of commendation, it was probably applied by the καλοὶ κἀγαθοὶ to themselves: so there is a political shade in the meaning here, as in [Xen.] *Pol. Ath.* 1. 6, 9 εἰ εὐνομίαν ζητεῖς, πρῶτα μὲν ὄψει τοὺς δεξιωτάτους αὐτοῖς τοὺς νόμους τιθέντας· ἔπειτα κολάσουσιν οἱ χρηστοὶ τοὺς πονηρούς: this is probably intended by Cleon in Thucyd. iii 37. 3. Like 'clever,' the word (in the metaphorical sense) was colloquial, and apparently quite rare except in Comedy. ὁ θεὸς is of course Apollo: the phrase was oracular, Thucyd. i 118. 3 and ii 54. 4 καὶ αὐτὸς (ὁ θεὸς) ἔφη ξυλλήψεσθαι: a common stimulus to self-help was τῷ γὰρ πονοῦντι καὶ θεὸς ξυλλαμβάνει Eurip. *fr.* 435, cf. Aesch. *Pers.* 742, Soph. *fr.* 666, Menander 572.

230—3. δέδια is allowed an imperative, as being present in meaning: see Rutherford on Babrius 15. 13. In the Old Comedy new masks would be required for many plays: they were carefully made as portraits, so that the person intended was recognisable by the mask alone (Platonius *de differ. com.* § 19: he adds that in the New Comedy the masks

ΑΛΛ. οἴμοι κακοδαίμων, ὁ Παφλαγὼν ἐξέρχεται.

ΠΑ. οὔ τοι μὰ τοὺς δώδεκα θεοὺς χαιρήσετον, 235
ὁτιὴ 'πὶ τῷ δήμῳ ξυνόμνυτον πάλαι.
τουτὶ τί δρᾷ τὸ Χαλκιδικὸν ποτήριον;
οὐκ ἔσθ' ὅπως οὐ Χαλκιδέας ἀφίστατον.
ἀπολεῖσθον, ἀποθανεῖσθον, ὦ μιαρωτάτω.

234. NIK., MSS. and old editions : but Nicias' final exit at 154 seems fairly certain.
ΑΛΛ. most editions since K. F. Hermann.   236. ξυνώμνυτον MSS. except R.

---

of types carefully avoided resemblance to real people). An actor without a mask, as in this case, was called αὐτοπρόσωπος (Lucian *Timon* 27, *pro imag.* 3), and in later times and styles this was more common: Athen. x 452 F Κλέων ὁ μίμαυλος ἐπικαλούμενος, ὅσπερ καὶ τῶν Ἰταλικῶν μίμων ἄριστος γέγονεν αὐτοπρόσωπος ὑποκριτής. The story that Aristophanes himself played the part of Cleon in the play is given in a scholium here, in the second argument, and in the *vita Aristoph.*: but it is not accepted by Kock p. iv, A. Müller *Bühnenalt.* 281, Denis *Comédie grecque* i 380. Pollux iv 115 explains σκευοποιός by προσωποποιός, and ii 47 says ἡ νέα κωμῳδία καὶ προσωποποιὸν εἴρηκεν ὃν ἡ ἀρχαία σκευοποιόν: but σκευοποιός was the regular word even in late times, Aristot. *Poet.* 6, Plut. *comp. Ar. et Men.* 2. 853 E, *adv. Colot.* 28. 1123 C, so σκευοποιεῖσθαι *masquerade* id. *quom. adul.* 17. 59 B. γε μήν, 'however,' see Appendix i. θέατρον, 'the house,' the only meaning the word has in literature till well on in the fourth century B.C. (Wilamowitz *Hermes* xxi 602).

234. οἴμοι κακοδαίμων, a comic exclamation of distress: see on 7 and 1243.

235—6. Is there a reason for the oath by the Twelve Gods? Their altar was set up, as a point from which distances were to be measured, by the younger Pisistratus, son of Hippias, Herod. ii 7, Thuc. vi 54. 7. It was thus a central point of Attic interests, and the Twelve Deities may have been appealed to when the heart of Attic feeling was to be touched. The only other case of the oath I know is Alciphron ii 3. 8, where Menander swears μὰ τοὺς δώδεκα θεοὺς that he will not think of leaving Athens for all Ptolemy's tempting offers in Egypt. As the Pisistratic arrangements

were so often in a democratic spirit, this too may have had a political meaning as against aristocratic particularism in religion and government. The altar was an asylum, Herod. vi 107; it was circled in Dionysiac festivals by the chorus, Xen. *Hipparch.* 3. 2 (and perhaps Pindar, *fr.* 53 Böckh, means it by the ὀμφαλὸν θυόεντα): and it was the scene of some striking appeals to popular sentiment, Plut. *Nicias* 13.

ξυνομνύναι ἐπί may take dat. of the enemy or of the object to be gained, as ξυνωμοσίας ἐπὶ δίκαις καὶ ἀρχαῖς Thucyd. viii 54. 4, *Lys.* 577. The word was mostly used of oligarchic combinations in ἑταιρεῖαι, and that is no doubt the meaning here, cf. on 475.

237—8. Χαλκιδεύς and Χαλκιδικός were used both of Chalcis and of Chalcidice. It is probable that here Χαλκιδικὸν means 'of Chalcis' and Χαλκιδῆς 'the people of Chalcidice': the audience would understand the absurd ignorance implied in this piece of συκοφαντία on Cleon's part. Chalcis' commercial and political league with Samos, Corinth and Croton against Eretria, Miletus, Athens and Sybaris had a most important influence on Greek history (see Curtius *Gesamm. Abhandl.* i 185, Holm in *Aufsätze gewidmet zu E. Curtius* 21—). Its aristocracy had made it revolt against Athens, and the decree of settlement passed on its reduction in B.C. 445 is extant (*CIA* iv 1 p. 10, Hicks, *Greek Hist. Inscr.* no. 28), the clause of the Chalcidian oath being ἐὰν ἀφιστῆ τις, κατερῶ 'Αθηναίοισι. ποτήρια Χαλκιδικά occur several times in the Parthenon inventories (one in a list for the year 425—4 *CIA* i 174): they were probably from Chalcis (Böckh *Staatsh.*² ii 168—), though Athenaeus xi 502 B and Eustathius on *Il.* ii 537 thought they

38   ΑΡΙΣΤΟΦΑΝΟΥΣ

Οἰ. Α. οὗτος, τί φεύγεις, οὐ μενεῖς; ὦ γεννάδα   240
ἀλλαντοπῶλα, μὴ προδῷς τὰ πράγματα.
ἄνδρες ἱππῆς, παραγένεσθε· νῦν ὁ καιρός. ὦ
Σίμων,
ὦ Παναίτι, οὐκ ἐλᾶτε πρὸς τὸ δεξιὸν κέρας;
ἄνδρες ἐγγύς· ἀλλ᾽ ἀμύνου, κἀπαναστρέφου
πάλιν.
ὁ κονιορτὸς δῆλος αὐτῶν ὡς ὁμοῦ προσκειμέ-
νων.   245
ἀλλ᾽ ἀμύνου καὶ δίωκε καὶ τροπὴν αὐτοῦ ποιοῦ.

240—1. A scholiast says that some copies omitted these two lines: also that some gave ἄνδρες ἱππῆς to ΑΛΛ., and some ἄνδρες ἐγγὺς to Θεράπων (meaning Demosthenes). **244.** ἄνδρες Dindorf for ἄνδρες.

---

might be from Chalcidice: they are usually described as ἀργυρᾶ, but here the ware is no doubt humbler, the slaves' *poteria* of Plaut. *Trin.* 1017, *Stich.* 694: so a scholium ἐχρῶντο τοῖς ὀστρακίνοις εἰς τὰ συμπόσια. Some of the Athenian allies in Chalcidice had revolted before, and others were looking forward to the Spartan aid that Brasidas brought them later in the year (Thucyd. iv 79).

240. γεννάδας (only nom. and voc.), in Comedy, Plato, Aristot. *Eth. Nic.* i 10 —12, and Lucian: the Dorism is peculiar and would be felt as a comic form of γενναῖος: so we have comic patronymics applied to humble individuals, as in *Ach.* 220, 612, *Pax* 1142, 1154—5.

242. The chorus is seen from the stage now, but it comes into the audience's full view in 247. The change from iambic to trochaic rhythm heightens the trepidation of the moment: so in other cases at the entrance of the chorus, *Pax* 298, cf. *Av.* 268: indeed the chorus always makes its appearance to trochaics when there is no lyric *parodos*. Members of chorus are often addressed individually: the Simon and Panaetius here may be the names of the two hipparchs of the time. The Simon whose book on horsemanship is quoted with respect by Xenophon *de re equestri* was probably contemporary, and may be the person mentioned here. Helbig thinks so and identifies his portrait on a vase (Daremberg-Saglio s.v. *Equitatio*).

The name, however, was not originally an honoured one: it was no doubt connected in the popular mind with σιμός, though the quantity makes the connexion doubtful: Lucian's cobbler, Simon, *Gallus* 14, changes his name to Simonides when he becomes rich: Phaedo's dialogue Σίμων ὁ σκυτεύς is in point: Simon in *CIA* i 321 is a mason, in *CIA* iv i p. 42 a fuller: the Simon of *Nub.* 351 is a swindler.

The order given to the hipparchs might be familiar on the battle-field as the cavalry were regularly posted on the wings.

They would naturally enter on the west side, as they would be supposed to come from the town: δεξιόν probably means to the other side of the stage, the actor's right, though 'right' and 'left' are ambiguous in stage-language (Haigh *Attic Theatre* 177).

244—6. ἐγγύς and ὁμοῦ form a climax, ὁμοῦ suggesting ὁμόσε χωρεῖν : Xen. *Hell.* iv 5. 15 ἀναχωρεῖν ἐκέλευε πρὶν τοὺς ὁπλίτας ὁμοῦ γίγνεσθαι: so ὁμοῦ is more than ἐγγύς in *Pax* 513 (where καὶ μὴν implies that Peace is just coming on to the stage), *Thesm.* 572: see Cobet *NL* 99. προσκεῖσθαι was specially used of cavalry charges, Herod. ix 40, 57, 60, Thucyd. vii 30. 2, 78. 3.

τροπὴν ποιεῖσθαι by the common periphrasis: Cobet *NL* 261 denies τροπὴν ποιεῖν and corrects Xen. *Hell.* vii 2. 20,

ΧΟΡ. παῖε παῖε τὸν πανοῦργον καὶ ταραξιππόστρατον
καὶ τελώνην καὶ φάραγγα καὶ Χάρυβδιν ἁρπαγῆς,
καὶ πανοῦργον καὶ πανοῦργον· πολλάκις γὰρ
αὖτ᾽ ἐρῶ.
καὶ γὰρ οὗτος ἦν πανοῦργος πολλάκις τῆς ἡμέρας.
ἀλλὰ παῖε καὶ δίωκε καὶ τάραττε καὶ κύκα   251
καὶ βδελύττου, καὶ γὰρ ἡμεῖς, κἀπικείμενος βόα·
εὐλαβοῦ δὲ μὴ ᾽κφύγῃ σε· καὶ γὰρ οἶδε τὰς ὁδούς,

---

248. φάλαγγα V: Zieliński *Märchenkomödie* 46 approves in the sense 'venomous spider': he has also the strange idea that τελώνης here has a modern Greek meaning of 'mischievous spirit.'

Eurip. *Heracl.* 743 (reading θείμην for θείην); but in Herod. i 30 τροπὴν ποιήσας τῶν πολεμίων ἀπέθανε κάλλιστα and Plut. *Philopoemen* 14 the active is used of the general or prominent individual; in Thuc. vi 69. 2 τροπὰς ἀλλήλων ἐποίουν the ἀλλήλων excuses the active.

247. The chorus divides at once into two squadrons: 247—250 come from one and 251—4 from the other, probably at the two ends of the orchestra. The first words of the chorus often fall into four lines, either trochaic as *Ach.* 204, *Pax* 301, or iambic tetr. as *Eccl.* 285, *Plut.* 257. παῖε is specially common in Aristophanic style, Rutherford *NP* 261. The coined word ταραξιππόστρατος is suggested by the Ταράξιππος, the bogey of horses on race-courses. Pausanias vi 20. 15—19 gives an account of various beliefs as to the origin of this daemon or form of Poseidon at Olympia and the Isthmus: something of the same kind caused ill-luck at the Pythia too (*id.* x 37. 4). In any case, the name stood for a δαίμων βάσκανος τοῖς ἱππεύουσι (Paus. vi 20. 17) and is so applied here. One of Pausanias' explanations (vi 20. 18), that the terror was something which Pelops buried in the earth at the spot, reminds us of the curious *devotiones* of horses found on race-courses at Carthage, *Demon...trado tibi os equos ut deteneas illos et implicentur.*

The τελῶναι in Athens farmed the various state-revenues. Some politicians, like Agyrrhius, tried to make money in this way (Böckh *Staatsh.*² i 452): Andoc. *Myst.* 133 Ἀγύρριος, ὁ καλὸς κἀγαθὸς (of course ironical here), ἀρχώνης ἐγένετο τῆς

πεντηκοστῆς. The abusive application was natural and became common: Philonides 5 πορνοτελῶναι, Μεγαρῆς δεινοί (the πορνικὸν τέλος being farmed like the rest), Theophr. *char.* 6 (16 Jebb) δεινὸς πανδοκεῦσαι καὶ τελωνῆσαι καὶ πορνοβοσκῆσαι, Apollod.com. 13. 12 ψεύδετ᾽ ἐπιορκεῖ μαρτυρεῖ δικορραφεῖ κλέπτει τελωνεῖ ῥᾳδιουργεῖ, Lucian *Pseudolog.* 30 προσαιτεῖ καὶ λωποδυτεῖ καὶ τελωνεῖ, Plut. *curios.* 7. 518 E τοὺς τελώνας βαρυνόμεθα καὶ δυσχεραίνομεν. The actual collection of taxes was sometimes made by underlings like ἐκλογῆς, but that word is rare, and the τελῶναι were collectors probably in Athens and certainly in the East under Roman rule: *publicanus* was wrongly used (instead of *portitor*) to translate the word in the New Testament. Pollux ix 32 gives a collection of abusive epithets, in high style and low, for use against the class.

ἁρπαγῆς must be taken with φάραγγα as well as with Χάρυβδιν. Χάρυβδις occurs in this sense as early as Hipponax 95 ποντοχάρυβδιν: ἐκχαρυβδίσαι Pherecrates 95. Cic. *de orat.* iii 163 thinks the phrase *Charybdim bonorum* rather too strong for *voraginem*.

251—4. τάραττε καὶ κύκα: the two verbs used so often of Cleon's conduct are here turned against him. βδελύττομαι is always middle until late times, the classical passive being βδελυγμίαν παρέχω, as Xen. *Mem.* iii 11. 13. βόα of a hopeful or triumphant cheer, as always in military affairs. We know nothing of the allusion in 254: Eucrates' (see on 129) 'flight straight to the bran' has been taken to mean (1) that he retired to enjoy the

ἄσπερ Εὐκράτης ἔφευγεν εὐθὺ τῶν κυρηβίων.

ΠΑ.   ὦ γέροντες ἡλιασταί, φράτερες τριωβόλου, 255
οὓς ἐγὼ βόσκω κεκραγὼς καὶ δίκαια κἄδικα,

255. φράτορες MSS., but the grammarian's note that φράτηρ was the Attic form (Aelius Dionys. ap. Eustath. 239. 30 &c.) is fully borne out by Inscriptions (Meisterhans § 50): it is also etymologically better, -τηρ, -τερος being the inflexion for nouns of relationship, -τωρ, -τορος for nouns of the agent.

wealth won as a miller (K. Hermann, Ribbeck, Müller-Strübing *Arist.* 583), (2) that he escaped a conviction by largesses of corn (Meineke *Fragm. Com.* ii 1003, Holden), (3) that he hid in his mills, or among his chaff (like the lover in Xenarchus 4. 12), till he could escape from a prosecution (Ranke *Arist. vita* 336, Mitchell). The proverb ὄνος εἰς ἄχυρα for unexpected good fortune (Apostol. 12. 78) may be in point (cf. *fr.* 76), as in *Vesp.* 1310 κλητῆρί τ' εἰς ἀχυρῶνας ἀποδεδρακότι. Nicknames, such as Κυρηβίων for a brother of Aeschines (Demosth. *FL* 329, Athen. vi 242 D, 244 A), Κύρηβος for a rich baker (Xen. *Memor.* ii 7. 6), may have been given to Eucrates: Donaldson *New Crat.* § 331 thought κυρήβια took its sense 'bran' from him. Aristot. *problem.* xi 25 and Plut. *non posse suav.* 13. 1096 B say that the orchestra was sometimes strewn with chaff and the like; so the reference may be to some scene in comedy. εὐθύ with gen. 'straight to' is a common Attic construction. Phrynichus' rule that εὐθύ is of place, εὐθύς of time, is accepted as holding for Attic prose and comedy by Rutherford: Lobeck gives instances to show that it was disregarded in Ionic and late Greek: Ammonius plainly was not convinced of its correctness. Shilleto thought that both forms might be used of place, the distinction being only in grammatical usage, εὐθὺ Ἀθηνῶν, εὐθὺς ἐς or πρὸς or ἐπὶ Ἀθήνας: but he had to correct εὐθὺ πρὸς in Soph. *OT* 1242 into εὐθὺς ἐς, and to allow Eurip. *Hipp.* 1197 τὴν εὐθὺς Ἄργους κἀπιδαυρίας ὁδόν as an exception. The latter passage stands alone in Attic, with the possible exception of Pherecrates 110: but in Epic and Ionic ἰθύς with gen. was common. Cases of εὐθύς with prep. meaning 'straight to' are Thucyd. iv 118. 3 (in a treaty), viii 96. 3 (not certain), Xen. *Cyrop.* ii 4. 24, vii 2. 1—2, *Ages.* 1. 29.
255—7. Cleon appeals to his partisans among the audience. Aristophanes' true democrat of the Philocleon type is

always old: his young man tends to oligarchy. The old φρατρία, a tie of blood and worship (ποία δὲ χέρνιψ φρατέρων προσδέξεται; Aesch. *Eum.* 655), has now given place to one of interest and pay, a creation of Cleon's.
βόσκω· πικρῶς ὡς θρέμμασιν αὐτοῖς κέχρηται ἀλόγοις schol. Cleon's use of the word shows his arrogant mastery over his supporters: βόσκω is properly used of beasts, and is transferred to men only with a sense of irksomeness or contempt. Note its contrast with the unobjectionable τρέφω in *Av.* 1356—9, the change in *Vesp.* from βόσκειν ἐθέλων 720 to καὶ μὴν θρέψω γ' αὐτόν 737 where Bdelycleon and his father understand each other, Eubulus 88 τρέφει με from the Πορνοβοσκός, Lucian *dial. meretr.* 6. 1—2 ἔβοσκον δὲ σὲ...θρέψεις ἐμέ. Serious prose writers sometimes use it, Herod. vi 39 of mercenary troops, and so Thucyd. vii 48. 5 where ξενοτροφοῦντας ἀναλίσκοντας βόσκοντας are felt as a climax, Plato *Rep.* ix 586 A. In Tragedy the use is more refined, and the food implied generally metaphorical: the person described may be despised, as in Soph. *fr.* 144 μὰ τὴν ἐκείνου δειλίαν ᾗ βόσκεται, Aesch. *Eum.* 302, but the contempt is generally pitying or kindly, as in such reflections on life generally as ἐλπὶς γὰρ ἡ βόσκουσα τοὺς πολλοὺς βροτῶν Soph. *fr.* 687, cf. *fr.* 518, or on the helplessness of children as Soph. *Trach.* 144, *Aj.* 558 where the contrast between ἐτράφης and βόσκου is of course intentional, or on one's own humble lot as Aesch. *Cho.* 26, Soph. *Ant.* 1246, *Elect.* 263, Eurip. *Phoen.* 405, *Ion* 127, 183.
καὶ δίκαια κἄδικα by a well-known idiom, where we should say *right or wrong*: cf. Aesch. *Sept.* 414—5 θεοῦ τε γὰρ θέλοντος ἐκπέρσειν πόλιν καὶ μὴ θέλοντός φησιν, *ib.* 1058 δράτω τι πόλις καὶ μὴ δράτω, Eurip. *Supp.* 895, *IA* 643 οὐκ οἶδ' ὅπως φῶ τοῦτο καὶ μὴ φῶ, τέκνον, Plut. *quaest. conv.* iv 2. 655 C ταῦτα ἔξεστι πιστεύειν καὶ μή.

παραβοηθεῖθ', ὡς ὑπ' ἀνδρῶν τύπτομαι ξυνωμοτῶν.

ΧΟΡ. ἐν δίκῃ γ', ἐπεὶ τὰ κοινὰ πρὶν λαχεῖν κατεσθίεις,
κἀποσυκάζεις πιέζων τοὺς ὑπευθύνους, σκοπῶν
ὅστις αὐτῶν ὠμός ἐστιν ἢ πέπων ἢ μὴ πέπων, 260
κἄν τιν' αὐτῶν γνῷς ἀπράγμον' ὄντα καὶ κεχηνότα,

ἀνδρῶν must not be neglected as otiose. ἀνήρ, especially in the plural, is very common in apposition: the effect generally is complimentary; a pleader would hardly venture to say δικασταί, or a general στρατιῶται, without the ἄνδρες, if he wished for a favourable hearing (in Cratinus 143. 5 ὦ στρατιῶται is contemptuous, as it is probably in Lucian *Zeuxis* 11): and so in comic speeches ὦ ἄνδρες θεοί Lucian *Jup. trag.* 15, ἄνδρες κύνες Athen. iv 160 B; but with a word of unfavourable meaning ἀνήρ deepens the dislike implied: we get cases of both applications, good and bad, in *Ach.* 707 ἄνδρα πρεσβύτην ὑπ' ἀνδρὸς τοξότου κυκώμενον, and in Plato *Euthyphro* 15 D ὑπὲρ ἀνδρὸς θητὸς ἄνδρα πρεσβύτην πατέρα διωκάθειν φόνου : so with ξυνωμοτῶν here the ἀνδρῶν emphasizes their villainy: cf. ὑπ' ἀνδρῶν βαρβάρων *Vesp.* 439 &c. The same word may of course in different mouths have different connotations : Medea says ἀνδρὸς Ἕλληνος λόγους πεισθεῖσα (Eurip. *Med.* 801) with hatred, cf. Aesch. *Pers.* 362, but Isocrates *Philipp.* 139 says ὑπ' ἀνδρὸς Ἕλληνος with pride : ἀνδρὶ δημότῃ is to 'a mere commoner' Soph. *Antig.* 690, but in *Nub.* 1219 'my worthy townsman.' ἀνὴρ βασιλεὺς is depreciatory in a defence of democracy Eurip. *Supp.* 444 (see on ἄνδρα τύραννον *inf.* 1114): so is μάντις ἀνὴρ *IA* 956. The enemy have become οἱ ξυνωμόται, a recognised factor in politics, by 452. τύπτομαι may be used in both senses of τύπτω, i.e. as *vapulo* or as *vulneror* : it is actually found, as might be expected, more commonly in the former sense (Cobet *VL* 330).

258—60. ἐν δίκῃ γε, as *Nub.* 1379 ΣΤ. ἀλλ' αὖθις αὖ τυπτήσομαι. ΦΕΙ. νὴ τὸν Δί' ἐν δίκῃ γε, *Vesp.* 508 νὴ Δί' ἐν δίκῃ γε. τὰ κοινά of the object of peculation, as *Plut.* 569 πλουτήσαντες ἀπὸ τῶν κοινῶν, Plato com. 14 κλέπτειν τὰ κοινά, Aristot. *Pol.* viii 6. 9 of ruined oligarchs ὁτὲ μὲν

ἐπιχειροῦσί τι κινεῖν, ὁτὲ δὲ κλέπτουσι τὰ κοινά. The charges are the natural ones, 'you steal state-moneys yourself, you persecute and black-mail other functionaries.' The audience probably cared little whether τὰ κοινά referred chiefly to the cleruch-lands, which were a special feature of Periclean policy and were fresh in mind in the case of Mitylene (Thucyd. iii 50. 2), or the other spoils of war, over which a general had great control : and we need not suppose that the poet was precise. The thought of συκοφαντία starts him on an elaborate metaphor of the trade : Cleon picks the fruit from the fig-tree of state, the ὑπεύθυνοι being the figs. ἀποσυκάζω, on the analogy of ἀποθριάζω, ἀποκαρπίζω &c., ought to mean 'pick off figs.' ὠμός and πέπων suggest also the two types of character : μὴ πέπων must mean 'ripening.'

261. Prof. Mahaffy's explanation of these lines in *Hermathena* i 237— is ingenious and probably right : he supposes that the metaphor of fig-gathering is carried on : more point is then given to κεχηνότα (gaping like a ripe fig) : the MS. διαβαλών stands, ' having hooked him by calumny,' and ἐγκολῃβάζω has its proper meaning acc. to Hesychius and the scholia, 'gulp down.' The only change from the MS. reading is ὠμόν for ὦμον. The other explanation, that 262—3 give a picture of a wrestling-match, is as old at least as the scholia: but, as Prof. Mahaffy says, they have an inkling of his rendering. ἀγκυρίζω was a wrestling term, but it would seem that a meaning 'throw heavily' or the like had to be forced on ἐγκολῃβάζω. The ordinary Athenian was apt to understand ἀπράγμων in a sense suggested by Solon's law, 'useless to the state' : but the moderates assumed it as a title to praise, 'a hater of πράγματα' in the Aristophanic sense of war abroad and συκοφαντία

καταγαγὼν ἐκ Χερρονήσου, διαβαλών, ἀγκυ-
ρίσας,
εἶτ' ἀποστρέψας τὸν ὠμὸν αὐτὸν ἐνεκολήβασας·
καὶ σκοπεῖς γε τῶν πολιτῶν ὅστις ἐστὶν ἀμνο-
κῶν,
πλούσιος καὶ μὴ πονηρὸς καὶ τρέμων τὰ πράγ-
ματα.   265

ΠΑ. ξυνεπίκεισθ' ὑμεῖς; ἐγὼ δ', ἄνδρες, δι' ὑμᾶς
τύπτομαι,
ὅτι λέγειν γνώμην ἔμελλον ὡς δίκαιον ἐν πόλει
ἱστάναι μνημεῖον ὑμῶν ἐστιν ἀνδρείας χάριν.

262. διαβαλών MSS. διαλαβών Casaubon and most editors, in the wrestling sense.
263. ὦ μόν MSS. ὠμόν Mahaffy. ἐνεκολάβησας MSS.
264—5. Transposed to after 260 by Brunck.
268. ἐστάναι MSS. ἱστάναι Elmsley on Eurip. *Heracl.* 937 and most editors since.

at home: in Plato *Rep.* viii 565 A the αὐτουργοί τε καὶ ἀπράγμονες are the best class in a democracy: *Nub.* 1007 ἀπραγμοσύνη is a feature of the ideal youth, but in the speeches of Pericles (Thucyd. ii 40. 2, 63. 2) and Alcibiades (vi 18. 6—7) it is a contemptible feebleness (see Appendix ii). The ἐκ Χερρονήσου probably is intended to remind people of some actual case, now beyond guessing, of someone, either an Athenian officer on duty in the north, like Thucydides, or a man of position in an allied city of Chersonesus. For ἀποστρέψας cf. *Anth. Pal.* v 227. 2.

αὐτὸν 'the one you want')(τὸν ὠμόν, cf. αὐτό in Plato *Rep.* iv 432 E.

264—5. ἐσόμεθ' ἀλλήλοισιν ἀμνοὶ τοὺς τρόπους *Pax* 935. κοέω was no doubt common in some dialects, as it is a common element in proper names (of Trojans and Spartans chiefly), like Λαοκόων. We are reminded of Xen. *Mem.* ii 9, where Crito is the sheep at the mercy of wolfish συκοφάνται.

266—8. He warns the knights that they are in danger if a new demagogue should arise to outbid him: they are unpopular already, and he has suffered on suspicion that he meant to propose an honour to them. ἔμελλον (which never takes ἠ- augment in Aristoph. except in

anapaests, see Rutherford on Babrius 7) has probably its very idiomatic sense 'I was going to, as they know,' 'they know I was going to.' This usage is not very uncommon in Homer (see instances collected by A. Platt in *Journ. Phil.* xxi 39—), nor in Attic, as Thucyd. i 107. 3 κατὰ θάλασσαν Ἀθηναῖοι ἔμελλον κωλύσειν, διὰ δὲ τῆς Γερανείας οὐκ ἀσφαλὲς ἐφαίνετο πορεύεσθαι, cf. *Ach.* 347, *Vesp.* 460, *Thesm.* 1177, Plato i *Alcib.* 110 B ἀλλὰ τί ἔμελλον ποιεῖν, ὦ Σώκρατες, ὁπότε τίς με ἀδικεῖ; 'what did you expect me to do?' γνώμην λέγειν 'to propose a motion' either in βουλή or ἐκκλησία was the formal phrase, cf. *inf.* 654, 931, Lysias 20. 7 ὁμοίας τὰς κατηγορίας ποιοῦνται τῶν τε εἰπόντων γνώμην τινὰ ἐν τῇ βουλῇ καὶ τῶν μή, Thucyd. viii 67. 1, 68. 1 &c.: so γνώμην νικᾶν 'carry a motion' *Nub.* 432, *Vesp.* 594)(μὴ τυχεῖν γνώμης Thucyd. iii 42. 5. In state-records, the mover's name is given with εἶπεν alone (very rarely γνώμην τοῦ δεῖνος is found instead, Swoboda *Griech. Volksbeschlüsse* 34).

ἐν πόλει 'on the acropolis': so πόλις without the article=ἡ ἀκρόπολις Thucyd. ii 15. 6 καλεῖται ἡ ἀκρόπολις μέχρι τοῦδε ἔτι ὑπ' Ἀθηναίων πόλις, Isaeus 5. 44 οὐδὲ τὰ ἀναθήματα εἰς πόλιν κεκόμικας, Pausanias i 26. 7 ἐν τῇ νῦν ἀκροπόλει, τότε δὲ

ΧΟΡ. ὡς δ' ἀλαζών, ὡς δὲ μάσθλης· εἶδες οἷ' ὑπέρχεται
ὡσπερεὶ γέροντας ἡμᾶς καὶ κοβαλικεύεται; 270
ἀλλ' ἐὰν ταύτῃ γε νικᾷ, ταυτηὶ πεπλήξεται·
ἢν δ' ὑπεκκλίνῃ γε δευρί, τὸ σκέλος κυρηβάσει.

270. γέροντας ἡμᾶς ἐκκοβαλικεύεται MSS. (but R omits ἡμᾶς). γέροντας ὄντας καὶ κοβ. Cobet *NL* 37 after Porson, κἀκκοβαλικεύεται Brunck. **272.** τὸ R. πρὸς other MSS., δευρὶ πρὸς σκέλος Piccolomini in *Studi ital. di filol.* ii 577.

ὀνομαζομένῃ πόλει: and so always in documents (as Thucyd. v 18. 10, 23. 5, 47. 11) and Inscriptions, which do not seem to give ἀκρόπολις at all till the fourth century. For cases where ἡ πόλις in the same sense appears in MSS. see Wyse ap. Sandys' Arist. *Pol. Ath.* 24. 15.
The monument 'for valour' would be in honour of their conduct at Solygeia. Among the many honorific decrees found in Athens and elsewhere, very few, if any, seem to bear such terms: the services rewarded are generally social and political, and the phrases run ὅτι ἄνδρες ἀγαθοί εἰσιν περὶ τὸν δῆμον, ἀνδραγαθίας ἕνεκα τῆς εἰς τὸν δῆμον and the like.
269—70. δὲ in indignant exclamations was allowed and could be repeated: Demosth. *Mid.* 209 is parallel οὐκ ἂν εὐθέως εἴποιεν 'τὸν δὲ βάσκανον, τὸν δὲ ὄλεθρον, τοῦτον δὲ ὑβρίζειν, ἀναπνεῖν δέ': cf. also *inf.* 397. There is no doubt an adversative meaning behind, as we might say 'But what nonsense!'
μάσθλης 'prepared leather,' Hippocr. *de morb.* ii 59 τρίζει τὸ αἷμα οἷον μάσθλης: from the idea of suppleness it was one of the many words used for 'rascal,' *Nub.* 449 μάσθλης, εἴρων, γλοιός, ἀλαζών.
εἶδες. This 'aorist of instantaneous action' is naturally much commoner in drama than elsewhere: comparison with Vedic Sanskrit shows it to be the original use. ὑπέρχομαι, for synonyms see on 47: this compound of ἔρχομαι has the strange peculiarity of being used in Attic, when it means 'fawn on,' in parts besides the pres. indic. as ὑπέρχεσθαι Andoc. *Alcib.* 21, Demosth. *Aristocr.* 8, ὑπερχόμενος Plato *Crito* 53 E, [Xen.] *Pol. Ath.* 2. 14 (Rutherford *New Phryn.* 110: there seem to be no other instances).
The knights' youth and the dramatic rule mentioned in 255 make them choose

the word γέροντας 'old drivellers' with special indignation.
κόβαλος, an apish imp (possibly akin to κοϜάλεμος, see on 221), was familiarly used of grotesque trickery. κοβαλεία· ἡ προσποιητὴ μετ' ἀπάτης παιδιὰ Harpocr.: *inf.* 332, 417, 635, Aristot. *Hist. Anim.* ix 12. 597ᵇ23 ἔστι δὲ (ὁ ὦτὸς) κόβαλος καὶ μιμητής, καὶ ἀντορχούμενος ἁλίσκεται. Hence came the Low-Latin *cobalinus*, French *gobelin*, our *goblin*. On verbs in -εύομαι, see Rutherford on Babrius 104. 5. I fancy that from a few rather pretentiously and officially serious words—μαντεύομαι, πολιτεύομαι, πρεσβεύομαι, ἐπικηρυκεύομαι—there arose in a kind of parody a large class of colloquial words applied to calling or manner, like ὀττεύομαι, δημοτεύομαι, ἀλαζονεύομαι: φιλανθρωπεύομαι for instance is not a word of the highest seriousness, any more than Strepsiades' ξυνωρικεύομαι, and Aristotle's ἀνθρωπεύομαι, *Eth. Nic.* x 8. 6, would enliven his lecture room: the habits implied are usually not respectable: βωμολοχεύομαι, βδελυρεύομαι, φορτικεύομαι show the type (see also on 279).
271—2. Only the performance could make these lines quite clear. The scholia show that some took ταύτῃ as for πονηρίᾳ, some as for χειρί. No doubt the chorus is divided, and the pronouns take definite meaning from the speakers and the action. Herwerden (*Hermes* xxiv 607) suggests that ταύτῃ answers to δευρί, and ταυτηί (sc. τῇ χειρί) to τὸ σκέλος. It is pretty certain that ταύτῃ and ταυτηί cannot have the same reference: so perhaps *Thesm.* 1218—: Blass shows in *Rhein. Mus.* xliv 1— that οὑτοσί is often nearer ὅδε than οὗτος. νικᾷ has been objected to (Zieliński *Gliederung* 268—9): but Cleon's partial victory is not regarded as unlikely. The phrases are military: πεπλήξεται seems to be *ferietur*, not *vapulabit* (Cobet *VL* 338), and the only other instance quoted of

ΠΑ.　ὦ πόλις καὶ δῆμ', ὑφ' οἵων θηρίων γαστρίζομαι.

ΧΟΡ.　καὶ κέκραγας, ὥσπερ ἀεὶ τὴν πόλιν καταστρέφει;

ΑΛΛ.　ἀλλ' ἐγώ σε τῇ βοῇ ταύτῃ γε πρῶτα τρέψο-
　　　　　μαι.　　　　　　　　　　　　　　　　　　275

ΧΟΡ.　ἀλλ' ἐὰν μὲν τόνδε νικᾷς τῇ βοῇ, τήνελλος εἶ·
　　　　ἢν δ' ἀναιδείᾳ παρέλθῃ σ', ἡμέτερος ὁ πυραμοῦς.

274. Most editors, following Sauppe, mark a lacuna of one verse between 273 and 274, thinking that the chorus should have two lines here corresponding to 276—7. ὅσπερ 5 MSS. and old editions: ᾧπερ Kock Mein. καταστρέφει R. -στρέφεις the other MSS. **275.** ΑΛ. MSS., ΠΑ. editors, surely without sufficient reason. **276.** μέντοι γε MSS. μὲν τόνδε Porson and editors since. τήνελλος εἶ MSS. τήνελλ' ἔσει Porson Vels. τηνελλάσει Mein. τήνελλά σοι Kock Ribb. **277.** παρέλθῃς MSS., except M which has παρέλθῃ σ'.

ὑπεκκλίνω (Plut. Camillus 18 τὸ δεξιὸν ὑπεκκλῖναν τὴν ἐπιφορὰν ἐκ τοῦ πεδίου πρὸς τοὺς λόφους) shows its use in tactics: κυρηβάζω was probably a 'sporting' word of the wrestling ground; can it be connected with κυρήβια (see on 254), 'bring him to the sawdust'?

273. πόλις is the common vocative in Attic tragedy and comedy alike: ὦ πόλις πόλις Ach. 27, Soph. OT 629, Eupolis 205, and so Ant. 842, Eurip. Hipp. 884, Phoen. 1213, Ar. Thesm. 839: πόλι seems to be confined to comedy and there to cretics, Ach. 971, fr. 162. 1 ἇ πόλι φίλη Κέκροπος, αὐτοφυὲς Ἀττική (quoted by Marcus Aurelius iv 23), and 'epionics,' Eupolis 290 ὦ καλλίστη πόλι πασῶν ὅσας Κλέων ἐφορᾷ. πόλις and δῆμος are associated even in Homer, as Od. viii 555 εἰπὲ δέ μοι γαῖάν τε τεὴν δῆμόν τε πόλιν τε: here Cleon means his demesmen, often invoked for protection (Lys. 685), though he extends it to the spirit of democracy.

γαστρίζω with the usual elasticity of verbs in -ίζω may have various meanings: it is found in two; (1) as here, punch in the stomach, so inf. 454, Vesp. 1529, Diog. Laert. vii 5. 172, which illustrates the ease with which such words might be formed, εἰ ὁ εἰς τὴν γαστέρα τύπτων γαστρίζει, καὶ (then) ὁ τοὺς μηροὺς τύπτων μηρίζει: (2) eat a bellyful, as Lucian rhet. praec. 24, Athen. iii 96 F &c., Alciphro iii 45. 3, 46. 4: Athen. x 421 A plays on both meanings: the former sense became rare, and Phrynichus 76 strangely denies it (see Rutherford there on this class of words).

274. καταστρέφω 'overturn,' καταστρέφομαι 'subdue,' is the distinction. I see no sufficient reason against the indignant καί, which some editors object to.

275. The Sausage-man now breaks in to challenge Cleon on his own ground. There is no awkwardness in the chorus addressing Cleon in the next sentence; surely σε need not always refer to the last speaker. The MS. arrangement seems to me to give more point to almost every word in the line, than it has if spoken by Cleon.

276—7. Apart from the question whether μέντοι γε is good Attic (see Appendix i), Porson's emendation of it improves the meaning: τόνδε has its proper meaning, 'this friend of ours.' The spirited onomatopoetic τήνελλα was of course very well known in the phrase τήνελλα καλλίνικε: the rather strange τήνελλος is given by Suidas and Hesychius and the scholia: the knights no doubt use phrases throughout the play that marked their sporting and social coteries of the day.

277. πυραμοῦς, formed from πυροί, perhaps on the analogy of σησαμοῦς. It was a cake, given as the prize to the banqueter who kept up the symposium all night (Pollux vi 108 τοῖς διαπαννυχίσασιν ἆθλα ἦν σησαμοῦς καὶ πυραμοῦς: so Athen. xiv 647 C, xv 668 C), as the ἑωλοκρασία was the punishment for those who failed. It became a symbol or phrase for success in general: τοῦ γὰρ τεχνάζειν ἡμέτερος ὁ πυραμοῦς Thesm. 94: Plut. quaest. conv. ix 15. 747 B πυραμοῦς is a prize for dancing, Artemid. Oneirocr. i 72 a sign in dreams of success at law.

ΠΑ. τουτονὶ τὸν ἄνδρ' ἐγὼ 'νδείκνυμι, καὶ φήμ' ἐξ-
ά́γειν
ταῖσι Πελοποννησίων τριήρεσι ζωμεύματα.

ΑΛΛ. ναὶ μὰ Δία κἄγωγε τοῦτον, ὅτι κενῇ τῇ κοιλίᾳ 280
ἐσδραμὼν ἐς τὸ πρυτανεῖον, εἶτα πάλιν ἐκθεῖ
πλέα.

ΟΙ. Α. νὴ Δί', ἐξάγων γε τἀπόρρηθ', ἅμ' ἄρτον καὶ κρέας
καὶ τέμαχος, οὗ Περικλέης οὐκ ἠξιώθη πώποτε.

278. δείκνυμι MSS. 'νδείκνυμι schol. Dobree.   282. ἐξαγαγών MSS.

278—9. Cleon begins with something which would be called συκοφαντία:
and the οὗτος and οὑτοσί of legal and
political opposition appear. An ἔνδειξις
was generally brought against a disqualified holder of office, but it might be
brought against a disqualified candidate
or speaker as well: it seems to have
ensured the arrest of the person charged,
Demosth. *Nicost.* 14 παρεσκευάζοντο ἐν-
δεικνύναι με καὶ ἐμβάλλειν εἰς τὸ δεσμω-
τήριον. For a similar case in history see
Andocides *de red.* 14 Πείσανδρος ἔφη
"ἐγὼ τὸν ἄνδρα τοῦτον ἐνδεικνύω ὑμῖν σῖτόν
τε εἰς τοὺς πολεμίους εἰσαγαγόντα καὶ
κωπέας." The penalty on conviction was
often death. φημί is almost technical,
cf. 445, Plato com. 14 εἰ Πάμφιλόν γε
φαίης κλέπτειν τὰ κοινά: it does not seem
that it was certain whether φημί or φαίνω
was the verb of φάσις: so Athenaeus iii
94 D quotes 300 with φήσω instead of
φαίνω: ἐνδείκνυμι καὶ φαίνω in the commercial treaty *CIA* ii 546. ἐξάγω, 'ex-
port,' has as correlative ἄγω as well as
εἰσάγω: Plato *Legg.* viii 847 C μήτε τις
ἀγέτω μήτε ἐξαγέτω (Kock on Cratinus
40).
The ἀπόρρητα, or forbidden exports,
of Athens were mainly corn and ship-
building materials, in both of which the
country was naturally so poor. ζωμεύματα is of course a comic invention;
'manufactured broth-stuffs' is hardly an
exaggerated translation. There were only
a few old words, used outside Attic,
in -ευμα, like στράτευμα, τόξευμα, βού-
λευμα: none of them seem to be older
than about Pindar's time, and even they
must have been felt as rather artificial at
first. Tragic style delighted in them,
a pupil was παίδευμα, a slave δούλευμα
and so on. Outside serious poetry the
words are used to denote artificial pro-
ducts of civilisation, as πολίτευμα ἀπο-
μνημόνευμα, of art, such as τόρευμα,
σμίλευμα *Ran.* 819, comically of the art
of cookery and the like, as καρύκευμα,
νωγάλευμα, χόρδευμα (*inf.* 315): sometimes more generally, but always with
the idea of being the result of trouble
or skill, even in πονήρευμα, θώπευμα,
διεντέρευμα (*Nub.* 166) &c.
The idea that there is a play on ὑποζώ-
ματα, 'cables for under-girding,' is as old
as the scholia, but does not help.
280—1. 'If smuggling is your charge
against me, we can all see what sort of
smuggling you carry on.' Public entertainment was provided at the Prytaneum
for envoys and those distinguished Athenians who had the σίτησις, at the Tholos
and Thesmotheteion for Prytaneis and
Archons.
282—3. Demosthenes is struck by
the new idea 'By Zeus, it *is* illegal to
take out...': ἀπόρρητα, 'contraband goods,'
as *Ran.* 362. He mentions what the ordinary Athenian would think invidiously
sumptuous fare, wheaten bread, meat
and fishes large enough to be sliced.
Athenaeus iv 137 E says that Solon prescribed only μᾶζα for the Prytaneum
meals, allowing ἄρτος besides on festivals.
τέμαχος is always of fish (τόμος of meat
and other eatables): L. and S. say *salt*-
fish, but there is no evidence for this:
Archestratus ap. Athen. vii 303 E θερμά
τ' ἔχειν τεμάχη βάπτων δριμεῖαν ἐς ἅλμην
is of fresh tunny with brine sauce: cf.
inf. 1177—8, Pherecrates 45 καὶ δῆθ'
ὑπάρχει τέμαχος ἐγχέλειον ἡμῖν, τευθίς,

ΠΑ.   ἀποθανεῖσθον αὐτίκα μάλα.

ΑΛΛ.   τριπλάσιον κεκράξομαί σου.   285

ΠΑ.   καταβοήσομαι βοῶν σε.

ΑΛΛ.   κατακεκράξομαί σε κράζων.

ΠΑ.   διαβαλῶ σ', ἐὰν στρατηγῇς.

287. "I have long suspected that Aristoph. gave the vastly more sonorous κατακεκράξομαι κεκραγώς," Shilleto on Thucyd. ii 4. 2. No doubt κράζω is hardly an Attic form (here and thrice in Aristotle), but it is excused as closer to βοῶν, and σε is necessary.

ἄρνειον κρέας, φύσκης τόμος κ.τ.λ., Strattis 44 κᾆτ' εἰς ἀγορὰν ἐλθόντες ἀδροὺς ὀψωνοῦσιν μεγάλους τε φάγρους καὶ Κωπᾴδων ἀπαλῶν τεμάχη, Ephippus ap. Athen. vii 322 D.

Kock gives a rule that Aristophanes contracts -κλέης into -κλῆς only when the resulting antepenult is long as in Θεμιστοκλῆς: for instances see his notes here and on Cratinus 15. The rule must have been one of metrical convenience only: Inscriptions lend it no countenance, giving Περικλῆς, Ἱεροκλῆς &c. as regular forms, with Ἡρακλέης and the like as rare exceptions, Meisterhans § 51. 7, Kretschmer *Griech. Vaseninschriften* 194.

The natural meaning of the words is that Pericles never had the σίτησις. From the mutilated inscription *CIA* i 8, it may be inferred that successful generals formed the last and rarest category of citizens so honoured.

284—. The Agon begins with lively trochaics dimeter, the resolution of the first foot adding to the spirited effect. This metre is rare, but occurs again *Av.* 387—398, *Thesm.* 524—8, *Ran.* 242—, 534—548, answered by 590—604, *Eccl.* 893—. Observe that Cleon is more political, less coarse and personal, and therefore less successful, than his rival.

The dual means of course that Demosthenes is included: he hardly threatens the chorus at all: and after the first line he practically ignores Demosthenes too except at 429. αὐτίκα μάλα is a favourite combination, cf. πηνίκα μάλιστα: even when αὐτίκα means *for example*, μάλα may be added, as Plato ii *Alcib.* 143 E, Demosth. i *Aristog.* 29.

286. καταβοᾶν τινος *shout against*, καταβοᾶν τινα *shout down*, is the regular distinction, applicable to all such κατα- compound verbs. L. and S. give instances for καταβοῶ, καταγλωττίζω, καταγελῶ, κατα-

λαλῶ (the meanings *rail at* and *talk down* should be distinguished), καταπαίζω, καταψευδομαρτυρῶ, κατορχοῦμαι. Like many other Attic refinements, this was lost in later Greek, where the gen. is used instead of the acc., see instances in L. and S. under καταδολεσχῶ, καταδυναστεύω, καταληρῶ, καταφλυαρῶ, καταφιλοσοφῶ, κατεπᾴδω: Theophrastus' καταυλεῖν τοῦ τόπου if correctly quoted by Athen. xiv 624 B would be the earliest case. So κατατρέχω, *run down*, *decry*, has acc. in Plato, but gen. in Athenaeus &c. (Cobet *VL* 629), καθιππάζω has gen. in Diog. Laertius: in 287 most MSS. give κατακεκράξομαί σου, though metre as well as good usage demand σε: Plutarch follows the rule in πολλοὶ καταδημαγωγοῦσι τοὺς ἀδελφούς *frat. am.* 482 E, as compared with καταψιθυρίζοντα τοῦ ἀδελφοῦ *ib.* 10. 483 C, though he sometimes neglects it. Cobet *NL* 97 positively denies καταγελῶ τινι in Herodotus (iii 37 and four other cases): but there are other instances of such κατα- verbs with dative in Ionic: Μασσαγετέων τριτημορίδι τοῦ στρατοῦ κατυβρίσας Herod. i 212, καταείδοντες τῷ ἀνέμῳ vii 191.

287. κράζω is more of an inhuman or inarticulate cry than βοῶ: hence Aristot. *Poet.* 22. 1458ᵇ31 reduces Homer's ἠϊόνες βοόωσιν to prose by substituting κράζουσιν. In good prose it is used only by orators attacking their opponents' style, generally in combination with βοῶ, Demosth. *Cor.* 132 βοῶν ὁ βάσκανος οὗτος καὶ κεκραγώς, *ib.* 199, ii *Aristog.* 47, Lysias 3. 15, Aeschin. *Ctes.* 218 σὺ ἀναλώσας ἐκέκραγας, Athen. x 420 E, xiii 601 B: Xen. *Cyrop.* i 3. 10, of drunken men.

288. The office of στρατηγός was of course the main object of the statesman: Thucydides uses διαβάλλω of Cleon's conduct to other στρατηγοί in iv 27. 4 and v 16. 1; it is the regular word for 'damaging' a political opponent.

ΑΛΛ. κυνοκοπήσω σου τὸ νῶτον.

ΠΑ. περιελῶ σ' ἀλαζονείαις.   290

ΑΛΛ. ὑποτεμοῦμαι τὰς ὁδούς σου.

ΠΑ. βλέψον εἴς μ' ἀσκαρδάμυκτος.

ΑΛΛ. ἐν ἀγορᾷ κἀγὼ τέθραμμαι.

ΠΑ. διαφορήσω σ', εἴ τι γρύξει.

ΑΛΛ. κοπροφορήσω σ', εἰ λαλήσεις.   295

ΠΑ. ὁμολογῶ κλέπτειν· σὺ δ' οὐχί.

ΑΛΛ. νὴ τὸν Ἑρμῆν τὸν ἀγοραῖον,
κἀπιορκῶ γε βλεπόντων.

---

289. τὸν R and most MSS.   **290.** ἀλαζονείαις Elmsley on Soph. *OC* 1454 for ἀλαζονείας.   **292.** ἀσκαρδαμυκτί Mein. from *Etym. Mag.*
294. γρύξει Elmsley on *Ach.* 278 for γρύξεις or γρύξεις of MSS.
298. γ' ἐμβλεπόντων Pors. on *Ach.* 739, Cobet *Mnemos.* n. s. ii 416 : RV &c. give 298 and 300 to ΠΑ., 299 to ΑΛΛ. ; so Piccolomini.

---

289. νῶτον Ἀττικῶς, νῶτος Ἑλληνικῶς is the grammarians' rule: the refinement that νῶτος might be used in Attic of animals is applicable to Xen. *de re equest.* 3. 3 and most of the cases in Aristotle. The ancients differed as to the exact meaning of the unique κυνοκοπῶ.

290. It is curious to notice how scholars have taken περιελῶ from περιαιρῶ (on 143), partly owing to the scholium. Cleon takes his metaphor from cavalry tactics: cf. Plut. *Nicias* 19 τοῖς ἱππεῦσι περιελαύνοντες πολλοὺς ἤρουν : so περιελαύνω came to mean *harass*, as *inf.* 887, Herod. i 60, Demosth. *Phaenipp.* 32.

291. ὑποτέμνομαι was also a word of tactics, military as Xen. *Cyrop.* i 4. 19, Plut. *Lucullus* 15, or naval as Xen. *Hell.* i 6. 15.

292. Aristot. ap. Athen. viii 353 C has some safe remarks on winking as a clue to character. Kock quotes Xen. *Cyrop.* i 4. 28 and Lucian in support of ἀσκαρδάμυκτί : and such adverbs became the regular usage, Lucian for instance being full of them. But in older Greek ἀσκαρδάμυκτος &c. would be more idiomatic, there being so many verbals in -τος with ἀ- privative that are active of persons, passive of things, ἄπρακτος, ἀπροσδόκητος, ἄθυτος, ἀνήκουστος, &c. ἀπείρατος and ἄγνωστος Pind. *Isthm.* 3. 48 are both active in sense: in *Nem.* 7. 45 the scholiast's

first interpretation, that ἀδόκητον = οὐ δοκέοντα, seems the best: and in Soph. *OT* 336 ἀτελεύτητος is possibly active, though ἄτεγκτος is of course passive.

294. διαφορῶ, *differo*, *rend.* Compounds of φορῶ as slight intensives of the φέρω forms are common in Herodotus, and known in Attic : Eurip. *Bacch.* 739, 746, 754 will illustrate the difference between διαφέρω and διαφορῶ : see on παρεφόρουν *inf.* 1215. γρύξει is confirmed by γρύξομαι in Alcaeus com. 22, and by Rutherford's reasoning on such futures *New Phryn.* 381—. The word is used only of human speech, and in negative or quasi-negative sentences, οὐδὲ γρύζω = *ne hisco quidem.* It does not seem to mean *grunt*, whether the other explanations given by Hesychius (γρῦ· ὁ ὑπὸ τῷ ὄνυχι ῥύπος. ἤδη καὶ τὸ ἐλάχιστον) and Clemm (*Curt. Studien* iii 293, γρῦ kin to *granum*) are right or not.

295. κοπροφορήσω in parody of the rather exceptional διαφορήσω. The acc. is found also after ψηφοφορῶ *vote for*, κωδωνοφορῶ, δορυφορῶ.

297. The oath is by the appropriate deity. Most cities had a Ἑρμῆς ἀγοραῖος : in Athens his bronze statue stood near the στοὰ ποικίλη (see Harrison and Verrall *Myth. and Mon.* 127—). For Ζεὺς ἀγοραῖος see on 410.

298. Arist. is fond of such genitives abs., *Vesp.* 882 κἀπιδακρύειν ἀντιβολούντων

ΠΑ. ἀλλότρια τοίνυν σοφίζει,
     καί σε φαίνω τοῖς πρυτάνεσιν,   300
     ἀδεκατεύτους τῶν θεῶν ἱ-
     ρὰς ἔχοντα κοιλίας.

ΧΟΡ. ὦ μιαρὲ καὶ βδελυρὲ καὶ κεκράκτα, τοῦ σοῦ
     θράσους

300. φανῶ MSS.: so *Ach.* 819 MSS. have φανῶ, edd. mostly φαίνω: Athen. iii
94 C quotes φήσω σε ἀδεκατεύτους κοιλίας πωλεῖν: φανῶ σε Pors. Dobr. Vels.: φανῶ
for φαενῶ, like ἀρῶ, is possible *a priori*, but is quite unsupported (φᾱνῶ *Ach.* 914
&c.). **301.** ἱερὰς MSS.
303. The MSS. reading καὶ κεκράκτα is excellent, except for the metre : there
ought to be a correspondence with 381. To suit this, Herm. proposed κατακεκράκτα,
adopted by Dind. Hold. Kock Blaydes ; then a lacuna is assumed in 386 : παγκατακε-
κράκτα E. S. Thompson.   βδελυρὲ κράκτα Dobree (entered in Madvig's copy), κράκτα
Mein. Ribb. Vels.: this suits the metre, but κράκτης is a late word : καὶ κράκτης in
Plut. *praec. ger. reip.* 9. 804 C and Pollux v 90 is a mere mistake for κεκράκτης.   The
scholiasts had the MSS. reading, which they scan carefully, 304 being a cretic and a
dochmius : such a combination is very rare but it occurs in Aesch. *Suppl.* 429—437.

&c. I keep βλεπόντων: γε͂ is allowable in Comedy before βλ, and my feeling is that a Greek would say ἐπιορκῶ
βλεπόντων but ἐπιορκῶ ἐμβλέπων: Aeschin.
Ctes. 94 τὰ δέκα τάλαντα ὁρώντων φρονούν-
των βλεπόντων ἔλαθον ὑμῶν ὑφελόμενοι, cf.
Epictet. iii 22. 52, but Demosth. *adv.*
Phorm. 19 εἰς τὰ ὑμέτερα πρόσωπα ἐμβλέ-
ποντα τὰ ψευδῆ μαρτυρεῖν.
299. ἀλλότρια σοφίζεσθαι was a common charge among comedians, repelled
by implication on Aristophanes' part *Nub.*
547 ἀεὶ καινὰς ἰδέας εἰσφέρων σοφίζομαι:
the word reflects the *artistic* sense of
σοφός and was helped to an unfavourable
meaning in that way.   It may be however that the phrase means here 'your
arts are *out of place* here': this would
give a better meaning to καί. The process
called φάσις was applicable to various
offences (Pollux viii 47), one class of which
was defrauding the customs.   The tithe
would be payable to the gods: but it is
well known that the Athenian state regarded the funds of Athena and the other
gods as reserves to be borrowed from, if
not appropriated at need.   It is not clear
whether τῶν θεῶν means 'the other
gods' whose funds were separately managed from those of Athena, Athena
having the right chamber of the Opis-
thodomos as treasury, the other gods the
left (I do not know of any certain case of

οἱ ἄλλοι θεοί in this sense) ; nor is it quite
clear that a φάσις would come before the
πρυτάνεις (Isocr. *Callim.* 6, *Trapez.* 42
do not prove it, see Meier and Schömann
*Att. Proc.*² 300), though the βουλή had
so much financial power.   The scholium
ἔθος γὰρ εἶχον τὰς δεκάτας τῶν θυομένων
τοῖς πρυτάνεσιν οἱ μάγειροι διδόναι is defended by Stengel from *CIA* ii 163. 11.
But the charge is probably made in a
confused manner intentionally : Cleon is
nervous and alarmed. 'Athena's tithe'
was very well known in Attic finance : it
was levied on confiscated estates : even
filibusters observed the custom Lysias
20. 24: Demosth. *Timocr.* 120 contrasts
it with 'the fiftieth of the other gods.'
303—. The 'enthusiastic' paeonic
rhythm, though no doubt common in
hymns, was in the drama almost confined to Comedy: only two cases are
quoted from Tragedy, Aesch. *Supp.* 417
—437 an ode of the Egyptian maidens in
chorus, and Eurip. *Orest.* 1415 in parts
of the commos of the Phrygian slave.
The 'first paeon' is the common resolved form in Aristophanes, the 'fourth
paeon' being allowed, though quite rare.
The distinction between θάρσος a virtue
and θράσος a fault (θράσος ἡ ἄλογος ὁρμή,
θάρσος ἔλλογος ὁρμή Ammonius), so far as
it existed at all, was apparently an Attic
refinement,   taking   advantage   of   the

πᾶσα μὲν γῆ πλέα, πᾶσα δ' ἐκκλησία,   305
καὶ τέλη καὶ γραφαὶ καὶ δικαστήρι', ὦ
βορβοροτάραξι καὶ
τὴν πόλιν ἅπασαν ἡμῶν ἀνατετυρβακώς,   310
ὅστις ἡμῶν τὰς Ἀθήνας ἐκκεκώφωκας βοῶν,
κἀπὸ τῶν πετρῶν ἄνωθεν τοὺς φόρους θυννο-
σκοπῶν.   313

312. ἐκκεκώφηκας R and most MSS. -φευκας A, -φωκας Reiske and most editors, Cobet *Mnemos*. n. s. ii 416: Plato *Lysis* 204 C ἐκκεκώφωκε but Anacreon 81 φρένες ἐκκεκωφέαται: the forms were disputed in the time of Aristoph. of Byzantium, who supported ω against η (schol. on Eurip. *Orest.* 1288).
313. θυννοσκοπεῖς Lenting Mein. Kock: but see expl. note.

optional αρ or ρα for vocalic *r*. For the tragic use see Verrall on Eurip. *Med.* 469. θάρσος seems foreign to Comedy, and θράσος, though generally a fault as here, is a virtue in *Lys.* 546. Our texts of Thucydides bear out Ammonius' distinction well. Plato and the Orators avoid both words, using ἀνδρεία for the virtue, and θρασύτης for the fault (yet θράσος does occur Plato *Legg.* iii 701 B, Demosth. *Mid.* 10, 20, 194). Aristotle keeps the distinction: θάρσος is the opposite of φόβος (*Rhet.* ii 5. 1383ᵃ 16), θράσος of αἰδώς (*de caelo* ii 12. 291ᵇ 26), *Eth. Eud.* iii 7. 1234ᵇ 12 οἷον πέπονθε τὸ θράσος πρὸς τὸ θάρσος καὶ ἀσωτία πρὸς ἐλευθεριότητα: so Lucian *musc. encom.* 5 οὐδὲ γὰρ θράσος ἀλλὰ θάρσος φησὶν αὐτῇ προσεῖναι.

305—9. All the earth, all our politics, finances, and business of law, public and private, have been muddled: cf. *inf.* 866, *Pax* 753 ἀπειλὰς βορβοροθύμους. βορβοροτάραξις is a word of a very rare type, a compound abstract noun of this form used as a concrete: almost the only other instance is ὠτοκάταξις 'ear-smasher' of a boxer *fr.* 72, Lucian *Lexiph.* 9.
310. τυρβάζω and its cognates are colloquial, if not coarse: τύρβα is found in a Satyric fragment (321) of Aeschylus, quoted by Athenaeus ix 375 E, δονοῦσα καὶ τρέπουσα τύρβ' ἄνω κάτω of a sow: τυρβάζω is confined to Comedy and Satyric fragments of Sophocles (720, 927): Xenoph. *Cyrop.* i 2. 3 has τύρβη to take up and illustrate the ἀπειροκαλίαι of the market, Polybius i 67. 3 makes some apology for using the word, Plut. *non posse suav.* 2. 1086 F gives ἡ ποιητικὴ τύρβη as a specimen of the rudeness of Epicurean phrase, Lucian has it in Charon's mouth (*Contempl.* 15)

and again *Peregr.* 32: we are surprised to find in Isocr. *Antid.* 130 τὰς ταραχὰς καὶ τὴν τύρβην ἐν ᾗ ζῶμεν of life's turmoil. The words were applied to Bacchus-worship Paus. ii 24. 6, and so in the Ionic forms with σ- συρβηνεύς Cratinus 84 &c. We can see from Plautine phrases that the Latin *turba, turbo*, had a narrow escape from a similar brand.
312—3. The paeonic system ends with trochaics, as in *Ach.* 233—5, 987= 999, *Vesp.* 1283=1291, *Pax* 356. All analogy supports ἐκκεκώφωκας. Verbs in -όω are always causals, except ῥιγόω and ἰδρόω whose forms show a different vocalism; verbs in -έω, -άω are denominatives. The distinction is no doubt connected with the Sanskrit rule that causals are formed by -áya-, denominatives by -ayá- or -āyá-. Although κωφόω is the right form for *deafen*, later Greek for whatever reason evidently used κωφέω or more likely κωφάω in that sense (L and S give ἐκκωφέω, Stephanus with more reason ἐκκωφάω): Porson on Eurip. *Orest.* 1288 leaves the question as to the better form open: several MSS. give ἐκκεκώφηται (the perfect is almost the only form extant) in Lucian *bis accus.* 1, *Timon* 2, *navig.* 10 &c. κωφάω seems to have been also old Ionic, cf. ἀτιμάω.

Cleon looking out from the Pnyx over the Aegean as an Attic lake with clusters of tributary islands is compared to a watcher for tunny-shoals from a high rock (θυννοσκοπεῖον). Literature made much use of metaphors from tunny-fishing: as was natural from its picturesqueness, the fish being trapped and speared in enormous nets, the migrations of the huge tunny-shoals and the wide-spread

ΠΑ.   οἶδ' ἐγὼ τὸ πρᾶγμα τοῦθ' ὅθεν πάλαι καττύεται.

ΑΛΛ.   εἰ δὲ μὴ σύ γ' οἶσθα κάττυμ', οὐδ' ἐγὼ χορ-
      δεύματα,   315
      ὅστις ὑποτέμνων ἐπώλεις δέρμα μοχθηροῦ βοὸς
      τοῖς ἀγροίκοισιν πανούργως, ὥστε φαίνεσθαι
      παχύ,
      καὶ πρὶν ἡμέραν φορῆσαι, μεῖζον ἦν δυοῖν δοχμαῖν.

ΟΙ. Α.   νὴ Δία κἀμὲ τοῦτ' ἔδρασε ταὐτόν, ὥστε κατά-
      γελων

---

318. δυεῖν R : this form does not occur in Inscriptions till 334 B.C. (Meisterhans p. 70—1).
319. ΧΟ. Beer (*Zahl d. Schausp.* 25) Mein. Dind. Bergk. ΝΙΚ. Elmsley *Class.*

---

commerce in 'tunnies steeped in brine' (P. Rhode *Thynnorum Captura* in *Neue Jahrb. supp.* xviii): some instances are Herod. i 62, Aesch. *Pers.* 424, *fr.* 297, Soph. *fr.* 446, Theocr. 3. 26, Hor. *Sat.* ii 5. 44. The stupid helplessness of the fish is often implied: θυννώδες τὸ ἐνθύμημα καὶ παχύ Lucian *Jup. trag.* 25. The full zoological and gastronomical details given about the tunny by Aristotle and Athenaeus (vii 301 E—) are not in point here: but something may be quoted from the descriptions of tunny-fishing given by Aelian and Philostratus; Aelian *Nat. Anim.* xv 5 σκοπιὰ ἐπί τινος αἰγιαλοῦ παγεῖσα ἀνέστηκεν ἐν περιωπῇ σφόδρα ἐλευθέρᾳ..., ὁ σκοπὸς ἰδὼν σοφίᾳ τινὶ ἀπορρήτῳ καὶ φύσει ὄψεως ὀξυωπεστάτῃ... διδοῦσιν ὥσπερ στρατηγὸς τὸ σύνθημα καὶ χορολέκτης τὸ ἐνδόσιμον...καὶ μάλα ὀξὺ ἐκβοήσας λέγει διώκειν...νωθεῖς δὲ ὄντες οἱ θύννοι πεπιεσμένοι μένουσι, οἱ δὲ ἐρέται αἱροῦσιν ἰχθύων, ποιητὴς ἂν εἶπε, δῆμον: Philostr. *Imag.* i 13 σκοπωρεῖταί τις ἀφ' ὑψηλοῦ ξύλου ταχὺς μὲν ἀριθμῆσαι, τὴν δὲ ὄψιν ἱκανός,...βοῆς τε ὡς μεγίστης δεῖ αὐτῷ πρὸς τοὺς ἐν τοῖς ἀκατίοις...οἱ δὲ ἀποφράξαντες αὐτοὺς βαθεῖ καὶ κλειστῷ δικτύῳ δέχονται λαμπρὰν ἄγραν ὑφ' ἧς καὶ πλουτεῖν ἕτοιμον τῷ τῆς θήρας ἡγεμόνι. The fishing is still very important in the Mediterranean, but chiefly in the French, Italian and Dalmatian waters.

314. '*I* know all about the cobbling up of this job.' The verb κασσύω became καττύω in Attic: this is probably due to false analogy, as is the perfect κεκάττυμαι Alexis 98. 8, the word being

for κατ(α)σύω: no other derivative of σύω = Latin *suo* is known. The καττύματα were the thick soles of the plebeian shoe or coarse sandal, ὑποδήματα ἀκάττυτα being the elegant wear (*inf.* 869, Antig. Caryst. ap. Athen. xiii 565 E, Teles 30. 4 Hense ἐξ ἀνάγκης ἔδει ὑπόδημα ἔχειν καὶ τοῦτο ἀκάττυτον ἥλους οὐκ ἔχον, *CIA* iv 834 b ii 18 ὑποδημάτων κάττυσις τοῖς δημοσίοις): in *Ach.* 300, *Vesp.* 1160 καττύματα are meant as a surprise.

315—8. χόρδευμα (here only) is a comic formation like ζώμευμα 279. ὑποτέμνω was no doubt a word of the shoe-making trade, as συντέμνω Xen. *Cyrop.* viii 2. 5: it may mean merely *cutting for a sole*, though editors follow the scholiast on 291 in taking ὑπο- to imply a dishonest trick. μοχθηρὸς in the common trade-sense of bad wares; here, as in all its meanings, synonymous with πονηρός. For the ellipse πρὶν (τινα) φορῆσαι, Eurip. *Med.* 182 σπεύσον δὲ πρίν τι κακῶσαι τοὺς εἴσω, *Plut.* 597 ἁρπάζειν πρὶν καταθεῖναι, Aeschin. *Ctes.* 116 ἀσπίδας ἀνέθηκεν πρὸς τὸν νεὼν πρὶν ἐξαράσασθαι are quoted. δύο δοχμά, no doubt a phrase in colloquial style, as *fr.* 721. δοχμή was a popular, not an official, style of reckoning (it is not quoted except from Aristophanes) : hence the different accounts of its exact meaning : etymology bears out the older authorities in the statement that it means *hand-breadth*, not *span*. δυοῖν apparently was never used with plural, except of abstract nouns, Rutherf. *New Phryn.* 290.

319. The dactyl in trochaics is con-

πάμπολυν τοῖς δημόταισι καὶ φίλοις παρασχέ-
θειν. 320
πρὶν γὰρ εἶναι Περγασῆσιν, ἔνεον ἐν ταῖς ἐμβάσιν.

ΧΟΡ. ἆρα δῆτ' οὐκ ἀπ' ἀρχῆς ἐδήλους ἀναί- 322
δειαν, ἥπερ μόνη προστατεῖ ῥητόρων;

Journ. vi 222 (see expl. notes on 154 and 321). νὴ Δία κἀμὲ R. καὶ νὴ Δία κἀμὲ the other MSS. κἀμὲ τοῦτ' ἔδρασε ταὐτὸ νὴ Δί' Porson Ribb. Vels. κἀμὲ νὴ Δί' αὐτὸ τοῦτ' ἔδρασεν ὥστε καὶ γέλων Elmsley Dind. Mein. &c. νὴ Δί Dindorf, holding from Photius 297. 23 and Choerob. in Bekk. *Anecd.* 1362 that this was a colloquial form.
325. τῶν ῥητόρων MSS.

---

fidently defended by Wilamowitz *Isyll.* 8: he quotes *Ach.* 318, *Av.* 396, *Thesm.* 436, *Eccl.* 1155, four cases from Epicharmus, and an express permission by rule from Hephaestion: the license was confined to Comedy.

320. The feeling that one's δημόται are one's chief critics as well as audience and allies is very Attic, *Lys.* 685, Susarion 1. 3: it is introduced with an almost comic effect into Eurip. *Alc.* 1057 διπλῆν φοβοῦμαι μέμψιν, ἔκ τε δημοτῶν, μή τίς μ' ἐλέγχῃ... The fiction of slavery is of course dropped here. The general opinion is that σχέθειν and such forms are presents; Brugmann *Morph. Unters.* i 78— collects similar cases; Arcadius *de accent.* 155—6 classes σχέθω with ἔθω φαέθω &c.: but Jebb on Soph. *OT* 651 is no doubt right in saying that the forms were sometimes felt as aorists (so Kühner-Blass *Griech. Gramm.* § 272).

321. Περγασῆσι is Attic locative pl., like Θήβησι Ἀθήνησι &c. (Gust. Meyer *Griech. Gramm.*² § 379): the form given is however Περγασή: I am not aware that it has been identified. Elmsley inferred from Heracl. Pont. ap. Athen. xii 537 C that Nicias' deme was Pergase: but inscriptions show that it was Cydantidae, and the Νικίας ὁ Περγασῆθεν of Athen. and Aelian *Var. Hist.* iv 23 must be a different person.

The ἐμβάς, as the name implies, was a shoe, not a sandal merely: it was worn by men only, and those of humbler station, εὐτελὲς τὸ ὑπόδημα, τὴν δὲ ἰδέαν κοθόρνοις ταπεινοῖς ἔοικεν Pollux vii 85; *Nub.* 858 Pheidippides is scornful of his father's ἐμβάδες, as Bdelycleon is *Vesp.* 1157 ἀποδύου τὰς καταράτους ἐμβάδας: so *Eccl.* 633 ἐμβάδ' ἔχων is the poor

man, Isaeus 5. 11 ὅτι ἐμβάδας καὶ τρίβωνα φορεῖ marks the poor; cf. *Plut.* 867, 941, Menander 109. 3, *Anth. Pal.* vi 21. 4. Anytus' nickname Ἐμβαδᾶς (Theopomp. com. 57) is more pointed than if it came from ὑπόδημα, which was the elegant wear, Athen. viii 351 A &c., see on 314. For the inelegance of wide shoes, editors quote Theophr. *char.* 4 (ὁ ἄγροικος) μείζω τοῦ ποδὸς τὰ ὑποδήματα φορεῖ, Hor. *Sat.* i 3. 30, Lucian *Gall.* 26; for this way of expressing it, Ovid *ars amat.* i 516 *nec vagus in laxa pes tibi pelle natet.*

322—5. ἀπ' ἀρχῆς, even in your trade before you became a politician. Ἀναίδεια, 'the sole patron-deity of public men,' is more than Impudence: it is the tyrant's quality as well as the demagogue's: the personification was helped by the stones on the Areopagus, called of Ὕβρις and Ἀναίδεια, whatever their original significance may have been: they were held apparently to be abodes of these two beings (Ister ap. Suidas s.v. θεός, Cic. *Legg.* ii 28). Xenoph. *Symp.* 8. 35, praising Sparta, at the expense of Athens no doubt, says θεὰν γὰρ οὐ τὴν Ἀναίδειαν ἀλλὰ τὴν Αἰδῶ νομίζουσι: the proverb θεὸς ἡ Ἀναίδεια is given in all the collections: and Menander *fr.* 257 has ὦ μεγίστη τῶν θεῶν νῦν οὖσ' ἀναιδεί' εἰ θεὸν καλεῖν σε δεῖ· δεῖ δέ. The metaphor is rather from the protecting deity (Eurip. *Heracl.* 349 τῶν μὲν γὰρ Ἥρα προστατεῖ, ἡμῶν δ' Ἀθάνα) than from the legal relation of προστάτης to μέτοικος. Lucian *bis accus.* 29 makes Rhetoric say ἐπιγράφονται με ἅπαντες προστάτιν ἑαυτῶν: but in later times Law and the like were more the source of phrases than Religion.

4—2

ἢ σὺ πιστεύων ἀμέργει τῶν ξένων τοὺς καρ-
πίμους,

πρῶτος ὤν· ὁ δ' Ἱπποδάμου λείβεται θεώ-
μενος.   327

ἀλλ' ἐφάνη γὰρ ἀνὴρ ἕτερος πολὺ
σοῦ μιαρώτερος, ὥστε με χαίρειν,

ὅς σε παύσει καὶ πάρεισι, δῆλός ἐστιν, αὐτόθεν,

πανουργίᾳ τε καὶ θράσει   331

καὶ κοβαλικεύμασιν.

ἀλλ' ὦ τραφεὶς ὅθενπέρ εἰσιν ἄνδρες οἵπερ εἰσίν,

326. ἀμέλγει R. ἀμέλγεις the other MSS. ἀμέργεις Bothe Vels. ἀμέργει Mein.
Dind. Kock Blaydes.

327. Many conjectures have been made to avoid the irregular quantity in the
penult of Ἱπποδάμου. Erdmann in *Philol.* xlii 199— thinks Archeptolemus was son,
not of the famous Hippodamus, but of an Athenian Hippodāmus: so Zacher.

---

326. The scholium ἀμέλγεις δὲ ἀπο-
δρέπῃ, ἀπανθίζεις, τρυγᾷς καὶ καρπίζῃ
points to ἀμέργει. The word is mostly
lyric and late Epic, but a comic fragment (Mein. v p. 122, Kock *adesp.* 437)
implies its use among Attic farmers for
the olive-harvest ὁ μέν τις ἀμπέλους τρυ-
γῶν, ὁ δ' ἀμέργων τὰς ἐλάας. It was
naturally confused with ἀμέλγω in all
parts and derivatives, as ἀμοργοὶ πόλεως
ὄλεθροι Cratinus 214, but ἀμολγοὶ in same
meaning *fr. adesp.* 1351 (Eustath. 838.
54). The reference is the usual one, to
the harassing of the rich, not only in
Athens, but in the allied cities, cf. *Pax*
639 τῶν δὲ συμμάχων ἔσειον τοὺς παχεῖς
καὶ πλουσίους: or possibly to the recent
raising of tribute (so Gilbert *Inn. Gesch.*
186).

327. The remarkable personality of
Hippodamus is commented on by Aristot.
Pol. ii 8. 1 as a natural introduction to
his political theories. His physics and
architecture had made him welcome from
Miletus to Athens, and his son Archeptolemus had gained the full franchise in the
deme Agryle. Bred a political idealist,
the son was sure to look with hatred on
the war and with friendliness on Sparta.
His fortunes are pathetic: his vain efforts
for peace (see on 794) led to dealings
with Sparta that were deemed traitorous:
he was executed along with Antiphon,

his house destroyed and his very name
and race blotted out, at the instance of
the moderate party (Plut. *vita Antiph.*
24—27): and a modern editor of Thucydides thinks he was a Spartan. Antiphon's
lost speeches on the tribute of Lindus and
Samothrace were expressions of the aristocratic feelings on such questions implied
here (Jebb *Att. Or.* i 5), and may have
been written about this time (Gilbert *Inn.
Gesch.* 187, Beloch *Att. Pol.* 41: Blass
Att. Bereds. i² 103 thinks 418 the probable date). λείβεται θεώμενος may imply
some reproach of his inactivity (Kock).
Ἱπποδάμου must be taken with the
other cases of lengthening a short vowel
before a liquid, such as Αἰσχινάδου *Pax*
254, Ἱππομέδοντος Aesch. *Sept.* 483, Παρ-
θενόπαιος *ib.* 542. This lengthening is
well-known and recognised in Homer:
it is only a rare survival in Attic.

328. ἀλλά...γάρ: the old clumsy
hypothesis of a long ellipse in such cases
seems to me quite unnecessary: the nearest
English is 'Ah, but': see Appendix i.

330. αὐτόθεν answers the ἀπ' ἀρχῆς
of 324: the new champion too shows at
once and on the spot his supremacy:
Kock quotes *Eccl.* 246 καὶ σε στρατηγὸν
αἱ γυναῖκες αὐτόθεν αἱρούμεθα, where αὐτόθεν refers to a successful speech of
Praxagora's: cf. Thucyd. i 141. 1 Shilleto.

333—4. Two lines, spoken by the

νῦν δεῖξον ὡς οὐδὲν λέγει τὸ σωφρόνως τρα-
φῆναι.

ΑΛΛ. καὶ μὴν ἀκούσαθ' οἷός ἐστιν οὑτοσὶ πολίτης. 335

ΠΑ. οὐκ αὖ μ' ἐάσεις; ΑΛΛ. μὰ Δί', ἐπεὶ κἀγὼ
πονηρός εἰμι.

ΧΟΡ. ἐὰν δὲ μὴ ταύτῃ γ' ὑπείκῃ, λέγ' ὅτι κἀκ
πονηρῶν.

ΠΑ. οὐκ αὖ μ' ἐάσεις; ΑΛΛ. μὰ Δία. ΠΑ. ναὶ
μὰ Δία. ΑΛΛ. μὰ τὸν Ποσειδῶ,
ἀλλ' αὐτὸ περὶ τοῦ πρότερος εἰπεῖν πρῶτα
διαμαχοῦμαι.

339. αὐτὸ R. αὐτὸ τοῦτο most MSS.: V and others place the line after 336.

Coryphaeus, beginning with ἀλλά, inviting discussion on the subject and written in the metre of the following debate, is regular at the beginning of portions of the Agon. The metre may be iambic, trochaic, or anapaestic, but always tetram. catalectic. Such lines are called κατακελευσμός by Zieliński, who gives all the instances, *Gliederung* 120: see also M. W. Humphreys in *Amer. Journ. Phil.* viii 199. The ἄνδρες would remind the house of 179. εἰσὶν οἵπερ εἰσίν is a sarcastic application of the oracular, mostly depreciatory, repetition, well-known in such phrases as βλαστοῦσ' ὅπως ἔβλαστε Soph. *OT* 1376, ἐσμὲν οἷόν ἐσμεν Eurip. *Med.* 889 &c., μέλει θεοῖσιν ὧνπερ ἂν μέλῃ πέρι Aesch. *Cho.* 776. 'Show us now what nonsense a decent breeding is.' οὐδὲν λέγεις *Nub.* 781 &c., the correlative being οὐδένα λόγον ποιοῦμαι: cf. on 204 *sup.* σώφρων of good up-bringing as *Nub.* 1006 &c.: the main idea being a proper restraint)(license or insolence: so σωφρονεῖς *Plut.* 1119 'you're learning your place': hence the political and social meaning it sometimes has, see Appendix ii.

335. καὶ μὴν opens the discussion or exposition as *Av.* 462, *Eccl.* 583, καὶ μὴν...γε *inf.* 624, *Nub.* 1036, *Ran.* 907.

336. αὖ emphasizes the other side 'allow *me*, please': *Vesp.* 28 ἀτὰρ σὺ τὸ

σὸν αὖ λέξον, 942 οὐκ αὖ σὺ παύσει; so οὐδ', αὖ is common. Xen. *Hell.* ii 3. 28 αὖ seems to emphasize the *first* of two sides αὐτὸς μὲν αὖ...ἡμεῖς δέ... .

337. The common reference to ancestry, giving the emphasis of heredity to a quality, even when already in the superlative, Soph. *Phil.* 384 κακίστου κάκ κακῶν 'Οδυσσέως, Eurip. *Androm.* 590.

338—9. The oath by Poseidon seems to be more powerful than one by other gods, so *Plut.* 395 ΒΛ. πρὸς τῆς 'Εστίας; ΧΡ. νὴ τὸν Ποσειδῶ. Zieliński and Humphreys lay down a curious rule, which they say Ar. keeps, that the first speaker in a comic Agon is always beaten in the end: here the struggle for the first word means that this part of the Agon is not to be decisive.

αὐτὸ τοῦτο is not uncommon as acc. of respect in such cases, and αὐτὸ μόνον occurs, as Lucian *vita Luc.* 9 αὐτὸ μόνον ἐργάτης καὶ τῶν ἐκ τοῦ πολλοῦ δήμου εἷς, Athen. v 192 E, vi 270 B λόγους αὐτὸ μόνον καταβροχθίσας (other cases in Schmid *Atticismus* i 249): but I do not know of any other case of αὐτὸ alone. Cf. Plato *Soph.* 241 D φαίνεται τὸ τοιοῦτον διαμαχητέον ἐν τοῖς λόγοις, Alexis 34 οὐ ταῦτ' ἀεὶ πίπτουσιν (οἱ κύβοι), and the Latin use of acc. neuter pronouns in such cases, where acc. of a noun would not be allowed.

ΠΑ. οἴμοι, διαρραγήσομαι. ΑΛΛ. καὶ μὴν ἐγὼ
      οὐ παρήσω.   340
ΧΟΡ. πάρες πάρες πρὸς τῶν θεῶν αὐτῷ διαρραγῆναι.
ΠΑ. τῷ καὶ πεποιθὼς ἀξιοῖς ἐμοῦ λέγειν ἔναντα;
ΑΛΛ. ὁτιὴ λέγειν οἷός τε κἀγὼ καὶ καρυκκοποιεῖν.
ΠΑ. ἰδοὺ λέγειν. καλῶς γ' ἂν οὖν σὺ πρᾶγμα προσ-
      πεσόν σοι

340. ἐγώ σ' οὐ MSS. σ' ἐγὼ οὐ Bentl. Pors. Dind.: but it is better Greek without σ', cf. Soph. *OC* 591 ἀλλ' οὐδ'...παρίεσαν.

342. ἐναντία MSS. ἔναντα Bothe and vulg.: where ἔναντα and similar forms are certain, -αντία is a constant MS. variant.

343. καρυκκο- R and several other MSS.: as the thing was Lydian originally (Athen. xii 516 C), so probably was the word, which may have meant *red* (cf. καρύκινος): the spelling with κκ is a constant variant, is prescribed by Herodian i 317. 19 Lentz, and is adopted by some editors as Kaibel in Athen. iv 160 A, 173 CD (but καρυκ- *ib.* xii 516 C), Wachsmuth *Sillogr.* p. 155.

344. σὺ Herm. and editors since, σοὶ R, τι B, om. V and most MSS.

340—1. καὶ μὴν without γε following is commonly used to bring a new person on the stage or a new feature into the action: sometimes however it serves to introduce a counterpart to what has just been said by another speaker; that counterpart may be an acquiescence as Soph. *Elect.* 556 ΗΛ. ἦν ἐφῇς μοι... ΚΛ. καὶ μὴν ἐφίημ', or a direct contradiction and challenge as here, *Lys.* 363, *Thesm.* 568, Soph. *Ant.* 1054. The comic curse διαρραγείης is of course in the mind of the chorus: cf. Lucian *Peregr.* 31 ἐγὼ δὲ ἀφεὶς αὐτὸν διαρρηγνύμενον ἀπῄειν.

342. The rule that καὶ before an interrogative word must raise an objection to the last thing said, whatever its reason, was quite distinct in Attic (see *sup.* 128): hence the numerous cases where καὶ follows the interrogative may be partly owing to it, and are sometimes clearly contrasted with it, as Eurip. *Phoen.* 1367 and 1373, *Alc.* 1049 and 1052. Porson's classic note on Eurip. *Phoen.* 1373 lays down that καὶ simply means *praeterea.* Paley there re-states the rule in this way: "καὶ πῶς asks an ironical question, πῶς καὶ a serious one." Hermann's note 320 on Viger proposes a curious refinement: "qui τί χρὴ λέγειν interrogat, is *quid* dici, non *an aliquid* dici debeat, quaerit. Sed qui τί χρὴ καὶ λέγειν, is non solum *quid*, sed etiam *an aliquid* dicendum sit, dubitat. Cujus

interrogationem plane sic proferemus: *quid dicendum est, si omnino aliquid dicendum est?* Εἴ τι πράσσειν θέλεις est, *si quid vis suscipere*, quibus certum relinquitur, utrum quis id velit, an non. Εἴ τι καὶ πράσσειν θέλεις significat, *vix suscipies aliquid, sed si aliquid tamen suscipere vis.*" The safest way of expressing the meaning of the καὶ is merely that the question is emphasized by it; the nearest parallel is the Irish use of *at all* in questions.

ἔναντα, like the similar forms κάταντα &c., is Epic and Lyric, Soph. *Antig.* 1299, Eurip. *Orest.* 1478, κατέναντα Cydias ap. Plato *Charm.* 155 D. There is probably a quotation or parody here.

343. The ellipse of the copula is common with οἷός τε, δύνατος and the like; though few instances are quoted with the first person, *Lys.* 719 ἐγὼ αὐτὰς ἀποσχεῖν οὐκέτι οἵα τ' ἀπὸ τῶν ἀνδρῶν, Soph. *OT* 92 ἕτοιμος (εἰμὶ) εἰπεῖν.

καρύκκη was a rich kind of soup, mentioned along with ὀνθόλευσις a rich way of preparing meat, in contrast with simple food, Alexis 163. 6, Menander 462. 7, 518. 7, Timon ap. Athen. iv 160 A, Plut. *quaest. conv.* iv 1. 664 A: the parallel passage to ours is Plut. *quom. adul.* 11. 55 A τοῦ κόλακος τοῦτ' ἔργον ἐστὶ ἀεί τινα παιδιὰν ἢ πρᾶξιν ἢ λόγον ἐφ' ἡδονῇ καὶ πρὸς ἡδονὴν ὀψοποιεῖν καὶ καρυκκεύειν.

344—5. ἰδού as in 87. The meaning of λέγειν becomes more precise each time

ὠμοσπάρακτον παραλαβὼν μεταχειρίσαιο χρηστῶς. 345
ἀλλ' οἶσθ' ὅπερ πεπονθέναι δοκεῖς; ὅπερ τὸ
πλῆθος.
εἴ που δικίδιον εἶπας εὖ κατὰ ξένου μετοίκου,
τὴν νύκτα θρυλῶν καὶ λαλῶν ἐν ταῖς ὁδοῖς
σεαυτῷ,

347. κατ' ἀξένου or κατὰ ξένου ἢ μετ. Meineke *Vind. Arist.* 56, κατ''Αξένου Vels., κατ' ἀπροξένου Müller-Strübing *Aristoph.* 610.
348. θρυλλῶν ΒΔΘ: this variant is constant, but θρυλῶ is recognised as right, see Cobet *Misc. Crit.* 221, Schanz Plato vii p. vii.

---

it is used. Cleon's furious scorn 'you'ld be more of a butcher than a cook in your oratory' is marked by the repeated pronoun and by the two adverbs καλῶς and χρηστῶς in the places of emphasis: καλῶς is vague, 'a pretty mess,' χρηστῶς more definite in its trade or business sense, not uncommon in cookery, as Archestratus ap. Athen. vii 311 C οὐ γὰρ ἐπίστανται χρηστῶς σκευάζεμεν ἰχθῦς, Alexis 149. 6 τὸν ὀψοποιὸν σκευάσαι χρηστῶς μόνον δεῖ τοὔψον. ὠμοσπάρακτος, like the ὠμοβόεια and ὠμοβύρσινα of tanner's trade, is of course as far removed from καρύκκη as possible. Gorgias' phrase ἔναιμα πράγματα, quoted without approval by Aristot. *Rhet.* iii 3. 4, does not seem to be parallel.

346. 'Look here—shall I tell you what I think of your case?' οἶσθα as in οἶσθ' οὖν ὃ δρᾶσον &c. is an example of the Greek use of active verbs for passive meanings.

347. εἴ που = if perhaps, not the same as εἴ ποτε (Verrall on Aesch. *Agam.* 524). δίκην λέγειν is not a common phrase: its meaning is not certain in the well-known Homeric scene *Il.* xviii 508: in Attic it may be used of a man conducting his own case (*Vesp.* 776 ἦν δίκην λέγῃ μακράν τις, Xen. *Mem.* iv 8. 1, Plut. *Demosth.* 12), or of advocates by profession (Isocr. *antid.* 40, 47 μᾶλλον ὠφελεῖν δυνάμενοι τῶν δίκας εὖ λεγόντων, Dinarch. *Demosth.* 111 λογογράφος καὶ μισθοῦ τὰς δίκας λέγων).

ξένου μετοίκου is strange: though ξένος μέτοικος was possibly the original full phrase for a μέτοικος, yet ξένος and μέτοικος are usually opposed, *Ach.* 505—8, *Pax* 297, *Lys.* 580, Isocr. *de pace* 21,

Aristot. *Pol.* iii 5. 1277ᵇ 39, *Pol. Ath.* 57: in Soph. *OT* 452 ξένος λόγῳ μέτοικος, the terms are not technical, and in Aristot. *Pol.* iii 2. 1275ᵇ 37 πολλοὺς ἐφυλέτευσε ξένους καὶ δούλους μετοίκους the meaning is doubtful. But ξένος may be used for a μέτοικος: Clerc *Métèques Athén.* 327 quotes Demosth. *Lept.* 21, 29, *Androt.* 21, Lycurg. *Leocr.* 41: and Cleon here probably is showing a contemptuous indifference to legal accuracy, 'some poor rustic stranger.' Such strangers were easy to attack; Xen. *Mem.* ii 1. 15 Socrates says to Aristippus, who proposes to go from city to city, σὺ τοιοῦτος ὢν οἵοις μάλιστα ἐπιτίθενται οἱ βουλόμενοι ἀδικεῖν, ὅμως διὰ τὸ ξένος εἶναι οὐκ ἂν οἴει ἀδικηθῆναι; cf. Aristotle's complaint in a letter to Antipater, quoted in the lives of Aristotle (*fr.* 667 Rose), "τὸ 'Αθήνησι διατρίβειν ἐργῶδες· ὄγχνη γὰρ ἐπ' ὄγχνη γηράσκει, σῦκον δ' ἐπὶ σύκῳ" τὴν διαδοχὴν τῶν συκοφαντούντων αἰνιττόμενος, Aesch. *Supp.* 994 πᾶς δ' ἐν μετοίκῳ γλῶσσαν εὔτυκον φέρει κακήν, Demosth. *Callipp.* 9 τὸν μέτοικον ἄνθρωπον καὶ ἐν Σκύρῳ κατοικοῦντα καὶ οὐδενὸς ἄξιον.

348. θρυλῶ of tiresome repetition: when a speaker uses it of himself, he has an apologetic tone, serious or humorous, as Eurip. *Elect.* 909, Plato *Phaedo* 76 D, Demosth. *FL* 156. λαλῶ)(λέγω as *loquor*)(*dico* : λαλεῖν ἄριστος, ἀδυνατώτατος λέγειν was said of Phaeax about this time, see on 1377. In later Rhetoric λαλιαί, *causeries*, were admitted as an irregular kind of λόγοι ἐπιδεικτικοί. Part of Cleon's charge against his adversaries in Thucyd. iii 38. 2 is τὸ εὐπρεπὲς τοῦ λόγου ἐκπονῆσαι. Lucian *Scytha* 6 αὐτὸς πρόσεισιν, ὁ ἐπὶ συννοίας, ὁ λαλῶν ἑαυτῷ.

ὕδωρ τε πίνων, κἀπιδεικνὺς τοὺς φίλους τ'
ἀνιῶν,
ᾦου δυνατὸς εἶναι λέγειν. ὦ μῶρε τῆς ἀνοίας. 350

ΑΛΛ. τί δαὶ σὺ πίνων τὴν πόλιν πεποίηκας, ὥστε
νυνὶ
ὑπὸ σοῦ μονωτάτου κατεγλωττισμένην σιωπᾶν;

ΠΑ. ἐμοὶ γὰρ ἀντέθηκας ἀνθρώπων τίν'; ὅστις εὐθὺς
θύννεια θερμὰ καταφαγών, κᾆτ' ἐπιπιὼν ἀκράτου
οἴνου χόα κασαλβάσω τοὺς ἐν Πύλῳ στρατηγούς.

ΑΛΛ. ἐγὼ δέ γ' ἤνυστρον βοὸς καὶ κοιλίαν ὑείαν 356

---

349. πίνεις κἀπιδεικνὺς τοὺς φίλους ἀνιᾷς Cobet *Mnemos.* n. s. ii 416.

---

349. Water-drinking during training for a speech was practised by some, scouted by others: Demosthenes 2 *Phil.* 30 admits that this practice had done harm to his reputation, λέγοντες ὅτι ἐγὼ μὲν ὕδωρ πίνων εἰκότως δύσκολος καὶ δύστροπός εἰμί τις ἄνθρωπος: Lucian *rhet. praec.* 9 πόνον καὶ ἀγρυπνίαν καὶ ὑδατοποσίαν καὶ τὸ λιπαρὲς ἀναγκαῖα ταῦτα καὶ ἀπαραίτητα φήσει. See on 89 *sup.* "ἀνιῶ in Epic and Tragedy, ἀνιῶ in Comedy" is the rule, broken only in this case: is the exception due to a reminiscence of Soph. *Ajax* 266 φίλους ἀνιῶν αὐτὸς ἡδονὰς ἔχειν?

351—2. τί δαί marks some surprise, as usual. τὴν πόλιν is 'accusative of anticipation,' here followed by a ὡς ὥστε clause: cf. *Av.* 652 where a ὡς clause follows, *Av.* 1269 an εἰ clause: in Thucyd. v 36. 2 τὸ Πάνακτον ἐδέοντο Βοιωτοὺς ὅπως παραδώσουσι Λακεδαιμονίοις, Shilleto held Βοιωτοὺς to be such an accus., quoting Eurip. *Bacch.* 286, Xen. *Cyrop.* ii 1. 5, Demosth. i *Aph.* 40, Plato *Rep.* iii 415 C, Aristot. *Rhet.* ii 9. 4 as other cases. μονώτατος is quoted not only from *Plut.* 182, Theocr. 15. 137, but from Lycurg. *Leocr.* 88 μονώτατοι ἐπώνυμοι τῆς χώρας εἰσίν: so that it is not one of the purely comic comparatives and superlatives spoken of by the grammarians, as Apollon. Dysc. *pronom.* 81 A (αὐτότερος and Δαναώτατος).
For καταγλωττίζω see on 286 *sup.*

353—5. The γὰρ 'Oh then' is a confident reply to the invidiousness of the μονωτάτου. θύννεια is the *menu* word, as in so many similar cases ἐγχέλεια, βόεια &c.; this is emphasized by the θερμὰ 'dressed,' 'cooked.' His food and drink are Gargantuan: θύννεια are large pieces of the huge tunny, and the χοῦς ἀκράτου (see on 95) a gigantic draught, like that of Polyphemus in Eurip. *Cycl.* 327. κασαλβάσω· λοιδορήσω· πρὸς δὲ τὸ ῥηθὲν ὑπὸ τοῦ ἑτέρου "κασαλβάσω τοὺς στρατηγοὺς" ἀντέθηκεν "καὶ Νικίαν ταράξω" schol. (as it should surely be written). It occurs again in Hermippus 71 (probably almost contemporary), but the meaning of this coarse word is not quite clear in either passage.

356—8. δέ γε, to cap the previous statement. Shilleto's remark on Dem. *FL* 102, "This use of δέ γε or δὲ...γε in continuation or retort is so frequent that it is remarkable how frequently it has been misunderstood" is still in point. His fare is stronger or coarser, and his words, arranged with some skill for the purpose, are harsh and alarming in sound. ἤνυστρον, *omasum*, the fourth of the cow's stomachs (κοιλία, κεκρύφαλος, ἐχῖνος, ἤνυστρον, Aristot. *part. anim.* iii 14. 7), was a plebeian food: Dioxippus ap. Athen. iii 100 E οἴων δ' ἐπιθυμεῖ βρωμάτων, ὡς μουσικῶν· ἤνυστρα, μήτρας, χόλικας, Hor. *Sat.* ii 5. 40, *Epist.* i 15. 34.

καταβροχθίσας, κᾷτ᾽ ἐπιπιὼν τὸν ζωμὸν ἀνα-
πόνιπτος
λαρυγγιῶ τοὺς ῥήτορας καὶ Νικίαν ταράξω.

ΟΙ. Α. τὰ μὲν ἄλλα μ᾽ ἤρεσας λέγων· ἐν δ᾽ οὐ προσίεταί με,
τῶν πραγμάτων ὁτιὴ μόνος τὸν ζωμὸν ἐκρο-
φήσει.   360

ΠΑ.   ἀλλ᾽ οὐ λάβρακας καταφαγὼν Μιλησίους κλο-
νήσεις.

359—60. ΧΟ. MSS. Dind., ΟΙ. A Enger and now most editors.
360. ἐκροφήσεις MSS. -σει Elmsley, see Rutherford *New Phryn.* 392—3·
361. MSS. and schol. continue the line to the Chorus. ΠΑ. Casaubon and vulg.

καταβροχθίσας, a colloquial word, of greedy or hasty eating, 826, Antiphanes 190. ὁ οἷοι καταβροχθίζειν ἐν ἀγορᾷ τὰ τεμάχη, Lucian *Prom.* 10, Alciphro iii 53. 4, in the mouth of a Cynic Athen. vi 270 B.

ἀπονίψασθαι in Attic of washing hands after dinner)(ὕδωρ κατὰ χειρὸς before, Athen. ix 408 F, Cobet *NL* 4. Athen. iv 148 F—describing the rude Arcadian feasts μάζας φησὶν εἶναι καὶ θεα κρέα... τοῖς ἐσθίουσι τῶν νέων ἀνδρικώτερον ζωμὸν τ᾽ ἐγχεῖν πλείω...μετὰ δὲ τὸ δεῖπνον σπονδὰς ἐποιοῦντο οὐκ ἀπονιψάμενοι τὰς χεῖρας.

λαρυγγίζω, like other verbs of the kind, was elastic in meaning: it may be intrans. *bawl*, or trans. *throttle* as here (Mitchell, Blaydes, Rutherford *New Phryn.* 180). Nicias' timidity exposed him to such attacks: Plut. *Nicias* 4 quotes this line (as said by Cleon), with others from Comedians, to show τὸ ἀθαρσὲς αὐτοῦ καὶ καταπεπληγμένον.

359—60. λέγων is intended, with reference to 350, 'the other points of your *speech*.' The old English 'it likes me not' is a well-known parallel to οὐ προσίεται με for οὐ προσίεμαι, which apparently was much more common (see Blaydes' collection of instances here): the Greeks may have felt some distinction between 'it does not attract me' and 'I do not take it to myself.' Some editors (Mitchell, Dindorf, Blaydes) take τῶν πραγμάτων with ἔν, but it gives more

point if taken with ζωμόν. For ζωμὸν ἐκροφεῖν see on 51.

361. λάβραξ, *lupus*, was the large sea-pike or bass; it is discussed by Athenaeus vii 311 A—, who quotes Archestratus as holding that Miletus produced the best specimens: λάβρακες Μιλήσιοι is given as a proverb by Suidas, Apostol. x 38 &c., though its meaning is not clear. Here it is impossible to be sure of the construction or sense: very possibly the line is meant to be awkward and confused. Miletus was an old ally of Athens (see on 237) and had done good service recently at Solygeia and Cythera (Thucyd. iv 42. 1, 53. 4): in 932 Cleon is speaking on a Milesian question, probably about tribute, which in the case of Miletus varied between 5 and 10 talents: though Miletus was democratic, the oligarchic faction was active and party-struggles sometimes very severe (the mutilated inscription *CIA* iv 22 *a* referring to something of the kind has been shifted back in date from about 425 to about 450 B.C.). It is possible that λάβρακες was a nickname for the oligarchic party in Miletus, where political nicknames flourished (see Gilbert *Griech. Staatsalt.* ii 139 quoting Plut. *quaest. graec.* 32. 298 C, Heraclid. Pont. ap. Athen. xii 524 A). κλόνος and its derivatives are epic and tragic for the most part, used of winds or waves or heroes driving all before them (of Love *Anth. Pal.* v 286. 2); in other styles the words are

ΑΛΛ. ἀλλὰ σχελίδας ἐδηδοκὼς ὠνήσομαι μέταλλα.

ΠΑ. ἐγὼ δ' ἐπεισπηδῶν γε τὴν βουλὴν βίᾳ κυκήσω.

ΑΛΛ. ἐγὼ δὲ κινήσω γέ σου τὸν πρωκτὸν ἀντὶ φύσκης.

ΠΑ. ἐγὼ δέ γ' ἐξέλξω σε τῆς πυγῆς θύραζε κύβδα. 365

ΟΙ. Α. νὴ τὸν Ποσειδῶ κἀμέ τἄρ', ἤνπερ γε τοῦτον
ἕλκῃς.

ΠΑ. οἷόν σε δήσω 'ν τῷ ξύλῳ.

ΑΛΛ. διώξομαί σε δειλίας.

365. ἐξέλξω Pors. for ἐξ' ἐλλέγξω R ἐξελῶ other MSS. κύβδα Mein. (as from κῦφός).

366. γὰρ MSS. γ' ἄρ' Brunck; τἄρα Bothe and vulg.: τἄρα is generally ironical but γ' ἄρα is very rare and doubtful. The line is given to ΘΕ. (θεράπων) by R, to ΧΟ. by most MSS.: the scholia record the difference.

367. 'ν is not in any MS. Elmsley on Ach. 343 proposed to introduce it, as it seems to be necessary in the phrase.

368. Wilam. Hermes vii 152 would arrange in the order 368, 370, 371, 369, 372.

used only of physiological effects of wind, Nub. 387, Plut. quaest. conv. v 7. 681 A.

362. He again caps his adversary's fish with meat: σχελίδες, sides of beef, were used naturally in large entertainments, as to choruses, fr. 249, Plut. glor. Ath. 6. 349 A.

The silver mines of Laurium were sold in lots to private persons who paid, besides purchase-price, a rent of a twenty-fourth of the produce: the words used of these transactions are ὠνοῦμαι Demosth. FL 293 παρὰ τῶν ἐωνημένων τὰ μέταλλα, ὠνητὴς CIA ii 780, πωλῶ Aristot. Pol. Ath. 47. Nicias hired a thousand slaves to Sosias, one of these contractors, for an obol a day per head, Xen. vectig. 4. 14. There may be some allusion here to a financial rivalry with Nicias.

363. The Council superintended the letting of taxes, mines &c. by the πωληταί: and this line is suggested by the Sausageman's financial pretensions. Some control of the Council was necessary for a demagogue, cf. 166.

365. κύβδα gives the sense of comic awkwardness that κύπτω and its compounds were evidently so often used in Attic conversation to bring out.

For ἕλκῃς after ἐξέλξω see on 98.

367—. A system of Iambic dimeters till 381, in some respects parallel to an anapaestic system. "Originating in the cult of Dionysus and Demeter, this rhythmic form passed into Comedy, where it appears mostly in close connexion with a group of Iambic tetrameters, especially in Agon-scenes, Eq. 367—, 441—56, 911—40, Nub. 1089—1104, 1385—90, 1446—52, Lys. 382—6, Ran. 971—91." Gleditsch Metrik (§ 62) in Iwan Müller's Handbuch ii.

For οἷον in exclamation cf. inf. 703: it is tempting to take it in both passages as masc. 'what a figure you'll be!' but this is forbidden by Vesp. 1329 οἷον ὑμᾶς σκευάσω, Thesm. 704. τὸ ξύλον means stocks or pillory of various forms: such punishments were inflicted sometimes on freemen for theft (Lysias 10. 16, Demosth. Timocr. 105) or failure to fulfil state-contracts (Andoc. myst. 92), but more commonly on slaves: here Cleon turns on Demosthenes with this threat.

368. After Sphacteria, a charge of δειλία would confound Cleon above everything. The offences of ἀστρατεία, λιποτάξιον, and δειλία were tried before the Strategi with taxiarchs or phylarchs as assessors, and the culprit's fellow-soldiers as jurymen: the nearest approach to martial law allowed by the Athenian spirit. A false charge of δειλία was a libel, punishable by a fine of 500 drachmae (Lysias 10. 12).

ΠΑ. ἡ βύρσα σου θρανεύσεται.

ΑΛΛ. δερῶ σε θύλακον κλοπῆς. 370

ΠΑ. διαπατταλευθήσει χαμαί.

ΑΛΛ. περικόμματ᾿ ἐκ σοῦ σκευάσω.

ΠΑ. τὰς βλεφαρίδας σου παρατιλῶ.

ΑΛΛ. τὸν πρηγορεῶνά σούκτεμῶ.

ΟΙ. Α. καὶ νὴ Δί᾿ ἐμβαλόντες αὐ- 375
τῷ πάτταλον μαγειρικῶς
εἰς τὸ στόμ᾿, εἶτα δ᾿ ἔνδοθεν
τὴν γλῶτταν ἐξείραντες αὐτοῦ σκεψόμεσθ᾿ εὖ κἀνδρικῶς
κεχηνότος 380

---

373. παρατιλῶ R and vulg. περιτιλῶ the other MSS.: παρα- is the common compound.
374. πρηγορεῶνα MSS. πρηγορῶνα most edd. after Bentley: so Av. 1113 MSS. give πρηγορεῶνας against the metre.

---

369. βύρσα would not be seriously used of the human skin any more than *corium*. θρανεύειν is from θρᾶνος, a tanning-bench: the passage is of course full of terms of trade.
370 would suit Cleon better. The prolepsis 'I'll flay you into a thieving-wallet' is derived from the common phrase ἀσκὸν δέρειν *Nub.* 441, ἀσκὸς δεδάρθαι Solon 33. 7: the construction seems to have been specially common in such comic threats derived from the leather trade, *inf.* 768, *Ach.* 300, Plato com. 164 σὲ παλινδορίαν παίσας καταθήσω.
371. In a description of flaying a man alive, Plut. *Artax.* 17 has τὸ μὲν σῶμα προσέταξε διὰ τριῶν σταύρων ἀναπῆξαι, τὸ δὲ δέρμα χωρὶς διαπατταλεῦσαι.
372 is a rhythmical equivalent to 371, and all the better as a retort. περικόμματα, loose scraps, trimmed off meat, are mentioned along with sausages and tripe, Metagenes 6. 7, Alexis 132 χορδαρίου τόμος ἧκεν καὶ περικομματίου: they are poor material made tolerable only by good cookery, Dionysius com. 3. 14, and hence Aristophanes *fr.* 180 applies the word, with others like it, to Euripides' poetry. For ἐκ σοῦ cf. *Nub.* 455 ἐκ μοῦ χορδὴν παραθέντων, and for the threat,

Plaut. *Mil.* 8 *gestit fartum facere ex hostibus*, *Truc.* 613 *ego ted offatim offigam*.
374. πρηγορεών is probably a noun of the class called by grammarians περιεκτικά (see Uhlig's index to Dion. Thrax), implying the place where things are collected, like ῥοδών, ἀνδρών &c.: if Furtwängler's theory as to the Parthenon (*Masterpieces* Eng. tr. 424) is correct, Παρθενών has its proper meaning. The affix for such nouns was ϝων (Brugmann *Grundriss* ii § 216): and the original type would be παρθενεϝών, becoming παρθενεών in Ionic, παρθενών in Attic. Phrynichus' rule 144, ἱστών λέγε, ἀλλὰ μὴ ἱστεών, suits most cases: the exceptions are given by Lobeck and Rutherford, see also for place-names Grasberger *Griech. Ortsnamen* 221—. The word seems to contain the same root as *gigeria*, whence our *gizzard*: this root may be that of ἀγείρω as the ancients supposed, Pollux ii 204.
375—. Demosthenes comes in as in 366. 'We'll treat him like a pig, and see if he's measly.' πάτταλος is a *gag*, as *Thesm.* 222 ἐμβαλῶ σοι πάτταλον, ἢν μὴ σιωπᾷς. μαγειρικῶς, 'in butcher's style,' as *Pax* 1017 ὅπως μαγειρικῶς σφάξεις τὸν οἶν, see 216 *sup.* εὖ κἀνδρικῶς, comic, 'so bold and gay,' as *Vesp.* 153, 450: εὖ κἀνδρείως in

τὸν πρωκτόν, εἰ χαλᾷ.

ΧΟΡ. ἦν ἄρα πυρός γ' ἕτερα θερμότερα, καὶ λόγων
ἐν πόλει τῶν ἀναιδῶν ἀναιδέστεροι·   385
καὶ τὸ πρᾶγμ' ἦν ἄρ' οὐ φαῦλον ὧδ' * * *
ἀλλ' ἔπιθι καὶ στρόβει,
μηδὲν ὀλίγον πόει. νῦν γὰρ ἕχεται μέσος·

382. πυρὸς R and most MSS.: πυρός γ' B and three other MSS., edd. vulg.:
the correspondence with 303— is not perfect as the systems stand: most editors
suppose a lacuna of one cretic in 386: Bergk and Blaydes supply οὐδ' ἐλαφρόν,
Hermann καὶ λόγοι τῶν in 383. Two scholia scan the system: the older one seems
to imply a cretic more than the later, lost rather in 386 than in 383.

more serious style, *Thesm.* 656, Plato
com. 109 (see on 81): all these passages,
and several in Plato (*Crat.* 440 D σκοπεῖ-
σθαι χρὴ ἀνδρείως τε καὶ εὖ) favour the
connexion with σκεψόμεσθα rather than
with κεχηνότος.

χαλαζάω (cf. λιθάω, ποδαγράω &c.), *to
have measles*, of pigs: Aristot. *hist. anim.*
viii 21 gives βραγχᾶν, κραυρᾶν, χαλαζᾶν,
as the three diseases of swine: of the last
he says χαλαζώδεις δ' εἰσὶ τῶν ὑῶν αἱ
ὑγρόσαρκοι...δῆλοι δ' εἰσὶν αἱ χαλαζῶσαι·
ἔν τε γὰρ τῇ γλώττῃ τῇ κάτω ἔχουσι
μάλιστα τὰς χαλάζας...ἔτι δὲ τὰ χαλα-
ζῶντα τοὺς ὀπισθίους πόδας οὐ δύνανται
ἡσυχάζειν...χαλάζᾳ δὲ μόνον τῶν ζῴων ὧν
ἴσμεν ὗς: id. *problem.* 34. 4 ἡ γλῶττα ση-
μαντικόν...ἐὰν χάλαζαι ἐνῶσιν. In Athen.
iii 93 C the disease is compared in appearance to pearls in oysters: it is called by
the Germans *Perlsucht* for this reason.
The tongue is always mentioned as the
chief seat of such morbid appearances:
Hippocr. *epidem.* iv 10 γλῶσσα ἐτραχύ-
νετο ὥσπερ χαλαζώδει πυκνῷ, Aretaeus p.
181. 1 Kühn γλῶσσα χαλαζώδεσι ἰόνθοισι
τρηχεῖα...καὶ γὰρ καὶ τοῖσι κακοχύμοισι
ἱερείοισι τὰ κρέα χαλάζης ἐστὶ ἔμπλεα,
Oribas *coll. med.* iv 2 χαλάζας ἐν τοῖς
κρέασι γινομένας ὡς ἐπὶ τοῖς ὑσὶν ἡγοῦ τὰς
μὲν ὀλίγας ἡδίω τὴν σάρκα ποιεῖν τὰς δὲ
πλείους ὑγροτέραν καὶ ἀηδεστέραν· δια-
γνώσῃ δὲ ἔτι ζῶντος τοῦ ἱερείου εἰ ἔνεισι
χάλαζαι παρά τε τὴν γλῶσσαν σκεπτόμενος
καὶ ἐν τοῖς ποσὶ τοῖς ὄπισθεν, οὐ γὰρ δύνανται ἀτρεμεῖν (see Bussemaker and
Daremberg on Oribas i 616). In *Philologus* li 377 Dr Hirschberg describes a
process like that in the text as still used
in Germany to detect the *cysticercus cel-
lulosae* in live pigs.

382. In the common idiom ἦν ἄρα,

it seems there is, the verb is rarely so
emphatic as to come first in the sentence:
Anthol. Pal. ix 359. 9 ἦν ἄρα τοῖνδε δυοῖν
ἐνὸς αἵρεσις: with ἄρα, Cratinus 24 ἦν ἄρ'
ἀληθὴς ὁ λόγος ὡς δὶς παῖς γέρων. I have
no other case of ἄρα...γε at hand, except
perhaps Hom. *Il.* iii 7: but οὐκ ἄρα...γε
and the like occur, as *Il.* i 93, 330, Plato
Laches 192 D.

Plut. *Demetrius* 12 ἦν δὲ ἄρα καὶ πυρὸς
ἕτερα θερμότερα κατὰ τὸν Ἀριστοφάνη:
but such phrases were probably well-
known and popular. Pausan. vii 12. 1
βεβαιοῖ δὴ τὸ λεγόμενον ὡς ἄρ' ἦν καὶ πῦρ
ἐς πλέον ἄλλου πυρὸς καῖον καὶ λύκος
ἀγριώτερος λύκων ἄλλων καὶ ὠκύτερος ἱέραξ
ἱέρακος πέτεσθαι εἴγε καὶ Καλλικράτην
ἀνοσιώτατον τῶν τότε Μενακλίδας ὑπερῆρεν
ἀπιστίᾳ, Eurip. *fr.* 432 (from the first
Hippol.) ἀντὶ πυρὸς γὰρ ἄλλο πῦρ μεῖζον
ἐβλάστομεν γυναῖκες.

386—. πρᾶγμα is meant in the dramatic sense of *action*, or *plot*, see on 36. For
ὧδε absolute, like οὕτως with a word of depreciation, cf. Cratinus 54 τοὺς ὧδε μόνον
στασιάζοντας καὶ βουλομένους τινὰς εἶναι.
στρόβει is apparently intrans. in *Vesp.*
1529, *whirl* in the dance called στρόβιλος:
but it is best taken here as trans., *harass*
the enemy: a scholium sees an allusion
also to a fuller's instrument called στρο-
βεύς.

οὐδὲν ὀλίγον ποιεῖν, πράσσειν, ἐπινοεῖν
were regularly used of high hopes and
schemes, political or military, Thucyd.
ii 8. 1, vii 59. 2, 87. 6, viii 15. 2.

ἔχομαι μέσος, the well-known wrestling
phrase, almost confined to Comedy. A
later use of μέσον ἔχειν or λαμβάνειν is
put in the place of honour, pay honour to,
as Plut. *Cato* 57, *praec. reip. ger.* 21. 6,
817 B.

ὡς ἐὰν νυνὶ μαλάξῃς αὐτὸν ἐν τῇ προσβολῇ,
δειλὸν εὑρήσεις· ἐγὼ γὰρ τοὺς τρόπους ἐπίσταμαι. 390

ΑΛΛ. ἀλλ' ὅμως οὗτος τοιοῦτος ὢν ἅπαντα τὸν βίον,
κᾆτ' ἀνὴρ ἔδοξεν εἶναι, τἀλλότριον ἀμῶν θέρος.
νῦν δὲ τοὺς στάχυς ἐκείνους, οὓς ἐκεῖθεν ἤγαγεν,
ἐν ξύλῳ δήσας ἀφαύει κἀποδόσθαι βούλεται.

ΠΑ. οὐ δέδοιχ' ὑμᾶς, ἕως ἂν ζῇ τὸ βουλευτήριον 395
καὶ τὸ τοῦ δήμου πρόσωπον μακκοᾷ καθήμενον.

ΧΟΡ. ὡς δὲ πρὸς πᾶν ἀναιδεύεται κοὐ μεθίστησι τοῦ χρώματος τοῦ παρεστηκότος.

394. ἀφαυει R. ἀφαίνει Ribbeck Zacher.

μαλάσσω may refer to tanning, but it was a phrase of the games as well, Pind. *Nem.* 3. 16 ἐν περισθενεῖ μαλαχθεὶς παγκρατίου στόλῳ. The emphatic ἐγὼ must imply a reference, caught by the audience, to some collision, such as we hear of, between Cleon and the Knights.

391—2. κᾆτα is a stronger form of εἶτα *indignantis*, as *Lys.* 560, Demosth. i *Olynth.* 21. ἀνήρ, as 179. For the metaphor of reaping without sowing cf. Eurip. *fr.* 423 ἀμᾶσθε τῶνδε δύστηνον θέρος, Hes. *Theog.* 599 drones ἀλλότριον κάματον σφετέρην ἐς γαστέρ' ἀμῶνται, Callim. *hymn. Dem.* 139 φέρβε καὶ εἰράναν ἵν' ὃς ἄροσε κεῖνος ἀμάσῃ.

393—4. στάχυς to keep up the metaphor of θέρος. The Sphacterian captives are of course meant: their 'parched' appearance was a bye-word, *Nub.* 186, and Cleon would be open to charges of using them to bargain with Sparta, Thucyd. iv 41. Plut. *Nicias* 9 speaks of Nicias' kindness to them.
ἀφαύει seems unique: Suidas quotes *Thesm.* 216 τὰ κάτω δ' ἀφαύειν, but ἀφεύω is the right reading there and *Pax* 1144, *Eccl.* 13; would the Attics use both ἀφαύω and ἀφεύω in the same meaning? The only certain compound of αὔω, *burn*, is ἐναύω: in the others ἐξαύω, καταύω, προσαύω, -αύω may as well or better mean *take*. On the derivation see Osthoff *Perfect* 484—. ἀφεῖναι διανοεῖται Schol. points to some other

word: for Ribbeck's ἀφαίνει see on 963.

395—6. 'I don't think you Knights and your champion dangerous, as long as the Council goes on, and the booby-face of the People is helpless before me in the Ecclesia': I control both powers of State. On the question whether Cleon was a member of Council this year or not, see on 626. For ζῇ cf. *Lys.* 696 οὐ γὰρ ὑμῶν φροντίσαιμ' ἂν ἦν ἐμοὶ ζῇ Λαμπιτώ. The timidity of Attic speech made expressions like τὸ βουλευτήριον for ἡ βουλή rare; but τὸ θέατρον was regular for the audience (see on 233): Cicero recommends such phrases to the Roman orator, *gravis modus in ornatu orationis et saepe sumendus...curiam pro senatu* &c. *de orat.* iii 167. The look on the mask of Demos is foretold: and there may be a flout, pointed by a gesture, at the spectators present, as καθῆσθαι was used of a theatrical audience, and Cleon uses it pointedly of the Athenian public in Thucyd. iii 38. 7 σοφιστῶν θεαταῖς ἐοικότες καθημένοις μᾶλλον ἢ περὶ πόλεως βουλευομένοις.

397. Answering to 322. For δέ in exclamation and ἀναιδεύομαι see on 269-70. μεθίστησι is transitive, χρώματος being partitive genitive; Eurip. *Alc.* 173 οὐδὲ τοὐπιὸν κακὸν μέθιστη χρωτὸς εὐειδῆ φύσιν. The comedian Nicolaus says of a parasite (the butt of the New Comedy, as the demagogue is of the Old) πλευρὰν ἔχειν πρώτιστον ἐν τούτοισι δεῖ, πρόσωπον ἰταμὸν, χρῶμα διαμένον, γνάθον ἀκάματον.

εἰ σὲ μὴ μισῶ, γενοίμην ἐν Κρατίνου κῴδιον, 400
καὶ διδασκοίμην προσᾴδειν Μορσίμου τραγῳδίαν.
ὦ περὶ πάντ' ἐπὶ πᾶσί τε πράγμασι
δωροδόκοισιν ἐπ' ἄνθεσιν ἵζων,
εἴθε φαύλως, ὥσπερ ηὖρες, ἐκβάλοις τὴν ἔνθεσιν.
ᾄσαιμι γὰρ τότ' ἂν μόνον·   405
πῖνε πῖν' ἐπὶ συμφοραῖς·
τὸν Ἰουλίου τ' ἂν οἴομαι, γέροντα πυροπίπην,
ἡσθέντ' ἱππαιωνίσαι καὶ Βακχέβακχον ᾆσαι.

400—1. ΘΕ. most MSS. ἐν MSS. (except B), Suidas s.v. κῴδιον: ἐν vulg. and probably rightly (Cobet *NL* 154—5): but *one* fleece was the mark of poverty or asceticism *Thesm.* 1180, Philemon 26, Plut. *x orat. Lycurg.* 19, M. Aurel. xi 28, Athen. x 420 A, Diog. Laert. ii 139)(κῴδια of luxury Plato *Protag.* 315 D, Plut. *Ages.* 12.
401. τραγῳδίᾳ Dind. &c., ὑπᾴδειν τραγῳδίαν Cobet *NL* 155.
407. Οὐλίου Bothe, Βουλίου Mein. Holden, Ἰωλκίου Droysen (Thucyd. v 19. 2), Ἰουλιήτην τ' οἴομαι Duker Vels. πυρροπίπην V and some other MSS. Kock Ribb. Vels.

400. The scholiasts' explanation (ὡς ἐνουρητὴν καὶ μέθυσον διαβάλλει τὸν Κρατῖνον, cf. the Summanus of Plaut. *Curc.* 416) has been accepted by all editors except Bergk, who sees an ellipse of κωμῳδία and a reference to the luxurious bedding of Dionysus in Cratinus' play *Dionysalexandros*. Ar. never attacks Cratinus' art; his work is of the inner circle of poetry *Ran.* 357. The imprecation is a professional one 'may we sink to minister to the drunken life of our poet's chief rival in Comedy or to the bad tragedy of Morsimus.'
401. προσᾴδω would naturally take the dative, but such words tend to take acc., like πρόσημαι -καθέζομαι, -κειμαι, -πίπτω, -πολῶ, -γελῶ, and especially προσκυνῶ: προσπαίζω takes both cases: and this would naturally happen first in the mouth of a chorus. Cobet's ὑπᾴδειν seems to be used not of a chorus, but of the musicians who perform to dancers Hom. *Il.* xviii 570, *Ran.* 366, Callim. *Hymn. Dian.* 242, Lucian *salt.* 33 πάλαι μὲν οἱ αὐτοὶ καὶ ᾖδον καὶ ὠρχοῦντο· εἶτ' ἄμεινον ἔδοξεν ἄλλους αὐτοῖς ὑπᾴδειν: προσᾴδω of a chorus Plato *Legg.* ii 670 B ὅσοι προσᾴδειν καὶ βαίνειν ἐν ῥυθμῷ γεγόνασι διηναγκασμένοι, cf. Soph. *Philoct.* 405, Eurip. *Phoen.* 1499.
Of Morsimus, whose personal supervision of rehearsals is part of the

curse, we hear from scholiasts that he was a grand-nephew of Aeschylus, and we know from Aristophanes (*Pax* 801, *Ran.* 151) that he was a tragedian of no merit or success, attacked along with his brother Melanthius for bad poetry and good living. Plato com. 128 seems to present him with an admirer.
402—3. The lines may be slightly altered from some lyric poem. ἵζω in ordinary Attic is not used of persons: *Ran.* 197 Dionysus says ἵζω 'πὶ κώπην, but is corrected by the καθεδεῖ of next line; Plato *Legg.* ix 855 D κατὰ πρέσβιν ἵζεσθαι is plainly antique in phrase.
404. φαύλως, 'easily' and also '*sans façons*' as 1292, *Pax* 25: for ἔνθεσις see on 51. 'Cleon disgorging' was an idea and phrase familiar to the audience *Ach.* 6. The ease with which he had won the σίτησις (see on 282) is implied by ηὖρες: ηὗρου would imply more effort or desert.
405—6. 'Our one song then would be Simonides' (*fr.* 14) *Drink, drink for this good luck.* συμφορά was originally a neutral word, and cases of a good meaning occur in Aesch. *Agam.* 24 and Soph. *Elect.* 1230: but the bad sense was by this time fixed in common speech, except when an adjective like ἀγαθὸς is added as 655, *Lys.* 1276, Eurip. *Alc.* 1155.
407—8. Metrically these lines answer

ΠΑ. οὔ τοί μ' ὑπερβαλεῖσθ' ἀναιδείᾳ μὰ τὸν Ποσειδῶ,
ἢ μή ποτ' ἀγοραίου Διὸς σπλάγχνοισι παραγε-
νοίμην. 410

ΑΛΛ. ἔγωγε νὴ τοὺς κονδύλους, οὓς πολλὰ δὴ 'πὶ
πολλοῖς
ἠνεσχόμην ἐκ παιδίου, μαχαιρίδων τε πληγάς,
ὑπερβαλεῖσθαί σ' οἴομαι τούτοισιν, ἢ μάτην
γ' ἂν
ἀπομαγδαλίας σιτούμενος τοσοῦτος ἐκτραφείην.

414. -δαλιᾶς most MSS. here and 415. -δαλιαῖς R, which omits 414, in 415: the
accent of the word was doubtful, Chandler *Accent.* § 76, but gen. with σιτεῖσθαι seems
late : -δαλίας Suidas.

to 333—4 and might be expected to contain a fresh κατακελευσμός; but there is no fresh aspect of the Agon, and the hint of public delight over Cleon's fall starts the altercation again. We know nothing of 'Iulius' son' who embodies this delight in hymns of triumph. 'Ιούλιος is not otherwise known except as = Julius in Roman times. τὸν Ἰουλιήτην would be Simonides, born at Iulis in Ceos, died 467; Βουλίας was the proverbial dilatory judge, Οὔλιος a name of Apollo at Miletus, ἴουλος a song of woolworkers or to Demeter Athen. xiv 618 D, 619 B: but no conjecture or explanation has been of service. Interpreters from the scholiasts downward hesitate between πυρο- and πυρρο-πίπης. The curious Homeric word παρθενοπίπης was followed by παιδοπίπης &c. (οἰνοπίπης *Thesm.* 393 is doubtful). I am not clear either that Curtius' etymology as a reduplication of οπ (adopted by Brugmann) is possible, or that πυρρο- could = παιδο-. The gods thanked are Apollo and Dionysus, invoked together as helpers against evil in Soph. *OT* 204. 'Ιὴ Παιάν or the like was regular in hymns to Apollo: cf. ἰηπαιηόν' ἀείδειν Hom. *hymn. Apoll.* 500, the opening of Isyllus' hymn at Epidaurus, the end of each stanza in the Delphic paean. For the form Βακχέβακχος cf. 'Ιόβακχος. Dithyrambic poetry, represented by this unknown old man, as well as the drama, represented by the young knights, would be joyful.

409—10. He accepts their charge of ἀναίδεια, and uses the oath by Poseidon (see on 551). Ar. keeps the general

Attic rule that, when used of persons, ὑπερβάλλομαι takes an acc., ὑπερβάλλω is absolute (*Plut.* 109) except in the phrase ὑπερβάλλω πάντας ἀνθρώπους Demosth. *Cor.* 275, Xen. *Hell.* vii 3. 6.

The σπλάγχνα ἀγοραίου Διός may mean the περίστια or καθάρσια sacrificed at the beginning of an Ecclesia-meeting; anyhow the phrase is equivalent to 'public life.' Ζεὺς ἀγοραῖος was the spirit of state-business in the different cities where he had altars (not statues apparently except at Thebes, Paus. ix 25. 4): in Athens *inf.* 500, Aesch. *Eum.* 973, Eur. *Heracl.* 70: other deities near at hand sometimes defined that spirit more clearly as Themis at Thebes, Ge and Poseidon Asphalios at Sparta, Paus. iii 11. 9. For similar phrases cf. *Vesp.* 654 κἂν χρῇ σπλάγχνων μ' ἀπέχεσθαι 'though I were excommunicated'; Plut. *an seni resp.* 17. 792 F μηδὲ σεαυτὸν οἴου δεῖν, τῶν πολιτικῶν ἱερῶν ἔξαρχον ὄντα καὶ προφήτην, ἀφεῖναι τὰς τοῦ Πολιέως καὶ 'Αγοραίου τιμὰς Διός, ἔκπαλαι κατωργιασμένον αὐταῖς. παραγίγνομαι implies taking an active or prominent part more than πάρειμι would.

411—4. 'My training has been very different from yours, but it has made me hard and stout enough to beat you in your own walk' (ταῦτα). πόλλ' ἐπὶ πολλοῖς 'many on many a time' *Vesp.* 1046, Aelian *Var. Hist.* iv 18 (Blaydes). μαχαιρίς (1) *a small cook's or carver's knife*, as here, Plut. *Artax.* 19, Pollux x 104, (2) *a razor*, as Eupolis 278, Lucian *adv. indoct.* 29, Alciphro iii 66. 1: *cultellus* has the same meanings in Latin. For ἤ...γε 'else'

ΠΑ. ἀπομαγδαλίας ὥσπερ κύων; ὦ παμπόνηρε, πῶς
οὖν   415
κυνὸς βορὰν σιτούμενος μάχει σὺ Κυνοκε-
φάλλῳ;
ΑΛΛ. καὶ νὴ Δί' ἄλλα γ' ἐστί μου κόβαλα παιδὸς
ὄντος.
ἐξηπάτων γὰρ τοὺς μαγείρους ἂν λέγων τοιαυτί·
σκέψασθε, παῖδες· οὐχ ὁρᾶθ'; ὥρα νέα, χε-
λιδών.

416. μάχει MSS. μαχεῖ Dind. and most editors: -κεφάλῳ MSS. -κεφάλλῳ Dind. after Photius 188, 11: -κεφάλῳ μαχεῖ σύ; Cobet *Mnemos.* n.s. ii. 417.
418. μαγείρους λέγων most MSS. N. ἂν λέγων Cobet *NL* 411, ἐπιλέγων ΒΔ (these MSS. similarly patch the metre in *Av.* 505).

cf. Plato *Theaet.* 178 E, Dem. *i Aristog.* 71, *Nausim.* 18, *Boeot. de nom.* 33, Lysias 3. 42, Isocr. *Phil.* 103. The use of ἐκτρα-φείην ἂν at first seems like the Homeric use of ἂν with the optative of a definite point in past time (instances best given in Monro's *Hom. Grammar* § 300 c): but the action here is only just finished, and the opt. is hardly more strange than in Eurip. *Heracl.* 282 μάτην γὰρ ἥβην ὧδέ γ' ἂν κεκτήμεθα πολλὴν ἐν Ἄργει, μή σε τιμωρούμενοι, or Herod. vii 161 μάτην γὰρ ἂν στρατὸν εἴημεν κεκτημένοι, εἰ συγχωρήσομεν τῆς ἡγεμονίης. ἀπομαγδαλίαι were lumps of dough or soft bread used as napkins at meals, after meals used sometimes by Spartans as ballots (Plut. *Lycurg.* 12), but generally thrown to the dogs or the like Athen. iv 149 C, Philost. *vit. Apoll.* vii 23 συκο-φάνται, οὓς ἔδει μειλίττεσθαι τῇ ἀπο-μαγδαλίᾳ ταύτῃ. σιτεῖσθαι implies regular food, and generally inferior position, as of pensioners or animals *Nub.* 491 κυνηδὸν τὴν σοφίαν σιτήσομαι, Poseidon. ap. Athen. iv 152 F ὑποκαθήμενος τῷ βασιλεῖ τὸ παραβληθὲν ὑπ' αὐτοῦ κυνιστὶ σιτεῖται, Aesch. *Agam.* 1668 contemptuously of exiles, Plut. *tranq. anim.* 3. 466 D of a man reduced to a spare diet, and so *quaest. conv.* iv 660 F, Epictet. iii 3. 26, Philemon 155 to a soldier σιτούμενε, ὥσπερ ἱερεῖον ἵν', ὅταν ᾖ καιρός, τυθῇς.
415—6. παμπόνηρος was specially used with contempt of the social or intellectual upstart, as of the caricaturist Pauson *Ach.* 854, of Euripides by Heracles *Ran.* 106, of some philosophers by society

Plato *Rep.* vi 487 D, 489 D. βορά in Comedy and Prose is very rare and used only of animals' food. κυνοκέφαλος was (1) a *baboon*, thought a specially savage kind of ape, Plin. *NH* viii 216, (2) one of a fabled half-human race in Africa, Herod. iv 191, credited to Aeschylus along with Στερνόφθαλμοι by Strabo i 2. 35, vii 3. 6, or an Anubis-like deity, Lucian *deor. conc.* 11. As Kock says, the nickname σχινοκέφαλος for Pericles may have suggested this counterpart for Cleon. The grammarians' statement that the λλ was specially Attic is unlikely: the forms with ᾶ or λλ were Epic (see Rzach on Hes. *Theog.* 287) and grotesque, used mainly in epithets of monsters, as here.
418. Cobet, after Porson on *Phoen.* 412, shows that the use of ἂν with past tenses to denote frequency was not understood by copyists, who often drop ἂν in such cases. But he condemns ἐπιλέγων too summarily: that compound means *utter a spell* or the like, ἐπειπὼν ἐπῳδὴν Lucian *Necyom.* 3, *philops.* 35, Athen. xi 496 B, and also *quote* as in *point* Aristot. *Eth. Nic.* ii 9. 6, Lucian *somn.* 3 ἐπειπὼν τὸ κοινὸν "ἀρχὴ δέ τοι ἥμισυ παντός," Athen. v 186 D, Alciphro iii 56. 2, Aelian *Var. Hist.* iv 18 and very often in late Greek: either meaning would be fairly in point here.
419. The connexion of the swallow with early spring was very familiar in usage and language (the song χελιδόνισμα, the wind χελιδονίας, the *celandine* χελι-δόνιον &c.): *Thesm.* 1 χελιδὼν ἆρα πότε φανήσεται; An amphora of Vulci shows a

οἱ δ' ἔβλεπον, κἀγὼ 'ν τοσούτῳ τῶν κρεῶν
ἔκλεπτον.   420

ΧΟΡ. ὦ δεξιώτατον κρέας, σοφῶς γε προὐνοήσω·
ὥσπερ ἀκαλήφας ἐσθίων πρὸ χελιδόνων ἔκ-
λεπτες.

ΑΛΛ. καὶ ταῦτα δρῶν ἐλάνθανόν γ'· εἰ δ' οὖν ἴδοι
τις αὐτῶν,
ἀποκρυπτόμενος εἰς τὼ κοχώνα τοὺς θεοὺς
ἀπώμνυν·
ὥστ' εἶπ' ἀνὴρ τῶν ῥητόρων ἰδών με τοῦτο
δρῶντα·   425
οὐκ ἔσθ' ὅπως ὁ παῖς ὅδ' οὐ τὸν δῆμον ἐπιτροπεύσει.

421—2. Zieliński (*Gliederung* 118) would give these lines, and 427—8 to OI.
A, holding that in the Agon the chorus is judge merely: so Vahlen in *Hermes* xxvi
169. ὡς σοφῶς MSS. προὐνοήθης Cobet *Mnemos.* n. s. ii 417, "barbarum est, opinor,
προὐνοησάμην in Attica pro προὐνοήθην": but Veitch quotes it from Antiphon *caed.*
Herod. 43, as well as from Eurip. *Hipp.* 399, 685, and the tone may be mock-tragic.
423—4. γ' om. MSS. except Δ sec. m.: ἐλάνθανον ἂν Lenting, Cobet *ib.*, scout-
ing γ', which seems to me exactly in point. MSS. vary between τὰ κόχωνα (R V N
schol.) and τὰ κοχώνα; but Cobet's rule (*VL* 70) that τὼ is the only Attic dual nom.
form is fully borne out by inscriptions (Meisterhans § 46, 17). ἀπώμνυον MSS. as *-νυμι*
forms disappeared in use, see Rutherf. Babrius p. 55.

youth pointing out the swallow to a man
and a boy, who answer ἔαρ ἤδη (given
in Baumeister's *Denkm.* fig. 2128, Schrei-
ber's *Atlas* lxiv 10). The proverb μία
χελιδὼν οὐκ ἔαρ ποεῖ implies that playing
tricks on the simple in this respect was
common: νέα χελιδὼν ἐπὶ ἐξαπατώντων
τινὰς Suidas (who, like the Scholiast here,
separates ὥρα from νέα): so probably *fr.*
499 πυθοῦ χελιδὼν πηνίκ' ἄττα φαίνεται,
and the comic use of ἔαρ ἤδη in Lucian
Nigrin. 13.
420. ἐν τοσούτῳ, of a brief opportunity seized, as Thucyd. vi 64. 1, Lucian
dial. marin. 5. 1, *dial. meretr.* 9. 1; so
ἐν ᾧ Thucyd. ii 11. 7, iii 39. 3, ἐν τῷ
τοιούτῳ Plato *Rep.* v 465 A.
421. Schol. on *Ran.* 191 (νεναυ-
μάχηκε τὴν περὶ τῶν κρεῶν) gives Aristarchus as authority that τὰ κρέα was often
used for τὰ σώματα: but in the few other
extant cases (here, *inf.* 457, Soph. *fr.* 650,
which is probably satyric), κρέας is a

humorous equivalent for λῆμα.
422. The young nettle is eatable (it
is much used in Scotland); it was thought
very wholesome (Athen. iii 90 A, Catullus 44. 15 Ellis, Plin. *NH* xxi 93), and
especially good with Athenian ἀφύαι
(Athen. vii 185 B): but the gatherers had
to come early in the year 'before the
swallow dares.'
423—4. εἰ δ' οὖν, ἢν δ' οὖν, introduce
a case emphatically marked as exceptional
or secondary: in English the meaning is
brought out by emphasis laid on the
auxiliary verb, 'if one of them *should, did,*
see me': Paley on Aesch. *Agam.* 1042
gives cases, *Vesp.* 92, Soph. *OT* 851 &c.;
add Lysias 9. 11, Plut. *amator.* 4. 750 F.
425—6. ἀνήρ is an example of the
use of this word for τις: Thucydides is
fond of ἄνδρες for τινες: there is a burlesque
shade of emphasis or compliment, as we
should expect, more than τις would have, *a
political gentleman.* ἐπιτροπεύσει, cf. on 212.

N. A.   5

ΧΟΡ. εὖ γε ξυνέβαλεν αὔτ'· ἀτὰρ δῆλόν γ' ἀφ' οὗ
ξυνέγνω·
ὁτιὴ 'πιώρκεις θ' ἡρπακὼς καὶ κρέας ὁ πρωκτὸς
εἶχεν.

ΠΑ. ἐγώ σε παύσω τοῦ θράσους, οἶμαι δὲ μᾶλλον
ἄμφω.
ἔξειμι γάρ σοι λαμπρὸς ἤδη καὶ μέγας κα-
θιείς,   430
ὁμοῦ ταράττων τήν τε γῆν καὶ τὴν θάλατταν
εἰκῆ.

ΑΛΛ. ἐγὼ δὲ συστείλας γε τοὺς ἀλλᾶντας εἶτ' ἀφήσω
κατὰ κῦμ' ἐμαυτὸν οὔριον, κλάειν σε μακρὰ
κελεύων.

428. RM omit θ' and give τὸ κρέας. **431.** θάλασσαν R alone, perhaps rightly : the tone is tragic. **433.** πολλὰ κελεύσας R.

427—8. ξυνέγνω does not here imply either agreement or concession or conscience, as the word usually does : L and S quote only Dion. Hal. *Antiq. Rom.* iv 4 for the sense *conclude from premises*. For the reasons given in 428 cf. *inf.* 878, *Nub.* 1093, *Eccl.* 112, Plato com. 186. 5, and Aristophanes' speech in Plato *Symp.* 192 A τελεωθέντες μόνοι ἀποβαίνουσιν εἰς τὰ πολιτικὰ ἄνδρες οἱ τοιοῦτοι.
429. ἄμφω, the Sausage-man and Demosthenes. I am not aware that any principle has been found regulating the use of οἴομαι and οἶμαι, except that οἴομαι is never used parenthetically.
430—1. The comparison of Cleon to a storm-wind is taken in 511 as a commonplace of the day. The words are all regular ones of wind : for ἔξειμι cf. 760, *Ran.* 848, Diphilus 67 ὡς ῥαγδαῖος ἐξελήλυθεν (Kock); for λαμπρὸς Herod. ii 96 ἦν μὴ λαμπρὸς ἄνεμος ἐπέχῃ, and the Latin *clarus;* for καθιεὶς the use of καθίημι ἐξίημι εἰσβάλλω of rivers. The new start, marked by ἤδη, promises a new vigour, fresh and formidable charges against his rival, but also a clearer recognition of the rival's position and power.
432—3. 'Oh, but your wind will only blow me fairly on with my sausage-

sails shortened.' δέ...γε marks opposition here as καί...γε in 434 support.
To shorten (συστέλλειν) or lower (ὑφίεσθαι) sail was a common metaphor of dealing with adversity or strong opposition in words or deeds, *Ran.* 999—, 1220, Eurip. *Med.* 522—, Soph. *Elect.* 335.
κατὰ κῦμα, of gay and confident speed, as Hom. *Il.* i 483 and *Od.* ii 489 ἡ δ' ἔθεεν κατὰ κῦμα διαπρήσσουσα κέλευθον, *hymn.* 5. 4 Ζεφύρου μένος ὑγρὸν ἀέντος ἤνεικεν κατὰ κῦμα πολυφλοίσβοιο θαλάσσης ἀφρῷ ἔνι μαλακῷ : there of course, as to a less extent here, the phrase exactly suits the metre. The tragic κατ' οὖρον on the other hand is generally of carelessness and despair, as Aesch. *Sept.* 690, 854, *Pers.* 481, Soph. *Trach.* 468. οὔριον goes with ἐμαυτόν, cf. Eurip. *Hel.* 147 νεὼς στείλαιμ' ἂν οὔριον πτερόν.
μακρὰ κλάειν, μακρὰ οἰμώζειν, a stronger form of πολλὰ χαίρειν, which is not used of friendly farewell. A scholiast remarks on the εἶδος ἀρχαῖον καὶ Ἀττικὸν τῆς συνθέσεως, and it seems to have died out : the index to Lucian gives no case : later Greek used μακρὰ χαίρειν of a 'long farewell'; τὸ μακρὰ χαίρειν φράσαι τὸ μηκέτι φροντιεῖν δηλοῖ Lucian *laps. inter salut.* 2.

ΟΙ. Α. κἄγωγ', ἐάν τι παραχαλᾷ, τὴν ἀντλίαν φυλάξω.

ΠΑ. οὔ τοι μὰ τὴν Δήμητρα καταπροίξει τάλαντα
πολλὰ 435
κλέψας Ἀθηναίων. ΟΙ. Α. ἄθρει, καὶ τοῦ
ποδὸς παρίει·
ὡς οὗτος ἤδη καικίας ἢ συκοφαντίας πνεῖ.

ΠΑ. σὲ δ' ἐκ Ποτειδαίας ἔχοντ' εὖ οἶδα δέκα τάλαντα.

437. ἤτοι κακίας ἢ R, Plut. comp. Ar. et Men. i. 853 B, ἤδη κακίας καὶ other MSS.
438—9. I keep the MSS. distribution of persons, altered needlessly by several editors.
438. Ποτιδαίας all MSS. Ποτειδαίας Thiersch &c. rightly (Meisterhans 41).

---

434. παραχαλᾷ (here only), 'there is a leak')(στέγει ἡ ναῦς, στεγανός &c.
For ἀντλίαν φυλάξω editors quote Soph. *Phil.* 481, Cic. *Epist. Fam.* ix 15. 3 (of his own position) *nunc vix in sentina locus est.*
435—6. L and S give the known cases (Archil. Herod. Arist. and late) of this curious word. The form was probably -προίξομαι Ionic, -προίξομαι Attic (Ruth. *NP* 160).
In Attic law κλοπή was peculation as well as theft, in the former case δημοσίων or ἱερῶν χρημάτων being generally added for definition as Ἀθηναίων is here. Meier and Schömann *Att. Process*² 454—6 give the methods of procedure and the punishments (tenfold restitution as in Demosth. *Timocr.* 112, 127 &c., or even death).
436. ἀθρεῖν is chiefly used in imperative: it is common in Tragedy and Plato, but occurs only once in Thucyd. (v 26. 2) and once in the Orators, Isocr. *Philipp.* 17, both times of historical survey. It has been connected with *wonder* (Kluge), but may be taken with ἀθρόος.
τοῦ ποδὸς παρίει 'slacken the sheet' to suit the gale; cf. Plut. *praec. ger. reip.* 24. 818 A ὁ περὶ πάντα λίαν ἀκριβὴς καὶ σφοδρός, οὐδὲν ὑποχωρῶν οὐδ' ὑπείκων, ἀντιφιλονεικεῖν τὸν δῆμον αὐτῷ καὶ προσδυσκολαίνειν ἐθίζει, μικρὸν δέον ποδὸς χαλάσαι μεγάλῃ κύματος ἀλκῇ.
437. Aristot. (*Meteor.* ii 6. 364ᵇ 12—) and Theophrastus (*de vent.* 37, *de sign.*

temp. 36) say that the καικίας or N.E. wind gathers clouds, instead of dispelling them, and that ἕλκων ἐφ' αὑτὸν (κακὰ) ὥστε καικίας νέφος was proverbial, cf. Plut. *de cap. util.* 4. 88 E, *praec. ger. reip.* 31. 823 B, A. Gell. ii 22, Plin. *NH* ii 126. The figure of Καικίας in the Athenian Tower of the Winds is the most savage of the eight. The name is probably Phocaean, meaning 'the wind from the Caicusmouth' to the N.E. The wind was disliked in Lesbos, the harbour of Mitylene being exposed to it, Aristot. ἀν. θεσ. 973ᵇ 8. As names of winds so often ended in -ίας (Φοινικίας, ἀπαρκτίας, Ὀλυμπίας &c.), we have the invented wind συκοφαντίας, like ὀρνιθίας *Ach.* 877, and perhaps γονίας Aesch. *Cho.* 1065.
In Plutarch's *comp. Aristoph. et Men.* i. 853 B this line is quoted with 454 as a specimen of our author's untimely and pointless puns: the pun is not explained, but Plutarch probably saw one on κακίας or αἰκίας.
438. The frank meeting of this charge as a blackmailing one is a new feature in the Sausage-man's dexterity.
Potidaea was taken by the Athenians in 430—29 (Gilbert, *Inn. Gesch.* 122, sees here a reference to the prosecution of the successful generals for making terms without authority, Thucyd. ii 70): the inhabitants dispersed and were replaced by Attic colonists, and the town was a centre of the Attic interest against Brasidas.

ΑΛΛ. τί δῆτα; βούλει τῶν ταλάντων ἓν λαβὼν
σιωπᾶν;

ΧΟ. ἀνὴρ ἂν ἡδέως λάβοι. τοὺς τερθρίους παρίει, 440
τὸ πνεῦμ᾽ ἔλαττον γίγνεται.

ΠΑ. φεύξει γραφὰς ἑκατονταλάντους τέτταρας.

ΑΛΛ. σὺ δ᾽ ἀστρατείας γ᾽ εἴκοσιν,
κλοπῆς δὲ πλεῖν ἢ χιλίας.

ΠΑ. ἐκ τῶν ἀλιτηρίων σέ φη-   445
μι γεγονέναι τῶν τῆς θεοῦ.

ΑΛΛ. τὸν πάππον εἶναί φημί σου

440. ἀνήρ MSS.
442. φεύξει γραφὰς σὺ δειλίας | ἑκατονταλάντους τ. Meineke, who supposes that
the passage was corrupted by a scribe who made one iambic trimeter of it: but the
scholiast notes the trimeter and Zieliński p. 121 allows it: besides, the only punishment under a γραφὴ δειλίας seems to have been ἀτιμία, Meier and Schömann *Att.
Proc.*² 465. **443—50.** R arranges the persons wrongly, continuing **443—4** to
Cleon, and omitting the γ᾽ after ἀστρατείας.

The expense of reducing it had been
enormous (2000 talents Thucyd. iii 17),
and it may have become a commonplace
in Athenian finance to refer to it.
439. Demosth. *Cor.* 82 ὦ βλασφημῶν
περὶ ἐμοῦ καὶ λέγων ὡς σιωπῶ μὲν λαβὼν
βοῶ δ᾽ ἀναλώσας, Aeschin. *Ctes.* 218 λαβὼν μὲν σεσίγηκας, ἀναλώσας δὲ κέκραγας.
440. τοὺς τερθρίους παρίει)(τοῦ ποδὸς
παρίει. Dind. sees an allusion to the
curious grammarians' usage of τερθρεία
for oratorical claptrap: cf. τερθρεύεται
Bergk's conjecture in *fr.* 1 for τηρεύεται.
442. The tenfold restitution (see on
435) of the ten talents peculated is
threatened in each of four actions. The
sum would seem monstrous and the sound
of the word ἑκατονταλάντους fearful: Pollux ix 52 remarks that such compounds
should be restricted to cases ὅπου μὴ τὸ
δύσφθεγκτον καὶ τὸ τραχὺ πρὸς τὴν ἀκοὴν
ἐμποδίζοι.
443—4. A charge of ἀστρατεία is
more outrageous even than the δειλία of
368 against the incorruptible hero. κλοπή
is given, *Nub.* 591, as an offence of which
Cleon ought to have been convicted.
445—6. After the murder of Cylon's
friends in sanctuary the murderers and
their descendants were called ἐναγεῖς καὶ
ἀλιτήριοι τῆς θεοῦ, Thucyd. i 126. 7: and
none of their race, alive or dead (Aristot.

Pol. Ath. 1), were secure from molestation
on this score: it is notorious how the
charge was used against Cleisthenes and
Pericles, and it may have been revived
now against Alcibiades. The guilt and
pollution fell mainly on the Alcmaeonidae,
and here the implication is that the Sausage-man is a member of that ancient
house. I have little doubt that the murder
of the suppliants was an intentional insult
to Athena-worship as the democratic cult:
the Alcmaeonidae traced their descent to
Poseidon through Neleus, see on 551.
ἀλιτήριος is always a grave word, implying pollution and danger to the com-
munity, τὸν τῆς Ἑλλάδος ἀλιτήριον Aeschin.
Ctes. 157, οὐ καταλεύσετε τὸν ἀλιτήριον;
Lucian *Jup. trag.* 36. A Megacles, son
of Megacles, doubtless an Alcmaeonid,
appears as γραμματεὺς ταμιῶν τῆς θεοῦ,
CIA i 122, 149, so that the goddess had
forgiven.
It is known that ἡ θεός is the only prose
form for *goddess*: ἡ θεά occurs on Inscriptions, but only for Persephone when
coupled with Pluto (Meisterhans § 47 a,
4).
447—9. δορυφόροι meant a *tyrant's*
lifeguard of *foreign* mercenaries: Pisistratus' Athenian guard are expressly distinguished as κορυνηφόροι, Herod. i 59.
The word, related to τύραννος as *satelles*

τῶν δορυφόρων. ΠΑ. ποίων; φράσον.

ΑΛΛ. τῶν Βυρσίνης τῆς Ἱππίου.

ΠΑ. κόβαλος εἶ. ΑΛΛ. πανοῦργος εἶ.   450

ΧΟΡ. παῖ᾽ ἀνδρικῶς. ΠΑ. ἰοὺ ἰού,

τύπτουσί μ᾽ οἱ ξυνωμόται.

ΧΟΡ. παῖ᾽ αὐτὸν ἀνδρικώτατα, καὶ

γάστριζε καὶ τοῖς ἐντέροις

καὶ τοῖς κόλοις,   455

χὤπως κολᾷ τὸν ἄνδρα.

ὦ γεννικώτατον κρέας ψυχήν τ᾽ ἄριστε πάντων,

καὶ τῇ πόλει σωτὴρ φανεὶς ἡμῖν τε τοῖς πολί-

ταις,

453. ἀνδρικώτατ᾽ αὖ Reisig, -κώτατ᾽, εὖ Elmsley, ἀνδρειότατα Dind. &c. : in such iambics synapheia holds, and a tribrach may end the line, as 931, *Nub.* 1386—9, though I have no other case of a final anapaest.

to *rex*, retained an invidious and sinister meaning, Aesch. *Cho.* 769 (where it suggests the δεσπότου στύγει of the next line), Thucyd. i 130 of Pausanias' oriental habits, vi 56. 2 of Hippias as here, Demosth. *Aristocr.* 123, several times in Plato *Rep.* ix where sinister conditions of the mental polity are implied, Lucian *dial. mort.* 30. 2 δῆμιος ἢ δορυφόρος, ὁ μὲν δικαστῇ πεισθείς, ὁ δὲ τυράννῳ, *tyrannoc.* 4: a rare exception is Isocr. *Helena* 37 τῇ τῶν πολιτῶν εὐνοίᾳ δορυφορούμενος. Hippias married Myrsine, daughter of a Callias: she is mentioned only by Thucydides vi 55 with some emphasis on her pedigree. The obscurity of women in Greek politics is not always the rule under tyrants. The play in Βυρσίνη is as in 59. The name was not uncommon among Greek women, but by this time was always Μυρρίνη, cf. Meisterhans § 34. 11, § 35.
451—2. For ἀνδρικῶς see on 82 : and for οἱ ξυνωμόται on 257.
455—6. Confusion between κόλον and κῶλον is constant in MSS.: κῶλον is regular in this sense in later medical writers and κωλικός seems the only extant form of the adjective: Latin has *cōlum* or *cōlus* always. Pollux ii 209 makes a serious etymology out of the pun here: κόλον...ἀφ᾽ οὗ τὸ κολάζεσθαι, διὰ τὸ φέρειν τὸ ἐν αὐτῷ πάθος τῶν σωμάτων ὀξείας τινὰς

ἀλγηδόνας. κολᾷ: there is no fixed rule for the Attic future of verbs in -άζω: κολωμένους *Vesp.* 244, but κολάσομαί σ᾽ ἐγώ Theopomp. com. 27. Veitch on δικάζω and κολάζω uses them as a reproach and challenge to uniformists. The syncopation is confined to a few verbs βιβάζω, κολάζω, πελάζω, σκευάζω, σκιάζω, and perhaps βιάζω and ἐξετάζω, with ἐλῶ, κρεμῶ, κερῶ, σκεδῶ. Except ἐλῶ, the only -ῶ future for -άσω found in Inscriptions is σκευῶ in the second century B.C. (Meisterhans § 64. 2). Grammarians disagree: Moeris says διαβιβῶ Ἀττικῶς, διαβιβάσω Ἑλληνικῶς (cf. Cobet *VL* 28), Choeroboscus ii 156 Hilgard ignorantly denies the syncopation of -άσω from -άζω altogether.
457—8. γεννικός is to γενναῖος as ἀνδρικός to ἀνδρεῖος, see on 81 (ἀνδρειότατα in 453 spoils the parallelism here, cf. Luc. *vit. auct.* 7). The word is comic and Platonic (*Theaet.* 144 D, *Phaedr.* 279 A). The absurdity of γεννικώτατε in the literal meaning here is softened by the ψυχήν τ᾽ ἄριστε: but the more serious γενναῖος is used of him later (511, 787 &c.), as he wins still greater admiration from the knights, who claim special patriotism in the ἡμῖν τοῖς πολίταις. For κρέας see on 421: γεννικός was used, like νεανικός, of eatables Eubulus 7. 8 κρέας βόειον ἑφθὸν ἀσόλοικον μέγα, ἀκροκώλιόν τε γεννικόν, Antiphanes 192. 3.

ὡς εὖ τὸν ἄνδρα ποικίλως τ' ἐπῆλθες ἐν λό-
γοισιν.

πῶς ἄν σ' ἐπαινέσαιμεν οὕτως ὥσπερ ἡδόμε-
σθα ;　　　　　　　　　　　　　　　　　　460

ΠΑ. ταυτὶ μὰ τὴν Δήμητρά μ' οὐκ ἐλάνθανεν
τεκταινόμενα τὰ πράγματ', ἀλλ' ἠπιστάμην
γομφούμεν' αὐτὰ πάντα καὶ κολλώμενα.

ΑΛΛ. οὔκουν μ' ἐν Ἄργει γ' οἷα πράττεις λανθάνει.
πρόφασιν μὲν Ἀργείους φίλους ἡμῖν ποεῖ·　465

459. θ' ὑπῆλθες all MSS. except R: in Eurip. *Hipp.* 1089 MSS. vary between
ὑπέρχεται and ἐπέρχεται.

464. MSS. except R omit γ' (οὔκουν· γε is very common, Eurip. *Hel.* 124 οὔκουν
ἐν Ἄργει γ' οὐδ' ἐπ' Εὐρώτα ῥοαῖς &c.): ἐν Ἀργείοις ἅ Porson, Cobet. πράττεις MSS.
πράττει Bentley and most edd., but Lenting quoted for the change of person *Lys.* 486,
Ran. 1007.

459. Though ποικίλως suits ὑπῆλθες in
the sense of *cajole*, ἐπῆλθες is much better
here, 'you have taken the offensive with
skill': in Thucydides ἐπέρχομαι constantly
has this meaning)(ἀμύνομαι, though it
takes the dative after it, except perhaps
ii 39. 2. The ποικιλία of the rivals is
compared in 686, and the passage similar
to this 758.

460. 'Oh that we could thank you
in a way worthy of the pleasure you give
us!' As ἐπαινῶ means 'no, thank you,'
ἐπαινεῖν often means *thank, give vote of
thanks*, cf. 595, Thucyd. ii 25 ἐπῃνέθη
(was *thanked officially*) ἐν Σπάρτῃ, ἐπαινεῖν
καὶ εἰς τὸ πρυτανεῖον καλεῖν Demosth. *FL*
31, 234, *Polycl.* 13 and often in Inscriptions; though it is characteristic of Greek
politics that the same word means *official
thanks* and *popular acclaim* (Plato *Rep.*
vi 492 c).

461—3. Cleon's one speech in Thucydides (iii 37—40) contains no such
metaphors as those, but rather protests
against the Athenian liking for them,
for the καινότης λόγου and the ξυνέσεως
ἀγών of their orators. The chorus here
behave as Cleon reproaches his hearers
with doing, ὑμεῖς κακῶς ἀγωνοθετοῦντες
οἵτινες εἰώθατε θεαταὶ μὲν τῶν λόγων
γίγνεσθαι..., caring for style more than
for matter: schol. on 480 says τὸ ὅλον
πρὸς τοὺς ῥήτορας ὡς τὸ πλῆθος καταπλησ-
σομένους ταῖς αὐτῶν ἀκυρολογίαις. It is a
commonplace that ancient oratory is to

our minds sparing and timid in metaphors,
but the power of using them was a main
point, πολὺ μέγιστον τὸ μεταφορικὸν εἶναι
Arist. *Poet.* 22, *Rhet.* iii 2. 8.

The three metaphors here form a climax
in art: τεκταίνομαι is not unfamiliar, but
metaphors with γόμφοι and κόλλη are very
rare (Aeschylus' γεγόμφωται σκάφος), except in criticism of literary style and the
like (συγκολλήτης ψευδῶν, *Nub.* 446,
Aristot. *Rhet.* iii 2. 12 in an αἴνιγμα or
extreme case of metaphor, Hermogenes
quoted by L and S, Longinus *de sublim.*
41 ὡσανεὶ γόμφοις τισὶν ἐπισυνδεδεμένα)
and of personal attachment. So there is
a climax in Plaut. *Bacch.* 693 *compara
fabrica finge quod lubes conglutina.*

465—7. The power and ancient
prestige of Argos, its rivalry with Sparta,
its non-Ionic democracy made it always
an important factor in Greek politics. At
this time its thirty years' truce with Sparta
was running out, Thucyd. v 14. 4: the
dispute about Cynuria was likely to be
revived, and Athenian statesmen like
Cleon and Alcibiades naturally were
working for Argive support. Changes in
Athenian feeling are reflected in Aeschylus'
Eumenides (458 B.C.) and Euripides' *Supplices* (probably 420), which urge an
Argive alliance, and the *Heraclidae*, whatever its date, which gives as its keynote
on this question φθείρου· τὸ σὸν γὰρ
Ἄργος οὐ δέδοικ' ἐγώ, 284. The feeling
in Comedy is generally one of irritation

ἰδίᾳ δ᾽ ἐκεῖ Λακεδαιμονίοις ξυγγίγνεται.

ΧΟΡ. οἴμοι, σὺ δ᾽ οὐδὲν ἐξ ἁμαξουργοῦ λέγεις;

ΑΛΛ. καὶ ταῦτ᾽ ἐφ᾽ οἷσίν ἐστι συμφυσώμενα
ἐγῴδ᾽· ἐπὶ γὰρ τοῖς δεδεμένοις χαλκεύεται.

ΧΟΡ. εὖ γ᾽ εὖ γε, χάλκευ᾽ ἀντὶ τῶν κολλωμένων. 470

ΑΛΛ. καὶ ξυγκροτοῦσιν ἄνδρες αὔτ᾽ ἐκεῖθεν αὖ,
καὶ ταῦτά μ᾽ οὔτ᾽ ἀργύριον οὔτε χρυσίον
διδοὺς ἀναπείσεις, οὔτε προσπέμπων φίλους,
ὅπως ἐγὼ ταῦτ᾽ οὐκ Ἀθηναίοις φράσω.

ΠΑ. ἐγὼ μὲν οὖν αὐτίκα μάλ᾽ εἰς βουλὴν ἰὼν 475
ὑμῶν ἁπάντων τὰς ξυνωμοσίας ἐρῶ,

467 is 464 in all MSS. Hermann made it 467 and so most editors: the scholiast pretty certainly read it as 467.

at Argos' trimming of the scale, *Pax* 475 —7, Pherecrates 19 οὗτοι γὰρ ἡμῖν οἱ κακῶς ἀπολούμενοι ἐπαμφοτερίζουσ᾽ ἐμποδὼν καθημένοι.

465—6. πρόφασιν μὲν answered not by τὸ δ᾽ ἀληθές as regularly (Thucyd. vi 33. 2, Lysias *Agorat.* 12): cf. Eurip. *Bacch.* 224, and a letter in Demosth. *Cor.* 77 πρόφασιν μὲν ὡς τὸν σῖτον παραπέμψοντα ἐκ τοῦ Ἑλλησπόντου, βοηθήσοντα δὲ Σηλυβριανοῖς.

467. The Chorus call for striking figures more than for definite facts: their champion has beaten Cleon in the latter, but his style lacks the metaphor of his rival: besides, ἁμαξιαῖα meant 'big words' (Diogenianus 3. 41). They use tragic rhythm by Zieliński's rule: and it seems to be a point of skill in the disputants at this crisis to bring in a line or two of the same kind.

468—9. τέκτων, χαλκεύς, σκυτεύς, were the main trades, Xen. *Memor.* i 2. 37, iv 2. 22, 4. 5: μηδεὶς χαλκεύων ἅμα τεκταινέσθω Plato *Legg.* viii 846 E. The metaphor would be unusual and striking, though Pindar *Pyth.* 1. 87 has χάλκευε γλῶσσαν and the Romans were fond of *conflo, procudo*, and the like in this sense. γάρ in 469 of course explains ἐφ᾽ οἷσιν: for the charge here cf. 393—4. *Pax* 480 may refer to something of the same kind.

470. 'Bravo, give him smith's work for his glue and stuff.'

471. ξυγκροτῶ became a favourite word to mean *organise* and the like: Thucyd. viii 95 ἀξυγκρότητα, of ships' crews. ἐκεῖθεν by the well-known idiom for ἐκεῖ, their action affecting matters outside: αὖ=on their side)(Cleon in Athens.

472—4. The non-poetic words ἀργύριον and χρυσίον (*Cycl.* 161 is the only case in Eurip.) often have the invidious sense of bribes, as βασιλικὸν χρυσίον, *Persian gold* &c. προσπέμπω, of confidants in intrigue of love (Herod. ix 108) or politics (Thucyd. viii 47. 2 a passage full of political phrases, Demosth. *FL* 167). φράσω is fut. indic. as Arist. avoids ὅπως with subj., Ph. Weber *Absichtssätze* 124.

475. He means to proceed by εἰσαγγελία before the Council as was regular in cases of treason, see Hager's article in Smith's *Dict. of Antiq.* (the first class of crime under the νόμος εἰσαγγελτικός being ἐάν τις τὸν δῆμον τὸν Ἀθηναίων καταλύῃ ἢ συνίῃ ποι ἐπὶ ᾽καταλύσει τοῦ δήμου ἢ ἑταιρικὸν συναγάγῃ): the Council also had a reviewing control of the knights.

476—9. ἐρῶ fut. to φημί in the sense of *inform, denounce*. The ξυν- in each line harps on the democratic fear of oligarchic combination: for ξυνωμοσία see on 236, for ξύνοδος of secret political meetings, Thucyd. iii 82. 6, Andoc. *Myst.*

καὶ τὰς ξυνόδους τὰς νυκτερινὰς ἐπὶ τῇ πόλει,
καὶ πάνθ' ἃ Μήδοις καὶ βασιλεῖ ξυνόμνυτε,
καὶ τἀκ Βοιωτῶν ταῦτα συντυρούμενα.

ΑΛΛ. πῶς οὖν ὁ τυρὸς ἐν Βοιωτοῖς ὤνιος;   480

ΠΑ. ἐγώ σε νὴ τὸν Ἡρακλέα παραστορῶ.

ΧΟΡ. ἄγε δὴ σὺ τίνα νοῦν ἢ τίνα γνώμην ἔχεις;
νυνὶ διδάξεις, εἴπερ ἀπεκρύψω τότε
εἰς τὼ κοχώνα τὸ κρέας, ὡς αὐτὸς λέγεις.
θεύσει γὰρ ἄξας εἰς τὸ βουλευτήριον,   485

477. ἐν τῇ π. R, ἐπὶ τῇ π. most MSS. schol.: the latter gives the meaning *treasonable*, which is wanted: τὰς ἐν πόλει Cobet (*Mnemos.* n.s. ii 418), but why should they meet on the acropolis?   **482.** Zieliński, *Glied.* 294, would give these lines to Demosthenes, as the metre is not tragic enough for the chorus by his rule; cf. crit. note on 490.   γνώμην R, ψυχήν the other MSS.   **483.** νυνί γε δείξεις Mein. after Cobet *Mnemos.* i 416: Elmsley on *Ach.* 108 pointed out that γε after -ί is very rare, yet νυνί γε is read *Nub.* 295, *Pax* 326, 337, *Ran.* 276.   **484.** τὰ κόχωνα R, τὰς κοχώνας other MSS.; see on 424.

47, Plato *Theaet.* 173 D, Isocr. *Nicocles* 54 ἑταιρείας μὴ ποιεῖσθε μηδὲ συνόδους (the verb is σύνειμι as Demosth. *Timarch.* 144). νυκτερινός *by night*, νυκτερήσιος *like night*, Rutherf. *NP* 125. Medism was a form of treason ever kept before the Athenian mind by the curse invoked at the ecclesia-meetings against it, *Thesm.* 337, Isocr. *Paneg.* 157 ἐν τοῖς συλλόγοις ἔτι καὶ νῦν ἀρὰς ποιοῦνται, πρὶν ἄλλο τι χρηματίζειν, εἴ τις ἐπικηρυκεύεται Πέρσαις τῶν πολιτῶν, Plut. *Aristides* 10: in *Pax* 108 as here, it is a comic ground of charge. Sparta had recently been intriguing with Persia, and Athens had shown some willingness to make a counter-bid, Thucyd. iv 50, *Ach.* 61—: Artaxerxes Longimanus was dying, and a new policy might be expected from his successor.

συντυρ., a phrase of common life, which became a literary metaphor, like *brew mischief*, Lucian *asin.* 31 κακὸν ἐμοὶ μέγα τυρεύων: Demosth. says ὁ δ' ἔνδον ἐτύρευε *FL* 295, but Pollux vi 130 says he cannot admit such a phrase among the many allowable forms of abuse πρὸς τὸν θορυβοῦντα τὸ δημόσιον. The rich pastoral country of Boeotia was famous for its cheese: Hesiod's μᾶζα ἀμολγαίη is probably a kind of cheese: the Athenian market for χλωρὸς τυρός was a rendezvous for Plataeans, Lysias 23. 6.

About this time, Demosthenes began

to intrigue actively with the Boeotian democrats for Athenian supremacy there, Thucyd. iv. 76—: but no evidence exists to show that the attempt had any success and the battle of Delium crushed it. For Βοιωτῶν cf. on δειλαῖος 139.

480. πῶς, not πόσου, ὤνιος is the Attic phrase, Cobet *VL* 110. Diocletian's edict gives 12 denarii per pound for τυρὸς ξηρός, and 10 denarii per sextarius for *caseus recens* (5. 11, 6. 96). 'Whatever may be doing in Boeotia, you know how to make money there': and Cleon has no answer except the bully's. The scholiast says παραστορέννυμι (a very rare word) is a tanner's phrase, and νὴ τὸν Ἡρακλέα is a form of oath suited to Boeotia.

483–4. The sentence is a simple conditional one, 'if you are the man you say you are, now you'll teach us (what policy you have).' τότε = ὡς εἶπες, giving a reference backwards, as often in Thucydides.

485–7. θεύσει and ἄξας to beat Cleon's ἰών in 475. εἰσπίπτω is rarely passive in meaning, (ἐκπίπτω nearly always), yet Thucyd. i 131. 2 ἐς τὴν εἱρκτὴν ἐσπίπτει ὑπὸ τῶν ἐφόρων. Here it strengthens the notion of violence or awkwardness in Cleon's conduct: cf. Soph. *Aj.* 55, *Ran.* 945 οὐκ ἐλήρουν ὅτι τύχοιμ' οὐδ' ἐμπεσὼν ἔφυρον, *Vesp.* 120, Hipponax 35,

ὡς οὗτος εἰσπεσὼν ἐκεῖσε διαβαλεῖ
ἡμᾶς ἅπαντας καὶ κράγον κεκράξεται.

ΑΛΛ. ἀλλ' εἶμι· πρῶτον δ', ὡς ἔχω, τὰς κοιλίας
καὶ τὰς μαχαίρας ἐνθαδὶ καταθήσομαι.

ΟΙ. Α. ἔχε νυν, ἄλειψον τὸν τράχηλον τουτῳί, 490
ἵν' ἐξολισθάνειν δύνῃ τὰς διαβολάς.

ΑΛΛ. ἀλλ' εὖ λέγεις καὶ παιδοτριβικῶς ταυταγί.

ΟΙ. Α. ἔχε νυν, ἐπέγκαψον λαβὼν ταδί. ΑΛΛ. τί
δαί;

ΟΙ. Α. ἵν' ἄμεινον, ὦ τάν, ἐσκοροδισμένος μάχῃ.

486. ἐμπεσών MSS. except R: ἐμπ. was commoner, see expl. note.
487. κεκραγὸν R, καὶ κραγὼν AN &c., καὶ κραγὸν V &c., schol. after Aristarchus
and Herodian, καὶ κράγον most edd.: Lobeck *Paralip.* 506 quoting Eustathius *epist.*
xix 164. 43 κραγὸν ὃ δὴ λέγεται ἀνακράζοντες suggested κράγον as right accent:
Hesychius κράγον· βόημα. **490.** XO. MSS.: OIK. A Enger (*Neue Jahrb.* lxix
365) and most editors: so 492, 493, 495 : this arrangement suits Zieliński's rule.

Apollodorus com. 24 δεδείπνηχ' ὡς ἔοικεν
ἐμπεσών of an uninvited guest, Herod. iii
81 ὠθέει ἐμπεσὼν τὰ πρήγματα ἄνευ νοῦ,
Aristot. *Pol.* ii 9. 19. 1270ᵇ 9 ἐμπίπ-
τουσιν ἄνθρωποι πένητες ἐς τὸ ἀρχεῖον,
Lucian *adv. indoct.* 9 ἀπορρήγνυσι τρεῖς
χορδὰς σφοδρότερον τοῦ δέοντος ἐμπεσὼν
τῇ κιθάρᾳ. The meaning is more that of
the middle of εἰσβάλλω than the passive,
so in the military sense *throw oneself into*
a position, Thucyd. ii 25. 3 ἐσπίπτει ἐς
τὴν Μεθώνην, iv 68. 5 : cf. ii 4. 1 τὰς
προσβολὰς ᾗ προσπίπτοιεν ἀπεωθοῦντο.
487. κράγον κεκραγέναι is a popular
or invented phrase, like βάδον βαδίζειν
Av. 42, where scholiasts say ἐν παιδιᾷ
παρεσχημάτισται, and οἱ κωμικοὶ παίζειν
εἰώθασι τὰ τοιαῦτα.
488. ὡς ἔχω, 'without more ado':
as *Eccl.* 533, Pherecrates 108. 21 κολυμ-
βᾷν ὡς ἔχετ' ἐς τὸν Τάρταρον, Thucyd. i
134· 3, iii 30· 1, viii 42. 1, Antiphanes
199 ἴωμεν ὥσπερ ἔχομεν; in the first
person the tone is rather apologetic, as
here and Eurip. *Hec.* 614, where it is
contrasted with ὡς μὲν ἄξια (εἰ).
490—1. ἄλειψον: the active in such
cases seems usual, when a part of the
body is mentioned, ἐστεφάνωσε χαῖταν
Pind. *Olymp.* 14. 24, κόμας ἀναδήσαντες
Pyth. 10. 40, but of the whole body, or
when no object is expressed, the middle,
ἀλειψαμένη τὸ σῶμ' ὅλον *Eccl.* 63, see on

910. Juvenal's *ceromatico fert niceteria
collo*, 3. 68, is in point.
The τουτῳί is probably oil : though
Enger's idea that it is the wine left in the
pitcher by Demosthenes is supported by
the ἐπέγκαψον of 493. ἀλείφεσθαι and
σκοροδίζεσθαι both come to mean *get
primed for fighting*, or for political action,
Plut. *Themist.* 3 ἑαυτὸν ὑπὲρ τῆς ὅλης
Ἑλλάδος ἤλειφε; σκοροδίζω (a metaphor
from cock-fighting) being, like *prime*, too
colloquial for serious writing, *Ach.* 166
&c.: the two are comically combined in
Pax 502 αὐτὴν τοῖς σκορόδοις ἠλείψατε.
διαβολάς is of course a pun on διαλαβάς
of wrestling.
492. παιδοτριβικῶς, 'in professional
style,' like μαγειρικῶς *Ach.* 1015, *Pax*
1017, μαντικῶς *Pax* 1026, and comically
τριβωνικῶς *Vesp.* 1132.
493. κάπτω and its compounds are
used of lower animals (as Herod. ii 93,
of birds οὐ σπῶντες οὐδὲ λάπτοντες ἀλλὰ
κάπτοντες Plut. *quaest. conv.* vii 1. 699 D)
and of men, but only in homely style,
Eccl. 687, Plut. *an seni resp.* 8. 788 A, or
parodies of tragic language, Eurip. *Cycl.*
629 σιγῶμεν ἐγκάψαντες αἰθέρα γνάθοις,
Eubulus 10. 7 κάπτοντες αὔρας ἐλπίσας
σιτούμενοι, Teleclides 33 ὦ δέσποθ' Ἑρμῆ,
κάπτε τῶν θυλημάτων. It seems to have
been a serious word in Laconian from
Athenaeus' quotations, iv 140 D—141 A.

καὶ σπεῦδε ταχέως. ΑΛΛ. ταῦτα δρῶ. ΟΙ. Α.
μέμνησό νυν   495
δάκνειν, διαβάλλειν, τοὺς λόφους κατεσθίειν,
χὤπως τὰ κάλλαι' ἀποφαγὼν ἥξεις πάλιν.
ΧΟΡ. ἀλλ' ἴθι χαίρων, καὶ πράξειας
κατὰ νοῦν τὸν ἐμόν, καί σε φυλάττοι
Ζεὺς ἀγοραῖος· καὶ νικήσας   500
αὖθις ἐκεῖθεν πάλιν ὡς ἡμᾶς
ἔλθοις στεφάνοις κατάπαστος.
ὑμεῖς δ' ἡμῖν προσέχετε τὸν νοῦν
τοῖς ἀναπαίστοις,
ὦ παντοίας ἤδη μούσης   505
πειραθέντες καθ' ἑαυτούς.

496. καταβάλλειν ΑΘ, Reifferscheid *meletem. Aristoph.*
503. πρόσχετε Bentl. and most editors, πρόσσχετε Dindorf. The proceleusmatic
προσέχετε is given by all mss., and occurs in the parabasis of *Av.* 688 προσέχετε τὸν
νοῦν τοῖς ἀθανάτοις ἡμῖν, and of *Vesp.* 1015: cf. *Nub.* 575 in the trochaic epirrhema
ὦ σοφώτατοι θεαταί, δεῦρο τὸν νοῦν προσέχετε. It was plainly allowable and seems to
me just the rhythm suited to a lively appeal. Another proceleusm. in anapaests is
Nub. 916 διὰ σὲ δὲ φοιτᾶν.
505—6. om. Herm. Mein. Vels.: a scholiast had only eight lines in the whole
κομμάτιον. καθ' ἑορτάς Deventer in *Mnemos.* i 416.

496—7. διαβάλλειν does not occur
among the quail- and cock-fighting
phrases given by Pollux and scattered
through literature; but it need not be
altered. λόφοι are the *comb*, κάλλαια the
wattles; so *crista* and *palea* are given
separately in Varro's points of a good bird
(*Res Rust.* iii 9. 5).
498. The parabasis is complete according to the scheme given by Pollux iv
111: the parts are κομμάτιον 498—506,
παράβασις 507—546, μακρόν or πνῖγος
547—550, ᾠδή 551—564, ἐπίρρημα 565—
580, ἀντῳδή 581—594, ἀντεπίρρημα 595—
610. One scholiast seems to begin the
parabasis proper at 503, the κομμάτιον
then would be 503—506.
498—9 come from Sophocles, according to the scholium, the play being
the Oecleus (Dindorf), or Iocles (Nauck):
but similar phrases recur *Nub.* 510, *Vesp.*
1009, *Pax* 729 at the beginning of the
parabasis and were very natural in the circumstances. For Ζεὺς ἀγοραῖος cf. on 410.

501—2. The victor in such an ἀγών
might expect the compliment of wreaths
and ribbons paid to popular statesmen
and athletes, Thucyd. iv 121. 1, Xen.
Hell. v 1. 3, Plut. *Pericles* 28 (Kock).
πάττω and its compounds mean (1)
sprinkle, (2) *bespangle*: cf. 99, 968, *Nub.*
1330: καταπάττω of plenteousness, Pherecrates 168 μηδὲν κοτυλίζειν ἀλλὰ κατα-
πάττειν χύδην.
504. ἀνάπαιστοι in Aristoph. are
always the long anapaestics of the
parabasis, *Ach.* 627, *Pax* 735, *Av.* 684.
505—6. For μούσης cf. Plut. *Cicero* 2
ἁπτόμενος ποικιλώτερον τῆς περὶ ταῦτα
μούσης. An appeal for attention in the
name of Attic taste and art is natural here,
cf. *Nub.* 521, *Vesp.* 1012—5: but it is oddly
expressed, and καθ' ἑαυτούς, though plainly
emphatic, is not clear. As καθ' ἑαυτόν
was a phrase used in criticism of Aristophanes for using other men's names as a
dramatist (*inf.* 513, *Vesp.* 1021), καθ'
ἑαυτούς may be a comic retort to such

εἰ μέν τις ἀνὴρ τῶν ἀρχαίων κωμῳδοδιδάσκαλος
ἡμᾶς
ἠνάγκαζεν λέξοντας ἔπη πρὸς τὸ θέατρον παρα-
βῆναι,
οὐκ ἂν φαύλως ἔτυχεν τούτου· νῦν δ' ἄξιός
ἐσθ' ὁ ποιητής,
ὅτι τοὺς αὐτοὺς ἡμῖν μισεῖ, τολμᾷ τε λέγειν
τὰ δίκαια,   510

---

criticism 'you have had experience of all kinds of art and artists *in your own names*, and had to bear all the brunt as critics.'

507—9. The true παράβασις begins, the chorus turn round, facing the house full: παραβαίνειν πρὸς τὸ θέατρον, παρελθεῖν ἐς τὸν δῆμον or ἐς τὴν ἐκκλησίαν is a constant distinction. The form of this conditional sentence, imperfect in protasis followed by aorist with ἄν in apodosis, is not common: the cases are of two classes, (1) where the apodosis refers to present time, generally εἶπον ἄν or the like, *I should have said*, as Plato *Euthyphro* 12 D, *Gorg.* 447 D, Soph. *Ant.* 755 and the other passages quoted by Goodwin *Syntax* § 414; add *Apol.* 38 AB, Isocr. *antid.* 139, Eurip. *IA* 1211, Menander 679 a general saw εἰ πάντες ἐβοηθοῦμεν ἀλλήλοις ἀεί, οὐδεὶς ἂν ὢν ἄνθρωπος ἐδεήθη τύχης: (2) where the protasis refers to past time, the imperfect being (*a*) ἦν, as Pind. *Nem.* 7. 24 εἰ γὰρ ἦν ἀλάθειαν ἰδέμεν, οὐ κεν Αἴας ἔπαξε διὰ φρενῶν λειρὸν ξίφος, Herod. iii 21 εἰ γὰρ ἦν δίκαιος, οὔτ' ἂν ἐπεθύμησε χώρης ἄλλης, οὔτ' ἂν ἐς δουλοσύνην ἀνθρώπους ἦγεν, Eurip. *Hipp.* 1042, *Alc.* 357, Lysias 3. 38, Aeschin. *Ctes.* 208 &c., or (*b*) where the imperfect is of continued or repeated action, and the aorist would not have been clear enough, as ἤθελον Plato *Lach.* 121 B, ἐβουλόμην Lysias 7. 21, 21. 5, ἐπειθόμην id. 13. 53, ἐπίστευον Demosth. *Leochar.* 4. 43, *Aphob.* 47, ἐνόμιζον *Eubul.* 6, εἶχον Lysias 1. 31, ἐχρῶντο Thucyd. iv 78. 3, Xen. *Anab.* v 8. 13 εἰ τοῦτο πάντες ἐποιοῦμεν, ἅπαντες ἂν ἀπωλόμεθα, or in inceptive meaning as Isaeus 11. 29, or conative as here. ἀναγκάζω tends towards the imperfect, cf. Plato com. 92 which however falls under (1), though it is very like our passage, εἰ μὴ λίαν ἠναγκαζόμην στρέψαι δεῦρ', οὐκ ἂν παρέβην εἰς λέξιν τοιάνδ' ἐπῶν.

Two cases in Homer, *Il.* xxiii 490, *Od.* xxiv 50, may be explained as falling under this last head: and so perhaps the case in *or. obl.*, Thucyd. iv 27. 5 καὶ αὐτός γ' ἄν, εἰ ἦρχε, ποιῆσαι τοῦτο. ἡμᾶς is emphasised by its position, a chorus *of knights*. ἀρχαίων here of the generation before the author, cf. Terence's *vetus poeta*: the opposite of ἀρχαῖος is generally καινός, the word Ar. uses so often of his originalities in art: so ἀρχ. means rather *old-fashioned* than *ancient*. For ἔπη cf. on 39.

Is any contrast intended between κωμῳδοδιδάσκαλος and ποιητής? Aristot. *Poet.* 5. 1449[b] 2 οἱ λεγόμενοι αὐτῆς ποιηταί would imply some slowness to grant the name ποιητής to comedians: yet *ib.* 4. 1449[a] 4 he contrasts κωμῳδοποιοί and τραγῳδοδιδάσκαλοι: *Pax* 734 and 737, *Thesm.* 30 and 88, *Ran.* 1021 and 1026 show an indifferent use of both words: so *inf.* 516 κωμῳδοδιδασκαλία is used as an honourable word in a serious and vigorous defence of the art. ἀνήρ is complimentary, see on 257. φαύλως as 404.

510—11. κωμῳδεῖν τὰ δίκαια *Ach.* 655. γενναίως 'like a knight.' χωρεῖν, like *vado*, stronger than *ἰέναι*, Thucyd. iii 64. 4, 66. 1—2.

Typhos, Typhon, or Typhœeus, an earth-born monster described by Hes. *Theog.* 820— as having a hundred snaky heads growing from his shoulders, all with hideous beast-voices of bull, lion, &c., and as cause or parent of irregular tempestuous winds. Zeus quelled his revolt against heaven (Aesch. *Prom.* 355) and confined him under Aetna (Hes. Pindar &c.) or among the Arimi (*Iliad* ii 782). This monstrous figure for Cleon is implied again *Vesp.* 1033 by the ἑκατὸν κεφαλαὶ κολάκων οἰμωξομένων. Poetry found the snaky heads most suitable, painting

καὶ γενναίως πρὸς τὸν Τυφῶ χωρεῖ καὶ τὴν
ἐριώλην.

ἃ δὲ θαυμάζειν ὑμῶν φησιν πολλοὺς αὑτῷ
προσιόντας,

καὶ βασανίζειν, πῶς οὐχὶ πάλαι χορὸν αἰτοίη
καθ᾽ ἑαυτόν,

ἡμᾶς ὑμῖν ἐκέλευε φράσαι περὶ τούτου. φησὶ
γὰρ ἀνὴρ

οὐχ ὑπ᾽ ἀνοίας τοῦτο πεπονθὼς διατρίβειν,
ἀλλὰ νομίζων   515

κωμῳδοδιδασκαλίαν εἶναι χαλεπώτατον ἔργον
ἁπάντων·

πολλῶν γὰρ δὴ πειρασάντων αὐτὴν ὀλίγοις
χαρίσασθαι·

513. ὡς MSS., πῶς Bentl. and vulg., Cobet *VL* 109, 'most felicitously' Shilleto on Dem. *FL* 28.
514. ἐκέλευσε MSS. except R.

preferred a figure "huge ending in snaky twine" below, as in the vase painting given in Baum. *Denkmäler*, fig. 2393, and the giant-figures generally and Aesch. *Sept.* 493, where the πλεκτάναι are probably the snaky legs. The 'Typhon-pediment' on the Acropolis shows a figure with three blue-bearded heads (figured in *Amer. Journ. Archaeol.* viii). Mythology gave sometimes Zeus, sometimes Heracles, as the victorious opponent of Typhon, see Wilam. on Eurip. *HF* 1272.

ἐριώλη here and *Vesp.* 1148 (for a pun on ἔριον, as on καυνάκη with καυνίας), and again in Apoll. Rhod. The schol. thinks ἐριώλη should have come first as the weaker word.

512—13. θαυμάζειν 'ask with surprise,' as Dem. *FL* 28 where Shilleto quotes 3 *Phil.* 75, Eurip. *Elect.* 516, *Ion* 44, Plato *Gorg.* 481 E.

προσιόντας implies Aristophanes' importance, as βασανίζειν does a certain resentment of interference. For πρόσειμι to a superior cf. *Vesp.* 553 where προσιών τις is surely right, Thucyd. i 130, Lysias 9. 4 προσελθὼν τῷ στρατηγῷ, Aeschin. *FL* 22 ὅταν προσίωμεν τῷ Φιλίππῳ, Aristot. *Pol.*

Ath. 11. 1, Lucian *Nigr.* 22 οἱ προσιόντες καὶ θεραπεύοντες (Latin *accedo*, as Hor. *Ep.* i 17. 12): ἐντυγχάνω is to an equal, id. *dial. deor.* 9. 1 Poseidon asks ἔστιν, ὦ Ἑρμῆ, νῦν ἐντυχεῖν τῷ Διί; Both words occur together in Strabo i 2. 2.

χορὸν αἰτεῖν, technical for *try to produce a play*: καθ᾽ ἑαυτόν, see on 506.

514. ἐκέλευε: the imperfect is regular in this word though the aorist seems more natural: Sauppe's *Lexil. Xenoph. s.v. Imperfecti* gives many cases from Xenophon. Blass in *Rhein. Mus.* xliv comments on instances in the Orators, concluding that the impf. is used especially when the answer to the request is doubtful, or when some difficulty in complying with it is implied.

γάρ of explanation, 'well then.'

515—6. In τοῦτο πάσχειν and such phrases, πάσχω often is intransitive '*be in such a state*,' not the passive of ποιῶ; no compulsion or external force is implied: cf. *Nub.* 234.

νομίζων *believing*, of conscientious ground of action: as νομίζω θεούς &c. *Fr.* 250 of older poets οὕτως αὐτοῖς ἀταλαιπώρως ἡ ποίησις διέκειτο.

ὑμᾶς τε πάλαι διαγιγνώσκων ἐπετείους τὴν
φύσιν ὄντας,
καὶ τοὺς προτέρους τῶν ποιητῶν ἅμα τῷ γήρᾳ
προδιδόντας·
τοῦτο μὲν εἰδὼς ἄπαθε Μάγνης ἅμα ταῖς πο-
λιαῖς κατιούσαις,   520
ὃς πλεῖστα χορῶν τῶν ἀντιπάλων νίκης ἔστησε
τροπαῖα·
πάσας δ᾽ ὑμῖν φωνὰς ἱεὶς καὶ ψάλλων καὶ
πτερυγίζων
καὶ λυδίζων καὶ ψηνίζων καὶ βαπτόμενος
βατραχείοις

518. Cobet *Mnemos.* n.s. ii 418 takes offence at διαγιγνώσκειν and conj. δὴ
γιγνώσκειν.

521. τρόπαια MSS.: τροπαῖα 'old Attic,' schol. on Thuc. i 30, and on *Thesm.* 697:
see similar cases in Chandler and in Wheeler *Griech. Nominalaccent* 113—.

---

517. πειράω with acc. has only this
meaning in Attic: this restriction was
noted by the grammarians Moeris s.v.,
Eustathius on *Il.* 338. 31 &c. In Thucyd.
ii 19. 1 πᾶσαν ἰδέαν is acc. of respect.
For the metaphor cf. Shelley *Peter Bell
the Third* iv 11—13.

518. ἐπέτειος of anything that varies
year by year, revenue, plants &c. (cf.
ἐφημέριος, ἐπιμήνιος). The schol. takes
the metaphor to be from birds of passage,
Kock from annual flowers. Cratinus 23
expressed the same complaint ἐτήσιοι γὰρ
πρόσιτ᾽ ἀεὶ πρὸς τὴν τέχνην: he applies a
still more slighting epithet to rival poets
in their relation to the audience 306
ἀφυπνίζεσθαι χρὴ πάντα θεατήν, ἀπὸ μὲν
βλεφάρων αὐθημερινῶν ποιητῶν λῆρον
ἀφέντα.

520. τοῦτο μέν is answered by εἶτα
526, as if it were πρῶτον μέν: Kock
quotes Soph. *Phil.* 1346—7, cf. *Antig.* 61.
Aristotle *Poet.* 3 marks the beginning
of Attic comedy by the names of Chioni-
des and Magnes. The inscription *CIA*
971 A mentions him as victor, along with
Aeschylus in tragedy. Anonym. *de Com.*
iii 24 (Dübner) says that he won eleven
times, and that the nine plays attributed
to him were not genuine. Athen. ix
367 F &c. quotes "Magnes or the author

of the plays attributed to him." Hesych.
and Phot. (s.v. λυδίζων) say that these plays
had been " edited," διεσκευασμένα. The
names of the plays mentioned here imply
that they were of the old beast-fable or
folk-lore kind.
Zieliński *Glied.* 241 thinks the names
of his plays mean, not the disguise of the
chorus, but the character of the music:
Magnes was a writer of 'Märchenkomödie'
and an Ionic musician.
πολιαῖς sc. θριξί: the same ellipse *inf.*
908, *fr.* 360, Pind. *Ol.* 4. 40, Aeschines *Timarch.* 49, αἱ πολιαὶ ἀδρανέες *Anth. Pal.*
ix 359. 8, ἤλυθον ἐς ἔλεγον xii 176. 4 and
τὰς φθονεράς *ib.* 21. 6: *cani* is common in
Latin poets.

521. τροπαῖον νίκης occurs, and τροπαῖον with gen. of the enemy is common:
but the combination seems unique.

522—3. The allusion is to the plays
Βαρβιτισταί, Ὄρνιθες, Λυδοί, Ψῆνες, Βάτρα-
χοι. His other plays seem to have been
of Attic country life (Ποάστριαι, Τιτα-
κίδαι). Ψήν is the animal instrumental in
'caprification.'
Schol. says βατραχεῖον, a green dye,
was smeared on actors' faces before the
invention of masks: cf. the stories of
wine-lees, white-lead, and vermilion
used in the same way, also fig leaves,

οὐκ ἐξήρκεσεν, ἀλλὰ τελευτῶν ἐπὶ γήρως, οὐ
γὰρ ἐφ᾽ ἥβης,
ἐξεβλήθη πρεσβύτης ὤν, ὅτι τοῦ σκώπτειν
ἀπελείφθη·   525
εἶτα Κρατίνου μεμνημένος, ὃς πολλῷ ῥεύσας
ποτ᾽ ἐπαίνῳ
διὰ τῶν ἀφελῶν πεδίων ἔρρει, καὶ τῆς στάσεως
παρασύρων

524—5. Herm. would omit ἀλλά...ἐξεβλήθη. **526.** βρίσας Bergk, ῥέψας
Fritzsche, πρέψας Kock, βρύσας (among other proposals) Blaydes, πνεύσας Piccolomini,
λάβρος Hultzsch in *Neue Jahrb.* cli 669.

A. Müller *Griech. Bühnenalt.* p. 270:
but the plural is strange. It became the
painter's word for *green*, Philostr. *vita
Apollon.* ii 22 1 ξυγκεράννυσι τὰ κυανᾶ
τοῖς βατραχείοις. Eupolis' *Baptae* does
not seem to be in point.
524. ἐξήρκεσε, cf. ἀντήρκει 540. The
dactyl in this foot is a rare rhythm (Blaydes
quotes five other cases from Ar.), and
probably intentional here. γάρ, pathetic
'ah never.'
Töpffer *Att. Geneal.* p. 202 sees here a
reference to the pathetic line in Cratinus'
Eunidae 65 ἥβης ἐκείνης νοῦ δὲ τοῦδε καὶ
φρενῶν: and indeed the following lines
are probably full of such parodies or
references.
525. We expect ἐξέπεσε as in the
famous Demosth. *Cor.* 265 ἐξέπιπτες, ἐγὼ δ᾽
ἐσύριττον, Arist. *Rhet.* iii 11. 13, *Poet.* 18,
Plato *Gorg.* 517 A &c. But passives direct
from βάλλω do occur, *fr.* 185ᵇ, Antiphon
Tetral. Γ γ. 1, and of actors hissed off,
Lucian *Nigr.* 8; of dead bodies, Soph.
Aj. 1064, Aristot. *Ath. Pol.* 1.
526. ῥεύσας is very doubtful Attic,
as well as awkward with ἔρρει following:
Eurip. *Dan.* 32 quoted carelessly by editors
from Lobeck *Phryn.* 759 (where see
collected cases) is of course from the
forged prologue, *fr.* 1117 Dind.: Lycurg.
Leocr. 96 περιρρεῦσαι is suspected: it
occurs in Hippocrates and in late Greek.
Blaydes' βρύσας is perhaps the best of
many conjectures, but the use of βρύω
for a well or spring (common in Modern
Greek) is not old seemingly, and the μέγας
ἔβρυεν said of Cratinus *Anth. Pal.* xiii 29.
5 is suggested by ὑπὸ στεφάνοις before.
The boldness and power of Cratinus

in attack and in language were univer-
sally acknowledged : but this is the finest
tribute to his genius. No fragments
remain of his Χειμαζόμενοι (second to the
Acharnians) or the Σάτυροι (second to
the *Knights*): but his renewed vigour
and success next year in the Πυτίνη (which
beat the *Clouds*) brilliantly showed that
his day was not yet past. The Lucianic
(Μακρόβιοι 25) story that he was now 95
is not well authenticated. The plot of
the Πυτίνη (Cratinus' desertion of his wife
Κωμῳδία for Μέθη) may have been suggested by 517: and the simile of our line
was taken up by Cratinus in the play ἄναξ
Ἄπολλον, τῶν ἐπῶν τῶν ῥευμάτων· κανα-
χοῦσι πηγαί, δωδεκάκρουνον τὸ στόμα,
Ἰλισὸς ἐν τῇ φάρυγι, 86.
527. ἀφελής seems unexampled in
this (presumably the original) sense of
open: it is used of *open, honest*, characters,
and of *plain* style, so the schol. here cannot
rid his mind of this use. Ar. may well be
imitating or quoting a phrase of Cratinus'
or of some non-Attic poet, which would
be the only defence for ῥεύσας.
Hor. *Od.* iv 2. 5 on Pindar is a well-
known case of the same metaphor.
παρασύρω was later a word of literary
criticism: Longinus *Subl.* 32. 4 τῷ ῥοθίῳ
τῆς φορᾶς ταυτὶ (τὰ σφοδρὰ πάθη) πέφυκεν
ἅπαντα τἆλλα παρασύρειν καὶ προωθεῖν, 33·
5 is Eratosthenes in his faultless *Erigone*
μείζων ποιητὴς Ἀρχιλόχου πολλὰ καὶ ἀνοι-
κονόμητα παρασύροντος, κἀκεῖνα τῇ ἐμβολῇ
τοῦ δαιμονίου πνεύματος? In both cases
the word implies a certain want of care
and self-control on the poet's part: and
Cratinus was criticised for rashness in
attack and for a want of unity in plot,

ἐφόρει τὰς δρῦς καὶ τὰς πλατάνους καὶ τοὺς
ἐχθροὺς προθελύμνους·
ᾆσαι δ᾽ οὐκ ἦν ἐν ξυμποσίῳ πλήν, Δωροῖ συκοπέδιλε,
καί, τέκτονες εὐπαλάμων ὕμνων· οὕτως ἤνθη-
σεν ἐκεῖνος.   530
νυνὶ δ᾽ ὑμεῖς αὐτὸν ὁρῶντες παραληροῦντ᾽ οὐκ
ἐλεεῖτε,
ἐκπιπτουσῶν τῶν ἠλέκτρων, καὶ τοῦ τόνου οὐκ
ἔτ᾽ ἐνόντος,

Platonius *de com.* 2. 1 εὔστοχος ὢν ἐν ταῖς
ἐπιβολαῖς τῶν δραμάτων καὶ διασκευαῖς,
εἶτα προιὼν καὶ διασπῶν τὰς ὑποθέσεις οὐκ
ἀκολούθως πληροῖ τὰ δράματα.

στάσις the schol. thought meant *em-
bankment.*

528. Here and *Pax* 1210 Ar. certainly
used προθέλυμνος=πρόρριζος: and so did
the later writers, whatever it may mean
in *Il.* xiii 130: cf. τετραθέλυμνος.

ἐχθρούς· τοὺς περὶ τὸν Καλλίαν αἰνίτ-
τεται, Schol. meaning the comic poet of
the name: it may be either political or
dramatic enemies.

529. The songs quoted were from
Cratinus' *Eunidae*, a play named after
that Dionysiac family (Töpffer *Att. Geneal.*
181—) and full of parodies (Ath. xv 698).
Its date is unknown: it was popular at
the time and a chief favourite with Alexander the Great according to the story
(in Photius) that it was found under his
pillow at his death.

The Δωροῖ συκοπέδιλε would be a
parody of such patriotic songs to deities
as are given among the scolia in Bergk
40. 2— (*Poet. Lyr. Graec.*[4] iii 643—):
χρυσοπέδιλος occurs as an epithet of Hera
and of Eos, and sandals with gilt straps
were used by Phidias for his Athena,
Pollux vii 92.

Hesychius gives Δεξώ and Ἐμβλώ as
other new Heroines of corruption invented
by Cratinus. Such fem. names in -ώ
(whether ampliatives like masc. in -ων or
hypocoristics) were common in mytho-
logical figures such as Κλωθώ, Αὐξώ,
Ἀκεσώ, Ἰασώ, especially bogies like Γοργώ,
Ἀκκώ, Ἀλφιτώ, Γελώ, Μορμώ, of which

class Cratinus was probably thinking. It
is curious that both Δεξώ and Δωρώ occur
on monuments, Δεξώ on a tombstone at
Copae in Boeotia (Röhl *Inscr. Gr. Ant.*
304) and Δωρώ as a Bacchant in a disreputable scene on a black-figured Chalcidian
vase *CIG* 7460, Roulez · *Vases peints de
Leyde* p. 18.

530. The Τέκτονες are probably the
Eunidae, whose special cult was of Dionysus Μελπόμενος (Töpffer *Att. Geneal.*
203): the phrase is in Pindar's style (*Pyth.*
3. 113, *Nem.* 3. 4: and παλάμη of poetic
skill, *Ol.* 9. 26).

ἀνθεῖν, as *Nub.* 897, 962, *species semper
florenti Homeri* Lucr. i 124. The aorist
emphasises the short life of his vogue,
as the ἐκεῖνος does the change in the man.

531. παραληρῶ, *drivel*, of bad acting
as *Ran.* 594 or of dotage. Cratinus 36
may be addressed to his Muse in her
days of ill-success ὅτε σὺ τοὺς καλοὺς
θριάμβους ἀναρύτουσ᾽ ἀπηχθάνου.

532. The rare fem. form ἡ ἤλεκτρος
(does it occur elsewhere?) is generally
taken to mean *amber* used for ornament
(after Lepsius). Blümner *Technologie* ii
384— supports this explanation, quoting
Lucian *adv. indoct.* 9 of an unsuccessful
citharist συλλέγων χαμόθεν τῆς κιθάρας τὰς
σφραγῖδας· ἐξεπεπτώκεισαν γὰρ κἀκείνης
ξυμμαστιγουμένης αὐτῷ.

Helbig has laid stress on the marked
rarity of amber in Greek art except in
Homeric and late times: but the sense
of *amber* is the most likely one; the
scholiast's explanation of ἠλέκτρων, τόνου
and ἁρμονιῶν from *bedding* is unnatural
and pointless.

τῶν θ᾽ ἁρμονιῶν διαχασκουσῶν· ἀλλὰ γέρων
ὢν περιέρρει,
ὥσπερ Κοννᾶς, στέφανον μὲν ἔχων αὖον, δίψῃ
δ᾽ ἀπολωλώς,
ὃν χρῆν διὰ τὰς προτέρας νίκας πίνειν ἐν τῷ
πρυτανείῳ,   535
καὶ μὴ ληρεῖν, ἀλλὰ θεᾶσθαι λιπαρὸν παρὰ
τῷ Διονύσου.

535. χρὴ MSS. except M.
536. Διονύσῳ MSS. Διονύσου Elm. on *Ach.* 1086, Kock, Vels., A. Müller
Bühnenalt. p. 295. Bos gives no similar case of ellipse except Demosth. *Mid.* 53 ὁ
τοῦ Διός in an oracle from Dodona : but the meaning would be obvious and could be
pointed by gesture.

Lexicons show how common τόνος was in later Greek for high-strung, well-braced, spirit and energy.

533. Editors quote Epicrates 2. 18 of Lais ἐπεὶ δὲ δόλιχον τοῖς ἔτεσιν ἤδη τρέχει | τὰς ἁρμονίας τε διαχαλᾷ τοῦ σώματος, and Lucian *bis accus.* 21 of lax Stoics χαλῶντες τοῦ τόνου.
The opposite is expressed by Lucian *rhet. praec.* 19 πεπληρωκέναι τὴν ἁρμονίαν. Ar. was fond of the pathetic assonance in γέρων ὢν and γέροντας ὄντας, *Ach.* 222 &c., Blaydes on *Plut.* p. 394.

534. Connus, the great musician, teacher of Socrates (Plato *Euthyd.* 272 C, *Menex.* 235 E), had fallen in his old age into poverty and neglect: the proverb Κόννου ψῆφος, *Vesp.* 675, is said to reflect the insignificance of his later years. Cratinus had taken him as an example of decay in the lines (*fr.* 317, probably from the *Eunidae*) ἔσθιε καὶ σῇ γαστρὶ δίδου χάριν, ὄφρα σε λιμὸς | ἐχθαίρῃ, Κοννᾶς δὲ πολυστέφανός σε φιλήσῃ, parodying Hes. *Op.* 299: Ar. here turns Cratinus' flout on himself. Connus' στέφανος, the mark of his bygone success, was proverbial, Eupolis 68 ἀναρίστητος ὢν κοὐδὲν βεβρωκώς, ἀλλὰ γὰρ στέφανον ἔχων, and the line on him Δελφὸς ἀνὴρ στέφανον μὲν ἔχων, δίψῃ δ᾽ ἀπολωλώς. The perversion of his name into Κοννᾶς is an insult: the rare termination -ᾶς was used (1) in names of birds like ἀτταγᾶς, πελεκᾶς, ἐλασᾶς, (2) in plebeian words of abuse like τρεσᾶς, χεσᾶς, and (3) in men's names: I believe such names were origi-

nally contemptuous, and in early times they hardly occur except in perversions like Κοννᾶς, or nicknames like Ἐμβαδᾶς for Anytus (Theopomp. com. 57), Ἀργᾶς for Demosthenes (Aeschines *FL* 99), the Delphian Τριχᾶς (Collitz no. 1683, Roberts no. 229), Στομᾶς, Κεφαλᾶς: Ἀλκᾶς seems to be the only case in *CIA* i (433): later they are more common, but still I think are apt to retain something of their original meaning: the Ἐπαφρᾶς, Δημᾶς, Σιλᾶς and others so common in the New Testament (Blass *Gram. neutest. Griech.* 71) would probably be understood to be in humble life.

535. Suidas says Cratinus gained nine victories in all: the inscription *CIA* ii 977 d gives him three, but the list refers only to the Great Dionysia. πίνειν of course a surprise for δειπνεῖν: cf. *Plut.* 972 where ἔπινες is for ἐδίκαξες.

536. 'not drivel (on the stage) but have a cosy seat by Dionysus' highpriest in the theatre.' θεάομαι, 'be in the theatre' as often: θέα, *a seat* in the theatre, Lucian *Hermot.* 39. Dionysus' priest had of course the seat of honour, the centre chair in the front row: it is marked with his name in the Dionysiac theatre of Athens (of Hadrian's time).

λιπαρός, *unctus, gay and sleek*)(αὐχμηρός Xen. *Mem.* ii 1. 31. It was specially applied to old men, see L and S: λιπαρὸν γῆρας in the patriotic prayer which Cratinus (*fr.* 1) puts into the mouth of Metrobius, Connus' father; of Xenophon in Plutarch *de exil.* 603 B.

οἵας δὲ Κράτης ὀργὰς ὑμῶν ἠνέσχετο καὶ στυ-
φελιγμούς·
ὃς ἀπὸ σμικρᾶς δαπάνης ὑμᾶς ἀριστίζων ἀπέ-
πεμπεν,
ἀπὸ κραμβοτάτου στόματος μάττων ἀστειοτά-
τας ἐπινοίας·
χοῦτος μέντοι μόνος ἀντήρκει, τοτὲ μὲν πίπτων,
τοτὲ δ' οὐχί.   540
ταῦτ' ὀρρωδῶν διέτριβεν ἀεί, καὶ πρὸς τούτοισιν
ἔφασκεν
ἐρέτην χρῆναι πρῶτα γενέσθαι, πρὶν πηδαλίοις
ἐπιχειρεῖν,

537. στυφελισμούς MSS. except R.   **539.** σταιτὸς Zacher.

---

537. The three poets are well chosen to mark different styles and stages of their art, Magnes the comedy of the old folk- or beast-tale, Cratinus the old comedy of personal attack, Crates a foreshadowing of the new comedy. Aristot. *poet.* 5. 1449ᵇ 7 says Κράτης πρῶτος ἦρξεν ἀφέμενος τῆς ἰαμβικῆς ἰδέας καθόλου ποιεῖν λόγους καὶ μύθους, evidently approving the innovation as Vahlen says, the *Equites* is a perfect instance τῆς ἰαμβικῆς ἰδέας. The few extant fragments of Crates are free from personality.

538—9. The metaphor of a banquet set forth by the poet was familiar: as Aeschylus' τεμάχη τῶν Ὁμήρου μεγάλων δείπνων (Athen. viii 347 E), Ar. *fr.* 313 ἢ μέγα τι βρῶμ' ἔτι τρυγῳδοποιομουσική, Metagenes 14 ὡς ἂν καιναῖσι παροψίσι καὶ πολλαῖς εὐωχήσω τὸ θέατρον, Astydamas ap. Athen. x 411 A. Here every phrase is chosen to suit Crates' characteristics: he gave the audience a light *lunch* of the most Attic wit, prepared with apparent ease. Plutarch's fanciful derivation in *quaest. conv.* viii 6. 4, 726 D τὸ ἄριστον αὐτόθεν ἀπραγμόνως προσφερόμενοι καὶ ῥαδίως ἀπὸ τῶν τυχόντων, τὸ δὲ δεῖπνον ἤδη παρεσκευασμένον, ἐκεῖνο μὲν ῥᾷστον τοῦτο δ' ὥσπερ διαπεπονημένον ἐκάλεσαν is in point: Ar. *fr.* 313 has ἀπόνως of Crates' art, μάττω is always of the less luxurious barley bread, and ἀστεῖος would specially suit this Athenian

N. A.

Terence. κράμβος is best taken as our *dry*)(the vinous flavour of Cratinus: the word occurs only here and in dictionaries. Wilam. *Antigonos* 96 takes it with κράμβη as an insipid sweetish taste.

540. There is no record of a prize gained by Crates either in the official lists, *CIA* ii 977, which do not mention him (nor Aristophanes), or in Eudocia &c. Bergk *Griech. Liter.* iv 59 thinks Crates' name should be supplied at the head of eight prizes won B.C. 440—434, in the list *CIG* i 229.

πίπτω = *cado* of a play, as Hor. *Epist.* ii 1. 176.

542—4. Comedy is a serious business and needs training: the metaphor is not undignified, and suits statesmanship: Plut. *praec. ger. reip.* 15—16. 812 A οἱ κυβερνῆται τὰ μὲν ταῖς χερσὶ δι' αὑτῶν πράττουσι, τὰ δ'...χρῶνται καὶ ναύταις καὶ πρωρεῦσι καὶ κελευσταῖς, καὶ τούτων ἐνίους ἀνακαλούμενοι πολλάκις εἰς πρύμναν ἐγχειρίζουσι τὸ πηδάλιον, cf. *Agis* 1, *an virt. doc.* 3. 440 A.

Aristophanes' way of putting it was well known: Appian *bell. civ.* i 94 says Sulla quoted this line over the body of young Marius, and Suidas gives Gregor. Nazianz. *Orat.* 43. 791 C as paraphrasing it, so Claudian *cons. Mall.* 42— (Kuster, and Gataker on M. Aurel. 11. 29).

πρὶν πηδαλίοις ἐπιχειρεῖν is not referred to by ἐντεῦθεν in 543: it might stand in

6

κᾆτ' ἐντεῦθεν πρωρατεῦσαι, καὶ τοὺς ἀνέμους
διαθρῆσαι,
κᾆτα κυβερνᾶν αὐτὸν ἑαυτῷ. τούτων οὖν εἵνεκα πάντων,
ὅτι σωφρονικῶς κοὐκ ἀνοήτως ἐσπηδήσας ἐφλυ-
άρει, 545
αἴρεσθ' αὐτῷ πολὺ τὸ ῥόθιον, παραπέμψατ'
ἐφ' ἕνδεκα κώπαις,

544. ἕνεκα R, εἵνεκα three MSS., οὕνεκα V and most MSS. Wackernagel (*Kuhn's Ztschr.* xxviii 126) would expel εἵνεκα from Attic as being pure Ionic, but it is found in poetical inscriptions of the fifth century B.C. (Meisterhans p. 176).

that line as well as in 542. The plural implies the difficulty of managing the two rudders in a Greek ship.

The steps of promotion in naval service were κελευστής, πρωράτης or πρωρεύς, κυβερνήτης. πρωρεύς is called διάκονος τοῦ κυβερνήτου, Xen. *Oecon.* 8. 14, cf. Aristot. *Pol.* i 4. 2, 1253ᵇ 29, Plut. *Agis* 1; while the κυβερνήτης takes orders from the τριήραρχος only, Demosth. *Polycles* 50: κυβερνήτης and πρωρεύς are first and second officer in Plut. *Theseus* 17, Moschion ap. Athen. v 209 A, cf. Lucian *Jup. trag.* 49: Xen. *Hell.* i 5. 11 the κυβερνήτης on the flagship is next to the Admiral: πρυμνήτης ἄναξ Aesch. *Eum.* 16 &c., is poetic for κυβερνήτης: Plaut. *Rud.* 1014 *si tu proreta isti navi is, ego gubernator ero.* Pollux i 95 gives οἱ ἐμπλέοντες κυβερνήτης, πρωράτης, ναύτης, ἐρέτης, presumably in order of rank: [Xen.] *rep. Ath.* 1. 2 has οἱ κυβερνῆται καὶ οἱ κελευσταὶ καὶ οἱ πεντηκόνταρχοι καὶ οἱ πρωρᾶται not so arranged.

545. ἐσπηδήσας on the stage, almost like ἐμπεσών, cf. on 486.

546. 'Raise the surge of his applause on high, speed it on with eleven oars a side, our good knights' festal shout.' ῥόθιον is regularly used of waves dashed up by oars, ταχεῖα κώπα ῥοθίοισι μάτηρ Eurip. *Hel.* 1454, κώπη ῥοθιάς Aesch. *Pers.* 396: but Plut. *praec. reip. ger.* 27. 819 F has it of the shout of a multitude, like ῥόθος and ῥοθῶ.

The phrase ἐφ' ἕνδεκα κώπαις has not been understood. Kock has abandoned his idea (suggested also by Walsh) that it might refer to the divisions (κερκίδες, *cunei*) of seats in the theatre: there is

no case of κώπη in this sense, and the Athenian theatre had thirteen κερκίδες. Diels (*Rhein. Mus.* xxx 138) takes κώπαι as *fingers*, and wishes to read παραπέμψαντες δέκα κώπαις uncritically: Merry's refinement ἕνδεκα κώπαις, 'with all your fingers and more,' is merely ingenious. I think it must refer to the number of the chorus: the twenty-four members of it would at this moment be dividing into two halves, and it is likely that the two leaders, considered as κελευσταί, are excepted, the eleven others on each side being compared to rowers. [The scholium on 589 says that ἡμιχόρια were not 12 and 12, but 13 and 11 (13 male to 11 female, 13 women to 11 boys, or 13 senior to 11 junior): but the statement has not been accepted, A. Müller *Bühn.* 220.] It was not out of the way of Athenian metaphor to call a man *an oar* in such circumstances. Such nautical phrases were almost limitless in their application: Kock quotes φίλον εἰρεσίῃ γλώσσης ἀποπέμψομεν εἰς μέγαν αἶνον from Dionysius Chalcus ap. Athen. xv 669 A: and the fragments of that curious poetaster, who was alive when the *Knights* appeared, contain similar phrases. (The explanations quoted from Suidas and Eustathius look like mere inventions.)

παραπέμπω may mean (1) *convey* a person, (2) *pass on* a phrase or sound, as Soph. *Phil.* 1459 π. στόνον, and here. The ἐπί is unusual: in the military meaning the case must be gen. or accus. The chorus is now included in the appeal: this is unusual, but there is no other instance of such a passing from the *parabasis* proper to the πνῖγος without a break.

θόρυβον χρηστὸν ληναΐτην,
ἵν' ὁ ποιητὴς ἀπίῃ χαίρων,
κατὰ νοῦν πράξας,
φαιδρὸς λάμποντι μετώπῳ.   550
ἵππι' ἄναξ Πόσειδον, ᾧ

---

547. χρηστόν defines the neutral
θόρυβον (cf. εὐμενῶς ἐπιθορυβεῖν Xen.
Hell. ii 3. 50), also a knight's word, see
Appendix ii.

ληναΐτην: the Lenaea retained its pre-
eminence as the chief occasion for comedy,
though the Great Dionysia attracted the
best tragedies.

Suidas gives ληναΐτης χορός: but otherwise the word seems unexampled, and
the form is odd: cf. πυκνίτης 42.

549. κατὰ νοῦν, *de animi sententia:*
Pax 762, 940.

550. The gaiety on the poet's brow
would be enhanced by his baldness,
which came on him young, and which
he likes to speak of (*Nub.* 540, *Pax* 767).
Eupolis 78 κἀκείνους τοὺς Ἱππέας συνε-
ποίησα τῷ φαλακρῷ τούτῳ κἀδωρησάμην.

551. The life and grace of this ode
make it almost worthy to be the literary
counterpart of the young knights' procession in the Parthenon frieze.

The strophe and antistrophe are invocations of Poseidon and Athena, 'our country
and its chief deities': the pride of Athens
was that its religion and patriotism were
unequalled in their combination (Lycurg.
Leocr. 15). Poseidon is invoked specially
as ἵππιος, and is put before Athena by
the knights. In the famous chorus of
Soph. *OC* 694—719 this order is reversed
and Athena comes first. Whatever the
original meaning of the struggle between
those two deities for the soil of Attica,
there is no doubt that the worship of
Athena was carefully fostered by democratic leaders, and there are indications
that conservatives resented and opposed
her supremacy, showing a preference for
Poseidon as the champion of aristocracy.
His antiquity was recognised *Plut.* 1050
ὦ Ποντοπόσειδον καὶ θεοὶ πρεσβυτικοί, Isocr.
Panath. 193 Eumolpus, son of Poseidon,
ἠμφισβήτησεν Ἐρεχθεῖ τῆς πόλεως, φάσκων
Ποσειδῶ πρότερον Ἀθηνᾶς καταλαβεῖν αὐ-
τήν. In the *Birds*, his political feeling
is strongly marked, 1570 ὦ δημοκρατία,
ποῖ προβιβᾷς ἡμᾶς ποτε; in the new order
of things Athena is expressly deposed

from her place (828—), and in the prayer
to the chief deities of state the line ὦ
Σουνιέρακε, χαῖρ' ἄναξ Πελαργικέ 869 is
put in with great emphasis to show
Peisetaerus' feeling that the bird-god
answering to Poseidon is of main importance, whereas no deity answering to
Athena is mentioned at all. In this play
inf. 839 the new ruler is to have Poseidon's attribute of the trident. Pausanias
vii 21. 7 says Poseidon had three universal
names over Greece, θαλάσσιος, ἵππιος and
ἀσφάλιος: the latter two would be felt
naturally as having a close connexion with
aristocratic politics (see Appendix ii on
ἀσφάλεια). It was no accident that under
the oligarchic rule in 411 B.C. the ecclesia
was held in the shrine of Poseidon Hippios
at Colonus, Thucyd. viii 67. 2. It seems
likely that the Erechtheum was built in
opposition to the Parthenon; Poseidon-
Erechtheus was placed on something like
equality with Athena within its walls:
Eurip. *Erechth. fr.* 362. 46—9 may be a
contemporary protest or explanation.
Many if not most of the great houses of
Athens traced descent from Poseidon.

A combination of Poseidon worship
with Athena's was effected in other Greek
states: in Sparta (where it would appear
from Plut. *Agis* 16 ὁ μὲν Ἄγις ἐπὶ τὴν
Χαλκίοικον κατέφυγεν, ὁ δὲ Κλεόμβροτος
εἰς τὸ τοῦ Ποσειδῶνος ἱερὸν ἐλθὼν ἱκέτευε
that the two royal families represented
the two religions), Troezen, Rhodes &c.
(see Wide *Lakon. Kulte* 37); for Corinth
see on 608: but I do not maintain that
in those states the deities were taken as
champions of political parties. Poseidon
often yielded with good grace to other
deities, Plut. *quaest. conv.* ix 6. 741 A.

The oath by Poseidon is the most common one in Aristophanes, and I have
said on 144 that there is, sometimes at
least, a political significance in it: *Ran.*
1430 Dionysus probably means that the
sentiment applauded is a good conservative one: see on 843.

A god is often appealed to by his
delight in something that the worshippers

χαλκοκρότων ἵππων κτύπος
καὶ χρεμετισμὸς ἀνδάνει,
καὶ κυανέμβολοι θοαὶ
μισθοφόροι τριήρεις,　　　　　　　　　　555
μειρακίων θ' ἅμιλλα λαμ-
πρυνομένων ἐν ἅρμασιν
καὶ βαρυδαιμονούντων,
δεῦρ' ἔλθ' ἐς χορόν, ὦ χρυσοτρίαιν', ὦ
δελφίνων μεδέων, Σουνιάρατε,　　　　　560

themselves represent or can offer : here it is natural that the horse comes before the ship.

552. The ring of the hoofs is to Poseidon's ear like the clash of cymbals to Demeter (Pind. *Isthm.* 6. 3): κτύπος would be used of cymbals (as Lucian *dial. deor.* 12. 1), and of horse-hoofs as in the splendid line *Il.* x 535 ἵππων μ' ὠκοπόδων ἀμφὶ κτύπος οὔατα βάλλει: this allusion is well borne out by Simon's test of a good horse ap. Xen. *de re eq.* i. 3 ὥσπερ κύμβαλον ψοφεῖ ἡ κοίλη ὁπλή. ἱππόκροτα γυμνάσια (Eurip. *Hipp.* 229, *Hel.* 207), χαλκόκροτος, χαλκόπους imply only the ring of the hoof, probably hardened artificially, but not shod : horse-shoes in our sense being unknown till after our era.

554—5. The ἔμβολον, an iron-tipped construction of beams, rising generally into three projections, was the trireme's weapon of attack in ramming (ἐμβολή). Why μισθοφόροι? Of course the crews of triremes were paid, and many of them were hired foreigners (Thucyd. i 121. 3, 143. 1 Athenian power was in danger if other states offered seamen higher pay): but that does not seem to give any point here. Mitchell and Kock hold that it means *winning prizes* at the regattas held at Sunium (Lysias 21. 5 νενίκηκα τριήρει ἁμιλλώμενος ἐπὶ Σουνίῳ ἀναλώσας πεντεκαίδεκα μνᾶς, Herod. vi 87), and also at Piraeus during the Panathenaea (Plato com. 183 ap. Plut. *Themist.* 32 of Themistocles' tomb ὁπόταν ἅμιλλ' ᾖ τῶν νεῶν θεάσεται): at the latter contest the prize was 300 drachmae *CIA* ii 965 a. For such races see P. Gardner in *Journ. Hell. Stud.* ii 91—: there may be allusion to them in Pind. *Isthm.* 4. 5—6 ἐριζόμεναι

ναῆς ἐν πόντῳ καὶ ὑφ' ἅρμασιν ἵπποι ὠκυδινάτοις ἐν ἁμίλλαισι θαυμασταὶ πέλονται.

556. At the Panathenaea, the chariot races for ζεύγη and ἅρματα πολεμιστήρια seem to have been open only to men, not to the classes of ἀγένειοι and boys ; yet μειρακίων is plainly emphatic here: throughout this passage there must be several points bearing on arrangement of games which escape us. For the part played by the knights in the Panathenaic and other games, see Martin *Cavaliers Athén.* Kock follows the scholiast in taking βαρυδαιμονούντων of men ruined by outlay on horses, which was great, hence the epithet ἀδήφαγος *CIA* ii 965 b: I prefer to take λαμπρ.)(βαρυδ. of winners and losers in the ἅμιλλα : Poseidon Taraxippus (see on 247) would have a hand in the loser's bad luck. There may be special allusion to Alcibiades, whose use of λαμπρύνω in Thucyd. vi 16. 3 (cf. § 5) is marked. λαμπρός was applied to horses, πομπικῷ καὶ μετεώρῳ καὶ λαμπρῷ ἵππῳ χρήσασθαι Xen. *de re eq.* 11. 1. βαρυδαίμων was not excluded from serious literature as κακοδαίμων was (see on 7), Eurip. *Alc.* 868, *Tro.* 112, in hexameters Diotimeus ap. Suidas s.v. Εὐρύβατος, Timon's epitaph ap. Plut. *Anton.* 70: so it is given as a stronger word than κακοδαίμων *Eccl.* 1102.

559—. The god is invoked in the form familiar from works of art, where the trident (originally a fish-spear or harpoon) and dolphin (sometimes tunny, sometimes hippocamp) are Poseidon's regular attributes.

The headlands of Sunium and Geraestus, along with Calauria and Tenos, formed a famous group of Poseidonic

ὦ Γεραίστιε παῖ Κρόνου,
Φορμίωνί τε φίλτατ', ἐκ
τῶν ἄλλων τε θεῶν Ἀθη-
ναίοις πρὸς τὸ παρεστός.
εὐλογῆσαι βουλόμεσθα τοὺς πατέρας ἡμῶν,
ὅτι   565
ἄνδρες ἦσαν τῆσδε τῆς γῆς ἄξιοι καὶ τοῦ
πέπλου,

564. παρεστώς MSS. except R.

worship: for some influences of this connexion on myths and rites, see Wide *Lakon. Kulte* 43. At Sunium (probably a Phoenician name) political reasons had exalted Athena over Poseidon: the famous temple there is hers: I do not know if Bursian's idea that there are remains of a temple of Poseidon there (*Geog. Griech.* i 355) has been confirmed. *Av.* 869 Σουνιέρακε in travesty. The promontory of Geraestus was in the territory of Carystus, whose coins sometimes bear Poseidon with dolphin and trident (Head *Hist. Num.* 302). Eurip. *Cycl.* 293— couples Sunium and Geraestus as holy to Poseidon: cf. Strabo x 1. 7, Lucian *Jup. trag.* 25. Carystians had served with the Athenian force in the recent campaign on the Isthmus, Thucyd. iv 42. 1.

562. Phormio is the type of the Athenian naval hero. He served with distinction at Samos in 440 B.C. (Thuc. i 117), in Chalcidice in 432 (i 64—5), in Acarnania in 430 (ii 68—69) and especially in the Corinthian Gulf in 429 (ii 83—4, 88—92). He was a favourite of Comedy: Ar. takes him as model of a captain *Pax* 348 (where ἔλαχε gives the idea that he is the *Hero* of Bivouacs), *Lys.* 804 (with Myronides): and he was the hero of Eupolis' *Taxiarchi.* There has been much debate over the circumstances of his disgrace (Pausan. i 23. 10) and the date of his death, probably before 428 Thuc. iii 7. 1: see Böckh *Staatsh.*² i 515, Müller-Strübing *Aristoph.* 671—689, Gilbert *Inn. Gesch.* 105, Wilam. *Kyd.* 65—67.
There seems no evidence to connect Phormio with Poseidon-worship: his father's name—Asopius (Thuc.) or Aso-

pichus (Pausan.)—looks Boeotian or Sicyonian.

563—4. This emphatic justification of the pre-eminence given to Poseidon may refer (as Kock says) to recent Athenian successes with ships and cavalry (595). So τὸ παρεστός would refer more to the interests of the state than εἴπερ ποτὲ καὶ νῦν in the answering line 594, which thinks only of the chorus' victory.

565—580. Chivalrous patriotism was the spirit of our fathers, and we knights still keep this, though others have a selfish spirit.

565. εὐλογῶ and εὐλογία generally imply some formal or set panegyric, 'eulogy,' *Ach.* 372, *Eccl.* 454, Eurip. *HF* 356.

566. τοῦ πέπλου means no doubt the Panathenaic procession. At the Great Panathenaea (and perhaps at the lesser as well) a new peplus was carried as a ship's sail on a mast through the city and offered to Athena Polias on the Acropolis. The peplus, wrought by girls and women of noble family (ἀρρηφόροι and ἐργαστῖναι), bore an embroidered picture of the Gigantomachia on a saffron ground Eurip. *Hec.* 466—: probably the picture was confined to a border in front as in the Dresden torso (Roscher's *Lex. d. Myth.* i 694, Baumeister's *Denkm.* fig. 370). At first sight our passage seems to mean that Athenian warlike exploits were represented (so schol. Ribbeck, A. Mommsen *Heortologie* 186): but, as was pointed out by Heyne on Verg. *Ciris* 20, it seems understood that contemporary figures or events were not introduced till Demetrius Poliorcetes ventured against the will of heaven to do so (Plut. *Demetr.* 12): so

οἵτινες πεζαῖς μάχαισιν ἔν τε ναυφράκτῳ
στρατῷ
πανταχοῦ νικῶντες ἀεὶ τήνδ' ἐκόσμησαν πόλιν·
οὐ γὰρ οὐδεὶς πώποτ' αὐτῶν τοὺς ἐναντίους
ἰδὼν
ἠρίθμησεν, ἀλλ' ὁ θυμὸς εὐθὺς ἦν ἀμυνίας· 570
εἰ δέ που πέσοιεν ἐς τὸν ὦμον ἐν μάχῃ τινί,
τοῦτ' ἀπεψήσαντ' ἄν, εἶτ' ἠρνοῦντο μὴ πεπτω-
κέναι,
ἀλλὰ διεπάλαιον αὖθις. καὶ στρατηγὸς οὐδ'
ἂν εἷς

569. οὐδὲ εἷς γὰρ Cobet *Mnemos*. n.s. ii 419.
570. Ἀμεινίας Ridgeway in *Camb. Philol. Trans*. i p. 210, with reference to Herod. viii 84.
571. ὠμόν Dind. Bergk by mistake.
572. τοῦτ' R, Suidas and edd. ταῦτ' most MSS. κάρτ' Bentl.

that our phrase means only the ceremony of presenting the peplus: 'worthy of Attica and of the knights' place in its great religious ceremony.' Though I believe the knights are careful to put Poseidon first, they fully recognise Athena's greatness. The knights were prominent figures in the procession, as is plain from the Parthenon frieze: and Xenophon (*Hipparch*. 2. 1) puts appearance in processions first among the objects of knights' training.

567—8. The colour here is tragic or serious: the omission of the preposition in the first member of 567 is illustrated by Monk on Eurip. *Alc*. 114 from tragedy only, cf. *inf*. 610, Blaydes n. cr. on *Ach*. 533; so τήνδε πόλιν for τήνδε τὴν πόλιν, though common enough in tragedy (Porson on Eurip. *Orest*. 659, Blaydes n. cr. on *Ach*. 454) is not found in comedy except in quotation or parody (*Lys*. 706, *Av*. 921) or ode; ναύφρακτος is Aeschylean.

In older times at least, knights served in the fleet.

569—70. There may be special allusion to such cases as that in Thucyd. ii 88. 2, where Phormio is said to have always impressed on his men that Peloponnesian superiority in numbers at sea was not to be regarded as of any moment.

An Amynias is mentioned, not flatteringly, *Nub*. 686, *Vesp*. 74, 466, 1267, Cratinus 212, Eupolis 209: another, a moneylender, *Nub*. 31, 1259: but there is no clue to the exact reference here. κομηταμυνία *Vesp*. 467 is a democrats' scoff at Bdelycleon. The meaning and form of the word, combined with some personal allusion, suggested antique manliness. The Ἀμυνομένη was an Athenian trireme.

571. As the riders had neither saddle nor stirrup, falls were not unusual. The phrase here is taken more particularly from the wrestling-ring: cf. the remark of Thucydides, son of Melesias, about Pericles, in Plut. *Per*. 8. The vague τοῦτ' is the English *it* in 'wiped *it* off': Greek idiom often uses the plural in such cases, as *Ran*. 1466.

572. For aorist with ἄν of frequency in past time cf. *Lys*. 511 ἠκούσαμεν ἄν, *Plut*. 982—6, *Nub*. 977 and Kock there: with εἰ in protasis, Thucyd. vii 71. 3 εἴ τινες ἴδοιεν τοὺς σφετέρους ἐπικρατοῦντας, ἀνεθάρσησάν τε ἂν καὶ πρὸς ἀνάκλησιν θεῶν ἐτρέποντο, where the moods and tenses are parallel to our passage.

573. διαπαλαίω *wrestle out*, Plut. *Eumen*. 7 ἐν λαβαῖς ἦσαν καὶ διεπάλαιον: *have a wrestling-match* would be διαπαλαίεσθαι.

τῶν πρὸ τοῦ σίτησιν ἤτησ' ἐρόμενος Κλεαί-
νετον·

νῦν δ' ἐὰν μὴ προεδρίαν φέρωσι καὶ τὰ σιτία, 575

οὐ μαχεῖσθαί φασιν. ἡμεῖς δ' ἀξιοῦμεν τῇ
πόλει

προῖκα γενναίως ἀμύνειν καὶ θεοῖς ἐγχωρίοις.

καὶ πρὸς οὐκ αἰτοῦμεν οὐδέν, πλὴν τοσουτονὶ
μόνον·

ἤν ποτ' εἰρήνη γένηται καὶ πόνων παυσώμεθα,

μὴ φθονεῖθ' ἡμῖν κομῶσι μηδ' ἀπεστλεγγισ-
μένοις.   580

---

574. The σίτησις and προεδρία, the recognised rewards for distinguished services, were conferred by decree, so that political influence might be needed to secure them. They were not conferred on Pericles (see on 283). Cleaenetus was Cleon's father: 'our fathers did not apply to Cleaenetus to procure them rewards, as we now do to Cleon.'

σιτία is contemptuous for σίτησις, 'that victual,' so 709: Lucian has it with some contempt of a sick-diet, *de merc. cond.* 5.

577. προῖκα (connected with Homeric προΐκτης), 'as a gift,' 'for the asking,' 'for nothing': ἀρετὴ τὸ προῖκα τοῖς φίλοις ὑπηρετεῖν, Antiphanes 210.

προῖκα here probably means only 'without special reward.' In Xenophon's time (*Hipparch.* 1. 19) the state spent about 40 talents yearly on the cavalry: and besides the κατάστασις, we hear of allowances given them, e.g. Thucyd. v 47. 6. For a discussion of the subject see Martin *Cav. Athén.* 346—: he thinks there must be some special foundation for the claim to γενναιότης made here.

578. πρός adverbially = *besides*, is used from Homer downwards, always with καί, δέ, or τε.

580. 'Don't grudge us our little ostentations and luxuries.'

Long hair in grown men was a mark of aristocratic or Laconizing sympathies, and was looked on with suspicion: Aristot. *Pol.* ii 8. 1 of Hippodamus περιττότερος διὰ τὴν φιλοτιμίαν ὥστε δοκεῖν ἐνίοις ζῆν περιεργότερον τριχῶν τε πλήθει καὶ κόσμῳ

πολυτελεῖ, Lysias 16. 18 χρὴ...οὐκ εἴ τις κομᾷ διὰ τοῦτο μισεῖν, in the defence of the young knight Mantitheus: cf. *inf.* 1121, *Nub.* 1101, *Vesp.* 466, 1317, *Lys.* 561 ἄνδρα κομήτην φυλαρχοῦντ' εἶδον ἔφιππον, and the proverb οὐδεὶς κομήτης ὅστις οὐ βινητιᾷ. Long hair was traditional among Pythagoreans (Lucian *vit. auct.* 2), whose aristocratic leanings were well-known. Monuments do not seem to show it as a feature in Athenian knights.

The bronze στλεγγίς (*stringo, strigil*) was employed in the bath as a rough towel to remove the unguents used in exercise: hence λήκυθος καὶ στλεγγίς, Plato *Hipp. min.* 368 C, *Charm.* 161 E, Ar. *fr.* 14. ξύστρα was the common word later (non-Attic acc. to Phrynichus, p. 299 Lob., p. 358 Rutherford, who strangely says neither word occurs in Attic): hence it is the scholiast's gloss here; Lucian *Lexiph.* 2 has στλεγγίδα καὶ βύρσαν καὶ φωσώνια, and *rhet. praec.* 17 recommends ἀποστλεγγίσασθαι as an affectation for ἀποξύσασθαι. So Herodian, ap. Lobeck *Phryn.* p. 460, does not understand our word (τὸ ἄνευ ἀλείμματος λούσασθαι). Lysippus' famous statue was known as the ἀποξυόμενος (Pliny alone seems to give the name).

Nothing is known of the sumptuary law against the luxury and long hair of youth, mentioned here by the scholiast as proposed by Κινέας καὶ Φρῖνος: I think we should read Κινησίας ὁ καὶ Φιλύρινος, a well-known butt of comedy (called χοροκτόνος by Strattis 15), cf. *Av.* 1377.

88 ΑΡΙΣΤΟΦΑΝΟΥΣ

ὦ πολιοῦχε Παλλάς, ὦ
τῆς ἱερωτάτης, ἀπα-
σῶν πολέμῳ τε καὶ ποιη-
ταῖς δυνάμει θ' ὑπερφερού-
σης μεδέουσα χώρας,   585
δεῦρ' ἀφικοῦ λαβοῦσα τὴν
ἐν στρατιαῖς τε καὶ μάχαις
ἡμετέραν ξυνεργὸν
Νίκην, ἢ χορικῶν ἐστιν ἑταίρα,

586. ἀφίκου MSS.
589. χορικῶν MSS. edd. Χαρίτων Wilam. (*Herm.* xiv 186), Kock.

581—. There is less spirit in the antistrophe than in the call to Poseidon. The appeals to *Athena* in Ar. are Cleon's *inf.* 763, the chorus' in *Nub.* 601—2, where she comes third in the antistrophe; the popular one quoted sarcastically *Pax* 218, and the bitter one over Cleon's death, *Pax* 271: to *Pallas* here, in quotation *Nub.* 1265, *Eccl.* 476, and *Thesm.* 1136, where she is expressly called to by a δῆμος (1145). The fragments show no case of either before Alexis.

This confirms what was said above, that the worship of Athena, though of course national, was largely democratic, and was supported and organised with this view by Pisistratus, Themistocles and Pericles. The combination Ἀθηνᾶ Δημοκρατία is an archaistic phrase of Herodes Atticus' time (*CIA* iii 165), but embodies the historic fact.

μεδέουσα was used in old formulae of Athena-worship, Plut. *Them.* 10, *inf.* 763, and an inscription at Samos (H. W. Smyth *Ionic Dialect* § 74): an attempt has actually been made to make Ἀθηνᾶ τῶν Ἀθηνῶν μεδέουσα a separate object of worship from Ἀθηνᾶ Πολιάς.

Athena was πολιοῦχος in many cities besides Athens—Troezen, Sparta &c., Preller *Griech. Myth.*[4] i 219.

Athens' claim to special sanctity was strengthened by its very numerous festivals, [Xen.] *Rep. Ath.* 3. 8 ἄγουσιν ἑορτὰς διπλασίους ἢ οἱ ἄλλοι, Paus. i 24. 3.

Recent campaigns and the present Dionysia confirm Athens' pre-eminence in war and poetry: Athena and the knights have a share in both. Athena's intellectual aspect was encouraged by Pericles:

his building of the Odeum, and the prominence he gave to musical and poetic contests at the Panathenaea, were probably somewhat resented by the upholders of the ἱππικὸς ἀγών and the more athletic events: it became more marked later, when she was associated with the Muses and became patroness of libraries, Preller *Griech. Myth.*[4] i 225. Plato *Crat.* 407 A takes her name from Θεονόα: Aristot. *Pol.* v 6.14 τῇ Ἀθηνᾷ τὴν ἐπιστήμην περιτιθέμεν καὶ τὴν τέχνην. The parabasis of the *Acharnians* shows how Ar. thinks poets had helped the power of Athens.

586. Athena νικηφόρος was a very early conception, Hes. *scut. Herc.* 339 νίκην ἀθανάτης χερσὶν καὶ κῦδος ἔχουσα: it was embodied in her statues, especially in Phidias' Parthenos, which held in the hand a Nike carrying a gold crown. Athena was actually called Νίκη, Soph. *Phil.* 134, Eurip. *Ion* 1528, Menand. 218: and the famous temple of Νίκη ἄπτερος is now recognised as Athena's, who is invoked (under the temple) by the chorus in *Lysist.* 297 as Δέσποινα Νίκη. This temple is explained as a work of the conservative party, by Cimon after Eurymedon (Benndorf), or more probably, by Nicias in 425 or 424 (Furtwängler *Masterp.* Eng. tr. p. 443).

There is no case of στρατεία in the extant lines of Ar., who has στρατιά for both στρατός and στρατεία (*Ach.* 251, *Lys.* 592): the scholiast on *Thesm.* 828 says Eupolis made the same confusion: cf. Shilleto on Thucyd. i 9. 3.

For ξυνεργός used by mortals of deities cf. Eurip. *Med.* 395, *Hipp.* 523, *Ion* 48.

χορικῶν ἑταῖρα, if right, expresses the

τοῖς τ' ἐχθροῖσι μεθ' ἡμῶν στασιάζει.　590
νῦν οὖν δεῦρο φάνηθι· δεῖ
γὰρ τοῖς ἀνδράσι τοῖσδε πάσῃ τέχνῃ πορίσαι σε νί-
κην εἴπερ ποτὲ καὶ νῦν.
ἃ ξύνισμεν τοῖσιν ἵπποις, βουλόμεσθ' ἐπαι-
νέσαι.　595
ἄξιοι δ' εἴσ' εὐλογεῖσθαι· πολλὰ γὰρ δὴ πράγματα
ξυνδιήνεγκαν μεθ' ἡμῶν, εἰσβολάς τε καὶ μάχας.
ἀλλὰ τὰν τῇ γῇ μὲν αὐτῶν οὐκ ἄγαν θαυμά-
ζομεν,
ὡς ὅτ' εἰς τὰς ἱππαγωγοὺς εἰσεπήδων ἀνδρικῶς,

---

feeling of the Euripidean ending (*Orest.*, *Phoen.*, *IT*), ὦ μέγα σεμνὴ Νίκη τὸν ἐμὸν βίοτον κατέχοις καὶ μὴ λήγοις στεφανοῦσα: but the use of the adj. is not easily paralleled.

Wilamowitz's Χαρίτων is tempting. Ar. often speaks of the Χάριτες as comrades of Love, Peace &c. *Ach.* 989, *Pax* 456, *Av.* 1320, and *fr.* 314 from the *second Thesm.* μήτε Μούσας ἀνακαλεῖν μήτε Χάριτας βοᾶν χορὸν Ὀλυμπίας is exactly in point.

ἑταίρα in the good sense seems almost confined to deities or abstractions.

590. Victory sides with us against the foe, and also against rival choruses, [Eurip.] *Rhes.* 995 τάχα δ' ἂν νίκην δοίη δαίμων ὁ μεθ' ἡμῶν.

591—. 'Now is the time, if ever, for you to bring victory, and we are the men.'

πάσῃ τέχνῃ, *quovis pacto*: it would appear that both phrases were phrases of contract, business or law, coming to be used colloquially as *anyhow* (*Nub.* 885, 1323, *Ran.* 1235): a fuller phrase was πάσῃ τέχνῃ ἢ μηχανῇ as Thucyd. v 18. 4, Lysias 13. 95, Demosth. *Neaer.* 16 (in a law), *Timocr.* 150 (in a heliastic oath).

595—. The antepirrhema is a eulogy of the horses who had served in the recent campaign of Nicias on the Isthmus, Thucyd. iv 42—44. The cavalry had

distinguished themselves in the battle (Solygeia), and the praise of the horses implies the services of their riders. The Corinthians had no cavalry in the campaign, which gives more point to 608—.

ξύνοιδα with a neut. acc. pron. and dat. of person='know about one': Herod. ix 58 ἐπαινεόντων τούτους, τοῖσί τι καὶ συνῃδέατε, Lysias 3. 3 ὑπὲρ ὧν ἐγὼ αἰσχυνόμενος εἰ μέλλοιεν πολλοί μοι συνείσεσθαι, Plato *Protag.* 348 B ἵνα τούτῳ ταῦτα συνειδῶμεν, Lucian *Somn.* 15 ἃ σύνοισθα τῷ βίῳ ἑκάστῳ.

ἐπαινῶ, *praise and thank*, see on 460: both this word and εὐλογεῖσθαι imply a set form of praise.

597. ξυνδ.: Herod. i 18 οἱ Μιλήσιοι τοῖσι Χίοισι τὸν πόλεμον συνδιήνεικαν. εἰσβολάς into the Megarid (Thucyd. ii 31. 3), Isthmus &c.

598. as if οὐχ οὕτως ἄγαν.

599. νῆες ἱππαγωγοί were peculiarly Persian (Herod. vi 48. 95, vii 97), until the Athenians converted some old triremes into such transports in 430, Thucyd. ii 56. 2. They are specially mentioned in this Corinthian campaign, Thucyd. iv 42. 1. The word in literature is ναῦς ἱππαγωγός or ἱππαγωγός alone, as here and Demosth. i *Phil.* 21: but the official word was ἱππηγός, see the documents quoted by Martin *Cav. Athén.* 364.

ἀνδρικῶς: see on 451.

πριάμενοι κώθωνας, οἱ δὲ καὶ σκόροδα καὶ
κρόμμυα·   600
εἶτα τὰς κώπας λαβόντες ὥσπερ ἡμεῖς οἱ
βροτοὶ
ἐμβαλόντες ἀνεβρύαξαν, ἱππαπαί, τίς ἐμβαλεῖ;
ληπτέον μᾶλλον. τί δρῶμεν; οὐκ ἐλᾷς, ὦ
σαμφόρα;

600. δὲ σκόροδα MSS. (exc. M), Athen. xi 483 d. δὲ καὶ σκ. M vulg. δέ γε ci
Blaydes. δὲ σκόροδ' ἐλάας κρόμμυα Bergk Mein. Vels.: cf. Ach. 550.
602. ἀνεφρύαξαν Herw. ἀνεφρύαξανθ' Walsh Blaydes Zacher. ἱππαπαί MSS.
ἱππαπαῖ Dindorf and edd. vulg.: see n. cr. on 1.

---

600. The κώθων is treated by Athenaeus xi ch. 66. Critias quoted there and
Plut. *Lycurg.* 9 explain its advantages as
a soldier's cup: the woman-soldier in
Theopomp. com. 54 shrinks from it.
It was used also at sea, Archiloch.
fr. 4 (ap. Ath. *l.c.*). So it would be a
requisite for campaigning, not kept in
the house (Alexis 176 is comic). Perhaps
from military habits κωθωνίζω came to
mean 'drink hard,' and κώθων was used
later to mean 'tippling.'
The suppression of οἱ μέν is common
enough: a good case is Eurip. *HF* 636
ἔχουσιν, οἱ δ' οὔ, see Wilam. there.
A decree of the people called out a
certain number of troops, horse and foot,
as required: the troops then had to pro-
vide three days' rations before marching,
Ach. 197, *Pax* 1181—2: these would
generally be found and carried by servants
to the cavalry and hoplites (Thucyd. vii
75. 5). Barley-meal, wine, oil, and onions
or garlic were the regular military food
(Xen. *Anab.* vii 1. 37): serious history
naturally insists on the meal, Thucyd. viii
100. 2 (ἄλφιτά τε καὶ τἆλλα ἐπιτήδεια),
comedy on the garlic, *Ach.* 1099, *Pax*
1129, Eupolis 255.
601. βροτός came from Aeolic (where
op, po for ϳ was regular) by epic to Ionic
and to Attic tragedy. There seem to be
three cases of the word in Attic prose,
Plato *Rep.* viii 566 D (where βροτός is
mock-tragic), Arist. *Top.* v 4, 133ᵃ 31
in a logical form (cf. Plut. *de virt. mor.*
2. 440 E) *ib.* vi 11. 149ᵃ 7 βροτὸς ἀργός
as an oddity for ἄνθρωπος λευκός. In

comedy it is fairly common, but always
I think either in mock-tragedy or, as we
use 'mortal,' colloquially. The Attics
never said οἱ βροτοί except with adj. or
pron. as here.
602. ἐμβάλλω for *row* was a sailors'
word, *Ran.* 206, Xen. *Hell.* v 1. 13, where
he gives the actual phrase used.
βρυάζω, 'teem' (cf. βρύω), and φρυάσ-
σομαι, 'snort,' 'neigh,' both came to
mean 'wax wanton.' Neither word is
known to have had a compound with ἀνα-
apart from this passage. Suidas and
schol. give ἀνεβρύαξαν· ἀνεθορύβησαν,
ἀνέκραγον. If βρ- were for φρ- in βρέμω
βλαστάνω &c., as some have supposed,
-βρυάζω and φρυάσσω might be connected:
but. Brugmann *Grund.* i § 495 denies β
for φ absolutely.
ἱππαπαί: Houyhnhnm (Merry) for the
sailors' ῥυππαπαῖ, *Ran.* 1073.
603. λαμβάνω in this sense)(κενὴν
παρέλκω, 'don't miss your stroke.' In τί
δρῶμεν; δρ. is indic., and the meaning is
almost 'this won't do.' Cf. τί πράττομεν;
Hermippus 58. 2. High-bred horses were
branded on the hind-quarters (Anacreont.
26 B). The brands we hear of were the
Doric letters San and Koppa in the forms
σαμφόρας *Nub.* 122, 1298 (our phrase),
κοππατίας *Nub.* 23, 438 *fr.* 135 or κοππα-
φόρος Lucian *adv. indoct.* 5, figures of a
wolf &c. (Becker's *Charicles*). The letters
Koppa Ϙ and San Ϻ occur in the writing
of Argos, Corinth and Sicyon, all of which
countries bred horses, down to the end of
the fifth century.

ἐξεπήδων τ᾿ ἐς Κόρινθον· εἶτα δ᾿ οἱ νεώτατοι
ταῖς ὁπλαῖς ὤρυττον εὐνὰς καὶ μετῆσαν στρώ-
ματα· 605
ἤσθιον δὲ τοὺς παγούρους ἀντὶ ποίας Μηδικῆς,
εἴ τις ἐξέρποι θύραζε, κἀκ βυθοῦ θηρώμενοι·
ὥστ᾿ ἔφη Θέωρος εἰπεῖν καρκίνον Κορίνθιον·
δεινά γ᾿, ὦ Πόσειδον, εἰ μηδ᾿ ἐν βυθῷ δυνή-
σομαι,
μήτε γῇ μήτ᾿ ἐν θαλάττῃ διαφυγεῖν τοὺς
ἱππέας. 610

ΧΟΡ. ὦ φίλτατ᾿ ἀνδρῶν καὶ νεανικώτατε,

604. εἶτα δ᾿ R, εἶτά γ᾿ the other MSS. as 377. νεώτατοι RM edd., νεώτεροι the
other MSS. Blaydes Zacher. βρώματα R.
609. μήτ᾿ MSS. μηδ᾿ Brunck vulg.
610. μήτ᾿ ἐν γῇ MSS. : so in Ach. 533: there and here the phrase comes from the
scolion of Timocreon, ὤφελές γ᾿, ὦ τυφλὲ Πλοῦτε, μήτε γῇ μήτ᾿ ἐν θαλάσσῃ μήτ᾿ ἐν
ἠπείρῳ φανῆμεν.

---

604. Κόρινθος for the territory of the
city.
605. εὐνή is hardly used in prose
except for bivouac or camp beds, Thucyd.
iii 112. 3, iv 32. 1, vi 67. 1, Plato Rep.
iii 415 E, Polit. 272 E: Xen. Cyrop. viii
8. 14 seems an exception.
μετῆσαν, the only Attic form according
to Cobet VL 32—, Rutherf. Babrius p.
82. Xen. Cyrop. viii 8. 19 στρώματα πλείω
ἔχουσιν ἐπὶ τῶν ἵππων ἢ ἐπὶ τῶν εὐνῶν.
Cavalry used horse-cloths for bedding,
Antiphanes 109 τὸ μὲν ἐφίππιον στρῶμ᾿
ἐστιν ἡμῖν.
606. πάγουρος (Athen. vii 319 A,
πάγουρος ἀμμοδύτωρ Anth. Pal. vi 176.
1) is said to be still a Greek word for a
crab: Arist. Hist. An. iv 2. 525ᵇ5 it was
a species of the καρκίνος, and another
species found in Phoenicia was called
ἱππεύς from its swiftness.
ποία Μηδική. Hehn Cult. und Haus.⁶
397 shows the high repute of this clover
(medicago, lucerne) in Persia, Greece and
Italy: it was introduced into Greece after
the Persian wars (Plin. NH xviii 144),
into Italy between Cato's time and Varro's.
The accent of both words was disputed;
some wrote μηδίκη to distinguish it from
the ordinary adjective, see Chandler Greek
Acc. § 115; both ποία and ποιά were used,

Chandler § 108. πόα seems the only prose
form: but ποία is necessary both here and
Epicrates 11. 26.
607. θύραζε of course means 'on
land': Kock quotes Il. xvi 408 ἕλκει
ἱερὸν ἰχθὺν ἐκ πόντοιο θύραζε and several
other cases from Homer.
608. The scholiast calls this Theorus
a poet. There is no other evidence about
him: he is probably not the Theorus,
Cleon's parasite, of Ach. 134, Nub. 400,
Vesp. 42 &c.
καρκίνος, an Athenian nick-name for a
Corinthian, as Kock says a Dane is called
Seekrebs in North Germany.
The appeal to Poseidon would be
natural to a Corinthian from the Isthmian
worship: at Corinth there was, as at
Athens, a joint-worship of Poseidon and
Athena (under the aspect Ἱππία), Pind.
Olymp. 13. 78—9.
διαφυγεῖν, of course not flee from, but
escape from, by the constant distinction
between φεύγω and its compounds with
ἀπο- δια- ἐκ-.
611—5. By Zielinski's rule these
lines are in tragic iambic, as being spoken
by the Coryphaeus : 612, however, breaks
Porson's rule of the cretic.
νεανικός, gay, dashing, was used by
young Athens of what they approved as

ὅσην ἀπὼν παρέσχες ἡμῖν φροντίδα·
καὶ νῦν ἐπειδὴ σῶς ἐλήλυθας πάλιν,
ἄγγειλον ἡμῖν πῶς τὸ πρᾶγμ᾽ ἠγωνίσω.
ΑΛΛ. τί δ᾽ ἄλλο γ᾽ εἰ μὴ Νικόβουλος ἐγενόμην; 615
ΧΟΡ. νῦν ἄρ᾽ ἄξιόν γε πᾶσίν ἐστιν ἐπολολύξαι.
ὦ καλὰ λέγων, πολὺ δ᾽ ἀμείνον᾽ ἔτι τῶν λόγων
ἐργασάμεν᾽, εἴθ᾽ ἐπέλ-
θοις ἅπαντά μοι σαφῶς·

614. ἠγώνισαι ci Bergk and Cobet *Mnemos.* i 416.
616. ἄξιόν γε B and edd. vulg. ἄξιον other MSS. The metre ought to be troch. trim. brachycat. =683, but γε cannot be regarded as certain. ἐπολολύξαι vulg. ἐπολολῦξαι Kock after Cobet *Mnemos.* n.s. ii 419. ὀλολύξαι RM.
617. ἀμείνον᾽ Bergler and vulg. for ἄμεινον of MSS.
618. ἐργασάμεν᾽ Bentl. for εἰργασμέν᾽.

'good style,' cf. *Vesp.* 1204—5, humourously in 1307 and 1362, Plato *Lysis* 204 E ὡς γενναῖον καὶ νεανικὸν τοῦτον τὸν ἔρωτα ἀνεῦρες.

σῶς, *incolumis*, not condemned or even arrested. ἠγωνίσω, with reference to the comic ἀγών, *inf.* 688, *Ach.* 481.

615. τί δ᾽ ἄλλο γ᾽ εἰ μή in off-hand style, making a matter of course of it, 'merely made myself Sir Council-master': for τί δ᾽ ἄλλο γ᾽ εἰ μή cf. Aesch. *Sept.* 851, *Nub.* 1287, *Pax* 103, 923, *Av.* 25, *Ran.* 198, Lysippus 1. 1 (from Ribbeck); and see note on 186.

Nicobulus was a natural enough name, and is found in Demosth. *Pantaen.* 22, Plautus *Bacch.* and inscriptions. Bergk thought *CIG* 174 (*CIA* ii 1995) Νικόβουλος Μυννίχου Εἰτεαῖος· Σῆς ἀρετῆς ἕστηκεν ἐν Ἑλλάδι πλεῖστα τροπαῖα might be the epitaph of the man alluded to, but it is more likely to be here an invented name like Λυσιμάχη, *Pax* 991, and those in *Thesm.* 806—8. The Sausage-man has not yet disclosed his real name.

616. Probably this call of the Coryphaeus is answered in the next lines, given as an ὀλολυγμός. ἄξιος with gen. and dat. means 'deserving something at someone's hands': for instances see Porson on Eurip. *Hec.* 309; closely akin is the usage of ἄξιος personally with dat. and infin., see Monk on Eurip. *Alc.* 433. ἄξιον impers. with dat. and inf. means 'it is the proper thing for so and so to...': cases are *Ach.*

205, Plato *Theaet.* 143 E, 145 AB, Lysias 2. 60, Heraclitus *fr.* 114 Byw., Xen. *Memor.* ii 1. 34, Demosth. *FL* 354 &c., negatively *Av.* 548, Xen. *Anab.* ii 3. 25 &c. ἄξιόν ἐστιν or ἄξιον alone, with dative of person and later absolutely like *est tanti*, became common in this sense, 'it is proper' or 'worth doing,' *inf.* 624, *Ach.* 8 from Eurip. *Tel. fr.* 718, Xen. *Anab.* vi 5. 13 and often in Plutarch.

ὀλολυγμός, properly the cry of women in triumphant or hopeful address to a god: Herod. iv 189, Aesch. *Sept.* 267 (to chorus of women) ἔπειτα σὺ ὀλολυγμὸν...παιώνισον, Ἑλληνικὸν νόμισμα θυστάδος βοῆς, *Lys.* 240 τίς ὀλολυγά; of women in the Acropolis, Xen. *Anab.* iv 3. 19 ἐπαιάνιζον πάντες οἱ στρατιῶται καὶ ἀνηλάλαξον, συνωλόλυζον δὲ καὶ αἱ γυναῖκες ἅπασαι. Thucyd. ii 4 has it of the cry of women and slaves in a street-fight: cf. Aesch. *Agam.* 1235 ἐπωλολύξατο ὥσπερ ἐν μάχης τροπῇ. It is rarely used of men as here and 1327 (*Anth. Pal.* vi 234. 2 of a eunuch). The cases quoted to show that it may be of a sorrowful cry in good authors do not hold (e.g. Aesch. *Cho.* 386): that use is late as *Anth. Pal.* vii 182. 5.

617. The hero transcends the usual contrast of λόγοι and ἔργα: ἐργάζομαι implies more effort and care than δρῶ.

ἐπέρχομαι, 'run over,' 'run through': Plato *Legg.* xii 967 E, *Polit.* 279 C διὰ βραχέων ταχὺ πάντ᾽ ἐπελθόντες, Arist. *Pol.* vii (vi) 1. 1317ᵃ15 πῶς δεῖ κατασκευάζειν

ὡς ἐγώ μοι δοκῶ   620
κἂν μακρὰν ὁδὸν διελθεῖν
ὥστ' ἀκοῦσαι. πρὸς τάδ', ὦ βέλ-
τιστε, θαρρήσας λέγ', ὡς ἅ-
παντες ἡδόμεσθά σοι.
ΑΛΛ. καὶ μὴν ἀκοῦσαί γ' ἄξιον τῶν πραγμάτων.
εὐθὺς γὰρ αὐτοῦ κατόπιν ἐνθένδ' ἱέμην·   625
ὁ δ' ἄρ' ἔνδον ἐλασίβροντ' ἀναρρηγνὺς ἔπη

ἐπέλθωμεν συντόμως, and often in Aristotle. ἐπεξέρχομαι and διεξέρχομαι imply more thorough discussion.

622. Cobet *NL* 271— showed that πρὸς ταῦτα and πρὸς τάδε imply that the speaker's mind is made up: the position is definite and must be carefully considered in action by the person addressed. So πρὸς τάδε or πρὸς ταῦτα βουλεύειν and the like, Aesch. *Prom.* 1030, Soph. *Elect.* 383, Thucyd. i 71. 7, iv 87. 6, Xen. *Cyrop.* ii 1. 4. Hence πρὸς ταῦτα is well known in a defiant sense, Aesch. *Prom.* 992, 1043, Soph. *Ajax* 971, 1065, 1115, 1313, *Ant.* 658, *OT* 426, *OC* 455, 956, *Elect.* 820, Eurip. *Med.* 1358, *Phoen.* 521, *Heracl.* 978, Ar. *Ach.* 659, *Vesp.* 1386: πρὸς τάδε is used rather in friendly appeal as here, *Nub.* 1030, *Pax* 305, Aesch. *Sept.* 312, *Pers.* 170, *Eum.* 545, Eurip. *Elect.* 693, *Hipp.* 304, Herondas 7. 92; Soph. *OT* 343 is less defiant than 426. Both phrases seem to be used in Attic at least only with the imperative Rutherf. Babrius, p. 23: see *inf.* 760.

624—682. In this brilliant comic narrative, the style of a tragic ἀγγελικὴ ῥῆσις would of course be parodied. Observe how the rhythm of 624 at once suggests this, and how tragic lines are brought in at appropriate instants. But observe also that the symmetry of the report preserves the symmetry of an acted *agon*: the whole is arranged thus—(1) one pair of eight lines each, (2) three pairs of six lines each, (3) the finale of seven lines. I do not find καὶ μήν or καὶ μήν...γε introducing a ῥῆσις in any tragedy: though Ar. has it several times to open the ἐπίδειξις, see on 335·

ἀκούω rarely takes gen. of thing in Attic, except when the word in gen. is practically a synonym for the speaker, as *inf.* 961.

625. γάρ, see on 40. The proceedings parodied are those of the Council, when an εἰσαγγελία on a treason-case came before it.

626. ἔνδον, in the βουλευτήριον (485), which was in or near the agora (Thucyd. viii 92. 2). The βουλή held its regular meetings here: they were generally public, as this one is supposed to be: the βουλευταί were separated from the public by δρύφακτα, and ἔνδον may mean *inside the bar*, here and Andoc. *myst.* 43 θεωρὰς ὄντας καὶ καθημένους ἔνδον. Is ἐντός in the doubtful speech Lysias 9. 10 the word for one of the public in the συνέδριον? The question whether Cleon was one of the Council at this time has been a good deal debated: Müller-Strübing (*Aristoph.* 139) and Beloch (*Att. Pol.* 355—6) think he was not, Gilbert (*Inn. Gesch.* 91) holds that he was, having been elected for several years running. I think it most likely that he is a member and takes regular part in their business: so γνώμην ἔλεξεν 654 is *formally moved*, and he says ἄνδρες, not ὦ βουλή; the Sausage-man's proceedings and victory are more remarkable if he begins with the disadvantage of being only a member of the public.

The scholiast says ἐλασίβροντ' comes from an exordium of Pindar's (*fr.* 108 Böckh = 144 Bergk⁴) ἐλασίβροντε παῖ 'Ρέας. ἀναρρηγνὺς like thunder or volcano. Pericles was often likened to Zeus: Cleon rather to a giant as in 511, and the rock-hurling here seems a carrying out of that idea, cf. Aeschylus in *Ran.* 823— ἥσει ῥήματα γομφοπαγῆ, πινακηδὸν ἀποσπῶν γηγενεῖ φυσήματι: 'with eruptions of

τερατευόμενος ἤρειδε κατὰ τῶν ἱππέων,
κρημνοὺς ἐρείδων καὶ ξυνωμότας λέγων
πιθανώταθ᾽· ἡ βουλὴ δ᾽ ἅπασ᾽ ἀκροωμένη
ἐγένεθ᾽ ὑπ᾽ αὐτοῦ ψευδατραφάξυος πλέα,   630
κἄβλεψε νᾶπυ, καὶ τὰ μέτωπ᾽ ἀνέσπασεν.
κἄγωγ᾽ ὅτε δὴ ᾽γνων ἐνδεχομένην τοὺς λόγους
καὶ τοῖς φενακισμοῖσιν ἐξαπατωμένην,
ἄγε δὴ Σκίταλοι καὶ Φένακες, ἦν δ᾽ ἐγώ,

628. ἐρείδων MSS. and vulg. ἐρείπων Brunck Dind. Mein. Vels. Hold. Blaydes.
ἐρείκων ci Bergk. ἐρεύγων Thiersch.
631. νᾶπυ MSS.: the word had passed out of use, so Crates ap. Athen. ix 366 F
quotes κάβλεπε σίναπυ, and the mason is puzzled by the word in the Apellas inscription
at Epidaurus, Wilam. *Isyll.* 123.

thunder-rolling phrases, he hurled his
monstrous bombast at the knights.'
627. τέρας of Typhoeus Aesch. *Prom.*
352. τερατεύομαι &c. came to be used of
strained or bombastic phrase or oratory,
Nub. 318, *Lys.* 762, *Ran.* 834: Aeschines
is fond of the word. ἐρείδω of violent
hurling or thrusting in combat, then of
violent debate, *Nub.* 1375 ἔπος πρὸς ἔπος
ἠρειδόμεσθα.
628. κρημνός was used of phrases that
were thought too 'steep': κρημνοποιός of
Aeschylus *Nub.* 1367. L and S quote
κρημνηγορῶ, κρημνογράφος &c.
ξυνωμότας, cf. on 236.
630. The plant ἀτράφαξυς (also written
ἀτράφαξις, ἀδράφαξυς, ἀνδράφαξις) is the
Latin *atriplex*, French *arroche* (both
names from the Greek), our *orach*. The
point here is explained by the scholiast
from the plant's rapid growth, ὡς τῆς
βουλῆς τοῖς ψευδομένοις καὶ διαβάλλουσι
πειθομένης εὐχερῶς καὶ ῥαδίως, ὥσπερ καὶ τὸ
λάχανον αὔξεται. Pliny *NH* xx 219 supplies
another point *atriplex...accusatum Pytha-
gorae tamquam faceret hydropicos morbos-
que regios et pallorem, concoqueretur diffi-
cillime, ac ne in hortis quidem juxta id
nasci quicquam nisi languidum culpavit*:
Cleon's claptrap at once prejudices the
Council against any other view. So Kock:
but Merry thinks the allusion is to seasoning of sausages with the herb.
It is curious that the ἀτράφαξυς, which
is constantly mentioned along with cori-
ander, occurs in a fragment of Pherecrates'
Κοριαννώ (75 Kock): and if Merry is

right, there may be a contrast intended between the ψευδατράφαξυς and the κορίαννα
which crown the hero's success (676, 682).
Theophr. *Hist. Plant.* vii 1. 2—3 says
the plant was sown, with parsley and
leeks, in Gamelion, and came up in a
week: so that it would be springing in
the gardens at the Lenaea.
631. βλέπειν νᾶπυ and such phrases
occur in great variety in Greek: Blaydes
on *Ach.* 95 gives a very large collection of
cases: βλ. κάρδαμα of a jury, *Vesp.* 455.
μετ. ἀνέσπ.: ἀνασπᾶν ὀφρῦς is more
common, see Blaydes on *Ach.* 1069, and
Ellis on Catullus 67. 46.
632. ἐνδέχομαι λόγον or λόγους is
regular of one enticed to accept a view,
Herod. v 92, Thucyd. iii 82. 7.
634. Pericles, on his way to the bema,
always prayed, silently, no doubt (Plut.
Per. 8). Some extant speeches of the
orators begin with a prayer, as Demosth.
Cor., Lycurg. *Leocr.*, Cic. *Mur.* and *post
Red. ad Quir.*: but these exordia, like
Cleon's *inf.* 763, are really protestations of
patriotism more than prayers. Here we
have a silent (φροντίζοντι 638) invocation
of strange goblins who inspire the speaker's
impudence and the hearers' dulness:
"fiends...of lust, as Obidicut, Hobbidi-
dence, prince of dumbness,...Flibberti-
gibbet, of mopping and mowing." We
know about as much of the Sausage-man's
goblins as of Edgar's: a scholiast says
Σκίταλοι and Βερέσχεθοι are names invented by Ar. and never explained,
though another says Σκίταλοι is formed

Βερέσχεθοί τε καὶ Κόβαλοι καὶ Μόθων, 635
ἀγορά τ᾽, ἐν ᾗ παῖς ὢν ἐπαιδεύθην ἐγώ,
νῦν μοι θράσος καὶ γλῶτταν εὔπορον δότε
φωνήν τ᾽ ἀναιδῆ. ταῦτα φροντίζοντί μοι
ἐκ δεξιᾶς ἀπέπαρδε καταπύγων ἀνήρ.
κἀγὼ προσέκυσα· κᾆτα τῷ πρωκτῷ θενὼν 640
τὴν κιγκλίδ᾽ ἐξήραξα, κἀναχανὼν μέγα

635. μόθωνες MSS. κοάλεμοί τε καὶ Μόθων Dobr. Zacher from schol.
637. γλῶσσαν three MSS.
639. ἐπέπαρδε Halbertsma Mein. Vels. Kock Blaydes Merry: that compound
might be expected on analogy of ἐπιπταίρω.
640. θένων MSS.

from a certain Σκίτων. For similar demons cf. Plato com. 174. Very likely the appeal here, like the homage to Κοάλεμος *sup.* 221, is meant to be the comic counterpart to such invocations as Aeschin. *Ctes.* 260 ὦ γῆ καὶ ἥλιε καὶ ἀρετὴ καὶ σύνεσις καὶ παιδεία, ᾗ διαγιγνώσκομεν τὰ καλὰ καὶ τὰ αἰσχρά...

ἄγε δή of course is common with plurals, but I do not suppose it would he used in devout prayer.

We find in Greek mythology and art instances of Ἀπάτη, Γέλως, Εὐήθεια &c., see *Personifikationen* in Baumeister's *Denkmäler*. The βουλευτήριον was adorned in Pausanias' time with statues of Zeus, Apollo and Demos, and probably also with paintings: there may be allusion here to certain divine or heroic figures in the hall. The beings invoked would be personifications of rhetorical πάθη in the most extreme form: these effects and the styles of oratory corresponding are often mentioned as allowed in democratic, forbidden in aristocratic, states, Arist. *Rhet.* i 1. 4, Plut. *de virt. mor.* 7. 447 F διὸ τοὺς ῥήτορας ἐν ταῖς ἀριστοκρατίαις οἱ ἄρχοντες οὐκ ἐῶσι παθαίνεσθαι.

635. Κόβ. See on 270. Μόθων is said to be a Spartan word: we hear of Μόθακες and Μόθωνες as foster-brothers of Spartiates, perhaps children of Spartiate fathers and Helot mothers; some distinguish μόθων *verna*, μόθαξ *libertinus*, see Hermann-Thumser *Griech. Staatsalt.* 175, Cantarelli *Riv. Filol.* xviii 465—. μόθων in Attic means (1) *impudent* (*vernilis*) *Plut.* 379, Ion of Chios called Pericles'

social bearing μοθωνικός (Plut. *Per.* 5), (2) a kind of dance *inf.* 697.

636. The ἀγορά was just outside and perhaps in view : note the emphatic confidence of ἐγώ. Observe the rhythm of 634—639: the first three lines attempt tragic style, which is fully reached in 637—8, with the sentence-ending in the third foot so marked in tragic ῥήσεις, then the comic rhythm breaks in exactly at the comic word in 639. The seriousness of 637 would be heightened by reading γλῶσσαν.

639. Thunder and sneezing were both favourable when heard on the right, Hom. *Il.* ii 353, Plut. *Themist.* 13, see Ellis and Baehrens on Catull. 45. 8.

640. προσκύνησις at a good omen, especially a sneeze, Xen. *Anab.* iii 2. 9 πτάρνυταί τις· ἀκούσαντες δὲ οἱ στρατιῶται πάντες μιᾷ ὁρμῇ προσεκύνησαν τὸν θεόν (apparently Zeus Soter), Aristot. *probl.* 33. 9, 662ᵃ 37 διὰ τὸ ἱερώτατον οὖν εἶναι τὸν τόπον (head) καὶ τὸ πνεῦμα τὸ ἐντεῦθεν ὡς ἱερὸν προσκυνοῦσιν, Athen. ii 66 c. For θείνω in Attic see Ruth. *NP* 10.

641. In the Council-hall and law-courts the council and the juries sat within a partition called δρύφακτος, δρύφακτοι (=Lat. *cancelli*, Plut. *Marius* 5; schol. here explains κ. by τὸ κάγκελον): the public stood outside ἐπὶ τοῖς δρυφάκτοις, *Vesp.* 552, Xen. *Hell.* ii 3. 50. [A similar partition is mentioned in lists of temple-furniture at Delos and Oropus (*Inscr. Graec. Septent.* 3498. 5) under the name τρύφακτος.] The lattice-door through this bar was called κιγκλίς; no one, except

ἀνέκραγον· ὦ βουλή, λόγους ἀγαθοὺς φέρων
εὐαγγελίσασθαι πρῶτος ὑμῖν βούλομαι·
ἐξ οὗ γὰρ ἡμῖν ὁ πόλεμος κατερράγη,
οὐπώποτ' ἀφύας εἶδον ἀξιωτέρας.   645
οἱ δ' εὐθέως τὰ πρόσωπα διεγαλήνισαν·
εἶτ' ἐστεφάνουν μ' εὐαγγέλια· κἀγὼ 'φρασα
αὐτοῖς ἀπόρρητον ποιησάμενος, ταχὺ

643. πρῶτον MSS. Ribb. Blaydes. πρῶτος V sec. m. Phryn. Dind. and now vulg.
646. οἱ δ' R and edd. vulg. τῶν δ'...-νισεν most MSS. Bergk. ἡ δ'...-νισεν
Fritzsche Kock.

---

councillors and jurymen, passed this door, *Vesp.* 775, Demosth. i *Aristog.* 23. 28. So Lucian *de merc. cond.* 21 ἐντὸς τῆς κιγκλίδος of one in the inner circle of a patron's friendship. Plutarch uses κιγκλίς for *the bar* as a profession. For ἐξήραξε cf. Lysias 3. 6 ἐκκόψας τὰς θύρας εἰσῆλθεν.

642. ὦ βουλή seems to have been regular, not ὦ ἄνδρες βουλευταί. See such speeches as Lysias 8 and 24 *passim*: but a βουλευτής might say ἄνδρες as 654: see on 626.

643. εὐαγγελίζομαι took acc. of person in late Greek (Phrynichus no. 235 Ruth.), in Attic dat. of person and sometimes acc. of thing.

Kock supports πρῶτος by Soph. *Trach.* 180, 190, Aeschin. *FL* 171: add Phryn. com. 44 acc. to Cobet's restoration ἵνα εὐαγγελίσωμαι πρῶτος ὑμῖν τἀγαθά: but there may be a reference to Cleon's despatch from Sphacteria, Lucian *pro laps. inter salut.* 3 ἐν ἐπιστολῆς ἀρχῇ Κλέων ἀπὸ Σφακτηρίας, πρῶτον χαίρειν προὔθηκεν εὐαγγελιζόμενος τὴν νίκην τὴν ἐκεῖθεν.

644. γάρ is not 'for,' but epexegetic of λόγους ἀγαθούς. κατερράγη: this metaphor of the storm of war was common, *Ach.* 528, Thucyd. i 66 οὐ μέντοι ὅ γε πόλεμός πω ξυνερρώγει.

645. The ἀφύη (*sprat,* indefinitely used for several kinds of small fish) was the favourite relish of the Athenian poor: it is discussed by Athen. vii 22—24, where Chrysippus the Stoic says it was called πτωχικὸν ὄψον at Athens.

ἄξιος, 'cheap' as 672, 895—6, *Vesp.* 491 ταρίχους ἀξιωτέρα, Pherecr. 16 ὅδ' ἔστ' ἐφ' οὗ ποτ' ἦν ὁ πυρὸς ἄξιος, Eubul. 10. 2 ἀξιωτέρους πωλοῦσιν τοὺς ἄρτους ἐκεῖ, Lysias 22. 8, 22, where τίμιος is the oppo-

site of ἄξιος, Xen. *Vect.* 4. 6, Lucian *dial. mort.* 4. 1 ἄξια ταῦτα ὠνήσω. See Cobet in *Mnemos.* ix 345, showing that later writers went back to the Homeric use of ἄξιος = *dear.*

For prices of fish in Athens see Böckh *Staatshaus.*[3] i 128—9.

646. διεγαλ., ἡ συννεφὴς ἕξις (τοῦ μετώπου) αὐθάδειαν ἐμφαίνει, ἥ τε γαλήνη κολακείαν Aristot. *physiog.* 812[a] 1, Plut. *de aud.* 45 Β ὄμματος πρᾳότητα καὶ γαλήνην προσώπου καὶ διάθεσιν εὐμενῆ ἐμπαρασχεῖν.

647. εὐαγγέλια (always plur. in Attic as gen. of feasts, sacrifices &c.), *an offering for good news,* generally a sacrifice to gods as 656, Xen. *Hell.* i 6. 37, iv 3. 14, Isocr. *Areop.* 10, but also a reward to men, *Plut.* 764.

The offering was voted by the council in either case, Aeschin. *Ctes.* 160 εἰς αἰτίαν εὐαγγελίων θυσίας τὴν βουλὴν κατέστησεν.

The reward to the bringer of good news was in Athens a garland or crown, as here, *Plut.* 764 ἀναδῆσαι βούλομαι εὐαγγέλιά σε, in Sparta meat from the mess, Plut. *de glor. Ath.* 347 D; the sacrifice and crowning together, *Demosth.* 22 ἔθυον εὐαγγέλια καὶ στεφανοῦν ἐψηφίσαντο Παυσανίαν, *reg. et imp. apophth.* 184 A εὐαγγέλια τοῖς θεοῖς ἔθυσε καὶ τὰς πόλεις τὰς ὑφ' ἑαυτοῦ στεφανηφορεῖν ἐποίησεν.

For double acc. cf. *Plut.* 764, Aesch. *Agam.* 167 Ζῆνα ἐπινίκια κλάζων, Plato *Phaedr.* 265 C ὕμνον προσεπαίσαμεν Ἔρωτα.

648. αὐτοῖς emphatically with ἀπ. ποιησ. 'making it a state-secret for *them* (the βουλή).' For ἀπόρρητον, 'a state-

ἵνα τὰς ἀφύας ὠνοῖντο πολλὰς τοὐβολοῦ,
τῶν δημιουργῶν ξυλλαβεῖν τὰ τρύβλια.   650
οἱ δ' ἀνεκρότησαν καὶ πρὸς ἔμ' ἐκεχήνεσαν.
ὁ δ' ὑπονοήσας, ὁ Παφλαγών, εἰδώς θ' ἅμα
οἷς ᾔδεθ' ἡ βουλὴ μάλιστα ῥήμασιν,
γνώμην ἔλεξεν· ἄνδρες, ἤδη μοι δοκεῖ
ἐπὶ συμφοραῖς ἀγαθαῖσιν εἰσηγγελμέναις   655
εὐαγγέλια θύειν ἑκατὸν βοῦς τῇ θεῷ.
ἐπένευσεν εἰς ἐκεῖνον ἡ βουλὴ πάλιν.
κᾆγωγ' ὅτε δὴ 'γνων τοῖς βολίτοις ἡττημένος,

650. τρυβλία six MSS., but see Chandler *Greek Acc.* § 350.
652. εἰδώς τ' ἅμα R, εἰδώς θ' ἅμα Dind.¹ Bergk Kock Blaydes. εἰδώς ἄρα the other MSS. vulg. εἰδώς τ' ἄρα Dind. Ribb. Zacher.
655. ἀγαθαῖσιν ἠγγελμέναις R : ἀγαθαῖσι ταῖς ἠγγελμέναις Cobet *NL* 327 : but εἰσαγγέλλω is used of information given to the βουλή or any similar body, as Thucyd. viii 92. 6, Andoc. *de red.* 3, 21 : he uses official style, answered 659.

secret,' cf. Herod. ix 45, 94, Xen. *Anab.* vii 6. 43 : especially a secret for the Council, not to be divulged in the Ecclesia, *Eccl.* 443, Demosth. i *Aristog.* 23 τὸ τὴν βουλὴν τοὺς πεντακοσίους ἀπὸ τῆς ἀσθενοῦς τοιαυτησὶ κιγκλίδος τῶν ἀπορρήτων κυρίαν εἶναι, Andoc. *de red.* 3 εἰσαγγείλαντός μου ἀπόρρητα εἰς τὴν βουλήν : so ἐν ἀπορρήτῳ is used of the βουλή acting on its own responsibility and secretly, Andoc. *Myst.* 45, *de red.* 21, Lysias 13. 21 εἰσελθὼν εἰς ταύτην τὴν βουλὴν ἐν ἀπορρήτῳ μηνύει, Plut. *garrul.* 11. 507 B, *quaest. symp.* vii 9. 714 B : of the senate at Rome, Aelian *Var. Hist.* xii 33.
ταχύ is probably to be taken with ξυλλαβεῖν.
649—50. This stroke of finance is a comic counterpart of the ' forestalling or engrossing' operations which were generally forbidden, but sometimes undertaken by states, Böckh *Staatsh.*³ i 66. Seizure of all the pots in the crockery-shops would paralyze the market in sprats. ξυλλαβεῖν is a serious word, gen. used of arresting persons: the line (in tragic rhythm) may be a parody.
Cleon's recent financial strokes—the raising of the φόρος and of the dicast's fee —would be in the minds of all.
δημιουργός, for a potter, Antiphanes

163 πολλὰ κἀγάθ' οἱ θεοὶ τῷ δημιουργῷ δοῖεν ὃς ἐποίησέ σε (κύλιξ). τρύβλια, for holding ἀφύας, as *Av.* 77 &c.
653—4. ᾔδεθ' for ᾔδεται. γνώμην ἔλ., cf. on 267, 626. Procedure in the βουλή, as far as we know, was like that in the ἐκκλησία, Gilbert *Gr. Staats.* i² 307- .
654—6. ἄνδρες, see on 642. ἤδη marks a crisis, as often. συμφ., cf. on 406. The βουλή had control of state sacrifices and festivals (cf. Aeschin. *Ctes.* 160). Cleon is an Athenist, see on 581 and 763. ἑκατὸν βοῦς : ἑκατόμβη seems not to occur in Attic literature except four times in Middle and New Comedy, in Inscr. *CIA* i 188. 7 where 5114 drachmae is the sum paid for the hecatomb at the Panathenaea, and ii 741. 36. Whatever the original meaning of the word (see Platt in *Journ. Phil.* xxii 46), the hecatomb was often less than a hundred animals : see L and S, and Athen. i 3 D of Conon after Cnidus ἑκατόμβην τῷ ὄντι θύσας καὶ οὐ ψευδωνύμως πάντας Ἀθηναίους εἱστίασεν (so it would be popular cf. Xen. *Pol. Ath.* 2. 9).
657. The asyndeton is echoed in 663.
658. βολ. as *Ach.* 1025. The schol. quotes βολίτου δίκη for a trifling law-suit, and says that the later form was βόλβιτος : and so in M. Aurel. 3. 3 βολβίτῳ κατακεχρισμένος, see Lobeck *Phryn.* 357.

διηκοσίῃσι βουσὶν ὑπερηκόντισα·
τῇ δ' Ἀγροτέρᾳ κατὰ χιλίων παρῄνεσα   660
εὐχὴν ποήσασθαι χιμάρων εἰσαύριον,
αἱ τριχίδες εἰ γενοίαθ' ἑκατὸν τοὐβολοῦ.
ἐκαραδόκησεν εἰς ἔμ' ἡ βουλὴ πάλιν.
ὁ δὲ ταῦτ' ἀκούσας ἐκπλαγεὶς ἐφληνάφα.
κᾆθ' εἷλκον αὐτὸν οἱ πρυτάνεις χοἰ τοξόται.   665
οἱ δ' ἐθορύβουν περὶ τῶν ἀφύων ἑστηκότες·
ὁ δ' ἠντεβόλει γ' αὐτοὺς ὀλίγον μεῖναι χρόνον·

659. διηκοσίῃσι, -ῃσι RV and most MSS. -ιοισι three MSS. -ιαισι Dind. and vulg.
Meisterhans § 46. 12 shows that such datives plural in Attic ended in -ῃσι after conso-
nants, -ασι after vowels, till 420 B.C., when -αις became regular. Here the Ionism in
official style is a point, as Ionic forms were sometimes used in Attic ritual, cf. 763,
Av. 867 Ὀλυμπίοις καὶ Ὀλυμπίῃσι, *Lys.* 642, μυρίῃσι *CIA* iv 1 53 a, p. 66.
660. χιλίων MSS. χιλιῶν schol. which is said to have been the Attic accentuation,
when δραχμῶν was understood, Chandler § 757.
667. ἠντιβόλει MSS. Dind. Bergk Kock, ἠντεβόλει Cobet *NL* 157; for γ' Lenting
Blaydes give 'τ', i.e. ἔτι.

---

660. Probably παρῄνεσα)(γνώμην
ἔλεξεν of 654, as γνώμην λέγειν would be
used only of a Councillor or Strategus.
The Persian loss at Marathon was so
great (over 6000) that the Athenians
were unable to pay their vow to Artemis
Agrotera of a goat for every enemy killed,
and commuted it for an annual sacrifice
of 500 yearling (and therefore eatable)
goats on the sixth of Boedromion
(Sandys gives the references on Aristot.
Pol. Ath. 58). Artemis was the chief
deity on the east coast of Attica, and
goats were a common offering to her, as
by the Spartans before a battle (Preller-
Robert *Griech. Myth.* i 302, 312), hence
δίκαν χιμαίρας of Iphigenia, Aesch. *Ag.*
232. The shrine of Artemis Agrotera,
Agraia, or Agra (Plato *Phaedr.* 229 C) at
Athens was at Agrae across the Ilissus.
κατά is idiomatic of the person or thing
vowed: as in the phrase κατὰ τέκνων or
παίδων ὀμνύειν in the orators, ὀμνύναι καθ'
ἱερῶν *Ran.* 101, Thucyd. v 47. 8, κατεύ-
χομαι τῶν ἱερῶν inscr. at Oropus in
Bechtel *Inschr. Ion. Dial.* 18. 25: then
by confusion ὀμνύειν κατ' ἐξωλείας &c.
εὐχή is not, like the Latin *votum*, always a promise to pay, but it often has
that meaning.
The cheapness of small fish would be
worth two Marathons.
662. τριχίς is said by Aristot. *HA* vi

15. 569ᵇ 25 to be descended from a kind
of ἀφύη. For instances of forms in -οιατο
see Ruth. *NP* 431, G. Meyer *Gr. Gram.*
§§ 470—1, Meisterhans § 61. 4.
663. καραδοκῶ occurs in Herod., often
in Eurip. (some of whose ῥήσεις Ar. probably is thinking of), once in Xen. *Mem.*
iii 5. 6 σιγῶσι καραδοκοῦντες τὰ προσταχ-
θησόμενα, ὥσπερ οἱ χορευταί, then often
in Polyb. and Plutarch.
In Eurip. *Orest.* 703 it is used of a
politician watching his opportunity.
665. The πρυτάνεις would preside over
the Council-meeting, and the police were
under their orders. *Thesm.* 923 προσέρχεται γὰρ ὁ πρύτανις χὠ τοξότης. For ἕλκω
cf. *Eccl.* 259 ἢν σ' οἱ τοξόται ἕλκωσιν,
Demosth. *Androt.* 53, Lucian *catap.* 9.
666. The accent of ἀφύων (cf. χρή-
στων) was intended to prevent confusion
with ἀφυῶν from ἀφυής (cf. the pun in
Lucian *pisc.* 48). ἑστηκότες, to mark
enthusiasm, *stantes plaudebant,* Cic. *Lael.*
24 and Reid's note.
667. For double augment of ἀντιβολῶ see Ruth. *NP* 84.
Blaydes rightly says δὲ...γε has a very
marked force (see on 356): but he fails to
see this force here and reads 'τ' for ἔτι
after Lenting. I believe the δὲ...γε is quite
right : the words are really a quotation;
Cleon said ἐγὼ δ' ἀντιβολῶ γ' ὑμᾶς...
If Shilleto on Thucyd. i 76. 4 was right

ἵν᾽ ἄτθ᾽ ὁ κῆρυξ οὐκ Λακεδαίμονος λέγει
πύθησθ᾽· ἀφῖκται γὰρ περὶ σπονδῶν· λέγων.
οἱ δ᾽ ἐξ ἑνὸς στόματος ἅπαντες ἀνέκραγον· 670
νυνὶ περὶ σπονδῶν; ἐπειδή γ᾽, ὦ μέλε,
ἤσθοντο τὰς ἀφύας παρ᾽ ἡμῖν ἀξίας;
οὐ δεόμεθα σπονδῶν· ὁ πόλεμος ἑρπέτω.
ἐκεκράγεσάν τε τοὺς πρυτάνεις ἀφιέναι·
εἶθ᾽ ὑπερεπήδων τοὺς δρυφάκτους πανταχῆ. 675
ἐγὼ δὲ τὰ κορίανν᾽ ἐπριάμην ὑποδραμὼν
ἅπαντα τά τε γήτει᾽ ὅσ᾽ ἦν ἐν τἀγορᾷ·

668—9. ἁτ᾽ R. ἄθ᾽ V &c. λέγῃ R. λέγει πάλιν V and four MSS. σπονδῶν λέγων or λόγων MSS. σπ. πάλιν Pors. on *Hec.* 1161 Blaydes.
674. ἀπιέναι MSS.
676. ὑπεκδραμών R. ἐγὼ δ᾽ ἐπριάμην τὰ κορίανν᾽ ὑπεκδραμών Fritzsche Mein. Kock Vels.

in his explanation of Xen. *Mem.* i 2. 12, γε is similarly taken there out of the speaker's words, ἀλλ᾽ ἔφη γε ὁ κατήγορος Σωκράτει... standing for ἀλλὰ Σωκράτει γε..., ἔφη ὁ κατήγορος: but the more obvious meaning is probably right there, as it certainly is in Demosth. *Mid.* 91 mentioned by Shilleto. I believe that ἀλλά in *Nub.* 1364 is explicable from the or. recta ἀλλὰ μυρρίνην λαβὼν τῶν Αἰσχύλου λέξον τί μοι. So γε in Aesch. *Agam.* 1240, *Vesp.* 1190, Plato *Charm.* 172 E in quotation of the actual words used: and cf. the two cases quoted from Plato by Riddell *Digest* § 295.

670. Plato *Rep.* ii 364 A, *Legg.* i 634 E μιᾷ φωνῇ καὶ ἐξ ἑνὸς στόματος πάντας συμφωνεῖν,...καὶ ἐάν τις ἄλλως λέγῃ, μὴ ἀνέχεσθαι τὸ παράπαν ἀκούοντας.

671. The γε is of ironical assent. ὦ μέλε of remonstrance, as often: the word is given once in Plato, once in Menander, eleven times in Ar.

673. It is an inference from this line and *Lys.* 129 that ὁ πόλεμος ἑρπέτω was a current phrase with the old and poetical ἕρπω, Ruth. *NP* 50.

674. ἐκεκράγη is of course imperfect in meaning; Xen. *Cyrop.* i 3. 10 has it among a number of imperfects. As the Council meeting was called by the πρυτάνεις, they also broke it up, as they are made to do here by the enthusiasm of the members. "Meminerint tirones λύεσθαι μὲν τὴν ἐκκλησίαν, ἀφίεσθαι δὲ τὴν βουλὴν καὶ τὰ δικαστήρια," Elms. on *Ach.* 173, quoting *Vesp.* 595, *Eccl.* 377: Demosth. *Timocr.* 26 ἀφειμένης τῆς βουλῆς. The distinction was forgotten later: Plutarch has ἀφῆκαν τὴν ἐκκλησίαν *Aemil.* 30, *Ti. Gracch.* 16, as well as διαλύειν.

675. A comparison of this line with 641 seems to support the distinction given on that line between κιγκλίς and δρύφακτοι, though the words are not distinguished by some, Gilbert *Staatsalt.* i² 307.

676. It is not easy to choose between ὑποδραμών and ὑπεκδραμών on the merits of the words themselves. The instances of ὑποτρέχω (so ὑποθέω), in a sense suitable here, imply *cutting off retreat*, as Xen. *Cyrop.* i 2. 12; ὑπεκτρέχω generally implies *outstripping* an enemy or pursuer, Soph. *Antig.* 1086, Eurip. *Phoen.* 887 &c. But ὑποδραμών needs no change in the rest of the line, and is probably right = *cutting in before*: Plut. *frat. am.* 10. 482 E has it of unfair rivalry.

677. γήτειον, γήθυον, γηθυλλίς, see Hehn *Culturp.*⁶ 194. The words became obsolete (Lucian *Lexiph.* 3), πράσον being used instead. κορίαννον, γήτειον, γήθυον occur in the lists of ἡδύσματα, quoted from Alexis by Athen. iv 170 A—B. γήτειον, as seasoning for sprats, *Vesp.* 496. ὀρίγα-

ἔπειτα ταῖς ἀφύαις ἐδίδουν ἡδύσματα
ἀποροῦσιν αὐτοῖς προῖκα, κἀχαριζόμην.
οἱ δ᾽ ὑπερεπήνουν ὑπερεπύππαζόν τέ με   680
ἅπαντες οὕτως ὥστε τὴν βουλὴν ὅλην
ὀβολοῦ κοριάννοις ἀναλαβὼν ἐλήλυθα.

ΧΟΡ. πάντα τοι πέπραγας οἷα χρὴ τὸν εὐτυχοῦντα·
ηὗρε δ᾽ ὁ πανοῦργος ἕτερον πολὺ πανουργίαις
μείζοσι κεκασμένον,   685
καὶ δόλοισι ποικίλοις,
ῥήμασίν θ᾽ αἱμύλοις.
ἀλλ᾽ ὅπως ἀγωνιεῖ φρόν-
τιζε τἀπίλοιπ᾽ ἄριστα·
συμμάχους δ᾽ ἡμᾶς ἔχων εὔ-
νους ἐπίστασαι πάλαι.   690

ΑΛΛ. καὶ μὴν ὁ Παφλαγὼν οὑτοσὶ προσέρχεται,

683. πάντα τοι R, Dind. Mein. Kock Ribb.   πάντα δή other MSS. Blaydes.

νον, ὃς δὴ σεμνύνει τὸ τάριχον ὁμοῦ μιχθεὶς κοριάννῳ Anaxandrides 50; ...τύρον, κορίαννον, οἷς ὁ Κρόνος ἀρτύμασιν ἐχρᾶτο Anaxippus 1. 8.

678. ἐδίδουν, the proper Attic form, Ruth. *NP* 316: inscriptions, so far as they go, bear the rule out, Meisterhans § 742.

680. Plato *Euthyd.* 303 A—B ὁ δὲ Κτήσιππος...πυππὰξ ὦ Ἡράκλεις, ἔφη, καλοῦ λόγου· καὶ ὁ Διονυσόδωρος, πότερον οὖν, ἔφη, ὁ Ἡρακλῆς πυππάξ ἐστιν ἢ ὁ πυππὰξ Ἡρακλῆς;...ἐνταῦθα μέντοι οὐδεὶς ὅστις οὐ τῶν παρόντων ὑπερεπήνεσε τὸν λόγον. πυππάξω, Cratin. 52.

681—2. 'I've come with the whole Council in my pocket for a pennyworth of coriander-seed.' Kock quotes a similar use of λαβών from Demosth. *Cor.* 40, *FL* 19. ἀναλαμβάνω was used in Rhetoric for *winning over* an audience, Arist. *Rhet.* i 1. 11, and in politics for *winning supporters*, Dinarchus *adv. Dem.* 28, Athen. vi 260 D, and often in Plutarch; of *winning* a lover Aeschin. *Tim.* 54.

683. 'Your fortune has been all that marks the successful man.' ὁ εὐτυχῶν

seems commoner than ὁ εὐτυχής, success being *of the time:* οἱ εὐτυχοῦντες διὰ τέλους οὐκ εὐτυχεῖς Eurip. *HF* 103. The word generally implies a contest and victory as in Pindar of athletes, in history of armies.

684—6. The colouring is poetic. κεκασμένος is Epic=*excelling*, *Il.* iv 339 κακοῖσι δόλοισι κεκασμένε, *Od.* xix 395 ἀνθρώπους ἐκέκαστο κλεπτοσύνῃ θ᾽ ὅρκῳ τε: the tragedians took it as = κεκοσμημένος and so perhaps did Ar. here. δόλος is barely an Attic prose word; indices quote it from Isocr. *Evag.* 36 and Plato *Legg.* x 908 D, xii 941 B, all passages of legend and poetry: so αἱμύλος in the fable Plato *Phaedr.* 237 B and in quotation *Legg.* vii 823 D. In Comedy δόλος seems confined to Epic (*Pax* 1099), lyric and tragic styles: αἱμύλος here and in the Spartan ode *Lys.* 1269.

687—90. ἀγωνίζομαι of the coming part as of the past (614): *fut.* cf. on 474.

691. καὶ μήν introducing a new figure on the stage is never followed by γε: in Soph. *OC* 1249—50 the ἀνδρῶν γε μοῦνος is an afterthought; see Appendix i.

ὠθῶν κολόκυμα καὶ ταράττων καὶ κυκῶν,
ὡς δὴ καταπιόμενός με. μορμὼ τοῦ θράσους.
ΠΑ. εἰ μή σ᾽ ἀπολέσαιμ᾽, εἴ τι τῶν αὐτῶν ἐμοὶ
ψευδῶν ἐνείη, διαπέσοιμι πανταχῇ.   695
ΑΛΛ. ἥσθην ἀπειλαῖς, ἐγέλασα ψολοκομπίαις,
ἀπεπυδάρισα μόθωνα, περιεκόκκυσα.

697. -κόκκαυσα R. -κόκκυσα other MSS. schol. and Suid. -κόκκασα Phot. and edd. vulg.

---

692. κολόκυμα was taken by one scholiast as κυλίον κῦμα, by another more sensibly as κόλον or κολοβὸν κῦμα, a *hornless* or *crestless* wave. Such a swell, presaging storm, was also called τυφλὸν or κῶφον (*Il.* xiv 16), or σκώληξ (ἡ κώφη τῶν κυμάτων ἐπανάστασις Bekk. *Anecd.* 62. 20, Plato com. 25).
ταρ. καὶ κυκῶν 251.
693. ὡς δή, sarcastic, the δή marking it as Cleon's thought: *Vesp.* 1315 and Aesch. *Ag.* 1633 (Paley). καταπίνω of swallowing solids, as often : of the sea swallowing a ship, Theognis 680 δειμαίνω μή πως ναῦν κατὰ κῦμα πίῃ: of a Charybdis-like ἑταίρα, τόν τε ναύκληρον λαβοῦσα καταπέπωκ᾽ αὐτῷ σκάφει Anaxilas 22.
μορμὼ τοῦ θράσους, 'Bo, what a swagger!' Μορμώ a bogey-name, cf. on 529: used as an interjection here and Theocr. 15. 40 μορμώ, δάκνει ἵππος. θρ., cf. on 304.
694—5. When the apodosis of a conditional sentence is the true optative of wish, the protasis is put in the indic. when a present or actual state is meant (κάκιστ᾽ ἀπολοίμην Ξανθίαν εἰ μὴ φιλῶ *Ran.* 579), but in the opt. when a future condition is expressed, as in threats (so here, *Od.* xvi 102, Theocr. 5. 149): see examples collected by Blaydes on *Ach.* 476.
It seems that the secondary conditional clause, εἴ τι...ἐνείη, is attracted by the opt. ἀπολέσαιμι: the simple sentence would be εἴ τι...ἔνεστι ('if my old lies have not deserted me'), ἀπολῶ σέ. The confusion is, I think, intended to show Cleon's alarm : cf. on 287, 299, 698.
διαπέσοιμι like διαρραγείην : the word was used of the bursting of bubbles.
696—7. 'Aorists of instantaneous action' are almost confined to dramatists. Ar. is fond of ἥσθην in this sense (*Nub.*

174, 1240, *Pax* 1066, *Av.* 570, 880), *I am amused at*)(ἥδομαι, *I feel happy.*
ψολοκομπίαι is intended to mean *harmless thunder, brutum fulmen.*
ψολ., 'smoke and noise' : ψόλος is sooty ashes, Aesch. *fr.* 22 a (perhaps akin to ἄσβολος). In Epic ψολόεις κεραυνός occurs *Od.* xxiii 330, xxiv 539, *Hymn. Aphr.* 289, Hes. *Theog.* 515, *Scut.* 422, *fr.* 49. 2 Göttl. The poets use ψολόεις κεραυνός for one kind of thunderbolt, ἀργὴς κ. for another, as we are told by schol. here (τῶν κεραυνῶν οἱ μὲν καταιβάται, οἱ δὲ ψολόεντες, οἱ δὲ ἀργῆτες καλοῦνται, ὡς Ὅμηρος ὠνόμασεν), Aristot. *Meteor.* iii 1. 371ᵃ 21 (where see Ideler's note) ὁ δὲ βραδύτερος (ψολόεις) ἔχρωσε μέν, ἔκαυσε δ᾽ οὔ, *de mundo* 4. 395ᵃ 26 τῶν κεραυνῶν οἱ μὲν αἰθαλώδεις ψολόεντες λέγονται, οἱ δὲ ταχέως διᾴττοντες ἀργῆτες, Plut. *de fac. lun.* 922 Α τυφόμενον ἀεὶ καὶ πυρίκαυστον, ὥσπερ τῶν κεραυνῶν τοὺς ἀλαμπεῖς καὶ ψολόεντας ὑπὸ τῶν ποιητῶν καλουμένους, Plin. *NH* ii 137. But the distinction does not seem to hold for Homer, cf. *Od.* v 131, vii 249 with xxiii 30. Cf. αἰθαλόεις, which is used of a thunderbolt and of a smoky hall.
697. Scholia give three explanations of the words in this line ; modern editors are agreed to adopt one. πυδαρίζω probably meant 'to leap,' *tripudiare;* and μόθων acc. to scholia here and *Plut.* 279, also Pollux iv 101, sometimes meant a coarse kind of dance (cf. Athen. xiv 618 c) ; in Eurip. *Bacch.* 1060 it is, by the conjectural reading, Pentheus' word for the Bacchants' dance. In this sense it may be connected with μέθυ. Why the rare word -κοκκάζω is preferred by editors is not clear : κοκκύζω means to *cry cuckoo,* or to *crow* (Aristoph. Byz. *fr.* 73 Nauck) ; either suits the passage well.

ΠΑ. οὔ τοι μὰ τὴν Δήμητρά γ᾽, εἰ μή σ᾽ ἐκφάγω
ἐκ τῆσδε τῆς γῆς, οὐδέποτε βιώσομαι.

ΑΛΛ. εἰ μὴ ᾽κφάγῃς; ἐγὼ δέ γ᾽, εἰ μή σ᾽ ἐκπίω,   700
κἀπεκροφήσας αὐτὸς ἐπιδιαρραγῶ.

ΠΑ. ἀπολῶ σε νὴ τὴν προεδρίαν τὴν ἐκ Πύλου.

ΑΛΛ. ἰδοὺ προεδρίαν· οἷον ὄψομαί σ᾽ ἐγὼ
ἐκ τῆς προεδρίας ἔσχατον θεώμενον.

ΠΑ. ἐν τῷ ξύλῳ δήσω σε νὴ τὸν οὐρανόν.   705

ΑΛΛ. ὡς ὀξύθυμος. φέρε τί σοι δῶ καταφαγεῖν;
ἐπὶ τῷ φάγοις ἥδιστ᾽ ἄν; ἐπὶ βαλλαντίῳ;

698. Δήμητρά γ᾽ εἰ R, Ribb. Bergk Mitch. Holden. Δήμητρ᾽ ἔτ᾽ εἰ Reis. Mein. Dind. Kock in note, Zacher. Δήμητρ᾽ ἐάν other MSS. Cobet Blaydes.
700. So R. ἢν μή all other MSS. both times: but their readings in other respects are unmetrical.
701. κἀπεκροφήσας MSS. κἂν ἐκρ. Bothe vulg. κᾶτ᾽ ἐκρ. Seager Mitch. Dind. Blaydes.
707. φαγὼν ἥδοι᾽ ἄν Enger Vels. φαγὼν ἥδοιτ᾽ ἄν Kock. βαλλαντίῳ R vulg., βαλαντίῳ V and most MSS.; see Schanz Plato vii p. vii.

698. R alone gives the two 'solecisms,' γ᾽ immediately after a deity's name (Pors. *Adv.* 23) and εἰ with subj. But in the former case MSS. give γε *inf.* 1350, *Av.* 11, *Thesm.* 225, *Eccl.* 748. In the latter Cobet's short way of altering either the verb termination or the particle is no doubt usually right in comedy and prose. Yet Sophocles found an elegance in using εἰ with subj. *OC* 1443 &c.: and probably so did Cratinus (28) and Crates (5). Ar. in *Thesm.* 870 puts Sophocles' extraordinary μὴ ψεῦσον into the mouth of the terrified Mnesilochus: and here he may have done something similar with the alarmed and angry Cleon. The retort seems to mock at something special in Cleon's words. The same threat in the well-known case of Cinadon's conspiracy at Sparta Xen. *Hell.* iii 3. 6 ἡδέως ἂν καὶ ὠμῶν ἐσθίειν αὐτῶν.
700—1. 'Drink you up and gulp you up too, though I burst myself for it': the sentence being constructed like those mentioned by Shilleto on Thucyd. i 20. 3. For ἐκροφεῖν see on 51; add Plato com. 149 τὸ ἔψημα ἐκροφήσας: also Posidon. ap. Athen. iv 152 C ἀπορροφοῦσι (mead), Clearchus com. 1 (ap. Athen. x 426 A) ἐπιρρόφει, Artemid.

Oneirocr. i 31 ἄνευ ὀδόντων οὐκ ἔστι χρήσασθαι ὑγιεινῇ τροφῇ ἀλλὰ ῥοφήματι καὶ χολῷ, and the cases of ῥυφέω ῥύφημα in Hippocrates: I do not see any point here except that he beats Cleon in the game of brag by using two to one of the three verbs applied to taking food and drink. Lucian *bis acc.* 15 πολλοὶ οἱ κᾶν ἐπὶ τριωβόλῳ διαρραγῆναι ἕτοιμοι.
703—4. ἰδού, see on 87. οἷον, see on 367. ἔσχατον θεώμ. 'in the back seats'; the price for unreserved seats was probably the same in all parts of the Attic theatre; but the audience may have been to some extent classified, Alexis 41 ἐνταῦθα περὶ τὴν ἐσχάτην δεῖ κερκίδα ὑμᾶς καθιζούσας θεωρεῖν ὡς ξένας: in Rome the back seats were like our gallery, Seneca *tranq. an.* 11. 8 *mimicas ineptias et verba ad summam caveam spectantia*, Plut. *Titus* 19 ἐπ᾽ ἐσχάτοις που καθήμενος ἀτίμως.
706—7. ὡς ὀξύθυμος is probably said to the chorus, cf. ὡς ἀλαζών 269, ὡς δριμύς *Pax* 257.
Attics always said ἐσθίειν ὄψον ἐπὶ σίτῳ, ἀλφίτοις &c. (Blaydes on *Ach.* 835): the exceptions are non-Attic, as the Megarian παίειν ἐφ᾽ ἁλὶ τὰν μάδδαν *Ach.* 835, and late, as Plut. *virt. et vit.* 101 D

ΠΑ. ἐξαρπάσομαί σου τοῖς ὄνυξι τἄντερα.

ΑΛΛ. ἀπονυχιῶ σου τὰν πρυτανείῳ σιτία.

ΠΑ. ἕλξω σε πρὸς τὸν δῆμον, ἵνα δῷς μοι δίκην. 710

ΑΛΛ. κἀγὼ δέ σ᾽ ἕλξω καὶ διαβαλῶ πλείονα.

ΠΑ. ἀλλ᾽, ὦ πόνηρε, σοὶ μὲν οὐδὲν πείθεται·
     ἐγὼ δ᾽ ἐκείνου καταγελῶ γ᾽ ὅσον θέλω.

ΑΛΛ. ὡς σφόδρα σὺ τὸν δῆμον σεαυτοῦ νενόμικας.

ΠΑ. ἐπίσταμαι γὰρ αὐτὸν οἷς ψωμίζεται. 715

ΑΛΛ. κᾆθ᾽ ὥσπερ αἱ τιτθαί γε σιτίζεις κακῶς.
     μασώμενος γὰρ τῷ μὲν ὀλίγον ἐντίθης,
     αὐτὸς δ᾽ ἐκείνου τριπλάσιον κατέσπακας.

711. διαβαλῶ γε V and seven other MSS., δέ γε being natural.
712. πόνηρε RV and most MSS. rightly. πονηρέ vulg.
716. καθῶσπερ R. καθώσπερ and κάθως περ most MSS., Suidas &c. κᾆθ᾽ ὥσπερ
V and vulg. τίτθαί γε R &c. τῖτθαί γε A. τιτθαί γε Bergk (on accent, see Chandler
Greek Acc. § 87).
717. μασσώμενος RV: the σσ is probably etymological (Bezzenb. in *Bezz. Beitr.*
vii 62), but unattic.

ἄρτον ἐπὶ τύρῳ ἔσθοντες, *tranq. an.* 3. 466 D
αὐτόπυρον ἐπ᾽ ἐλαίαις σιτεῖται; except the
comic absurdity *fr.* 528 ἐπὶ τῷ ταρίχει τὸν
γέλωτα κατέδομαι. 'What *bread* would
you like best?' Cf. on 1140.
708—9. Cf. 205: ἀπονυχίζω, *claw
out*, for the retort: elsewhere ὀνυχίζω, ἀπονυχίζω, ἐξονυχίζω mean either *pare nails*
or *test closely*: σιτία, cf. on 575.
712—3. ὦ πόνηρε was the commonest vocative of contempt: ὦ κακέ
never occurs: see on 181. καταγελῶ,
'make a fool of.' The Ionic θέλω is
hardly used by Ar. except in quotation or
parody (H. W. Smyth *Ionic Dialect* § 588):
Lys. 1216 and this passage seem to be
exceptions: Van Leeuwen on *Vesp.* 493
would alter them.
714—5. ὡς σφόδρα as *Ran.* 41, *fr.*
198. 11. νομίζω, *hold, believe*, as ground
for action; answered by the strong word
ἐπίσταμαι. Editors quote Ter. *Adelphi*
898 *plebem facio meam*, Ovid *ars am.* ii
259 *fac plebem, mihi crede, tuam.*
ψωμίζω (akin to *spuo, spuma* probably),
explained in 717: cf. *Lys.* 19, *Thesm.*
692. Aristot. *Rhet.* iii 4. 3 quotes from
Pericles a metaphor comparing the Sa-
mians to infants at nurse, and from a
certain Democrates the metaphor in our

passage slightly coarsened. Democrates
was a contemporary of Demosthenes, and
one would think must have stolen the
idea from Aristophanes, whose credit
Aristotle does not much care to uphold.
Sextus Emp. *adv. math.* ii 42 also gives
the metaphor of demagogues.
716. κᾆτα (*indignantis*)...γε is just
what is required.
σιτίζω, a rare word, used of feeding
children (Herod. vi 52 ὀκότερον τῶν παίδων πρότερον λούει καὶ σιτίζει), cocks (Xen.
Symp. 4. 9), dogs (Isocr. *Demon.* 29),
young ravens (Aristot. *HA* vi 6. 563ᵇ 12):
the military *provision* is always ἐπισιτί-
ζομαι. Cf. Theophr. *Char.* 20 τὸ παιδίον
τῆς τίτθης ἀφελόμενος μασώμενος σιτίζειν
αὐτός. The word seems to have died
out: Dion. Hal. *de Isaeo* 4 (592. 5 Reiske)
only quotes it from an ἀρχαῖος ῥήτωρ
attacking Demosthenes, and Athenaeus
xii 530 C has σιτεῖσθαι where an Attic
would have used the more pointed σιτίζεσθαι (yet ix 376 B λαρινεύεσθαι ὅπερ ἐστὶ
σιτίζεσθαι).
717—8. ἐντίθης, see on 51.
κατέσπακας, gnomic perfect, rare compared to the aorist: *Vesp.* 561, *Ran.* 970,
Kock on Antiphanes 204. 3.
Antiphanes 204. 12 ὅταν τὴν ἔνθεσιν

ΠΑ. καὶ νὴ Δί' ὑπό γε δεξιότητος τῆς ἐμῆς
δύναμαι ποεῖν τὸν δῆμον εὐρὺν καὶ στενόν. 720

ΑΛΛ. χὠ πρωκτὸς οὑμὸς τουτογὶ σοφίζεται.

ΠΑ. οὐκ, ὦγάθ', ἐν βουλῇ με δόξεις καθυβρίσαι.
ἴωμεν ἐς τὸν δῆμον. ΑΛΛ. οὐδὲν κωλύει·
ἰδού, βάδιζε, μηδὲν ἡμᾶς ἰσχέτω.

ΠΑ. ὦ Δῆμε, δεῦρ' ἔξελθε. ΑΛΛ. νὴ Δί', ὦ πάτερ,   725
ἔξελθε δῆτ'. ΠΑ. ὦ Δημίδιον ὦ φίλτατον,
ἔξελθ', ἵν' εἰδῇς οἷα περιυβρίζομαι.

ΔΗ. τίνες οἱ βοῶντες; οὐκ ἄπιτ' ἀπὸ τῆς θύρας;
τὴν εἰρεσιώνην μου κατεσπαράξατε.

---

723. ἐς RM. εἰς other MSS. ὡς Mein. Dind. Vels. Kock.
724. βαδίζω B Blaydes. ΠΑ. βάδιζε. ΑΛΛ. μηδέν Kock: Wilam. *Herm.* xiv
185 arranges ΠΑ. ἰδού, βαδίζω. ΑΛΛ. μηδέν.
726. , ὦ Δημίδιον. ΠΑ. ὦ φίλτατε Cobet *NL* 53 Vels.: Kock gives the whole
line to ΑΛΛ. Wilam. omits it. MSS. omit the second ὦ.
727. Elm. and vulg. for οἷάπερ ὑβρ.: the line comes after 729 in MSS. except R
and two others: so Kock Wilam.   **728.** ἐκ τῆς R.
729. κατασπαράξετε Cobet *Mnemos.* n.s. ii 421.

ἐντὸς ἤδη τῶν ὀδόντων τυγχάνῃς κατ-
εσπακώς.

719—20. εὐρύς is curiously rare in
Attic: it is almost confined to passages of
epic reference, as Soph. *Trach.* 115, *Av.*
693, Aeschin. *Ctes.* 135, and of express
contrast to στενός as here, Plato *Phaedo*
111 D, *Tim.* 66 D, *Legg.* v 737 A, Aristot.
Meteor. iii 1. 370ᵇ 18.
721. σοφίζομαι of political artifice,
Aristot. *Pol.* vi (iv) 13. 1 ὅσα σοφίζονται
πρὸς τὸν δῆμον.
722. 'You won't get the credit of
bullying me in the council.' καθυβρίζω
may take gen. or acc., and it is difficult
to see any distinction in meaning, such as
would hold in the case of κατα- compounds of intransitive verbs (see on 286):
ὑβρίζω is sometimes transitive.
723. Ar. has κωλῦω in iambics (972,
fr. 156: so Antiphanes 125. 4, Anaxilas
25. 2, Menander 367. 2 in trochaics),
κωλύω in anapaests, *Pax* 499, *Av.* 463,
Lys. 607.
724. ἰδού, as 121.

725—6. πάτερ, to mark στοργή (769)
and kinship: Cleon's tone is insolently
familiar. Other arrangements of the
speakers (as old as the scholiast) spoil
this contrast of tone. Cobet *NL* 52—3
denies ὦ δέσποτ' ὦναξ and the like, but
Blaydes on *Ach.* 475 quotes *Pax* 1198 ὦ
φίλτατ' ὦ Τρυγαῖε, *Vesp.* 1512, *Thesm.*
210, *Eccl.* 1129, Soph. *Phil.* 799, Eurip.
Cycl. 266.
729. At the Pyanopsia and the Thargelia the εἰρεσιώνη, an olive-twig decked
with wool and various harvest-produce,
was offered to Apollo, after a procession
and song, given by schol. here and Plut.
Theseus 22: similar twigs were placed at
the doors of private houses (cf. *Vesp.* 399).
It seems to have also been offered to the
dead as an honour, Eupolis 119, Alciphro
iii 37. 1, *CIA* iii 1337. 10. Mannhardt
Antike Wald- und Feldkulte ch. iv first
described the usage fully, and showed its
connexion with similar usages (*Erntemai*
&c.). If, as Mannhardt thinks (p. 221),
the symbol was set only at the doors of
farmers or landowners, Demos would be

τίς, ὦ Παφλαγών, ἀδικεῖ σε; ΠΑ. διὰ σὲ
τύπτομαι 730
ὑπὸ τουτουὶ καὶ τῶν νεανίσκων. ΔΗ. τιή;
ΠΑ. ὁτιὴ φιλῶ σ᾽, ὦ Δῆμ᾽, ἐραστής τ᾽ εἰμὶ σός.
ΔΗ. σὺ δ᾽ εἶ τίς ἐτεόν; ΑΛΛ. ἀντεραστὴς τουτουί,
ἐρῶν πάλαι σου, βουλόμενός τέ σ᾽ εὖ ποιεῖν,
ἄλλοι τε πολλοὶ καὶ καλοί τε κἀγαθοί. 735
ἀλλ᾽ οὐχ οἷοί τ᾽ ἐσμὲν διὰ τουτονί. σὺ γὰρ
ὅμοιος εἶ τοῖς παισὶ τοῖς ἐρωμένοις·
τοὺς μὲν καλούς τε κἀγαθοὺς οὐ προσδέχει,
σαυτὸν δὲ λυχνοπώλαισι καὶ νευρορράφοις
καὶ σκυτοτόμοις καὶ βυρσοπώλαισιν δίδως. 740

737. om. Wilam.
739—40. -πώλαισι-ν R and vulg. -πώλησι-ν or -πώλησι-ν other MSS., perhaps rightly, see crit. note on 659.
740. -πώλαις ἐπιδίδως Mein. after Cobet *Mnemos.* i 416 : ἐπιδίδωμι 'se donner,' though the usage seems to be late, Plut. *Her. malign.* 11. 856 E, Alciphro iii 8. 2, 64. 3.

marked at once by this exclamation as more of a countryman than a cockney.

730—1. Cleon thinks to damage the Sausage-man by classing him with the young bloods, and his rival makes no objection, but adopts their tone. The young knights were specially called νεανίσκοι, a colloquial equivalent to ἔφηβοι: Thucydides used the word in this application only, viii 92. ὁ τῶν ἱππέων νεανίσκοι, and viii 69. 4 where οἱ εἴκοσι καὶ ἑκατὸν νεανίσκοι are no doubt knights (is Ἕλληνες their name as a Panhellenic ἑταιρεία?): on both occasions they are strongly anti-democratic: so the oligarchic νεανίσκοι in Xen. *Hell.* ii 3. 23 are knights. In Sparta κόροι was the regular name for ἱππῆς, Inscr. in Roberts no. 245 : and *juvenes* often means *young knights* in Livy (ii 12. 15 &c.). Droysen suggests *Junkern* as an equivalent: cf. Walpole's 'the Boys.'

732. Pericles had used ἐραστὴς τῆς πόλεως of the true Athenian patriot, Thucyd. ii 43. 1 : see on 1341 *inf.*

733. ἀντεραστής, like *pelex*, takes gen. of the rival: ἀντεράω takes dat. of the rival, gen. of the person loved.

735. The forms allowed were καλὸς

κἀγαθός and (much more rare) καλός τε κἀγαθός, as *Nub.* 101, *Ran.* 728 : crasis was necessary (Schanz Plato *Theaet.* prolegg. v).

737—8. The lover's tone of 732—5 gives at once an opportunity for expostulation. προσδέχομαι implies the special sense as in Plut. *quaest. conv.* ix 1. 737 B, *soll. anim.* 35. 983 A, Aristot. *HA* vi 23. 577ᵇ 15 (Latin *admitto*): cf. Aeschines *FL* 166 οὐ προσδέχεται δίκαιος ἔρως πονηρίαν.

739—40. The common complaint of καλοὶ κἀγαθοί in a democracy, echoed by Comedy, as Eupolis 117. There was some surprise at Sophocles' election as στρατηγός with Pericles, Gilbert *Inn. Gesch.* 4. λυχν. means Hyperbolus, the other three words are probably variations of contempt for Cleon (schol. adds Lysicles for no reason). νευρορράφος is *a cobbler*: Plato *Rep.* iv 421 A selects this trade to contrast with statemanship. The sedentary nature of such work (σκυτοτομεῖ καθήμενος *Plut.* 162) seemed specially 'unsportsmanlike.' For discussion of the leather-trade and its branches see Blümner *Gewerbe und Künste* i 268.

ΠΑ. εὖ γὰρ ποιῶ τὸν δῆμον. ΑΛΛ. εἰπέ μοι, τί
δρῶν;
ΠΑ. ὅτι τῶν στρατηγῶν ὑποδραμὼν τῶν ἐκ Πύλου,
πλεύσας ἐκεῖσε, τοὺς Λάκωνας ἤγαγον.
ΑΛΛ. ἐγὼ δὲ περιπατῶν γ' ἀπ' ἐργαστηρίου
ἕψοντος ἑτέρου τὴν χύτραν ὑφειλόμην. 745
ΠΑ. καὶ μὴν ποήσας αὐτίκα μάλ' ἐκκλησίαν,
ὦ Δῆμ', ἵν' εἰδῇς ὁπότερος νῷν ἐστί σοι
εὐνούστερος, διάκρινον, ἵνα τοῦτον φιλῇς.
ΑΛΛ. ναὶ ναὶ διάκρινον δῆτα, πλὴν μὴ 'ν τῇ πυκνί.

741. εἰπέ μοι νῦν RM. εἰπέ νυν and εἰπὲ νῦν rest: εἰπέ νυν never occurs in
Comedy exc. Vesp. 996 (Kock). εἰπέ μοι vulg.
742. This is practically the reading of all good MSS. Editors have wished to
introduce more point. ὅ, τι; Elm. Blaydes Kock. ἀποδραμόντων K. F. Hermann. τοὺς
στρατηγοὺς ὑποδραμὼν τοὺς Brunck. τῶν στρατηγῶν ὑποδραμὼν τοὺς Bentl. ὑποδρα-
μόντων Mein. (withdrawn in Vind. Aristoph. 61). ὑποτρεμόντων Kock Merry. τὸν
στρατηγὸν ὑποδραμὼν τὸν B Vels. except that he has ὑπεκδραμὼν from six MSS.
747—8. ὦ Δημίδιον, εἶθ' ὁπότερος Herw.: the slight awkwardness of the double
ἵνα may be intentional, cf. on, 694. ἵνα τοῦτον RM vulg. ἵν' ἐκεῖνον other MSS.
Brunck.

741. Cleon puts on the cap and claims that he can beat the καλοὶ κἀγαθοί on their own ground of military affairs.
742. Kock's ὑποτρεμόντων expresses what Cleon and many others did say of Nicias, and would be a very pointed answer to the καλούς τε κἀγαθοὺς of 738. A scholium καταδραμὼν τοὺς ἐν Πύλῳ στρατηγούς· ἅμα δὲ ὅτι καὶ συνεχῶς μέμνη-ται τοῦ ἐν Πύλῳ κατορθώματος seems to imply a different reading from any in the MSS. ὑποτρέχω could not take gen. : ἐν σχήματι εἶπεν ἀντὶ τοῦ στρατηγούς schol. wrongly : στρατηγῶν must depend on Λά-κωνας in the MS. reading, which is satisfac-tory enough : the idea of running in before the generals is required, and is taken as a characteristic of Cleon in 1161. 743 looks tragic.
744—5. 'That's no better than to loaf and steal other men's pots and por-ridge at home as I've done.' ἕψω χύτραν ἔτνους is regular, Ran. 505, Eccl. 845. ἐργαστήριον, 'work-shop,' perhaps of slaves, or 'barber's shop,' as Athen. xii 518 A. The ἐργαστήρια are spoken of as meeting places for lounging and gossip, Isocr. Areop. 15, Callim. 9, Antiphanes

240, Plut. Nicias 12: the incident is trivial and easy in every way.
746. καὶ μὴν (without γε) to introduce a new proposal or detail, cf. inf. 970, 1232, see App. i.
ποεῖν ἐκκλησίαν generally implies that the ἐκκλησία is σύγκλητος or specially summoned : the nominative may be the name of an important magistrate or οἱ Ἀθηναῖοι. Cases are Thucyd. i 139. 3, ii 22. 1, iv 118. 14, vi 8. 2, viii 76. 2, Aeschin. Ctes. 66—7, Demosth. FL 185, Mid. 9, CIA i 40. 53—4 συνεχῶς ποεῖν τὰς ἐκκλησίας ἕως ἂν διαπραχθῇ, Ach. 169, Thesm. 301, Xen. Hell. i 7. 9, ii 2. 4, 19, vi 5. 33. ἐκκλησίαν ποεῖσθαι seems rare : I have noticed it of Athenians only in the doubtful Demosth. Syntax. 1, and in Cor. 213 of Boeotians.
748. εὔνους τῷ δήμῳ was synonymous with 'orthodox Athenian patriot,' cf. inf. 779, 788, 874.
διακρίνειν, not technical, decide: said of events, battles, persons &c. : especially as here of deciding between two rivals, Plato Legg. ii 659 B, Xen. Symp. 4. 20.
749. It is singular that so much discussion should have been required to

ΔH.   οὐκ ἂν καθιζοίμην ἐν ἄλλῳ χωρίῳ·   750
       ἀλλ' ὡς τὸ πρόσθε χρὴ παρεῖν' ἐς τὴν πύκνα.
ΑΛΛ.   οἴμοι κακοδαίμων, ὡς ἀπόλωλ'. ὁ γὰρ γέρων
       οἴκοι μὲν ἀνδρῶν ἐστι δεξιώτατος,
       ὅταν δ' ἐπὶ ταυτησὶ καθῆται τῆς πέτρας,
       κέχηνεν ὥσπερ ἐμποδίζων ἰσχάδας.   755
ΧΟΡ.   νῦν δή σε πάντα δεῖ κάλων ἐξιέναι σεαυτοῦ,
       καὶ λῆμα θούριον φορεῖν καὶ λόγους ἀφύκτους,

750. καθεξοίμην Bergk. **751.** ἐς RM Dind. Ribb. εἰς most MSS. ὡς S edd. vulg. ἀλλ' ἐς τὸ πρόσθε. χρῆν Mein. Zacher (with χρὴ). **754.** κάθηται MSS. **755.** ἐνστομίζων conj. Zacher. **756.** νῦν δή σε πάντα δεῖ VM edd. vulg. νῦν δὴ σε πάντα δὴ R. νῦν δεῖ σε παντά δὴ most MSS., Cobet *Misc. Crit.* 294 quoting Eurip. *Med.* 278: but Blaydes gives cases on the other side, as *Vesp.* 526, *Eccl.* 571.

identify the Pnyx: see Milchhöfer in Baumeister's *Denkm.* i 152—, Lolling in Iwan Müller's *Handbuch* iii 331—, Harrison and Verrall *Myth. and Mon.* 107—, Crow in *Papers of Amer. School at Athens* iv, Frazer on Pausan. i 29. 1. Before 400, meetings not on the Pnyx either were held during the rule of the 400 as those at Colonus (Thucyd. viii 67. 2), at Munychia (93. 1), the Dionysiac theatre (93. 3), or were called to decide questions of Ostracism, and perhaps other personal questions (Gilbert *Staatsalt.* i² 321).
750. Proposals to sit anywhere but in the Pnyx looked suspicious. The question of καθίζομαι and καθέζομαι may be settled by epigraphy some day. Meisterhans mentions only καθίζω, but that does not affect the middle forms. καθέζομαι and καθίζομαι are of course both found frequently, and both are inceptives (*take seat*) of κάθημαι (*sit*) in meaning. Demosth. *Mid.* 162 πρὶν καὶ προέδρους καθίζεσθαι.
751. πάριτ' ἐς τὸ πρόσθεν was an order at meetings (*Ach.* 43, *Eccl.* 129: hence παρελθεῖν of speakers?): this may have led to the reading of most MSS.
752. οἴμοι κακοδαίμων, comic exclamation, see on 1243 *inf.*
753. δεξιός, as often, of critics, cf. on 228: add Epicharmus 99. 2 Kaibel.
754. πέτρας: the Pnyx has still three rows of seats cut in the rock.
755. The simile is unexplained: and the inconsistent scholia show that the phrase was obscure even to the Alexan-

drians. It has been taken to mean (1) *stringing figs* for packing, πούς or πόδιον being part of the fig: cf. Varro *Res Rust.* i 41 *resticulas per ficus perserunt et eas cum inaruerunt complicant ac quo volunt mittunt* (Casaubon, Brunck, Bergk, Ribbeck), (2) *playing bob-fig* (Bergler, Mitchell, Merry, Piccolomini), (3) *trampling figs* into cases (Sir C. Newton after Hesychius), (4) *chewing figs*, like bee-keepers for bees in winter (Aristarchus, Symmachus). The last has the highest ancient authority and seems the least possible.
756. The main Agon, before Demus as judge, has two parts, the first in anapaests, 763—822, the second in iambic tetrameters, 843—910, as in the *Clouds* and *Frogs*, Ziel. *Gliederung* 19. The chorus introduces both parts in seven lines, 756—762=836—842: the asynartete metre of 757—8=837—8 is used by the chorus in *Vesp.* 249—, *Lys.* 256—8, as here in advice and in alternation with tetram. catalectics.
'Now spread all the sail you have': cf. Eurip. *Med.* 278 ἐχθροὶ γὰρ ἐξιᾶσι πάντα δὴ κάλων, *HF* 837 φόνιον ἐξίει κάλων, where see Wilam.: Plato *Protag.* 338 A πάντα κάλων ἐκτείνειν of argument, Lucian *Alex.* 57.
757. λῆμα, a favourite word of lyric and tragic poetry (not found in Epic and no doubt closely connected with the verb λάω so much used by the Dorians). Aristoph. has it in criticisms by the chorus of the dramatis personae, as *Nub.*

ὅτοισι τόνδ᾽ ὑπερβαλεῖ. ποικίλος γὰρ ἀνὴρ
κἀκ τῶν ἀμηχάνων πόρους εὐμήχανος πορίζειν.
πρὸς ταῦθ᾽ ὅπως ἕξει πολὺς καὶ λαμπρὸς ἐς τὸν
ἄνδρα.   760
ἀλλὰ φυλάττου, καὶ πρὶν ἐκεῖνον προσκεῖσθαί
σοι, πρότερον σὺ
τοὺς δελφῖνας μετεωρίζου καὶ τὴν ἄκατον παρα-
βάλλου.

759. Bentley for εὐμηχάνους of MSS.
760. ἔς MSS. and vulg. ἐπὶ Cobet *Mnemos.* i 416 Mein. Dind. Vels. Blaydes.
761. προσικεσθαί σου R. πρότερον R Dind. Vels. πρότερος other MSS. Bergk Mein. Kock.

457, 1350, *Thesm.* 459, and in the mock-heroics of Bacchus and Xanthias in *Ran.* 463, 500, 603. It is used by Herod., never in Attic prose (in an epigram, Demosth. *Cor.* 289). Dionys. Hal. has it in the phrase ὑπὸ λήματός τε καὶ προθυμίας (*Ant. Rom.* vi 12, ix 63). Lucian *Soloec.* 5 shows that after being revived in prose-writing it was apt to be confused with λῆμμα (see Hemsterhuis there).
So θούριος is tragic (*Ran.* 1289 from Aeschylus).
ἄφυκτος (often written ἄφευκτος after φεύγω, cf. ζευκτὸς, δεικτὸς &c.) is rightly act. of persons in *Nub.* 1047 σ᾽ ἔχω μέσον λαβὼν ἄφυκτον. In the passive sense it is specially used of questions (Plato *Theaet.* 165 B, *Euthyd.* 276 E) and arguments, Aeschin. *Ctes.* 17 πρὸς τὸν ἄφυκτον λόγον ὅν φησι Δημοσθένης, Lucian *Hermot.* 79 οἶδεν ὡς χρὴ ἐρέσθαι καὶ σοφίσασθαι καὶ πανουργῆσαι καὶ ἐς ἄφυκτα ἐμβαλεῖν.
758. οἷς τισι in hexameters, *Pax* 1279.
759. Blomfield on Aesch. *Prom.* 59 δεινὸς γὰρ εὑρεῖν κἀξ ἀμηχάνων πόρους, and Ribbeck here give parallels, which show that jingles like πόροι ἐξ ἀπόρων became common : *Eccl.* 236, Alexis 234.
760. πρὸς ταῦτα, not defiant as usual, nor with an imperative, though ὅπως ἕξει is equivalent to one : cf. on 622 and add Aesch. *Sept.* 57.
ἕξει..., see on 430 : Demosth. i *Aristog.* 57 ὡς πολὺς ἔπνει καὶ λαμπρός.
761. ἐν ἐκθέσει ἐστὶ τὸ ἔθιμον, διπλῆ ἀνάπαιστος τετράμετρος καταληκτικὴ schol.: cf. on 333.

The common military πρόσκειμαι as in 245 might be used of naval ship-to-ship encounters.
762. δελφῖνες were fish-shaped masses of iron or lead hung from yards and thence dropped on the enemies' ship. The schol. here quotes from Pherecrates' Ἄγριοι (12):

ὅδε δὴ δελφίς ἐστι μολυβδοῦς δελφινο-
φόρος τε κερούχος,
ὃς διακόψει τοὔδαφος αὐτῶν ἐμπίπτων
καὶ καταδύων.

They are not mentioned in naval history except in Thucyd. vii 41. 2, where the Syracusan triremes are stopped from pursuit by αἱ κεραῖαι αἱ ἀπὸ τῶν ὁλκάδων δελφινοφόροι ἠρμέναι. Pollux i 86 says the δελφίς was hung over the ἔμβολον (as masts were lowered for action), and Assmann (art. *Seewesen* in Baumeister's *Denkmäler*, p. 1613) gives a representation from a coin of Samos. So the Rhodians dropped fire on the enemy's deck, Polyb. xxi 5, Liv. xxxvii 30. 3, and Hiero's ship dropped stones, Athen. v 208 B.
τὴν ἄκ. παρ., 'get the boat ready for lowering,' 'lay it alongship.' The boat of a ship is generally λέμβος or ἐφόλκιον, Plut. *Pomp.* 73 ἐκέλευσε τοὺς ναύτας τὸ ἐφόλκιον παραβαλεῖν : but ἄκατος, which is generally an independent vessel of small size, was also used in this sense, Heliod. *Aethiop.* v 27, Agathias *Hist.* iii 21 (Dar. and Saglio). Breusing's explanation (*Nautik* 70) 'lay yourself alongside the enemy,' would imply, I suppose, that ἄκατος here is a pirate craft

ΠΑ. τῇ μὲν δεσποίνῃ Ἀθηναίῃ, τῇ τῆς πόλεως με-
δεούσῃ,
εὔχομαι, εἰ μὲν περὶ τὸν δῆμον τὸν Ἀθηναίων
γεγένημαι
βέλτιστος ἀνὴρ μετὰ Λυσικλέα καὶ Κύνναν καὶ
Σαλαβακχώ, 765
ὥσπερ νυνὶ μηδὲν δράσας δειπνεῖν ἐν τῷ πρυ-
τανείῳ·
εἰ δέ σε μισῶ καὶ μὴ περὶ σοῦ μάχομαι μόνος
ἀντιβεβηκώς,

763. Ἀθηναίᾳ VM edd. vulg. Ἀθηναίῃ R and MSS. vulg. Bentl. Kock Wecklein
curae epigr. 12.
764. τῶν Ἀθ. MSS.
767. ἀντιβεβηκὼς R and edd. vulg. ἀντιβεβληκὼς MSS. vulg.

as it sometimes is : but the laying the trireme's boat alongside, whether for precaution or defence, is a more likely metaphor. Cf. the naval sense of παραβολή and παράβλημα. Epicrates 10 κατάβαλλε τἀκάτια is not parallel, as ἀκάτιον means a *sail*.

763. His elaborate periodic exordium is interrupted before the first μὲν is answered. Cf. on 581—5 and 654: Athena is the democratic deity. Such protestations are criticised by Aeschines (*Ctes.* 248) ἡ γὰρ εὔνοια καὶ τὸ τῆς δημοκρατίας ὄνομα κεῖται μὲν ἐν μέσῳ, φθάνουσι δ' ἐπ' αὐτὰ καταφεύγοντες τῷ λόγῳ ὡς ἐπὶ πολὺ οἱ τοῖς ἔργοις πλεῖστον ἀπέχοντες. The longer form of the goddess' name in this serious protestation, and so *Pax* 271, *Av.* 828, with some of her titles: Ἀθηνᾶ in less formal appeal, *Pax* 218. Meisterhans, § 14. 1, shows that though Ἀθηνᾶ occurs early, Ἀθηναία is the regular form in inscriptions till the fourth century. Ἀθηναίη is unknown to ordinary Attic (Reinach *Épig. gr.* 260, Smyth *Ionic Dialect* § 78) : it no doubt marks an old ritual formula, like μεδέουσα, see on 585 and 659, and Paton and Hicks, *Inscr. of Cos*, no. 148, Foucart *Bull. Corr. Hell.* xii 133. Whether accidentally or not, μεδέουσα occurs generally when very strong appeals are made to the deity, Athena here and in the famous case Plut.

Themistocles 10, Artemis Eurip. *Hipp.* 167, Aphrodite *Lys.* 833.

764. This use of περὶ is chiefly found in the orators: Lysias 13. 2 ἄνδρας ὄντας ἀγαθοὺς περὶ τὸ πλῆθος τὸ ὑμέτερον, 60 οὕτω χρηστὸς ἦν περὶ τὸν δῆμον, 14. 31 τοῦ πατρὸς χρηστοῦ περὶ τὴν πόλιν γεγενημένου, 31. 30: it is common (alternating with εἰς and πρὸς) in inscriptions recording decrees of thanks and honour (Meisterhans § 83. 44, Reinach *Épigr. gr.* 359).

765. 'Since Lysicles—and Aspasia' (cf. on 132) is expected, but he brings out the names of two notorious courtesans. This idea of Müller-Strübing's (*Arist.* 586) is reasonable. Cleon's eyes are called Κύννης ὀφθαλμοὶ *Vesp.* 1032 = *Pax* 755 : the Κυννίδαι were a respectable family (Töpffer *Att. Geneal.* 301—), but our name is probably a nickname like Salabaccho (cf. *salaputium* : though some take it as Semitic and compare Salambo). Cynna is found again as the name of an Amazon (Pauly-Wissowa *Encycl.* i 1758), of a daughter of Philip of Macedonia and of an Illyrian princess.

766. For μηδὲν δράσας cf. the οὐδὲν ἠδικηκόσιν of *Plut.* 805.

767. μισόδημος)(εὔνους τῷ δήμῳ, *Vesp.* 474.
As the Epic ἀμφιβεβηκὼς means 'standing as protector,' ἀντιβεβηκὼς means 'standing as adversary' of attacking enemies.

ἀπολοίμην καὶ διαπρισθείην κατατμηθείην τε
λέπαδνα.

ΑΛΛ. κἄγωγ᾽, ὦ Δῆμ᾽, εἰ μή σε φιλῶ καὶ μὴ στέργω,
κατατμηθεὶς
ἑψοίμην ἐν περικομματίοις· κεἰ μὴ τούτοισι
πέποιθας,   770
ἐπὶ ταυτησὶ κατακνησθείην ἐν μυττωτῷ μετὰ
τυροῦ
καὶ τῇ κρεάγρᾳ τῶν ὀρχιπέδων ἑλκοίμην ἐς
Κεραμεικόν.

ΠΑ. καὶ πῶς ἂν ἐμοῦ μᾶλλόν σε φιλῶν, ὦ Δῆμε,
γένοιτο πολίτης;
ὃς πρῶτα μέν, ἡνίκ᾽ ἐβούλευόν σοι, χρήματα
πλεῖστ᾽ ἀπέδειξα

768. διατμηθείην MSS. vulg. except R.   **774.** ἐβούλευον, σοὶ χρ. Kock.

---

768. A wish taken from his trade, as the Sausage-man's (771) from his.

λέπαδνα, the breast-bands fastening the yoke: hence ἀνάγκας λέπαδνον, Aesch. *Agam.* 217. The phrase looks like a reminiscence of *Ach.* 300 ὃν (Κλέωνα) κατατεμῶ τοῖσιν ἱππεῦσι καττύματα. The second accus. (without εἰς, which the schol. supplies) after κατατέμνω and other verbs of the kind seems regular in Attic: cf. 370 δερῶ σε θύλακον κλοπῆς, and similar cases quoted by Elmsley and Blaydes on *Ach.* 300; add Herod. i 180 τὸ ἄστυ κατατέτμηται τὰς ὁδοὺς ἰθείας.

769—. στέργω, cf. ὦ πάτερ 725. περικομμ. cf. on 372: they are mentioned with ἀκροκώλια, which were boiled, Athen. iii ch. 48—9, 95 A—96 C.

ταυτησὶ Mitchell thinks means the rock: but editors are agreed to understand the table or dresser which the Sausage-man brought with him (152): then τῇ κρεάγρᾳ means his own flesh-hook. If this is right, it is an argument against supposing a change of scene. μυττωτὸς κατασκευάζεται ἀπὸ τυροῦ (grated) καὶ σκορόδου καὶ ᾠοῦ καὶ ἐλαίου καὶ πράσου schol.: the grating of cheese (at least as old as *Il.* xi 639) was thought to bring it into artistic cookery.

772. κρεάγρα is a cook's flesh-hook, *Vesp.* 1155, Anaxippus 6 κρεάγραν θύειαν τυρόκνηστιν, *Anth. Pal.* vi 101. 6, 305. 5 : then a hook for buckets *Eccl.* 1002, Pollux x 31.

It is natural to see a reference to the dragging of executed criminals to exposure or burial; κρεάγρᾳ ἕλκομαι would answer exactly to the Roman *unco trahi* (Mayor on Juv. 10. 66), and Casaubon quotes from the *Apocolocyntosis* Seneca's joke on Claudius "unco tractus est in caelum" (this is given, not in the *Apocol.*, but by Dio Cass. lx 35. 3 as Gallio's jest: and the Greek for *uncus* there is ἄγκιστρον). I can find no mention of such dragging in Greek usage; but the line is a comic combination of wishes for the utmost ignominy (*Plut.* 955) and a patriot's burial in the Ceramicus. ἀπάτησις τοῦ δήμου was a recognised offence (Meier and Schöm. *Att. Process*[2] 424), punishable by the barathrum (as in Miltiades' case, Herod. vi 136, Plato *Gorg.* 516 D).

773. καὶ πῶς ἄν, cf. on 128. πολίτης in a place of emphasis.

774. 'When I was only a Councillor, not Strategus.' The Council controlled finance in the way of letting the customs &c., exacting payment of state-debts, and

ἐν τῷ κοινῷ, τοὺς μὲν στρεβλῶν, τοὺς δ' ἄγχων,
τοὺς δὲ μεταιτῶν,   775
οὐ φροντίζων τῶν ἰδιωτῶν οὐδενός, εἰ σοὶ χαριοίμην.

ΑΛΛ. τοῦτο μέν, ὦ Δῆμ', οὐδὲν σεμνόν· κἀγὼ γὰρ
τοῦτό σε δράσω.
ἁρπάζων γὰρ τοὺς ἄρτους σοι τοὺς ἀλλοτρίους
παραθήσω.
ὡς δ' οὐχὶ φιλεῖ σ' οὐδ' ἔστ' εὔνους, τοῦτ' αὐτό
σε πρῶτα διδάξω,
ἀλλ' ἢ διὰ τοῦτ' αὔθ' ὁτιή σου τῆς ἀνθρακιᾶς
ἀπολαύει.   780

---

fixing the tribute payable by the allies: and their strictness in business varied, Lysias 30. 22 εἰδὼς ὅτι ἡ βουλὴ ἡ ἀεὶ βουλεύουσα, ὅταν μὲν ἔχῃ ἱκανὰ χρήματα εἰς διοίκησιν, οὐδὲν ἐξαμαρτάνει, ὅταν δὲ εἰς ἀπορίαν καταστῇ, ἀναγκάζεται εἰσαγγελίας δέχεσθαι καὶ δημεύειν τὰ τῶν πολιτῶν καὶ τῶν ῥητόρων τοῖς τὰ πονηρότατα λέγουσι πείθεσθαι.

ἀποδείκνυμι λόγον, 'render account,' Herod. vii 118, 119; ἀποδείκνυμι χρήματα 'show a profit' (there was no regular budget); cf. Demosth. i *Aph*. 19 οὐδ' ὁτιοῦν ἀποδείκνυσιν, Alexis 105 σφαῖραν ἀπέδειξε τὴν πατρῴαν οὐσίαν, a Delphian inscription (Collitz 1683, Roberts 229) οἱ πεντεκαίδεκα ἀπέδειξαν μνᾶς δεκατέτορες. ἀποφαίνω, which runs along with ἀποδείκνυμι in most meanings, is more common in this sense.

Gilbert (*Inn. Gesch.* 131) is probably right in referring this to the εἰσφορά, first raised in 428—7. Resistance to such a tax would be natural with the peace-party: and this boast, implying the setting of poor against rich, brings out just what the poet wants to condemn in Cleon. στρεβλῶν must not be taken literally: at least we have no right to suppose that men were compelled to pay εἰσφορὰ under torture, which was illegal in the case of Athenian citizens by the psephism of Scamandrius (Andoc. *myst.* 43). ἄγχω of harassing debtors, as Lucian *Symp.* 32 οὐδὲ ἄγχω τοὺς μαθητὰς ἢν μὴ κατὰ καιρὸν ἀποδῶσι τοὺς μισθούς (πνίγω was Hellen-

istic S. Matth. 18. 28). μεταιτῶ, a rare compound, generally means 'blackmail,' 'claim a share' as an accomplice or partner in some dubious transaction, Herod. iv 146, vii 150, *Vesp.* 972, Demosth. *FL* 222: later it means 'beg' (μεταίτης *beggar*), Lucian *Necyom.* 17, Plut. *Stoic. absurd.* 5. 1058 C: does it mean more than '*dunning*' here?

776. The defence of συκοφάνται, cf. *Plut.* 907—919.

χαριοίμην, fut. opt. as quasi-oblique, cf. Xen. *Anab.* i 4. 7 ᾧκτειρον εἰ ἁλώσοιντο.

777. οὐδὲν σεμνόν, 'nothing to brag about,' correlative to σεμνύνομαι, Arist. *Eth. Nic.* iv 8. 1124^b 20 τῶν μὲν γὰρ ὑπερέχειν χαλεπὸν καὶ σεμνόν, τῶν δὲ ῥᾴδιον, καὶ ἐν ἐκείνοις μὲν σεμνύνεσθαι οὐκ ἀγεννές, ἐν δὲ τοῖς ταπεινοῖς φορτικόν: often colloquial or mock-serious, Plato *Crat.* 392 A οὐκ οἴει τοῦτο σεμνόν τι εἶναι, γνῶναι ὅπῃ ποτὲ ὀρθῶς ἔχει ἐκεῖνον τὸν ποταμὸν Ξάνθον καλεῖν μᾶλλον ἢ Σκάμανδρον; Arist. *Eth. Eud.* iii 1. 1228^b 11 εἰ μὲν δὴ τὰ ἑτέρῳ φοβερά, οὐθὲν σεμνὸν φαίη ἄν τις εἶναι, *Pol.* vii (vi) 3. 1325^a 26 οὐθὲν γὰρ τό γε δούλῳ, ᾗ δοῦλος, χρῆσθαι σεμνόν, Plut. *frat. am.* 479 E, *de seips. laud.* 17. 545 F.

778. γάρ, of explanation as 644 &c.

779—80. διδάσκω, often of proving one's contention in the Agon, *Vesp.* 519, *Plut.* 582. οὐκ (μὴ) ἀλλ' ἤ, as *Pax* 475 οὐδ' οἶδε γ' εἵλκον οὐδὲν ἀργεῖοι πάλαι ἀλλ' ἢ κατεγέλων τῶν ταλαιπωρουμένων, Plato *Crat.* 438 B εἴπερ μὴ ἔστι τὰ πράγματα

σὲ γάρ, ὃς Μήδοισι διεξιφίσω περὶ τῆς χώρας
Μαραθῶνι,
καὶ νικήσας ἡμῖν μεγάλως ἐγγλωττοτυπεῖν
παρέδωκας,
ἐπὶ ταῖσι πέτραις οὐ φροντίζει σκληρῶς σε
καθήμενον οὕτως,
οὐχ ὥσπερ ἐγὼ ῥαψάμενός σοι τουτὶ φέρω.
ἀλλ' ἐπαναίρου,

781. ἐν Μαραθῶνι MSS.

μαθεῖν ἀλλ' ἢ ἐκ τῶν ὀνομάτων: so after interrog. *Ran.* 438 τουτὶ τί ἦν τὸ πρᾶγμα ἀλλ' ἢ Διὸς Κόρινθος ἐν τοῖς στρώμασιν; The ἀλλ' in such phrases may have developed out of ἀλλ' ἢ with οὐδὲν preceding, as in *Lys.* 427 οὐδὲν ποιῶν ἀλλ' ἢ καπηλεῖον σκοπῶν, then with ἄλλο...ἀλλ' ἢ as Plato *Phaedo* 97 D οὐδὲν ἄλλο σκοπεῖν προσήκει...ἀλλ' ἢ τὸ ἄριστον. Anyhow the phrase uses to mean *simply, merely*, but only after a negative or its equivalent, *inf.* 1397, Thucyd. vii 50. 3 οὐδὲ ὁ Νικίας ἔτι ὁμοίως ἠναντιοῦτο, ἀλλ' ἢ μὴ φανερῶς γε ἀξιῶν ψηφίζεσθαι, cf. v 60. 1, Xen. *Hell.* i 7. 15 οὗτος δ' οὐκ ἔφη ἀλλ' ἢ κατὰ νόμον πάντα ποιήσειν and cases in Aristotle (see Bonitz's index). 'Except merely for the one reason of enjoying your fire': ἀνθρακιὰ is the heap of charcoal on the hearth or an ἀνθράκιον.

781. διαξιφίζομαι, middle by the rule illustrated in Cobet's *NL* 625—6 that compounds with δια- implying *contest* are put in the middle. ξιφίζω, ξιφισμός, ξίφισμα, ξιφίνδα all mean a dance or game with swords: and possibly διαξιφίζομαι, which is not quoted except from this passage, means 'played the sword-game with' the Persian. Plutarch *de genio Socr.* 597 F has ἀγὼν δὲ ἦν τῷ Πελοπίδᾳ πρὸς τὸν Λεοντίδην καὶ διαξιφισμός.

ἐν Μαραθῶνι, all MSS. of course wrongly. Such a strong case of interpolation goes far to justify Cobet *VL* 30, 201, *NL* 95, 321 in condemning ἐν in all such cases, Μαραθῶνι being exactly parallel to οἴκοι: so ἐν has had to be omitted in Eupolis *fr.* 216 ὃς τὴν Μαραθῶνι κατέλιφ' ἡμῖν οὐσίαν. Meisterhans § 82. 23 quotes no case of ἐν before 315 B.C., but the Index to vol. i of *CIA* shows that ἐν

Κολλυτῷ, ἐν Μελίτῃ, ἐν 'Ελαιεῖ were not uncommon in the fifth century. See on 785 and 1334. The Athenian Demos is always in his ideal condition the Demos of τὰ Μηδικά (τὰ Περσικά not before Plato *Legg.* i 642 D).

782. ἐγγλωττοτυπεῖν: the ἐν- is idiomatic, cf. Cobet *NL* 476, 775, *Av.* 38 πᾶσι κοινὸν ἐναποτῖσαι χρήματα, and Blaydes there: Eurip. *Supp.* 535 ἐνοικῆσαι, Plato *Phaedr.* 228 E ἐμαυτόν σοι ἐμμελετᾶν παρέχειν: Cope on Arist. *Rhet.* ii 4. 12. The metaphor is from 'minting' or 'moulding' phrases: cf. γνωμοτυπεῖν. μεγάλως, see on 151.

783. πέτραι, of the Pnyx, as elsewhere in this play, 313, 754, 956.

φροντίζω with ταῦτα, ἄλλο οὐδὲν &c. is well known: but no other case of an ordinary acc. construction is quoted. Kühner-Gerth *Griech. Gram.* § 417. 6 shows that such verbs as κήδω, ἐπιμελοῦμαι, φροντίζω tended to take accus.: cf. τὰ μετέωρα φροντιστής Plato *Apol.* 18 C.

784. The Greek idiom is different here from the English, 'unlike me, who bring,' or 'but I on the other hand': cf. Plato *Gorg.* 522 A τοὺς νεωτάτους ὑμῶν διαφθείρει τέμνων τε καὶ κάων...οὐχ ὥσπερ ἐγὼ πολλὰ καὶ ἡδέα καὶ παντοδαπὰ ηὔσχουν ὑμᾶς, *Symp.* 179 E, 189 C, *Rep.* iii 410 B, where μεταχειρίζονται is right, *epist.* 7, 333 A, Eurip. *Bacch.* 728—9, Eubulus 42, Demosth. i *Phil.* 34, *Mid.* 218, cases from Aristotle in Bonitz *Index* s.v. ὥσπερ, Hyperides *Euxen.* 20. 15, Lucian *Hermot.* 60 (references chiefly from Heindorf): Shilleto on Thucyd. ii 42. 1.

τουτὶ sc. προσκεφάλαιον, which like ποτίκρανον (Theocr. 15. 2) was sometimes placed on the seat: so in the theatre

κᾶτα καθίζου μαλακῶς, ἵνα μὴ τρίβῃς τὴν ἐν
Σαλαμῖνι. 785
ΔΗ. ἄνθρωπε, τίς εἶ; μῶν ἔγγονος εἶ τῶν Ἁρμοδίου
τις ἐκείνων;
τοῦτό γέ τοί σου τοὔργον ἀληθῶς γενναῖον
καὶ φιλόδημον.
ΠΑ. ὡς ἀπὸ μικρῶν εὔνους αὐτῷ θωπευματίων γεγένησαι.

786. ἔγγονος RV and MSS. vulg.   ἔκγονος PM edd. vulg.
787. γέ τοι R.   γε rest of MSS.

Theophrast. *char.* 2. As bearing on the
next line, cf. Pollux x 40 οὐ μὴν φαῦλον
τετηρηκέναι ὅτι τὸ ναυτικὸν ὑπηρέσιον ἰδίως
Κρατῖνος ἐν ταῖς Ὥραις (269) προσκεφάλαιον, and so Hermippus 54 τὸν κωπητῆρα
λαβόντα καὶ προσκεφάλαιον. ῥαψάμενος,
'got sewn': the cushion is of leather
(Pollux), and Cleon the more confounded.
785. 'her of Salamis,' 'your Sala-
minian,' sc. τὴν πυγήν. For the voice of
τρίβῃς see on 490 and 910. 'The heroes
of Marathon,' 'the heroes of Salamis,'
were phrases so common as to invite
caricature. The difference οἱ Μαραθῶνι,
οἱ ἐν Σαλαμῖνι is curious, but seems certain: ἐκείνην τὴν Μαραθῶνι *Thesm.* 806,
Thucyd. i 73. 4 φαμὲν γὰρ Μαραθῶνι
τε μόνοι προκινδυνεῦσαι καί...ἐν Σαλαμῖνι
ξυνναυμαχῆσαι, Demosth. *Cor.* 208 μὰ
τοὺς Μαραθῶνι προκινδυνεύσαντας...καὶ τοὺς
ἐν Σαλαμῖνι ναυμαχήσαντας, *Syntax.* 21,
Aristocr. 196, cf. *Neaer.* 97, Isocr. *Philipp.*
147 ἐκ τῆς Μαραθῶνι μάχης καὶ τῆς ἐν Σαλαμῖνι ναυμαχίας, Plato *Menex.* 241 B—C:
it has confirmation from inscriptions,
Meisterhans § 82. 23, but was often neglected, as Plato *Menex.* 245 A τὰ τρόπαια
τά τε...Μαραθῶνι καὶ Σαλαμῖνι καὶ Πλα-
ταιαῖς, so Lucian *Dem. Enc.* 36, Demosth.
FL 312: Aeschin. *FL* 74—5, *Ctes.* 181 ἐν
Μαραθῶνι and ἐν Σαλαμῖνι, so Arist.
Rhet. ii 22. 6: see on 1334: Athen. ix
380 c misquotes Demosth. *Cor.* 208 with
ἐν Μαραθῶνι, and so does Dion. Hal. *de
adm. vi* 31. 1055. 10 Reiske.
At the time of Salamis, rowers in triremes were all Athenian citizens: this line
would not be so appropriate of Demos if
a contemporary battle were substituted for
Salamis.

786. Attempts to distinguish between
ἔκγονος, *son or near descendant,* and ἔγγονος, *more distant descendant* (Shilleto
n. cr. on Demosth. *FL* 53), or to insist on
the definition of ἔγγονος as *grandson,* lack
support from the one source of certain
evidence, epigraphy: inscriptions of fifth
and fourth centuries B.C. give both words
in same meaning: then ἔγγονος disappears
from 300 B.C. to the second century A.D.
(Meisterhans § 40 A 4). Herwerden (*lap.
test.* 50) suspects that ἔγγονος is merely a
misspelling of ἔκγονος, and so G. Meyer,
Gr. Gram.[3] § 275. In this case it is not
likely that the youthful Harmodius had
any descendants: but his kin and those of
Aristogeiton had the σίτησις *CIA* i 8.
They were both of the family Gephyraei
(Töpffer). It is rare to find them mentioned separately (Shilleto on Demosth.
FL 321).
787. γέ τοι is necessary, meaning, as
it regularly does, 'at all events,' 'all I
can say is,' *Plut.* 424.
'Your service is worthy of a true gentleman and patriot.'
788—9. ὡς ἀπὸ μικρῶν = ἀφ' ὡς μικρῶν: the particle comes before the prep.
in such cases regularly. ἀπὸ at expense
of, as *decr. ap.* Demosth. *Cor.* 92, Plut.
praec. ger. reip. 4. 800 F.
εὔνους γεγ., have gained the position of
εὔνους, cf. on 767.
Plut. *praec. ger. reip.* 31. 823 C, 'the
true patriot' προσάγεται τοὺς πολλούς,
νόθα καὶ κίβδηλα τὰ τῶν ἄλλων θωπεύματα
καὶ δελεάσματα πρὸς τὴν τούτου κηδεμονίαν
καὶ φρόνησιν ὁρῶντας. Liv. xli 23. 8 *nos
caeci specie parvi beneficii inescamur.*

N. A. 8

ΑΛΛ. καὶ σὺ γὰρ αὐτὸν πολὺ μικροτέροις τούτων
δελεάσμασιν εἶλες.

ΠΑ. καὶ μὴν εἴ πού τις ἀνὴρ ἐφάνη τῷ δήμῳ μᾶλλον ἀμύνων   790
ἢ μᾶλλον ἐμοῦ σε φιλῶν, ἐθέλω περὶ τῆς
κεφαλῆς περιδόσθαι.

ΑΛΛ. καὶ πῶς σὺ φιλεῖς, ὃς τοῦτον ὁρῶν οἰκοῦντ' ἐν
ταῖς πιθάκναισι
καὶ γυπαρίοις καὶ πυργιδίοις ἔτος ὄγδοον οὐκ
ἐλεαίρεις,

789. συνεῖλες MSS.: see crit. note on 867.
790. εἰ πώποτ' ἀνὴρ Cobet *Mnemos.* n.s. ii 421, cf. *Vesp.* 1226.
792. πιθάκναισι MSS. and so *Plut.* 546. φιδάκναισι Brunck Vels.

μικρότερος and μικρότατος, which are rare compared with μείων ἐλάσσων &c., seem nearly always to imply contempt: cases are *Vesp.* 1511, Plato *Soph.* 248 C, *Rep.* iii 395 B, iv 428 E, v 465 C, 475 B, *Legg.* x 904 C, Xen. *Cyrop.* ii 2. 3, *Rep. Ath.* 2. 7, *Mem.* iii 11. 12, Demosth. *Mid.* 138, Critias ap. Athen. xi 483 B, Plut. *praec. ger. reip.* 17. 813 D, *curios.* 5. 517 E, *fort. Alex.* 2. 1, 334 C, *Pyth. orac.* 15. 401 C, Lucian *calumn.* 3, *quom. hist. scrib.* 27, *apolog.* 9, *adv. indoct.* 8, Dion. Hal. *ars rhet.* 10. 374. 16 Reiske: but cases where contempt or disparagement is not implied do occur, as Plato *Protag.* 356 C, *Phaedo* 93 B, Plut. *quaest. conv.* vii 3. 702 A, Athen. ii 50 A, ix 390 B, 391 B, 398 C, Stobaeus *phys. ecl.* i 17, and several cases in *script. physiogn.* (see Förster's index).

790—1. This rare use of περιδόσθαι (always fut. or 2 aor. mid.) takes εἰ of the thing bet against, *Ach.* 773, *Nub.* 645: in *Il.* xxiii 485, *Ach.* 115 it takes πότερος: in *Odyss.* xxiii 78 αἴ κέν σ' ἐξαπάφω may depend on περιδώσομαι. The gen. may be one of price, but the usage is unexplained; cf. *perdo*?

ἐθέλω, 'I don't mind,' weaker than βούλομαι, see Shilleto on Demosth. *FL* 26.

792. The crowding of the country people in Athens during the Spartan invasions was a main cause of the plague, Thucyd. ii 52. 2 οἰκιῶν οὐχ ὑπαρχουσῶν, ἀλλ' ἐν καλύβαις πνιγηραῖς διαιτωμένων, *ib.*

17 οἱ πολλοὶ τά τε ἔρημα τῆς πόλεως ᾤκησαν καὶ τὰ ἱερὰ καὶ τὰ ἡρῷα...κατεσκευάσαντο δὲ καὶ ἐν τοῖς πύργοις τῶν τειχῶν πολλοὶ καὶ ὡς ἕκαστός που ἐδύνατο (on the long walls down to the Piraeus). To Ar. the Demos is always the country-people mainly.

Moeris' rule φιδάκνη Ἀττικῶς, πιθάκνη Ἕλληνες is so far confirmed by φιδάκνιον on an Attic inscription of B.C. 330 (Meisterhans § 38. 5): the variation is an instance of 'Grassmann's law,' and probably dialectic; Eubulus 132 speaks of Μεγαρικὰ πιθάκνια. Suidas &c. call it a diminutive of πίθος (the term. seems unexampled): but Lucian *quom. hist. scrib.* 4 uses πιθάκνιον for dimin., and Aelian *Nat. Anim.* xii 41 speaks of a πιθάκνη holding twenty amphoreis. Diogenes' abode is always spoken of as a πίθος. The πίθος (answering to *fidelia* and *dolium* in meaning) was the huge earthen cask in which wine was first put.

793. γυπάριον, dimin. of γύπη, which Hesychius explains by καλύβη (cf. Thucyd. above), θαλάμη, or κατὰ γῆν οἴκησις, for which cf. Hehn *Cult. und Haust.*[6] 517. The connexion with γύψ is uncertain.

πυργίδια comic for πύργοι in Thucyd. *sup.*: later the word meant little more than *farm-houses* as in *CIA* iii 61.

The last half of the line is a quotation or parody, as ἐλεαίρω is found only in Epic, here, and Lucian *Tragop.* 305: he says ἕκτῳ ἔτει of the war in *Ach.* 267, 890.

ἀλλὰ καθείρξας αὐτὸν βλίττεις; Ἀρχεπτολέμου
δὲ φέροντος
τὴν εἰρήνην ἐξεσκέδασας, τὰς πρεσβείας τ᾿ ἀπε-
λαύνεις   795
ἐκ τῆς πόλεως ῥαθαπυγίζων, αἱ τὰς σπονδὰς
προκαλοῦνται.

ΠΑ.   ἵνα γ᾿ Ἑλλήνων ἄρξῃ πάντων. ἔστι γὰρ ἐν
τοῖς λογίοισιν
ὡς τοῦτον δεῖ ποτ᾿ ἐν Ἀρκαδίᾳ πεντωβόλου
ἡλιάσασθαι,

794. εἶτα N.
798. πεντώβολον MSS. πεντωβόλου Kuster and edd. vulg.

---

794. Shilleto held that, in Thucyd. at least, καθείργω is literal, κατείργω metaphorical: so Thucyd. iv 47. 3)(iv 98. 6, vi 6. 2: epigraphy, I believe, gives no light. For καθείρξας here Kock quotes Demosth. 3 *Olynth.* 31 οἱ πολιτευόμενοι ἐν αὐτῇ τῇ πόλει καθείρξαντες ὑμᾶς τιθασεύουσι.

βλίττω for μ(ε)λίτιω=take honey from bees: it is used by Plato in his well-known elaboration of the bee-metaphor, *Rep.* viii 564 E πλεῖστον δὴ τοῖς κηφῆσι μέλι καὶ εὐπορώτατον ἐντεῦθεν (from the rich) βλίττεται: Philost. *vita Apoll.* vi 36 τοὺς τοιούτους (rich) ὑποβλίττουσιν οἱ συκοφάνται κέντρα ἐπ᾿ αὐτοὺς ἡρμένοι τὴν γλῶτταν.

On Archeptolemus see on 327 *sup.* The allusion is of course to the rejection of the Spartan proposals after a keen debate before Sphacteria (Thucyd. iv 21— 22, Philochorus *Fragm. Hist. Gr.* i 401), and the ill-success of pacific attempts just after (iv 41): cf. *Pax* 665. We have no other information that Archeptolemus was prominent in the negotiations, but he would of course be anxious for peace; his name is put forward here partly for the pun (*Delawarr brought peace in his hands*).

795—6. ἐκσκεδάννυμι is not quoted elsewhere.

ῥαθαπ. (ῥοθοπ. Suidas) is defined by Pollux ix 126 as the game σιμῷ τῷ ποδὶ τὸν γλουτὸν παίειν (Nauck on Aristoph. Byz. p. 224).

προκαλεῖσθαι, *make an offer* in the course of a dispute, is not confined to legal phrase: Thucyd. has it several times

of these same negotiations, iv 19. 1 Λακεδαιμόνιοι ὑμᾶς προκαλοῦνται ἐς σπονδάς, 20. 1 ἀνάγκη...ὑμᾶς στερηθῆναι ὧν νῦν προκαλούμεθα, cf. 22. 3, v 37. 5. The word may take two accusatives, *Ach.* 652 ὑμᾶς Λακεδαιμόνιοι τὴν εἰρήνην προκαλοῦνται.

797—8. The undisputed empire of Athens is his object: the jury-courts would still be supreme (cf. 1089), and the end of all would be another two obols to the dicast's fee. This is the condition of Cleon's Panhellenism. The form of the pretended oracle parodies no doubt some of the many Delphic responses to emigrants in search of a settlement: and Athens is to be more successful than Sparta, which had for answer Ἀρκαδίην μ᾿ αἰτεῖς· μέγα μ᾿ αἰτεῖς· οὔ τοι δώσω Herod. i 66. Cleon's negotiations with Argos would lead to relations with democratic Mantinea and schemes of policy in North Arcadia, Thucyd. v 29, 47. Five obols seems to have been common daily wages for labour (Böckh *Staatsh.* book i ch. 21), and four is spoken of as a competence by a dicast or soldier in a fragment of Theopompus com. 55: but the main point probably is that this prospect raises the dicast's pay to that of the βουλευτής, which was five obols, Aristot. *Ath. Pol.* 62.

ἡλιάζομαι seems hardly to have been a serious word: it occurs in a law ap. Demosth. *Timocr.* 50, and Harpocration quotes it from Lysias *c. Philonides* with reserve as to the genuineness of the speech.

8—2

ἢν ἀναμείνῃ· πάντως δ᾽ αὐτὸν θρέψω ᾽γὼ καὶ
θεραπεύσω,
ἐξευρίσκων εὖ καὶ μιαρῶς ὁπόθεν τὸ τριώβολον
ἕξει.   800

ΑΛΛ. οὐχ ἵνα γ᾽ ἄρχῃ μὰ Δί᾽ Ἀρκαδίας προνοούμενος,
ἀλλ᾽ ἵνα μᾶλλον
σὺ μὲν ἁρπάζῃς καὶ δωροδοκῇς παρὰ τῶν πό-
λεων· ὁ δὲ δῆμος
ὑπὸ τοῦ πολέμου καὶ τῆς ὁμίχλης ἃ πανουργεῖς
μὴ καθορᾷ σου,
ἀλλ᾽ ὑπ᾽ ἀνάγκης ἅμα καὶ χρείας καὶ μισθοῦ
πρός σε κεχήνῃ.
εἰ δέ ποτ᾽ εἰς ἀγρὸν οὗτος ἀπελθὼν εἰρηναῖος
διατρίψῃ,   805

804. χρείας τοῦ μισθοῦ Cobet *Mnemos.* n.s. ii 421.
805. εἰ MSS. ἢν Dobree. Sobolewski *sentent. condic. Ar.* 18 defends subj. in anapaests from *Eccl.* 687.

Kock sees a reference here to the ἁλιασταί of Tegea, mentioned on inscriptions, though not early : this is unlikely (Wilam. *Arist. und Athen* i 159).

799. θρέψω, see on 255. θεραπεύω of courting political support, see on 59.

800. εὖ καὶ μιαρῶς, see on 256.
ἕξει 'shall keep': σχήσει could not be used here, see on 130.

801. 'Yes, though your thought was not...': οὐ...γε sometimes allows the previous statement, bringing in at once a reservation, so Soph. *Ant.* 570, Eurip. *HF* 857, *Ion* 1290. See App. i.
προνοεῖν, προνοεῖσθαι take inf. Eurip. *Hipp.* 399, inf. with μὴ *Nub.* 975, τοῦ with inf. Alexis 9. 6, ὅπως with fut. Diocles com. Meineke ii p. 841 = Kock i p. 769, Lysias 3. 41, μὴ with subj. Xen. *Oecon.* 9. 66, ὡς μὴ Xen. *Cyrop.* i 6. 24.
Notice from here to 835 the great freedom and variety of metaphor and phrase on the Sausage-man's part: his εὐγλωττία is meant to be marvellous (837).

802. αἱ πόλεις, the Athenian allies, as often : but there also may be a contrast implied to Arcadia, which was rather an ἔθνος than a πόλις.

803. ὁμίχλη is ἀτμώδης ἀναθυμίασις ἄγονος ὕδατος, ἀέρος μὲν παχυτέρα, νέφους δὲ ἀραιοτέρα, Aristot. *de mundo* 4: the phrase would be comic for Homer's νέφος πολέμοιο.
ἃ πανουργεῖς with σοῦ as = τὰ πανουργή- ματά σου: cf. Plato *Gorg.* 517 C ἀγνοοῦντες ἀλλήλων ὅ τι λέγομεν.

804. The μισθός, as the μισθοφορά in 807, is best taken of the dicast's pay. Cleon's claim in 800 is being replied to. Cf. μισθός in 903, 1019 &c.

805. 'The country,' as opposed to 'the town,' is in Attic comedy and prose ἀγρὸς or οἱ ἀγροί. ὁ ἀγρός always means a particular farm or part of the country : in *Ach.* 32 this meaning gives point to ἀποβλέπων and τὸν ἐμὸν δῆμον· so *Pax* 1318, Philemon 98. 1, Demosth. 3 *Aph.* 3, Xen. *Anab.* v 3. 9, *Oecon.* 20. 4, Lucian *philops.* 11, Epictetus iii 3. 1 ὁ ἀγρὸς γεωργοῦ ὕλη &c. So ἀγρός and ὁ ἀγρός are expressly contrast- ed as general and particular, Alciphro iii 20. 4 μὴ γένοιτο κατ᾽ ἀγρὸν τοιοῦτο θηρίον, πάντα γὰρ ὑφαιρούμενος φροῦδά μοι τὰ κατὰ τὸν ἀγρὸν ἀπεργάσεται, cf. Ar. *fr.* 344. 2 οἰκεῖν ἐν ἀγρῷ ἐν τῷ γηδίῳ : so οἱ ἀγροί and

καὶ χῖδρα φαγὼν ἀναθαρρήσῃ καὶ στεμφύλῳ ἐς
λόγον ἔλθῃ,
γνώσεται οἵων ἀγαθῶν αὐτὸν τῇ μισθοφορᾷ
παρεκόπτου,
εἶθ' ἥξει σοι δριμὺς ἄγροικος, κατὰ σοῦ τὴν
ψῆφον ἰχνεύων.
ἃ σὺ γιγνώσκων τόνδ' ἐξαπατᾷς, καὶ ὀνειροπολεῖς περὶ σαυτοῦ.

ΠΑ. οὔκουν δεινὸν ταυτί σε λέγειν δῆτ' ἔστ' ἐμὲ καὶ
διαβάλλειν   810
πρὸς Ἀθηναίους καὶ τὸν δῆμον, πεποιηκότα
πλείονα χρηστὰ

806. χῖδρα MSS. here and *Pax* 595: but the ι is long. ἐλθών Hirschig, Cobet
&c. : then εἰ would stand with διατρίψει and -ρήσει : this seems the best solution.
808. τε for τήν (Palmer in) *Quart. Rev.* clviii 365.
811. πρὸς τὸν δῆμον τὸν Ἀθηναίων Cobet *Mnemos.* n.s. ii 421 : that would be the
form in an official document, but not necessarily here : the MS. reading gives more
point, 'before citizens of Athens and Mr Demos.'

ὁ ἀγρός Athen. xii 554 D. [οἱ ἀγροί may
be pl. of ὁ ἀγρὸς as Thucyd. ii 22. 2, Arist.
Pol. Ath. 2.] Tragedy uses ἀγροί for οἱ
ἀγροί, which it avoids : and we have ἀγροί
'country-places' in phrases like Διονύσια
κατ' ἀγρούς, and οἷα δὴ ἐν ἀγροῖς Plato *Rep.*
ii 372 C, κατ' ἀγρούς iii 399 D (so Cratinus
318), ἐπ' ἀγρῶν *Legg.* i 637 A, πρὸς ἀγρούς
vii 789 E : but ἀγροί usually means *farms*,
as Eupolis 153, Plato *Rep.* v 470 D, Xen.
Vect. 4. 5, Lucian *ep. Saturn.* 1. 20, *merc.
cond.* 20, Athen. iv 130 D.
806. χῖδρα, a porridge explained by
Athenaeus xiv 648 B as ἐφθοὶ πυροί, by
Pollux vi 62 as ἔτνους ἰδέα ἐκ πυροῦ
χλωροῦ : κυρίως ἀπὸ χλωρᾶς κριθῆς according to one scholiast; and this may be
etymological : χ[ρ]ῖδρα and κριθή would be
from the same root by Grassmann's law.
Cato *agric.* 86 gives the recipe for *granea*,
the corresponding Roman farmer's food.
στέμφυλον, in Attic *pressed olives*, Hellenic (as in Hippocrates and late) *pressed
grapes or raisins* (Attic βρύτεα), Athen.
ii 56 D, Phrynichus 384, except where
ἐλάας is expressed as *Geoponica* ix 14. 2,
xii 30. 8. στέμφυλον and σταφυλή are the
same word, varying in accent and termination only. This seems to be the
only case of the singular except *Geop.* ix

14. 2, cf. Lat. *floces*, *fraces*.
For χῖδρα and στέμφυλα as mainstay
and type of Attic country life cf. *Pax* 595
τοῖς ἀγροίκοισιν γὰρ ἦσθα χῖδρα καὶ σωτηρία, *Nub.* 45, Alciphr. iii 29. 1 ἄνθρωπον
...ἀγροῖκον, ὄξοντα στεμφύλων καὶ κόνιν
πνέοντα, Plut. *an seni resp.* 4. 785 D.
ἐς λόγον ἰέναι, 'have a good talk with,'
comic for 'eat': so ξυγγίγνομαι Eupolis 38,
108, σπλάγχνοισι συγγενώμεθα.
807. παρακόπτω in the sense 'cheat'
is quoted only here, *inf.* 859, *Nub.* 640.
παρακρούω is more common and lasted late.
808. ἥξει, as in κακὸν ἥκει *Ran.* 552,
606.
δριμύς is specially used of the dicast
keen for condemnation *Vesp.* 146, 278,
Pax 349, and generally of the democratic
temper (*shrewd* in the old sense) as often
in Plato, *Rep.* viii 564 D &c.; the ἄγροικος
here corrects any disparagement conveyed
by the adjective. The last five words read
like a parody with ψῆφον introduced.
809. ὀνειροπολεῖς, taken as transitive by schol. and L and S, needlessly:
rather 'deal in dreams,' 'work oracles,'
though ὀνειροπολεῖν generally means
'dream and deceive oneself.'
810—11. διαβάλλω τινά is the regular phrase for *damage* an opponent : it

νὴ τὴν Δήμητρα Θεμιστοκλέους πολλῷ περὶ
τὴν πόλιν ἤδη ;

ΑΛΛ. ὦ πόλις Ἄργους, κλύεθ᾽ οἷα λέγει. σὺ Θεμιστοκλεῖ ἀντιφερίζεις ;
ὃς ἐποίησεν τὴν πόλιν ἡμῶν μεστὴν εὑρὼν ἐπιχειλῆ,
καὶ πρὸς τούτοις ἀριστώσῃ τὸν Πειραιᾶ προσέ-
μαξεν,   815
ἀφελών τ᾽ οὐδὲν τῶν ἀρχαίων ἰχθῦς καινοὺς
παρέθηκεν.
σὺ δ᾽ Ἀθηναίους ἐζήτησας μικροπολίτας ἀπο-
φῆναι

---

may be followed by dat., εἰς, or πρός: πρός
probably implying a present audience, εἰς
an absent one, as Thucyd. iii 109. 2, iv 22.
3, Plato *Rep.* vii 539 C.

812. For περί see on 764. Both
πολλῷ and ἤδη are brought in late to
mark the climax in Cleon's pretensions.
Pericles is not to be mentioned with him,
and he has beaten Themistocles easily
already. We hear from Aelian, *Var. hist.*
x 17, that the oligarch Critias in his
writings coupled Themistocles and Cleon
as men who began public life poor and
made themselves rich by politics.

813. ὦ πόλις Ἄργους. The exact point
of this scoffing appeal, given again in *Plut.*
601, is not clear, any more than the reason
of Aristophanes' constant quotation from
Euripides' *Telephus*, from which it comes.
It may be in the speaker's mind that Cleon
was working for an Argive alliance (cf. in
465), or that Themistocles was exiled to
Argos first: for the curious parallel between the stories of Telephus and of
Themistocles at Admetus' court (Thucyd.
i 136) see Robert, *Bild und Lied* 146.
σὺ Θεμ. ἀντ. is probably parody, ἀντιφε-
ρίζω being an Epic word.

814. The attempts to emend this line
arise from ignorance of the meaning of
ἐπιχειλῆ. Pollux v 133 πλῆρες, ἰσοχειλές,
μεστόν..., τὸ δὲ μικρῷ ἐνδεέστερον ἀπλή-
ρωτον καὶ ἐπιχειλές: cf. ii 89, iv 170,
Suidas s.v.: the χεῖλος being the *lip* in
the proper sense, the saucer-like part

above the neck of the vessel, the width
of which is regulated in the case of certain
vessels by *CIA* ii 476. 20: so ὑπερχειλής
means *quite full*, not *running over*, *Anth.*
Pal. xii 168. 7 μεστὸν ὑπὲρ χείλους πίομαι,
a *full bumper.*

προσέμαξε looks as if he thought, as
the scholiasts do, that Themistocles
built the Long Walls. Plutarch, *Themist.*
19, from the conservative standpoint of
the later historical criticism, would reverse the statement: Θεμιστοκλῆς δ᾽ οὐχ,
ὡς Ἀριστοφάνης λέγει, τῇ πόλει τὸν Πειραιᾶ προσέμαξεν, ἀλλὰ τὴν πόλιν ἐξῆψε τοῦ
Πειραιῶς καὶ τὴν γῆν τῆς θαλάττης. He
plainly took προσμάττω in its ordinary
sense, *make to adhere.* Shilleto thought
πρὸς τούτοις προσέμαξε here meant merely
πρὸς τούτοις ἔμαξε, quoting for the redundant prep. in the compound verb Thucyd.
v 103. 1 and Eurip. *El.* 609 ἐλλείπει ἐν=
λείπει ἐν, Plato *Rep.* vii 521 D προσέχειν
πρός, Soph. *El.* 736: this is probably right,
as πρὸς ἀριστώσῃ gives no point. Taking
a set lunch implied comfortable or luxurious circumstances, *Nub.* 416, Antipho
ap. Athen. x 423 A πράγματα τὰ ἑαυτοῦ ἢ
τὰ τῶν φίλων κατηρίστηκεν, Hippocr. *aer.*
1 φιλοπόται καὶ ἀρισταὶ καὶ ἀταλαίπωροι.

816. καινός and ἀρχαῖος are generally
opposed, as νέος and παλαιός, πάλιν χρόνῳ
τἀρχαῖα καινὰ γίγνεται Nicostratus 30.
Themistocles gave Athens both new bread
and new fish, a new harbour and new
trade.

διατειχίζων καὶ χρησμῳδῶν, ὁ Θεμιστοκλεῖ
ἀντιφερίζων.
κἀκεῖνος μὲν φεύγει τὴν γῆν, σὺ δ᾽ Ἀχιλλείων
ἀπομάττει.
ΠΑ. οὔκουν ταυτὶ δεινὸν ἀκούειν, ὦ Δῆμ᾽, ἐστίν μ᾽
ὑπὸ τούτου, 820
ὁτιή σε φιλῶ; ΔΗ. παῦ᾽ οὑτωσί, καὶ μὴ
σκέρβολλε πονηρά.
πολλοῦ δὲ πολύν με χρόνον καὶ νῦν ἐλελήθης
ἐγκρυφιάζων.

821. παῦ᾽ οὑτοσί MSS. παῦ᾽ οὑτωσί Kuster Cobet *Mnemos.* n.s. ii 421: παῦ᾽ οὗτος καὶ μή μοι Porson Dobree, παῦ παῦ᾽ οὗτος Elmsley Dind. Mein. &c. (παῦ is vouched for by Photius 403. 4 and Aelius Dionysius 275 Schwabe). παῦ᾽ ὦ οὗτος Bentl. Mein. *Vind. Arist.* 62.
822. ἐλελήθεις MSS. See Rutherf. *NP* 237.

817—8. Pollux ix 25 quotes τὸ μικροπολιτικόν from Aristophanes (*fr.* 649): it would be interesting to know the context. Xen. *Hell.* ii 2. 10 says the Athenians after Aegospotami feared the fate they had wantonly brought on ἀνθρώπους μικροπολίτας: Aeschines *FL* 120 quotes it from a Chalcidian speaking of his townsmen: so Athen. viii 351 D, Dion. Hal. *de Thucyd.* 41 (919. 3 R.), Dio Chrys. *or.* 34. 46 all in the most obvious sense. We might expect a further meaning answering to our 'Little-England' party; but there is no need to look for this. The words πόλιν ποιῆσαι μεγάλην ἐπίσταμαι were connected with Themistocles' name in the story given by Plut. *Cimon* 9. The point here is partly Cleon's 'setting class against class,' looking to a single ἔθνος rather than to the whole πόλις, as Plato puts it *Rep.* iv 420 B &c., and partly some building operation, now unknown. Wachsmuth thinks (*Stadt Athen* i 342. 5, 572, ii 203) that Cleon built a wall across the Pnyx, which would make that side of Athens defensible, even though the Long Walls fell: this wall, partly traced by Pervanoglu, might be the διατείχισμα of the inscription *CIA* ii 167. 53, and alluded to here. This measure would seem a falling off from the confidence in Athens' strength displayed by her older leaders Curtius *Stadtgesch.* 195.
A similar charge is implied against Cleon by the διστάναι of *Vesp.* 41, and

made against Pericles by Teleclides 42 λάινα τείχη τὰ μὲν οἰκοδομεῖν, τὰ δὲ αὐτὰ πάλιν καταβάλλειν.
819. 'And there he is—an exile from the country, and you—in the prytaneum.' The tomb of Themistocles at the Piraeus (Plut. *Themist.* 32) was probably later: Aristot. *Hist. Anim.* vi 15. 569ᵇ 12 is the earliest mention of that Θεμιστόκλειον as he calls it: Plut. *ib.* says that Andocides in his oligarchic days used the fate of Themistocles as a charge against Athenian democracy.
The ἀχιλληΐς was a variety of barley)(ἐτεόκριθος, Theophr. *caus. plant.* iii 22. 2, dry and easily blighted, *ib.* i 21. 3, *hist. plant.* viii 10. 2: Ἀχίλλειον is the fine bread made of this grain (Athen. iii 114 F), regular in the prytaneum (schol.), as in Pherecrates' land of cokayne *fr.* 130. 4. It is not too good for Cleon to wipe his hands on (414). The gen. Ἀχιλλείων is odd and may imply a parody.
821. The history of παῦε in such cases is given by Rutherford on Babrius 28.
σκερβόλλω, perhaps from σκῶρ βάλλω (Corssen), occurs only here and in dictionaries: κερβόλλω Bacchyl. 1 d 6 (Blass). The schol. quotes from Callimachus the unique σκέρβολα μυθήσαντο.
πονηρά is meant as an answer to Cleon's χρηστά in 811.
822. πολλοῦ πολύς, as *Ran.* 1046 πολλοῦ πολλή: without another part of πολύς, *Nub.* 915 θρασὺς εἶ πολλοῦ, Eupolis

ΑΛΛ. μιαρώτατος, ὦ Δημακίδιον, καὶ πλεῖστα παν-
οῦργα δεδρακώς,
ὁπόταν χασμᾷ, καὶ τοὺς καυλοὺς
τῶν εὐθυνῶν ἐκκαυλίζων 825
καταβροχθίζει, κἀμφοῖν χειροῖν
μυστιλᾶται τῶν δημοσίων.

ΠΑ. οὐ χαιρήσεις, ἀλλά σε κλέπτονθ᾽
αἱρήσω ᾽γὼ τρεῖς μυριάδας.

ΑΛΛ. τί θαλαττοκοπεῖς καὶ πλατυγίζεις, 830
μιαρώτατος ὢν περὶ τὸν δῆμον
τὸν Ἀθηναίων; καί σ᾽ ἐπιδείξω

826. χεροῖν MSS. : inscriptions give only χειροῖν, χειρῶν, Meisterhans § 56. 17, and the forms with short penult seem not to be used in Comedy, except in paratragedy as *Ran.* 1348, *Vesp.* 1193, *Thesm.* 912.

---

74. 2. Suidas mentions the use πολλοῦ πάνυ.

ἐγκρυφιάζω seems to mean ' hoodwink.' The rare ἐγκρύπτω and its derivatives seem to be used mostly of fire : the ἄρτος ἐγκρυφίας (for references see Blümner *Technologie* i 75) was baked in hot ashes: it was indigestible (Athen. iii 115 E) and apt to contain ashes (Lucian *dial. mort.* 20. 4), and it is possible that the verb here is a word of the baker's trade, *palming off inferior bread.* Athenaeus iii 110 B says that the Alexandrians used this bread in the worship of Cronus.

823. The Δημακίδιον is a comic combination of a magnificative Δημᾶκ- and a diminutive, in contrast to the familiar Δημίδιον 726. -ᾱκ is not common in literary Greek, but πλούταξ, σύρφαξ, ῥύαξ &c. show I think that its use was the reverse of diminutive (θύνναξ, Eriphus com. 3, is most likely ampliative), and cases like θαλάμαξ, φλύαξ &c. show that it could be used colloquially with freedom.

A similar combination is the Laconian Αττικίων in *Pax* 214, which is also the name of Lexiphanes' slave in Lucian *Lexiph.* 3 : there the ampliative -ων follows the diminutive; cf. μαλακίων, *Eccl.* 1058.

824—8. χασμάω is not used in act. καυλός was used specially of the silphium stalk (see on 894), so I suppose it means

here 'delicate titbits.' ἐκκαυλίζω is invented, as so many verbs of this termination are.

μυστίλη, bread used to sop up broth &c., was the oldest form of spoon : the purist in Athenaeus iii 126 A, who prefers μυστίλη to μύστρον for a real spoon, is refuted. λίστριον, another word for a spoon, gave way to the Latin *cochleare* under the form κοχλιάριον, Pollux vi 87, x 89, Phrynichus 293 Ruth.: so μυστιλῶμαι (cf. 1168, *Plut.* 627) is an oddity in Lucian *Lexiph.* 5.

828—9. Cleon becomes more helpless in the face of the vigour and variety of his adversary's language: he is no more forward than at 435 q.v.

830. θαλαττοκοπεῖν and πλατυγίζειν are either invented, or rowers' words for useless beating and splashing with the oar.

832—5. ἐπιδείξω, not technical like ἐνδείξω, but merely = *show* : Antipho *caed. Her.* 61 ἐπέδειξεν ἀδικοῦντα ἐκεῖνον, socr. 3 ἐὰν ἐπιδείξω τὴν τούτων μητέρα φονέα οὖσαν τοῦ ἡμετέρου πατρός.

Very little seems to be known of Lesbian history after the revolt of 428 and the settlement described by Thucydides iii 50, which began with the execution on Cleon's motion of over a thousand men : the movements of the exiles on the Asiatic coast mentioned in iv 52 are later than our play. The sum of 40 minae seems small : but the Sausage-man is almost pitying now.

νὴ τὴν Δήμητρ᾽, ἢ μὴ ζῴην,
δωροδοκήσαντ᾽ ἐκ Μυτιλήνης
πλεῖν ἢ μνᾶς τετταράκοντα.　　　　835

ΧΟΡ. ὦ πᾶσιν ἀνθρώποις φανεὶς μέγιστον ὠφέλημα,
ζηλῶ σε τῆς εὐγλωττίας. εἰ γὰρ ὧδ᾽ ἐποίσεις,
μέγιστος Ἑλλήνων ἔσει, καὶ μόνος καθέξεις
τἀν τῇ πόλει, τῶν ξυμμάχων τ᾽ ἄρξεις ἔχων
τρίαιναν,
ἢ πολλὰ χρήματ᾽ ἐργάσει σείων τε καὶ ταράττων.　　　　840
καὶ μὴ μεθῇς τὸν ἄνδρ᾽, ἐπειδή σοι λαβὴν δέ-
δωκεν·

834. Μιτυλήνης MSS. Μυτιλ- is invariable on inscriptions B.C. (Meisterhans § 13. 7) and coins.
835. μυριάδας (Μδας) τεττ. conj. Zacher.
837. ἐποίσεις MSS. ' put blow on blow' Shilleto in MS. note. ἐποίσει Kock.

Kock quotes from a scholiast on Lucian *Timon* 30 the story that a bribe of 10 talents was given to Cleon by Lesbians resident in Athens.
836—842 answer to **756—762**.
836—7. The order of compliments and prophecies is curious—blessing to the world, greatest of Greeks, sovereign over Athens and her allies: and the tone descends from the tragic style of 836 to the comedy of 842. εὔγλωττος is generally 'glib' more than 'eloquent': the chorus of καλοὶ κάγαθοί is not too complimentary to the coming tyrant. The ζηλῶ or ἄγαμαι of the chorus often points out to the house the main feature of the protagonist's excellence, Eurip. *Alc.* 602, *Ach.* 1008, *Vesp.* 1450 &c.: so in Thucyd. v 105. 3 οὐ ζηλοῦμεν is one of the dramatic touches of the Melian debate. There seems to be no other case of ἐπιφέρω meaning 'lay on' absolutely in the active: and Kock is perhaps right in reading ἐποίσει, ἐπιφέρομαι meaning 'rush on,' 'attack.'
838. καθέξεις. For the distinction between the ἕξω and σχήσω forms see on 130. Other cases of καθέξω *shall hold, hold in check*, are Soph. *OC* 381, 874, *Ajax* 1167, Eurip. *Phoen.* 720, *Hipp.* 883 (οὐκέτι κατασχήσω would be inconsistent), *Andr.* 348, *Hec.* 526, Xen. *Symp.* 8. 26,

Demosth. 2 *Olynth.* 9, Aristot. *de anima* i 4. 409ᵃ 23: of κατασχήσω *shall get hold* Thucyd. vi 11. 1, Demosth. *Aristocr.* 12, Aristot. *Pol.* viii (v) 7. 12. 1307ᵇ 10, 10. 27. 1312ᵃ 33, or *shall put in to land* Thucyd. iv 42. 3, Soph. *Elect.* 501 Jebb.
839—40. The chorus think of Poseidon as the proper divine type, cf. on 551. ἐργάζεσθαι χρήματα, 'make money' in a business way, Plato *Hipp. mai.* 282 C, Aristot. *Oecon.* ii 1346ᵇ 23,'*Anth. Pal.* vi 248. 2 εἰργάσατο χλανίδα *earned* the cloak: cf. ἐργασία, ἀργός in business sense. σείω in two senses, (1) making earthquakes, and (2) squeezing money (almost =συκοφαντῶ), as *Pax* 639, Dicaearchus in *Fr. Hist. Gr.* ii 255 διατρέχουσι δέ τινες ἐν τῇ πόλει λογογράφοι, σείοντες τοὺς παρεπιδημοῦντας καὶ εὐπόρους τῶν ξένων; cf. διασείω in S. Luke 3. 14 and elsewhere in late Greek.
841—2. The κατακελευσμός is of two lines as always (Zieliński *Gliederung*, p. 120), here introduced by καὶ instead of the regular ἀλλά.
The common wrestling metaphor in λαβή determines πλευράς to mean *stout ribs*: it does not seem to have the sense of the Latin *latus, latera, lungs, strong voice.* Aristot. *physiogn.* 6. 810ᵇ 12 οἱ εὔπλευροι εὔρωστοι τὰς ψυχάς· ἀναφέρεται

κατεργάσει γὰρ ῥᾳδίως, πλευρὰς ἔχων τοιαύτας.

ΠΑ. οὔκ, ὦγαθοί, ταῦτ᾽ ἐστί πω ταύτῃ μὰ τὸν
Ποσειδῶ.
ἐμοὶ γάρ ἐστ᾽ εἰργασμένον τοιοῦτον ἔργον ὥστε
ἀπαξάπαντας τοὺς ἐμοὺς ἐχθροὺς ἐπιστομί-
ζειν,   845
ἕως ἂν ᾖ τῶν ἀσπίδων τῶν ἐκ Πύλου τι λοιπόν.

ΑΛΛ. ἐπίσχες ἐν ταῖς ἀσπίσιν· λαβὴν γὰρ ἐνδέδωκας.
οὐ γάρ σ᾽ ἐχρῆν, εἴπερ φιλεῖς τὸν δῆμον, ἐκ
προνοίας
ταύτας ἐᾶν αὐτοῖσι τοῖς πόρπαξιν ἀνατεθῆναι.

ἐπὶ τὸ ἄρρεν...ὅσοι δὲ ἐκ τῶν πλευρῶν
περίογκοί εἰσιν, οἷον πεφυσημένοι, λάλοι
καὶ μωρολόγοι· ἀναφέρεται ἐπὶ τοὺς βοῦς
ἢ ἐπὶ τοὺς βατράχους.

τοιοῦτος, properly *such as yours*, τοιόσδε
such as mine or *ours* (as Soph. *OC* 391): so
with τοσοῦτος, τοσόσδε, cf. Herod. vii 160,
Pind. *Ol.* 1. 115—6 οὗτος *yours*, τοσσάδε
all mine: the Euripidean τοιόνδ᾽ ἀπέβη
τόδε πρᾶγμα is defiant, 'Such is *my* way
of working out this plot.'

843. The ὦγαθοί is sarcastic to the
knights, and the μὰ τὸν Ποσειδῶ a defiant
reference to their metaphor in 839 and
their Tory religion. ταῦτα ταύτῃ, 'your
ideas in your way')(the emphatic ἐμοί
of 844 in his usual style, and the ἔργον
following their phrases in 840 and 842.
Eurip. *Medea* 365 ἀλλ᾽ οὔτι ταύτῃ ταῦτα,
μὴ δοκεῖτέ, πω, Aesch. *Prom.* 511 οὐ ταῦτα
ταύτῃ Μοῖρά πω τελεσφόρος κρᾶναι πέπρω-
ται, both in answer to the chorus.

845. ἐπιστομίζειν, 'shut up,' 'gag,'
Demosth. *Halonn.* 33 ἐπιστομεῖν ἡμᾶς ἔφη
τοὺς αὐτῷ ἀντιλέγοντας, Plut. *praec. ger.
reip.* 13. 810 E. The phrase probably
came from horsemanship, 'curb,' as in
Philost. *imag.* 18, cf. the elaborate metaphor in Plut. *gen. Socr.* 22. 592 B—, of wild
geese ἐπιστομίζοντες αὐτῶν καὶ χαλινοῦντες
τὸ φιλόφωνον καὶ λάλον *sollert. anim.* 10.
967 B: of men bribed, Plut. *Philopoemen*
15, or merely silenced, Lucian *Jup. trag.*
35 ἰχθὺν σε ἀποφανεῖ ἐπιστομίζων.

846. These shields from Sphacteria
were painted with pitch and preserved in
the Stoa Poecile, where Pausanias (i 15. 4)
saw them along with others from Scione,

captured in 423 and also of course connected with Cleon: so Persian shields
were dedicated at Delphi after Plataea,
Aeschin. *Ctes.* 116. Votive shields were
hung round the Parthenon architrave by
bronze pins, the stumps of which still
remain.

847. Generally ἐπίσχες αὐτοῦ, Soph.
OC 856, Cratinus 66.

849. Whatever was the exact difference between the πόρπαξ and the ὀχάνη
or ὄχανον, the former was characteristic
of the Spartan shield till the time of
Cleomenes (Plut. *Cleomenes* 11). The
word is very rare in literature: Tragedians
use it of heroic armour (probably taking
that to be like the Spartan): Arist. has it
here of Spartan shields, and in *Lys.* 106
πορπακίζομαι in the Spartan woman's
mouth: Critias quoted by Libanius *or.* 24.
ii 86 Reiske ἐξαιρεῖ Σπαρτιάτης οἴκοι τῆς
ἀσπίδος τὸν πόρπακα. Xen. has it as the
name of a dog, *Cyneg.* 7. 5. It seems to
have become extinct; Pollux has ὄχανον
only i 133. There seems no sufficient
evidence for the idea of scholiasts and
editors that handles were usually taken
off votive shields, though such offerings
when made for the purpose of dedication
(Paus. vi 23. 7, x 19. 4) might well have
no handles: the bronze shields at Olympia
showed remains of handles (Furtwängler,
Bronzefunde aus Olymp. p. 80), and the
Parthenon inventory *CIA* ii 720 mentions
πόρπακες on certain shields presumably
Spartan: Plut. *Timoleon* 31 tells of Car-
thaginian shields dedicated with all their
ornaments.

ἀλλ' ἐστὶ τοῦτ', ὦ Δῆμε, μηχάνημ', ἵν', ἢν σὺ
βούλῃ 850
τὸν ἄνδρα κολάσαι τουτονί, σοὶ τοῦτο μὴ
'γγένηται.

ὁρᾷς γὰρ αὐτῷ στῖφος οἷόν ἐστι βυρσοπωλῶν
νεανιῶν· τούτους δὲ περιοικοῦσι μελιτοπῶλαι
καὶ τυροπῶλαι· τοῦτο δ' εἰς ἕν ἐστι συγκε-
κυφός.

ὥστ' εἰ σὺ βριμήσαιο καὶ βλέψειας ὀστρακίνδα, 855
νύκτωρ κατασπάσαντες ἂν τὰς ἀσπίδας θέοντες
τὰς εἰσβολὰς τῶν ἀλφίτων ἂν καταλάβοιεν
ἡμῶν.

851. 'γγένηται R, 'κγένηται rest.
856. κατασπάσαντες R, καθαρπάσαντες V and most MSS, Zacher.

---

851. Blaydes says "ἐγγένεσθαι τί τινι valet *licere alicui aliquid*, ἐκγένεσθαι contingere ut in *Pac.* 346. Cf. *Ran.* 690": but can a distinction be drawn between ἔξεστι, ἐκγίγνεται and ἔνεστι, ἔνι, ἐγγίγνεται?

852—4. The trades in the agora were congregated in κύκλοι of the same craft, see Wachsmuth *Stadt Athen* ii 461—, and no doubt the sellers of leather, honey and cheese were near together. Tanneries were generally outside city walls, as malodorous, Blümner *Technologie* i 262: but βυρσοπῶλαι are the retail-dealers in the agora. στῖφος implies a packed body, usually of soldiers massed together, *globus*. συγκύπτω, 'make common cause,' 'put their heads together': in Attic a comic word, like κύπτω generally, though Herodotus uses it seriously in two well-known passages, iii 82 οἱ κακοῦντες τὰ κοινὰ συγκύψαντες ποιεῦσι in Darius' criticism of democracy, and vii 145.

855—7. βριμάομαι βριμόομαι seemingly 'snort' or 'bellow' originally: then 'be angry,' as here and Xen. *Cyrop.* iv 5. 9: ἐμβριμάομαι &c. are not uncommon in Christian Greek.
Like other words in -ινδα, ὀστρακίνδα

is an adverb of a game; Pollux ix 110 gives a list and description of a dozen or so. In this game, two sides of boys threw up a potsherd, blackened on one side, with the cry 'νὺξ ἢ ἡμέρα' (black or white): according to the fall of the potsherd, the sides had to run and pursue. The game is alluded to in Plato *Phaedr.* 241 B, ὀστράκου μεταπεσόντος, 'the pursuer runs now,' and described in Plato com. 153 probably with the reference to ostracism which is so plain here. Potsherds used in the ostracism of Xanthippus, Megacles and Themistocles have been found, *Class. Rev.* v 277, *Mitt. arch. Inst.* xxii 345. Cratinus 415 coined a word of the kind, ἐποστρακισμός, 'the appeal-game.'

ἐποστρακισμός was 'ducks and drakes,' Pollux ix 119.

These trades, being in the agora, were naturally near the Stoa Poecile, where the shields were hanging ready, handles and all, for use. Near this was the στοὰ ἀλφιτοπωλίς, the only regular meal-market of Athens; 'they would occupy the passes into the meal-market,' and starve the state. The idiom by which τὰ ἄλφιτα means the meal-market is well known: it is called by the grammarians a specially Attic elegance.

ΔΗ. οἴμοι τάλας· ἔχουσι γὰρ πόρπακας; ὦ πόνηρε,
ὅσον με παρεκόπτου χρόνον τοιαῦτα κρουσι-
δημᾶν.

ΠΑ. ὦ δαιμόνιε, μὴ τοῦ λέγοντος ἴσθι, μηδ᾽ οἰηθῇς
ἐμοῦ ποθ᾽ εὑρήσειν φίλον βελτίον᾽· ὅστις εἷς
ὢν   861
ἔπαυσα τοὺς ξυνωμότας, καί μ᾽ οὐ λέληθεν οὐδὲν
ἐν τῇ πόλει ξυνιστάμενον, ἀλλ᾽ εὐθέως κέκραγα.

ΑΛΛ. ὅπερ γὰρ οἱ τὰς ἐγχέλεις θηρώμενοι πέπονθας.
ὅταν μὲν ἡ λίμνη καταστῇ, λαμβάνουσιν οὐ-
δέν·   865
ἐὰν δ᾽ ἄνω τε καὶ κάτω τὸν βόρβορον κυκῶσιν,

858—9. γὰρ, *Oh, then.* παρεκόπτου, on 807. κρουσιδημῶν, 'by tricks of the political trade,' is invented from κρουσιμετρεῖν, 'to cheat in selling corn by *knocking* the measure and spilling the grain,' cf. Pherecrates 105 λαβοῦσα μὲν τῆς χοίνικος τὸν πύνδακ᾽ εἰσέκρουσεν. The word occurs only in dictionaries and scholiasts: cf. κρούω in such cases as Eupolis 184 κρούων γε μὴν αὐτὰς ἐωνούμην ἐγώ, Soph. *fr.* 926 A ὡς μήτε κρούσῃς μηθ᾽ ὑπὲρ χεῖλος βάλῃς, quoted by Harpocration s.v. παρακρούομαι.

860—1. ὦ δαιμόνιε in expostulation, as usual: in answer to imprecation or abuse as *Av.* 961. τοῦ λέγοντος εἶναι, 'be of the opinion of the last speaker': as Soph. *OT* 910, cf. *Phil.* 386 ἀεὶ τοῦ διδόντος εἶναι, Alciphro i 38. 3 τοῦ προστυχόντος, Lucian *Toxaris* 13; the reproach is made by the historical Cleon to the δῆμος in the Mitylene speech, Thucyd. iii 37, especially in his harping on the dangers of the ἀγών.

861—2. The change from ὅστις to μ᾽, not ὅντινα, is idiomatic, as is εἷς ὤν, cf. Hermippus 45. 3 πέμπειν Νόθιππον ἕν᾽ ὄντα.—See on 476 for the point in ξυνωμότας, ξυνιστάμενον. In κέκραγα he gives the obvious metaphor of the housedog as before: this is to be beaten by a new figure of the enemy.

864—. The stem ἐγχελυ sometimes had -ῠ: hence the accent ἐγχέλῠς and the declension ἐγχέλυος &c. Athenaeus vii 299 A quotes cases to prove that the Attics in the plural at least used ἐγχέλεις &c. as from -ῠ stem, and forms like ἐγχέλυες seem to come in with Aristotle. θήρα θηρεύω &c. are regular of fishing. Similar accounts of the taking of eels are given by Aristotle, *Hist. Anim.* viii 2. 592ᵃ 6—, and *fragm.* 311 Rose, translated by Pliny *NH* ix 74.

λίμνη means a freshwater marshy lake here: Athenaeus viii 355 D ἡ δὲ λιμναία ἔγχελυς τῆς θαλασσίας εὐστομωτέρα καὶ πολυτροφωτέρα: and the most famous eels came from the λίμναι of Copais and the Strymon above Amphipolis. ταράττειν, κυκᾶν, βόρβορον were phrases so commonly used of Cleon (see *sup.* 251 &c.) that this simile came naturally. ἔγχελυς was connected by some etymologically with ἰλύς, Athen. vii 299 D.

καταστὰς καθεστηκώς, 'calm,' of water, wind, expression of feature, political situation &c.

Both λαμβάνειν and αἱρεῖν were used of success in hunting or fishing, and also in business 'make something': cf. the proverb of fishermen εὕδοντι κύρτος αἱρεῖ, parodied by Cratinus 4.

In *Nub.* 559 Aristophanes says this figure was stolen by other comedians and applied to Hyperbolus. It spread and lived, 'fishing in troubled waters.'

αἱροῦσι· καὶ σὺ λαμβάνεις, ἢν τὴν πόλιν τα-
ράττῃς.

ἐν δ' εἰπέ μοι τοσουτονί· σκύτη τοσαῦτα
πωλῶν,

ἔδωκας ἤδη τουτωὶ κάττυμα παρὰ σεαυτοῦ

ταῖς ἐμβάσιν, φάσκων φιλεῖν; ΔΗ. οὐ δῆτα

μὰ τὸν Ἀπόλλω.   870

ΑΛΛ. ἔγνωκας οὖν δῆτ' αὐτὸν οἷός ἐστιν; ἀλλ' ἐγώ
σοι

ζεῦγος πριάμενος ἐμβάδων τουτὶ φορεῖν δίδωμι.

ΔΗ. κρίνω σ' ὅσων ἐγᾦδα περὶ τὸν δῆμον ἄνδρ'
ἄριστον

εὐνούστατόν τε τῇ πόλει καὶ τοῖσι δακτύλοισιν.

867. om. Cobet *Mnemos.* n.s. ii 422, saying that the line is a versified scholium, and that αἱρεῖν in this sense is not Attic. Against this Kock quotes Ephippus 5. 2 ὁπόταν ἰχθύν τιν' ἕλωσ': that passage however contains several tragic expressions. Add Xen. *Mem.* iii 11. 11 βίᾳ μὲν οὐκ ἂν ἕλοις φίλον, εὐεργεσίᾳ δὲ τὸ θηρίον τοῦτο ἁλώσιμόν ἐστιν, and the proverb quoted in expl. note: and cf. 789.
872. ἐμβάδων MSS. ἐμβάδοιν Dind. and most editors: Meineke *Vind. Arist.* 62 says "sic constanter Attici ζεῦγος cum duali coniungunt": this is entirely wrong: ζεῦγος ἐμβάδοιν is as unnatural as 'a pair of two shoes': the gen. pl. is regular, though editors perversely give the dual sometimes: *fr.* 52 βοιδαρίων ζεῦγος, Alcaeus com. 14 ζεῦγος βοῶν, Antiphanes 205 ταῶν ζεῦγος, Andoc. *Alcib.* 26 ζεῦγος ἵππων, and so Isocr. *big.* 25, κυλίκων ζεῦγος Ister ap. Athen. xi 478 B (*Fr. Hist. Gr.* i 423), ζεῦγος σπυρίδων *Anth. Pal.* vi 28. 5, ζεῦγος χηνῶν *ib.* 231. 4, ζεῦγος δημαγωγῶν Plut. *Agis* 2, ζεῦγος δρακόντων *Ti. Gracch.* 1, στροφίγγων ζεῦγος *CIA* ii 834 b, ζεῦγος σκύφων *ib.* iii 60, ὀρνειθίων ζεῦγος &c. Diocletian's *Tariff* 4. 23—31. The only case I know of the dual is Ar. *fr.* 344. 4 ζευγάριον οἰκεῖον βοοῖν, where there is special emphasis on the ordinary farmer's two oxen and no more. In Aesch. *Agam.* 44 there is more to be said for Dindorf's ζεῦγος Ἀτρειδαιν than for most of such duals: but MSS. have Ἀτρειδᾶν.
873. ὅσον R and most MSS. ὅσων γ' B, ὅσον γ' X. ἄνδρ' R, ὄντ' the rest.

---

868. 'With so many hides in your stock': τοσαῦτα of the second person as properly, see on 842: σκύτος, like βύρσα, δέρμα, διφθέρα, may mean tanned or untanned hide, but it was usually 'leather,' cf. σκυτοτόμος &c. For κάττυμα, 'a piece to patch his old shoes,' and ἐμβάδες, see on 314—. παρὰ σεαυτοῦ (cf. Xen. *Mem.* iii 11. 13 χαρίζοιο δ' ἂν μάλιστα, εἰ δεομένοις δωροῖο τὸ παρὰ σεαυτῆς), to point the contrast in πριάμενος 872. For prices of shoes at Athens see Böckh *Staatsh.* i 134 and Fränkel's note 188, and later Diocletian's *Tariff* 9.
871—2. γιγνώσκω 'see through,' as

Thucyd. vi 89. 6 δημοκρατίαν καὶ ἐγιγνώσκομεν οἱ φρονοῦντές τι, *Nub.* 918 γνωσθήσει. φορεῖν ready for wear)(κάττυμα. τουτί of course deictic, else the article would be necessary.
873—4. These lines parody the formulae regularly used in decrees of thanks, προξενία, εὐεργεσία, or the like: ἀνὴρ ἀγαθὸς περὶ τὴν πόλιν, ἀρετὴ καὶ εὔνοια &c. constantly occur. A document beginning in this way would lead up to a decree of special honour and reward.
τοῖσι δακτύλοισιν, 'toes': Alexis 148, the inventor of lamps ἦν τις κηδεμὼν τῶν δακτύλων.

ΠΑ. οὐ δεινὸν οὖν δῆτ᾽ ἐμβάδας τοσουτονὶ δύνασθαι,
ἐμοῦ δὲ μὴ μνείαν ἔχειν ὅσων πέπονθας; ὅστις
ἔπαυσα τοὺς βινουμένους, τὸν Γρύττον ἐξα-
λείψας. 877

ΑΛΛ. οὔκουν σε ταῦτα δῆτα δεινόν ἐστι πρωκτοτηρεῖν,
παῦσαί τε τοὺς βινουμένους; κοὐκ ἔσθ᾽ ὅπως
ἐκείνους
οὐχὶ φθονῶν ἔπαυσας, ἵνα μὴ ῥήτορες γένοιντο.
τονδὶ δ᾽ ὁρῶν ἄνευ χιτῶνος ὄντα τηλικοῦτον, 881
οὐπώποτ᾽ ἀμφιμασχάλου τὸν Δῆμον ἠξίωσας,
χειμῶνος ὄντος· ἀλλ᾽ ἐγώ σοι τουτονὶ δίδωμι.

ΔΗ. τοιουτονὶ Θεμιστοκλῆς οὐπώποτ᾽ ἐπενόησεν.
καίτοι σοφὸν κἀκεῖν᾽ ὁ Πειραιεύς· ἔμοιγε μέντοι
οὐ μεῖζον εἶναι φαίνετ᾽ ἐξεύρημα τοῦ χιτῶνος. 886

877. Suidas says Γρύττον was read, and under βινέω he quotes Γρῖττον.   γρυπὸν
conj. Bergk Mein.   Γρύλλον conj. Blaydes.
878. So M : other MSS. omit δῆτα : edd. δῆτα ταῦτα from Aldine.
881. τηλικουτονί MSS.

875—7. He rises to the tone of the moral reformer. οὖν δῆτα *Nub.* 791, *Av.* 969 and cf. οὔκουν δῆτα. Conviction on a γραφὴ ἑταιρήσεως entailed ἀτιμία and was especially intended to prevent such men *speaking.* Γρύττον is probably a nickname, if anything : but we know no more than the scholia, one of which says γρύττον means γρῦ, τὸ τυχόν. Γρύλλον is possible : Xenophon's father and son bore the name : and the father was no doubt a conservative. The καλοὶ κἀγαθοί were certainly very open to such a charge (Eupolis 100): and the political effect of such connexions on their side was quite recognized in some states, Athenaeus xiii 601 E παρὰ τὰς ἄλλας ταῖς εὐνομουμέναις (conservative) πόλεσιν ἐπὶ τῆς Ἑλλάδος σπουδασθῆναι τόδε τὸ ἔθος : he goes on to give instances of such connexions being instruments against tyranny.
878—80. 'Scandalous! it is scandalous that your vigilance takes such a form!' For the common remark about ῥήτορες in 880 cf. *Eccl.* 112—4, *Nub.* 1093, Plato com. 186, and especially Aristophanes in Plato *Symp.* 192 A.
881—3. Spartans usually wore the χλαῖ-

να alone (doubled), and so did humbler Athenians (not artisans), calling the garment τρίβων : Demos wears this dress, which suggested the dicast or the loafer. Socrates went ἀνυπόδητος καὶ ἀχίτων (Xen. *Mem.* i 6. 2), and this style was affected by Stoics like Cleanthes, and especially by the Cynics. Portrait-statues often have the ἱμάτιον alone, as the Lateran Sophocles; but probably this is owing to artistic effect, not to actual truth. The (χιτών) ἀμφιμάσχαλος covered the whole body below the neck)(the ἑτερομάσχαλος or ἐξωμίς, which left the right shoulder bare, and was worn by slaves and artisans as convenient for manual labour. The names ἔσθος, ἱμάτιον, εἶμα show that the upper garment was more essentially 'the dress' than the χιτών, and so γυμνὸς means 'without *the* dress,' wearing the χιτών only. χειμῶνος of course at the Lenaea.
884—6. ἐπινοεῖν of a practical notion, cf. on 90. In *Lys.* 1150— the advance from smock-frocks (κατωνάκαι) to χλαῖναι is spoken of as a great thing in Athenian history. ἐξεύρημα implies more thought and invention than εὕρημα, which often means 'piece of luck.'

ΠΑ. οἴμοι τάλας, οἵοις πιθηκισμοῖς με περιελαύνεις.

ΑΛΛ. οὔκ, ἀλλ᾽ ὅπερ πίνων ἀνὴρ πέπονθ᾽ ὅταν χεσείη,
τοῖσιν τρόποις τοῖς σοῖσιν ὥσπερ βλαυτίοισι
χρῶμαι.

ΠΑ. ἀλλ᾽ οὐχ ὑπερβαλεῖ με θωπείαις· ἐγὼ γὰρ αὐ-
τὸν   890
προσαμφιῶ τοδί· σὺ δ᾽ οἴμωζ᾽, ὦ πόνηρ᾽.

ΔΗ. ἰαιβοῖ.

---

887. His boast in 290 περιελῶ σ᾽ ἀλαζονείαις is changed to complaint and fear.

πιθηκισμοῖς: Suidas says the word was taken by some to mean ἀπάταις, by others μιμήμασιν, the pet-name for a monkey being μιμώ.
The retort implies that it is taken in the latter sense by the adversary.

888—9. 'I only take your ways as a man at a wine-party might take another's slippers for the convenience of the moment.'

πίνω, as the verb of συμπόσιον, Nub. 1358, Vesp. 1198, Eupolis 351. 5, Plato com. 51. 2, Athenaeus xv 675 B πινόντων ὄμβρος τὸ συμπόσιον διέλυσεν. Cleon was not unknown as a guest at such parties (Vesp. 1220): and now the Sausage-man takes a tone of society.

βλαῦται were light slippers worn by guests on the way to and from banquets, though in the host's house they were laid aside for the time. They are the mark of luxurious ease, Hermippus 47. 4, Plato Symp. 174 A Σωκράτη λελουμένον τε καὶ τὰς βλαύτας ὑποδεδεμένον, ἃ ἐκεῖνος ὀλιγάκις ἐποίει (and was blamed for by Diogenes, Aelian Var. Hist. iv 11), Lysippus 2, Anaxilas 18. 2, Plut. Marcellus 22 πεζὸς ἐν βλαύταις...ὡς ἀπόλεμος καὶ ἡδύς, Athen. viii 338 A, xii 543 F (Aelian Var. Hist. ix 11), Philost. epist. 18, Pollux vii 87. It was an affectation in Cynics to wear them, Anth. Pal. vi 293. 1.

890—1. θωπεία he thinks a more creditable word than πιθηκισμός.

The χιτών and χλαῖνα or ἱμάτιον were so different in material and wear that we should expect different verbs to be attached to each: and so ἐνδύω is used of

putting on the χιτών, and ἀμπέχομαι, ἀμφιέννυμι, ἀναβάλλομαι of the χλαῖνα or ἱμάτιον, which is the τοδί here.

Heraclides Pont. ap. Athen. xii 512 B ἀλουργῆ ἠμπίσχοντο ἱμάτια, ποικίλους δ᾽ ὑπέδυνον χιτῶνας. The scholium προσαμφιῶ· πρὸς οἷς ἔχει ἐνδύσω· παρεπιγραφὴ δέ· δίδωσι γὰρ αὐτῷ ὁ Κλέων χιτῶνα shows the loss of feeling for the distinction common in later times and the consequent mistake as to the action: so Thomas Magister s.v. ἀνεβαλόμην χιτῶνα ἢ ἐνεδύθην.

In Eccl. 332 Blepyrus has put on his wife's shift instead of a ἱμάτιον (315): hence the point in the verbs τὸ κροκωτίδιον ἀμπισχόμενος οὐνδύεται, cf. 374 τὸ τῆς γυναικὸς ἀμπέχει χιτωνίον; Xen. Cyrop. i 3. 17 could not have written ἐκδύσας αὐτὸν τὸν μὲν ἑαυτοῦ ἐκεῖνον ἠμφίεσε, τὸν δ᾽ ἐκείνου αὐτὸς ἐνέδυ without meaning that the big boy threw his own tunic over the small boy and put the small boy's tunic properly on himself. ἐνδύω is used of the upper garment worn in a particular way (probably without a χιτών) at religious services: Aesch. Eum. 1028 φοινικοβάπτοις ἐνδυτοῖς ἐσθήμασι, Soph. Trach. 674 and Jebb's note, 759, Theophr. ap. Athen. x 423 F: so ἔνδυτον of religious attire Eurip. Bacch. 111, 138, Anth. Pal. vi 237. 1.

Philetaerus ap. Athen. i 21 C does not use ἀμπέχεσθαι of the tunic (as L and S say) but of the φᾶρος, though there again Eustathius comments ἀμφέξει ἤγουν ἐνδύσῃ.

We expect two different words also for taking off the ἱμάτιον and the χιτών: ἀποδύομαι τὸ ἱμάτιον, ἐκδύομαι τὸν χιτῶνα is the proper distinction, clearly marked in Lysias

οὐκ ἐς κόρακας ἀποφθερεῖ, βύρσης κάκιστον
ὄζων;

ΑΛΛ. καὶ τοῦτό γ᾽ ἐπίτηδές σε περιήμπεσχεν, ἵν᾽ ἀπο-
πνίξῃ·
καὶ πρότερον ἐπεβούλευσέ σοι. τὸν καυλὸν
οἶσθ᾽ ἐκεῖνον
τοῦ σιλφίου τὸν ἄξιον γενόμενον; ΔΗ. οἶδα
μέντοι.   895

892. ὄζων MSS. and vulg. ὄζει Kock Vels.
893. τοῦτό γ᾽ Bentl. and vulg. for τοῦτ᾽. περιήμπεσχεν R. -ισχεν rest: the aorist is required, see Ruth. *NP* 85 for the form.

---

10. 10 φάσκων θοιμάτιον ἀποδεδύσθαι ἢ τὸν χιτωνίσκον ἐκδεδύσθαι, Bekk. *Anecd.* 218. 3, Polyb. xv 27. 9: the verbs are used in these senses respectively in Anacreon 41, Herod. i 8, v 106, Ar. *Thesm.* 214, 656, *Eccl.* 536, Archippus 40, Xen. *Hell.* iv 3. 19, *Ages.* 1. 28 : so Aristotle has ἀποδύεσθαι of the nautilus losing its shell, *Hist. Anim.* x 37. 622ᵇ 18, but ἐκδύεσθαι of a lizard casting its skin, *mirab. ausc.* 66. 835ᵃ 27. So it is probable that the chorus of old men in the *Lysistrata* threw off their ἱμάτια at the word ἐπαποδυώμεθα 615, as they do their ἐξωμίδες at the word ἐκδυώμεθ᾽ 662 (then are the women too naked after 686?). But ἀποδύομαι seems to mean *strip naked* of athletes in Thucyd. i 6. 5 and so probably Plato *Rep.* v 457 A, Xen. *symp.* 2. 18, Lysias *fragm.* 75. 1 : it is not clear how ἀποδύω and ἐκδύω differ in Xen. *Anab.* iv 3. 12 and 17: and Demosth. *Conon* 32 and 35 has ἐκδεδύσθαι θοιμάτιον. Perhaps either word was used of the ἱμάτιον worn as the τρίβων (see on 881—3): but I can only quote ἀποδύω, as *Vesp.* 1121. In *Av.* 934 and 947 it is possible to take the first ἀπόδυθι as said to the slave, 'take off your σπολάς,' and the second as to the poet, 'take off the σπολάς you have just got, as you are going to get the χιτωνίσκος to put under it.' The distinction is not kept in Homer (*Il.* ii 262, *Od.* xiv 341 &c.), or in later writers, as Athen. vii 281 D ἀποδὺς τὸν χιτῶνα, xi 507 D, Plut. *garrul.* 9. 506 D.

I think τοδί would sound more arrogant than the Sausage-man's τουτονὶ in 883 : and ὦ πόνηρε is the swaggerer's retort to his illustration from social usage. The ἱμά-

τιον is probably one of the leather garments mentioned by Pollux vii 70.

892. This use of φθείρομαι = ἰέναι with a curse occurs in the compounds with ἀνα- ἀπο- εἰσ- ἐκ- περι- προσ- συν-. Though it was hardly a dignified expression, Euripides has it four times, φθείρομαι *Heracl.* 284, *Androm.* 708, 715, and ἀποφθ- *HF* 1290.

Vesp. 38 ὄζει κάκιστον τοὐνύπνιον βύρσης σαπρᾶς of a dream about Cleon : see Blümner *Technol.* i 262 for details of tanning in point.

893—5. Compare Philocleon's struggles against a change in his dress, *Vesp.* 1122—. 'He is trying to stink you out, as he has done before.' The ἐκεῖνον and the τότε in 900 may refer to some actual case of recent interest. καυλός, properly the *stalk* of the silphium, Pollux vi 67: καυλὸς καὶ σίλφιον mentioned separately in Eubulus 7. 3, 19. 3, Alexis 127. 5. The silphium plant is fully described by Theophrastus *Hist. Plant.* vi 3, followed by Pliny *NH* xix 38—, xxii 101 : it seems to have been the main condiment of Greek cookery, and it was much used in medicine. It must have been the chief article in the large trade between Athens and Cyrene : Theophrastus implies that it mostly came to the Piraeus. Its decay, whether owing to ravages of barbarians (Strabo xvii 3. 22), the conduct of Roman *publicani* (Plin. *NH* xix 39), or merely a change of taste (Hehn), is one of the curiosities of commerce. A Persian inferior variety is supposed to be asafoetida (*stercus diaboli*). We cannot tell why it was cheap at this time in Athens : the fall in price may

ΑΛΛ. ἐπίτηδες οὗτος αὐτὸν ἔσπευσ᾽ ἄξιον γενέσθαι,
ἵν᾽ ἐσθίοιτ᾽ ὠνούμενοι, κἄπειτ᾽ ἐν Ἡλιαίᾳ
βδέοντες ἀλλήλους ἀποκτείνειαν οἱ δικασταί.

ΔΗ. νὴ τὸν Ποσειδῶ καὶ πρὸς ἐμὲ τοῦτ᾽ εἶπ᾽ ἀνὴρ
Κόπρειος.

ΑΛΛ. οὐ γὰρ τόθ᾽ ὑμεῖς βδεόμενοι δήπου ᾽γένεσθε
πυρροί ;   900

ΔΗ. καὶ νὴ Δί᾽ ἦν γε τοῦτο Πυρράνδρου τὸ μηχάνημα.

ΠΑ. οἵοισί μ᾽, ὦ πανοῦργε, βωμολοχεύμασιν ταράτ-
τεις.

ΑΛΛ. ἡ γὰρ θεός μ᾽ ἐκέλευσε νικῆσαί σ᾽ ἀλαζονείαις.

ΠΑ. ἀλλ᾽ οὐχὶ νικήσεις. ἐγὼ γάρ φημί σοι παρέξειν,
ὦ Δῆμε, μηδὲν δρῶντι μισθοῦ τρύβλιον ῥοφῆσαι.
905

899. Κόπριος MSS. except R which has Κοπρεῖος. **900—1.** πυρροί and
Βυρσάνδρου Müller-Strübing *Arist.* p. 70. **903.** Dind. for ἀλαζονείας R, -νείᾳ rest.

possibly have had something to do with
the recent establishment of democracy in
Cyrene (Head *Hist. Num.* p. 729), or
with Cleon's interest in hides, the other
article from Cyrene mentioned in Hermippus' well-known list of Athenian
imports (*fr.* 63. 4 Kock): that list is
nearly contemporary with the *Knights*,
and Cyrene comes first, no doubt owing
to some temporary importance. The
comic charge here depends on the flatulent
and purgative qualities of the plant, which
are given in detail by Theophrastus and
Pliny. For ἄξιος *cheap* see on 645. The
Attic μέντοι 'of eager assent' generally
goes with the emphatic word of the
question repeated as here.

896—8. σπεύδω σπουδή of political
influence put in force, generally invidious,
as *inf.* 1370, σοφοὶ σιγῶσι κοὐ σπεύδου-
σιν εἰς τὰ πράγματα Eurip. *Ion* 599,
σπουδαὶ ἑταιρειῶν ἐπ᾽ ἀρχὰς Plato *Theaet.*
173 D, οὐ καταγνοὺς αὐτὸς αὑτοῦ ἀλλὰ
τὴν σπουδὴν τῶν κατηγόρων φοβηθεὶς
ὑπαπέστη Antipho *tetral.* iii 8. 1: cf.
σπουδαρχίδης *Ach.* 595, σπουδαρχίας Xen.
Symp. 1. 4.
The second plur. here and 900 seems
to mean an appeal to the general audience.

899. Κόπρος was a deme: the ad-

jective Κόπρειος occurs in *CIA* i 185 A
38 &c.

900. οὐ δήπου is *nonne*, οὐ τί που
num. For πυρροί cf. *Eccl.* 1061.

901. There is practically no ground
for the ingenious guesses that Πύρρανδρος
means Cleon, that he was red-haired,
and that the epithet αἴθων in the well-
known fragment of Hermippus 46, δηχθεὶς
αἴθωνι Κλέωνι, means 'red-haired.' Πύρρανδρος was a fairly common name Aeschin.
Ctes. 139, *CIA* i 447, ii 19. The proverb
Πυρράνδρου μηχάνημα (Suidas and Apostol.
15. 16) was probably invented by grammarians.

902—3. Cleon has failed to do what
he threatened in 290, περιελῶ σ᾽ ἀλαζονείαις.
βωμολόχος combines the ideas of buffoon
and parasite: Plutarch uses it of Cleon,
Nicias 3. It is the goddess of democracy
who gives the advice against her own
champion, cf. 1203.

904—5. παρέξειν as it is to be permanent, see on 130, 838, 912. 'Payment
for nothing' is a dish of φακῆ or some
common food, the verb with which was
ῥοφῶ as in 51, cf. *Ach.* 278, *Vesp.*
1118. It appears from Aristot. *Pol.
Ath.* 41 that ecclesiasts were not paid
till Agyrrhius' time: but a scheme for
such payment may have been broached

N. A.   9

ΑΛΛ. ἐγὼ δὲ κυλίχνιόν γέ σοι καὶ φάρμακον δίδωμι
τὰν τοῖσιν ἀντικνημίοις ἑλκύδρια περιαλείφειν.
ΠΑ. ἐγὼ δὲ τὰς πολιάς γέ σοὐκλέγων νέον ποιήσω.
ΑΛΛ. ἰδοὺ δέχου κέρκον λαγὼ τὠφθαλμιδίω περιψῆν.
ΠΑ. ἀπομυξάμενος ὦ Δῆμέ μου πρὸς τὴν κεφαλὴν
ἀποψῶ.   910
ΑΛΛ. ἐμοῦ μὲν οὖν. ΠΑ. ἐμοῦ μὲν οὖν.
ἐγώ σε ποιήσω τριη-
ραρχεῖν, ἀναλίσκοντα τῶν

913. ἀναλίσκοντα τῶν σαυτοῦ om. Cobet (*Mnemos.* n.s. ii 422), as a scholium which has crept into the text: but the system seems to be in sets of four lines.

---

as early as Cleon's day; or more probably the reference is to state-support of the poor, who had an allowance of one obol in Lysias' time (24. 13), afterwards raised to two Aristot. *Pol. Ath.* 49.

906—7. Free medicine is the next bid, and it is given, not merely promised. κυλίχνιον is a box of medicine, called also κυλιχνίς, as by Antiphanes 208, Athen. xi 480 c, and πυξίδιον. Free medical attendance was an old idea in Greek states, older than free education, Diodor. Sic. xii 13. 4.

Ulcers on the shins, arising from varicose veins, are common in medical practice, especially among the old and poor: cf. Theophrastus *char.* 19, Pollux iv 196, 206. κυλίχνιον, ἑλκύδριον, ὀφθαλμίδιον in 909 are all quoted from this passage only: the terminations have different meanings, 'a nice little pipkin for your nasty little sores,' 'your dear little pair of eyes.'

908. *fr.* 360 ἐκλέγει τ᾽ ἀεὶ ἐκ τοῦ γενείου τὰς πολιὰς (cf. *sup.* 520): and so Theophrast. *char.* 2 of the flatterer. I cannot agree with Rutherford that ἐκλέγω can mean 'speak out,' even in Thucyd. iv 59.

909. The modern use is the hare's foot for cosmetics.

910. The rule for the voice of verbs in such cases is given *sup.* 490, 785: for the active in this verb cf. οὐ δύναται τῇ χειρὶ Πρόκλος τὴν ῥῖν᾽ ἀπομύσσειν *Anth. Pal.* xi 268. 1. ἀποψῶ=ἀποψῇ τὴν χεῖρα.

912—8. Iambic dimeters, as usual in close connexion with tetrameters catal. in

the Agon: synapheia holds and the system ends with a catalectic (Gleditsch, *Metrik* § 62, and cf. *sup.* 367—, 441—). Cleon takes his adversary as a man of wealth and position now, to be annoyed as such by trierarchies and income-taxes. Cleon as strategus would appoint the trierarchs. Till B.C. 412 a trierarchy fell on each individual on the roll: the burden was in later times shared between two or more people. The state provided the hull and the main part of the tackle, which were made under contracts arranged for by the Council (Aristot. *Pol. Ath.* 46), the trierarch having only to keep the ship in good repair. The cost was 40 to 60 minae a year (Böckh). The grumbler about the hardships of the rich man's life at Athens (Antiphanes 204) says ἢ γὰρ εἰσφορά τις ἥρπακεν τἄνδοθεν πάντ᾽...ἢ χορηγὸς αἱρεθεὶς ἱμάτια χρυσᾶ παρασχὼν τῷ χορῷ ῥάκος φορεῖ ἢ τριηραρχῶν ἀπήγξατο.

ἀναλίσκοντα 913 and ἀναλῶν 915 seem inconsistent. The only other case of ἀναλίσκω in Arist. is in a tragic speech by Euripides *Thesm.* 1131. ἀναλίσκω seems to have prevailed in the end, but both were certainly used in 5th century prose (Meisterhans gives both from inscriptions). *Fr.* 15 εἰς τὰς τριήρεις δεῖν ἀναλοῦν ταῦτα καὶ τὰ τείχη.

The distinction between ἐφέξω and ἐπισχήσω is the same as between ἕξω and σχήσω (see on 130 and 838): ἐφέξω intrans. here and Soph. *Elect.* 1369, trans. Eurip. *Hec.* 1283, Plut. *quom. adul.* 20. 62 A : ἐπισχήσω trans. Plato *apol.* 39 D, Demosth. 1 *Steph.* 88, Eurip. *Andr.* 160, *Hec.* 692. [For

σαυτοῦ, παλαιὰν ναῦν ἔχοντ',
εἰς ἣν ἀναλῶν οὐκ ἐφέ- 915
ξεις οὐδὲ ναυπηγούμενος·
διαμηχανήσομαί θ' ὅπως
ἂν ἱστίον σαπρὸν λάβῃς.

ΑΛΛ. ἀνὴρ παφλάζει, παῦε παῦ'
ὑπερζέων· ὑφελκτέον 920
τῶν δᾳδίων, ἀπαρυστέον
τε τῶν ἀπειλῶν ταυτηί.

ΠΑ. δώσεις ἐμοὶ καλὴν δίκην,
ἱπούμενος ταῖς εἰσφοραῖς.

918. τὸν ἱστὸν ἂν conj. Kock (ed. 1); cf. *CIA* iv 834 ii 94 τούτων (ἱστῶν) εἷς μέν ἐστι τριπήδεστος.
919. ΧΟ. MSS. vulg. ΑΛΛ. Bergk Ribb. Blaydes Zieliński p. 117 (as the chorus must here be judicial merely).
921. δαίδων or δάδων MSS., δᾳδίων Pors. δαλίων Bentley Dind. &c.: but δάλιον, restored from Suidas in *Pax* 959, is a ritual word for the brand dipped in the χέρνιψ.

cases of -έξω and -σχήσω from other compounds of ἔχω see Blass in *Rhein. Mus.* xlvii 285—7.] The derived nouns were distinguished: the rare ἔφεξις meant *excuse, reason*, as *Vesp.* 338, ἐπίσχεσις meant a *check*, ἐποχή came in later and was specially used in the philosophical sense of *suspense of judgment*. Plato i *Alcib.* 107 C illustrates the difference between ναυπηγεῖν (*be a ship-carpenter*) and ναυπηγεῖσθαι (*have ships built*): the active is naturally much the less common.
ὅπως ἂν, see on 80 *sup.*, and Shilleto on Thucyd. ii 60. 1.
919— παφλάζει, 'bubbles,' *fr.* 423 τὸ δ' ἔτνος τοὐν ταῖς κυλίχναις τουτὶ θερμὸν καὶ τοῦτο παφλάζον. The senses of *bubble* and *babble* may be combined, as here, Eubulus 109 προσγελῶσά τε λοπὰς παφλάζει βαρβάρῳ λαλήματι, Timocles 15 of Hyperides (Kock), and in Παφλαγών. 'Pull the firewood from below, and skim the froth from above.' For ἀπαρύω 'skim' cf. Herod. iv. 2 (of cream), Alexis 45 man is like wine, οἶνον τὸν νέον πολλή 'στ' ἀνάγκη καὶ τὸν ἄνδρ' ἀποξέσαι......ἀπαρυθέντα τὴν ἄνω ταύτην ἄνοιαν ἐπιπολάζουσαν, τότε πότιμον γενέσθαι καὶ καταστῆναι πάλιν, Plut. *ser. num. vind.* 5. 551 B λόγοι μνημονευόμενοι καὶ πράξεις λεγόμεναι τὸ τραχὺ καὶ σφοδρὸν ἀπαρύουσι τῆς ὀργῆς,

and for the metaphor of firewood Teleclides 40 (Εὐριπίδης) ᾧ καὶ Σωκράτης τὰ φρύγαν' ὑποτίθησι.
ταυτηί sc. τῇ ἀρυταίνῃ, cf. Antiphanes 25 ἀρύταιναν ἐκ μέσου βάψασα τοῦ λέβητος ζέοντος ὕδατος; or ἐπηνρύσει as *Ach.* 245, ζωμηρύσει as Athen. iii 126 D ζῶμον τῇ ζωμηρύσει καταμίγνυε...αὐτὸν ἀπ' αὑτοῦ ἀρυόμενος πρὸς τὸ μηδὲν ὑπερξέσαι, *Anth. Pal.* vi 101. 5 ζωμήρυσίν τε τὴν λίπους ἀφρηλόγον.
Observe the regular usage of plur. in the diminutive, δᾷς δᾴδια, cf. λαγὼς λαγῷα &c. Cf. on 100.
923—6. Trierarchy gave exemption from the προεισφορά, which was a kind of liturgy, but not from the εἰσφορά, which was levied on all citizens and metics worth over 25 minae, as a progressive income-tax on property. Under the system of Nausinicus 378 B.C. the richest class consisted of 300 men. Lysias 28. 3 of Athenians generally, πιεζόμενοι ταῖς εἰσφοραῖς. Though the εἰσφορά was not a liturgy strictly, yet it fell so much on the rich, that it is spoken of as a special burden which it was creditable to have undertaken honourably, Lysias 2. 31 τριηραρχῶν καὶ εἰσφορὰς εἰσφέρων καὶ χορηγῶν καὶ τἆλλα λῃτουργῶν οὐδενὸς ἧττον πολυτελῶς τῶν πολιτῶν. As a war-tax,

ἐγὼ γὰρ εἰς τοὺς πλουσίους   925
σπεύσω σ' ὅπως ἂν ἐγγραφῇς.
ΑΛΛ. ἐγὼ δ' ἀπειλήσω μὲν οὐδέν, εὔχομαι δέ σοι ταδί·
τὸ μὲν τάγηνον τευθίδων
ἐφεστάναι σίζον· σὲ δὲ   930
γνώμην ἐρεῖν μέλλοντα περὶ
Μιλησίων καὶ κερδανεῖν
τάλαντον, ἢν κατεργάσῃ,
σπεύδειν ὅπως τῶν τευθίδων
ἐμπλήμενος φθαίης ἔτ' εἰς   935
ἐκκλησίαν ἐλθών· ἔπει-
τα πρὶν φαγεῖν, ἀνὴρ μεθή-

935—6. ἔτ' ἢ 's ἐκ. ἐλθεῖν Zacher.   ἐλθεῖν R and most MSS.   ἐλθών V and edd.

---

falling on the richer classes, and fixed as to amount by vote of the ecclesia, it would be just the field for Cleon's σπουδή.

ἵπος ἵπόω were originally either of fulling or of a mousetrap (Pollux vii 41): yet they were used seriously by Pindar and Aeschylus.

927—. The comic curse is the proper answer to the serious threats of Cleon. For similar short comic curses in lyric metres cf. *Ach.* 1156. The construction is the acc. and inf. idiomatic in prayers, even without εὔχομαι expressed (as *Ach.* 248—&c.), changing later to the more common and direct optative.

The τευθίς, smaller and more delicate than the τεῦθος and σηπία, was broiled as a rule Antiphanes 217. 21, Metagenes 6. 6, Anaxandr. 41. 46 (τευθίδες ὀπταί, σηπίαι ἐφθαί), Athen. iii 108 A—C (Sotades 1. 15 ἀστεῖον ἐφθὴ τευθίς is exceptional and condemned by Athen. viii 356 E): it does not seem to have been thought a dainty dish except when served very hot in the frying pan as here, Alexis 187 ἐπὶ τὸ τάγηνον σίζον ἐπεισιὼν φέρω: and so with ἀφύαι Pherecrates 104: the Sausage-man is now on a higher level than Cleon in luxury.

The variation between τάγηνον and τήγανον is curious and unexplained: τήγανον is illustrated as the exceptional form by Athenaeus vi 228 C and Pollux x 98: it is opposed to λοπὰς as *frying-pan* to *boiling-pot*, Eubulus 109.

930—. Miletus is assessed on the tribute-lists to pay ten talents B.C. 449—446, five B.C. 445—439, and ten B.C. 424. Gilbert (*Inn. Gesch.* p. 187) supposes that the tribute was raised to ten talents in 424, that Cleon opposed this rise and was thought to be bribed to do so.

935—. φθαίης, 'be in time,' as Thucyd. iv 96. 1 τοιαῦτα τοῦ Ἱπποκράτους παρακελευομένου καὶ μέχρι μὲν μέσου τοῦ στρατοπέδου ἐπελθόντος, τὸ δὲ πλέον οὐκ-έτι φθάσαντος: 'have time,' Lucian *Dial. Mort.* 13. 2 οὐ γὰρ ἔφθασα ἐπισκῆψαί τι περὶ αὐτῆς, which seems to support ἐλθεῖν of MSS.: but φθάνω with inf. is not unusual in late Greek (Cobet *VL* 316), and the inf. in *Nub.* 1384 and Thucyd. iii 82. 7 has not been corrected. On the tendency of φθάνω to take a participle of the same tense after it (φθάνω κελεύων, ἔφθασα κελεύσας), see Gildersleeve, *Amer. Journ. Phil.* xii 76.

Archestratus cf. Athen. vii 327 A ἐπείγου οὕτως ὡς πνίγεσθαι ὑπὸ σπουδῆς καταπίνων.

κοι, καὶ σὺ τὸ τάλαντον λαβεῖν
βουλόμενος ἐ-
σθίων ἀποπνιγείης. 940
ΧΟΡ. εὖ γε νὴ τὸν Δία καὶ τὸν Ἀπόλλω καὶ τὴν
Δήμητρα.
ΔΗ. κἀμοὶ δοκεῖ καὶ τἄλλα γ' εἶναι καταφανῶς
ἀγαθὸς πολίτης, οἷος οὐδείς πω χρόνου
ἀνὴρ γεγένηται τοῖσι πολλοῖς τοὐβολοῦ. 945
σὺ δ', ὦ Παφλαγών, φάσκων φιλεῖν μ' ἐσκορό-
δισας.
καὶ νῦν ἀπόδος τὸν δακτύλιον, ὡς οὐκ ἔτι

940. ἀποπνιγείης MSS., ἐπαποπνιγείης Elmsley, ἄμ' ἀποπνιγείης Mein., ἐναποπνιγείης Bergk: ὅπν is of course impossible in ordinary comic iambic trimeter: but such things are allowed in lyric metres, and I cannot think there is sufficient reason to introduce any conjecture: tragic scansion would give burlesque emphasis to the curse.

941. Aristophanes very seldom uses prose: a scholiast here says Eupolis often did. The cases in Ar. are chiefly formal oaths, as here, *Av.* 865, *Thesm.* 295. The formula here is the ancient and solemn one prescribed for the heliastic oath, Pollux viii 122 ὤμνυσαν ἐν Ἀρδήττῳ δικαστηρίῳ Ἀπόλλω πατρῷον καὶ Δήμητρα καὶ Δία Βασιλέα· ὁ δὲ Ἄρδηττος...ὠνόμασται ἀπό τινος ἥρωος, ὃς στασιάζοντα τὸν δῆμον ὑπὲρ ὁμονοίας ὥρκισεν (the combination of deities probably implies the reconciling of tribes): it occurs also in the oath imposed on the βουλή of Erythrae *CIA* i 9 (Hicks no. 23), in the treaty between Athens and Corcyra BC. 375 *CIA* ii add. 49ᵇ, and a magistrate's oath *CIA* ii 578. After the 'great oath' of Homer by Zeus, Apollo and Athene the omission of Athena seems strange: it may be due to a desire that no deities of party should be mentioned (see *sup.* on 551). A suspected copy of the oath in Demosth. *Timocr.* 151 gives Poseidon for Demeter. Draco ordered the invocation of Zeus, Poseidon and Athena (Schol. Ven. on *Il.* xv 36). Zeus, Athena, Poseidon, Demeter are the powers sworn by in the treaty with Ceos (Dittenberger no. 79). Demosth. *Callipp.* 9 uses the appeal in the text as witness to his truth: in *Mid.* 198 he uses νὴ τὸν Δία καὶ τὸν Ἀπόλλω καὶ τὴν Ἀθηνᾶν in an appeal to democratic feeling against Midias' insolence. Plato *Legg.* xi 936 E prescribes to a witness an oath by τοὺς τρεῖς θεοὺς Δία καὶ Ἀπόλλωνα καὶ Θέμιν. For collections and theories on the heliastic oath, see Fränkel in *Hermes* xiii 452—, E. Curtius *Gesamm. Abhandl.* i 384, Wilam. *Aus Kyd.* 95, Ott *Griech. Eid*, Drerup xxiv *Suppt. Jahrb. Kl. Phil.*

943. Genitives of 'time since when' are common with a numeral or vaguer adjective, πέντε ἐτῶν, πολλοῦ χρόνου &c.: χρόνου alone is partly excused by the πω (see Rutherf. *NP* 345), but no parallel is quoted except the curiosity χρόνου ἤδη ἀκάθαρτον in Lucian *Lexiph.* 19 by Kock: id. *Demosth. enc.* 36 ἤδη διὰ χρόνου does not seem suitable, and ἤδη χρόνου may be right. χρόνου is not uncommon 'for some time' in affirmative clauses and χρόνου with a negative is of course very parallel.

945. 'The great three-halfpence worth': τοὺς χύδην διακειμένους ἄνδρας, Eust. on *Odyss.* p. 1382. 18, cf. τῆς δὲ πλείστης τοὐβολοῦ μάχης Antiphanes 135, τὰ δέκα τοῦ ὀβολοῦ ἐπὶ τῶν μηδενὸς ἀξίων Prov. in Gaisford's *Paroem.* p. 130.

946. σκοροδίζω, 'anger' up to fighting point: cf. 494.

ἐμοὶ ταμιεύσεις. ΠΑ. ἔχε· τοσοῦτον δ' ἴσθ' ὅτι,
εἰ μή μ' ἐάσεις ἐπιτροπεύειν, ἕτερος αὖ
ἐμοῦ πανουργότερός τις ἀναφανήσεται. 950

ΔΗ.　οὐκ ἔσθ' ὅπως ὁ δακτύλιός ἐσθ' οὑτοσὶ
οὑμός· τὸ γοῦν σημεῖον ἕτερον φαίνεται·
ἀλλ' ἢ οὐ καθορῶ; ΑΛΛ. φέρ' ἴδω, τί σοι
σημεῖον ἦν;

ΔΗ.　δημοῦ βοείου θρῖον ἐξωπτημένον.

954. θρίον MSS. except R corr.

948—9. The words ταμίας and
ἐπίτροπος with their derivatives are
used of honourable positions of trust,
generally of freemen, but also sometimes
of slaves: so they exactly suit the case in
the play as a representation of history.
It is hardly possible to mark a distinction
in meaning between the two words:
ταμίας is the older, less specially Attic,
less legal, word, and there were state-
functionaries called ταμίαι of departments,
while ἐπίτροπος is more of private ward-
ship: but the two are often used together,
as *Eccl.* 212 ταύταις ἐπιτρόποις καὶ ταμί-
αισι χρώμεθα, and the *fr.* from the second
Peace, πιστή τροφός, ταμία, σύνεργος,
ἐπίτροπος. Later ταμίας was used for
quaestor, and ἐπίτροπος for *procurator*, in
Roman imperial business.

The idea that there is special reference
to the ταμίας τῆς κοινῆς προσόδου here was
held by Valesius (on Harpocr. s.v. ταμίας),
approved by Böckh *Staatsh.*[3] i p. 204, and
insisted on by Müller-Strübing *Aristoph.*
p. 136, but it has not been confirmed by
recent discovery or accepted by scholars
generally. ταμίαι of other departments
certainly existed before **400**, but of the
common Revenue apparently not.

A ταμίας or ἐπίτροπος was a necessary
part of an ideal Greek household, Aristot.
Pol. i 7. 1255[b] 35 ὅσοις ἐξουσία μὴ αὑτοὺς
κακοπαθεῖν, ἐπίτροπος λαμβάνει ταύτην τὴν
τιμήν, αὐτοὶ δὲ πολιτεύονται ἢ φιλοσοφοῦ-
σιν.

A seal-ring would be held by the ταμίας
in both meanings, public and private: the
imitation of a seal was a danger to all
business, and Solon commanded that seal-
makers should destroy the casts of seals
supplied to individuals, Diog. Laert. i 57.

The δημοσία σφραγὶς or δημόσιον σή-
μαντρον was kept by the ἐπιστάτης for
the time, Aristot. *Pol. Ath.* 44: it might
be used by him (*CIA* iv 104[a] 30) or by the
Strategi (*CIA* ii 443). Its device was no
doubt the owl, or the gorgoneion (E.
Curtius in *Ges. Abhandl.* ii 86).

δακτύλιος is the whole ring, σφραγίς or
ψῆφος the engraved gem in it, σῆμα or
σημεῖον the device engraved.

949. εἰ μή with fut. in a threat.
Plato com. 186 ἦν γὰρ ἀποθάνῃ εἷς τις
πονηρός, δύ' ἀνέφυσαν ῥήτορες. ἀναφανήσεται looks colloquial, like *invenietur*.

951—3. οὑτοσί)(ἐμός, γοῦν giving an
instance or proof, as often.

ἀλλ' ἦ is common as an interrogative in
tragedy, see Elmsley on Eurip. *Heracl.*
425 and Blaydes' crit. note here. It
generally means 'Perhaps?', 'I hope
not,' asking a question in hope of a negative answer)(μέν interrog.: such cases
outside tragedy are *Thesm.* 97 ἀλλ' ἦ
τυφλὸς μέν εἰμι; *Vesp.* 8 and *fr.* 178 ἀλλ'
ἦ παραφρονεῖς; Xenoph. *Symp.* i. 15 ἀλλ'
ἦ ὀδύνη σε εἴληφε; *Anab.* vii 6. 4 ἀλλ' ἦ
δημαγωγεῖ ὁ ἀνὴρ τοὺς ἄνδρας; Plato *Gorg.*
447 A ἀλλ' ἦ κατόπιν ἑορτῆς ἥκομεν; Lucian
Necyom. 1 οὗτος, ἀλλ' ἦ παραπαίεις; and
perhaps *inf.* 1162, *Lys.* 928. The MSS.
generally seem to give ἀλλή or ἀλλ' ἦ, as
here: and Suidas and Bekk. *Anecd.* 376. 8
attest the use of ἀλλ' ἦ for εἰ μή, ἤ, ἀλλ'
ἄρα or ἄρα. Yet ἀλλ' ἦ seems to suit the
meaning and usage better: and the usage
must in any case be carefully distinguished
from the ἀλλ' ἤ after negatives, as in 780.

954. This is an early instance of
'canting heraldry.' Ar. repeats the joke
Vesp. 40, the whale (Cleon) ἴστη βόειον
δημόν.

ΑΛΛ. οὐ τοῦτ᾽ ἔνεστιν. ΔΗ. οὐ τὸ θρῖον; ἀλλὰ τί;
ΑΛΛ. λάρος κεχηνὼς ἐπὶ πέτρας δημηγορῶν.   956
ΔΗ. αἰβοῖ τάλας. ΑΛΛ. τί ἔστιν; ΔΗ. ἀπόφερ᾽
　　　ἐκποδών.
　　　οὐ τὸν ἐμὸν εἶχεν, ἀλλὰ τὸν Κλεωνύμου.
　　　παρ᾽ ἐμοῦ δὲ τουτονὶ λαβὼν ταμίευέ μοι.
ΠΑ. μὴ δῆτά πώ γ᾽, ὦ δέσποτ᾽, ἀντιβολῶ σ᾽ ἐγώ,
　　　πρὶν ἄν γε τῶν χρησμῶν ἀκούσῃς τῶν ἐμῶν.
ΑΛΛ. καὶ τῶν ἐμῶν νυν. ΠΑ. ἀλλ᾽ ἐὰν τούτῳ πίθῃ,
　　　μολγὸν γενέσθαι δεῖ σε. ΑΛΛ. κἄν γε τουτῳί,
　　　ψωλὸν γενέσθαι δεῖ σε μέχρι τοῦ μυρρίνου.

962. νῦν MSS.　　　　**963—4.** δῆ R.

In the accounts of the curious omelette, called θρῖον, given by Suidas, Pollux vi 57, and Hesychius, hog's lard is mentioned specially: the scholiasts here say βόειος implies the stupidity of Demos: 'he is a great eater of beef, and it does harm to his wits.' The tragic rhythm of course heightens the absurdity of the device.

955. ἔνεστι is technical for the device on the gem: σφραγίς· ἔνι ταῦρος, and the like, occur often in the inventories.

956. λάρος is the *cormorant* in metaphor, if not in strict fact, καθάπερ ὁ λάρος ὅλον περιχανὼν τὸ δέλεαρ Lucian *merc. cond.* 3. It is the greedy Heracles of the bird-world, *Av.* 567: and the greedy demagogue, Cleon here and *Nub.* 591, Hyperides in a fragment of Timocles.

πέτρα, the *bema*, cf. πέτραι 313.

δημηγόρος and derivatives are generally, as we should expect, seriously used in the orators, sarcastically in Comedy and Plato.

957—8. αἰβοῖ τάλας, *Pax* 544. Cleonymus, the Falstaff of Attic comedy, glutton and coward, liar and parasite: as to his politics, *Vesp.* 592 represents him as a professed democrat: cf. Andoc. *Myst.* 27: his recent motion in favour of Methone *CIA* i 40 (second decree) might come from either party.

960—1. For the eager double γε cf. *Eccl.* 856 and the conjectural reading μήπω γε, πρὶν γ᾽ ἂν στῶ τρέχων, *Ach.* 176.

ἀκούω with gen., cf. on 624.

962. A well-known oracle had promised Theseus that Athens should always keep above water like a skin-bottle: Plutarch *Thes.* 24 ἀσκὸς γὰρ ἐν οἴδματι ποντοπορεύσει, and (from the Sibyl) ἀσκὸς βαπτίζῃ· δῦναι δέ τοι οὐ θέμις ἐστίν. This was repeated from Delphi to reassure Athens when threatened by Sulla, Pausan. i 20. 7 ἔχρησεν ἡ Πυθία τὰ ἐς τὸν ἀσκὸν ἔχοντα. Synesius was probably thinking of this when he wrote of Athens in decay (*epist.* 135 Migne) καθάπερ ἱερείου διαπεπραγμένου τὸ δέρμα λείπεται γνώρισμα τοῦ πάλαι ποτὲ ζῴου.

Scholia show complete helplessness before μολγός. Symmachus alone shows sense in connecting the phrase with the fragment (157 Dind.) from the Γεωργοί, probably not much later than the *Knights*, which contains the word μολγόν seemingly in a current phrase applied to Athens. Pollux x 187 alone gives the right meaning of the word, viz. βόειος ἀσκός; he quotes Aristophanes for another comic oracle, μή μοι Ἀθηναίους αἰνεῖν, οἱ μολγοὶ ἔσονται. μολγός then seems to be a contemptuous synonym for ἀσκός in the oracle of Theseus. In both fragments Bergk is probably right in proposing to read αἴνειν, the curious word (found in τρίαινα according to Brugmann in *Indog. Forsch.* iii 259) which Cobet *Mnemos.* x 61 says has been lost in our MSS. without leaving *vola aut vestigium.*

963—4. μέχρι τοῦ μυρρίνου, *pube tenus*, the expression μύρρινος and the like coming probably from such representa-

ΠΑ. ἀλλ' οἵ γ' ἐμοὶ λέγουσιν ὡς ἄρξαι σε δεῖ 965
χώρας ἁπάσης ἐστεφανωμένον ῥόδοις.
ΑΛΛ. οὑμοὶ δέ γ' αὖ λέγουσιν ὡς ἀλουργίδα
ἔχων κατάπαστον καὶ στεφάνην ἐφ' ἅρματος
χρυσοῦ διώξεις Cμικύθην καὶ κύριον.

969. διώξεις MSS. διώξει Elmsl. on *Ach.* 278 &c.: see Ruth. *NP* 377.

tions as early Cyprian terracottas: the line is quoted in *Paroemiogr. Bodl.* 953. ψωλός no doubt was often used in comic contempt, *Plut.* 267, *Av.* 507. Herod. ii 104 mentions circumcision as practised among 'Syrians' on the Parthenius; these would be in Paphlagonia, and this might be referred to here.

965—6. Notice the difference between ἀλλά· γε and δέ γ' 967. The rose-wreath marks of course the feaster, not the victor: but Demos' sway will be like the great king's.

967—9. The promise here is of greater and more outlandish pomp. Democracy had only recently levelled the dress of Athenians to the μετρία ἐσθής mentioned by Thucydides i 6. 3, as the French Revolution did in Europe. Heraclides of Pontus, who was a pupil of Plato, held that a luxurious dress lent a high spirit to the upper classes of Athens in the Persian wars, ἀλουργῆ μὲν γὰρ ἡμπίσχοντο ἱμάτια ποικίλους δ' ὑπέδυνον χιτῶνας (Athen. xii 512 B). But a purple dress was now held to be un-Hellenic, except as uniform or on festal occasions, and even then it was exceptional, Athen. xii 534 C of Alcibiades. It is coupled with διάδημα and the like Xen. *Cyrop.* viii 3. 13, Plut. *Demetr.* 41 &c.

For κατάπαστος, 'spangled,' cf. Democr. Ephes. ap. Athen. xii 525 D of a Persian robe, καταπέπασται χρυσοῖς κέγχροις, μίτρα χρυσόπαστος *ib.* 536 A: and χρυσόπαστος of theatrical tinsel (Lucian *Icarom.* 29) or offensive display (Demosth. *Polycl.* 34), Plut. *quaest. conv.* iv 6. 672 A μιτροφόρος καὶ νεβρίδα χρυσόπαστον ἐνημμένος of a high-priest at a Dionysiac orgie, Strabo iv 4. 5 of Celtic chiefs, cf. *chlamys aurata* Tac. *Ann.* xii 56, *chlamys distincta stellis aureis* Suet. *Nero* 25. The gold leaf was fastened or sewn on: a different art, now lost, was to weave gold thread into silk or fine cloth, χιτῶνες

χρυσοϋφεῖς Athen. v 196 F, *chlamys auro intertexta* Verg. *Aen.* viii 167. He is to have not the man's στέφανος, but the woman's στεφάνη, a metal ornament, sometimes of gold and elaborate diadem-form, Baumeister *Denkm.* p. 792. The στεφάνη was familiar on the head of Hera and Nike, *CIA* ii 652: in the Delphian inventory *CIG* 1688 it seems to be exceptionally a soldier's ornament. στεφανηφορῶ by a common change of stem in compounds is to *wear the στέφανος*.

968—9. ἅρμα a four-horse car for racing and processions only. *Vesp.* 1427 ἀνὴρ Συβαρίτης ἐξέπεσεν ἐξ ἅρματος. Instead of διώξει πολεμίους he turns off to the legal sense of διώκω (Scotch *pursue*) and 'Smicythe and consort' would be the legal phrase in an action against a woman, who could be represented only by her κύριος. Σμικύθη appears to be for Σμίκυθος, and the action would be one of the kind implied in 877. For such opprobrious feminine forms of men's names cf. Συστράτη and Κλεωνύμη *Nub.* 678—80, τὴν Ἀμυνίαν 690, *Thesm.* 373—4, Cic. *de orat.* ii 277, Hor. *Sat.* i 8. 39; and for a similar phrase in an actual case see Aeschines *Tim.* 128.

A Smicythus was secretary to the ταμίαι τῶν ἱερῶν χρημάτων, under the presidency of Thucydides of Acherdus, in this or the following year (*CIA* i 139). A Smicythus, perhaps the same, is among the women in *Eccl.* 293. The name looks at first barely serious: all names beginning with Σμικ- or Μικ- seem to be 'Kosenamen.' But the indices to inscriptions show that it was not very rare at Athens, one man of the name being son of a Cratinus, and another father of an Aristophanes: and Σμικύθη, an Athenian washerwoman, has also been found (Roberts *Greek Epigr.* p. 83). A Smicythus occurs twice on vases of Euthymides, perhaps a favourite of his (Brunn *Gesch. d. Künstler²* ii 469).

ΔΗ. καὶ μὴν ἔνεγκ' αὐτοὺς ἰών, ἵν' οὑτοσὶ 970
αὐτῶν ἀκούσῃ. ΑΛΛ. πάνυ γε. ΔΗ. καὶ σύ
νυν φέρε.
ΠΑ. ἰδού. ΑΛΛ. ἰδοὺ νὴ τὸν Δί'· οὐδὲν κωλύει.
ΧΟΡ. ἥδιστον φάος ἡμέρας
ἔσται τοῖσι παροῦσι καὶ
τοῖσιν εἰσαφικνουμένοις, 975
ἢν Κλέων ἀπόληται.
καίτοι πρεσβυτέρων τινῶν
οἵων ἀργαλεωτάτων
ἐν τῷ δείγματι τῶν δικῶν

970. ΔΗ. most MSS. ΚΛ. V. ΧΟ. Enger, Zacher.
974. παροῦσι καὶ τοῖσιν ἀφικνουμένοισιν MSS. παροῦσι πᾶσιν καὶ τοῖς Dobree, who points out that parts of πᾶς are often omitted in MSS. καὶ τοῖς ἀποῦσιν, ἱκνουμένως Bergk. καὶ τοῖσιν εἰσαφικνουμένοις Cobet *Mnemos.* i 417, n.s. ii 422 : Madvig has entered this emendation in his copy : τοῖς ἀφιξομένοισι Bentley : τοῖσιν ἀνταφικνουμένοις Kaibel, Steurer *de Ar. carm. lyr.* 29.

970. καὶ μὴν without γε as if a new character were coming on, cf. on 691.
972. ἰδού, 'very well,' see on 121.
973—. The metre of these six stanzas, each of three Glyconics and a Pherecratic, is very song-like in effect: this may be felt in fragments of Anacreon of the same metre, cf. *inf.* 1111—, *Ran.* 450—. The same form of stanza occurs in Tragic choruses of serious import, Soph. *OT* 1189—1203, *Phil.* 687—690, Eurip. *HF* 668—672 (a scholium here says ταῦτα παρὰ τὰ Εὐριπίδου), and in the Delphian Paean by Aristonous.
εἰσαφικνουμένοις is the best correction. The word in Attic means 'arrive at a place, not one's original home, where one is to be allowed to settle for a time': Plato *Meno* 92 B αἱ πόλεις ἐῶσαι αὐτοὺς εἰσαφικνεῖσθαι καὶ οὐκ ἐξελαύνουσαι, *Legg.* viii 848 A : hence it is used of visitors attracted to Athens by its trades, art and hospitality, Xenoph. *vectig.* 3. 12, 15. 1, Isocr. *Paneg.* 45, Demosth. *adv. Phorm.* 1 : it may mean here 'those who come for the festal season' as *CIA* iv 574. e 17 ἡ πανήγυρις τῶν εἰσαφικνουμένων Ἑλλήνων Ἐλευσῖνάδε.
This is the only express mention of Cleon's name in the play.
977—. Even his old partizans of the

Philocleon type defend him only as a necessary evil. οἵων by regular attraction, Plato *Symp.* 220 B ὄντος πάγου οἵου δεινοτάτου.
ἀργαλέος, specially of the litigious temper *Nub.* 450, Alciphron iii 22. 2, and perhaps in Demosthenes' nickname Ἀργᾶς (cf. on 534) given him on his first litigation Aeschin. *FL* 99, Plut. *Demosth.* 4. It was natural to connect it with πονηρός in meaning, so we have Aeschin. *Tim.* 61 οὐδέπω ὥσπερ νῦν ἀργαλέος τὴν ὄψιν, ἀλλ' ἔτι χρήσιμος (almost = χρηστός), Plut. *glor. Ath.* 5. 348 B Κινησίας ἀργαλέος ποιητής.
979. δεῖγμα (1) *a sample*, (2) *sample-shop*, or mercantile Exchange in the Piraeus and other ports (Demosth. *Polycl.* 24, Xen. *Hell.* v 1. 21 : at Rhodes Polyb. v 88. 8: generally Plut. *curios.* 8. 519 A, εἰς τὸ δεῖγμα καὶ τὴν ἀγορὰν καὶ τοὺς λιμένας ὠθοῦνται): so here comic for the old dicasts' business-resort, the law-courts. It may be more definitely the place where plaints at law were advertised before the statues of the eponymous heroes, Wachsmuth *Stadt Athen* ii 389. ἀντιλέγω 'argue' as against any other view, always apparently with ὡς, *Plut.* 593, Thucyd. viii 24. 5, Herod. viii 77.
χρήσιμος, often of serviceable citizens, almost like χρηστός, cf. Eupolis 118,

ἤκουσ' ἀντιλεγόντων,   980
ὡς εἰ μὴ 'γένεθ' οὗτος ἐν
τῇ πόλει μέγας, οὐκ ἂν ἤ-
στην σκεύη δύο χρησίμω,
δοῖδυξ οὐδὲ τορύνη.
ἀλλὰ καὶ τόδ' ἔγωγε θαυ-   985
μάζω τῆς ὑομουσίας
αὐτοῦ· φασὶ γὰρ αὐτὸν οἱ
παῖδες οἱ ξυνεφοίτων
τὴν Δωριστὶ μόνην ἂν ἁρ-
μόττεσθαι θαμὰ τὴν λύραν,   990
ἄλλην δ' οὐκ ἐθέλειν μαθεῖν·

981. Scal. for γένοιθ' of MSS.   **989.** MSS. omit ἄν, as often in this
usage Cobet *NL* 410. ἐναρμ. Dind. Kock, but this seems unexampled. μὲν ἁρμ.
Bernhardy Vels.

Alexis 247. Dionysius the elder went too far with the word in his tragic line οἴμοι γυναῖκα χρησίμην ἀπώλεσα, Lucian *adv. indoct.* 15.

δοῖδυξ and τορύνη as κύκηθρον καὶ τάρακτρον *Pax* 654, and the famous figure of the two pestles, Cleon and Brasidas, in *Pax* 259—: Lucian *Char.* 7 of Poseidon ἐτάραξε τὸν πόντον ὥσπερ τορύνην τινὰ ἐμβαλὼν τὴν τρίαιναν ..κυκῶν τὴν θάλατταν. Athen. iv 157 A speaks of a hetaera nicknamed θεατροτορύνη. Cf. the συκοφάντης as a household utensil in *Ach.* 934.

986— pointed as a retort to Cleon's contempt of culture expressed in such speeches as Thucyd. iii 37 : there (38. 2) he says the main dangers to Athens come from cultured eloquence selling itself for gain. He is answered apologetically by Diodotus in Thucyd. iii 42. 3, and here by turning the tables on himself. Themistocles had never learned to play or sing, Plut. *Cimon* 9. ὑομουσία, 'son éducation de cochon': the oxymoron is suggested by such phrases as ὗς πρὸς Ἀθηνᾶν, ὗς ἐκώμασε: it is the comic equivalent for ἀπαιδευσία in Diodotus' speech.

988. As φοιτῶ means 'go to school,' so συμφοιτῶ 'be schoolfellow': Plato *Euthyd.* 272 C Socrates going to Connus to learn music speaks of οἱ παῖδες οἱ συμφοιτηταί μοι, Lucian *adv. indoct.* 3.

It is well known that the Greeks, like the Chinese, gave great weight to music in education (*Vesp.* 959), and attributed ethical effects to the various ἁρμονίαι, which were classified in this view by Damon, if not before him : theorists on education agreed, as probably did parents and masters, that the Dorian scale, ἡ Δωριστὶ (ἁρμονία), a minor mode, was most manly and moral Plato *Rep.* iii 399, Arist. *Pol.* v (viii) 5. 22, 7. 8 : it was practically the only mode used in Tragic choral music. [Xen.] *Pol. Ath.* i. 13 says democracy disliked music in education.

ἁρμόττω takes acc. of instrument and cognate acc. of the tune or mode as well, Plato *Laches* 188 D ἁρμονίαν καλλίστην ἡρμοσμένος λύραν.

990. The λύρα was the simpler form, the κιθάρα the more elaborate : the former was naturally the more used in schools. The derivatives of κιθάρα are commoner : λυριστής is not classical, κιθαριστής being the master who taught the lyre, the cithara if required, and singing. θαμά is very rare in Comedy and Attic Prose : the cases quoted are *Av.* 234 (lyric), *Plut.* 1166, *fr.* 198. 4, Plato *Phaedo* 72 E, Isocr. *Panath.* 102, Xen. *Memor.* ii 1. 22 : it is never used by Thucydides, the orators (except the case in Isocrates), Aristotle ; it is not given in the index to Plutarch, and Lucian has it only in the *Lexiphanes*.

κᾷτα τὸν κιθαριστὴν
ὀργισθέντ᾽ ἀπάγειν κελεύ-
ειν, ὡς ἁρμονίαν ὁ παῖς
οὗτος οὐ δύναται μαθεῖν 995
ἢν μὴ δωροδοκιστί.

ΠΑ. ἰδού, θέασαι, κοὐχ ἅπαντας ἐκφέρω.

ΑΛΛ. οἴμ᾽ ὡς χεσείω, κοὐχ ἅπαντας ἐκφέρω.

ΔΗ. ταυτὶ τί ἐστι; ΠΑ. λόγια. ΔΗ. πάντ᾽;

ΠΑ. ἐθαύμασας,
καὶ νὴ Δί᾽ ἔτι γέ μοὔστι κιβωτὸς πλέα. 1000

ΑΛΛ. ἐμοὶ δ᾽ ὑπερῷον καὶ ξυνοικία δύο.

ΔΗ. φέρ᾽ ἴδω, τίνος γάρ εἰσιν οἱ χρησμοί ποτε;

996. So RV¹. δωροδοκηστί V² MSS. vulg. Dind. &c.
998. οἴμοι R.
1001. δύω RV and most MSS. as usual: but δύο is the only good form, Meister-hans § 60. 1.

---

993. The master's ἄπαγε might be transitive, addressed to the παιδαγωγός in attendance on Cleon, or intrans., addressed to Cleon himself, see on 1151: it is here transitive, as is plain from the ὁ παῖς οὗτος. The transition from ἀπάγειν to the or. recta is quite common in Greek.

994—6. *All his knowledge was tips,* Quart. Review clxiii 14.

997—. Oracles were so much run after in the early part of the Peloponnesian war that such a scene as this was a natural part of the Agon. The state appointed three ἐξηγηταί of sacred law and the like, but men like Lampon, Hierocles of Oreus, and Stilbides, reached great fame and influence by undertaking on their own account to work on men's minds by such means. There may be a good deal of allusion to current methods of interpretation, quite lost to us, throughout the scene. Demos is intentionally made sillier here than elsewhere.

997. ἰδού, θέασαι, cf. Ach. 366, to mark the arrangement of a new scene. The rhythm is tragic, cf. Soph. Trach. 1079, Eurip. HF 1131.

ἅπαντας sc. χρησμούς, here used as synonymous with λόγια, which would be more precise, see on 61.

998. Ran. 1—20 is one of several protests made by Aristophanes against comic 'effects' (σοφίσματα) of this kind in other poets.

999. τί οὖν δή ἐστιν ἄττα εἶπεν ὁ ἀνήρ; Plato Phaedo 57 A and Stallbaum's note there.

1000. A collection of oracles bearing on the history of Athens was made by the Pisistratidae, and after their expulsion fell into the hands of Cleomenes, King of Sparta, Herod. v 90. Such an oracle as Demosth. FL 297 reads and makes much of was no doubt taken from a collection apparently in possession of the state, cf. the λόγια of Bacis &c. κιβωτός is a chest for clothes and valuables generally Vesp. 1056 &c., κίστη a box, usually for eatables, as 1211: Vesp. 529 is a rare exception.

1001. The Sausage-man has acted the capitalist for some time: he is making public life pay already: he has not only a two-storied house but two lodging-houses to let. For a case where sudden prosperity is seen by owning συνοικίαι see Athen. xii 542 F. The συνοικία (insula) was a common form of investment for money, and would naturally be larger than the οἰκία.

1002—3. γάρ, see Appendix i: Bacis, see on 123.

ΠΑ. οὑμοὶ μέν εἰσι Βάκιδος. ΔΗ. οἱ δὲ σοὶ τίνος;
ΑΛΛ. Γλάνιδος, ἀδελφοῦ τοῦ Βάκιδος γεραιτέρου.
ΔΗ. εἰσὶν δὲ περὶ τοῦ; ΠΑ. περὶ Ἀθηνῶν, περὶ
Πύλου, 1005
περὶ σοῦ, περὶ ἐμοῦ, περὶ ἁπάντων πραγμάτων.
ΔΗ. οἱ σοὶ δὲ περὶ τοῦ; ΑΛΛ. περὶ Ἀθηνῶν, περὶ
φακῆς,
περὶ Λακεδαιμονίων, περὶ σκόμβρων νέων,
περὶ τῶν μετρούντων τἄλφιτ' ἐν ἀγορᾷ κακῶς,
περὶ σοῦ, περὶ ἐμοῦ· τὸ πέος οὑτοσὶ δάκοι.
ΔΗ. ἄγε νυν ὅπως αὐτοὺς ἀναγνώσεσθέ μοι, 1011
καὶ τὸν περὶ ἐμοῦ 'κεῖνον ὧπερ ἥδομαι,
ὡς ἐν νεφέλαισιν αἰετὸς γενήσομαι.
ΠΑ. ἄκουε δή νυν καὶ πρόσεχε τὸν νοῦν ἐμοί.
Φράζευ, Ἐρεχθείδη, λογίων ὁδόν, ἥν σοι Ἀπόλλων 1015

1010. So R and five MSS. περὶ ἁπάντων πραγμάτων V and the rest.
1013. νεφέλῃσιν MSS. except R. αἰετὸς R and vulg.: ἀετὸς is not found on inscriptions before 300 B.C., Meisterhans § 141.

1004. The fish γλάνις, a kind of shad, is known from Aristotle and comic fragments: but nothing is understood that throws light on the name here.

1005—10. 'Athens and Pylus, you and me &c.,' is all his table of contents: his rival again has a finer range, bringing in the material comfort of the masses as well as high politics, 'Athens and Sparta, lentil-porridge and fresh mackerel, the corn-question, and you and me': and Cleon is coarsely cast aside. φακῆ is fem. adj. from φακός. The mackerel is said to be still the commonest fish in the Black Sea and Hellespont, where the σκόμβρος was caught and exported in large quantities pickled or salted, ἐκ δ' Ἑλλησπόντου σκόμβρους καὶ πάντα τάριχη Hermippus 63. 5. So σκόμβρος was a nickname for a fish-curer, Alexis 77, 168. νέων· νεωστὶ τεταριχευμένων schol.
The corn-trade in Athens was under the strictest state-control, exercised through

officials called σιτοφύλακες and μετρονόμοι, and underlings called προμετρηταί: their functions are defined in Aristot. Pol. Ath. 51.

1011—3. The scholiast quotes the oracle, mentioned he says by Aristophanes also in the Banqueters and the Birds (979),

εὔδαιμον πτολίεθρον Ἀθηναίης ἀγελείης,
πολλὰ ἰδὸν καὶ πολλὰ παθὸν καὶ πολλὰ μογήσαν,
αἰετὸς ἐν νεφέλῃσι γενήσεαι ἤματα πάντα.

1015. He gives a Delphian oracle, though one of Bacis was expected. This is no doubt meant to be a mistake in policy on his part, as is the bearing of the oracle on himself without the expected compliment to Demos. The oracular style is well imitated, at least at first.

ἴαχεν ἐξ ἀδύτοιο διὰ τριπόδων ἐριτίμων.
σώζεσθαί σ' ἐκέλευσ' ἱερὸν κύνα καρχαρόδοντα,
ὃς πρὸ σέθεν χάσκων καὶ ὑπὲρ σοῦ δεινὰ κεκραγὼς   1018
σοὶ μισθὸν ποριεῖ, κἂν μὴ δρᾷς ταῦτ', ἀπολεῖται.
πολλοὶ γὰρ μίσει σφε κατακρώζουσι κολοιοί.
ΔΗ.   ταυτὶ μὰ τὴν Δήμητρ' ἐγὼ οὐκ οἶδ' ὅ τι λέγει.
τί γάρ ἐστ' Ἐρεχθεῖ καὶ κολοιοῖς καὶ κυνί;

1018. πρόσθε or πρόσθεν MSS. πρὸ σέθεν Hotib. Dobr. χάσκων R. λάσκων
and δάκνων most MSS. 1019. δρᾷ MSS. δρᾷς Hotib. Dobr. and vulg.
1022. Ἐρεχθείδῃ κολοιοῖς Bentley.

Part of the effect of the whole scene
depends on the occasional breaking off
from oracular into ordinary Attic language,
even in the hexameters, a metre so ill-
fitted to Attic as a rule. φράζεο was
common in oracles: the god φράζει, and
bids the mortal φράζεσθαι, as often *infra*.
ὁδός is almost technical of the oracular
form and purport, Aesch. *Agam.* 1154,
Soph. *OT* 311, Eurip. *Phoen.* 911.
ἰάχω is not used in Homer of divine
voices: there probably it means the shriek
of the Pythia coming from the holy place
through the collection of tripods dedicated
to the god. Hom. *hymn. Apoll.* 443 ἐς δ'
ἀδυτον κατέδυνε διὰ τριπόδων ἐριτίμων,
Paean of Aristonous ἀπὸ τριπόδων θεοκτή-
των μαντοσύναν ἐποιχνεῖς.
1017. Dogs attached to deities and
temples and were well known in parts of the
ancient world: Aelian gives some curious
tales of their habits in Sicily, *Nat. Anim.*
xi 3. 20.
καρχαρόδους was both the poetical and
the scientific name for beasts of the cat-
and dog-kinds. In literature it is almost
confined to dogs. Possibly enough Cleon
called himself the κύων καρχαρόδους of the
state: anyhow Aristophanes calls him ὁ
καρχαρόδους in the passage *Vesp.* 1031,
repeated *Pax* 754. Athenaeus vi 251 E
speaks of one Thraso, a court parasite,
who was nicknamed ὁ κάρχαρος, Lucian
de merc. cond. 35 ῥήτωρ τῶν καρχάρων,
salt. 3 ὡς κάρχαρον ἔλυσας ἐφ' ἡμᾶς τὸν
σαυτοῦ κύνα.
For demagogues claiming the title of
κύων τοῦ δήμου see *Vesp.* 895, Demosth. i
Aristog. 40, Theophr. *char.* 29 (30 Jebb),

where the φιλοπόνηρος uses the phrase
of a συκοφάντης, Plut. *Demosth.* 23 Δημ.
αὐτὸν μὲν εἴκασε καὶ τοὺς σὺν αὐτῷ κυσὶν
ὑπὲρ τοῦ δήμου μαχομένοις. *Aboyeur* was
used for the συκοφάνται of the Terror in
the French Revolution (Zieliński *Cicero* 53).
1018. χάσκων gives more variety
than the other readings. Applied to a
savage animal, the word is more Epic
than Attic, but this is in its favour: τὸ
χάσμα τοῦ λέοντος M. Aurel. vi 36, Ovid's
Cerberei rictus, though χάσκω is rather
hio than *ringor*. δεινὰ κεκραγώς: Cleon
thinks this will identify him.
1020. σφε κατακρ. 'croak him *down*,'
see on 287. σφε in sing. is post-homeric.
Pindar *Nem.* 3. 82 has κραγέται κολοιοί of
detractors, cf. Plut. *bruta rat.* 5. 989 A.
1021. By the distinction given *sup.*
204, φημι should have reference to the
words, λέγω to their meaning: and so
I think in 1025, 1060 and 1070 φησι
should be translated *say*, and the correction in each case is one of accurate
quotation.
1022. Herod. v 33 σοὶ δὲ καὶ τούτοισι τοῖσι πρήγμασι τί ἐστί; and similar
phrases occur very often in late Greek,
though in classical times it is more
common to have τί πρᾶγμα or the like.
Demus' silliness is, even in this scene,
relieved by occasional shrewdness. He
sees the right objection: dogs were not
allowed on the Acropolis, Plut. *comp.*
Demetr. & Anton. 4; nor were ravens,
Aelian *Nat. Anim.* v 8 (see *inf.* on 1051),
Plut. *Pyth. orac.* 8. 397 F ἐν τοῖς Σικελι-
κοῖς τῶν Ἀθηναίων ἀτυχήμασι...τὴν ἀσπίδα
τοῦ Παλλαδίου κόρακες περιέκοπτον.

ΠΑ.   ἐγὼ μέν εἰμ' ὁ κύων· πρὸ σοῦ γὰρ ἀπύω·
      σοὶ δ' εἶπε σώζεσθαί μ' ὁ Φοῖβος τὸν κύνα.

ΑΛΛ. οὐ τοῦτό φησ' ὁ χρησμός, ἀλλ' ὁ κύων ὁδὶ   1025
      ὥσπερ θύρας σου τῶν λογίων παρεσθίει.
      ἐμοὶ γάρ ἐστ' ὀρθῶς περὶ τούτου τοῦ κυνός.

ΔΗ.   λέγε νυν· ἐγὼ δὲ πρῶτα λήψομαι λίθον,
      ἵνα μή μ' ὁ χρησμὸς ὁ περὶ τοῦ κυνὸς δάκῃ.

ΑΛΛ. Φράζευ, Ἐρεχθείδη, κύνα Κέρβερον ἀνδραποδι-
      στήν,   1030
      ὃς κέρκῳ σαίνων σ', ὁπόταν δειπνῇς, ἐπιτηρῶν,
      ἐξέδεταί σου τοὖψον, ὅταν σύ ποι ἄλλοσε
      χάσκῃς·
      ἐσφοιτῶν τ' ἐς τοὐπτάνιον λήσει σε κυνηδὸν
      νύκτωρ τὰς λοπάδας καὶ τὰς νήσους διαλείχων.

ΔΗ.   νὴ τὸν Ποσειδῶ πολύ γ' ἄμεινον, ὦ Γλάνι. 1035

1026. θύρας MSS., ἀθάρης Hermann; I have thought of λαθύρας as a possible word and one likely to be corrupted: but the only form given is λάθυρος, which was a synonym for ἀθάρα.

1029. τὸ πέος οὑτοσὶ δάκῃ V.   **1032.** που MSS. ποι Cobet *Mnemos.* i 417.

1023. ἠπύω is fairly common in Homer, ἀπύω in Pindar and tragic chorus (once in dialogue *Rhes.* 776: in an iambic dedication *CIGS* 1818): this is unique in Attic.

1024. The Greek idiom in such sentences gives the double emphasis better than English: the fourfold repetition of parts of σύ in the oracle justifies σοί coming first.

1025—6 seem to mean that Cleon suppresses parts of oracles unfavourable to himself. But the reading is uncertain and the full meaning obscure. θύρας is explained by the scholium: the watchdog (usually chained up in the πρόθυρον by day) tries to gnaw his way out.

ὀρθῶς, the critic's word for a correct reading or rendering.

1030—2. If Cleon called himself κύων τοῦ δήμου, his enemies perverted the figure to Κέρβερος, cf. *Pax* 313 and schol. there.

ἀνδραποδιστής, like its cognate words, may mean (1) kidnapper, as *Plut.* 521,

(2) stealer of slaves from their owners, as Lycurg. ap. Harpocr. s.v., or (3) one who condemns free persons to slavery, as Cleon had done at Mitylene (Thucyd. iii 36. 2). ἀνδραποδίστην καλῶν καὶ τύραννον Plut. *quaest. conv.* ii 1. 632 F, cf. Xen. *Symp.* 4. 36. The notion of making money by traffic in human flesh was implied, and the law gave its sanction to the hatred expressed in the word by punishing the offences implied in meanings (1) and (2) with death.

ποι ἄλλοσε = πρὸς ἄλλο τι.

1033—4. ὀπτάνιον *culina*, μαγειρεῖον *forum coquinum*, is the Attic distinction as far as we have evidence. λοπάς was of earthenware)(πίναξ, a wooden platter, cf. Athen. iv 137 F. *Vesp.* 904 (again of Cleon) διαλείχειν τὰς χύτρας. νῆσοι the allies as usual. Lysias *fr.* 58 ἐλυμαίνοντό μου τὸν καρκίνον εἰσφοιτῶσαι αἱ κύνες. The καὶ τὰς νήσους, artistically obscure to previous hearers of the λόγιον, would now be clear in its reference.

ΠΑ. ὦ τάν, ἄκουσον, εἶτα διάκρινον τότε.

'Έστι γυνή, τέξει δὲ λέονθ' ἱεραῖς ἐν 'Αθήναις,

ὃς περὶ τοῦ δήμου πολλοῖς κώνωψι μαχεῖται,

ὥστε περὶ σκύμνοισι βεβηκώς· τὸν σὺ φύλαξαι,

τεῖχος ποιήσας ξύλινον πύργους τε σιδηροῦς.

ταῦτ' οἶσθ' ὅ τι λέγει; ΔΗ. μὰ τὸν 'Απόλλω

'γὼ μὲν οὔ.   1041

ΠΑ. ἔφραζεν ὁ θεός σοι σαφῶς σώζειν ἐμέ·

ἐγὼ γὰρ ἀντὶ τοῦ λέοντός εἰμί σοι.

ΔΗ. καὶ πῶς μ' ἐλελήθεις 'Αντιλέων γεγενημένος;

ΑΛΛ. ἐν οὐκ ἀναδιδάσκει σε τῶν λογίων ἑκὼν 1045

ὃ μόνον σιδηροῦν ἐστι τεῖχος καὶ ξύλων,

ἐν ᾧ σε σώζειν τόνδ' ἐκέλευσ' ὁ Λοξίας.

1036. τόδε Meineke, ποτε? εἶτα τότε would correspond to δὴ νῦν.
1039. φύλαξαι RMN. φυλάξαι V Meineke Kock Ribb. Vels. φύλασσε five MSS.
Dind. Bergk.
1044. 'Αντικλέων Reifferscheid.
1045—6. ἐν δ' οὐκ, and ὅ τι τὸ σιδηροῦν Cobet *Mnemos.* n.s. ii 423.
1046. ξύλων R and most MSS. ξύλον Γ Dindorf Blaydes.

1037. Cleon is claiming the honour
of being referred to in oracular prophecy,
like the oracles and dreams of lion-births
that foreshadowed the births of Cypselus
(Herod. v 92. 2) and Pericles (Herod. vi
131, Plut. *Pericl.* 3).
1038—9. κώνωψι, of enemies beneath
notice, as Apostol. *prov.* x 37 κώνωπος
ἐλέφας 'Ινδὸς οὐκ ἀλεγίζει (given also by
pseudo-Phalaris *epist.* 29): Martial xii 61.
5 *in tauros Libyci ruunt leones, non sunt
papilionibus molesti :* cf. ἀποσοβεῖ τοὺς ῥήτορας, *sup.* 60.
περί with dat. as *Il.* xvii 133 ὣς τίς τε
λέων περὶ οἷσι τέκεσσιν, and especially
βαίνω περί, as *ib.* 137. *Od.* xx 14 ὡς δὲ
κύων ἀμαλῇσι περὶ σκυλάκεσσι βεβηκώς.
1039. In strict Attic φυλάσσω is
'guard,' φυλάσσομαι 'guard against.' But
there are cases of the middle used to
mean 'guard': Shilleto on Dem. *FL* 287,
where Solon's poem has οὐδὲ φυλάσσονται
σεμνὰ δίκης θέμεθλα, quotes Aesch. *Supp.*
1012 μόνον φύλαξαι τάσδ' ἐπιστολὰς πατρός,
and Herod. vii 172 δεῖ φυλάσσεσθαι τὴν
ἐσβολήν, though that may be passive.
The use would cause just the ambiguity

that the oracular style loved, cf. the
oracle in Herod. vii 148 εἴσω τὸν προβό-
λαιον ἔχων πεφυλαγμένος ἧσο, καὶ κεφαλὴν
πεφύλαξο.
1040. Suggested by the famous Delphian advice to Athens to trust to a
wooden wall, Herod. vii 141 τεῖχος Τριτογενεῖ ξύλινον διδοῖ εὐρύοπα Ζεὺς μοῦνον
ἀπόρθητον τελέθειν τὸ σὲ τέκνα τ' ὀνήσει.
1043. 'I am as good as a lion for
you,' or 'I am all you have for a lion':
this use of ἀντί is epic and Ionic, as Hom.
Od. viii 546 ἀντὶ κασιγνήτου ξεῖνός θ'
ἱκέτης τε τέτυκται, Herod. iv 75 τοῦτό
σφι ἀντὶ λουτροῦ ἐστί· οὐ γὰρ δὴ λοῦνται
ὕδατι. The τοῦ is, as the article so often
is, for reference or quotation-marks.
1044. καὶ πῶς, see on 128 *sup.*
Nothing is known of the point in question: Antileon is evidently somebody or
something contemptible.
1045—6. ἀναδιδάσκω, cf. on 153.
'The only thing that is fort of iron
and timber': for ξύλων gen. of material
Shilleto in MS. note quotes Herod. ii 63,
schol. on Soph. *OC* 57.

ΔΗ.   πῶς δῆτα τοῦτ᾽ ἔφραζεν ὁ θεός; ΑΛΛ. τουτονὶ
     δῆσαί σ᾽ ἐκέλευσ᾽ ἐν πεντεσυρίγγῳ ξύλῳ.

ΔΗ.   ταυτὶ τελεῖσθαι τὰ λόγι᾽ ἤδη μοι δοκεῖ. 1050

ΠΑ.   μὴ πείθου· φθονεραὶ γὰρ ἐπικρώζουσι κορῶναι.
     ἀλλ᾽ ἱέρακα φίλει, μεμνημένος ἐν φρεσίν, ὅς σοι
     ἤγαγε συνδήσας Λακεδαιμονίων κορακίνους.

ΑΛΛ.   τοῦτό γέ τοι Παφλαγὼν παρεκινδύνευσε μεθυ-
     σθείς.

     Κεκροπίδη κακόβουλε, τί τοῦθ᾽ ἡγεῖ μέγα τοὔρ-
     γον;   1055
     καί κε γυνὴ φέροι ἄχθος, ἐπεί κεν ἀνὴρ ἀναθείη·

1049.   ἐκέλευσε R, ἐκέλευε the other MSS.: ἐν Pors. from *Etym. Mag.* 346. 16.
1052.   ὥς σοι Bergk and now vulg.
1056.   ἀναθείη Cobet *VL* 324.   ἐπειδὴ Madv. *Adv.* i 275.

1048—9. 'The stocks' is what the god must mean. As σῦριγξ meant almost any kind of hole, πεντεσύριγγον ξύλον meant pieces of wood made with holes for head, arms and legs, used in prison, Pollux viii 72. A cruel jest is quoted by Aristot. *Rhet.* iii 10. 7, by which a paralytic is called πεντεσυρίγγῳ νόσῳ δεδεμένος.

1050. ἤδη with fut. denoting immediate result, cf. 104 n., from this time on.' ταυτὶ emphatic ' in that sense I fancy the oracle will be fulfilled very soon.'

1051—3. The raven was tabooed on the Acropolis (see on 1022), and was thought to be an enemy of the owl, Aristot. *Hist. Anim.* xi 608ᵃ 8, Plut. *de inv. et odio* 4. 537 B μισοῦσι δ᾽ ἄλληλα καὶ πολεμοῦσιν ὥσπερ ἀσπείστους τινὰς πολέμους ἀετοὶ καὶ δράκοντες, κορῶναι καὶ γλαῦκες, αἰγιθαλλοὶ καὶ ἀκανθυλλίδες, Thompson *Greek Birds* 98—9. The hawk was sacred to Apollo. The allusion to hawking is probably only apparent, as that sport is not mentioned before Aristotle and then as a Thracian peculiarity (Hehn *Cult. und Haust.*⁶ 363). It does not seem to be clear for what reason Antiochus Hierax was so called. κορακίνος was a small fish *Lys.* 560, Athen. ii 63 A, vii ch. 81: it does not occur as the diminutive of κόραξ except here, and possibly *fr.* 452 ap. Athen. vii 308 F: and no doubt this mistake in the meaning is intentionally absurd.

1054. This might mean either 'the Pylus business was a drunken adventure of Cleon's,' and such language was no doubt used of it : or 'that last oracle is a last desperate venture in the altercation, and the man's drunk.' In either case, γέ τοι 'anyhow,' 'all I can say is,' suits well enough to depreciate the last speaker. παρακινδυνεύω is known in both senses : (1) of a bold deed, as the Helots running the blockade of Sphacteria, Thucyd. iv 26. 6, cf. *Ach.* 645, (2) of a bold phrase, as *Ran.* 99 and Dion. Hal. *ep. ad Pomp.* 2. p. 765. 18 R.: in Lucian *Alex.* 32 it means *risqué, compromising,* to the writer.

1055. The epic equivalents for Athenian are varied each time. Κεκροπίδαι occurs in a serious narrative, but as a comic touch, in Posidonius ap. Athen. v 212 B (*Fragm. Hist. Gr.* iii p. 267). ταχύβουλος μετάβουλος δυσβουλία are all used frankly to Athenians by Aristophanes, especially in parabasis. The scholion on *Nub.* 587 gives the explanation, probably current among aristocrats, that Poseidon, when defeated by Athena, imposed the curse of δυσβουλία on the country.

1056. The scholiast explains that this line is quoted from the *Little Iliad:*— a Trojan maiden was overheard using this argument against Ajax's carrying off

ἀλλ᾽ οὐκ ἂν μαχέσαιτο· χέσαιτο γάρ, εἰ μαχέ-
σαιτο.

ΠΑ. ἀλλὰ τόδε φράσσαι, πρὸ Πύλου Πύλον ἤν σοι
ἔφραζεν.
"Εστι Πύλος πρὸ Πύλοιο ΔΗ. τί τοῦτο λέγει,
πρὸ Πύλοιο;

ΑΛΛ. τὰς πυέλους φησὶν καταλήψεσθ᾽ ἐν βαλανείῳ.

ΔΗ. ἐγὼ δ᾽ ἄλουτος τήμερον γενήσομαι.   1061

ΑΛΛ. οὗτος γὰρ ἡμῶν τὰς πυέλους ἀφήρπασεν.
ἀλλ᾽ οὑτοσὶ γάρ ἐστι περὶ τοῦ ναυτικοῦ
ὁ χρησμός, ᾧ σε δεῖ προσέχειν τὸν νοῦν πάνυ.

ΔΗ. προσέχω· σὺ δ᾽ ἀναγίγνωσκε, τοῖς ναύταισί μου
ὅπως ὁ μισθὸς πρῶτον ἀποδοθήσεται.   1066

ΑΛΛ. Αἰγείδη, φράσσαι κυναλώπεκα, μή σε δολώσῃ,

1058. φράσαι RM (and so with most MSS. in 1067), φράξεν the other MSS.
1059. λέγει τὸ π. R.   1062. αὐτὸς MSS. except RM : Zacher would omit the line.

Achilles' body and this was taken as proving his superiority to Ulysses. 'Any one can carry a load if another puts it on,' Demosthenes here being the ἀνήρ. The phrase was probably often used in historical estimates of character, Plut. de Alexandri fort. 5. 337 E.

1057. The form χέσαιτο is a comic 'datismus' (cf. 115), and is meant, with the omission of ἄν, to mark a complete breakdown into vulgar burlesque, cf. Eccl. 808, Ran. 574.

1059. ἔστι Πύλος πρὸ Πύλοιο, Πύλος γε μὲν ἔστι καὶ ἄλλη was a well-known line bearing on the three cities named Pylus in western Peloponnesus (Strabo viii 3. 7), Pylus Oenoe in North Elis, Pylus Lepreaticus in South Elis, and Pylus, opposite Sphacteria, in Messenia. It was parodied in the line about usury ἔστι τόκος πρὸ τόκοιο, τόκος γε μέν ἐστι καὶ ἄλλος, Plut. de vit. aere al. 5. 829 D. The πρὸ is not clear in meaning, cf. the proverb δοῦλος πρὸ δούλου, δεσπότης πρὸ δεσπότου in Aristot. Pol. i 7. 3. Cleon's anxiety to bring home this old verse to his own case is cut short by the question of Demus, and the enemy's absurd interpretation in 1060.

1060. Puns on πύελος and Πύλος, as in 55, were no doubt common enough at the time, and used to cheapen Cleon's campaign down to the triviality given here. 'He speaks of going to seize the tubs at a public bath,' the last place for heroic adventure in Athenian street wit. I suppose (φησὶν) καταλήψεσθαι may be oblique for καταλήψομαι, καταλήψει or καταλήψεται, but not for καταλάβοι or καταλαβέτω.

1061. The tragic rhythm is counteracted by the colloquial τήμερον: so Av. 1045, Eccl. 1021, Plut. 232, 433, 947 would all be tragic except for this form : see Appendix iii.

1063. ἀλλὰ. γὰρ as of a new person entering the scene : 'Ah but here's the oracle about the fleet for you.'

1065—6. Cf. 1367 : Demus feels the special interest of this oracle, and an honest desire to do right to the seamen : the Sausage-man meets his wishes 1079.

1067—8. The Laconian breed of hounds were said to be hybrids of dog and fox, Aristot. Hist. Anim. viii 28. 607ᵃ 3, but these hybrids were called ἀλωπεκίδες, Xen. Cyneg. 3. 1, Pollux v 38, not κυναλώπεκες (except in Hesychius

λαίθαργον, ταχύπουν, δολίαν κερδώ, πολύϊδριν.
οἶσθ᾽ ὅ τί ἐστιν τοῦτο; ΔΗ. Φιλόστρατος ἡ
κυναλώπηξ.

ΑΛΛ. οὐ τοῦτό φησιν, ἀλλὰ ναῦς ἑκάστοτε   1070
αἰτεῖ ταχείας ἀργυρολόγους οὑτοσί·
ταύτας ἀπαυδᾷ μὴ διδόναι σ᾽ ὁ Λοξίας.

ΔΗ. πῶς δὴ τριήρης ἐστὶ κυναλώπηξ; ΑΛΛ. ὅπως;
ὅτι ἡ τριήρης ἐστὶ χὠ κύων ταχύ.

ΔΗ. πῶς οὖν ἀλώπηξ προσετέθη πρὸς τῷ κυνί;   1075

ΑΛΛ. ἀλωπεκίοισι τοὺς στρατιώτας ἤκασεν,
ὁτιὴ βότρυς τρώγουσιν ἐν τοῖς χωρίοις.

---

s.v.). κυναλώπηξ occurs only as a nick-name and in two sham-oracles, here and Lucian's Bacis-oracle against the Cynics, *Peregr.* 30 ; there it is masc.

λαίθαργος, a quaint word natural in this good imitation of (Hesiodic) oracular style. It is defined as a fawning, biting cur, and then a secret mischief-maker: the scholiast quotes as a proverb the line σαίνουσα δάκνεις καὶ κύων λαίθαργος εἶ, which is attributed to Sophocles *fr.* 902 (*fr.* 800 Nauck, who gives all the references to the word). Another form, probably a mere confusion with a better-known word, is λήθαργος, Rutherf. Babrius p. xlvi. The word was popularly supposed to be from λαθεῖν, cf. Plaut. *Bacch.* 1146 *clam mordax canis*, Lucian *bis accus.* 33 τὸ δῆγμα λαθραῖος. Babrius 87 is a short fable to illustrate the phrase. The word is a dog's name in the epigram *Anth. Pal.* vii 304, quoted by Pollux v 46. As λάθαργος occurs for *a leather paring* there is probably a special application to Cleon intended here.

κερδώ, the 'Reynard' or 'Brer Fox' of Greek story: it is the fem. hypocoristic of κερδαλέος.

ἴδρις and its compounds died out in Attic: they are words of the quaint kind proper in folk-lore: ἴδρις is *the ant* in Hes. *Op.* 778: cf. Arist. *Hist. Anim.* x 14. 615^b 23 ἡ σίττη λέγεται φαρμάκεια εἶναι διὰ τὸ πολύϊδρις εἶναι, where he is quoting a folk-tale.

1069. λέγει αὐτὸν καὶ (ὡς?) πορνο-βοσκὸν καὶ καλλωπιστήν schol.: he is no doubt the Κυναλώπηξ of *Lys.* 957.

1070. Measures of sending out νῆες ἀργυρολόγοι to collect arrears of tribute, or levy forced contributions from allies, were sometimes adopted, no doubt usually by the war party. We hear of them mostly when unsuccessful, Thucyd. ii 69, iii 19 (Lysicles killed on such an expedition). They must always have been invidious: Callicratidas refused ἀργυρολογεῖν τὰς πόλεις (Plut. *Lysander* 6), and Aeschines attacks Demosthenes because τοὺς Ἕλληνας ἠργυρολόγησε (*Ctesiph.* 159).

1072. The Sausage-man uses Λοξίας of his own oracles: his interpretation is certainly very forced and poor: as at 207, the principles are not much above Fluellen's. ἀπαυδῶ is in tragic style: it is not used in prose except =*fail, give up* in later writers as Theophr. *Hist. Plant.* v 6. 1, Plut. *ser. num. vind.* 13. 558 C, Lucian *merc. cond.* 39.

1076—7. He means soldiers on board triremes, who often made descents and ravages on the coasts as recently, Thucyd. iv 45, cf. *Pax* 626—7.

τὰ χωρία, in one of its regular senses, *small farms*.

"The little foxes that spoil the vines, for our vines have tender grapes," were themselves eaten by Greeks, Keller *Thiere des class. Alt.* p. 180. Mnesimachus 4. 49 gives in a list of meats at a banquet (κρέα) κίττης πέρδικος ἀλωπεκίου.

ΔΗ. εἶέν·

τούτοις ὁ μισθὸς τοῖς ἀλωπεκίοισι ποῦ ;

ΑΛΛ. ἐγὼ ποριῶ καὶ τοῦτον ἡμερῶν τριῶν.

ἀλλ' ἔτι τόνδ' ἐπάκουσον, ὃν εἶπέ σοι ἐξαλέα-

σθαι   1080

χρησμὸν Λητοΐδης Κυλλήνην μή σε δολώσῃ.

ΔΗ. ποίαν Κυλλήνην; ΑΛΛ. τὴν τούτου χεῖρ' ἐποί-

ησεν

Κυλλήνην ὀρθῶς, ὁτιή φησ', ἔμβαλε κυλλῇ.

ΠΑ. οὐκ ὀρθῶς φράζει· τὴν Κυλλήνην γὰρ ὁ Φοῖβος

1078. εἶέν R alone: see Wilam. on Eurip. *HF* 451, Uhlig in *Rhein. Mus.* xix
33— , Norden in *Hermes* xxvii 621— .
1080. τῶνδ' R. τοῦδ' Cobet *Mnemos.* i 417, on his rule ἐπακούω τινός, ὑπακούω
τινί (*NL* p. 521).
1084. φράζεις mss. except R.

1078. It is understood now that εἶ ἐν
was the proper spelling and pronunciation,
and that εἶέν : εἶα :: ἔνεκεν : ἔνεκα, though
the other explanation that it is opt. of
εἰμι was also held in antiquity (Bekk.
Anecd. 243. 24): see Uhlig on Dion.
Thrax pp. 82—3, where a scholiast says
it had two accents, and seems to add that
the last syllable was sometimes circum-
flexed (it is long in Aesch. *Cho.* 657, *Pax*
663). Moeris 127 says it was Attic for
the Hellenic ἄγε δή; the Atticists Dio
Chrysostom, Lucian &c. are very fond of
it.
1079. σιτί' ἡμερῶν τριῶν was the
commonest of soldier's phrases : here
there is a combination of that and 'within
three days,' as Cleon had engaged to take
Sphacteria within three weeks.
1081. The curious aorist forms ἀλέασθαι (apparently for ἀλέϝασθαι ἀλεύα-
σθαι) are not unusual in Homer and epic
generally: Hesiod has them several times
in moral warnings against things to be
avoided. The construction is not clear,
but probably χρησμὸν ὃν εἶπέ σοι, ἐξαλ.
Κυλλ. being epexegetic.
There is nothing to show whether
Cyllene is the celebrated Arcadian moun-
tain or the port of Elis (the modern
Cyllene has been so named only recently,
it is the mediaeval Clarence): the name
leads up to the κυλλῇ of 1083, but no

doubt there are allusions unknown to us.
Possibly Cleon had schemes of Attic
influence in Arcadia: cf. on 798.
1082. ποῖος in such cases means generally scornful rejection, 'Cyllene indeed !'
ποιεῖν may mean not only 'write poetry,'
but 'use a phrase' in poetry: τὰ ὑπὸ τῶν
ποιητῶν λεγόμενα ξυνιέναι ἅ τε ὀρθῶς πε-
ποίηται καὶ ἃ μή, Plato *Protag.* 339 A: so
ποίημα may mean a line of poetry, or a
poetical phrase, as in Cratinus 186. 5,
and in later Greek not unfrequently, as
Polyb. iv 31. 5, Lucian *Nigr.* 8.
1083. κυλλὸς is *bent, deformed*, mainly
a surgical word: Hephaestus is Κυλλο-
ποδίων in Homer, Cinesias has κυλλὸν
πόδα, *Av.* 1379. ἔμβαλε κυλλῇ was a
beggar's phrase, 'alms for a useless
hand' with a play on κοίλη, as in κοίλην
προτείνειν *Thesm.* 937)(ἐμβάλλει μοι
τὴν χεῖρ' ἁπαλὴν *Vesp.* 553: for ἔμβαλε
cf. the female demon of bribery Ἐμβλώ,
Cratinus 69.
1084. ὀρθῶς, the regular critic's
phrase. Diopithes had a deformed hand,
apparently. He was a leader of the conservatives in religious usage against the
philosophers, prosecuted Anaxagoras, and
had much influence with Nicias. Forgers
of oracles circulated them by means of
him, Amipsias 10. He moved one part
of the decree, in favour of Methone
(about 427 B.C.), which has been pre-

ἐς τὴν χεῖρ' ὀρθῶς ἠνίξατο τὴν Διοπείθους. 1085
ἀλλὰ γάρ ἐστιν ἐμοὶ χρησμὸς περὶ σοῦ πτερυ-
γωτός,
αἰετὸς ὡς γίγνει καὶ πάσης γῆς βασιλεύεις.

ΑΛΛ. καὶ γὰρ ἐμοί· καὶ γῆς καὶ τῆς ἐρυθρᾶς γε θαλάσσης,
χὥτι γ' ἐν Ἐκβατάνοις δικάσεις, λείχων ἐπίπαστα.

ΠΑ. ἀλλ' ἐγὼ εἶδον ὄναρ, καί μοὐδόκει ἡ θεὸς αὐτὴ
τοῦ δήμου καταχεῖν ἀρυταίνῃ πλουθυγίειαν. 1091

ΑΛΛ. νὴ Δία καὶ γὰρ ἐγώ· καί μοὐδόκει ἡ θεὸς αὐτὴ
ἐκ πόλεως ἐλθεῖν καὶ γλαῦξ αὐτῇ 'πικαθῆσθαι·
εἶτα κατασπένδειν κατὰ τῆς κεφαλῆς ἀρυβάλλῳ
ἀμβροσίαν κατὰ σοῦ, κατὰ τούτου δὲ σκοροδάλμην. 1095

1087. βασιλεύσεις MSS. except R.   **1089.** Dind. and Cobet *Mnemos.* n.s.
ii 411 would omit γ', but it marks the speaker's eagerness.

---

served (*CIA* i 40, Hicks no. 44), as Cleonymus did the other.

1086. Now he gives up his own personal glorification for the flattery of Demos demanded in 1012.

For γίγνει and βασιλεύεις in prophecy cf. on 127. The eagle, the attendant and armour-bearer of Zeus, was a natural symbol of sovereignty: but the regular use of an eagle-figure for this purpose does not seem to have been common in Greece; it was the bearings rather of Persian kings, whose power it symbolises in Aesch. *Pers.* 244: from them it was adopted by the Ptolemies, and from them by Augustus.

1088—9. These aspirations carry him eastwards instead of the westward movement already talked of. *Av.* 144 implies dreams of a Happy Land by the Indian Ocean (always the meaning of ἐρυθρὰ θάλασσα), which is the open way to India, Lucian *dial. marin.* 15. 1.

Ecbatana, the Athenian Eldorado, *Vesp.* 1143: for δικάσεις see on 798, and for ἐπίπαστα on 103.

1090—1. τὰ τῶν βαλανείων ἀγγεῖα

ἀρύβαλλος ἀρύταινα· ἄμφω δ' Ἀριστοφάνης λέγει, Pollux vii 166 and x 63. The shape of the aryballos is probably implied in the second half of the word =βαλλάντιον. Water was poured over the bathers with these vessels by the βαλανεύς, Theophr. *char.* 9: this *douche* is called καταιόνησις by Athen. i 24 D.

πλουθυγίεια sums up a list of blessings, *Vesp.* 677, *Av.* 731: the word seems to have been invented by Aristophanes, and does not occur except in him.

1092—5. The tone is studied to surpass Cleon's dream in picturesqueness and fullness of meaning: Athena coming from the Acropolis (see on 267) has an owl perched on her head or shoulder. This seems hardly to occur in art. "It has been often noted that on the Parthenon image, as we know of it, no place was found for the sacred bird of Athene, the owl: on the medallion (of the Hermitage) she is most happily introduced, perched on the right-hand cheek-piece," Harrison and Verrall *Myth. and Mon.* p. 455.

1095. ἀμβροσία is often spoken of as liquid, and the ambrosia of ritual was

ΔΗ. ἰοὺ ἰού.

οὐκ ἦν ἄρ' οὐδεὶς τοῦ Γλάνιδος σοφώτερος.

καὶ νῦν ἐμαυτὸν ἐπιτρέπω σοι τουτονὶ

γεροναγωγεῖν κἀναπαιδεύειν πάλιν.

ΠΑ. μήπω γ', ἱκετεύω σ', ἀλλ' ἀνάμεινον, ὡς ἐγὼ   1100

κριθὰς πορίῶ σοι καὶ βίον καθ' ἡμέραν.

ΔΗ. οὐκ ἀνέχομαι κριθῶν ἀκούων· πολλάκις

ἐξηπατήθην ὑπό τε σοῦ καὶ Θουφάνους.

ΠΑ. ἀλλ' ἄλφιτ' ἤδη σοι πορίῶ 'σκευασμένα.

ΑΛΛ. ἐγὼ δὲ μαζίσκας γε διαμεμαγμένας   1105

καὶ τοὔψον ὀπτόν· μηδὲν ἄλλ' εἰ μὴ 'σθιε.

ΔΗ. ἀνύσατέ νυν, ὅ τι περ ποιήσεθ'· ὡς ἐγώ,

ὁπότερος ἂν σφῶν εὖ με μᾶλλον ἂν ποῆ,

τούτῳ παραδώσω τῆς πυκνὸς τὰς ἡνίας.

1108. So MSS. Editors have altered the reading on a canon given by Elmsley, and explained by Hermann (*de part. ἄν* 191), that ἄν is not repeated in subjunctive clauses. For the second ἄν Reisig and Dind. give αὖ, Hermann ἄν. Vulg. εὖ με μ. and νῦν or νῦν με μ. εὖ.

water, oil and παγκαρπία, Athen. xi 473 C.

σκοροδάλμη, as 199.

1097. The article implies that Glanis is now well-known and respected: cf. Τρυγαῖος Ἀθμονεύς, Pax 190, but ἀθμονεὺς 919 (Shilleto).

1098. ἐγὼ οὑτοσί: such phrases are used when the favour or regard of the person addressed is asked, *Ach.* 367 ὁ δ' ἀνὴρ ὁ λέξων οὑτοσὶ τυννουτοσί, *Nub.* 141 ἐγὼ γὰρ οὑτοσὶ ἥκω μαθητής.

1099. This line was taken from Sophocles' *Peleus* (*fr.* 434), Πηλέα τὸν Αἰάκειον οἰκουρὸς μόνη γεροναγωγῶ κἀναπαιδεύω πάλιν. Plutarch twice (*Nicias* 2, and *praec. ger. reip.* 13. 807 A) says that Cleon gained power over the commons γεροναγωγῶν κἀναμισθαρνεῖν διδούς.

1100—1. Observe the climax in offers, κριθαί, ἄλφιτα, μᾶζαι. κριθαί is either the barley grain (as Aristot. *Pol. Ath.* 51 ὅπως οἱ μυλωθροὶ πρὸς τὰς τιμὰς τῶν κριθῶν τὰ ἄλφιτα πωλήσουσιν), or an inferior barley-meal: this is the point of the bitter κριθῶν at the end of the grievance about state-largesses of corn in *Vesp.* 718, cf. ἐσθίοι κριθὰς μόνας Pax 449, κρι-

θινον κόλλικα, δούλιον χόρτον Hipponax 35. 6.

1100. For state-largesses of corn at Athens, see Böckh *Staatsh.*[3] i p. 112: a distribution was made of corn from Egypt in 445 B.C., and an insufficient largess is grumbled at in *Vesp.* 715—, probably the result of such promises as Cleon makes here.

1102—3. κριθῶν may depend either on ἀνέχομαι or on ἀκούων.

The scholiast calls Thuphanes a κόλαξ and ὑπογραμματεὺς of Cleon's, this last post perhaps being that of the ἐπιγραφεῖς mentioned by Pollux viii 103 as employed in state-largesses. Θουφάνης is not merely *metri gr.* for Θεοφάνης: both names occur on the inscription *CIA* i 447.

1104. ἐσκευασμένα, ready for baking.

1105—6. μαζίσκη, a dainty cake of barley, here and *inf.* 1166. διαμάττω here and *Av.* 463, 'baked to a turn.' The article in τοὔψον, as if this further gift (whatever it was) was only natural, is meant as a reproach to his enemy.

1109. The metaphor of 'reins of state' occurs again, *Eccl.* 466, Plato *Polit.* 266 E, Plut. *Pericles* 11 τῷ δήμῳ

ΠΑ.   τρέχοιμ᾽ ἂν εἴσω πρότερος.   ΑΛΛ. οὐ δῆτ᾽, ἀλλ᾽

      ἐγώ.   1110

ΧΟΡ.   ὦ Δῆμε, καλήν γ᾽ ἔχεις

      ἀρχήν, ὅτε πάντες ἄν-

      θρωποι δεδίασί σ᾽ ὥσ-

      περ ἄνδρα τύραννον.

      ἀλλ᾽ εὐπαράγωγος εἶ,   1115

      θωπευόμενός τε χαί-

      ρεις κἀξαπατώμενος,

      πρὸς τόν τε λέγοντ᾽ ἀεὶ

      κέχηνας· ὁ νοῦς δέ σου

      παρὼν ἀποδημεῖ.   1120

1110. εἴσω RM. ἤδη the rest.

τὰς ἡνίας ἀνεὶς ἐπολιτεύετο πρὸς χάριν, *Numa* 16, *an seni sit ger.* 12. 790 D, Alciphro iii 61. 3 Δοσιάδης τὴν Πνύκα καταλαμβάνει δημηγορῶν...καὶ τὰς ἡνίας ἔχει τοῦ δήμου.

1111. In these brilliant little political songs (cf. on 973) are embodied the patriotic conservative's dislike of demagogues, and democracy's cynical self-defence. The metrical arrangement of 3 Glyconics and a Pherecratic, then 5 Glyconics and a Pherecratic, is found again in the parodos of *Eccl.* 290—. Similar, though shorter stanzas, occur *Pax* 856, 909, 1333, *Av.* 1731, *Ran.* 450. The metrical form was sometimes called προσοδιακόν, and is found, though rarely, in tragedy, Soph. *OT* 466, *OC* 1044 (Gleditsch *Metrik* § 96).

1112. ὅτε for *quandoquidem* is not unfrequent, though almost confined to present tenses : there is no etymological reason why this should not be the normal meaning of the word, but its correlative τότε seems to be confined to the temporal sense. There is some natural malice in pointing out the tyranny of Demus : the *imperium* and *libertas*, which Pericles' great speech insists on as the fate to which Athens is called, do not mean *liberty* for everybody. ἀνὴρ τύραννος is an intensification of τύραννος, good or evil as may be (see on 257) : in Eurip.

Med. 308, 700 ἄνδρες τύραννοι is bitterly ironical, in Menander 538. 4 serious, in Lucian *catap.* 13 and *dial. mort.* 10. 4 boastful in the tyrant's own mouth. That Athens' power was a τυραννίς was frankly proclaimed by Pericles Thucyd. ii 63. 2, and by Cleon iii 37. 2 : ὁ δῆμος εἶναι βούλεται μόναρχος Aristot. *Pol.* viii (v) 11. 11, vi (iv) 4. 26, ὥσπερ τυράννῳ τῷ δήμῳ χαριζόμενοι *ib.* ii 22. In later writers it is almost a commonplace to bring together these extreme forms of government and their instruments, δήμιος ἢ δορυφόρος Lucian *dial. mort.* 30. 2, δικασταὶ καὶ τύραννοι *Charon* 17.

1115—7. ὁ κόλαξ παρ᾽ ἀμφοτέροις (tyranny and democracy) ἔντιμος, παρὰ μὲν τοῖς δήμοις ὁ δημαγωγός (ἔστι γὰρ ὁ δημαγωγὸς τοῦ δήμου κόλαξ), παρὰ δὲ τοῖς τυράννοις οἱ ταπεινῶς ὁμιλοῦντες, ὅπερ ἐστὶν ἔργον κολακείας, Aristot. *Pol.* viii (v) 11. 12. 1313ᵇ 40. ἐξαπατώμενος forms the climax as in 48. The chorus' criticism here is almost exactly the same as Cleon's in Thucyd. iii 38. 5 μετὰ καινότητος μὲν λόγου ἀπατᾶσθαι ἄριστοι κ.τ.λ.

1120. ἀποδημεῖ νοῦς as *peregrinatur, peregre est, animus* in Latin, as Hor. *epist.* i 12. 13, Cic. *Tusc.* v 114 of philosophers : cf. S. Paul 2 *Corinth.* 5. 8 ἐκδημῆσαι ἐκ τοῦ σώματος. A similar metaphor is taken from the house, as in ἔνδον γενοῦ Aesch. *Cho.* 232, ἐντὸς and ἐκτὸς ἑαυτοῦ.

ΔΗ.   νοῦς οὐκ ἔνι ταῖς κόμαις
      ὑμῶν, ὅτε μ’ οὐ φρονεῖν
      νομίζετ’· ἐγὼ δ’ ἐκὼν
      ταῦτ’ ἠλιθιάζω.
      αὐτός τε γὰρ ἥδομαι   1125
      βρύλλων τὸ καθ’ ἡμέραν,
      κλέπτοντά τε βούλομαι
      τρέφειν ἕνα προστάτην·
      τοῦτον δ’, ὅταν ᾖ πλέως,
      ἄρας ἐπάταξα.   1130
ΧΟΡ. χοὔτω μὲν ἂν εὖ ποιοῖς,

1131. οὕτω most MSS. χ’οὕτω RV (from χο. οὕτω Blaydes). ἄρ’ εὖ ποιεῖς καί
σοι Mein. Vels. καὶ τοῦτο μὲν Wecklein.

1121—4. κόμαις, as the Knights' hair
is long and not yet turned grey : I suppose
κόμη was hardly used except of long hair,
τρίχες being the general word (cf. *Vesp.*
1065): *Av.* 911 δοῦλος ὢν κόμην ἔχεις; The
phrase looks like a proverb or adaptation
of one : and Suidas says it comes from νοῦς
οὐ παρὰ Κενταύροισι which is quoted by
the Paroemiographi.

Verbs in -άζω are formed from stems in
-ιο with the same freedom as verbs in -ίζω
from other stems.

1125. αὐτός has the same meaning
as ἐκών, and this is reiterated by the
βούλομαι of 1127.

βρύλλων. Σύμμαχος, ὑποπίνων, ἐκ μιμήσεως τῆς τῶν παίδων φωνῆς schol., the
φωνὴ being βρῦν as in *Nub.* 1382. The
word is not found elsewhere: like other
words in -ύλλω it was hardly literary at
all (see on 224). Its meaning was not clear
to the scholiasts, and it may mean *dozing*
(cf. βρίζω: E. S. Thompson). Demos is
fed like a child, ψωμίζεται, cf. 715. τὸ
καθ’ ἡμέραν may be either adverbial or
direct accus., as Epicrates 2. 6 (Λαῒς) τὸ
καθ’ ἡμέραν ὁρῶσα πίνειν κἀσθίειν μόνον.

1127—8. τρέφειν, not βόσκειν, because ironical respect for a time is implied,
see on 255 and 1136. No special office
or pay is meant: the προστάτης τοῦ δήμου
was merely the democratic leader, recognised by public opinion. Aristotle gives
a historical list of Athenian προστάται

Ath. Pol. 28. The title is given to
democratic leaders in Corcyra, Megara
and Elis by Thucydides and Xenophon
(Gilbert *Inn. Gesch.* 78): and Xen. *Hell.*
v 2. 6 speaks of προστάται τοῦ δήμου
at Mantinea. Προστάτης was however a
title of office in some cities (=πρύτανις in
Opus, Dyme &c.), and προστάται τοῦ
δάμου were magistrates at Tegea (Gilbert
Griech. Staatsalt. ii 129, 328). We find
προστάτης τῆς πόλεως of an Argive, Theopomp. ap. Athen. vi 252 A (*Fragm. hist.
Gr.* i 301), and Critias calls himself προστάτης Xen. *Hell.* ii 3. 51.

1129. 'When he has had his fill of
peculation I hoist and thrash him': αἴρω
as *Ach.* 565 εἰ θενεῖς, αὐτὸς ἀρθήσει, and
tollo, rapio, sublimem in Latin ; see on
1362 *inf.*
Vespasian is said to have promoted
rapacious procurators purposely, to "use
them as sponges," Sueton. *Vesp.* 16.

1131. If the reading is right, the
sentence is oddly constructed: the first
εἰ clause explains the state of things assumed in order to produce the effect
described in the second εἰ clause. I
believe οὕτω μὲν means 'if so,' 'that being
so,' *Av.* 656 οὕτω μὲν εἰσίωμεν, 1503 οὕτω
μὲν ἐκκαλύψομαι, Soph. *Aj.* 823 (so οὕτω
γάρ, 'on your principles then,' as Plut.
quaest. conv. iii 1. 646 B): then the
first εἰ clause expands οὕτω μέν, and the
second gives the apodosis to εὖ ἂν ποιοῖς,

εἴ σοι πυκνότης ἔνεστ'
ἐν τῷ τρόπῳ, ὡς λέγεις,
τούτῳ πάνυ πολλή,
εἰ τούσδ' ἐπίτηδες ὥσ-   1135
περ δημοσίους τρέφεις
ἐν τῇ πυκνί, κᾆθ' ὅταν
μή σοι τύχῃ ὄψον ὄν,
τούτων ὃς ἂν ᾖ παχύς,
θύσας ἐπιδειπνεῖς.   1140

ΔΗ. σκέψασθε δέ μ', εἰ σοφῶς
αὐτοὺς περιέρχομαι,
τοὺς οἰομένους φρονεῖν
κἄμ' ἐξαπατύλλειν.
τηρῶ γὰρ ἑκάστοτ' αὐ-   1145

1134. οὕτω Dobree.

---

though irregularly in indicatives. After their charge of weakness, the chorus accept Demos' cunning with ironical iteration.

ποιοῖς stands alone in Aristophanes for ποιοίης Ruth. *NP* 444, La Roche *Beitr. zur griech. Gram.* i 141: in iambics it would be inadmissible.

πυκνός in the sense of *cunning, shrewd* is in Attic rare and used to convey some irony: cf. Critias *Sisyphus* 12, Plato *Rep.* viii 568 A, Amphis 33. 5.

1135—. 'If you fatten them on public life as victims for sacrifice.' The two human victims sacrificed annually at the Attic Thargelia show how this method of propitiation, so often implied in legends, lasted in civilised times. Writers give very little information on this subject, and we know nothing of how the victims were selected and treated before the sacrifice. Other countries had the habit of human sacrifices and fattened the victims systematically (Frazer *Golden Bough*[1] ii 212). τρέφειν is the word used in such cases, Lucian *Timon* 17, *pisc.* 34. A good Latin parallel is Liv. vi 17. 2 *saginare plebem populares suos ut iugulentur.*

1139. παχύς, 'bloated,' was the retort-phrase used by the lower orders to the ὀλίγοι: it occurs seriously in Herodotus, colloquially in *Vesp.* 287, *Pax* 639: it is intended here to imply 'your demagogue can become as bloated as the man he attacks.'

1140. ἐπεσθίω τι properly means 'to eat as an ὄψον with bread' (*Plut.* 1005, Xen. *Memor.* iii 143, Athen. iv 164 AB, 170 D, cf. note on 706 *sup.*), so ἐπιδειπνῶ here following on the ὄψον above implies something of a *bonne bouche:* cf. *Eccles.* 1177, Alexis 242. The noun ἐπιδειπνίς means *supper*, and so ἐπιδειπνῶ in Hippocrates.

1141—4. 'My σοφία is greater than their φρόνησις': they are mere men of the world, I have the artist's temperament. This use of περιέρχομαι, 'circumvent,' 'trick,' is natural, but very rare, and seemingly avoided in serious Attic; Herod. iii 4, Plut. *Nicias* 10 Ἀλκιβιάδης περιῆλθεν αὐτοὺς δι' ἀπάτης.

ἐξαπατύλλω, as *Ach.* 657 οὐ θωπεύων οὐδ' ὑποτείνων μισθοὺς οὐδ' ἐξαπατύλλων. The word like others in -ύλλω is almost coarsely colloquial, see on 224, 1125 *sup.*

τούς, οὐδὲ δοκῶν ὁρᾶν,
κλέπτοντας· ἔπειτ' ἀναγ-
κάζω πάλιν ἐξεμεῖν
ἅττ' ἂν κεκλόφωσί μου,
κημὸν καταμηλῶν.   1150

ΠΑ. ἄπαγ' ἐς μακαρίαν ἐκποδών. ΑΛΛ. σύ γ', ὦ
φθόρε.

ΠΑ. ὦ Δῆμ', ἐγὼ μέντοι παρεσκευασμένος
τρίπαλαι κάθημαι, βουλόμενός σ' εὐεργετεῖν.

ΑΛΛ. ἐγὼ δὲ δεκάπαλαί γε καὶ δωδεκάπαλαι

1150. κημῷ Blaydes Zacher.   **1154.** γε om. R.

1145—50. οὐ δοκῶ=*pretend not to*...
Plut. 837 &c., also in Euripides, as *Hippol.*
462: so δοκῶ, *pretend to*, Eupolis 159. 10
δοκῶν τοῖσι λόγοισι χαίρειν.

ἐξεμεῖν, 'disgorge' as *Ach.* 6 τοῖς πέντε
ταλάντοις, οἷς Κλέων ἐξήμεσε: 'Cleon disgorging' was a familiar phrase and is
assumed here, see *sup.* 404.

La Roche *Beitr. zur griech. Gram.*
i 164 gives a list of perfect subjunctives,
showing that the periphrastic forms (κε-
κλοφὼς ᾇ) are more common, at least in
prose.

κημός is the wicker-work funnel at the
mouth of the ballot-jars as used in voting
at this time: it seems to have been afterwards replaced by a lead top (Hager in
Smith's *Dict. Antiq.* s.v. *Psephus*): both
arrangements being intended to guarantee
secrecy.

μήλη was a *probe*, such as those found
among the surgical instruments of Pom-
peii (Smith's *Dict.* s.v. *Chirurgia*): the
verbs μηλόω, καταμηλόω, apparently could
take accusative of the part treated (τὴν
φάρυγα μηλῶν *fr.* 515), or of the thing
used as instrument, so here, *use the ballot-
box as an emetic*. I do not know of any
other instance of this construction: Hippocrates more naturally has the dative of
the instrument, προμηλώσας μήλη iii 333
Kühn. Phrynichus 62 uses it absolutely,
ἔμει καταμηλῶν· φλέγματος γὰρ εἶ πλέως.

1151. ἄπαγε and βάλλε were common
in Greek imprecations as intransitives:
βάλλ' ἐς κόρακας &c.: Epicharmus ap.
Athen. ii 63 c (p. 281 Lorenz) ἄπαγ' ἐς τὸν

φθόρον: cf. also σόβει ἐς "Αργος Lucian
dial. deor. 24. 2. βάλλω intransitive in
various parts gave a meaning like the
Latin *ilicet*, as in the well-known phrase
of Alcman 8 βάλε δὴ βάλε κηρύλος εἴην,
Epictet. ii 20. 10 βαλὼν κάθευδε καὶ τὰ
τοῦ σκώληκος ποίει, iv 10. 29 τί οὖν οὐ
ῥέγκω βαλών; Μακαρία, the place of
the blessed dead, occurs in euphemistic
phrases as here, βάλλ' ἐς μακαρίαν, Plato
Hipp. ma. 293 A and Alciphron (Ruhnken
on Timaeus under this phrase), ἐς μακαρίαν
τὸ λουτρόν Antiphanes 245.

Timaeus, Zenobius (*Prov. Cent.* ii 61),
and the scholiast here all give the story
that the phrase arose from Macaria's self-
sacrifice, and was once complimentary.

φθόρος and ὄλεθρος of men, like *pestis*.
The distinction drawn by Cobet *VL* 245
—6 "veteribus κάθαρμα odium, ὄλεθρος
contemtum significat" seems over-refined:
in *Coll. Crit.* 110 he appears not to insist
on it. φθόρος noun, φθορός adj., would
be a natural distinction, and the analogy
of ὄλεθρος decides the accentuation to be
φθόρος.

1152—4. μέντοι is not adversative,
but has the original meaning, as in Homer.
The stage-arrangement and acting would
show the full point of κάθημαι: it is probably meant to imply Cleon's presumption
and haughtiness. The -πάλαι forms are
found also to some extent in comic fragments and Lucian's *Lexiphanes*: the one
serious instance of such a form is τετρά-
παλαι in the famous Heraclitus epigram
of Callimachus *Anth. Pal.* vii 80.

καὶ χιλιόπαλαι καὶ πρόπαλαι πάλαι πάλαι. 1155
ΔΗ. ἐγὼ δὲ προσδοκῶν γε τρισμυριόπαλαι
βδελύττομαί σφω, καὶ πρόπαλαι πάλαι πάλαι.
ΑΛΛ. οἶσθ᾽ οὖν ὃ δρᾶσον; ΔΗ. εἰ δὲ μή, φράσεις
γε σύ.
ΑΛΛ. ἄφες ἀπὸ βαλβίδων ἐμέ τε καὶ τουτονί,
ἵνα σ᾽ εὖ ποιῶμεν ἐξ ἴσου. ΔΗ. δρᾶν ταῦτα
χρή. 1160
ἄπιτον. ΠΑ. ἰδού. ΔΗ. θέοιτ᾽ ἄν. ΑΛΛ. ὑποθεῖν οὐκ ἐῶ.

1158. So R. εἰ γε μή, φράσῃς and φράσεις other MSS. εἴσομ᾽ ἦν φράσῃς Porson.

1157. βδελύττομαι, 'am sick of,' in impatience as *Av.* 1501.

1158. This common phrase used to occasion much unnecessary and mistaken explanation. The Greek imperative was used in a subordinate clause with perfect ease: if this is understood, there is no difficulty. The usage is clearly determined by Jebb on Soph. *OT* 543, Postgate in *Trans. Camb. Phil. Soc.* iii 50—, Rutherford on Babrius 32, and *First Greek Syntax* p. 23—4. A good instance is Lysias *fragm.* 75. 3 ἐδεήθη ἥκειν αὐτὸν ἐπὶ κῶμον, λέγων ὅτι μεθ᾽ αὑτοῦ καὶ τῶν οἰκετῶν πίετω. On Demos' reply Porson and Dobree (Porson *Aristoph.* p. 101) collect instances to show that the proper answer in such cases is of the type εἴσομαι ἢν λέγῃς. But their quotations illustrate the form for a courteous answer: here the answer is sulky.

1159—60. ἀφίημι, 'start a race,' so ἄφεσις and ἀφετηρία are synonyms for βαλβίς or ὕσπληξ: ἐξ ἴσου was the phrase for starting fair.

The article in Hesychius shows the difference in details of the meanings of βαλβίς: this arises partly from the different starts for different contests. So here, one scholium, almost identical with the articles in Suidas and Harpocration, says the βαλβίς was a line, γραμμή, and so Aelius Dionysius p. 127. 6 Schwabe: another says it was a stick put across before the runners: the article in *Etym. Mag.* = Bekk. *Anecd.* 220. 31, says it was a rope

stretched across between two sticks, and so Lycophron 13 ἐγὼ δ᾽ ἄκραν βαλβῖδα μηρίνθου σχάσας: Philost. *Imag.* i 24, describing a picture of Hyacinthus' death by Apollo's quoit, makes it a raised bank of earth, βαλβὶς διακέχωσται μικρά...: and Hippocrates has βαλβιδώδης meaning *with projecting edges*. The stadium at Olympia still shows a raised stone starting-line, divided by posts into places for twenty runners, Curtius and Adler *Olympia* ii 64—5.

1161. The want of stage directions and the uncertainty of marks for the speakers make this line a matter of guess-work.

In the compound ὑποθεῖν, the ὑπο- has the meaning 'before' as in ὑποτρέχω (see 676), ὑπειπεῖν, ὑποσαλπίζειν, &c.: so the word means 'cross the path,' as Pind. *Pyth.* 2. 155, and is used of eclipses when the moon crosses the sun's path, σελήνης ὑποδραμούσης Dio Chrysost. *orat.* 40. 38 (Cobet *Coll. Crit.* 92). Here some trick in running must be meant.

οὐκ ἐῶ, 'I bar,' 'you mustn't': at the beginning of a contest, as Plato com. 46. 6 ἀγεννῶς οὐκ ἐῶ παίζειν.

1162—3. It is not easy to say whether these lines form an ordinary disjunctive sentence, or two interrogative ones. I prefer the latter, taking ἀλλ᾽ ἤ almost as in 953; Demos is sulky and suspicious, and he does not expect much as yet.

'I wonder if I'm going to get some

ΔΗ. ἀλλ᾽ ἦ μεγάλως εὐδαιμονήσω τήμερον
ὑπὸ τῶν ἐραστῶν; νὴ Δί᾽ ἦ 'γὼ θρύψομαι;

ΠΑ. ὁρᾷς; ἐγώ σοι πρότερος ἐκφέρω δίφρον.

ΑΛΛ. ἀλλ᾽ οὐ τράπεζαν, ἀλλ᾽ ἐγὼ προτεραίτερος. 1165

ΠΑ. ἰδοὺ φέρω σοι τήνδε μαζίσκην ἐγὼ
ἐκ τῶν ὀλῶν τῶν ἐκ Πύλου μεμαγμένην.

ΑΛΛ. ἐγὼ δὲ μυστίλας μεμυστιλημένας
ὑπὸ τῆς θεοῦ τῇ χειρὶ τηλεφαντίνῃ.

1162. ἦ R, ἢ two MSS. ἤ MSS. and edd. vulg. 1163. ἢ 'γὼ MSS. εἰ
'γὼ Bentley. ἢ 'πιτρίψομαι Kock Mein. εἰ 'πιτρίψομαι; conj. Zacher. εἴ τι Hartman.
1168. γε μεμ. Cobet NL 435: δέ γε suits the meaning, but the rhythm should be
tragic as in Cleon's lines, see App. iii.

wondrous bliss at my lovers' hands.
Shall I play the coquette with them?'
and so he does till 1188 when he frankly
allows he is pleased with the wine. The
emphatic ἐγώ is needed—'shall *I*, an
elderly farmer, play the young beauty?'

μεγάλως, see on 151.

θρύπτομαι means (1) to get spoilt by
luxury or petting: the rare active θρύπτω
= to spoil slaves by treating them as freemen, Plato *Legg*. vi 778 A: (2) to coquet,
refuse what one likes, like ἀκκίζομαι,
Plato *Phaedrus* 228 C, especially of lovers'
offers, Xen. *Symp*. 8. 8, Alciphro iii 8.
2, Plut. *Gryllus* 7. 990 C, Aristaen. ii 16.
From the same root comes τρυφάω, which
is used of a difficult lover, as Xen. *Memor*.
iii 11. 10. of Demos in Demosth. *Chers*.
34 δημαγωγοῦντες ὑμᾶς οὕτως διατεθείκασιν
ὥστε ἐν ταῖς ἐκκλησίαις τρυφᾶν καὶ κολα-
κεύεσθαι.

Plutarch describes Pericles (*Pericl*. 15)
as ἐκ τῆς ἀνειμένης καὶ ὑποθρυπτομένης ἔνια
δημαγωγίας ὥσπερ ἀνθηρᾶς καὶ μαλακῆς
ἁρμονίας ἀριστοκρατικὴν καὶ βασιλικὴν ἐν-
τεινάμενος πολιτείαν.

1164. The δίφρος had no back or
arms, and, though it was sometimes highly
ornamented, was the common, undis-
tinguished, seat. Athenaeus v 192 E,
speaking of the Homeric age, ὁ θρόνος·
ἐλευθέριός ἐστιν καθέδρα...ὁ δὲ κλισμὸς
περιττοτέρως κεκόσμηται ἀνακλίσει· τούτων
δ᾽ εὐτελέστερος ὁ δίφρος· τῷ γοῦν Ὀδυσσεῖ
ἐπαίτῃ εἶναι δοκοῦντι 'δίφρον ἀεικέλιον,
φησί, καταθεὶς ὀλίγην τε τράπεζαν' (*Od*.
xx 259): *id*. x 428 B of Greeks growing
luxurious ἐπεὶ δὲ τρυφᾶν ἤρξαντο καὶ χλι-
δῶσι, κατερρύησαν ἀπὸ τῶν δίφρων ἐπὶ τὰς

κλίνας. Still the διφροφόροι on the Panathenaic frieze imply that the δίφρος had a
place in ceremony (Furtwängler *Masterp*.
428—30): in the Parthenon Inventories are
mentioned 12 θρόνοι, 4 δίφροι, 9 ὀκλαδίαι.

1165. προτεραίτερος, no doubt a comic
formation for the passage, but such forms
are not confined to comedy, πρώτιστος,
ἐσχατώτερος, κυντερώτερος, μειζονώτερος,
Aesch. *frag*. 351 &c.

1166. μαζίσκη, see on 1105. They
set out food in something like the natural
order of a dinner: this determines the
order also in Pherecrates·108, and *Ran*.
504—511, Alexis 163 and similar passages. Observe that Cleon's dishes and
phrases suggest war more than his rival's,
and also that Demos receives them in
silence.

The ὀλαί (οὐλαί or οὐλοχύται in Homer
&c.) meant barley used in sacrifice to
place on the victim's head. It is not
certain whether the barley was used in
grains, or bruised or ground: but there
seems to be no other mention of ὀλαί
made into bread (see on next line). A
pedantic cook speaks of οὐλοχύται for
κριθαί in Strabo ap. Athen. ix 383 A, but
sacrifice is in hand there: and Herod. i
160 seems to make an opposition between
οὐλαί and anything baked (πέμμα).

1168—9. μυστίλη, cf. on 827. μυστιλῶμαι as pass. seems to be unique. The
crusts are here to be used as spoons for
the thick soup, which begins the feast.

In chryselephantine work (the schol.
here is said to be the earliest or only
authority for χρυσελεφάντινος in Greek),
the flesh was represented by ivory. The

ΔΗ.   ὡς μέγαν ἄρ᾽ εἶχες, ὦ πότνια, τὸν δάκτυλον. 1170
ΠΑ.   ἐγὼ δ᾽ ἔτνος γε πίσινον εὔχρων καὶ καλόν·
      ἐτόρυνε δ᾽ αὖθ᾽ ἡ Παλλὰς ἡ Πυλαιμάχος.
ΑΛΛ. ὦ Δῆμ᾽, ἐναργῶς ἡ θεός σ᾽ ἐπισκοπεῖ,
      καὶ νῦν ὑπερέχει σου χύτραν ζωμοῦ πλέαν.

1171. γε om. R.
1172. αὖθ᾽ RV : Πυλαίμαχος V, Πυλαιμάχος R and vulg.: see Chandler *Greek Accent.* § 491.

---

idea that a feast and a sacrifice are one runs through the passage: but here the goddess almost waits upon Demos with offerings, and gets little thanks or respect. Probably the scene is suggested by the banquet given to the citizens of Athens at the Panathenaea after the hecatomb offered to Athena on the Acropolis, *CIA* ii 307.

The various epithets given to her do not include the old ritual names, πολιάς, ἐργάνη &c. One epithet after another, especially Cleon's, merely gives her warlike attributes : at this time her other features were not so prominent ; in the Panathenaic procession more emphasis was given as time went on to array of war, Aristot. *Pol. Ath.* 18 οὐ γὰρ ἔπεμπον τότε μεθ᾽ ὅπλων· ἀλλ᾽ ὕστερον τοῦτο κατεσκεύασεν ὁ δῆμος. But Τριτογενής at the end is not warlike, and it is her influence which first makes Demos content.

1170. A kind of exclamation usual at a revelation of divine presence or power, cf. *Vesp.* 821, but here not very respectful. The Parthenos was 26 cubits high, Plin. *NH* xxxvi 18.

πότνια has become strictly confined to voc.

1171—2. ἀθάρη was made with meal, ἔτνος with pease or pulse, ζωμός with fat meat : so the Sausage-man's dish caps Cleon's. For the manner of serving ἔτνος, cf. ἔτνους ἐπιθυμεῖ· δεῖ τορύνης καὶ χύτρας *Av.* 78, Plato *Hipp. ma.* 290 D. In this contest there is probably a parody of invocations of Athena by demagogues: Cleon takes her warlike aspects as most germane to his military exploits. Πυλαιμάχος is his own invention, to give the play on Πύλος (suggesting Πυλοιμάχος on the analogy of Πυλοιγενής): it occurs again in Callim. *fr.* 503 ἱλαθί μοι φαλαρῖτι πυλαιμάχε. Πυλαμάχος is quoted from

Stesichorus (*fr.* 48 Bergk⁴) by Athenaeus iv 154 F, meaning apparently Ares.

The colossal bronze Athena by Phidias, known as Athena Promachus, stood on the Acropolis west from the Parthenon, and probably in such a position that she might be said to guard the Propylaea, as appears on a type of coin quoted by Miss Harrison, *Myth. and Mon.*, p. 523. The only name we find for this statue in early times is ἡ χαλκῆ ἡ μεγάλη Ἀθηνᾶ, Demosth. *FL* 272. Ἀθηνᾶ Πρόμαχος seems to occur first in Alciphro iii 51. 4, and even then it is not certain that the statue is meant. For what is known of this statue and its copies, see Busolt *Gr. Gesch.* iii 499, and Furtwängler *Masterpieces* i —36, who thinks the artist was the elder Praxiteles, not Phidias : but the strong tradition in favour of Phidias should not be set aside, Farnell *Cults* i 357—9, 377 and Dümmler in Pauly-Wissowa *Encycl.* ii 2016. I think it probable that the two Phidian statues are intentionally alluded to successively.

1173—4. Solon's lines, quoted by Demosth. *FL* 255, would occur to the audience :

ἡμετέρα δὲ πόλις κατὰ μὲν Διὸς οὔ ποτ᾽ ὀλεῖται

αἶσαν καὶ μακάρων θεῶν φρένας ἀθανάτων·

τοίη γὰρ μεγάθυμος ἐπίσκοπος ὀβριμοπάτρη Παλλὰς Ἀθηναίη χεῖρας ὕπερθεν ἔχει.

The Sausage-man's rhythm is tragic, Demos' is comic in his sulky reply. ὑπερέχω χεῖρα of divine protection often. Theognis 757 Ζεὺς μὲν τῆσδε πόληος ὑπειρέχει χεῖρα, and so of Pericles' protection of Anaxagoras, Lucian *Timon* 10 ὑπερέσχε γὰρ αὐτοῦ τὴν χεῖρα Περικλῆς, cf. *Anth. Pal.* vi 155. 6. Schol. on *Nub.* 386 says the poorer citizens got only some bread and ζωμὸς at the Panathenaic feast.

ΔΗ.　οἴει γὰρ οἰκεῖσθ᾽ ἂν ἔτι τήνδε τὴν πόλιν,　1175
　　　εἰ μὴ φανερῶς ἡμῶν ὑπερεῖχε τὴν χύτραν;
ΠΑ.　τουτὶ τέμαχός σοὔδωκεν ἡ Φοβεσιστράτη.
ΑΛΛ.　ἡ δ᾽ Ὀβριμοπάτρα γ᾽ ἐφθὸν ἐκ ζωμοῦ κρέας
　　　καὶ χόλικος ἠνύστρου τε καὶ γαστρὸς τόμον.
ΔΗ.　καλῶς γ᾽ ἐποίησε τοῦ πέπλου μεμνημένη.　1180
ΠΑ.　ἡ Γοργολόφα σ᾽ ἐκέλευε τουτουὶ φαγεῖν
　　　ἐλατῆρος, ἵνα τὰς ναῦς ἐλαύνωμεν καλῶς.
ΑΛΛ.　λαβὲ καὶ ταδί νυν.　ΔΗ. καὶ τί τούτοις χρή-
　　　σομαι
　　　τοῖς ἐντέροις; ΑΛΛ. ἐπίτηδες αὔτ᾽ ἔπεμψέ σοι
　　　εἰς τὰς τριήρεις ἐντερόνειαν ἡ θεός·　　1185
　　　ἐπισκοπεῖ γὰρ περιφανῶς τὸ ναυτικόν.
　　　ἔχε καὶ πιεῖν κεκραμένον τρία καὶ δύο.

1185. ἐντερονείαν most MSS. -όνεια Herodian ap. schol.

1175. οἰκεῖσθαι πόλιν and similar phrases always imply civilised life and progress, not merely occupation of a settled home: but Demos is still sulky and not particularly respectful to Athena.

1177. τέμαχος)(τόμος, see on 282.

1178. The epithet Ὀβριμοπάτρα for Athena connects her intimately with Zeus and his might: the epithet was Epic, Ionic, and poetic, as Solon 2. 3 quoted on 1173, an inscription at Ceos (Roberts 32) εἰκόν᾽ Ἀθηναίης χρυσαιγίδος ὀβριμοπάτρης, also in Didot's *Anthol.* iii add. i 319 b: ὀβριμοδερκὴς Ἀθάνα Bacchyl. 15. 20.

ἠνύστρου, see on 356.

1180. 'Oh, that's all right: she's thinking of her peplus': a grudging acknowledgment. καλῶς ποιῶν and εὖ ποιῶν were often used of malicious or sulky satisfaction at another's misfortune, *Pax* 271, 285, *Eccl.* 803, *Plut.* 863, Lucian *dial. mort.* 11. 3. Yet sometimes simply = 'Thank you, you're very kind,' Plato *Lysis* 204 A, Lucian *Catap.* 27.

1181. Γοργολόφα means merely 'fierce plumed,' as of Lamachus *Ach.* 567 (where he is invoked as divine). The Gorgoneion appears of course constantly on Athena's shield and breast, but apparently not among all the elaborate paraphernalia of the helmet which the Parthenos wore—sphinx, horses &c. So the Gorgon-shield and the plume together make up the terror of warlike array in *Ach.* 964, *Pax* 561 &c.

Cleon remembers Demos' interest in the navy (1065), and makes a point, but his pun on ἐλατήρ ἐλαύνω is capped by two from the Sausage-man, whose gift is also typical of something more substantial than Cleon's.

1183—5. Demos objects to the coarse food offered: he is answered by a pun with the rare word ἐντερόνεια, 'belly-timber,' ἡ τῶν ἐγκοιλίων ὕλη, the Latin *interamenta*, Liv. xxviii 45. 15.

1186. This again suits Athena's democratic aspect.

1187. The wine was not usually brought on till the meat-course was over: and only τραγήματα were eaten with it.

The scholiast here says that the proportion mentioned was the best: so in Plut. *quaest. symp.* iii 9. 657 B in the comparison of wine and water to musical harmonies, ἡ δὲ δυεῖν πρὸς τρία μουσικωτάτη. It was a test of good wine to stand mixing with much water, to be

ΔΗ.   ὡς ἡδύς, ὦ Ζεῦ, καὶ τὰ τρία φέρων καλῶς.
ΑΛΛ. ἡ Τριτογενὴς γὰρ αὐτὸν ἐνετριτώνισεν.
ΠΑ.   λαβέ νυν πλακοῦντος πίονος παρ' ἐμοῦ τόμον.
ΑΛΛ. παρ' ἐμοῦ δ' ὅλον γε τὸν πλακοῦντα τουτονί. 1191
ΠΑ.   ἀλλ' οὐ λαγῷ ἕξεις ὁπόθεν δῷς· ἀλλ' ἐγώ.

1189. Τριτογένει' ἄρ' Cobet *Mnemos.* i 417.

πολυφόρος: ἄρ' οἴσει τρία; Cratinus 183, τὸν ἴσον ἴσῳ φέροντα 184, Pollux vi 18 ἐπήνουν οἶνον τὸν τρία φέροντα τουτέστιν ὕδατος τὸ τριπλοῦν (surely his explanation is wrong).

1189. Τριτογενὴς, a variant for the common Τριτογένεια, occurring Hom. *hymn.* 27. 4, Herod. vii 141 in the famous oracle quoted on 1040, and in the *Anthology:* Τριτωνίς (*Attic hymn at Delphi* 2. 11) and Τριτώ also occur. This curious epithet of Athena was usually explained to mean, "born at the stream or lake Triton" (Farnell *Cults* i 266–9), which was often identified with the lake of Gabes in Libya, by a myth connected with the wanderings of Jason in that region, and the high hopes once entertained of great Greek colonies there (Herod. iv 179): Delphi had spoken of a hundred Greek cities round the lake, and in Aesch. *Eum.* 293 Athena is supposed to be watching over the expansion of Attic empire in Africa, Τρίτωνος ἀμφὶ χεῦμα. There were several other explanations current: these are given by Suidas in his article on the word. Bruchmann's *Epitheta Deorum* shows how much the word was used, especially in later poetry: and so in the inscription in the Appian Way by Herodes Atticus *CIG* 6280, and at Pergamus *CIG* 3538. Comparative philologers favour a derivation from an Aryan word meaning 'water,' which appears as Τρίτων 'Αμφιτρίτη in Greek, tritan triath in Irish; this connects it with the Vedic deity Trita and the Zend Thrito, Thraêtaonô Âthwajânô (Osthoff *Morph. Unters.* iv 195): this passage and *Lys.* 347 make it probable that the Athenians gave the word some such meaning. So schol. on 886 gives the oracle on Athens' sea-power τεῖχος Τριτογενεῖ ξύλινον διδοῖ εὐρύοπα Ζεύς. The word was very widely connected with the number *three:* at Athens the third day of the month was said to be Athena's birthday (Harpocr. s.v. τριτόμηνις): and philosophers used it in symbolical and mystical applications, Democritus of the three bonds of human society (Diog. Laert. ix 46), Pythagoras of the equilateral triangle (Plut. *Is. et Osir.* 75. 381 D), Zeno of the three-fold division of philosophy, *fr.* 1 Pearson.

Athena's services are finished off with this pun: in Alexis 226, Kaibel's conjecture ἐγχέω Τρίτωνα πολύν ; is ingenious and in point.

The elasticity in meaning of verbs in -ίζω and the ease with which new and comic formations naturally took it have been mentioned several times above. For the ἐν- cf. Lucian *Menipp.* 20 ἐνεβριμήσατο ἡ Βριμώ, and so Eudocia *violarium* 216 ἡ δὲ (Περσεφόνη) ἐνεβριμήσατο...καὶ ἐντεῦθεν Βριμὼ προσηγορεύθη.

1190. πλακοῦς was the generic name for a rich cake, generally baked with honey: lists of species are given by Athenaeus xiv 643— and Pollux vi 77— 79. The Athenian πλακοῦντες were the best, Archestratus ap. Athen. iii 101 D ἀλλὰ πλακοῦντα αἴνει 'Αθήνησιν γεγενημένον. The appearance of the πλακοῦς marked a point in a liberal entertainment, Lucian *Gallus* 12 ἤδη τοῦ πλακοῦντος ἐσκομιζομένου, cf. Plut. *quaest. conv.* vii 6. 707 B: it was a mark of a good host to give special attention to the game and other dishes sent in with the wine, Archestratus *loc. cit.* The word became *placenta* in Latin: and Cato *Res Rust.* 76 gives directions for making a cake of the kind with cheese and honey. τόμος is specially used of sausages and cheese.

1192. λαγῷα, the menu word for hare, cf. ὀρνίθεια, ἐγχέλεια &c. (see on 353). Pieces of hare and of wild birds came with the wine as τραγήματα, not in the first part of dinner, Athen. xiv 641 F ἐδίδοτο δὲ καὶ ᾠὸν ἐν τῇ δευτέρᾳ τραπέζῃ, ὥσπερ καὶ λαγῷα καὶ κίχλαι κοινῇ μετὰ τῶν μελιπήκτων εἰσεφέρετο, Alexis 357

ΑΛΛ. οἴμοι· πόθεν λαγῷά μοι γενήσεται;
ὦ θυμέ, νυνὶ βωμολόχον ἔξευρέ τι.

ΠΑ. ὁρᾷς τάδ', ὦ κακόδαιμον; ΑΛΛ. ὀλίγον μοι
μέλει· 1195
ἐκεινοὶ γὰρ ὡς ἔμ' ἔρχονται. ΠΑ. τίνες;

ΑΛΛ. πρέσβεις ἔχοντες ἀργυρίου βαλλάντια.

ΠΑ. ποῦ ποῦ; ΑΛΛ. τί δέ σοι τοῦτ'; οὐκ ἐάσεις
τοὺς ξένους;
ὦ Δημίδιον, ὁρᾷς τὰ λαγῷ ἅ σοι φέρω;

ΠΑ. οἴμοι τάλας, ἀδίκως γε τἄμ' ὑφήρπασας. 1200

ΑΛΛ. νὴ τὸν Ποσειδῶ, καὶ σὺ γὰρ τοὺς ἐκ Πύλου.

ΔΗ. εἴπ', ἀντιβολῶ, πῶς ἐπενόησας ἁρπάσαι;

ΑΛΛ. τὸ μὲν νόημα τῆς θεοῦ, τὸ δὲ κλέμμ' ἐμόν.

ΠΑ. ἐγὼ δ' ἐκινδύνευσ'. ΑΛΛ. ἐγὼ δ' ὤπτησά γε.

ΔΗ. ἄπιθ'· οὐ γὰρ ἀλλὰ τοῦ παραθέντος ἡ χά-
ρις. 1205

1196—7. ἐκεῖνοι γὰρ RV and most MSS.: ἀλλὰ γὰρ ἐκεῖνοί γ' B, ἐκεινοὶ γὰρ Elmsl. The two lines are given continuously to ΑΛΛ. by Mein. Vels. after the second schol.

1200. ὑφαρπάσας, suggested (without confidence) by Dobree, has been wrongly adopted by some editors.

1203. Bergk assumes a lacuna after this line.

1204. Bothe and most editors give the whole line to Cleon.

τραγήματ' ἄμητας καὶ λαγῷα καὶ κίχλας, Teleclides 32 χαίρω λαγῴοις ἐπ' ἀμύλῳ καθημένοις. Hares were rare in Attica, and since the war they were very difficult to get, *Ach.* 520, 878.

1193—4. The lines are in part a parody of something in tragedy, or at least of tragic style: the νυνὶ βωμολόχον becomes comic in phrase and rhythm. From here to the end of the scene the rhythm often plainly implies parody: some whole scene of Euripides may be in view, see on 1229.

1195—. The scholiast explains: τάδε are pieces of hare that Cleon has got, the Sausage-man pretends that foreign envoys are coming with purses of money for him, and steals the hare, while Cleon is

intent on the purses. For κακόδαιμον *confounded fool*, see on 7. ξένους is of course respectful, as often.

1203. A parody, or quotation with the comic idea and rhythm δὲ κλέμμ' substituted for τοὔργον δ' or the like. The parody is continued in the next line, where the division between the speakers, as in the MSS., is clearly right: the meaning is *Cleon*. 'Mine was the daring deed (at Pylus).' *Saus.* 'Yes, but mine was the roasting (here).'

1205. οὐ γὰρ ἀλλά. Blaydes on *Nub.* 232 gives cases of this idiom, which was common colloquially: in literature it seems almost confined to Euripides, Old Comedy and Plato. The οὐ γὰρ answers to 'Oh, no, no,' 'Nay' of an English sentence.

ΠΑ. οἴμοι κακοδαίμων, ὑπεραναιδευθήσομαι.

ΑΛΛ. τί οὐ διακρίνεις, Δῆμ', ὁπότερός ἐστι νῷν
ἀνὴρ ἀμείνων περὶ σὲ καὶ τὴν γαστέρα;

ΔΗ. τῷ δῆτ' ἂν ὑμᾶς χρησάμενος τεκμηρίῳ
δόξαιμι κρίνειν τοῖς θεαταῖσιν σοφῶς;   1210

ΑΛΛ. ἐγὼ φράσω σοι. τὴν ἐμὴν κίστην ἰὼν
ξύλλαβε σιωπῇ, καὶ βασάνισον ἅττ' ἔνι,
καὶ τὴν Παφλαγόνος· κἀμέλει κρινεῖς καλῶς.

ΔΗ. φέρ' ἴδω, τί οὖν ἔνεστιν; ΑΛΛ. οὐχ ὁρᾷς
κενὴν
ὦ παππίδιον; ἅπαντα γάρ σοι παρεφόρουν. 1215

ΔΗ. αὕτη μὲν ἡ κίστη τὰ τοῦ δήμου φρονεῖ.

1206. ὑπεραναιδεσθήσομαι MSS. -ισθήσομαι Dindorf from Bekk. *Anecd.* 80. 30,
Rutherf. *NP* p. 140. -ευθήσομαι Elmsl. on Eurip. *Heracl.* 387.
1207. οὔκουν κρινεῖς ὦ Δῆμ' Zacher.

1206. οἴμοι κακοδαίμων, see on 1243.
1207. The aorist was the proper idiom in interrogative sentences beginning with τί οὐ. The present is sometimes found when another interrog. clause without οὐ precedes, as *Lys.* 1159—60 τί... μάχεσθε κοὐ παύεσθε τῆς μοχθηρίας (but next line τί δ' οὐ διηλλάγητε), and sometimes independently as here, *Lys.* 1103, Eurip. *Hippol.* 1060, Plato com. 69. 2, Lucian *dial. marin.* 12. 2.
1208. Cf. 874.
1209—10. κρίνειν may be for διακρίνειν by the usage mentioned on 98 *sup.*, or it may=*test*, as often with acc. case. Eur. *IA* 71 ὁ τὰς θεὰς κρίνων of Paris.
σοφῶς, 'wisely,' with the idea, common in the word, of 'effective artistically': he feels he has seemed stupid and vulgar.
1211. κίστη, see on 1000 *sup.*
1212. ξύλλαβε, cf. on 650.
1215. Though πάππος means only *grandfather*, its diminutive forms are used only of *father:* πάππας (Homer), παππίας, παππίδιον; so παππάζω and παππίζω 'to coax one's father.' Russians use 'Little Father' in respectful address: Turkish 'baba.'
Athenaeus ix 380 D thinks it worth while to give some quotations to illustrate παραφέρω. Generally παρατίθημι is used of the first course, παραφέρω of

dessert and wine; as is natural from the way of serving them, παρατιθέμενα being of course set on the table, παραφερόμενα carried along and handed by servants. So of *hors-d'œuvre* before dinner παραφέρω is used Athen. iii 101 B, but of τραγήματα served by some with the first course παρατίθημι id. ii 53 A; iii 120 B εἰθισμένα προπαρατίθεσθαι περιφοράς is an innovation. In Plato *Rep.* i 372 C τραγήματα παραθήσομεν αὐτοῖς is intentionally odd: there are to be no servants: I think Plut. *quaest. conv.* iv 1. 664 A misses this point when he refers to the passage. παρατίθημι may be used of wine in large vessels set on the table as Crates ap. Athen. xi 495 B. So παρετίθει 1223 of his booty in general. For παρεφόρουν see on 294 *sup.*: Herod. i 133 has παραφορεῖν and παραφέρειν in successive clauses: in the same inscription *CIA* iv 834 b i 76 and ii 80 we find τοῖς ἐκφέρουσι τὸν σῖτον and τῷ τὰ λιθολογήματα ἀνελόντι καὶ ἐκφορήσαντι. The imperfect of course denotes habit.
1216. A good instance of the force, sometimes modest, sometimes minatory as here, of μὲν with no δὲ clause expressed. τὰ τοῦ δήμου φρονεῖ as an orthodox Athenian who passes his δοκιμασία, 'genuine democrat,' as Plut. *Alcib.* 27. The rhythm is intentionally pompous.

ΑΛΛ. βάδιζέ νυν καὶ δεῦρο πρὸς τὴν Παφλαγόνος.
ὁρᾷς; ΔΗ. ἰώ μοι, τῶν ἀγαθῶν ὅσων πλέα.
ὅσον τὸ χρῆμα τοῦ πλακοῦντος ἀπέθετο·
ἐμοὶ δ' ἔδωκεν ἀποτεμὼν τυννουτονί. 1220
ΑΛΛ. τοιαῦτα μέντοι καὶ πρότερόν σ' ἠργάζετο·
σοὶ μὲν προσεδίδου μικρὸν ὧν ἐλάμβανεν,
αὐτὸς δ' ἑαυτῷ παρετίθει τὰ μείζονα.
ΔΗ. ὦ μιαρέ, κλέπτων δή με ταῦτ' ἐξηπάτας;
ἐγὼ δέ τυ ἐστεφάνιξα κἀδωρησάμαν. 1225

1217. γ' οὖν RV, γοῦν other MSS., νυν Cobet *Mnemos.* i 418, δ' οὖν Sauppe.
1218. οἴμοι MSS. ὁρᾷς τάδ'; οἴμοι Elmsl., not so well, as τάδ' should be of the first person as 1195.
1221. εἰργάζετο all MSS. except R. Inscriptions show that Attic used ἠργ- in impf. and aor., εἰργ- in perf. Meisterhans § 62. 11.
1225. τοι R: -άμην MSS. except M.

1217. γ' οὖν is just possible in its original sense 'Oh well, then,' but this is rare.
1219. χρῆμα 'thing' as used in Scotch, 'what a thing of cake!' χρῆμα in this sense was rather colloquial; it is not found in Aeschylus: in Sophocles once in *fr.* 357 (probably satyric) συὸς μέγιστον χρῆμα; several times in Eurip., generally depreciatory and in the mouths of women or a παιδαγωγός as *Phoen.* 198 φιλόψογον δὲ χρῆμα θηλειῶν ἔφυ: often in Comedy and once or twice in Plato, as *Theaet.* 209 E ἡδὺ τὸ χρῆμα τοῦ λόγου. See Starkie on *Vesp.* 933·
ἀποτίθεσθαι is naturally used of birds, bees &c. storing up food; Plato *Legg.* x 887 C of men bringing out all their powers of argument, μηδὲν ἀποθέμενοι διεξέλθωμεν.
1222. προσδίδωμι is meant offensively, being used of superiors giving to inferiors as in charity. This (and not *give in addition*) seems to be its usage in good Greek: it is correlative to προσαιτῶ *beg*: Soph. *Phil.* 309, Eurip. *Supp.* 351, *Hel.* 700, *Cycl.* 531, Xen. *Mem.* i 2. 29, *Anab.* i 9. 19, Isocr. *de pace* 23, Menand. 926 (v.l. προσεδόκας). It was used also of priests handing part of the victim to worshippers or bystanders, *Pax* 955, 1111, Plut. *Crassus* 19: in this sense too προσαιτῶ was the correlative, see Harpocration s.v. βωμολοχεύεσθαι. In later Greek it is used more vaguely, Plut. *Cato* 24, *Brutus* 5,

Anton. 83, *quaest. conv.* v 3. 11, Lucian *de merc. cond.* 20.
1225. μιμεῖται δὲ τοὺς Εἴλωτας ὅταν στεφανῶσι τὸν Ποσειδῶνα schol. A play called *The Helots* is quoted seven times, sometimes as by Eupolis, sometimes as by an unknown author, Kock *Com. fr.* Eupolis 138—144: K. O. Müller thought there were two plays of the name, one by Eupolis, one satyric; Nauck seems to think that the satyric one was the 'Heracles at Taenarum' of Sophocles (Nauck *Trag. fr.* Soph. 205—). Anyhow the line is a quotation from a Doric protest, no doubt by Helots, against Poseidon's disregard of their offerings. Poseidon's famous shrine at Taenarum was an asylum for Helots (see 1312 for the significance of this), and several of the inscriptions found there are enfranchisement - deeds in the form of dedications of Helots to Poseidon, Cauer *Delect. Inscr. Gr.* no. 19, 21—23, Roberts *Epigr.* 265: no. of these is dated to the year 427—6 B.C. It is probable that the Helots continued to worship the old pre-Dorian Poseidon rather than the newer Dorian deities; Poseidon avenged their wrongs, Aelian *Var. Hist.* vi 7, cf. Pausan. iv 24. 6: and it would be interesting to know what gods the Mainotes, whose non-Slavonic blood and pagan manners were noted, worshipped down to the ninth century when they became Christians (Constant.

N. A. 11

ΠΛ. ἐγὼ δ' ἔκλεπτον ἐπ' ἀγαθῷ γε τῇ πόλει.
ΔΗ. κατάθου ταχέως τὸν στέφανον, ἵν' ἐγὼ τουτῳὶ
      αὐτὸν περιθῶ. ΑΛΛ. κατάθου ταχέως, μα-
      στιγία.
ΠΛ. οὐ δῆτ', ἐπεί μοι χρησμός ἐστι Πυθικὸς
      φράζων, ὑφ' οὗ 'δέησέ μ' ἡττᾶσθαι μόνου.   1230
ΑΛΛ. τοὐμόν γε φράζων ὄνομα καὶ λίαν σαφῶς.
ΠΛ. καὶ μήν σ' ἐλέγξαι βούλομαι τεκμηρίῳ,
      εἴ τι ξυνοίσεις τοῦ θεοῦ τοῖς θεσφάτοις.
      καί σου τοσοῦτο πρῶτον ἐκπειράσομαι·
      παῖς ὢν ἐφοίτας ἐς τίνος διδασκάλου;   1235
ΑΛΛ. ἐν ταῖσιν εὔστραις κονδύλοις ἡρμοττόμην.

1230. φράζων ὑφ' οὗ δεήσει (or δεήσειν) μ' MSS. unmetrically. 'δέησέ μ' Bentl.
δίκη 'στί μ' Kock. ὑφ' οὗ δεήσει μ' ἀνδρὸς Herm.   1236. εὔστραις V¹.

Porphyr. *de adm. imper.* 50). Gibbon gives 'Neptune and Venus' without quoting authority. The gifts found near the shrine are mostly figures of bulls or horses, both likely gifts to Poseidon (bulls were his favourite offering, Athen. vi 261 D &c.).

1226. Both the ἐγώ and the δὲ...γε show that this line is a retort to 1225 more than a self-defence.

ἐπ' ἀγαθῷ with dat. as *Ran.* 1487—8, *Plut.* 888 οὐκ ἐπ' ἀγαθῷ γὰρ ἐνθάδ' ἐστὸν οὐδενί.

1227—8. The rhythm is much resolved to imply haste and to contrast with the tragic parody of 1229—. For κατάθου cf. on 155.

The στέφανος was official as well as social in its meaning: in *Nub.* 625 it marks a holy office: Aeschin. *Timarch.* 19 στεφανηφόρος ἡ ἀρχή of the archonship as religious: cf. Demosth. 2 *Aristog.* 5 πέπαυνται ἄρχοντες καὶ τοὺς στεφάνους περιήρηνται, *Theocrin.* 27, *Mid.* 32—3, Lysias *Euandr.* 8, Lycurg. *Leocr.* 122.

The στέφανος is a more obvious mark of office even than the δακτύλιος, which was taken from Cleon 947.

περιτίθημι στέφανον, not ἐπιτίθημι, is the idiom in good Greek, Cobet *VL* 190: the corresponding word for *take off* a wreath is περιαιρῶ, Demosth. 2 *Aristog.* 5

and Lycurg. *Leocr.* 122 quoted above: cf. περισπάσας τὸ διάδημα Plut. *garrul.* 12. 508 D: Lucian *Anach.* 23 has κράνη ἐπικείμενοι, but 32 κράνη περιθήσεσθε.

μαστιγίας, cf. στιγματίας, ἀλωπεκίας: the termination was used of winds (see *sup.* 437), of animals as ξιφίας, κνακίας, of plants as ὀμφακίας, of wines as ἀνθοσμίας, and of men contemptuously as τομίας, ἐξωμίας, λαισποδίας, φρονηματίας, or hypocoristically, as Νικίας &c.

1229. The parody of a tragic ἀναγνώρισις from here to 1253 is heightened by the rhythm, which is comic only in a few lines, and those probably with intent.

1232—. καὶ μήν of a fresh start as 970. The language is carefully tragic, as τεκμηρίῳ, ἐλέγχειν εἰ (cf. a similar crisis, Aesch. *Cho.* 851), and ἐκπειράσομαι is in the tragic style of compounds. In 1235—7 the words are common, and the tragic rhythm is all the more marked.

1235. ἐς τίνος διδασκάλου, cf. *fragm.* 5 b σοὶ γὰρ σοφίσμαθ' εἴ τιν' εἰσηγησάμην, οὐκ εὐθὺς ἀπεδίδρασκες ἐκ διδασκάλου;

1236. εὔστραι δὲ οἱ βόθροι ἐκαλοῦντο, ἐν οἷς εὔεται τὰ χοιρίδια· τὰ δὲ ἐγκαύματα εὔσανα, Pollux vi 91.

'Keeping in order' was not much in favour in Attic politics or education: Soph. *OC* 908 Theseus retorts on Creon's harshness νῦν δ' οὕσπερ αὐτὸς τοὺς νό-

ΠΛ. πῶς εἶπας; ὡς μού χρησμὸς ἅπτεται φρενῶν.
εἶέν.
ἐν παιδοτρίβου δὲ τίνα πάλην ἐμάνθανες;
ΑΛΛ. κλέπτων ἐπιορκεῖν καὶ βλέπειν ἐναντία.
ΠΛ. ὦ Φοῖβ' Ἄπολλον Λύκιε, τί ποτέ μ' ἐργάσει; 1240
τέχνην δὲ τίνα ποτ' εἶχες ἐξανδρούμενος;
ΑΛΛ. ἠλλαντοπώλουν καί τι καὶ βινεσκόμην.
ΠΛ. οἴμοι κακοδαίμων· οὐκέτ' οὐδέν εἰμ' ἐγώ.
λεπτή τις ἐλπίς ἐστ' ἐφ' ἧς ὀχούμεθα.
καί μοι τοσοῦτον εἰπέ· πότερον ἐν ἀγορᾷ 1245

1238. εἶέν, so R: see on 1078 *sup.*   **1239** ἐναντίον MSS. except R.

μους εἰσῆλθ' ἔχων, τούτοισι κοὺκ ἄλλοισιν ἀρμοσθήσεται : among Dorians it was more approved and familiar, hence ἀρμοστής &c.

1237. μού as οὐκτὸς *Vesp.* 1287.

ἅπτεται φρενῶν, quotation or parody, see Ruth. *NP* 9 on φρήν : so the Cyclops becomes tragic in the line αἰαῖ, παλαιὸς χρησμὸς ἐκπεραίνεται Eurip. *Cycl.* 696.

1238—9. Cleon's line has comic rhythm, for whatever reason, and it is an elegance in the game for the response to follow in similar rhythm.

πάλη must suggest 'trick' as well as 'wrestling': from similarity to παλάμη Παλαμήδης, παιπάλη παιπάλημα, παλεύω: Plut. *quaest. conv.* ii 4 τεχνικώτατον καὶ πανουργότατον τῶν ἀθλημάτων ἡ πάλη... ἡ γὰρ πάλη μοι δοκεῖ τῷ παλεύειν, ὅπερ ἐστὶ δι' ἀπάτης καὶ δόλου καταβάλλειν, κεκλῆσθαι.

1240. From Euripides' *Telephus* (schol.): Apollo appeared in that story as giving the oracle ὁ τρώσας ἰάσεται. Apollo Lycius in Athens was the patron of the Lyceum and the gymnasia there.

ἐργάσει, cf. on 145. The future in such cases was specially Euripidean, see Monk on *Hippol.* 353.

1241. ἐξανδρούμενος is Ionic and tragic: in both the extant cases in Euripides the weight of the word is relieved by a trisyllabic foot earlier in the line, *Phoen.* 32 ἤδη δὲ πυρσαῖς γένυσιν ἐξανδρού-

μενος, *Supp.* 703 λόχος δ' ὀδόντων ὄφεος ἐξηνδρωμένος.

1242. Mock-tragic of course in rhythm and expression. καί τι καί was 'precious,' and imperfects of the -σκο- form seem confined in Attic writers to three instances in chorus, one in a mock-oracle, *Pax* 1070, this case, and Aesch. *frag.* 298. Curtius *Griech. Verb.* cap. xxii says these forms are always more or less experiments in language by the author.

1243. οἴμοι κακοδαίμων (as if 'I'm damned' came in a tragic passage on our stage) was probably a favourite comic effect in parodies of tragic lines, cf. *fr.* 308, Antiphanes 282.

οὐδέν εἰμι, 'I am brought to nought,' is tragic, Eurip. *Hel.* 1194 &c.

1244. Porson on Eurip. *Orest.* 68 says "ὁρμεῖν sive ὀχεῖσθαι ἐπὶ ἀγκύρας dicunt Graeci...et cum spes aptissime per ancoram significetur, facillima translatione dicunt ἐπ' ἐλπίδος ὀχεῖσθαι, unde in proverbium abiit" (cf. *fragm.* 198. 11, Blaydes on *Lys.* 31); and Eurip. *Hel.* 277 has ἄγκυρα τὰς τύχας ὤχει: but it is more likely that, as Casaubon said, the metaphor came from a man who has had to relinquish his ship for a raft: so evidently in Plato *Phaedo* 85 D ἐπὶ τούτου ὀχούμενος ὥσπερ ἐπὶ σχεδίας, and Plut. *non posse suav.* 23. 6. 1103 D νεὼς μὲν ἐκπεσὼν ἐπ' ἐλπίδος ὀχεῖται τινος. The rhythm breaks down next line into a comic triviality.

II—2

ἠλλαντοπώλεις ἐτεὸν ἢ 'πὶ ταῖς πύλαις;
ΑΛΛ. ἐπὶ ταῖς πύλαισιν, οὗ τὸ τάριχος ὤνιον.
ΠΛ. οἴμοι πέπρακται τοῦ θεοῦ τὸ θέσφατον.
κυλίνδετ' εἴσω τόνδε τὸν δυσδαίμονα.
ὦ στέφανε, χαίρων ἄπιθι, κεί σ' ἄκων ἐγὼ 1250
λείπω· σὲ δ' ἄλλος τις λαβὼν κεκτήσεται,
κλέπτης μὲν οὐκ ἂν μᾶλλον, εὐτυχὴς δ' ἴσως.
ΑΛΛ. Ἑλλάνιε Ζεῦ, σὸν τὸ νικητήριον.

1247 ἐν ταῖς N. **1250.** καὶ MSS.

1246—7. ἐτεόν of appealing questions as always. The gates are those between the outer and inner Ceramicus : the population here was disreputable, Hesych. Κεραμεικός· ἔνθα οἱ πόρνοι προεστήκεσαν, and Δημίαισι πύλαις...πρὸς αὐτάς φασιν ἑστάναι τὰς πόρνας : cf. Isaeus 6. 20 τὴν Ἀλκὴν καθίστησιν ἐπιμελεῖσθαι τῆς ἐν Κεραμεικῷ συνοικίας, τῆς παρὰ τὴν πυλίδα οὗ ὁ οἶνος ὤνιος, Ran. 1095 οἱ Κεραμῆς ἐν ταῖσι πύλαις παίουσ' αὐτοῦ γαστέρα, Alciphro iii 25. 2, 49. 2.

πωλεῖσθαι in passive is very rare, and ὤνιός ἐστι was probably used instead in Attic (Rutherford NP 213) : cf. πῶς ὤνιος ; sup. 480, Plato Legg. viii 848 A πάντων τῶν ἀναγκαίων ἀπονεμηθὲν τρίτον μέρος ὤνιον ἔστω μόνον, τῶν δὲ δύο μερῶν μηδὲν ἐπάναγκες ἔστω πωλεῖν ; so οὗ τὰ βύβλι' ὤνια Eupolis 304, Aristot. Pol. Ath. 51 ὅπως ὁ ἐν ἀγορᾷ σῖτος ὤνιος ἔσται δικαίως, ἔπειθ' ὅπως οἱ μυλωθροὶ πρὸς τὰς τιμὰς τὰ ἄλφιτα πωλήσουσιν, Alexis 76 τῆς οὐσίας γάρ εἰσιν ἡμῶν ὤνιοι ; but the participle occurs Xen. Oecon. 1. 11 μὴ πωλούμενοι οὐ χρήματά εἰσιν οἱ αὐλοί, Antiphanes 100. 4 πλεῖς τὴν θάλατταν σχοινίων πωλουμένων, Menander 195, Plut. tranq. an. 4. 466 E Διογένης πωλούμενος ἔσκωπτε τὸν κήρυκα, Epictet. iii 3. 4 προέσθαι αὐτὸν δεῖ τὸ ἀντὶ νομίσματος πωλούμενον : and other parts, Xen. Hiero 1. 13 τοιαῦτα πωλεῖται τοῖς τυράννοις, Eubulus 74. 1 ἐν τῷ γὰρ αὐτῷ πάνθ' ὁμοῦ πωλήσεται, Plut. Solon 23 ὅσαι πεφασμένως πωλοῦνται, Anth. Pal. v 177. 1 πωλείσθω but fut. πεπράσεται.

The ταριχοπώλης was among the lowest of tradesmen, Plato Charm. 163 B ὄνειδος εἶναι σκυτοτομοῦντι ἢ ταριχοπωλοῦντι ἢ ἐπ' οἰκήματος καθημένῳ, Lucian necyom. 17 πτωχεύοντας καὶ ἤτοι ταριχοπωλοῦντας ὑπ' ἀπορίας ἢ τὰ πρῶτα διδάσκοντας γράμ-

ματα. Plut. quaest. conv. ii 1. 631 D ὁ εἰπὼν ταριχοπώλην αὐτόθεν ἐλοιδόρησεν, ὁ δὲ φήσας ' μεμνήμεθά σε τῷ βραχίονι ἀπομυττόμενον ' ἔσκωψε. It is to be distinguished from ἰχθυοπώλης, as τάριχος from ἰχθύς, cf. Plut. an virt. doc. 2. 440 A ἐνὶ δακτύλῳ τὸ τάριχος ἀρασθαι, δυσὶ τὸν ἰχθύν, σῖτον, κρέας.

1248—9. Both lines are obviously tragic : the second, according to the scholiast, is from Euripides' Bellerophon (fr. 312) with κομίζετ' altered to κυλίνδετ' : probably the Sthenoboea is meant, from which the lines are quoted (fr. 673) κομίζετ' εἴσω τήνδε· πιστεύειν δὲ χρὴ γυναικὶ μηδέν, ὅστις εὖ φρονεῖ βροτῶν. For such words in colloquial usage cf. μετακυλίνδω Ran. 536, παλάθαν σὺ προκύκλει ἐκ πίονος οἴκου in the Rhodian Swallow-song. There is no special reference to the machinery of the ἐκκύκλημα, of which εἰσκυκλεῖν and ἐκκυκλεῖν are used, Ach. 408, Thesm. 96, 265 : though Pollux iv 128 mentions Bellerophon specially in connexion with the μηχανή.

1250—2. Parody of Alcestis' farewell to her marriage-bed, Eurip. Alc. 177 — σὲ δ' ἄλλη τις γυνὴ κεκτήσεται, σώφρων μὲν οὐκ ἂν μᾶλλον, εὐτυχὴς δ' ἴσως. He speaks no more, like Iago.

1253. Whatever was the origin of this Aeginetan surname of Zeus, it had become by the Persian wars a symbol of Greek unity and a Panhellenic call, as in the Athenian protest, Herod. ix 7, ἡμεῖς Δία τε Ἑλλήνιον αἰδεσθέντες καὶ τὴν Ἑλλάδα δεινὸν ποιεύμενοι προδοῦναι. So this line is the keynote of the play: Cleon's fall will be the victory of Panhellenism. The Dorian form was the original, and here enhances the Panhellenic effect. It is found also in the Ionic island of Tenos

ΧΟΡ. ὦ χαῖρε καλλίνικε, καὶ μέμνησ᾽ ὅτι
ἀνὴρ γεγένησαι δι᾽ ἐμέ· καί σ᾽ αἰτῶ βραχύ, 1255
ὅπως ἔσομαί σοι Φανὸς ὑπογραφεὺς δικῶν.

ΔΗ. ἐμοὶ δέ γ᾽ ὅ τι σοι τοὔνομ᾽ εἴπ᾽. ΑΛΛ. Ἀγορά-
κριτος·
ἐν τἀγορᾷ γὰρ κρινόμενος ἐβοσκόμην.

ΔΗ. Ἀγορακρίτῳ τοίνυν ἐμαυτὸν ἐπιτρέπω,

1254. ΔΗΜ. RA Bekk. Zieliński *Glied.* p. 294. ΧΟ. vulg.
1256. γένωμαι MSS. except RM. Φανὸς MSS. Φᾶνος Mein. &c. by the rule that
such proper names are distinguished from adjectives by throwing back the accent:
for cases see Lehrs *Arist. stud. Hom.*³ p. 276— and Chandler.

(Preller-Robert, *Griech. Mythol.* i 126).
It is significant that we hardly hear of the
idea except in the Persian wars, here, and
(as implied) in Isocrates *Evagoras* 15.
Hadrian personified in Ζεὺς Πανελλήνιος
his ideal of a Panhellenism centred in
Athens. Euripides uses Ἑλλανία for
Ἑλλὰς several times in lyrics (*Hippol.*
1121, *Ion* 796 &c.): but otherwise the adjective Ἑλλήνιος is rare and confined to
religious phrases θεοὶ Ἑλλήνιοι Herod. v
49, Lucian *Herc.* 2, Aelian *Var. Hist.*
xii 1, πὰρ βωμὸν πατέρος Ἑλλανίου Pind.
Nem. 5. 10, τὸ τέμενος τὸ Ἑλλήνιον at
Naucratis Herod. ii 178, Athena Ἑλληνία
Aristot. *mirab. ausc.* 108. 840ᵃ 28.
1254—. Zieliński's rule, that the
Chorus speaks in tragic iambics, seems
right generally, and certainly these lines
are more in place if Demosthenes is the
speaker. Yet if Demosthenes is still on
the stage, who acted the part? Zieliński
says a 'parachoregem.'
1255—6. ἀνὴρ 179: 'let me be to
you what Phanus is to Cleon': Phanus is
mentioned with Cleon, but as a silent
guest, at the comic party in *Vesp.* 1220.
Nothing else is known of him.
ὑπογραφεὺς has nothing to do with
ὑπογραμματεύς, but comes straight from
ὑπογράφω, ὑπογραφή (cf. ἀντιγραφεύς, ἀπο-
γραφεύς): it would not mean *under-
secretary* any more than συγγραφεύς would
mean *joint-secretary* (except perhaps
where γραφεύς was used for *secretary* as
in some Dorian states). ὑπογραφεὺς was
an office at Acrae in Sicily. The office
of ὑπογραμματεὺς was by no means

admired, *Ran.* 1083, Lysias *Nicom.* 27.
ὑπογραφεὺς in Plutarch and later Greek
seems to mean amanuensis or short-hand
writer, *notarius.* ὑπογράφω δίκην does
not seem to occur: but the ὑπογραφὴ of
Plato *Theaet.* 172 E and the ὑπογράφω of
Demosth. *Pantaen.* 23 imply the drawing
up of a *brief* regulating the further proceedings in a law-case.
Symmachus' scholion is sensible (φαίνεται τις γραμματεὺς οὗτος· τῶν πάνυ σπα-
νίων ὄνομα κύριον), and we know little
more than he did. The other scholia
are foolish, and their distinction ὑπογραφεὺς ἐπὶ τοῦ δήμου, ὁ δὲ τοῦ βουλευ-
τηρίου ἀντιγραφεύς, is unsupported. Pha-
einus took φανὸς as an adjective, and
probably puns on Phanus and φαίνω were
common: cf. Φαναῖσι, *Av.* 1694.
1257. Both ἐμοὶ and δέ γε contrast
Demus' request with the previous one,
and imply his claims to be answered first.
1257—8. The -κριτος in names really
means 'approved by,' as in Δημόκριτος,
Λάκριτος (for Λεώκριτος?), Θεόκριτος: the
derivation given is of course comic: from
κρίνομαι, '*quarrel, brawl.*' Euripides
sometimes refined in a like manner, *fr.*
521 Μελέαγρε, μελέαν γάρ ποτ᾽ ἀγρεύεις
ἄγραν. Names beginning with Ἀγορα-
are quite rare: Pape gives only Ἀγό-
ραισος, Ἀγορακλῆς, Ἀγοράκριτος, Ἀγορά-
ναξ, Ἀγόρανδρος, Ἀγοράνομος, Ἀγόρατος,
none of them occurring often. For ἐβοσκόμην see on 256 *sup.*
The sculptor Agoracritus of Paros,
Phidias' favourite pupil, must have been
well-known at Athens during this time.

καὶ τὸν Παφλαγόνα παραδίδωμι τουτονί. 1260
ΑΛΛ. καὶ μὴν ἐγώ σ᾽, ὦ Δῆμε, θεραπεύσω καλῶς,
ὥσθ᾽ ὁμολογεῖν σε μηδέν᾽ ἀνθρώπων ἐμοῦ
ἰδεῖν ἀμείνω τῇ Κεχηναίων πόλει.
ΧΟΡ. τί κάλλιον ἀρχομένοισιν
ἢ καταπαυομένοισιν 1265
ἢ θοᾶν ἵππων ἐλατῆρας ἀείδειν μηδὲν ἐς Λυσί-
στρατον,
μηδὲ Θούμαντιν τὸν ἀνέστιον αὖ λυπεῖν ἑκούσῃ
καρδίᾳ;
καὶ γὰρ οὗτος, ὦ φίλ᾽ Ἄπολλον, ἀεὶ πεινῇ,
θαλεροῖς δακρύοις 1270
σᾶς ἁπτόμενος φαρέτρας Πυθῶνι δίᾳ μὴ κακῶς
πένεσθαι.

1270. οὑτοσί MSS.: ἀεὶ om. MSS. added by Dindorf.
1271. Πυθῶνι ἐν δίᾳ MSS.: μὴ om. MSS. except P.

1259—60 repeats and confirms 1098—9 in a more official style.
παραδίδωμι, 'hand over,' 'give up,' usually with a dative of the magistrate or power to whom the surrender is made. Here the τουτονί practically implies σοί.
1261—3. καὶ μὴν, see on 746.
κέχηνα, of the gullible Athenian populace, 755 &c.: Κεχηναῖος was near enough to ᾿Αθηναῖος for this mock-tragic exit in procession.
1264—. The first six extant plays of Aristophanes have a second parabasis, consisting generally of a συζυγία ἐπιρρηματική as here (ode, epirrhema, antode, antepirrhema), Zieliński Glied. 176—180. A close parallel to the second parabasis here is given by that in the Wasps 1265—, though there the antode is lost. The dramatic situation generally is that the final festal scene of display is being prepared and an interlude is convenient.
The metre (dactylo-epitrite) is a favourite one of Pindar's; it is seldom used in Tragedy, and by Aristophanes only in parody, Nub. 457, Vesp. 273, Pax 775, Eccl. 571 (Gleditsch).
The ode, being religious in origin and theory, begins with the first words of a

προσόδιον of Pindar's, quoted by the scholiast here (fr. 59 Bergk): τί κάλλιον ἀρχομένοισιν ἢ καταπαυομένοισιν ἢ βαθύζωνόν τε Λατὼ καὶ θοᾶν ἵππων ἐλάτειραν ἀεῖσαι; Böckh thought this προσόδιον was that written by Pindar for the Aeginetan worship of Artemis Aphaia, whose shrine was on the way to that of Zeus Panhellenius (Pausan. ii 30. 3). It was a likely phrase to become common, and so it ends the extant work of Athenaeus (Deipn. xv 702 C).
The ἐλατῆρας, changed from ἐλάτειραν with a slight profanity, may be subject or object to ἀείδειν, better I think the former. In Pindar θοᾶν ἵππων means 'of swift chariots,' but the Knights would not perhaps be critical on this point. An explanation or excuse is needed for leaving former butts, the unsuccessful buffoon Lysistratus (fr. 1 from the Δαιταλῆς, Ach. 855—, Vesp. 788, 1302) and the superstitious starveling Thumantis (Hermippus 35), for men like Ariphrades.
1270—3. Of course θαλεροῖς δακρύοις and Πυθῶνι δίᾳ are in lyric style: Ariphrades is treated in ordinary Attic λοιδορία. ἅπτομαι φαρέτρας is construed with inf. as if it were εὔχομαι: so προσ-

λοιδορῆσαι τοὺς πονηροὺς οὐδέν ἐστ' ἐπίφθονον,
ἀλλὰ τιμὴ τοῖσι χρηστοῖς, ὅστις εὖ λογί-
ζεται. 1275
εἰ μὲν οὖν ἄνθρωπος, ὃν δεῖ πόλλ' ἀκοῦσαι
καὶ κακά,
αὐτὸς ἦν ἔνδηλος, οὐκ ἂν ἀνδρὸς ἐμνήσθην
φίλου.
νῦν δ' Ἀρίγνωτον γὰρ οὐδεὶς ὅστις οὐκ ἐπί-
σταται,
ὅστις ἢ τὸ λευκὸν οἶδεν ἢ τὸν ὄρθιον νόμον.
ἔστιν οὖν ἀδελφὸς αὐτῷ τοὺς τρόπους οὐ
συγγενής, 1280
Ἀριφράδης πονηρός. ἀλλὰ τοῦτο μὲν καὶ βού-
λεται·
ἐστὶ δ' οὐ μόνον πονηρός, οὐ γὰρ οὐδ' ἂν
ᾐσθόμην,
οὐδὲ παμπόνηρος, ἀλλὰ καὶ προσεξεύρηκέ τι.
τὴν γὰρ αὐτοῦ γλῶτταν αἰσχραῖς ἡδοναῖς
λυμαίνεται,

πίτνω, ἱκνοῦμαι and similar verbs (cases collected by Blaydes here). κακῶς πένεσθαι, 'cursed poverty,' cf. on 1 sup.: Epicrates fr. 3 eagles, when old, ἐπὶ τοὺς νεὼς ἵζουσι πεινῶντες κακῶς.

1274—5. Slightly apologetic in tone, as sentences with ἀνεπίφθονον often are. The ὅστις with antecedent suppressed, where εἴ τις would be clearer, by an idiom not uncommon, αἴσχιστον ὅστις...Eurip. IT 606, Thucyd. ii 62. 4 ἐγγίγνεται καταφρόνησις, ὃς ἂν πιστεύῃ τῶν ἐναντίων προέχειν, vii 68. 1 νομίσωμεν νομιμώτατον εἶναι, οἳ ἂν δικαιώσωσιν ἀποπλῆσαι τὸ θυμούμενον.

1276—. Of Automenes' three sons, Arignotus was a famous citharist, a second was a good actor, and Ariphrades a disgrace (though a pupil of Anaxagoras), Vesp. 1275—83, Pax 883, Athenaeus v 220 B, Lucian Pseudolog. 3.

νῦν δ' is of course not temporal, but as it is. ἐπίσταμαι of a person is rare, and means 'know quite well who he is,' Eurip. Ion 51, Plutarch Cicero 44.
τὸ λευκὸν (ἢ τὸ μέλαν) schol. and editors, calling it a common proverb: but it is not quoted from Paroemiographi nor from literature (Matro ap. Athenaeus iv 135 C is doubtful). One scholium takes it of a certain νόμος, and λευκός has a musical sense clear in timbre. The ὄρθιος νόμος is what everyone knows in music, like the National Anthem. Its exact meaning seems to have been a piece of music in cretic or paeonic time, with all the five notes to the bar (Crusius Delph. Hymn. 52).

1281. Andoc. myst. 95 Ἐπιχάρης ὁ πάντων πονηρότατος καὶ βουλόμενος εἶναι τοιοῦτος: Blaydes here collects other instances of the phrase in this connexion.

ἐν κασαυρίοισι λείχων τὴν ἀπόπτυστον δρό-
σον,   1285
καὶ μολύνων τὴν ὑπήνην, καὶ κυκῶν τὰς ἐσχάρας,
καὶ Πολυμνήστεια ποιῶν, καὶ ξυνὼν Οἰωνίχῳ.
ὅστις οὖν τοιοῦτον ἄνδρα μὴ σφόδρα βδελύτ-
τεται,
οὔ ποτ᾽ ἐκ ταὐτοῦ μεθ᾽ ἡμῶν πίεται ποτηρίου.
ἢ πολλάκις ἐννυχίαισι   1290
φροντίσι συγγεγένημαι,
καὶ διεζήτηχ᾽ ὁπόθεν ποτὲ φαύλως ἐσθίει Κλεώ-
νυμος.
φασὶ μὲν γὰρ αὐτὸν ἐρεπτόμενον τὰ τῶν ἐχόν-
των ἀνέρων   1295
οὐκ ἂν ἐξελθεῖν ἀπὸ τῆς σιπύης· τοὺς δ᾽ ἀντι-
βολεῖν ἂν ὅμως·

1285. κασωρείοισι Cobet *Mnemos.* i 418.   **1293.** Bentl. for φασὶ γάρ.
1296. So Zacher for ὁμοίως.   ὅμως Bergk.

1287. From Cratinus 305, καὶ Πο-
λυμνήστει᾽ ἀείδει μουσικήν τε μανθάνει,
Πολυμνήστεια would appear to be a kind
of songs with music. Polymnestus of
Colophon is mentioned by Pindar, Alcman, and by Plutarch *music.* 5—12 as
having developed flute-music in important
ways and applied it to the ὄρθιος νόμος
invented by Terpander for the lyre. His
songs and music were probably erotic,
Crusius in *Philol.* xlvii 40. Oeonichus is
mentioned again by Hesychius, Οἰωνίχου
μουσεῖον : but we have no further clue.
The name is Boeotian in form: not the
only case of proverbial blackguards being
Boeotian, cf. Φρυνώνδας *Thesm.* 861.
1288—9. A form of excommunication, such offences not being a matter for
civil law. For similar phrases in curses,
see *CIA Defixiones* p. x, Inscr. at Cnidos
Collitz 3536–. πίεται Plato com. 9, where
Kock gives the cases of both πῑ- and πῐ-
in the word. Here begins the part said
to be by Eupolis; schol. ἐκ τοῦ "ὅστις
οὖν τοιοῦτον ἄνδρα" φασί τινες Εὐπόλιδος
εἶναι τὴν παράβασιν, εἴ γε φησὶν Εὔπολις
"ξυνεποίησα τῷ φαλακρῷ."

1290—. Εὐριπίδεια ἡ παρῳδία ἐξ Ἱπ-
πολύτου schol. in V : the reference being
no doubt to Phaedra's lines 374—5, but
the parody is not obvious in form and, as
in the ode, the reference is probably to
some lost lyric. In the ode Thumantis
prays to Apollo to save him from the curse
of starvation: here Cleonymus' (cf. on
958) hosts pray to him not to eat them
out.
φαύλως *sans façons*, as *Pax* 25, Agathocles ap. Athen. xiv 650 A.
οἱ ἔχοντες became very common for
'the rich,' especially in passages of reflections on the relations of class and class,
patron and parasite: the addition of ἀνέρων
is a point both in metre and in dialect.
ἐρέπτομαι ἀλόγοις μόνοις οἰκεῖον Eustathius : here in burlesque of a man. The
word occurs only in the participle. As
ἀνέρων is of course Epic or Lyric, and so
is ὦ ἄνα πρὸς γονάτων, there is no doubt a
parody running through the lines, possibly
of a beast-fable about a mouse, as σιπύη is
a *meal-tub* or chest. There was also some
tale about Cleonymus' household meal
matters, *Nub.* 675.

ἴθ᾽ ὦ ἄνα, πρὸς γονάτων, ἔξελθε καὶ σύγγνωθι
τῇ τραπέζῃ.
φασὶν ἀλλήλαις ξυνελθεῖν τὰς τριήρεις εἰς λόγον, 1300
καὶ μίαν λέξαι τιν᾽ αὐτῶν, ἥτις ἦν γεραιτέρα·
οὐδὲ πυνθάνεσθε ταῦτ᾽, ὦ παρθένοι, τὰν τῇ
πόλει;
φασὶν αἰτεῖσθαί τιν᾽ ἡμῶν ἑκατὸν ἐς Καρχηδόνα
ἄνδρα μοχθηρὸν πολίτην, ὀξίνην Ὑπέρβολον·
ταῖς δὲ δόξαι δεινὸν εἶναι τοῦτο κοὐκ ἀνα-
σχετόν, 1305
καί τιν᾽ εἰπεῖν, ἥτις ἀνδρῶν ἆσσον οὐκ ἐλη-
λύθει·
ἀποτρόπαι᾽, οὐ δῆτ᾽ ἐμοῦ γ᾽ ἄρξει ποτ᾽, ἀλλ᾽
ἐάν με χρῇ,

1303. Καλχηδόνα Casaub. &c. following a scholium: but see on 174 *sup.*

σύγγνωθι τῇ τραπέζῃ, probably 'don't eat the table too.' Mnesimachus 8. 2 τῶν Φαρσαλέων ἥκει τις ἵνα καὶ τὰς τραπέζας καταφάγῃ;

1300. The antepirrhema is a spirited personification of the fleet as protesting in conference against demagogues and the war-policy. Here the political πονηρία of Hyperbolus is attacked, as the moral πονηρία of Ariphrades in the epirrhema. Names of Greek ships seem to have always been feminine: the lists in *CIA* ii 789— offer no exception: names of interest are Δημοκρατία, Ἀνδραγαθία, Τριτογενής, Κωμῳδία, Τραγῳδία.

A conference is λόγος, not σύλλογος, as συλλέγω comes from λέγω *to gather*, not *to speak.*

1301. γεραιτέρα because considered as human, else παλαιοτέρα, cf. 914. Triremes soon decayed, but were of course repaired as long as possible.

1302. From the *Alcmaeon* (fr. 67), the earlier of the two plays by Euripides under this name.

1303—4. For Athenian operations in Sicily B.C. 427—424 see Freeman's *Sicily* iii pp. 27—65. When the *Knights*

appeared, the question would lie between a recall and a reinforcement of the fleet that had been sent out in 427. The conference at Gela in the summer of 424 determined the commanders to return to Athens, where popular feeling punished them, Thuc. iv 65. The more daring advocates of a Western Policy no doubt had an eye to a conquest of Carthage.

Hyperbolus has had few defenders in history: Thucydides allows himself to use the words μοχθηρὸς ἄνθρωπος of him viii 73. 3, and he is coupled with Cleon as a by-word in later times, Lucian *Timon* 30, Aristides *or.* 46, p. 176.

ὀξίνης, wine turned sour (so τροπίας *fr.* 13), neither wine nor vinegar Plut. *stoic. repugn.* 30. 1047 E: so *vappa*, Plin. *Nat. Hist.* xiv 125 of new wine re-fermenting deperit sapor, vappaeque accipit nomen, probrosum etiam hominum cum degeneravit animus, Hor. *Sat.* i 1 104 vappam ac nebulonem.

1305. The wording of their resolution is a little feminine.

1307. Apollo was ἀποτρόπαιος as god of healing and plague. An altar at Athens bears the inscription Ἀγαθῇ τύχῃ· Ἀπόλ-

ὑπὸ τερηδόνων σαπεῖσ᾽ ἐνταῦθα καταγηράσο-
μαι·

οὐδὲ Ναυφάντης γε τῆς Ναύσωνος, οὐ δῆτ᾽,
ὦ θεοί,

εἴπερ ἐκ πεύκης γε κἀγὼ καὶ ξύλων ἐπη-
γνύμην.   1310

ἢν δ᾽ ἀρέσκῃ ταῦτ᾽ Ἀθηναίοις, καθῆσθαί μοι
δοκεῖ

εἰς τὸ Θησεῖον πλεούσαις ἢ 'πὶ τῶν σεμνῶν
θεῶν.

οὐ γὰρ ἡμῶν γε στρατηγῶν ἐγχανεῖται τῇ
πόλει·

1311. δοκῶ...πλεούσαις MSS.: δοκεῖ...πλεούσας Reiske, Cobet *NL* 436—7.

λωνι Προστατηρίῳ Ἀποτροπαίῳ Ἀγυιεῖ
Corp. Inscr. Gr. i 464. So these three
attributes are all mentioned in the oracles
ap. Demosth. *Mid.* 52—53. But the
epithet is comparatively rare in serious
books (not at all in Pausanias) and was no
doubt more common in colloquial than in
ritual style.

1308. κατα- adds to γηράσκω a sense
of failure or uselessness : contrast Solon's
γηράσκω δ᾽ ἀεὶ πολλὰ διδασκόμενος and
Plato *Rep.* vii 536 D γηράσκων τις πολλὰ
δυνατὸς μανθάνειν with *Theaet.* 202 D
πολλοὶ τῶν σοφῶν ζητοῦντες πρὶν εὑρεῖν
κατεγήρασαν: *Legg.* xii 958 D ἀνδρὶ ἐν
μοίρᾳ γηράσαντι of a well-spent life, but
Menander 281. 10 ἀπόρῳ συγκαταγηράσκει
βίῳ, Eurip. *Med.* 124, Duris ap. Athen. iv
167 D, Athen. xi 509 A ἐπέμενε καταγεγηρα-
κώς, ἀτίμως καὶ ἀδόξως διαζῶν, Plut. *Herod.
malign.* 13. 857 D, *brut. rat.* I. 986 E.

1309—10. She quotes the support
of a friend, or else that friend speaks her-
self (κἀγὼ rather supports this). Ναύσων
is given as invented by Cratinus (*fr.* 349
Kock) in Hesychius and Suidas: but it
would have been a common contraction
for names like Ναυσικράτης or Ναυσίνικος:
this is the origin of names like Παύσων,
which look like future participles.

Pine was the chief material in ship-
building: Eurip. *Med.* 4, Plato *Legg.* iv
705 C, Theophrastus *Hist. Plant.* v 7. 1,

where the ἐλάτη, πεύκη and πίτυς are
distinguished as good or convenient for
various kinds of ships, Blümner *Technologie* ii 272.

1311—2. 'I vote we take sanctuary
sailing to the shrines of Theseus or the
Eumenides,' both being of course *asyla*.

For the Theseum as a sanctuary cf. *fr.*
477 of runaway slaves κράτιστόν ἐστιν ἐς
τὸ Θησεῖον δραμεῖν (hence Θησειότριψ),
Plut. *Theseus* 36: if the ships refused to
serve they would be in the position of run-
aways. For the Eumenides' altar by the
cleft in the Areopagus, cf. *Thesm.* 224 ἐς
τὸ τῶν Σεμνῶν Θεῶν, Frazer on Pausan. i
28. 6.

The right of asylum has probably a
bearing on the political arrangements
connected with certain deities, Theseus
and the Eumenides being good cases in
Athens; see on 445 and 551 *sup.* It
seems likely that the precincts of the
deity of a subdued race were allowed to
be *asyla*, as a concession to that race; so
precincts of Poseidon are especially often
heard of as *asyla*, *sup.* 1225.

For the controversy as to whether the
great temple known as the Theseum is
rightly so called, see Miss Harrison *Myth.
and Mon.* 113 ff., Curtius *Stadtgeschichte*
122, Frazer on Pausan. i 17. 2.

1313. He shan't make a fool of his
country with us behind him.

ἀλλὰ πλείτω χωρὶς αὐτὸς ἐς κόρακας, εἰ βούλεται,

τὰς σκάφας, ἐν αἷς ἐπώλει τοὺς λύχνους, καθ-
ελκύσας. 1315

ΑΓΟΡ. εὐφημεῖν χρὴ καὶ στόμα κλήειν, καὶ μαρτυριῶν
ἀπέχεσθαι,

καὶ τὰ δικαστήρια συγκλήειν, οἷς ἡ πόλις ἥδε
γέγηθεν,

ἐπὶ καιναῖσιν δ' εὐτυχίαισιν παιωνίζειν τὸ θέατρον.

ΧΟΡ. ὦ ταῖς ἱεραῖς φέγγος Ἀθήναις καὶ ταῖς νήσοις
ἐπίκουρε,

τίν' ἔχων φήμην ἀγαθὴν ἥκεις, ἐφ' ὅτῳ κνισῶμεν
ἀγυιάς; 1320

1316—7. κλείειν and συγκλείειν MSS.: but see Meisterhans.
1319. So R: the other MSS. have ὦ ταῖς ἱεραῖς νήσοις ἐπίκουρε καὶ φέγγος
Ἀθήναις.

1315. Hyperbolus had made a fortune in the lamp-trade, and σκάφαι would be deep trays in which lamps would be set out for sale, with a reference to the other sense of *skiffs*.

ἕλκω, ἕλξω, εἵλκυσα were the Attic forms: see Ruth. on Babrius 72.

1316—8. Anapaests are similarly used to herald the entrance of an important figure in *Nub.* 263— εὐφημεῖν χρὴ τὸν πρεσβύτην καὶ τῆς εὐχῆς ἐπακούειν, *Av.* 658, *Lys.* 1673, 1108. Zieliński *Gliederung* 354 thinks there is an intentional symmetry in the arrangement: three lines of warning, then eight lines before Demos appears 1319—1326, and eight after his entrance 1327—34.

A special festival is proclaimed, and the law-courts must be shut, ἑορτὰς ἄγειν ἐν αἷς οὐχ οἷόν τε δικάζειν [Xen.] *Rep. Ath.* 3. 8. μαρτυριῶν is probably a surprise for some word implying pollution in word or deed.

θέατρον, cf. on 233.

1319. The Chorus' outburst marks the religious and imperial feeling of the play drawing to its climax. In prose and

comedy φέγγος nearly always means (1) a light at night, as of the moon, stars, a comet (Aristot. *meteor.* i 6. 343^b 13), torches &c. (see L and S), or a light under water as Plut. *de primo frig.* 13. 950 C τοὔλαιον ἐν τῇ θαλάττῃ φέγγος ἐνδίδωσιν, *aet. phys.* 12. 915 A, or (2) a light, real or metaphorical, to which we should attach the ideas implied in the word *mystic, Ran.* 344 φλογὶ φέγγεται δὲ λειμών in the chorus of *mystae*, and so 350, 447, 455, Plato *Phaedr.* 250 B δικαιοσύνης καὶ σωφροσύνης οὐκ ἔνεστι φέγγος ἐν τοῖς τῇδε ὁμοιώμασιν, Plut. *amator.* 19. 764 C Ἔρως μόνων τῶν καλῶν φέγγος ἐστί, *ad princ. inerud.* 3. 780 F τοιοῦτον ἐν πόλεσι μίμημα (θεοῦ) καὶ φέγγος ἄρχων, *an seni resp.* 15. 792 A ἐκεῖνο τῆς ψυχῆς τὸ γάνωμα καὶ τὸ φέγγος: for the connexion of the word with the mysteries, see Bury on Pind. *Nem.* 9. 42.

νῆσοι, as 170, for *allies of Athens.*

1320. φήμη is also a word of religious import: ἀγαθὴ φήμη in connexion with a religious service occurs again *Vesp.* 864.

ὅτῳ is said not to occur elsewhere for ᾗτινι: here it may be adverbial or a quo-

ΑΓΟΡ. τὸν Δῆμον ἀφεψήσας ὑμῖν καλὸν ἐξ αἰσχροῦ
πεποίηκα.

ΧΟΡ. καὶ ποῦ 'στιν νῦν, ὦ θαυμαστὰς ἐξευρίσκων
ἐπινοίας;

ΑΓΟΡ. ἐν ταῖσιν ἰοστεφάνοις οἰκεῖ ταῖς ἀρχαίαισιν
Ἀθήναις.

ΧΟΡ. πῶς ἂν ἴδοιμεν; ποίαν τιν' ἔχει σκευήν; ποῖος
γεγένηται;

1324. ποίαν ἔχει σκευὴν καὶ ποῖος MSS.

tation of some well-known command to sacrifice.

The phrase κνισᾶν ἀγυιάς occurs again *Av.* 1233, Demosth. *Mid.* 51, an oracle ap. Demosth. *Macart.* 66, Lucian *Prom.* 19. The article in Harpocration, Suidas and Bekker's *Anecdota*, recommends ἀγυιᾶς, acc. pl. of ἀγυιεύς, the sacred stone called Apollo, and set up by the doors of houses: but Lucian certainly understood ἀγυιάς, ἀκνίσωτοι αἱ ἀγυιαί *bis accus.* 2, and moderns generally agree with him (Cobet *VL* 224). Neither κνισάω nor ἀγυιά was used in ordinary Attic: the phrase is oracular in style and always implies a divine command that a whole city should join in religious festivity: the command generally came from Delphi, ἡ Πυθία καὶ κνισᾶν ἀγυιὰς ἀνῆρει Pollux i 28. ἀγυιά nearly always implies festal dance or procession through the street, hence εὔρυχόροι ἀγυιαί Pind. *Pyth.* 8. 55, Eurip. *Bacch.* 87, orac. ap. Demosth. *Mid.* 52: this suggestion gives point to Pindar's εὐστεφάνων ἀγυιᾶν *Pyth.* 2. 58 and λευκίπποισι Καδμείων ἀγυιαῖς 9. 83, and to such passages as Bacchyl. 3. 16, Soph. *Antig.* 1135, Eurip. *HF.* 782 ξεστᾶ θ' ἑπταπύλου πόλεως ἀναχορεύσατ' ἀγυιαί, Hom. *hymn.* ap. Thucyd. iii 104. 4, Xen. *Cyrop.* ii 4. 3. As Ἀπόλλων Ἀγυιεύς would naturally be intimately connected with festal public dances and songs, Horace appeals to him in *Od.* iv 6. 28 to favour his *Carmen Saeculare.*

1321. The meaning of ἀφέψω is derived from metallurgy or magic. The story of Medea gathering the 'enchanted

herbs, that did renew old Aeson' is as old as the Νόστοι and was well-known in Art. The ὑμῖν implies the Chorus' pleasure in τὸ καλόν, physical or social, expressed by themselves in 1324.

1322. Of course some incredulity is implied in καὶ ποῦ (see on 128).

1323. The epithets ἰοστέφανοι and λιπαραί, which so flattered the Athenian taste (*Ach.* 637—), were first bestowed on Athens by Pindar in a dithyramb; the two lines that are in point are preserved by scholiasts ὦ ταὶ λιπαραὶ καὶ ἰοστέφανοι καὶ ἀοίδιμοι, Ἑλλάδος ἔρεισμα, κλειναὶ Ἀθᾶναι, δαιμόνιον πτολίεθρον. Every word seems to have been treasured and quoted in Athens for centuries: see references in Bergk's *Poet. Lyr. Graeci* i p. 396. The brightness of the air and the plenty of flowers were glories of Attica: the ἴον (whether *violet* or *iris*) is dwelt on as a material for festal wreaths in the Athenian festival so splendidly celebrated by Pindar in another (or is it the same?) dithyramb, (*fr.* 75 Bergk) ἰοδετᾶν λάχετε στεφάνων... τότε βάλλεται, τότ' ἐπ' ἀμβρόταν χέρσον ἔραται ἴων φόβαι: and the 'violet-bed beside the well' of *Pax* 577 is also specially Attic, so *fr.* 476 of the Attic winter ὄψει δὲ χειμῶνος μέσον σικύους, βότρυς, ὀπώραν, στεφάνους ἴων.

1324. σκευή generally implies dress of a special kind, such as stage or official attire, or some 'fashion' of apparel: so Thucyd. i 6. 3, speaking of the same dress as is worn by Demos here, Ἰώνων τοὺς πρεσβυτέρους κατὰ τὸ ξυγγενὲς ἐπὶ πολὺ αὕτη ἡ σκευὴ κατέσχεν.

ΑΓΟΡ. οἷός περ Ἀριστείδη πρότερον καὶ Μιλτιάδη
ξυνεσίτει. 1325
ὄψεσθε δέ· καὶ γὰρ ἀνοιγνυμένων ψόφος ἤδη
τῶν προπυλαίων.
ἀλλ᾽ ὀλολύξατε φαινομέναισιν ταῖς ἀρχαίαισιν
Ἀθήναις
καὶ θαυμασταῖς καὶ πολυύμνοις, ἵν᾽ ὁ κλεινὸς
Δῆμος ἐνοικεῖ.
ΧΟΡ. ὦ ταὶ λιπαραὶ καὶ ἰοστέφανοι καὶ ἀριζήλωτοι
Ἀθῆναι,
δείξατε τὸν τῆς Ἑλλάδος ἡμῖν καὶ τῆς γῆς
τῆσδε μόναρχον. 1330

1325. The military, not the political, heroes of the Persian War period. "These two names summed up in themselves the ideals of the conservative peace party," Furtwängler *Masterpieces* 445 (Engl. trans.). ξυνεσίτει to mark that the dress is for peaceful festal occasions.

1326. I cannot think προπύλαια could be used of anything but the great buildings at the top of the ascent to the Acropolis. In *Vesp.* 875, quoted by Dörpfeld and Reisch *Griech. Theater* 208 as of a private house the readings are conjectural and prove nothing for the usage of προπύλαια. Whatever anachronism there was in supposing the Propylaea in ταῖς ἀρχαίαισιν Ἀθήναις might be excused by Attic pride in their splendour (see Miss Harrison *Myth. and Mon.* 371): and there were of course propylaea to the Acropolis long before the Periclean building. It had five gateways, each closed by massive gates. ψόφος corresponding to ψοφοῦσιν αἱ θύραι, of gates opened from within: Plato *Symp.* 212 c τὴν αὔλειον θύραν κρουομένην ψόφον παρασχεῖν, of a door being opened from without.

1327—8. ὀλολύξατε, see on 616.
κλεινὸς would not be used except in the high style, cf. *Ach.* 1184, *Thesm.* 29, *Plut.* 772, Eupolis 104 ἅπασα γὰρ ποθοῦμεν ἡ κλεινὴ πόλις, Eubulus 10 κλεινὰς Ἀθήνας ἐκπερᾶν Ἀμφίονα: it never occurs in Thucydides or the orators, and only twice in Plato.

1329. ὦ ταὶ λιπαραί, the famous words of Pindar's dithyramb : in serious literature of this time λιπαρὸς is rarely used except of Athens : *Nub.* 300, *fr.* 162, Eurip. *Alc.* 452, *IT* 1130, *Tro.* 803 ἵν᾽ ἐλαίας ἔδειξε κλάδον Ἀθάνα, οὐράνιον στέφανον λιπαραῖσί τε κόσμον Ἀθήναις, which confirms the traditional view that the allusion is specially to the olive : in a few cases it is a complimentary epithet of other cities, but generally is quite a colloquial word, as in Eurip. *Cycl.* 501 and often in Comedy.

1330. Δῆμος μόναρχος is an idea found as an ideal also in Eurip. *Supp.* 352 in the mouth of Theseus, the citizen-king, καὶ γὰρ κατέστησ᾽ αὐτὸν (δῆμον) εἰς μοναρχίαν ἐλευθερώσας τήνδ᾽ ἰσόψηφον πόλιν; in Arist. *Pol.* vi (iv) 4. 27. 1292ᵃ 11—17 the phrase has a bad sense ὁ τοιοῦτος δῆμος ἅτε μόναρχος ὤν, ζητεῖ μοναρχεῖν διὰ τὸ μὴ ἄρχεσθαι ὑπὸ νόμου, καὶ γίνεται δεσποτικός, ὥστε οἱ κόλακες ἔντιμοι. The word is the neutral one for absolute power, inclining to a good or bad sense with the context : *Vesp.* 474 μισόδημε καὶ μοναρχίας ἐραστά in the mouth of ordinary Athenian democrats, Thucyd. i 122. 3 (the only case in him of the word) Corinthians say τύραννον ἐῶμεν ἐγκαθεστάναι πόλιν, τοὺς δ᾽ ἐν μιᾷ μονάρχους ἀξιοῦμεν καταλύειν, in order to mark their feeling the tyranny of Athens is worse than that of any individual : it must have been well remembered that Pericles had compared Athens' position to a τυραννίς (Thucyd ii

ΑΓΟΡ. ὅδ' ἐκεῖνος ὁρᾶν τεττιγοφόρας, ἀρχαίῳ σχήματι
λαμπρός,
οὐ χοιρινῶν ὄζων, ἀλλὰ σπονδῶν, σμύρνῃ κατά-
λειπτος.

ΧΟΡ. χαῖρ', ὦ βασιλεῦ τῶν Ἑλλήνων· καί σοι ξυγ-
χαίρομεν ἡμεῖς.
τῆς γὰρ πόλεως ἄξια πράττεις καὶ τοῦ Μαρα-
θῶνι τροπαίου.   1334

1331. τεττιγοφόρας Porson from Hesychius for τεττιγοφόρος.
1334. τοὐν Μαραθῶνι MSS. τοῦ Bentley and most editors : see on 781, 785.
The MSS. give ἐν M. in Thucyd. i 18. 1, ii 34. 5, Ar. *fr.* 363, Plato *Gorg.* 516 D,
Lycurg. *Leocr.* 104.

---

63. 2), and that Cleon had repeated the words (iii 37. 2): the position here is comparable to Peisetaerus' marriage with Basileia at the end of the *Birds*.

1331. Demus wears the old Ionian dress which Thucydides speaks of in the famous passage i 6. 3 οἱ πρεσβύτεροι τῶν εὐδαιμόνων οὐ πολὺς χρόνος ἐπειδὴ χιτῶνάς τε λινοῦς ἐπαύσαντο φοροῦντες καὶ χρυσῶν τεττίγων ἐνέρσει κρωβύλον ἀναδούμενοι τῶν ἐν τῇ κεφαλῇ τριχῶν: the description is repeated with verbal variations by Heraclides Pont. ap. Athen. xii 512 C ἡ Ἀθηναίων πόλις, ἕως ἐτρύφα, μεγίστη τε ἦν καὶ μεγαλοψυχοτάτους ἔτρεφεν ἄνδρας. ἀλουργῆ μὲν γὰρ ἡμπίσχοντο ἱμάτια, ποικίλους δ' ὑπέδυνον χιτῶνας, κορύμβους δ' ἀναδούμενοι τῶν τριχῶν χρυσοῦς τέττιγας περὶ τὸ μέτωπον καὶ τὰς κόμας (κόρρας Birt Kaibel) ἐφόρουν. ὀκλαδίας τε αὐτοῖς δίφρους ἔφερον οἱ παῖδες, ἵνα μὴ καθίζοιεν ὡς ἔτυχεν. καὶ οὗτοι ἦσαν οἱ τὴν ἐν Μαραθῶνι νικήσαντες μάχην καὶ μόνοι τὴν τῆς Ἀσίας ἁπάσης δύναμιν χειρωσάμενοι, where the writer is plainly thinking of our passage and reflects its spirit: cf. Xenophanes 3, Lucian *Navig.* 3, Aelian *Var. Hist.* iv 22. At Sybaris, with its reflection of Ionic luxury, ἔθος καὶ τοὺς παῖδας ἦν μέχρι τῆς τῶν ἐφήβων ἡλικίας ἀλουργίδας τε φορεῖν καὶ πλοκαμῖδας ἀναδεδεμένους χρυσοφορεῖν, Athen. xii 518 E: at Samos χιονέοισι χιτῶσι πέδον χθονὸς εὑρέος εἶχον· χρύσειαι δὲ κόρυμβαι ἐπ' αὐτῶν τέττιγες ὥς· χαῖται δ' ἠωρεῦντ' ἀνέμῳ χρυσέοις ἐνὶ δεσμοῖς, Asius ap. Athen. xii 525 F. Tettichus is found as a name in the Attic epitaph (sixth century, probably of an aristocrat) *CIA* i 463, Roberts no. 36.

τεττιγοφόρας shows the termination of heroic import like γοργολόφας *Ach.* 567, λευκολόφας Eurip. *Phoen.* 119, *Eccl.* 645, ἑκατογκεφάλας *Nub.* 336. The golden τέττιξ bound the hair gathered into the form called κρωβύλος or κόρυμβος : the latter word implies a horn-shape (κορυμβ =corn(g)u-), cf. the possible meaning of κέρας applied to Paris' hair, *Il.* xi 385. Archaeologists disagree as to the exact meaning of κρωβύλος. Early sculpture shows hair gathered in a roll or knot at the neck behind (as in the Apollo on the pediment of the Zeus-temple at Olympia, where a hole is left for a pin of some kind), rather than in a top-knot, such as is common in later works, as in a simple form in the Boy with a Goose, and in a more elaborate shape in the Pourtalés Apollo, the Apollo Belvedere, the Venus of the Capitol. See Studniczka in Classen's Thucyd. i⁴ p. 330. The change in treatment of hair in art which came in in Phidias' time does not seem to correspond to the change in actual wear (Furtwängler *Masterpieces*, Eng. tr., 8, 19).

λαμπρός suits the linen material and also the bright colour of his dress.

1332. The χοιρίνη was a musselshell, used as a voting-counter in the Attic jury-courts: it seems to be mentioned only here and *Vesp.* 333, 349, and its use may have been only for a short period, as the scholia, Pollux, &c. would imply. There is of course the common play on both meanings of σπονδαί, *peace* and *festal libation*, the second meaning leading on to the mention of *festal array*.

1333—4. βασιλεῦ, see on 1330: the

ΔΗ.   ὦ φίλτατ' ἀνδρῶν, ἐλθὲ δεῦρ', Ἀγοράκριτε.
      ὅσα με δέδρακας ἀγάθ' ἀφεψήσας. ΑΓΟΡ.
      ἐγώ;
      ἀλλ', ὦ μέλ', οὐκ οἶσθ' οἷος ἦσθ' αὐτὸς πάρος,
      οὐδ' οἷ' ἔδρας· ἐμὲ γὰρ νομίζοις ἂν θεόν.
ΔΗ.   τί δ' ἔδρων πρὸ τοῦ, κάτειπε, καὶ ποῖός τις
      ἦ;   1339
ΑΓΟΡ. πρῶτον μέν, ὁπότ' εἴποι τις ἐν τἠκκλησίᾳ,
      ὦ Δῆμ', ἐραστής τ' εἰμὶ σὸς φιλῶ τέ σε
      καὶ κήδομαί σου καὶ προβουλεύω μόνος,
      τούτοις ὁπότε χρήσαιτό τις προοιμίοις,

1337. μέλε R, μέλε' most MSS.: this is very common in all cases where μέλ' is
found, owing to the idea that the word was connected with μέλεος.
1339. ἦν MSS. except R.

emphatic ἡμεῖς implies their general dislike of one-man power, as the reason given in the next line implies their pride in what they think the great days of their country.

1335. ὦ φίλτατ' ἀνδρῶν, a mode of address found in Tragedy, as Aesch. *Agam.* 1654, Soph. *Elect.* 23, *Trach.* 232, Eurip. *Hec.* 953, and in Comedy where the rhythm and tone are serious, *sup.* 611, *Plut.* 788, Phrynichus 80 ὦ φίλτατ' ἀνδρῶν, μή μ' ἀτιμάσας γένῃ.

1337—8. ὦ μέλ' in friendly remonstrance and the like, as *sup.* 671. πάρος is not used in prose, and in Comedy occurs only here and *Vesp.* 1536. νομίζω θεόν implies action taken in consequence of the belief, cf. on 515.

1339. κατειπεῖν as usual of disclosing information that may be harmful to someone.

1340. πρῶτον μέν is carried on by καὶ νὴ Δία γ' 1350, the form being changed to suit the turn of the dialogue.

1341—2. Tragic in rhythm and no doubt pronounced in suitable style. ἐραστής, see on 732. I do not know if Pericles was the first political orator who ventured to put this passionate expression of patriotism, but it was taken up as a form of flattery to Demos: *Ach.* 142 Sitalces φιλαθήναιος ἦν ὑπερφυῶς, ὑμῶν τ'

ἐραστὴς ἦν ἀληθής, cf. *Av.* 1279. Plato says with warning and some ridicule, i *Alcib.* 132 A τοῦτο μάλιστ' ἐγὼ φοβοῦμαι, μὴ δημεραστὴς ἡμῖν γενόμενος διαφθαρῇς· πολλοὶ γὰρ ἤδη κἀγαθοὶ αὐτὸ πεπόνθασιν Ἀθηναῖοι. εὐπρόσωπος γὰρ ὁ τοῦ μεγαλήτορος δῆμος Ἐρεχθέως· ἀλλ' ἀποδύντα χρὴ αὐτὸν θεάσασθαι. Otherwise prose writers used ἐρῶ in politics only of the ambition of tyrants and the like : Herod. i 96 ἐρασθεὶς τυραννίδος, iii 53 πολλοὶ τυραννίδος ἐρασταί εἰσι, Isocr. *de pace* 65 δυναστείας ὑπὸ πάντων ἐρωμένης καὶ περιμαχήτου γεγενημένης κατηγορεῖν, 113 οἱ πρωτεύοντες τοσούτων κακῶν ἐρῶσι.

Most of the cases of κήδομαι used in prose of political feeling imply some such protestation as we have here: Thucyd. vi 14, Plato *Apol.* 24 C, Demosth. 3 *Phil.* 73, *Timocr.* 173, 192, Isocr. *de pace* 51 τοὺς τὸν πόλεμον ἀγαπῶντας ὡς τῆς δημοκρατίας κηδομένους εὔνους εἶναι νομίζομεν, Dinarch. *Demosth.* 100 ὑμεῖς οἱ φάσκοντες τοῦ δήμου κήδεσθαι, Aeschin. *FL* 8 μόνος ἐν τῷ λόγῳ φαίνεται κηδεμὼν τῆς πόλεως Δημοσθένης.

προβουλεύω μόνος might be said in the technical sense by an arrogant member of the council, but of course προβουλεύω in the original meaning of *think for* gives sufficient point.

ἀνωρτάλιζες κἀκερουτίας. ΔΗ. ἐγώ;

ΑΓΟΡ. εἶτ᾽ ἐξαπατήσας σ᾽ ἀντὶ τούτων ᾤχετο. 1345

ΔΗ. τί φῄς;

τουτί μ᾽ ἔδρων, ἐγὼ δὲ τοῦτ᾽ οὐκ ᾐσθόμην;

ΑΓΟΡ. τὰ δ᾽ ὦτα γάρ σου νὴ Δί᾽ ἐξεπετάννυτο

ὥσπερ σκιάδειον καὶ πάλιν ξυνήγετο.

ΔΗ. οὕτως ἀνόητος ἐγεγενήμην καὶ γέρων;

ΑΓΟΡ. καὶ νὴ Δία γ᾽ εἴ σοι δύο λεγοίτην ῥήτορε,

ὁ μὲν ποιεῖσθαι ναῦς μακράς, ὁ δ᾽ ἕτερος αὖ

καταμισθοφορῆσαι τοῦθ᾽, ὁ τὸν μισθὸν λέγων

τὸν τὰς τριήρεις παραδραμὼν ἂν ᾤχετο.

1346. ᾔδειν for ᾐσθόμην MSS.
1347. γ᾽ ἄν R. γὰρ the other MSS., ὦτ᾽ ἄγαν Kock, ὦτά σου νὴ τὸν Δί᾽ Cobet *Mnem.* n.s. ii 423.
1352. τοῦθ᾽ A edd. vulg. τούτων R, τοῦτον most MSS. τούτοιν Elmsley, τῶνδ᾽ Kock.

1344. ἀνορταλίζω and κερουτιῶ do not occur elsewhere in literature, whether they were invented on the spot or words in common use for the childish delight of chickens flapping their wings and calves trying and tossing their horns. The denominative and desiderative terminations lend themselves easily to comic formations. κερουτιάω is apparently a desiderative from the stem of κέροεις.

1345. *Eccl.* 195 τῶν δὲ ῥητόρων ὁ τοῦτ᾽ ἀναπείσας εὐθὺς ἀποδρὰς ᾤχετο, Demosth. *Cor.* 40 ἐκ τούτων ᾤχετ᾽ ἐκείνους λαβὼν (*winning*) εἰς τὸ μηδ᾽ ὁτιοῦν προορᾶν ἀλλ᾽ ἐᾶσαι πάντα ἐκεῖνον ὑφ᾽ ἑαυτῷ ποιήσασθαι, *FL* 19 εἶπε τοιούτους λόγους ὥσθ᾽ ἅπαντας ὑμᾶς λαβὼν ᾤχετο.

1347—8. 'Your ears used to open like a parasol and flap to again,' according as you wished to hear or not.

1349. Soph. *Ant.* 281 μὴ ᾽φευρεθῇς ἄνους τε καὶ γέρων ἅμα.

1350—3. An accusative is needed after καταμισθοφορῆσαι, and τοῦθ᾽ is quite intelligible, *to spend it* (*i.e. the same sum*) *on fees*, cf. on 571. The verb καταμισθοφορῶ is of a type not uncommon in Greek: Demosth. *pro Phorm.* 39 δεινὰ πέπονθας πολλὰ καταλελητουργηκώς, Isaeus *Dicaeog.* 43 ἀλλὰ μὴν οὐδὲ καθιπποτρόφηκας...οὔτε κατεζευγοτρόφηκας; Blaydes here gives many other verbs of the same kind. κατα-

μισθοφορῶ may of course mean (1) *spend on mercenaries*, as Aeschin. *FL* 131, (2) *spend on fees* as here and Theopompus ap. Athen. iv 166 E (*Fragm. Hist. Gr.* i 293) ὁ μὲν δῆμος τῶν Ταραντίνων περὶ τὰς ἑστιάσεις εἶχε μόνον ἀκρατῶς, ὁ δὲ τῶν Ἀθηναίων καὶ τὰς προσόδους καταμισθοφορῶν διατετέλεκε. The rival proposals were no doubt actually pitted against each other sometimes, and Demus would be tempted to neglect his fleet : *fr.* 15 ἐς τὰς τριήρεις δεῖ μ᾽ ἀναλοῦν ταῦτα καὶ τὰ τείχη, εἰς οἶ᾽ ἀνάλουν οἱ πρὸ τοῦ τὰ χρήματα. Diodorus xi 43 says that twenty new war-ships were to be built every year : from Demosth. *Androt.* we see that the Council sometimes neglected or were unable to carry out this regulation. The decree *CIA* i 32. 30 laid down that after moneys due to the gods were paid, the balance should be expended εἰς τὸ νεώριον καὶ τὰ τείχη ; the νεώριον may include ship-building : but no doubt decree of the Ecclesia might regulate details from time to time (Gilbert *Greek Const. Antiq.* 335). In Arist. *Pol.* viii (v) 5. 2 the same question caused difficulties and a revolution in Rhodes, μισθοφορὰν γὰρ οἱ δημαγωγοὶ ἐπόριζον καὶ ἐκώλυον ἀποδιδόναι τὰ ὀφειλόμενα τοῖς τριηράρχοις· οἱ δὲ διὰ τὰς ἐπιφερομένας δίκας ἠναγκάσθησαν συστάντες καταλῦσαι τὸν δῆμον.

οὗτος, τί κύπτεις; οὐχὶ κατὰ χώραν μενεῖς;

ΔΗ.   αἰσχύνομαί τοι ταῖς πρότερον ἁμαρτίαις. 1355

ΑΓΟΡ. ἀλλ' οὐ σὺ τούτων αἴτιος, μὴ φροντίσῃς,
      ἀλλ' οἵ σε ταῦτ' ἐξηπάτων. νυνδὶ φράσον·
      ἐάν τις εἴπῃ βωμολόχος ξυνήγορος·
      οὐκ ἔστιν ὑμῖν τοῖς δικασταῖς ἄλφιτα,
      εἰ μὴ καταγνώσεσθε ταύτην τὴν δίκην· 1360
      τοῦτον τί δράσεις, εἰπέ, τὸν ξυνήγορον;

ΔΗ.   ἄρας μετέωρον ἐς τὸ βάραθρον ἐμβαλῶ,
      ἐκ τοῦ λάρυγγος ἐκκρεμάσας Ὑπέρβολον.

1354. κύπτεις, 'hang your head' in shame, as *Thesm.* 930, Demosth. *Cor.* 323, Plut. *Brutus* 27 λέγεται τὸ μὲν πλῆθος ἐπιδήλως στενάξαι, τοὺς δ' ἀρίστους κύψαντας εἰς γῆν ἡσυχίαν ἄγειν, *Ages.* 12. κατὰ χώραν, 'as you were'; so *Plut.* 367-ἀλλ' οὐδὲ τὸ βλέμμ' αὐτὸ κατὰ χώραν ἔχει.

1355. αἰσχύνομαι with dat. is rare: the acc. with this verb is generally of a person or personal quality, and the meaning is generally *be ashamed before*, the dat. is of action or conduct, *Nub.* 992 τοῖς αἰσχροῖς αἰσχύνεσθαι, Eurip. *HF* 1160 αἰσχύνομαι τοῖς δεδραμένοις κακοῖς, Lysias 3. 9.

1358. Aristophanes never mentions ξυνήγοροι except with some dislike *Ach.* 686, 705, *Nub.* 1089, *Vesp.* 482, *fr.* 362, from the Ὁλκάδες, ἔστι τις πονηρὸς ἡμῖν τοξότης ξυνήγορος: in all these cases they are prosecutors in vexatious charges against quiet or respectable men of position: in *fr.* 1 (from the Δαιταλῆς) their new-fangled phrases are the point: it may be no accident that all the passages are from early plays. These men were appointed to prosecute in the State's interest in cases of εἰσαγγελία.

1359—60. We are slow to believe that such an argument as this 'the ex-chequer is empty: the only way of getting your jurymens' pay is to fine the accused' could ever be heard in an Athenian court: but Lysias 27. 1 says that the accused persons in the case had often used the argument, πολλάκις ἠκούσατε τούτων λεγόντων, ὁπότε βούλοιντό τινα ἀδίκως ἀπολέσαι, ὅτι, εἰ μὴ καταψηφιεῖσθε ὧν αὐτοὶ κελεύουσιν ἐπιλείψει ὑμᾶς ἡ μισθοφορά: apparently they had been συνήγοροι themselves, and a συνήγορος now reminds the jury of their misdeeds in that capacity. Cf. Lysias 30. 22 ἡ βουλὴ ἡ βουλεύουσα, ὅταν μὲν ἔχῃ ἱκανὰ χρήματα εἰς διοίκησιν, οὐδὲν ἐξαμαρτάνει, ὅταν δὲ εἰς ἀπορίαν καταστῇ, ἀναγκάζεται εἰσαγγελίας δέχεσθαι καὶ δημεύειν τὰ τῶν πολιτῶν καὶ τῶν ῥητόρων τοῖς τὰ πονηρότατα λέγουσι πείθεσθαι. If the reference is to a case of εἰσαγγελία tried before a heliastic court, the heliasts numbered a thousand. Aristot. *Pol.* vii (vi) 5 (see on 103) thinks such risks as these proceedings imply are the most formidable dangers of democracy in general: Demosth. *Aristocr.* 209 is evidence of the straits to which the treasury of Athens was sometimes reduced. For ἄλφιτα meaning 'daily bread,' cf. *Nub.* 106, *Vesp.* 301, *Pax* 636 &c. εἰ μή with fut. is of course the regular form of conditional sentence in warning: for καταγιγνώσκω δίκην cf. Antiphon *caed. Herod.* 12 κελεύεις τοὺς δικαστὰς φόνου δίκην καταγνῶναι, Demosth. i *Onetor* 32 κατεγνωσμένης ἤδη τῆς δίκης, Plut. *Alcib.* 22 ἐρήμην αὐτοῦ καταγνόντες καὶ τὰ χρήματα δημεύσαντες.

1362—3. αἴρειν μετέωρον was said of the hoisting of slaves or criminals or captives for punishment, as Plut. *Camillus* 4: there is a comic point in Trygaeus' slave saying (*Pax* 80) ὁ δεσπότης γάρ μου μετέωρος αἴρεται: and if the hoisting is not of this kind the phrase is altered, as Eurip. *Alc.* 609 νέκυν πρόσπολοι φέρουσιν ἄρδην εἰς τάφον τε καὶ πυράν, Araros 17 τὴν νύμφην ἐπὶ τὸ ζεῦγος ἀναθήσεις φέρων. The *rapio sublimem*, so common in Plautus, is a translation. The βάραθρον was formed by rocks about 60 feet in height on the western

N. A.   12

ΑΓΟΡ. τουτὶ μὲν ὀρθῶς καὶ φρονίμως ἤδη λέγεις·
τὰ δ᾽ ἄλλα, φέρ᾽ ἴδω, πῶς πολιτεύσει φράσον.
ΔΗ. πρῶτον μὲν ὁπόσοι ναῦς ἐλαύνουσιν μακράς,
καταγομένοις τὸν μισθὸν ἀποδώσω 'ντελῆ.
ΑΓΟΡ. πολλοῖς γ᾽ ὑπολίσποις πυγιδίοισιν ἐχαρίσω.
ΔΗ. ἔπειθ᾽ ὁπλίτης ἐντεθεὶς ἐν καταλόγῳ
οὐδεὶς κατὰ σπουδὰς μετεγγραφήσεται,   1370
ἀλλ᾽ ὥσπερ ἦν τὸ πρῶτον ἐγγεγράψεται.

1368. δ᾽ R, γ᾽ all other MSS. rightly: ὑπολίποις R, ὑπολίσφοις Brunck, Dind.,
Mein., Vels. on the tradition that the Attics said λίσφος as ἀσφάραγος (*Phrynichus* 89)
&c. : *Ran.* 826 all MSS. have λίσπη (in chorus). **1369.** ὁπλίτης V, ὁ πολίτης R and the other MSS.
1371. ὅσπερ RV.

---

declivity of the Pnyx: it lay outside the
city, in the angle formed by the town-wall
and the northern long wall: hence Plato
Rep. iv 439 E ἀνιὼν ἐκ Πειραιέως ὑπὸ τὸ
βόρειον τεῖχος ἐκτός, αἰσθόμενος νεκροὺς
παρὰ τῷ δημίῳ κειμένους. The threat
is precise, for this was the punishment
assigned ἐάν τις τὸν Ἀθηναίων δῆμον
ἀδικῇ, Xen. *Hell.* i 7. 20, cf. Plato
Gorg. 516 D. But generally the word
βάραθρον is not used except in vague
threats and imprecations: *Nub.* 1450, *Ran.*
574, *Plut.* 1109, Alexis 155 καὶ τοὺς
ἁλιέας ἐς τὸ βάραθρον ἐμβαλῶ, Lucian
Icarom. 33 ἐς τὸ βάραθρον, ἐς τὸν Τάρταρον,
Plut. *Aristides* 3 εἶπεν ὡς οὐκ ἔστι σωτηρία
τοῖς Ἀθηναίων πράγμασιν, εἰ μὴ καὶ Θε-
μιστοκλέα καὶ αὐτὸν ἐς τὸ βάραθρον ἐμβά-
λοιεν. It is altogether avoided by Thucydides and the Orators (Demosth. has it
twice in metaphor, *Chers.* 45, i *Aristog.*
76): ὄρυγμα is used in describing the
executioner's function by Lycurg. *Leocr.*
121, Dinarch. *Demosth.* 62. Hyperbolus
is to be used to weight the criminal, cf.
Pax 687.
1366—7. The oarsmen in the triremes were paid by the State, though the
trierarchs on special occasions gave something additional to the θρανῖται (Thucyd.
vi 31. 3). These oarsmen were in the
main Athenian citizens and might have
to serve as soldiers: they had done so at
Sphacteria (Thucyd. iv 32. 2). Their
pay varied seemingly from 2 obols to a
drachma, the latter rate being given only
exceptionally: there might be competition

between the Greek states in the pay
offered (see on 554). Arrears were probably common enough; they are to be
paid the instant the ships come into port
(καταγομένοις). ἐντελής is the regular
and official word, for pay, supplies, forces,
provided in full: Thucyd. viii 29. 1, 45. 6,
78. 1, 83. 3 οὔτε μισθὸν ἐντελῆ πώποτε
λάβοιεν τό τε διδόμενον βραχὺ καὶ οὐδὲ τοῦτο
ξυνεχῶς, Demosth. *Polycl.* 35 τρυφῶντας
ἐπιβάτας καὶ ὑπηρεσίαν ὑπὸ μισθοῦ πολλοῦ
καὶ ἐντελοῦς, Isocr. *Philippus* 91 τοῖς
στρατιώταις ἐντελῆ τὸν μισθὸν ἀποδούς,
CIA ii 787 τριήρης δόκιμος καὶ ἐντελής,
808—9 *passim* σκεύη ἐντελῆ &c. of ships'
fittings.
1368. οἱ ἐνδεῶς πυγῶν ἔχοντες λίσποι
καὶ ὑπόλισποι καλοῦνται καὶ λισπόπυγοι,
ἐφ᾽ ᾧ μάλιστα Ἀθηναῖοι κωμῳδοῦνται,
Pollux ii 184. The κῶας or ὑπηρέσιον is
mentioned by Thucyd. ii 93. 2 along with
the oar as necessary for the rowers and
carried by them as such: we find jests
at the habit, Hermippus 54, Isocr. *de
pace* 48.
ἐχαρίσω is the dramatic aorist of
'instant action,' like ἔδακε in 1372.
1369—71. 'A man once entered on
the muster-roll for infantry service shall
never be transferred by using private influence.' A κατάλογος is any official list,
of the Knights (Aristot. *Pol. Ath.* 49. 2,
Lysias 16. 13), of those who were to have
civic rights under the Thirty (*Pol. Ath.*
36), of those liable for naval service
(Dem. *Polycl.* 6), but especially of those
liable for service as hoplites: so that

ΑΓΟΡ. τοῦτ' ἔδακε τὸν πόρπακα τὸν Κλεωνύμου.
ΔΗ.   οὐδ' ἀγοράσει γ' ἀγένειος οὐδεὶς ἐν ἀγορᾷ.
ΑΓΟΡ. ποῦ δῆτα Κλεισθένης ἀγοράσει καὶ Στράτων;
ΔΗ.   τὰ μειράκια ταυτὶ λέγω, τὰν τῷ μύρῳ, 1375

1373. ἀγοράσει τ' R, ἐν τ' ἀγορᾷ οὐδεὶς R, οὐδεὶς ἐν τ' ἀγορᾷ the other MSS, οὐδ' ἐν τἀγορᾷ G. Herm. Bergk, οὐδ' ἀγορασἀγένειος οὐδεὶς ἐν ἀγορᾷ Dind., ἐν τἀγορᾷ τ' ἀγένειος οὐδεὶς ἀγοράσει Kock Holden.
1374—81 Madvig *Advers.* i 275 thinks is a single speech of the sausage-man's.

---

phrases like στρατιῶται ἐκ καταλόγου were opposed to volunteers or mercenaries. Aristotle *Pol.* viii (v) 3. 7. 1303ᵃ 9, *Pol. Ath.* 26, says that this method of compulsory service caused great loss of life among the upper classes of Athens. But we hear complaints on the other side that influence might be used to have a man's name removed or transferred *Pax* 1180, and Thucyd. vi 31. 3 speaks of the landforce for the Sicilian expedition as καταλόγοις χρηστοῖς ἐκκριθέν, implying it would seem that this was exceptional. So καταλέγω and κατάλογος were used when an emphasis is laid on doing or shirking the patriotic duty of military service, as Xen. *Mem.* iii 4. 1 ἐκ καταλόγου στρατευόμενος κατατέτριμμαι, Lysias 14. 7 καταλεγεὶς ὁπλίτης οὐκ ἐξῆλθε μεθ' ὑμῶν. For σπουδὴ see *sup.* 896. The difference in meaning between the fut. and the fut. perfect in the continued sense is well seen; ἐγγεγράψεται is fut. of ἐγγέγραπται 'shall have been entered,' 'shall stand enrolled,' see Jebb on Soph. *O.T.* 411: cf. τιμωρηθήσεται...τετιμήσεται 'shall be punished,' 'shall *remain* honoured,' Lysias 31. 24, οὐκ ἀχθεσθήσομαι· ἀλλ' εὐεργέτης παρ' ἐμοὶ ἀναγεγράψει Plato *Gorg.* 506 c (see Blass in *Rhein. Mus.* xlvii). The rare μετεγγράφω occurs again in Lucian *quom. hist. scrib.* 5 μετεγγράψουσί τε τῶν ἅπαξ κεκυρωμένων, of historians.
1372. 'That's a hit at Cleonymus' shield-handle': for him see on 959: there may be a special point in πόρπαξ, see on 849.
1373. ἀγοράζω is the verb of ἀγόραιος *loafer* Cratinus 239, *Lys.* 556. It was a new thing for youth to frequent the agora, and conservatives disapproved of it. *Nub.* 991 ἐπιστήσει μισεῖν ἀγοράν, Isocr. *Areop.* 48 οὕτω ἔφευγον τὴν ἀγορὰν (οἱ νεώτεροι), ὥστ' εἰ καί ποτε διελθεῖν

ἀναγκασθεῖεν, μετὰ πολλῆς αἰδοῦς καὶ σωφροσύνης ἐφαίνοντο τοῦτο ποιοῦντες.
1374. γύννιδες οὗτοι καὶ πιττούμενοι τὰ γένεια schol. Cleisthenes is constantly the effeminate *Ach.* 118, *Nub.* 335, *Av.* 821, *Lys.* 1092, *Thesm.* 635, Pherecrates 135 ὦ περιστέριον ὅμοιον Κλεισθένει: Straton makes a pair with him in *Ach.* 122. Apparently they broke the custom, almost universal at Athens till Macedonian times, and shaved or used pitch to remove the hair: this was considered disgraceful *Thesm.* 218, Theopomp. ap. Athen. vi 260 E τί τῶν αἰσχρῶν δεινῶν αὐτοῖς οὐ προσῆν; οὐ ξυρούμενοι καὶ λεαινόμενοι διετέλουν ἄνδρες ὄντες; The earliest portrait statue with shaven face is said to be one of Aristotle.
1375. He means the true ἀγένειοι, who lounge in the perfumers' quarter of the agora, Pherecrates 2 λουσάμενοι πρὸ λαμπρᾶς ἡμέρας ἐν τοῖς στεφανώμασιν, οἱ δ' ἐν τῷ μύρῳ λαλεῖτε περὶ σισυμβρίων κοσμοσανδάλων τε, 64 κᾆτα μυροπωλεῖν τί παθόντ' ἄνδρ' ἐχρῆν καθήμενον ὑψηλῶς ὑπὸ σκιαδείῳ κατεσκευασμένον συνέδριον τοῖς μειρακίοις ἑλλαλεῖν δι' ἡμέρας, Eupolis 209 κλαύσεται ὅτι ὢν ἄγροικος ἵσταται πρὸς τῷ μύρῳ, Lysias 24. 20 ἕκαστος γὰρ ὑμῶν εἴθισται προσφοιτᾶν ὁ μὲν πρὸς μυροπωλεῖον, ὁ δὲ πρὸς κουρεῖον, ὁ δὲ πρὸς σκυτοτομεῖον, ὁ δ' ὅποι ἂν τύχῃ where probably a descending social scale is implied. For τῷ μύρῳ see on 857.
μεῖραξ was fem. in good Greek, Rutherford *NP* 291, for the masculine word was μειράκιον, μειρακίσκος, or μειρακύλλιον (the last depreciatory as *Ran.* 89, Demosth. *Mid.* 78, *Aristocr.* 163, Epicrates 5. 3, Eubulus 75. 3). In the Hippocratic division of man's life into seven periods (Pollux ii 4), μειράκιον comes third between παῖς and νεανίσκος, being the age from 14 to 21: μειράκιον ὢν ἔτι καὶ μήπω γενειῶν Plut. *Cicero* 28.

ἃ στωμυλεῖται τοιαδὶ καθήμενα·
σοφός γ ὁ Φαίαξ, δεξιῶς τ᾽ οὐκ ἀπέθανεν.
συνερκτικὸς γάρ ἐστι καὶ περαντικός,

1376. ἃ τοιαδὶ στωμύλλεται Herwerden Velsen Blaydes.
1377. τ᾽ ἐμάνθανε ΑΘ, τε κατέμαθεν Dind. Kock Ribbeck: καταμανθάνω does sometimes mean *learn thoroughly, by heart*, as Plato *Theaet.* 178 D, Timocles 6. 16 γέρων τις ἀτυχεῖ, κατέμαθεν τὸν Οἰνέα.
1378. συνερτικὸς Dind. Mein. Vels. from schol. συνείρειν τοὺς λόγους καὶ συντιθέναι δυνάμενος εὐκόλως.

1376. στωμύλλομαι (rare in active, as *Nub.* 1003) seems almost confined to Comedy: στωμυλεύομαι is late, as Alciphron ii 2. 3. The future seems out of place, and no στωμυλέομαι is quoted. Hesychius gives στωμυλῶν (so MSS.)· λαλῶν, which editors have altered to στωμύλλων.

1377. Phaeax, son of Erasistratus, a young man of good family, may have derived his curious name from Phaeax, son of Poseidon, the father of Alcinous (see on 551). He was sent on an important mission to Sicily in 422, but had little success there (Thucyd. v 4): and we have no other information as to the reasons for his being mentioned as a rival to Nicias and Alcibiades, except that he had control of a club or ἑταιρεία Plut. *Nicias* 11, *Alcib.* 13. He was plainly much discussed and admired at this time by the Athenian youth, though Plutarch says ἐντευκτικὸς (*a pleasant talker*) ἰδίᾳ καὶ πιθανὸς ἐδόκει μᾶλλον ἢ φέρειν ἀγῶνας ἐν δήμῳ δυνατός· ἦν γάρ, ὡς Εὔπολίς φησι, λαλεῖν ἄριστος, ἀδυνατώτατος λέγειν. The theory that he is the author of the speech against Alcibiades attributed to Andocides has found considerable support, but is generally rejected now, see Blass *Att. Beredsamkeit* i² 336, Jebb *Att. Orators* i 34, Pauly-Wissowa *Real-Encycl.* s.v. *Andokides*. The poetaster Dionysius Chalcus, a man of some political importance at this time, compliments him in *fr.* 4 Bergk δεξιότης τε λόγου Φαίακος Μουσῶν ἐρέτας ἐπὶ σέλματα πέμπει.
The only explanation of the οὐκ ἀπέθανε is the scholiast's obvious remark δεινὸς ῥήτωρ ὁ Φαίαξ ὡς καὶ ἀποφυγεῖν ἐπὶ θανάτῳ ἐπ᾽ αὐτοφώρῳ κρινόμενος. The phrase is odd, but it may have been one of the current phrases of the day (cf. *Eccl.* 202), and cf. Lucian *Peregr.* 19 ἐπὶ τὸν Δία καταφυγὼν ὁ γενναῖος εὗρε τὸ μὴ ἀποθανεῖν.

1378—. Adjectives in -ικὸς were fashionable, as rising from the growing tendency to philosophise and perhaps from the rhetoric of Gorgias: Strepsiades attempts them *Nub.* 1172 νῦν μέν γ᾽ ἰδεῖν εἶ πρῶτον ἐξαρνητικὸς κἀντιλογικός, Bdelycleon in *Vesp.* 1209 προμάνθανε ξυμποτικὸς εἶναι καὶ ξυνουσιαστικός, and τρόπους φρυαγμοσεμνάκους τινάς is an attempt to imitate his fashions of speech: Eupolis in the Δῆμοι (produced about this time) invented ἀριστητικός (130) in the same style: Lucian *Demosth. encom.* 32 gives among Demosthenes' excellences τὸ συνακτικὸν καὶ κρουστικόν. The adjectives in the first two lines are reasonable enough, and mostly lived and were found useful: but καταληπτικός *seizing* does not reappear till the Stoics, who used it so much in their psychology, and θορυβητικός is the climax of the affectation.
A similar fashion would be the use of abstract nouns, as *Nub.* 317—8 αἵπερ γνώμην καὶ διάλεξιν καὶ νοῦν ἡμῖν παρέχουσι καὶ τερατείαν καὶ περίλεξιν καὶ κρούσιν καὶ κατάληψιν.
συνερτικὸς is a tempting emendation, as συνείρειν λόγους was such a common phrase: but it is dangerous to interfere with what is meant to be a specimen of a passing fashion, and συνέργω might mean 'drive into a corner.'
περαίνω, used later of syllogistic formal reasoning, was open to an objectionable meaning, probably intended to be suggested here and no doubt often played upon, as in Lucian *Demonax* 15; so with κρούω and its derivatives.
The use of γνῶμαι or general maxims of life and conduct was of course a great thing in rhetoric: the principles regulating it were elaborated; γνωμολογία, the schoolword for the use (cf. Plato *Phaedrus* 267, Aristot. *Rhet.* ii 21), applied rather to the use of old maxims than to the invention of new ones. For the use in

καὶ γνωμοτυπικὸς καὶ σαφὴς καὶ κρουστικός,
κατάληπτικός τ' ἄριστα τοῦ θορυβητικοῦ. 1380
ΑΓΟΡ. οὔκουν καταδακτυλικὸς σὺ τοῦ λαλητικοῦ;
ΔΗ.   μὰ Δί', ἀλλ' ἀναγκάσω κυνηγετεῖν ἐγὼ
        τούτους ἄπαντας, παυσαμένους ψηφισμάτων.
ΑΓΟΡ. ἔχε νυν ἐπὶ τούτοις τουτονὶ τὸν ὀκλαδίαν,
        καὶ παῖδ' ἐνόρχην, ὅσπερ οἴσει τόνδε σοι· 1385
        κἄν που δοκῇ σοι, τοῦτον ὀκλαδίαν ποίει.
ΔΗ.   μακάριος ἐς τἀρχαῖα δὴ καθίσταμαι.
ΑΓΟΡ. φήσεις γ', ἐπειδὰν τὰς τριακοντούτιδας
        σπονδὰς παραδῶ σοι. δεῦρ' ἴθ' αἱ Cπονδαὶ ταχύ.

1381. MSS. give the line to the chorus, except R which has no mark of new speaker.

---

literature see Plut. *quaest. conv.* vii 8.
712 B, in political oratory *praec. ger.
reip.* 6. 803 A. γνωμοτύπος implies origi-
nality in striking out such maxims: Ar.
has it always of sophistic or rhetorical
display, *Nub.* 950, *Ran.* 877, *Thesm.*
55 where it occurs in a string of phrases,
something like our lines, coarsely interrupted as here, and, as here, probably
inspired by the rhetorical teaching and example of Gorgias (Blass *Att. Bereds.* i² 87).
1381. A MS. note of Madvig's (at
end of volume) is "καταδακτυλικός est qui
cum admiratione digito demonstrat. V. a
1374 ad 1381 omnes sunt Agoracriti, cui
Δῆμος respondet v. 1382": but I fear few
will agree with him in either view.
1382—3.   Editors quote Isocr.
Areop. 45 the men of old τοὺς βίον ἱκανὸν
κεκτημένους περὶ τὴν ἱππικὴν καὶ τὰ γυμνάσια καὶ τὰ κυνηγέσια καὶ τὴν φιλοσοφίαν
ἠνάγκασαν διατρίβειν, Xen. *Cyneg.* 12. 6
εἰδότες οἱ πρόγονοι ἡμῶν ὅτι ἐντεῦθεν (ἐκ
τοῦ κυνηγετεῖν) εὐτύχουν πρὸς τοὺς πολέμους
κ.τ.λ. Plato *Legg.* vii 823 B— holds the
legislator must recognise that hunting
may have both good and evil effects, and
make rules accordingly.
ψηφίσματα is used for the worse aspects
of political interests and activity *Lys.* 704
οὐχὶ μὴ παύσησθε τῶν ψηφισμάτων τούτων:
the contrast between the stable νόμος and
the shifting and temporary ψηφίσματα is
well known, as expressed by Aristot. *Pol.*
vi (iv) 4. 25. 1292ᵃ 5 ἕτερον (the extreme)

εἶδος δημοκρατίας τἄλλα μὲν εἶναι ταὐτά,
κύριον δ' εἶναι τὸ πλῆθος, καὶ μὴ τὸν νόμον,
τοῦτο δὲ γίνεται ὅταν τὰ ψηφίσματα κύρια
ᾖ ἀλλὰ μὴ ὁ νόμος· συμβαίνει δὲ τοῦτο διὰ
τοὺς δημαγωγούς· ἐν μὲν γὰρ ταῖς κατὰ νόμον
δημοκρατουμέναις οὐ γίνεται δημαγωγὸς
&c. This contrast may have gained a
more definite meaning in the fourth century B.C.
1384. ἐπὶ τούτοις 'on this under-
standing' marks that the position is
settled henceforward. Heraclides Pont. in
his curious defence of luxury as a condition of high spirit ap. Athen. xii 512 A
gives, as the points of luxury among the
Athenians of the Persian wars, the wearing of purple and coloured garments,
long hair wound up and the use of the
golden.tettix (see on 1331), the use
of camp-stools, ὀκλαδίας τε αὐτοῖς δίφρους
ἔφερον οἱ παῖδες, ἵνα μὴ καθίζοιεν ὡς ἔτυχεν.
Another point of connexion with old
Athens was the δίφρος ὀκλαδίας, said to
be the work of Daedalus, kept in the
Erechtheum, Pausan. i 27. 1. For the
shape of the ὀκλαδίας, see Baumeister's
Denkmäler 1650—1.
1385. Schol. ἐπειδὴ παρὰ τοῖς βαρ-
βάροις σπάδωνες, οὗτος ἐνόρχην δίδωσι.
1387. ἀρχαῖα see on 507, a word of
time-honoured customs, here much
strengthened by δὴ. καθίσταμαι, the
inceptive of a settled state.
1388—9. φήσεις γ' as *Pax* 916 &c.
The σπονδαί appear in bodily shape as

ΔΗ. ὦ Ζεῦ πολυτίμηθ᾽, ὡς καλαί· πρὸς τῶν θεῶν,
ἔξεστιν αὐτῶν κατατριακοντουτίσαι; 1391
πῶς ἔλαβες αὐτὰς ἐτεόν; ΑΓΟΡ. οὐ γὰρ ὁ
Παφλαγὼν
ἀπέκρυπτε ταύτας ἔνδον, ἵνα σὺ μὴ λάβῃς;
νῦν οὖν ἐγώ σοι παραδίδωμ᾽ εἰς τοὺς ἀγροὺς
αὐτὰς ἰέναι λαβόντα. ΔΗ. τὸν δὲ Παφλαγόνα, 1395
ὃς ταῦτ᾽ ἔδρασεν, εἴφ᾽ ὅ τι ποιήσεις κακόν.
ΑΓΟΡ. οὐδὲν μέγ᾽ ἀλλ᾽ ἢ τὴν ἐμὴν ἕξει τέχνην·
ἐπὶ ταῖς πύλαις ἀλλαντοπωλήσει μόνος,
τὰ κύνεια μιγνὺς τοῖς ὀνείοις πράγμασιν,

1392. ταύτας MSS.: R has ἔλαβε. **1393.** λάβοις Brunck Dind. Ribbeck.

---

females, like so many other symbolic figures in Aristophanes. Here again there is only a return to the old state of things when the thirty years' truce, conconclued in 445 B.C., was still in force. As in *Ach.* 194, this is regarded as ideal.

1390. The distinction between πολύτιμος *high-priced* and πολυτίμητος *venerated* was clear: Cobet *NL* 56 gives it from Ammonius and illustrates it : in *Ach.* 759 πολυτίματος ἅπερ τοὶ θεοί of corn during famine at Megara is of course intentional, as πολύτιμος would not be strong enough, so Epicharmus 71. 1, Kaibel. The word is sometimes ironical as *Ran.* 851, Plato *Euthyd.* 296 D, ἡ πολυτίμητος ἐπιγλωττὶς Plut. *quaest. conv.* vii 1. 699 C.

1391. κατατριακοντουτίσαι τούτεστιν εἰς συνουσίαν λαβεῖν schol. ; the genitive is probably in imitation of κατελαύνω.

1394. εἰς τοὺς ἀγροὺς see on 805 *sup.*: Demos is essentially a countryman see on 41 and 729.

1397. οὐδὲν μέγ᾽ ἀλλ᾽ ἢ see on 779. ἕξει implies a settled state, see on 130.

1398. ἐπὶ ταῖς πύλαις)(ἐν τῇ ἀγορᾷ, see on 1247. μόνος gives the idea of 'solitary,' 'unheeded,' 'unsuccessful.'

1399. τὰ κύνεια, τὰ ὄνεια, would be *menu*-words for dog-flesh and donkey-flesh : πράγμασιν is something of a surprise and would be more in place if

politics were still to occupy Cleon with the material and audience on a lower level than before: cf. χόρδευε τὰ πράγματα 214. Of course the bad quality of his sausages is meant: but asses' flesh was sold and eaten, Pollux ix 48 μεμνόνεια δὲ ἐκάλουν οὗ τὰ τῶν ὄνων κρέα ἐπιπράσκετο, Lucian *asinus* 33 ἀποσφάξατε αὐτόν, καὶ τὰ μὲν ἔγκατα τοῖς κυσὶ δότε, τὰ δὲ κρέα τοῖς ἐργάταις φυλάξατε, Hesychius μίμαρκυς· ὁ Φερεκράτης παίζων καὶ ἐπὶ ὄνου φησί, Sophilus 4 τὰς ὀνείας ματτύας: and for Roman usage Plin. *NH* viii 170 says the fashion of eating young asses' flesh was confined to Maecenas' time ; the *Corinthius asellus in promulsidari* of Petronius 31 refers of course to a Corinthian bronze.

For the use of dogs' flesh as food, see Daremberg and Saglio `at end of art. *Canis*, Bussemaker and Daremberg on Oribas i p. 586. From Plin. *NH* xxix 58 it appears that in Rome this use was a religious survival, as it is said to be to some extent in China. Hippocrates *de diaeta* ii 46 gives the qualities of ὄνεια and κύνεια in successive sentences: he recommends κύνεια or σκυλάκεια on several occasions for a sick-diet. Jerome Cardan treated Hamilton, Archbishop of St Andrews, with the flesh of whelps (about 1553).

μεθύων τε ταῖς πόρναισι λοιδορήσεται,   1400
κἀκ τῶν βαλανείων πίεται τὸ λούτριον.

ΔΗ. εὖ γ' ἐπενόησας οὗπέρ ἐστιν ἄξιος,
πόρναισι καὶ βαλανεῦσι διακεκραγέναι,
καί σ' ἀντὶ τούτων ἐς τὸ πρυτανεῖον καλῶ
ἐς τὴν ἕδραν θ', ἵν' ἐκεῖνος ἦν ὁ φαρμακός.
ἕπου δὲ ταυτηνὶ λαβὼν τὴν βατραχίδα·   1406
κἀκεῖνον ἐκφερέτω τις ὡς ἐπὶ τὴν τέχνην,
ἵν' ἴδωσιν αὐτόν, οἷς ἐλωβᾶθ', οἱ ξένοι.

1401. Elmsley for λοῦτρον of MSS.   **1408.** οἷς R. οὓς V and most MSS.

1400. λοιδορεῖν takes acc., λοιδορεῖσθαι dat. It is not easy to define any difference in meaning; but the middle generally implies wrangling, speaking back, bad language on both sides: Demosth. ii *Aristog.* 19 πρὸς ἅπαντας ἀεὶ προαιρεῖται λοιδορεῖσθαι καὶ διαβοᾶσθαι, Pherecrates 143. 8 εἶθ' ὅταν αἰτιώμεθα, λοιδοροῦνται, Alexis 156. 4 ἢν δ' εἴπῃς ἅπαξ, ἀντήκουσας· ἤδη λοιδορεῖσθαι λείπεται· εἶτα τύπτεσθαι δέδεικται καὶ παροινεῖν. In such cases as Ar. *fr.* 87 ὅστις φακῆν ἥδιστον ὄψων λοιδορεῖς, the middle would not be used. But the distinction is certainly not always very clear, and it was neglected in later writers.

1401. Dependence on the public baths for warmth was a mark of the poorest classes (*Plut.* 535 &c.): this is probably a slang phrase.

1402. ἐπινοεῖν as always with the idea of a practical hit, see on 90.

1403. βαλανεύς and πόρνη were the lowest of callings for the respective sexes: so βαλανεύς may be used merely as a term of abuse or insult, as *Ran.* 710.

διακέκραγα is a rare instance of the active in verbs compounded with δια- and signifying rivalry: see Cobet *NL* 625.

1404—5. The σίτησις and προεδρία combined as usual to mark the men whom the state delights to honour. φαρμακός was the name for the human victims offered at the Thargelia, see on 1136: so the word, like κάθαρμα, became an expression of hate and contempt, ὦ

φαρμακέ *fr.* 532. It is quoted twice from the orators, but both cases are in speeches of doubtful authenticity: Demosth. i *Aristog.* 80, Lysias 6. 53 of Andocides.

1406. βατραχίς was a green dress, Pollux vii 55, who adds that the φοινικίς and βατραχίς were for men, the κροκώτιον and ὀμφάκινον for women, though Alexander liked to wear the last-mentioned, and two βατραχίδες are among the treasures presented to Artemis Brauronia by women *CIA* ii 754. 16, 48. The colour was the same as that which became so well-known in the Roman circus as *prasinus*, Dio Cass. lix. Wilamowitz Eurip. *Her.* ii p. 5 says that Lycus in that play appeared in a green dress.

1407—8. λωβάομαι, like λυμαίνομαι, may take either acc. or dat., and it is not clear that there is any difference in meaning.

The play ends with this appeal to a wider Greek feeling than Cleon cared for.

Editors mostly assume that the *finale* was choral, as in all other extant plays of the author: but there is no trace of anything being lost and we are not forced to suppose that Aristophanes confined himself to a single form of ending for his comedies.

The leading off of Cleon to his fate is the dramatic conclusion. How the musical and spectacular effects may have modified or added to this we cannot tell. Cic. *Cael.* 65 implies that mimes had a stock farcical ending, regular plays had not.

APPENDIX I.

THE PARTICLE ΓΕ.

The particle γε is not now regarded by scholars as a word to be inserted or omitted at pleasure in any part of a Greek sentence: but I hope it may be of some service if I bring together certain principles that regulate its use.

Its origin is from an enclitic particle of the Aryan tongue, from which are descended the Sanskrit particles *gha* and *ha*, and the Gothic *k* in *mi-k*. The aspirates in the Sanskrit forms stand in the same relation to the unaspirated media of γε, as in *ahám* ἐγώ, *hánus* γένυς, *mahá* μέγας, and possibly a few other cases. The relation is of course exceptional, and it is not yet fully explained. The double form in Sanskrit is also strange, but its existence, probably caused by some obscure accentual conditions, is not a sufficient reason to cause serious doubt as to the connexion between *ha* and *gha* on the one side and γε on the other (though Wackernagel *Altind. Grammatik* i § 216b and Delbrück *Vergleich. Syntax* ii §§ 165–7 do not regard the connexion as certain).

gha is hardly found except in Veda: it is used with the negative *na*, with demonstrative and personal pronouns, and in combination with other particles: eight cases also occur of its use after prepositions, two after adjectives, and one after a verb. Its place is nearly always immediately after the first word in a line or half-line: the exceptions are mostly when another particle precedes it. Its meaning is to introduce a sentence or clause, marking a connexion of thought with what goes before. In one case it introduces the apodosis to a conditional clause (*Ṛg Veda* i 166. 8).

ha in Veda is used with pronouns, interrogative, relative, personal and demonstrative: there are also 36 cases of it with nouns, 9 with verbs, 10 with prepositions connected with verbs, and 10 with adverbs. Here again there are only quite a few cases of *ha* except after the first word of a line or half-line, and those cases are nearly all *ha* – – forming a bacchius at the end of a line.

It seems impossible to draw any distinction of meaning between *gha* and *ha*: except that *ha* has acquired the meaning of *quippe* with relative pronouns, and once at least with a participle (*Ṛg Veda* i 151. 7).

The use of *ha* in early prose is discussed by Delbrück *Altind. Syntax* § 251, and summed up as "emphasizing the first word of clauses attached to the preceding sentence." Some distinction is drawn between explanatory and narrative styles, and the curious remark made that the particle is used in the latter chiefly with the perfect tense (which is restricted to the narration of facts not witnessed by the speaker. Pāṇini expressly allows *ha* with imperfect iii 2. 116). In later Sanskrit it is used more freely and with less rule: at the end of a heroic verse it is extremely convenient and common, especially after a verb in the perfect of the metrical value ∪ – ∪ : the meaning is so vague that native grammarians give the note *pādapūraṇe* 'to fill up the line.' The subtle Pāṇini gives certain rules on the accent of verbs in a *ha*-clause, implying that such a clause is more or less subordinate, and gives a special case (viii 1. 60) where *ha* quotes a breach of good manners. Its connexion with story-telling style is implied in the word *itihāsa* (*iti ha āsa, so said he*) for an epic poem[1].

The Greek γε inherits that remarkable peculiarity of enclitics, fully dealt with by Wackernagel in his article *über ein Gesetz der indogermanischen Wortstellung* (*Indogerm. Forschungen* i 332–), the tendency to come as near the beginning of their clause as possible, i.e. generally as the second word. Wackernagel says (p. 371) that γε escapes any sweeping rule, because it is confined to the word which bears the chief weight of the affirmation. But the tendency is as clear in γε as in any other enclitic in the Greek language: early position in the clause is really more stringently required than a place after an emphatic word, and when γε comes later than the second or third place in the clause, there is nearly always another particle, or a combination of particles, preceding.

As regards meaning, γε answers more nearly to *well* than perhaps to any other English word: but of course its enclitic nature makes an important difference in its use. Being an enclitic, it is felt as intimately associated with the preceding word, to which it often gives an emphasis: but this association with a single word is not by any means the whole matter.

In Homer, γε occurs after pronouns much oftener than in other combinations. It is not very often second in the Homeric sentence or line: for here the favourite use is to have γε with the second of two pronouns, as

Il. ii 55   τοὺς ὅ γε συγκαλέσας πυκινὴν ἠρτύνετο βουλήν,
iii 391   κεῖνος ὅ γ᾽ ἐν θαλάμῳ καὶ δινωτοῖσι λέχεσσι,
v 301   τὸν κτάμεναι μεμαώς, ὅς τις τοῦ γ᾽ ἀντίος ἔλθοι,
v 554   οἵω τώ γε λέοντε δύω ὄρεος κορυφῇσιν,
Od. i 47   ὣς ἀπόλοιτο καὶ ἄλλος, ὅτις τοιαῦτά γε ῥέζοι,

---

[1] I am indebted to Mr E. H. Minns of Pembroke College for a careful statement of the uses of the cognate Russian particle *zhe*: they shew a remarkable similarity to those of *ha* and γε.

or with a pronoun preceded by a particle, as

Il. i 116   εἰ τό γ᾽ ἄμεινον,

    i 320 (and often)   ἀλλ᾽ ὅ γε...

   ii 314 (and often)   ἔνθ᾽ ὅ γε...

    v 812   οὐ σύ γ᾽ ἔπειτα,

    i 190   ἦ ὅ γε φάσγανον ὀξὺ ἐρυσσάμενος παρὰ μηροῦ,

or by particles, as

Il. i 342   ἦ γὰρ ὅ γ᾽ ὀλοιῆσι φρεσὶ θύει,

    i 295   μὴ γὰρ ἐμοίγε

σήμαιν᾽· οὐ γὰρ ἐγώ γ᾽ ἔτι σοὶ πείσεσθαι ὀΐω,

χερσὶ μὲν οὔ τοι ἐγώ γε μαχήσομαι εἵνεκα κούρης,

    i 286   ναὶ δὴ ταῦτά γε πάντα γέρον κατὰ μοῖραν ἔειπες,

Od. vi 120   ἦ ῥ᾽ οἵ γ᾽ ὑβρισταί τε καὶ ἄγριοι οὐδὲ δίκαιοι,

    x 350   γίγνονται δ᾽ ἄρα ταί γ᾽ ἔκ τε κρηνέων ἀπό τ᾽ ἀλσέων,

Il. ix 425   ἐπεὶ οὔ σφισιν ἥδε γ᾽ ἑτοίμη.

These are types of hundreds of other instances.

When γε follows a word which is not a pronoun, we find nearly always before it, not as a rule immediately, a particle or combination of particles, as

Il. iii 453   οὐ μὲν γὰρ φιλότητί γ᾽ ἐκεύθανον, εἴ τις ἴδοιτο,

   iv 372   οὐ μὲν Τυδεΐ γ᾽ ὧδε φίλον πτωσκαζέμεν ἦεν,

  iii 223   οὐκ ἂν ἔπειτ᾽ Ὀδυσῆΐ γ᾽ ἐρίσσειε βροτὸς ἄλλος,

Od. xi 430   ἦ τοι ἔφην γε,

   xi 447   ἦ μέν μιν νύμφην γε νέην κατελείπομεν ἡμεῖς,

Il. i 60   εἴ κεν θάνατόν γε φύγοιμεν,

   vi 128   εἰ δέ τις ἀθανάτων γε κατ᾽ οὐρανοῦ εἰλήλουθας,

  xvi 573   ἀτὰρ τότε γ᾽ ἐσθλὸν ἀνεψιὸν ἐξεναρίξας,

   v 380   ἀλλ᾽ ἤδη Δαναοί γε καὶ ἀθανάτοισι μάχονται,

   xi 107   δὴ τότε γ᾽ Ἀτρείδης εὐρὺ κρείων Ἀγαμέμνων.

πρίν γε is common, though some hold that in nearly all cases γε was inserted later, and πρῖν alone is right (Leaf on *Il.* v 288). Combinations where γε comes first are very rare in Homer: I am not sure that any occur except γε μὲν = Attic γε μήν, as *Il.* ii 703 πόθεόν γε μὲν ἀρχόν, v 516 μετάλλησάν γε μὲν οὔ τι, and the formula πάρος γε μὲν οὔ τι θαμίζεις. γ᾽ οὖν occurs *Il.* v 258, xvi 30, but with other particles.

There are a few cases where γε comes after a preposition in a short clause which is really an afterthought, as *Il.* xiii 325 ἔν γ᾽ αὐτοσταδίῃ, *Od.* viii 207 πλήν γ᾽ αὐτοῦ Λαοδάμαντος, xvi 447 ἔκ γε μνηστήρων.

In Pindar γε generally has the support of other particles: instances are γε μὰν *Pyth.* 7. 20 &c., γε μὲν *Ol.* 12. 5 &c., καὶ μὰν ἁ Σαλαμίς γε *Nem.* 2. 13, ἀτὰρ λευκωλένῳ γε *Pyth.* 3. 98, ἐπεὶ τό γε λοιδορῆσαι θεούς *Ol.* 9. 37. Two cases occur of κείνου γε unsupported in the middle of a sentence: *Pyth.* 4. 125, *Nem.* 8. 10. In one or two passages an un-supported γε has been introduced by mere conjecture : *Nem.* 6. 58 γ' is in no MS.; *Ol.* 9. 76 the readings γ' οὐλίῳ, γ' ἷνις, have no authority. Certain classes of the MSS. of Pindar seem to introduce γ' to make an end-syllable long, others introduce γε even where it makes a syllable too much, and it is likely that in some passages a γε has been wrongly adopted in our texts from these sources. I had expected that Pindar would sometimes use γε responsive (see below) at the beginning of an antistrophe, but there is no certain case of this (*Ol.* 1. 99 and *Nem.* 2. 11 are possible cases).

In Attic the conditions are slightly different, and I may be allowed to put down under headings the uses recognised and allowed. The gain may be small, but I believe that there is a certain vagueness in the prevalent ideas on the matter, and that the rules are more definite than is often imagined.

(1) With personal pronouns, I am not sure that restrictions can be proved in all cases. No doubt ἔγωγε and σύ γε are usually near the beginning of a sentence or clause, or are closely connected with other particles : but ἔγωγε at all events occurs independently and late in a clause, as if it were regarded as a single word and the γε were no longer subject to its ordinary conditions. This would be helped by the curious change of accent from ἐγώ γε to ἔγωγε, which was specially Attic. σύ γε is specially used in second alternative clauses (as *tu, ille* are sometimes in Latin), Soph. *OT* 1101 Jebb, Eurip. *Orest.* 1528 οὔτε γὰρ γυνὴ πέφυκας οὔτ᾽ ἐν ἀνδράσιν σύ γ᾽ εἶ.

With demonstrative pronouns, I have not found any certain case of γε merely emphasizing. There are a few possible cases in votive inscriptions, e.g. no. 1369 Collitz (from Dodona) Πολυξένα τά γεν ἀντίθητι if γεν is for γε, and no. 229 Roberts (742 Kaibel, 314 Röhl) τάσδε γ᾽ Ἀθαναίᾳ...ἔθηκε. Soph. *Phil.* 231 may be a case.

(2) After the first word in a sentence, γε emphasizes the word and gives an emotional or 'pathetic' colour to the whole phrase. The English equivalent is *Oh* or *Ah* : but in γε the logical significance to mark connexion is the original and main thing : it is little used in lyrics and never I think at the beginning of a *first* sentence. The first word may be

(*a*) a noun, rarely, as Eurip. *HF* 1403 ζεῦγός γε φίλιον, *Phoen.* 608 ἀδικίᾳ γ᾽, ὦ θεοί; in *Cycl.* 283 αἰσχρὸν στράτευμά γε, if right, is unique in the position of γε:

(*b*) an adjective, as Aesch. *Prom.* 953 σεμνόστομός γε καὶ φρονή-ματος πλέως, Soph. *OT* 1035 δεινόν γ᾽ ὄνειδος σπαργάνων ἀνειλόμην, Eurip. *Andr.* 909 κακόν γ᾽ ἔλεξας, ἄνδρα δίσσ᾽ ἔχειν λέχη, Thucyd. iii 63. 2 ἱκανή γε ἦν, Plato *Charm.* 172 E ἄτοπά γ᾽ ἔφην μοι προφαίνεσθαι (wrongly altered by Badham), Demosth. *Timocr.* 181 ὅμοιόν γε, οὐ γάρ; τοῦτο τοῖς προτέροις. In apodosis Eurip. *Bacch.* 445 ἃς δ᾽ αὖ σὺ Βάκχας εἶρξας...φροῦδαί γ᾽ ἐκεῖναι:

(*c*) an adverb, as Soph. *Ant.* 739 καλῶς γ᾽ ἐρήμης ἂν σὺ γῆς ἄρχοις μόνος, εὖ γε very common, Eurip. *Orest.* 99 ὀψέ γε φρονεῖς εὖ, τότε λιποῦσ' αἰσχρῶς δόμους, Aesch. *Prom.* 696 πρῴ γε στενάζεις καὶ φόβου πλέα τις εἶ, Soph. *Aj.* 589 ἄγαν γε λυπεῖς, καλῶς γε ποιῶν Ar. *Ach.* 1050, Plato *Symp.* 174 E:

(*d*) a verb, rare, in imperative as Soph. *Elect.* 411 ὦ θεοὶ πατρῷοι, συγγένεσθέ γ᾽ ἀλλὰ νῦν, Eurip. *Andr.* 589 ψαῦσόν γ᾽ ἵν᾽ εἰδῇς, καὶ πέλας πρόσελθέ μου, *Alc.* 1127, *Supp.* 842, Plato *Rep.* i 336 c οἵου γε σύ, or optative, as Ar. *Ach.* 93 ἐκκόψειέ γε κόραξ πατάξας, or indicative, as *ib.* 836 εὐδαιμονεῖ γ᾽ ἄνθρωπος:

(*e*) a participle, Eurip. *Supp.* 458 κλαίων γ᾽ ἂν ἦλθες, Plato *Rep.* iii 399 E σωφρονοῦντές γε ἡμεῖς.

(3) γε means *yes*: the use is extremely common in drama and in prose dialogue. The emphatic word of the reply is generally put first, and γε second: but γε may come later, especially if another particle begins the reply, as Aesch. *Prom.* 378 ἐάν τις ἐν καιρῷ γε μαλθάσσῃ κέαρ. Sometimes a question is answered in this way, even though it is not directly put: so Soph. *OT* 680 μαθοῦσά γ᾽ ἥτις ἡ τύχη answers τί μέλλεις κομίζειν; as if it were κομιεῖς; cf. Eurip. *Cycl.* 107. The affirmative character of the reply is often emphasized by πάνυ γε, κομιδῇ γε, and the like: ναὶ..γε Plato *Rep.* v 450 B.

Clauses with εἰ μὴ · γε meaning *yes, unless &c.* sometimes form a snare as Eurip. *Alc.* 493, *Andr.* 254, *Heracl.* 272.

Closely connected with this meaning is the use of γε in responses. There are cases when the first speaker gives a clause containing a nominative without a verb to complete the sentence: the sentence is completed by the second speaker in response with γε. These cases have the optative in the final clause, and are mainly parodies of prayers: it seems likely that religious services sometimes took this form, the priest beginning the sentence and giving the subject of the prayer, and the congregation finishing it with the appropriate verb and wish. Plain cases are Aristoph. *Plut.* 180 KAP. ὁ Τιμοθέου δὲ πύργος ΧΡΕ. ἐμπέσοι γέ σοι, Plato com. 173. 21 A. σκόρπιος αὖ B. παίσειέ γέ σου τὸν πρωκτὸν ὑπελθών. Another case, which has been curiously mistaken, is Aristoph. *Pax* 441–452. The scholiast plainly tells us the proper arrangement of these lines: δύο πρόσωπα ταῦτά φησιν, ὧν ὁ μὲν εὔχεται, ὁ δὲ ἕτερος ἀκόλουθα τῇ εὐχῇ καταρώμενος λέγει: but Richter seems to be the only editor, following Dobree, who has taken the scholiast's view. Trygaeus speaks two lines, the chorus responds and finishes the prayer with the third: this is repeated four times. The two prayers that concern us here are

ΤΡ.	κεἴ τις ἐπιθυμῶν ταξιαρχεῖν σοι φθονεῖ	444
	ἐς φῶς ἀνελθεῖν, ὦ πότνι᾽, ἐν ταῖσιν μάχαις	
ΧΟ.	πάσχοι γε τοιαῦθ᾽, οἷάπερ Κλεώνυμος.	
ΤΡ.	κεἴ τις στρατηγεῖν βουλόμενος μὴ ξυλλάβῃ	450
	ἢ δοῦλος αὐτομολεῖν παρεσκευασμένος	
ΧΟ.	ἐπὶ τοῦ τροχοῦ γ᾽ ἕλκοιτο μαστιγούμενος.	

(In 450 all MSS. have ξυλλάβῃ, and the imitation of ritual style may very well intend the archaic εἰ with subj.)

In the other two response-lines 443 and 449 the MSS. give no γε: but it is tempting to read ἐκ τῶν γ᾽ ὀλεκράνων ἀκίδας ἐξαιρούμενον (taking this line alone as the response for symmetry), and ληφθείς γ᾽ ὑπὸ ληστῶν ἐσθίοι κριθὰς μόνας.

Again in a religious service, though there is here no prayer, *Pax* 1074 IEP. ἀλλὰ τόδε πρότερον TΡΥ. τοῖς ἀλσί γε παστέα ταυτί.

It seems to me not unlikely that γε implies some response or change of speakers in several cases. This is clear in Eurip. *Supp.* 805 ΑΔ. ἰὼ ἰὼ ΧΟ. τῶν γ᾽ ἐμῶν κακῶν ἐγώ: in *Phoen.* 1740–2 Paley and others rightly follow the scholiast in reading ΟΙ. φεῦ τὸ χρήσιμον φρενῶν. ΑΝ. εἰς πατρός γε συμφορὰς | εὐκλεᾶ με θήσει, otherwise γε is absurd. In Aristoph. *Av.* γε in 1327 probably means that the speaker is Peisetaerus, as in the corresponding line 1315, where the MSS. give ΠΕ. It is possible that in Aesch. *Cho.* 94–5 Electra is parodying a prayer in response-form at her father's grave: and in 490, 492, 494 γε would certainly be more in place than δέ and τε.

(4) With relative pronouns and adverbs, γε, like *quippe* in Latin, implies a reason given. ὅς γε is too common to need illustration, but a few cases of the usage with other relatives may be given: Eurip. *Cycl.* 195 ἔσω πέτρας τῆσδ᾽, οὗπερ ἂν λάθοιτέ γε, *Orest.* 544 ἐγώ τοι πρός σε δειμαίνω λέγειν, ὅπου γε μέλλω σήν τι λυπήσειν φρένα, Soph. *Trach.* 444 χἀτέρας οἵας γ᾽ ἐμοῦ, Plato *Laches* 196 D τοῦτο δὲ οὐ παντὸς δὴ εἶναι ἀνδρὸς γνῶναι, ὁπότε γε μήτε ἰατρὸς μήτε μάντις αὐτὸ γνώσεται, Demosth. *Phaenipp.* 1 and *Timoth.* 57 ὅπου γε, Plato *Phaedo* 84 E χαλεπῶς ἂν τοὺς ἄλλους πείσαιμι, ὅτε γε μηδ᾽ ὑμᾶς δύναμαι πείθειν, Soph. *Aj.* 715 κοὐδὲν ἀναύδατον φατίσαιμ᾽ ἄν, εὐτέ γ᾽ ἐξ ἀέλπτων Αἴας μετανεγνώσθη.

In other cases, however, γε with certain relatives has a restrictive force, as with οἷος and ὅσος: *quidem* is exactly parallel.

Under this head (of γε = *quippe*) come instances of ὡς...γε, as Aesch. *Prom.* 77, Eurip. *Med.* 1278 (more than twenty cases in Euripides), Ar. *Ach.* 346, Thucyd. ii 102. 7 ὡς τῆς γε ἄλλης αὐτῷ μεμιασμένης, Xen. *Symp.* 4. 8, Lysias 12. 13 &c.: but ὡς γ᾽ may also be restrictive: both senses occur together in Eurip. *Alc.* 800– ὡς τοῖς γε σεμνοῖς καὶ συνωφρυωμένοις ἅπασιν ἐστὶν ὡς γ᾽ ἐμοὶ χρῆσθαι κριτῇ, οὐ βίος ἀληθῶς ὁ βίος, ἀλλὰ συμφορά. It seems to be a rule that ὡς γε is restrictive (as Herod. ii 10, Thucyd. vi 11. 2, 92. 1: I have not observed this in Tragedy), ὡς...γε explanatory. So ὥσπερ γε as Xen. *Hiero* 1. 24, Herod. ii 70 (explanatory): ὥστε..γε Plato *Rep.* ix. 582 C, *Phaedo* 67 C, Soph. *OC* 565.

A reason is also implied by γε with a participle, ὧν γε = *quippe qui sit*: Aesch. *Eum.* 435 σέβουσαί γ᾽ ἀξίαν, Eurip. *Supp.* 756 διδούς γε τῶν δεδραμένων δίκην, Thucyd. iii 63. 2 ὑπάρχον γε ἡμῖν, Ar. *Plut.* 21 οὐ γάρ με τυπτήσεις στέφανον ἔχοντά γε, Antiph. *Caed. Herod.* 95 τί ἔσται πλέον τῷ γε ἀποθανόντι; γε comes second in the participial clause; the participle may precede, as it usually does, or follow, as Epicharmus 87 Kaibel where Πέλοπί γ᾽ ἔρανον ἱστιῶν is allowable even without the pun on γέρανον which is the chief intention, Soph. *OT* 930 ἐκείνου γ᾽ οὖσα παντελὴς δάμαρ, Plato *Charm.* 154 E πρέπει δέ που τοιοῦτον αὐτὸν εἶναι, τῆς γε ὑμετέρας ὄντα οἰκίας, *Hipp. ma.* 289 E καλὸν φανεῖται, χρυσῷ γε κοσμηθέν, Demosth. *Pantaen.* 25 οὔτε γὰρ καθίστην ἐγώ, ὅ γε ὢν ἐν τῷ Πόντῳ. In a few cases γε comes later than the second place, if the preceding words are very closely connected, as Aristot. *Eth. Nicom.* iii 1. 13. 1110ᵇ 21 ἑκὼν μὲν οὐ πέπραχεν, ὅ γε μὴ ᾔδει, οὐδ᾽ αὖ ἄκων, μὴ λυπούμενός γε.

In a few cases, the participle ὤν seems to be omitted and γε with noun or adj. gives the reason. Eurip. *IA* 84 κἀμὲ στρατηγεῖν δῆτα Μενέλεω χάριν εἵλοντο, σύγγονόν γε.

(5) γε is used in connexion with other particles.

The variety of combinations observed is very great, and the delicate shades of meaning often difficult to appreciate, and still more difficult to express in English.

I give most of these combinations, noting some points of interest.

καί . γε is very common; it answers in meaning to *yes, and,* but is much more often used than the English phrase, and of course the γε generally comes after some word which is meant to be emphasized. Eurip. *Cycl.* 684 καί σε διαφεύγουσί γε; Soph. *OC* 65 καὶ κάρτα, τοῦδε τοῦ θεοῦ γ᾽ ἐπώνυμοι. καί γε is apparently not used in Classical Greek, though it appears later, as *Acts* 2. 18 = Septuag. Joel 2. 29 (where the best MSS. omit γε).

δέ γε or δὲ . γε is common in retort, where the second speaker, accepting the statement of the first, wishes to cap it or to bring in a consideration on the other side.

Aesch. *Agam.* 938 ΑΓ.　φήμη γε μέντοι δημόθρους μέγα σθένει.

ΚΛ.　ὁ δ᾽ ἀφθόνητός γ᾽ οὐκ ἐπίζηλος πέλει.

ΑΓ.　οὔτοι γυναικός ἐστιν ἱμείρειν μάχης.

ΚΛ.　τοῖς δ᾽ ὀλβίοις γε καὶ τὸ νικᾶσθαι πρέπει.

Eurip. *Andr.* 238 ΑΝ.　νέα πέφυκας καὶ λέγεις αἰσχρῶν πέρι.

ΕΡ.　σὺ δ᾽ οὐ λέγεις γε, δρᾷς δέ μ᾽ εἰς ὅσον δύνῃ.

It is commonest in the altercation of στιχομυθία of tragedy and of comedy (as in this play, see on 356), but it may also introduce a long retort to a set speech, as Aesch. *Sept.* 1026, Soph. *Aj.* 1150. It appears in the answers of a part-chorus in lyrics Aesch. *Sept.* 1057, or iambics *Agam.* 1350: in *Eum.* 257 a part-chorus replies with the extraordinary combination ὁ δ᾽ αὐτέ γ᾽ οὖν ἀλκὰν ἔχων. In Plato's dialogue, it often introduces in question-form what is really a minor premiss in a syllogism, the major having been admitted, as *Phaedo* 65 C, 93 D, *Rep.* i 335 D &c. In the Orators, it often implies an imaginary conversation or debate, as Demosth. *FL* 279 "καὶ ἠλέγχθησάν τινες αὐτῶν ἐν τῇ βουλῇ οὐ τἀληθῆ ἀπαγγέλλοντες." οὗτοι δέ γε καὶ ἐν τῷ δήμῳ, *Leochar.* 55 &c., so Thucyd. iii 63. 3 λέγετε ὡς αἰσχρὸν ἦν προδοῦναι τοὺς εὐεργέτας· πολὺ δέ γε αἴσχιον τοὺς πάντας Ἕλληνας καταπροδοῦναι.

The combination may also be used in all styles, without change of speaker, to continue an argument or ordered statement, especially to mark that the thought is now concerned with a different person or persons, Soph. *Elect.* 558 φαίη δ᾽ ἂν ἡ θανοῦσά γ᾽ εἰ φωνὴν λάβοι, Eurip. *Hec.* 1247 τάχ᾽ οὖν παρ᾽ ὑμῖν ῥᾴδιον ξενοκτονεῖν· ἡμῖν δέ γ᾽ αἰσχρὸν τοῖσιν Ἕλλησιν τόδε, Thucyd. ii. 54. 3, Antiph. *Caed. Herod.* 67, Plato *Phaedo* 82 A—B, Demosth. *Timocr.* 128–9.

Or, to change the address to a new person who is specially import-ant, Soph. *Aj.* 1409 παῖ, σὺ δὲ πατρός γ᾽ ὅσον ἰσχύεις φιλότητι θιγών.., *Elect.* 1367.

Of course a μέν-clause often precedes, and the δέ γε may mark simply that the δέ-clause is more important, as Soph. *Phil.* 559, Plato *Parm.* 128 C.

The corresponding negatives also occur (*no, nor*):

οὐδὲ. γε Soph. *OT* 1378,

Eurip. *IT* 569 ΙΦ. ψευδεῖς ὄνειροι, χαίρετ᾽· οὐδὲν ἦτ᾽ ἄρα.
OP. οὐδ᾽ οἱ σοφοί γε δαίμονες κεκλημένοι
πτηνῶν ὀνείρων εἰσὶν ἀψευδέστεροι.

Xen. *Symp.* 8. 21, 27 &c.

οὐδέ γε Eurip. *IA* 307 ΠΡ. οὐ χρῆν σὲ λῦσαι δέλτον, ἣν ἐγὼ ᾽φερον.
ΜΕ. οὐδέ γε φέρειν σε πᾶσιν Ἕλλησιν κακά.

Soph. *Elect.* 1347 OP. οὐχὶ ξυνίης; ΗΛ. οὐδὲ γ᾽ εἰς θυμὸν φέρω.

Plato *Charm.* 163 B, 165 E, *Rep.* i 341 B, Demosth. *Pantaen.* 59.

μηδέ γε Soph. *OC* 1743, Ar. *Pax* 457, Plato *Laches* 197 D.
μηδὲ. γε Soph. *Trach.* 305.

In μέν γε, the γε is not connected with the μέν-clause as contrasted with the δέ-clause, but introduces the whole statement consisting of the two clauses.   γε in this combination is just like the γὰρ of introduction. Instances of μέν γε are Ar. *Nub.* 1382, *Vesp.* 564, *Av.* 1136, *Lys.* 589, 720, *Thesm.* 804, *Ran.* 290, *Eccl.* 60, *Plut.* 665, Thucyd. i 70. 2, 74. 1, ii 38. 1, vi 86. 3, Antipho *socr.* 21, *caed. Her.* 14, Plato *Symp.* 180 D, 215 C, *Rep.* viii 559 B, Demosth. *Mid.* 73, *Timocr.* 44, 123, *Polycles* 60, Isaeus 4. 10, Aeschin. *Timarch.* 26, Isocr. *Paneg.* 153, Xen. *Cyrop.* i 6. 21, *Memor.* iii 14. 5, *Symp.* I. 9, *Hiero* I. 11 &c.   This use does not seem to occur in Tragedy, except Eurip. *fr.* 901. 4 πρῶτα μέν γε τοῦθ᾽ ὑπάρχει, and *Med.* 1094, if Reiske's μέν γ᾽ is right, but see Verrall.

In a few cases μέν γε, with τοῦτο or νῦν, has no δέ-clause to follow, and means *well, anyhow*, as Ar. *Ach.* 154 τοῦτο μέν γ᾽ ἤδη σαφές, *Nub.* 1172, *Lys.* 1165: so πρωὶ μέν γε Epicharmus 124 Kaibel.

μέν . γε Eurip. *Heracl.* 648, 692, in both cases the γε going with a pronoun.

μέν γε.. δέ γε in Lucian *Demosth. encom.* 23 is probably unique: in Plato *Phaedo* 75 D—E, *Rep.* viii 549 B a change of speakers excuses it?

In the rare τέ γε, there is again no close connexion between the particles: γε introduces the whole statement, as Plato *Phaedo* 59 C ναί, Σιμμίας τέ γε καὶ Κέβης.., i *Alcib.* 107 B, Xen. *Memor.* i 2. 54. [τε . γε Ar. *Av.* 823 seems to be wrong.]   So with οὔτε γε, as Plato *Rep.* viii 556 A.

ἀλλὰ . γε ought to mean *yes, but*, and this is its usual meaning, Aesch. *Supp.* 342, Soph. *OT* 1440, 1518, *Ant.* 556, Eurip. *Hec.* 264, *IA* 674, 1013, Lysias 6. 40, Plato *Charm.* 174 C.   We should in some cases rather use *Well, but* or *Nay, but*, as Eurip. *Andr.* 762 (which should begin a sentence), *Med.* 1247, Soph. *Aj.* 291, *OC* 590, *Ant.* 217, *Elect.* 1023, Ar. *Nub.* 401, *Eq.* 965, Antiph. *Caed. Herod.* 71, Demosth.

Timocr. 129 : or *Oh, but* Ar. *Nub.* 33. The strong adversative sense of ἀλλά naturally gives sometimes the meaning *Ah, no,* as Soph. *Aj.* 469, Eurip. *Andr.* 762, Plato *Phaedo* 58 D, *Rep.* i 340 E (?).

Sometimes we find it not at the beginning of a sentence, when ἀλλά answers μέν as Xen. *Hiero* 6. 9, or when ἀλλά has its meaning of entreaty with imperatives, as Soph. *OC* 1276 πειράσατ᾽ ἀλλ᾽ ὑμεῖς γε κινῆσαι πατρὸς στόμα, or in the combination ἀλλὰ νῦν γε (generally in entreaty), Andoc. *de red.* 26, Demosth. 3 *Olynth.* 33, Plut. *Timoleon* 4 καθικέτευον ἀλλὰ νῦν γε μεταβαλέσθαι.

For ἀλλά . γε in apodosis, see *infra* p. 200.

ἀλλά γε is very doubtful. It may be possible in Epic, but has been corrected, e.g., Hom. *Il.* i 82 is now read ἀλλά τε καὶ μετόπισθεν : Archestratus ap. Athen. vii 319 D ἀλλά γε χρὴ ῥίνης λόγον ἢ πλατυνώτου (ἀλλὰ τί χρὴ Wilam.), in Epicharmus (87 Kaibel) ap. Athen. viii 438 D Porson read ἀλλὰ οὔτι γέρανον ἀλλά γ᾽ ἔρανόν τοι λέγω, but MSS. have ἀλλ᾽ ἔρανόν γά τοι λέγω : in *Anth. Pal.* iii 6. 3 ἀλλά γε τόξῳ. But in Attic authority is against it : supposed cases can be read ἀλλ᾽ ἄγε, as Plato *Rep.* viii 543 C with the second best MS., so *Phaedo* 86 E, or otherwise altered with authority, as *Rep.* i 331 B, where Stobaeus quotes ἀλλ᾽ ἕν γε ἀνθ᾽ ἑνός, though all MSS. have ἀλλά γ᾽ ἕν : *Phaedr.* 262 A the Bodl. MS. has ἀλλά γε δή, but the Venetian ἀλλὰ δή : Aristot. *Eth. Eudem.* i 6. 1216ᵇ 20 οὐ μὴν ἀλλά γε περὶ ἀρετῆς is read without remark. The restriction was certainly removed in later Greek, Polybius, Pausanias, &c. : S. Luke 24. 21 ἀλλά γε καὶ σὺν πᾶσιν τούτοις, 1 *Corinth.* 9. 2 εἰ ἄλλοις οὐκ εἰμὶ ἀπόστολος, ἀλλά γε ὑμῖν εἰμι. The fact that ἀλλὰ γάρ is common would seem to be an argument in favour of the view that ἀλλά γε was at one time allowed.

So ἀτάρ . γε must be separated, as Aesch. *Prom.* 1011, Eurip. *Hipp.* 728, Ar. *Thesm.* 207, Xen. *Oecon.* 21. 1.

μήν is very often followed by γε, if another particle precedes μήν and some word or words intervene before γε. μήν γε was forbidden : Valckenaer in ignorance of this gave οὐ μήν γ᾽ against the MSS. in Eurip. *Phoen.* 1622. καὶ μήν never takes γε when it introduces a new character on the stage (see on 691) : or when it marks a new sight or the like, *Eq.* 340, 746, 970, 1232, Eurip. *Bacch.* 918, *Cycl.* 151, Aesch. *Sept.* 456. In other cases, γε follows more often than not : it is difficult to see whether it then does more than emphasise a particular word (Jebb on Soph. *Aj.* 531).

Soph. *OT* 1004 ΟΙ. καὶ μὴν χάριν γ᾽ ἂν ἀξίαν λάβοις ἐμοῦ.
      ΑΓ. καὶ μὴν μάλιστα τοῦτ᾽ ἀφικόμην, ὅπως
        σοῦ πρὸς δόμους ἐλθόντος εὖ πράξαιμί τι.

But when the καὶ μήν clause takes up and repeats a word from the previous speaker, γε does not seem to be generally used :

Soph. *Elect.* 554 ΗΛ. ἀλλ᾽ ἦν ἐφῆς μοι...
    556 ΚΛ. καὶ μὴν ἐφίημ᾽.

Plato *Theaet.* 143 E ΣΩ. εἰ δὴ οὖν τινὶ ἐνέτυχες ἀξίῳ λόγου, ἡδέως ἂν πυθοίμην. ΘΕΟ. καὶ μήν, ὦ Σώκρατες, ἐμοί τε εἰπεῖν καὶ σοὶ ἀκοῦσαι πάνυ ἄξιον οἵῳ μειρακίῳ ἐντετύχηκα.

Yet Soph. *Elect.* 1044 ΧΡ. ἀλλ᾽ εἰ ποήσεις ταῦτ᾽, ἐπαινέσεις ἐμέ.
                    ΗΛ. καὶ μὴν ποήσω γ᾽ οὐδὲν ἐκπλαγεῖσά σε.
See on *Eq.* 335, 340.

The γε may have as many as five or six words between μὴν and itself, Ar. *Av.* 639 καὶ μὴν μὰ τὸν Δί᾽ οὐχὶ νυστάζειν γ᾽ ἔτι (γ᾽ restored by Porson from Plut. *Nicias* 8), *Ran.* 1198 καὶ μὴν μὰ τὸν Δί᾽ οὐ κατ᾽ ἔπος γέ σου κνίσω.

οὐ μὴν . γε Aesch. *Prom.* 268, *Agam.* 1279, Soph. *OT* 810, *OC* 152, Eurip. *Alc.* 518, Plato *Rep.* i 344 D, Xen. *Memor.* i 2. 5, 27. Without γε Ar. *Ran.* 262 (with γε 263).

οὐ μὴν ἀλλά . γε Demosth. 2 *Aristog.* 20, Isocr. *Nicocl.* 8, Eurip. *IT* 630—1 οὐ μήν, ἐπειδὴ τυγχάνεις Ἀργεῖος ὤν, ἀλλ᾽ ὧν γε δυνατὸν οὐδ᾽ ἐγὼ λλείψω χάριν.

οὐ μὴν οὐδὲ . γε Xen. *Memor.* i 2. 5, Demosth. 3 *Olynth.* 14. Without γε Thucyd. i 3. 3, 82. 1, Plato *Rep.* vi 486 C.

ἦ μὴν . γε Eurip. *Alc.* 692 : without γε very common in solemn oaths.

ἀλλὰ μὴν . γε Aesch. *Pers.* 226, Eurip. *IA* 1368, Plato *Charm.* 160 A, *Phaedo* 58 D, 74 C, Demosth. 2 *Aphob.* 8, 3 *Aphob.* 28, adv. *Phorm.* 40, *pro Phorm.* 32, Xen. *Memor.* i 2. 63 : without γε Ar. *Av.* 385 : cases from Aristotle with and without γε are collected by Euchen *de Aristot. dicendi ratione* i pp. 8—9 : the combination often introduces the second horn of a dilemma and nearly always the second half of a conjoint argument.

Thucydides seems never to have μὴν with γε following, except perhaps iv 86. 1 ἦ μὴν οὖς ἂν ἔγωγε προσαγάγωμαι.

The use of γε with μέντοι is very parallel to its use with μὴν : μέντοι . γε, however, is very rare in poetry. Soph. *Phil.* 524 ἀλλ᾽ αἰσχρὰ μέντοι σοῦ γέ μ᾽ ἐνδεέστερον is the only case I can quote from tragedy. Ar. *Nub.* 126 ἀλλ᾽ οὐδ᾽ ἐγὼ μέντοι πεσών γε κείσομαι, Xen. *Cyrop.* iii 1. 16 ἀλλὰ σὺ μέντοι μεγάλα γ᾽ ἂν ζημιοῖο, Plato *Charm.* 162 A, *Rep.* i 331 E, v 473 C &c. οὐ μέντοι . γε is common in Thucydides, Xenophon, the Orators and Plato : it is indeed the regular way of answering a μέν-clause where the answer begins with οὐ (οὐ δὲ being felt as awkward), as Thucyd. i 142. 4, ii 13. 1, 47. 3.

Porson on Eurip. *Med.* 675 held that the Attics did not allow γε after τοι, except with a word intervening. This restriction has been denied by Lobeck on Phrynichus, p. 342, Hermann on Eurip. *IT* 720, Heindorf on Plato *Phaedo* 108 D, Meineke *Vindiciae Aristoph.* 197, Stallbaum on Plato *Rep.* i 329 E, and more recently by Kock in *Rhein. Museum* for 1891, p. 304. It seems to have been accepted by Dobree, *Observ. Aristoph.* on *Thesm.* 716, and is taken as a principle by Cobet *VL* 60, *NL* 684, and by Wilamowitz *Herakles* [1] i 247 ("all that was gained in the Porson-Hermann period is at stake if καίτοιγε is allowed for the fifth century &c."). Blaydes on *Thesm.* 709 would allow μέντοι γε if another particle precedes (so Holden on Xen. *Oecon.* 14. 3), but not καίτοι γε. Cases of τοί γε are collected by Blaydes and Kock : Eurip. *IT* 729 καίτοι γ᾽ ἐγγὺς ἔστηκας φόνου, *Tro.* 1015 καίτοι γ᾽ ἐνουθέτουν σε, Ar. *Ach.* 611, *Thesm.* 709 κοὖπω μέντοι γε πέπαυμαι, and a number from the Orators, Plato and Xenophon.

καίτοι. γε is common, as Soph *Aj.* 441, *OT* 855 καίτοι νιν οὐ κεῖνός γ’ ὁ δύστηνός ποτε κατέκταν’, Eurip. *Orest.* 77. So οὗτοι. γε as Soph. *Ant.* 747, *OC* 650, Eurip. *Alc.* 54 : μήτοι. γε as Soph. *Aj.* 472, *Elect.* 518, Eurip. *Med.* 178 : Soph. *Elect.* 298 ἀλλ’ ἴσθι τοι τίσουσά γ’ ἀξίαν δίκην : Eurip. *Cycl.* 198 ἐπεί τἂν μεγάλα γ’ ἡ Τροία στένοι.

As with ἀλλὰ γὰρ so τοίγαρ might be used in support of τοί γε.

γε μὴν and γε μέντοι are strong adversatives : γε μέντοι is a favourite phrase in στιχομυθία, as Aesch. *Sept.* 716, Soph. *Elect.* 398, Eurip. *Orest.* 196 &c. : not common apparently in prose, Plato *Charm.* 164 A.

γε μὴν, *all the same, for all that,* Aesch. *Agam.* 1378 σὺν χρόνῳ γε μήν, Eurip. *Elect.* 754, Herod. vi 129. 4 : rare in στιχομυθία as Soph. *Elect.* 587, Eurip. *Alc.* 516 : it may also be used like γοῦν to introduce a case in proof of a general statement, as Plato *Symp.* 197 A. Xenophon often has γε μὴν simply to introduce a new paragraph : so Plato *Rep.* i 332 E, *Phaedr.* 267 C. Plato has it sometimes like μέντοι of assent, *Theaet.* 208 E. We find it also answering to μὲν and practically = δέ, as Plato *Legg.* iv 705 A πρόσοικος γὰρ θάλαττα χώρᾳ τὸ μὲν παρ’ ἑκάστην ἡμέραν ἡδύ, μάλα γε μὴν ὄντως ἀλμυρὸν καὶ πικρὸν γειτόνημα, Xen. *Cyrop.* iii 3. 63 &c. Epicharmus 170. 13 Kaibel has ὁ μὲν γὰρ αὔξεθ’, ὁ δέ γα μὰν φθίνει.

γέ τοι has definitely the meaning so often attributed to γε alone, *at least* : Soph. *OC* 1323 ἐγὼ δὲ σός, κεἰ μὴ σός, ἀλλὰ τοῦ κακοῦ πότμου φυτευθείς, σός γέ τοι καλούμενος introduces a fact which goes some way to prove a previous statement : *at any rate, all I can say is,* as Eurip. *Cycl.* 224, Ar. *Eq.* 787, *Plut.* 424, Soph. *Phil.* 823.

Sophocles has it in its original meaning, as *Antig.* 1064 ἀλλ’ εὖ γέ τοι κάτισθι, *Trach.* 1107 ἀλλ’ εὖ γέ τοι τόδ’ ἴστε, *OT* 1171 κείνου γέ τοι δὴ παῖς ἐκλῄζετο.

γε after οὖν ought to have an intervening word : οὔκουν · γε, Aesch. *Prom.* 518 οὔκουν ἂν ἐκφύγοι γε τὴν πεπρωμένην, Soph. *Ant.* 321, Eurip. *Ion* 746, Thucyd. ii 43. 1 &c. : οὐκοῦν. γε Plato *Charm.* 159 A, Demosth. 2 *Onetor* 9 but οὔκουν γε is read Plato *Phaedo* 70 B : ἀλλ’ οὖν · γε, Aesch. *Prom.* 1058, Soph. *Aj.* 535 ἀλλ’ οὖν ἐγὼ ’φύλαξα τοῦτό γ’ ἀρκέσαι, Eurip. *Cycl.* 652.

οὐκ ἂν οὖν · γε Plato *Rep.* i 333 E.

μὲν οὖν · γε Eurip. *Hel.* 1022, Plato *Phaedr.* 277 C &c. : μὲν οὖν γε became common in later Greek (often written μενοῦνγε), as *epist. Rom.* 9. 20, 10. 18.

δ’ οὖν · γε Eurip. *Elect.* 508.

μὴ οὖν · γε Demosth. *Timocr.* 48.

μήτ’ οὖν γε Eurip. *IA* 1438 is now read, after Elmsley, μήτ’ οὖν σύ.

ἵν’ οὖν · γε Ar. *Thesm.* 755.

γ’ οὖν of course was so common as to become a single word, see on *Eq.* 87.

So γε δῆτα was allowed in answers, Eurip. *Supp.* 1098, *Phoen.* 1717 ; but δῆτα. γε had to be separated, see cases on *Eq.* 6. γε δὴ was not uncommon and γε μὲν δὴ was used, as Aesch. *Supp.* 241, 273, *Agam.* 661, 1213, *Eum.* 419, but δή. γε nearly always, e.g.

Eurip. *Heracl.* 269 πειρώμενος δὴ τοῦτό γ᾽ αὐτίκ᾽ εἴσομαι.

    Elect. 36 οὐ δὴ τοῦτό γ᾽ ἐξελέγχομαι.

    Elect. 424 ἔστιν δὲ δὴ τοσαῦτά γ᾽ ἐν δόμοις ἔτι.

Soph. *Ant.* 659 εἰ γάρ δὴ τά γ᾽ ἐγγενῆ φύσει.

    OT 294 ἀλλ᾽ εἴ τι μὲν δὴ δείματός γ᾽ ἔχει μέρος.

    Phil. 246 οὐ γὰρ δὴ σύ γ᾽ ἦσθα ναυβάτης.

Eurip. *Tro.* 210 μὴ γὰρ δὴ δίναν γ᾽ Εὐρώτα.

Thucyd. i 81. 6 μὴ γὰρ δὴ ἐκείνῃ γε τῇ ἐλπίδι ἐπαιρώμεθα.

Demosth. 1 *Aristog.* 19 ὕβρις γὰρ δὴ τοῦτό γε.

Plato *Symp.* 197 A καὶ μὲν δὴ τήν γε τῶν ζῴων ποίησιν.

    Phaedr. 268 A ἐῶμεν δὴ τά γε σμικρά.

δή γε is always suspicious. Eurip. *IT* 943 ἐς τὰς Ἀθήνας δή γ᾽ ἔπεμψε Λοξίας, *HF* 1146 τί δή γε φείδομαι ψυχῆς ἐμῆς; *IA* 1207 μὴ δή γε κτάνῃς, *Supp.* 162 ὃ δή γε πολλοὺς ὤλεσε στρατηλάτας, are all generally condemned: δή γε has disappeared from Ar. *Nub.* 681, 786, *Vesp.* 355, *Eccl.* 195: Eurip. *Heracl.* 632 πάρεσμεν, οἷα δή γ᾽ ἐμοῦ παρουσία is the most likely case, but the apologetic use of οἷος δή (generally in neuter pl., as *Orest.* 32, Ar. *Ach.* 753, Plato *Phaedo* 60 A) never has γε elsewhere. Xen. *Oecon.* 17. 2 ἐγνώκασι δή γε Holden, δέ γε Dindorf.
Later it is certain, as Moschus 4. 71.

ἐπειδή γε is certain, Eurip. *Hipp.* 946, Thucyd. vi 18. 1, Demosth. *Conon* 29, Plato *Phaedo* 77 D &c. : ἐπειδὴ . γε Soph. *Elect.* 631, Plato *Phaedo* 87 C.

γε που is found Ar. *Ach.* 896 ἀγορᾶς τέλος ταύτην γέ που δώσεις ἐμοί, Plato *Hipp. ma.* 298 A and που . γε, as Plato *Charm.* 168 B πάντως δὴ ἄν που ἐκεινό γ᾽ αὐτῷ ὑπάρχοι, δήπου . γε, Soph. *Antig.* 381, Antipho *socr.* 28, Demosth. 3 *Aphob.* 32, ἤπου . γε Lysias 13. 57, Demosth. *Timocr.* 53, οὐ γάρ που . γε Plato *Rep.* i 338 C: but πού γε is doubtful, Antipho *Caed. Herod.* 24.

γε may follow γὰρ either singly or with another particle preceding, but here again a word must intervene:

Eurip. *Ion* 1069 οὐ γὰρ δόμων γ᾽ ἑτέρους.

    Hipp. 640 μὴ γὰρ ἔν γ᾽ ἐμοῖς δόμοις.

    Elect. 243 οἴμοι, τί γάρ μοι τῶνδέ γ᾽ ἐστὶ φίλτερον;

    Cycl. 694 κακῶς γὰρ ἂν Τροίαν γε διεπυρώσαμεν.

    Hel. 1056 παλαιότης γὰρ τῷ λόγῳ γ᾽ ἔνεστί τις.

    Tro. 1247 ἔχει γὰρ οἷα δεῖ γε νερτέρων στέφη.

Aesch. *Pers.* 168 ἔστι γὰρ πλοῦτός γ᾽ ἀμεμφής, ἀμφὶ δ᾽ ὀφθαλμῷ φόβος.

Soph. *OT* 80 ὦναξ Ἄπολλον, εἰ γὰρ ἐν τύχῃ γέ τῳ.

Thucyd. ii 43. 6 ἀλγεινότερα γὰρ ἀνδρί γε φρόνημα ἔχοντι.

Demosth. 1 *Aristog.* 79 πῶς γὰρ τῷ γε μηδ᾽ ἐλευθέρῳ;

Plato *Phileb.* 12 D πῶς γὰρ ἡδονή γε ἡδονῇ μὴ οὐχ ὁμοιότατον ἂν εἴη;
Rep. i 339 B.

As γοῦν is parallel to γὰρ in formation, we find sometimes γοῦν. γε, as Plato *Apol.* 21 D ἔοικα γοῦν τούτου γε σοφώτερος εἶναι.

There does not seem to be any instance of γε in an ἄν-clause, unless some other particle also occurs in the clause. It is said to be a rule that ἄν γε never came together. This is certainly true for the most part :

Soph. *OC* 977 πῶς ἂν τό γ᾽ ἆκον πρᾶγμ᾽ ἂν εἰκότως ψέγοις;

Eurip. *IA* 324 οὔ, πρὶν ἂν δείξω γε Δαναοῖς πᾶσι τἀγγεγραμμένα.

Soph. *Aj.* 1342 ὥστ᾽ οὐκ ἂν ἐνδίκως γ᾽ ἀτιμάζοιτό σοι.

Thucyd. iii 60. 3 εἱλόμεθα γὰρ ἂν πρό γε τούτου λιμῷ τελευτῆσαι.

Demosth. 1 *Onetor* 10 ὥστ᾽ οὐκ ἂν διὰ τοῦτό γ᾽ εἶεν οὐκ εὐθὺς δεδωκότες.

But γ᾽ ἂν is allowed Ar. *Av.* 585 μὴ, πρίν γ᾽ ἂν ἐγὼ τὼ βοιδαρίω τὠμὼ πρώτιστ᾽ ἀποδῶμαι, Thucyd. i 77. 6 ὑμεῖς γ᾽ ἂν οὖν..., Plato *Rep.* i 345 D &c., and there are a few cases of ἄν γε (see Elmsley on Eurip. *Med.* 836), such as :

Eurip. *Heracl.* 966 οὐχ ὄντιν᾽ ἂν γε ζῶνθ᾽ ἕλωσιν ἐν μάχῃ.

So *Orest.* 784, *Phoen.* 1215.

Ar. *Vesp.* 720 πρὶν ἄν γ᾽ ἀκούσῃς ἀμφοτέρων (see Starkie there). Cf. *Eq.* 961.

Xen. *Oecon.* 7. 2 οὐδὲ ἂν γε νῦν.

In conditional clauses εἰ. γε is not unusual : Soph. *Aj.* 583 εἰ δίκης γε τυγχάνοις, Eurip. *IA* 654 εἰ σέ γ᾽ εὐφρανῶ, *Med.* 512, *Phoen.* 1562.

εἰ γε is also allowed Eurip. *Orest.* 1106 εἰ γ᾽ ἔσται καλῶς, Thucyd. vi 18. 2, Demosth. 2 *Onetor* 6, 12 &c., Plato *Laches* 192 B—C ΛΑ. εἰ τό γε διὰ πάντων πεφυκὸς δεῖ εἰπεῖν. ΣΩ. ἀλλὰ μὴν δεῖ, εἴ γε τὸ ἐρωτώμενον ἀποκρινούμεθα ἡμῖν αὐτοῖς.

It tends, like *si quidem*, to mean *since* ; so Soph. *Aj.* 1268, *OT* 383, *OC* 260 : or almost *for example* as Eurip. *Med.* 88.

So εἴπερ γε with or without an intervening word :

Aesch. *Cho.* 198 εἴπερ γ᾽ ἀπ᾽ ἐχθροῦ κρατὸς ἦν τετμημένος.
499 εἴπερ κρατηθείς γ᾽ ἀντινικῆσαι θέλεις.

Soph. *Aj.* 84 πῶς, εἴπερ ὀφθαλμοῖς γε τοῖς αὐτοῖς ὁρᾷ;

ἐάν γε, ἤν γε, ἐάν. γε. Eurip. *Orest.* 1593 ἀλλ᾽ οὔτι χαίρων, ἤν γε μὴ φύγῃς πτεροῖς, Plato *Phaedr.* 253 C ἐάν γε διαπράξωνται.

ἐὰν τῷ ὄντι γ᾽ ᾖ Plato *Phaedo* 68 B.

ἤνπερ γε Ar. *Eq.* 366, ἐάνπερ γε Plato *Phaedo* 89 B.

For a peculiar use of εἰ μὴ.. γε see on *Eq.* 186.

In disjunctive clauses ἢ. γε is found, no doubt where emphasis is put on a point in one of the alternatives :

Eurip. *Hel.* 973 ἢ νῦν ἐκείνους ἀπόδος ἐμψύχους πάλιν,
ἢ τήνδ᾽ ἀνάγκασόν γε.

Rhes. 622 Διόμηδες, ἢ σὺ κτεῖνε Θρήκιον λεών,
ἢ 'μοὶ πάρες γε, σοὶ δὲ χρὴ πώλους μέλειν.

Cobet *VL* 571 would read παράσχες for πάρες γε.

Thucyd. iii 45. 4 ἢ δεινότερόν τι τούτου δέος εὑρετέον ἐστὶν ἢ τόδε γε
οὐδὲν ἐπίσχει.

Plato *Hipp. ma.* 301 A γενναῖοι ἢ σοφοὶ ἢ τίμιοι ἢ γέροντές γε ἢ νέοι,
Phaedo 65 B, *Phaedr.* 272 D and cases given on *Eq.* 413.

When only one ἤ-clause is given, i.e. when ἤ means *otherwise*,
Demosth. *Nausim.* 48, *Boeot. de nom.* 33, Aeschin. *Ctesiph.* 203 ἢ πάντων γ' ἂν εἴην ἀπορώτατος.

With ἤτοι:

Eurip. *Ion* 431 ἤτοι φιλοῦσά γ' ἧς ὑπερμαντεύεται,
ἢ καί τι σιγῶσ' ὧν σιωπᾶσθαι χρεών.

Cf. Plato *Phaedo* 76 A.

In interrogative or exclamatory sentences, the 'pathetic' meaning of
γε is natural, and we find it in combination with ἆρα and ἤ.

Eurip. *Hec.* 745 ἆρ' ἐκλογίζομαί γε πρὸς τὸ δυσμενές.

Soph. *Phil.* 106 οὐκ ἆρ' ἐκείνῳ γ' οὐδὲ προσμῖξαι θρασύ;

Theocr. 3. 36 ἄλλεται ὀφθαλμός μευ ὁ δεξιός· ἆρά γ' ἰδησῶ
αὐτάν;

Ar. *Eq.* 616?

So ἆρά γε Ar. *Plut.* 546, Andoc. *Myst.* 41, Plato *Charm.* 174 B,
Demosth. *Timocr.* 94 &c.

ἆρα . γε occurs very rarely: Ar. *Eq.* 382, Plato *Rep.* v 468 D, *Phaedo*
87 C οὐκ ἆρα . γε *Rep.* i 342 C, E, *Phaedo* 76 C : γ' ἆρα Plato *Charm.* 159 B
(MS. Bodl., τἆρα Cobet). I do not know of ἆρα γε in Attic : later, as in
New Testament (S. Matth. 7. 20 &c.), it was common.

ἤ . γε: Aesch. *Agam.* 1064 ἢ μαίνεταί γε καὶ κακῶν κλύει φρενῶν.

τίς γε is doubtful if alone, though καὶ τίς · γε occurs Eurip. *Ion* 558,
Orest. 784, Aeschin. *FL* 163. Elmsley's note on Eurip. *Med.* 1334
(1367) disposed of many supposed cases of τίς . γε, cf. Plato *Phaedr.*
268 B. It is certain in the curious combination μή τί γε δή, *nedum*
(Demosth. 2 *Olynth.* 23, Plut. *de fac. in orbe lunae* 5. 922 C), or μή τί γε
(Demosth. *Androt.* 45, 1 *Corinth.* 6. 3), whatever its origin.

ἰδού γε *Eq.* 87 q.v.

Akin to these sentences are the cases where γε is used when an oath
by some deity is taken. Here the γε very seldom follows immediately
after the god's name : the obvious reason being that it is needed to
emphasise the first word in the main sentence, as Plato *Phaedr.* 230 A
νὴ τὴν Ἥραν, καλή γε ἡ καταγωγή, so Xen. *Memor.* iii 11. 5, *Symp.* 4.
54 &c.: yet see on *Eq.* 698, and add Demosth. *Syntax.* 16 καὶ νὴ Δία
γ', Plato *Theaet.* 155 C καὶ νὴ τοὺς θεούς γε, Xen. *Apol.* 20.

In merely negative clauses, οὐ or μὴ may be strengthened by a γε
following, not immediately. The common μὴ σύ γε in earnest appeal is
a case of this (Soph *OC* 1441, Eurip. *Ion* 439 &c.: μὴ ὑμεῖς γε Antiph.

Caed. Herod. 86): so is μή μοί γε *Eq.* 19, μήπω γε Aesch. *Prom.* 631, Ar. *Ach.* 176 μηδαμῶς ταύτας γ᾽ ἕλη μου, Soph. *OT* 1522, μή μόνον γε Plato *Meno* 71 C.

οὐ . γε in reply: οὐ σύ γε Eurip. *IA* 1441.

No, not.. Soph. *OT* 360 ΤΕ. οὐχὶ ξυνῆκας πρόσθεν; ἢ 'κπειρᾷ λέγων;
            ΟΙ.   οὐχ ὥστε γ᾽ εἰπεῖν γνωστόν· ἀλλ᾽ αὖθις φράσον·

    Ant. 770 ΧΟ. ἄμφω γὰρ αὐτὼ καὶ κατακτεῖναι νοεῖς;
              ΚΡ. οὐ τήν γε μὴ θιγοῦσαν· εὖ γὰρ οὖν λέγεις.

So Aesch. *Prom.* 258, Soph. *OT* 1131, Eurip. *Hec.* 399, *Hel.* 818, *Heracl.* 966, Plato *Charm.* 163 B &c.

For οὐ .. γε meaning *Yes, but not*, see on *Eq.* 801 : add οὐ μόνον γε as Plato *Legg.* vi 752 A.

οὐδείς γε Eurip. *Ion* 404, *IT* 564, Plato *Rep.* i 337 C.

οὐ . γε not in reply is very rare, but it occurs in a parenthesis in Soph. *OT* 711.

So ἥκιστά γε Soph. *OT* 1386, Eurip. *Hipp.* 1014, Plato *Rep.* i 340 C &c.

οὐ μή . γε Soph. *OT* 771.

πῶς οὐ . γε Xen. *Hipparch.* 5. 10.

τί (δὲ) ἄλλο γε .., as Plato *Phaedo* 63 D, *Meno* 73 C, is a common form of sentence.

(6) There is still left a certain number of cases, which do not strictly fall under any of the heads given.   The meaning in these cases develops out of the original meaning *Oh, Well*: such a meaning would easily become clearly restrictive and approach to the definite sense of *at least*, which is so often used to translate γε.   But this use of γε standing alone without other particles is confined to the following cases:

(*a*) where γε comes immediately after prepositions and similar words, and a short independent clause, restricting the main sentence, is formed.   Clauses of this kind are not uncommon in Attic Greek of all periods.

Solon 1. 4 ἀντί γ᾽ Ἀθηναίου, Aesch. *Prom.* 162 δίχα γε Διός, περί γε τῶν τοιούτων Plato *Euthyphro* 7 B &c.

πλήν γε often occurs (see on *Eq.* 27) and πλήν . γε as πλήν ἔτι γε καὶ νῦν in Philip's letter to Larissa, and a short restrictive clause beginning with πρίν γε is not unusual : so ὥς γ᾽ ἐμοὶ δοκεῖ and the like : in ἕνεκα-clauses that word is generally put later as τοῦδέ γ᾽ οὕνεκα Soph. *Elect.* 387 &c.

(*b*) where γε follows the article in cases like Soph. *OT* 90 τῷ γε νῦν λόγῳ, Eurip. *Elect.* 101, ὅ γε ὄντως φιλομαθής Plato *Rep.* vi 490 A, Demosth. 1 *Olynth.* 27 τοῖς γε σώφροσιν.

A last class of cases is (*c*) where γε marks the apodosis of a sentence. After a conditional clause or the like, 'well' introduces the main clause naturally enough, and the usage is to be expected.   Instances are

Soph. *Ant.* 655   ἐπεὶ γὰρ αὐτὴν εἷλον ἐμφανῶς ἐγὼ
                    πόλεως ἀπιστήσασαν ἐκ πάσης μόνην,
                    ψευδῆ γ᾽ ἐμαυτὸν οὐ καταστήσω πόλει.

Eurip. *Ion* 673 καθαρὰν γὰρ ἦν τις εἰς πόλιν πέσῃ ξένος,
       κἂν τοῖς νόμοισιν ἀστὸς ᾖ, τό γε στόμα
       δοῦλον πέπαται κοὐκ ἔχει παρρησίαν.

Thucyd. i 32. 1 ἀναδιδάξαι μάλιστα μὲν ὡς καὶ ξύμφορα δέονται, εἰ δὲ μή, ὅτι γε οὐκ ἐπιζήμια, Demosth. *Phaenipp.* 1 εἰ μὴ τότ' ἐβούλετο, τῇ γ' ἕκτῃ δοῦναι τοῦ Βοηδρομιῶνος, Plato *Laches* 190 A εἰ γὰρ μηδ' αὐτὸ εἰδείημεν, σχολῇ ἂν σύμβουλοί γ' ἄξιοι λόγου γενοίμεθα, Xen. *Cyrop.* v 5. 20 ἀλλ' εἰ πρὸς τοῦτο σιωπᾶν ἥδιόν σοι ἢ ἀποκρίνασθαι, τόδε γ' ἔφη, εἰπὲ.., Aeschin. *Timarch.* 48 &c. ἀλλὰ . γε may be used when appropriate in apodosis, as Aeschin. *Ctes.* 155, Isocr. 20. 11 &c. γέ τοι in such a case Xen. *Hiero* 1. 14. The word before γε is generally the article or a pronoun. So where the protasis is a relative, not a conditional, clause, as Eurip. *Bacch.* 443—5 ἃς δ' αὖ σὺ Βάκχας εἶρξας..., φροῦδαί γ' ἐκεῖναι.

Similar is the use after a suspense, *well*, as Soph. *Ajax* 476 τί γὰρ παρ' ἦμαρ ἡμέρα τέρπειν ἔχει προσθεῖσα κἀναθεῖσα τοῦ γε κατθανεῖν; Demosth. 1 *Aristog.* 93 (the long sentence is worth reading as an instance of this use).

We now and then find γε used in meanings where γὰρ is much more clear and more common, though all rise without any difficulty out of the original sense, and all may be rendered by our *well*.

To explain, when we should say *i.e.* and expect γάρ:

Eurip. *Orest.* 531 ἐν δ' οὖν λόγοισι τοῖς ἐμοῖς ὁμορροθεῖ·
       μισεῖ γε πρὸς θεῶν καὶ τίνεις μητρὸς δίκας.

Cf. the use of γε after a neuter pronoun, as Plato *Legg.* vi 752 B δῆλον τὸ τοσοῦτον...τὸ μὴ ῥᾳδίως γε αὐτοὺς προσδέξασθαι &c.

To open a statement of a case, where γὰρ is so common : Aesch. *Prom.* 700, Eurip. *Heracl.* 987, Ar. *Ach.* 628 (opening of the parabasis proper).

Sometimes it is used, like γοῦν, to give an example of a rule, as Ar. *Av.* 720.

The limits within which γε may be used have been given : though wide, they are real limits, and cases beyond them must be regarded as suspicious. In older books, like Hartung's *Partikeln*, we find a good many cases where these limits are disregarded : but on reference to modern texts, the γε will generally be found to have disappeared, and on MS. authority. A good case of the way in which γε has often crept into texts is Ar. *Av.* 1078: the MSS. have ἦν δὲ ζῶντ' or ζῶντα ἀγάγῃ unmetrically: Burges proposed ζῶντά γ' ἀγάγῃ, which Dindorf and Blaydes adopt, and the particle could fairly be defended and explained : but the fragment of papyrus published by Weil in *Revue de Philol.* vi 179 has ζῶντ' ἀπαγάγῃ, of course rightly. A good case of another kind is Eurip. *Cycl.* 401, where scribes not knowing the word στόνυξ wrote ὀξύν γ' ὄνυχα for ὀξὺν στόνυχα.

But MSS. on the other hand often give γε wrongly. Eurip. *HF* 1228 φέρει τὰ τῶν θεῶν γε πτώματ' οὐδ' ἀναίνεται MSS.: editors omit τῶν, but the γε should be omitted and τῶν kept. Hundreds of cases could be quoted where MSS. insert it or omit it wrongly (Soph. *Phil.* 594, Eurip. *Cycl.* 202 &c.): often the scribes inserted it for mistaken metrical reasons, e.g. in Ar. *Plut.* 481 a dozen inferior MSS. have ἐάν γ' ἀλῷς, because the writers did not know that α in ἐάν was long. [Insertion of γε for metrical reasons merely has been a device of many modern editors also: even Elmsley's fine sense for Greek idiom sometimes failed him here, cf. his notes on Ar. *Ach.* 48, 570.] Cobet in *VL* p. 570 and *NL* pp. 58, 210 makes short work of more than thirty cases of γε wrongly put in: in *NL* p. 435 he points out that in Aristophanes both R and V often omit γε against the metre, as *Eq.* 1150, 1167. In a few cases I venture to think Cobet misses a point in the use of the particle: in *Eq.* 423 γ' occurs in none of Velsen's MSS. except in Δ as a correction: something is necessary for the metre: Cobet reads ἐλάνθανον ἄν. Zacher says γ' is a conjecture of Triclinius': well, it is a restoration by a good Greek scholar in the thirteenth century of a particle which was dropped by careless scribes centuries earlier, and it seems to me a conjecture of the best kind. γ and ν were very much alike at one period of Greek writing: in Athen. xiii 579 E a line of Machon is given in the form εἰς αὐτό γ' αἰεὶ δραμάτων ἐμβάλλομεν; in 580 A the same line is written εἰς αὐτὸν αἰεί.

Collitz reads γε in several Cypriote inscriptions as nos. 56, 60. 29, 69: but other editors rightly give κε or other readings.

The refinements and real uses of γε became forgotten, along with so much of what was definitely regulated in good Greek. In the New Testament it is used about thirty times: nearly half the cases (καί γε, ἀλλά γε, μενοῦνγε, &c.) break the rules observed in earlier times. Wilamowitz on Eurip. *HF* 631 points out that in the Scaptoparene inscription of Gordian's time (*Mittheil. archäol. Inst.* xvi 275) it is used like τοίνυν as a connecting particle merely. In the *Christus Patiens* it is never used rightly except in the quotations from ancient writers. It has long been extinct, like all postpositives, in modern Greek, Jannaris, *Hist. Greek Grammar* § 1700[1]. I believe its loss came along with the change of accent from pitch to stress: the meaning could then be given by emphasis of pronunciation.

γάρ is γ' ἄρ, γ' ἄρα: it meant originally *oh, then*, or *well, then*: and this original sense remained in full use after the meaning *for* had become common. Recognition of this frees us from having to assume the strange ellipses in meaning so often supposed by editors (cf. on *Eq.* 328). It also explains at once why γάρ is so often used to open the statement of a case, legal or otherwise, why it is regular after τεκμήριον δὲ and the like, and why it can be used naturally in such cases as Soph. *Phil.* 433, *Eq.* 1002, Xen. *Symp.* 3. 4 &c.

So it might obviously be used, when *for* is so awkward, in interrogative clauses. And it would be a natural particle to introduce a new point as Pind. *Ol.* 13. 20, in transition as Xen. *Symp.* 3. 7, 8, 9 or even to begin a new paragraph as Aristot. *Pol.* ii 7 (Bekker p. 37. 6, and p. 46. 21).

---

[1] I am indebted to Mr J. C. Lawson of Pembroke College for the information that it is retained as a part of the interrogative ἄραγε.

APPENDIX II.

POLITICAL USE OF MORAL TERMS.

It is known that certain words, which usually bear a moral meaning, were used by the Greeks in a political or social sense as well. This usage of ἀγαθός, ἐσθλός, χρηστός and some other words was treated by Welcker in his *Prolegomena* to Theognis and by Grote *Hist. of Greece* ch. ix (near the end). Both these scholars seem to have thought that the usual sense of these words grew up after the social sense[1]. However that may be, the social and political use was certainly common at one period: it was no doubt more common in the conversation of political circles than in literature. I subjoin a number of cases, chiefly from Athenian writers of the late fifth and early fourth centuries B.C. It will be noticed that in the case of the more question-begging and offensive terms, serious writers (as Grote noticed in some instances) are careful to give the words as quotations or in speeches.

The political use of καλὸς κἀγαθός is found only twice in Thucydides, who in both cases is particular to mark that he is quoting; viii 48. 6 τοὺς καλοὺς κἀγαθοὺς ὀνομαζομένους is a quotation within a quotation and in iv 40. 2 a democratic ally of Athens puts to a Spartan who had not been killed at Sphacteria the bitter question εἰ οἱ τεθνεῶτες αὐτῶν καλοὶ κἀγαθοί[2].

The corresponding verb in use was ἀνδραγαθίζομαι. Notice how Pericles and Cleon bring in the word when they wish to sneer at their opponents who would claim its honourable colour for their peace policy. Thucyd. ii 63. 2 Pericles says "Athens cannot now resign her empire, εἴ τις καὶ τόδε ἐν τῷ παρόντι δεδιὼς ἀπραγμοσύνῃ ἀνδραγαθίζεται": and Cleon echoes his words in iii 40. 4 "We must punish Mytilene, or else we shall have to give up our empire καὶ ἐκ τοῦ ἀκινδύνου ἀνδραγαθίζεσθαι."

---

[1] It is interesting to find that the strange ethical speculations of Nietzsche took rise from this observation: "all pointed to the same *shifting of concepts*, 'superior,' 'noble' in its caste sense was in every case the fundamental concept for which 'good' in the sense 'superior in sentiment,' 'noble' in the sense 'privileged in sentiment,' necessarily developed: while 'mean,' 'moblike,' 'common' turn at last to the concept 'bad'." (*Genealogy of Morals* i 4.)

[2] See *Introduction* p. vii.

The noun ἀνδραγαθία generally means high personal merit in war or otherwise : but it seems to bear something of a political or social reference in Thucydides iii 57. 1, 64. 4, v 101, where the point is the special Dorian claim to an aristocratic strain of feeling and conduct. From other sources we can see that it was a test-word among Dorian aristocratic ideals: Aristot. *Pol.* ii 9. 25. 1270ᵇ 38 (of the Spartan γερουσία) ἐπιεικῶν ὄντων καὶ πεπαιδευμένων ἱκανῶς πρὸς ἀνδραγαθίαν τάχα ἂν εἴπειέ τις συμφέρον τῇ πόλει, Xen. *Pol. Lac.* 4. 2 Lycurgus ἐνόμιζεν οὕτως ἂν καὶ τούτους ἐπὶ πλεῖστον ἀφικνεῖσθαι ἀνδραγαθίας, Isyllus 1. 1

> δᾶμος εἰς ἀριστοκρατίαν ἄνδρας αἱ προάγοι καλῶς
> αὐτὸς ἰσχυρότερος· ὀρθοῦται γὰρ ἐξ ἀνδραγαθίας.
> αἱ δέ τις καλῶς προαχθεὶς θιγγάνοι πονηρίας
> πάλιν ἐπαγκρούων, κολάζων δᾶμος ἀσφαλέστερος.

The last passage, where δᾶμος means the *republic*, is a praxis of political terms.

Hippocrates is thinking of the social respect due to his profession when he says *de artic.* iii p. 262 Kühn ἀνδραγαθικώτερον τοῦτο καὶ τεχνικώτερον, ὅστις μὴ ἐπιθυμέει δημοειδέος κιβδηλίης.

In the fourth century B.C. ἀνδραγαθία was generally used in honorific decrees in the vague sense of ἀρετή, cf. Demosth. *Androt.* 72, Aeschines *Ctes.* 42, 49, 189 ἐφικόμενος τῆς ἀνδραγαθίας, οὕτω τὰς χάριτας τὸν δῆμον ἀπαιτεῖ.

It was natural that ἀσφάλεια should be a watchword of conservatism in Greece, as elsewhere. A hold of this political reference gives a fuller appreciation of many cases where a Greek writer is thinking of the opposite tendencies of parties and ideals of his day. Pind. *Ol.* 13. 6, praising Corinth as a home of Dorian aristocratic politics,

> ἐν τᾷ γὰρ Εὐνομία ναίει, κασιγνήτα τε, βάθρον πολίων, ἀσφαλὴς
> Δίκα, καὶ ὁμότροφος Εἰράνα, τάμι᾽ ἀνδράσι πλούτου,
> χρύσεαι παῖδες εὐβούλου Θέμιτος.

In Thucydides, a rhetorical point in a speech is often made by this meaning of the word. The Corinthians say to Spartans (i 69. 5) καίτοι ἐλέγεσθε ἀσφαλεῖς εἶναι. The Mytilenaeans (iii 13. 1) say their reasons for forsaking Athens ἱκανὰς (εἶναι) ἡμᾶς ἐκφοβῆσαι καὶ πρὸς ἀσφάλειάν τινα τρέψαι. In the Melian debate the Athenians open proceedings by a sarcastic reference to the Dorian fear of public discussion, ὑμεῖς οἱ καθήμενοι ἔτι ἀσφαλέστερον ποιήσατε (v 85), and in ch. 97, 98 there is some echo of the same meaning, as there probably is also in viii 24. 4, 66. 5. Archidamus uses the word three times in his short speech to his allies' officers (ii 11). In ii 63. 3 Pericles is retorting this conservative catch-word on his Athenian opponents, whom he reminds that "it is a subject, not an imperial, state that should adopt the 'security' which really means slavery" (οὐδὲ ἐν ἀρχούσῃ πόλει ξυμφέρει, ἀλλ᾽ ἐν ὑπηκόῳ, ἀσφαλῶς δουλεύειν).

There is no certain case in Tragedy, though Eurip. *Hipp.* 785 τὰ πολλὰ πράσσειν οὐκ ἐν ἀσφαλεῖ βίου may have a political reference (Hadley), and Soph. *fr.* 606 might be a conservative's protest against demagogues.

In Comedy, Aristophanes has Ποσειδῶν 'Ασφάλειος *Ach.* 682, and there may be an intended contrast in κοινόν, ἀσφαλῆ *Av.* 316, 'the plan is both liberal and conservative.' Eupolis 117 of the better times gone by ὥστ' ἀσφαλῶς ἐπράττομεν.

Though the original meaning of 'Ασφάλιος or 'Ασφάλειος applied to Poseidon was no doubt 'protector from earthquakes' or 'giver of safe voyages,' I believe that in the fifth century at least, the political significance of Poseidon as conservative was often in people's minds when they heard the phrase. See on 551.

σώφρων and σωφροσύνη were naturally used of constitutions which resisted extreme democracy: Shilleto on Thucyd. i 84. 3 gives the other cases in Thucydides iii 62. 4 where Boeotians say that a very narrow oligarchy is τῷ σωφρονεστάτῳ ἐναντιώτατον ἐγγυτάτω δὲ τυράννου, iii 82. 8 where the 'specious phrases' on either side are πλήθους ἰσονομία πολιτική and ἀριστοκρατία σώφρων, viii 24. 4 Χῖοι μόνοι μετὰ Λακεδαιμονίους ηὐδαιμόνησάν τε ἅμα καὶ ἐσωφρόνησαν, viii 53. 3, 64. 5. Cf. σωφρονισταὶ of an aristocratic party in the difficult passage iii 65. 3: though in viii 48. 6 we have the paradoxical phrase τὸν δῆμον ἐκείνων (καλῶν κἀγαθῶν) σωφρονιστήν.

In Ar. *Av.* 1540—1 τὴν εὐνομίαν, τὴν σωφροσύνην, τὰ νεώρια,

τὴν λοιδορίαν, τὸν κωλακρέτην, τὰ τριώβολα,

the first line gives conservative points, the second democratic.

Cf. *Ran.* 727—732.

So with κόσμος, which Pythagoras applied to politics as well as to other things, if his letter to Anaximenes in Diog. Laert. viii 49 is genuine. κόσμος and ἀσφάλεια occur together of Dorian discipline Thucyd. i 33. 2, ii 11. 8. Clear cases of its political sense are Thucyd. iv 76. 2 μεταστῆσαι τὸν κόσμον καὶ ἐς δημοκρατίαν τρέψαι, viii 24. 4; but it might be used of any settled constitution, even a democratic one Thucyd. viii 48. 4, 67. 3. It is not merely fanciful to suppose that the arrangements connected with the Attic ἔφηβοι were more or less of an aristocratic nature and came from the organisation of the Knights. Hence σωφρονισταὶ and κοσμηταὶ were their superintendents (Aristot. *Pol. Ath.* 42 &c.).

εὐνομία and its cognates were always used of a conservative 'order.' The use was specially associated with the 'good order' imposed on Sparta, with the divine sanction of Delphi, by Lycurgus (Herod. i 65, Plut. *Lycurg.* 5).

Pind. *Ol.* 9. 15 of Opus,

ἂν Θέμις θυγάτηρ τέ οἱ Σώτειρα λέλογχεν
μεγαλόδοξος Εὐνομία.

Ol. 13. 6 of Corinth, *Isth.* 4. 20 of Aegina. *Nem.* 9. 29 is a conservative's prayer for Aetna

μοῖραν δ' εὔνομον
αἰτέω σε παισὶν δαρὸν Αἰτναίων ὀπάζειν :

cf. *Pyth.* 1. 60 for the Dorian principles on which the constitution of Hiero's new state was laid.

So Bacchylides 13. 153 (12. 186 Blass) Εὐνομία σαόφρων of Aegina. εὐνομία is emphatic in the metrical inscription of Opus, *Corp. Inscr. Graec. Sept.* iii 270.

Tyrtaeus' poems were headed Εὐνομία, the watchword of Spartan patriotism : Aristotle implies that the title was a protest against a redistribution of land, v (viii) 7. 4. 1307ᵃ 1. Solon's praise of εὐνομία 2. 33 would be thought conservative by Athenians of later times. Thucyd. i 18. 1 ἡ Λακεδαίμων ἐκ παλαιοτάτου καὶ ηὐνομήθη καὶ ἀεὶ ἀτυράννευτος ἦν. Plato *Crito* 52 E Sparta and Crete ἃς δὴ ἑκάστοτε φῇς εὐνομεῖσθαι, *ib.* 53 B Θήβαζε ἢ Μέγαράδε, εὐνομοῦνται γὰρ ἀμφότεραι (all four states contrasted with Athens), *Hipp. ma.* 283 E εὔνομος ἡ Λακεδαίμων, [Xen.] *Pol. Ath.* 1. 8 ὁ γὰρ δῆμος οὐ βούλεται εὐνομουμένης τῆς πόλεως αὐτὸς δουλεύειν ἀλλ' ἐλεύθερος εἶναι καὶ ἄρχειν, τῆς δὲ κακονομίας αὐτῷ ὀλίγον μέλει· ὃ γὰρ σὺ νομίζεις οὐκ εὐνομεῖσθαι, αὐτὸς ἀπὸ τούτου ἰσχύει ὁ δῆμος καὶ ἐλεύθερός ἐστιν (the frank expression of what is implicit in many cases where εὐνομία is the emphatic word). Xen. *Hell.* iv 4. 6 εὐνομίᾳ χρωμένην (remaining an aristocracy), *Oecon.* 9. 14 where the εὐνομούμεναι πόλεις with their νομοφύλακες are Sparta and states like it. So in Aristot. *Rhet.* i 1. 4 the practice in εὐνομούμεναι πόλεις is opposed to that usual in Athens except in the conservative Areopagus court : the Athenian practice is dangerous (iii 1. 4) διὰ τὴν τοῦ ἀκροατοῦ μοχθηρίαν. Other passages in Aristotle are instructive : *Pol.* iv (vi 8. 5) 1294ᵃ 2 quoted on πονηρός, *ib.* vii (iv 6. 1) 1327ᵃ 11 where the question is πότερον ὠφέλιμος ἢ πρὸς τὴν θάλατταν κοινωνία ταῖς εὐνομουμέναις πόλεσιν ἢ βλαβερά, *ib.* ii 1 where the πόλεις εὐνομεῖσθαι λεγόμεναι are Sparta, Crete, and Carthage. Even the orators usually confine this particular word of praise to conservative states : Demosth. *Timocr.* 139 points his audience to Locri, οὐδὲν γὰρ χείρους ἔσεσθε παράδειγμά τι ἀκηκοότες, ἄλλως τε καὶ ᾧ πόλις εὐνομουμένη χρῆται, 1 *Aristog.* 11 he appeals to εὐνομία in a passage of warning against the dangers of democracy. Lycurg. *adv. Leocr.* 128 defends himself for quoting Sparta as a precedent, καλὸν γάρ ἐστι πόλεως εὐνομουμένης παραδείγματα λαμβάνειν. In Aeschin. *Tim.* 5, *Ctes.* 154, however, the word does not seem to have such associations.

In the fine lyric fragment (*fr. adesp.* 140 Bergk, 80 Hiller-Crusius), discussed by Wilamowitz *Isyllus* p. 16, the prayer for Εὐνομία to come along with her sister Horae Δίκα and Εἰρήνα probably marks the poem as an expression of aristocratic feeling (cf. Pind. *Ol.* 13. 6—8 for the same combination at Corinth). A good instance from a late writer is Athen. xiii 601 E quoted on *Eq.* 875. The priest of Eunomia at Athens does not appear till Roman times, *CIA* iii 623. 24, 738.

For χρηστός, we find ὀνήιστος in Ionic politics : Heraclitus 114 Bywater Ἑρμόδωρον ἄνδρα ἑωυτῶν ὀνήιστον ἐξέβαλον, φάντες· ἡμέων μηδὲ εἷς ὀνήιστος ἔστω, Pythagoras in the letter to Anaximenes in Diog. Laert. viii 49 εἰ ὑμεῖς οἱ ὀνήιστοι τὰς πόλεις ἐκλείψετε.

δεξιός may sometimes have borne the same sense. See on *Eq.* 228.

ἐπιτήδειος was also an aristocratic term, see Shilleto on Thucyd. i 19. 1, Whibley *Greek Oligarchies* p. 56 note 8. Ἐπιτάδας was a Spartan man's name Thucyd. iv 8. 31, Plut. *Ages.* 5.

πονηρός, μοχθηρός.

These words are as nearly synonymous as any two words in the Greek language. I do not know of any attempt to distinguish them, unless Aristotle's definition *Eth. Nicom.* vii 9. 1. 1150ᵇ 32 ἡ μὲν (μοχθηρία) συνεχής, ἡ δ᾽ (ἀκρασία) οὐ συνεχὴς πονηρία be taken to imply that πονηρία was the vaguer, as it probably was rather the more common, word.

Neither word is found in Homer. πονηρός occurs first in a fragment of Hesiod (95 Göttling, 159 Rzach), where Alcmena applies to Heracles a combination of adjectives which Athenians would think impossible :

ὦ τέκος, ἦ μάλα δή σε πονηρότατον καὶ ἄριστον
Ζεὺς τέκνωσε πατήρ.

πονηρός, *toiling, full of labours*, is the first meaning: and Heracles is the typical πονηρός: so Epicharmus (fr. 78 Kaibel, 56 Ahrens) makes him say

ἀλλὰ μὰν ἐγὼν ἀνάγκᾳ ταῦτα πάντα ποιέω·
οἴομαι δ᾽ οὐδεὶς ἑκὼν πονηρὸς οὐδ᾽ ἄταν ἔχων.

Next πονηρός is used of things, *involving toil or hardship or pain* : Theognis 274 πασέων νούσων ἐστὶ πονηρότερον, Aesch. *fr.* 86 βίου πονηροῦ θάνατος εὐκλεέστερος. μοχθηρός from its first appearance has this sense, Aesch. *Sept.* 257, *Cho.* 752.

By the latter half of the fifth century both words had come to mean *bad* in all the senses of the English word, *bad* wares, *bad* coin, *bad* symptoms in disease (often in Hippocrates), *bad* character, *bad* man.

The social and political use of πονηρός and μοχθηρός as opposed to καλὸς κἀγαθός or χρηστός appears chiefly from 430 to 350 B.C. It may be connected with πόνος, πένομαι as *working-class* (Whibley *Parties in Athens* p. 48, cf. Heracleides Pont. ap. Athen. xii 512 B) : and πόνῳ πονηρός was a kind of superlative (Ar. *Vesp.* 466, *Lys.* 350). It seems to have been specially Attic : and a reason can be assigned for this restriction. The words πόνος and μόχθος often mean athletic *training* and military *drill* : Pindar regularly uses them for the careful training of his heroes, *Ol.* 5. 15, *Isthm.* 1. 38, *Ol.* 10. 22 ἄπονον δ᾽ ἔλαβον χάρμα παῦροί τινες, *Nem.* 10. 30 οὐδ᾽ ἀμόχθῳ καρδίᾳ προσφέρων τόλμαν παραιτεῖται χάριν, *his heart's prayer for Olympian victory has his daring and his training to back it.* Training and drill seemed honourable to the disciplined Dorian, but repulsive to the Ionian and the Attic : Herod. vi 12 οἱ Ἴωνες ἀπαθέες ἐόντες πόνων τοιούτων, Thucyd. ii 39. 4 Pericles contrasts the Attic ῥᾳθυμία with the πόνων μελέτη of the Spartans τῶν ἀεὶ μοχθούντων, Aristot. *Pol.* v (viii) 4. 1 οἱ Λάκωνες θηριώδεις ἀπεργάζονται (τοὺς παῖδας) τοῖς πόνοις : the Corinthians' complaint of the Athenians in Thucyd. i 70. 8 καὶ ταῦτα μετὰ πόνων δι᾽ ὅλου τοῦ αἰῶνος μοχθοῦσι is a Dorian way of putting their enemies' formidable energy : Eurip. *Heracl.* 932 Eurystheus marches against Athens ἐκ Μυκηνῶν πολυπόνῳ σὺν ἀσπίδι. So the adjectives to a Dorian would not naturally be used of a man in any contemptuous sense.

Clear cases in Aristophanes are : of πονηρός *Eq.* 181, 186, 336, 415 (παμπόνηρος), *Nub.* 102, *Pax* 684, *Ran.* 731, *Plut.* 920 : of μοχθηρός *Ach.* 517, *Eq.* 1304 : the best instance of all is *Lys.* 576 where the μοχθηροί are the extreme democrats, as the συνιστάμενοι in the next line are the oligarchs.

The certain cases of πονηρός in Thucydides are all in the mouth of Alcibiades when he is speaking of his exile and attempting to please Spartans (vi 89. 5, 92. 3), or Athenian oligarchs (viii 47. 2 ἐπ᾽ ὀλιγαρχίᾳ βούλεται καὶ οὐ πονηρίᾳ οὐδὲ δημοκρατίᾳ κατελθὼν αὐτοῖς ξυμπολιτεύειν), by bitter references to democracy. μοχθηρός occurs only once in Thucydides: he describes the demagogue Hyperbolus (viii 93. 3) as μοχθηρὸς ἄνθρωπος (so Plato com. 166 refers to him as πονηρῷ καὶ ξένῳ). In vi 53. 2 and viii 97. 2 πονηρός may have a political as well as a moral reference.

The use is nowhere so clear as in the "Old Oligarch's" Ἀθηναίων πολιτεία included in Xenophon's minor works. He uses the contemptuous words of his party without reserve, and makes no attempt to see in his radical opponents anything but what is 'low.'

In the real Xenophon the cases are quotations from extreme oligarchs speaking to Spartan sympathisers (*Hell.* ii 3. 13, 14) or to each other (*ib.* § 27). The Socratic circle spoke much of καλοκἀγαθία as an ideal, but they do not seem to have used the rather offensive πονηρία. In *Memor.* ii 9. 8 the word is applied to συκοφάνται by Archedamus, Crito's "wolfhound": he is φιλόχρηστος and adopts the tone of a χρηστός. In iii 5. 18 πονηρία is used of the indiscipline of the Athenian δῆμος.

Euripides gives a few interesting cases. In that most political play, the *Supplices*, extreme democracy is criticised from the Dorian point of view by the Argive herald, and from the Athenian "moderate" point of view by Theseus: πονηρός in our sense occurs in both criticisms, 243 γλώσσαις πονηρῶν προστατῶν φηλούμενοι, and in 423—5

> ἦ δὴ νοσῶδες τοῦτο τοῖς ἀμείνοσιν,
> ὅταν πονηρὸς ἀξίωμ᾽ ἀνὴρ ἔχῃ
> γλώσσῃ κατασχὼν δῆμον, οὐδὲν ὢν τὸ πρίν.

In the *Ion* 634—7, Ion tells Xuthus that in Delphi 'low' persons always give him the wall,

> οὐδέ μ᾽ ἐξέπληξ᾽ ὁδοῦ
> πονηρὸς οὐδείς· κεῖνο δ᾽ οὐκ ἀνασχετόν,
> εἴκειν ὁδοῦ χαλῶντα τοῖς κακίοσιν.

Euripides must have heard the καλοὶ κἀγαθοί grumbling, as the Old Oligarch does (*Pol. Ath.* I. 10), πλείστη ἐστὶν Ἀθήνησιν ἀκολασία, καὶ οὔτε πατάξαι ἔξεστιν αὐτόθι οὔτε ὑπεκστήσεταί σοι ὁ δοῦλος.

In all these writers however, the usage we are discussing is not the common one or is plainly a matter mainly of quotation from the language of a coterie. The meaning *bad* is the normal one and so the word could be easily retorted on the party which claimed for itself the words χρηστὸς and καλὸς κἀγαθός. This retort-use we find in such cases as Ar. *Vesp.* 466 where the chorus call Bdelycleon ὦ πόνῳ πονηρὲ καὶ κομηταμυννία, Andoc. *Myst.* 95 where Epichares a supporter of the Thirty is called πάντων πονηρότατος καὶ βουλόμενος εἶναι τοιοῦτος, and Lysias 12. 5 where the phrase used of the Thirty, πονηροὶ καὶ συκοφάνται ὄντες (cf. *ib.* 76), would be felt as an experiment[1]. The moderating influence

---

[1] So Lysias 30. 14 uses καλοὶ κἀγαθοί of democrats executed by the Thirty.

of Theramenes is described as πονηρία by both parties, by Critias Xen. *Hell.* ii 3. 27, and by Lysias 12. 78.

Plato is very sparing in his use of πονηρός and μοχθηρός except in a moral sense. The vocative ὦ πονηρέ, ὦ μοχθηρέ, so common in Attic conversation, when some anger or contempt was implied (Ar. *Ach.* 165, *Av.* 3, *Ran.* 1175, *Plut.* 265), is a mark of rude ill-temper in *Phaedr.* 826 E. He is careful to mark that πονηροὶ and καλοὶ κἀγαθοὶ are phrases of certain parties, *Rep.* vii 519 A τῶν λεγομένων πονηρῶν, viii 569 A ἀπὸ τῶν πλουσίων τε καὶ καλῶν κἀγαθῶν λεγομένων, *Legg.* iii 701 A. So he is quoting, with a humorous appreciation of its bigotry, the phrases of average "Athenian society" in *Rep.* vi 488 D, where παμπόνηροι means *quite unpresentable, social outcasts, brutes* (Dr Jackson).

The orators naturally shew hardly any instance of the use : they and their audiences were themselves too near being "πονηροί." A case is given by Isocrates *Antid.* 316—7 in an attack on συκοφάνται.

Aristotle seldom has this usage. In the passage *Pol.* iv 8. 1293ᵇ 38— he is giving the view of the Greek aristocrats in their own question-begging phrases, and he marks by the repeated δοκοῦσι, φασι, δοκεῖ that he is quoting : δοκοῦσιν ἔχειν οἱ εὔποροι ὧν ἕνεκεν οἱ ἀδικοῦντες ἀδικοῦσιν· ὅθεν καὶ καλοὺς κἀγαθοὺς καὶ γνωρίμους τούτους προσαγορεύουσιν...καὶ τὰς ὀλιγαρχίας εἶναί φασιν ἐκ τῶν καλῶν κἀγαθῶν μᾶλλον. δοκεῖ δ' εἶναι τῶν ἀδυνάτων τὸ μὴ εὐνομεῖσθαι τὴν ἀριστοκρατουμένην πόλιν, ἀλλὰ πονηροκρατουμένην. It is the opinion and the language of the Old Oligarch, which Aristotle proceeds to pick to pieces. In the only other instance I can quote with confidence from Aristotle (*Pol. Ath.* 35) τοὺς συκοφάντας καὶ τοὺς τῷ δήμῳ πρὸς χάριν ὁμιλοῦντας παρὰ τὸ βέλτιστον καὶ κακοπράγμονας ὄντας καὶ πονηροὺς ἀνῄρουν he is thinking naturally of the phrases used by the Thirty : though *ib.* 37. 2 he uses πονηρία of the Thirty themselves.

By Theophrastus' time such usages were nearly worn out : his Oligarch has hardly any of such phrases as we are considering, though his φιλοπόνηρος shews that πονηρὸς still had some political associations (see on *Eq.* 1017).

Aristocrats, weary of the bustle and harassing interference of Athenian politics, used **πολλὰ πράττειν, πράγματα** and the like in impatience. The Argive herald (an interesting figure) in Eurip. *Supp.* 576 says to Theseus πράσσειν σὺ πόλλ' εἴωθας ἥ τε σὴ πόλις. The Athenian speaker in Thucyd. vi 87. 3 allows that πολυπραγμοσύνη is a character of his country.

Conservatives accordingly took **ἀπράγμων** as a word of praise : Ar. *Av.* 44 πλανώμεθα ζητοῦντε τόπον ἀπράγμονα. Pericles regards the ἀπράγμων as a hostile critic Thucyd. ii 64. 4, whose "playing the Greek gentleman" is ineffectual *ib.* 63. 2, and who is summarily regarded in Athens as ἀχρεῖος *ib.* 40. 2 : so Plato repeats average opinion as calling the best of the 'intellectuals' ἄχρηστοι, *Rep.* vi 487 D, 490 E.

In Doric **ἁσυχία** had the same significance as the Attic ἀπραγμοσύνη, and is even more definite as an ideal of Dorian politics. Epicharmus 72 Ahrens, 101 Kaibel

> ἁ δ' Ἀσυχία χαρίεσσα γυνά,
> καὶ Σωφροσύνας πλατίον οἰκεῖ.

Pindar *Ol.* 4. 16 αἰνέω νιν...καὶ πρὸς ἀσυχίαν φιλόπολιν καθαρᾷ γνώμᾳ τετραμμένον, *Pyth.* 1. 70 (Hiero) δᾶμον γεραίρων τράποι σύμφωνον ἐς ἀσυχίαν, *Pyth.* 8. 1, *fr.* 109 Bergk. The Corinthians in Thucyd. i 70. 8 well express the Dorian feeling towards Athenians who ξυμφορὰν οὐχ ἧσσον ἡγοῦνται ἡσυχίαν ἀπράγμονα ἢ ἀσχολίαν ἐπίπονον. The Happy Land in the *Birds* 1320—2 combines the culture and charm of Athenian life with the restfulness of a Dorian state, Σοφία, Πόθος, ἀμβροσίαι χάριτες, τό τε τῆς ἀγανόφρονος Ἡσυχίας εὐάμερον πρόσωπον. In ordinary Attic, however, this connotation of ἡσυχία is very rare: Dem. i *Aristog.* 24 ἰταμὸν γὰρ ἡ πονηρία καὶ τολμηρὸν καὶ πλεονεκτικόν, καὶ τοὐναντίον ἡ καλοκαγαθία ἡσύχιον κ.τ.λ. is not specially political: Eurip. *Supp.* 321— 325 contrasts the headstrong fiery spirit of Athens with other states:

αἱ δ᾽ ἡσύχοι σκοτεινὰ πράσσουσαι πόλεις
σκοτεινὰ καὶ βλέπουσιν εὐλαβούμεναι.

ἐπιεικής is commonly applied to the reasonable and moderate mind of the educated man: but it may have a political tinge of meaning in such cases as Thucyd. viii 93. 2, Xen. *Hell.* i 1. 30. In some well-known passages of Aristotle, ἐπιεικής, like γνώριμος, refers to social position more than to political opinion, *Pol.* viii (v) 10. 3 p. 1310ᵇ 10 ἡ βασιλεία πρὸς βοήθειαν τὴν ἀπὸ τοῦ δήμου τοῖς ἐπιεικέσι γέγονεν...ὁ δὲ τύραννος ἐκ τοῦ δήμου καὶ τοῦ πλήθους ἐπὶ τοὺς γνωρίμους, *ib.* 8. 14 p. 1308ᵇ 27 λέγω δ᾽ ἀντικεῖσθαι τοὺς ἐπιεικεῖς τῷ πλήθει.

All the words discussed, whether of praise or of blame, are used from the aristocratic point of view. Hardly any phrase can be quoted from the other side, except παχύς 'bloated,' which was used of aristocrats in several states, and possibly all over the Greek world. It is used quite seriously by Herodotus (v 30, 77, vi 91, vii 156), but in Attic occurs only in comedy (*Vesp.* 288, *Pax* 639).

There were no doubt many words and phrases used locally with a social sense, as κατωνακοφόρος in Sicyon, κονίποδες in Epidaurus, Γέργιθες in Miletus of the labouring or humbler farming class: cf. on *Eq.* 361 for references to such nicknames prevalent in Miletus.

APPENDIX III.

TRAGIC RHYTHM IN COMEDY.

The ἦθος of metre was a matter ever present to Greek theorists on education and poetry : and we may be sure that poets did not neglect it. We may never quite understand, without music or even with it, why the dramatists chose the particular rhythm they did for each choral ode : but we may make reasonable guesses on this subject. In dialogue it is usually plain why trochaics are chosen instead of iambics; the effect of hurry or trepidation is heightened unmistakeably. Each of the three Attic tragedians has his own way of managing the iambic trimeter, and no one with an ear can fail to feel how the character of the poet's thought or style is reflected in his rhythm.

The comic iambic trimeter has an entirely different effect from the tragic line of Æschylus and of Sophocles : the line of Euripides, especially in the plays written after about 421 B.C., is, as is well known, lighter and more colloquial in style, but is still separated by a great gulf from Aristophanes'. The comic iambic uses the anapaest in any foot except the sixth. That certain delicate restrictions were imposed on this license was made probable by Reisig (*Conject. ad Aristophanem*) : and the question has been treated elaborately by C. Bernhardi *de incisionibus anapaesti in trimetro comico Graecorum* : the results are given by Starkie in the introduction to his edition of the *Wasps*. I do not find it easy to believe that the rules given by these scholars were present in such definite forms to the ancient comic poets : these rules forbid rhythms which are no doubt exceptional, but might be used by the poets in exceptional cases for sufficient reasons of their own.

I believe that Aristophanes seldom if ever uses a purely tragic iambic line without an intention. By "purely tragic" I mean a line (not divided between speakers) containing only iambi and spondees, and containing a spondee in the fifth foot only under the well-known restrictions laid down by Porson. This definition of course excludes a large number of lines, containing trisyllabic feet, that may be looked on as either comic or tragic in rhythm. The restrictions which comedy and tragedy respectively imposed on the use of dactyls in the first and third feet, and of tribrachs throughout the first five feet are so far discoverable. Cobet (*Nov. Lect.* p. 207—) lays down the 'certa lex metrica' that a dactyl in the third foot of a tragic iambic must have all its three syllables in the same word (a rare occurrence), or must have its first syllable a final one and its two short syllables either two monosyllables or in one word. He quotes as very rare exceptions Eurip. *Hel.* 263, 826, *Hec.* 345. (Add three from a single scene of the *Bacchae*, 808, 816, 844 and *Phoen.* 509.) He holds that comedy kept the same rule (he corrects two exceptions, *Plut.* 174, 176, and expunges *Av.* 182 as a gloss). As to tribrachs, Tragedy, he continues, has practically the same rule as for dactyls : Comedy only avoids the second syllable being the final of a hyperdisyllabic word : *Nub.* 884 ὃς τἄδικα λέγων ἀνατρέπει τὸν κρείττονα he thinks spurious. See also Starkie, *Introd.* to *Wasps* p. xl, who gives O. Bachmann's results. Here again I confess to some scepticism.

Tragic rhythm in comedy is sometimes a point in religious ceremony and phrase, serious or parodied, as *Ach.* 259—60, *Vesp.* 862, 868, *Pax* 868 (cf. Phrynichus 9 ἀνὴρ χορεύει καὶ τὰ τοῦ θεοῦ καλά), *Lys.* 205—7, *Thesm.* 331, &c.

It is plainly used intentionally in formal statement of a case or in serious narrative or argument, though in such instances it is the habit to break off into comic rhythm, generally at appropriate words or places, cf. on *Eq.* 637. Instances are *Ach.* 136, 513— , *Eq.* 40— , 164, 179— 189, *Nub.* 94— , *Vesp.* 18 (where Starkie's explanation is probably right), 907— , *Pax* 50— , 1212—3, *Av.* 13— , 30—35, 639— , 995—6, *Lys.* 42— , 405— , 866— , 1112— , *Thesm.* 372— , *Eccl.* 1— , *Plut.* 6— . In these and other passages it seems to me clear that the tragic style is begun and purposely altered suddenly to a comic rhythm where the idea is suitable.

Tragic rhythm is naturally used in solemn exhortation or appeal, as *Eq.* 156, *Nub.* 88—9, 824, *Vesp.* 988, *Pax* 292—8, &c.: to give weight, serious or burlesque, to an important pithy statement, as *Eq.* 141, 143, *Nub.* 94, 831, 1153, *Vesp.* 994, *Lys.* 466, *Ran.* 533, or to the line that clinches and ends a speech, as *Eq.* 72, 96, *Nub.* 99, *Vesp.* 135, 930, 1261, 1386, *Av.* 1509, *Ran.* 82, 622, *Eccl.* 240, 407, *Plut.* 92, 831.

It has been noticed that Aristophanes often uses this rhythm for the last line before the exit of the speaker or the last line before a choral ode, as *Eq.* 1262, *Vesp.* 1325, *Pax* 288, *Av.* 1057, *Lys.* 780, *Ran.* 518, 578, 671, *Eccl.* 936, *Plut.* 228, 769, 950, 954.

In a reply, when the first speaker has used a line of tragic rhythm, it is often plainly a point that the answer should imitate it : *Ach.* 797—8, *Eq.* 18—9, 36—7, 72—3, 715—6, 997—8, 1235—6, *Nub.* 36—7, 486 —7, 691—2, *Vesp.* 13—4, 23—4, 197—8, 855—6, 1367—8, 1433—4, *Pax* 401—2, *Av.* 157—8, 160—1, 264—5, 911—2, *Eccl.* 156—7, *Plut.* 1128—9, &c.: Cobet failed to see this in *Eq.* 1168.

It is remarkable how often tragic lines occur in pairs, even when otherwise it is not easy to see any special reason for tragic rhythm. I have counted quite 220 lines in Aristophanes of this kind, not including the large number explicable by the principle of like rhythm in reply.

I allow that a certain number of lines remain, where no particular reason for the tragic rhythm appears to me : but the number is not great.

It may be merely accidental, but about 50 of such lines contain the non-tragic forms in -ί, όδί, ούτωσί or the like, and a few others have τήμερον (see on *Eq.* 1061) or ότιή, as *Eq.* 1077, or are otherwise marked as colloquial by their vocabulary. Sometimes the inconsistency is intentionally burlesque.

The other comedians seem to have followed the same principle in the main. Cratinus' wish for the blessings of youth and age together

$$\text{ἥβης τ' ἐκείνης νοῦ τε τοῦδε καὶ φρενῶν}$$

gains pathos and seriousness from the rhythm: and many similar cases might be quoted from the fragments. I fancy that even in Plautus and Terence we may notice the tendency to use a less resolved rhythm when dignity or pathos is a desired effect.

INDICES.

I. GREEK.

ἀγαθά colloquial retort 98
ἀγαθοῦ δαίμονος 85
ἄγε δή with plurals 634
ἀγκυρίζω 262
ἀγορά 636
'Αγορα-, names beginning with 1257
ἀγοράζω 1373
ἀγόραιος, ἀγοραῖος 218 (cr. n.)
ἄγροικος, ἀγροῖκος 41 (cr. n.)
ἀγρός, οἱ ἀγροί the country 805, 1394
ἀγυιά 1320
ἀετός, compounds of 203
-άζω, verbs in 1124; Attic future of
    verbs in 456
'Αθηναίη 763
ἀθρῶ 436
αἴ κα 201 (cf. 210 cr. n.)
αἰκάλλω 211
αἱματοπώτης 198
αἱμύλος 687
αἱρετώτερος 84
αἴρω 1129; αἴρω μετέωρον 1362
αἱρῶ 867 (and cr. n.)
αἰσχύνομαι, construction with 1355
-ᾱκ ampliative 823
ἄκατος 762
ἀκούω)(μανθάνω 204; with gen. of thing
    624
ἀκράχολος 41
ἀλέασθαι 1080
ἀλείφω active of part of body 490; ἀλεί-
    φομαι 490
ἀληθες ironical interrogative 89

ἀλιτήριος 445
ἀλλά . γάρ 328, 1063; ἀλλά . γε, δέ γε
    965; ἀλλά injunctive 197; ἀλλά μή
    12; ἀλλ' ἤ interrogative 953
ἀλλᾶς 143
ἄλφιτα 1359; τὰ ἄλφιτα the meal market 857
ἀμαξουργός 467
ἀμβροσία 1095
ἀμέργω 326
ἀμπέχομαι 891
ἀμφιέννυμι 891
ἀμφιμάσχαλος 881
ἄν with optative 413; with past tenses
    to denote frequency 418
ἀναβαίνω 149
ἀναβάλλομαι 891
ἀναγκάζω 508
ἀναδιδάσκω 153, 1045
'Αναίδεια 322
ἀναλαμβάνω 682
ἀναλίσκω 913
ἀνάπαιστοι 504
ἀναπείθω 68
ἀνασπῶ μέτωπα 631
ἀνδραγαθία p. 203
ἀνδραγαθίζομαι p. 202
ἀνδραποδιστής 1030
ἀνδρικός 81
ἀνεπίφθονος 1274
ἀνήρ 179, 392, 1255; emphasising praise
    or abuse 257, 507; ὁ ἀνήρ of an ad-
    versary 222; ἀνήρ for τις 425; ἀνήρ
    τύραννος 1114

κοκκύζω 697
κολόκυμα 692
κόλον and κῶλον confused in MSS. 455
κόμη 1121
κομψευριπικῶς 18
κομψός used by Euripides 18
Κόπρειος 899
κοπροφορῶ with acc. 295
κοράκινος 1053
Κόρινθος 604
κόροι 731
κοσκυλμάτια 49
κόσμος p. 204
κράγον κέκραγα 487
κράζω 137, 287
κράμβος 539
κρεάγρα 772; κρεάγρᾳ ἕλκεσθαι of criminals 772
κρέας 421
κρημνός 628
κριθαί 1101
κρίνω 1210
-κριτος, names in 1257
κρουνός 89
κρουνοχυτρολήραιον 89
κρουσιδημῶ 859
κρούω 1379
κρωβύλος 1331
κτύπος 552
κυαμοτρώξ 41
κύβδα 365
κυβερνήτης 544
Κυκλοβόρος 137
κυλίχνιον 906
κυλλός 1083
κυναλώπηξ 1067
κύνεια 1399
κυνοκέφαλος 416
κύπτω 1354
κυρηβάζω 272
κυρήβια 254
Κυρηβίων, nickname 254
κύων τοῦ δήμου 1017
κώθων 600
κωλύω 723
κωμῳδοδιδάσκαλος 507
κώνωψ 1038
κωφόω 311

λάβραξ 361
λαγῷα 1192
λαίθαργος 1068
λαικάζω 167
λαλῶ)(λέγω 348
λαμβάνω 867;)(κενὴν παρέλκω 603
λαμπρός 556; of wind 430
λάρος 956
λαρυγγίζω 358
λέγω 344
λείχω 103
λέπαδνα 768
λευκόν, τὸ 1279
λεώς, ὁ πένης 224
λῆμα 757
ληναΐτης 547
λίμνη 865
λιπαρός 536, 1323, 1329
λόγια 120, 153, 197, 997
λόγοι)(ἔργα 617
λόγος *conference* 1300
λοιδορῶ, λοιδοροῦμαι 1400; λοιδορῶ εἰς 90
Λοξίας 1072
λοπάς 1034
λόφοι 496
λύρα 990
λωβῶμαι, construction with 1408
λῷστος 83

μαγειρικός 216
μαγειρικῶς 376
μάγειρος 216
μάζαν μάττω 55
μαξίσκη 1105, 1166
Μακαρία 1151
μακάριος)(εὐδαίμων 157
μακκοάω 62
μακρὰ κλάειν 433; μακρὰ χαίρειν 433
μαλάσσω 389
Μαραθῶνι 781
μάσθλης 269
μαστιγίας 1228
μάττω 539
μαχαιρίς 412
μεγάλως 151, 782, 1162
μεδέουσα 585, 763
μεθίστημι 397
μειράκιον 1375

μέλλω 267
μέν with no δέ clause expressed 1216
μέντοι 1152; of eager assent 895; μέντοι
  γε 276
μεταιτῶ 775
μετεγγράφω 1371
μετῇσαν 605
μή μοί γε 19
μὴ πέπων 260
μήλη 1150
μικροπολῖται 817
μικρότερος, μικρότατος implying contempt
  789
μισθός 804
μισθοφόροι τριήρεις 555
μισθόδημος 767
Μόθων 635
μόθων 697
μολγός 963
μολεῖν tragic 21
μόνος 1398; μονώτατος 352
μορμὼ τοῦ θράσους 693
μοῦσα 505
μουσική 188
μουσικός 191
μοχθηρός 316, 1304, p. 206
μύρρινος 964
μυστίλη 827, 1168
μυστιλῶμαι 1168
Μυτιλήνη 834 (cr. n.)
μυττωτός 771

νᾶπυ 631 (cr. n.)
ναυπηγοῦμαι 916
Ναύσων 1309
ναύφρακτος 567
νεανικός 611
νεανίσκοι 731
νευρορράφος 739
νεώνητος 2
νὴ τὸν Ἡρακλέα 481
νῆες ἀργυρολόγοι 1070
νῆσοι, αἱ 170, 1034, 1319
νοίδιον diaeresis lost 100
νομίζω 515, 714, 1338
νυκτερινός)(νυκτερήσιος 477
νῦν δέ 1278
νῶτον, νῶτος 289

ξένος 1198; ξένος μέτοικος 347
ξυγγιγνώσκω 427
ξυγκροτῶ 471
ξυλλαμβάνω 21, 650, 1212
ξύλον, τό 367
ξυναυλία 9
ξυνεργός 588
ξυνήγοροι 1358
ξύνοδος 477
ξύνοιδα 595
ξυνόμνυμι ἐπί of oligarchic combinations
  236, 476, 628
ξυνωμόται 257

Ὀβριμοπάτρα 1178
ὅδε of first person, οὗτος of second 133, 276
ὁδός 1015
οἱ μέν suppressed 600
οἶδα for passive meaning 346
οἰκοῦμαι πόλιν 1175
οἴμοι of sarcastic anger 183; οἴμοι κακοδαίμων 234, 752, 1206, 1243
οἷον in exclamation 367, 703
οἶσθ' οὖν ὃ δρᾶσον; 1158
ὀκλαδίας 1384
ὀλαί 1167
ὀλκάδες 171
ὀλολυγμός 616, 1327
ὀμίχλη 803
ὁμοῦ 214, 245
ὄνεια 1399
ὀνειροπολῶ 809
ὀνήιστος p. 205
ὀξίνης 1304
ὀπάζω 200
ὀπτάνιον 1033
ὅπως with fut. ind. 474, 688; ὅπως ἄν
  with subj. 81, 917, 926; ὅπως μή after
  verbs of fearing 112
ὄρθιος νόμος 1279
ὀρθῶς 1027, 1084
ὅστις with antecedent suppressed 1275
ὀστρακίνδα 855
ὅτε quandoquidem 1112
ὅτῳ for ᾗτινι 1320
οὐ γὰρ ἀλλά 1205; οὐ...γε 801; οὐ δήπου,
  οὐ τί που 900; οὐ δοκῶ pretend not to
  1146; οὐ προσίεταί με 359; οὐ χεῖρον

37; οὐκ (μὴ) ἀλλ' ἤ 779, 1397; οὐκ ἐῶ
1161
οὐδέν εἰμι 1243; οὐδὲν ὀλίγον ποιῶ 388
οὗτος, οὑτοσί of legal and political opposition 278
οὑτοσί 203, 271; οὑτοσί)(ἐμός 951
οὕτω μέν 1131
ὀφθαλμίδιον 907
ὀχοῦμαι 1244
ὄψον ἐπὶ σίτῳ 707
-όω, verbs in 311

πάγουρος 606
παιδοτριβικῶς 492
παῖε 247
-παλαι forms 1153
πάλη 1238
παμπόνηρος 415, p. 206
πάντα ταυτί)(πάντα ἐκεῖνα 99
παππίδιον 1215
παραγίγνομαι 410
παραδίδωμι 1260
παρακινδυνεύω 1054
παρακόπτω 807
παραληρῶ 531
παραπέμπω 546
παραστορέννυμι 481
παρασύρω 527
παραφέρω)(παρατίθημι 1215
παραχαλᾷ)(στέγει ἡ ναῦς 434
παρέξω 904
πάριτ' ἐς τὸ πρόσθεν 751
πόρος 1338
πάσῃ τέχνῃ 592
πάσσω 99, 103
πάσχω intransitive not passive 515
πάτταλος 376
πάττω 502
Παφλαγών p. 6
παφλάζω 919
παχύς 1139, p. 209
πειράω with acc. 517
πεντεσύριγγον ξύλον 1049
πέπλος 566
περαίνω 1378
Περγασῆσι Attic locative pl. 321
περί with dat. 1038; περὶ τὴν πόλιν 812;
περί τινος ἔστι τινί 87; περὶ τὸν δῆμον 764

περιδόσθαι 791
περιελῶ 290
περιέρχομαι 1142
περικόμματα 372, 770
περιτίθημι στέφανον 1228
πέρναται 176
πέτραι, of Pnyx 313, 754, 783, 956
πεύκη 1310
πηδάλια 542
πίεται 1289
πιθάκνη 792
πιθηκισμός 887
πίνω 888
πίπτω 540
πλακοῦς 1191
πλατυγίζω 830
πλήν γε 27
πλουθυγίεια 1091
ποδὸς (τοῦ) παρίημι 436
ποεῖν 38 (cr. n.)
ποι ἄλλοσε 1032
ποία Μηδική 606
ποικίλος of oracles 196
ποιοῖς for ποιοίης 1131
ποῖος 32, 1082
ποιῶ 1082
πόλις = ἡ ἀκρόπολις 267; πόλις and δῆμος
associated 273; πόλις vocative 273;
πόλεις, αἱ 802
πολιτεία 219
πολλὰ πράττω p. 208; πόλλ' ἐπὶ πολλοῖς
411; πολλοῦ πολύς 822
Πολυμνήστεια 1287
πολυτίμητος 1390
πονηρός 181, 186, 336, p. 206
πόρπαξ 849, 1372
ποτήρια Χαλκιδικά 237
πότνια 1170
πρᾶγμα *action*, *story* of a play 56, 386;
πράγματα 117, p. 208
πρακτικός 91
πρηγορεών 374
προβατοπώλης 132
προβουλεύω 1342
προεδρία 574, 1404
προθέλυμνος 528
προῖκα 577
προκαλοῦμαι *make an offer* 796

II. NAMES OF PERSONS AND PLACES.

III. GENERAL.

accusative, double 647; of anticipation 351

Agon p. xiii *n.* 1, 756

agora, trades in 852, 857, 1375

amber 532

anapaests, proceleusmatic in 503 (*cr. n.*)

aorist in interrogative sentences 1207; of instantaneous action 269, 696, 1368, 1372; with ἀν of frequency in past time 572

Argive alliance 813

article omitted 166; employed to mark quotation 23, 73 (*cr. n.*), 124, 1043

assembly, payment for attending 905; place of meeting of 749

asses' flesh as food 1399

assonance, pathetic 533

asylum, right of 1312

Athena's tithe 300

Attic literature on the side of moderate democracy p. x

beans in elections 41

bull's blood believed to be poisonous 83

caesura wanting 100, 141

cavalry, maintenance of 577; posted on the wings 243

chariot-races at the Panathenaea 556

cheese, Boeotian 479

chorus divided into two squadrons 247 (cf. 271); entrance of 242

chryselephantine work 1169

cleruch lands 258

compound verbs, preposition dropped in repetition 98, 365

conditional sentence, apodosis expressing a wish 694; uncommon form of 507

confiscation of goods 103

corn, state-largesses of 1100

corn-trade in Athens 1009

coryphaeus 333

Council and control of finance 774, of knights 475, of state sacrifices and festivals 654; letting taxes, mines etc. 363; place of meeting of 626; procedure in 653

curse, comic 179, 927

Datismus 115, 1057

decrees of thanks 873

demagogues, conservative dislike of 1111

Δῆμος μόναρχος 1330

dicasts, corrupt appeals to 1359; payment of 50; their pay 798

dogs attached to deities 1017; not allowed on Acropolis 1022; their flesh as food 1399

Dorisms 201, 240

dress, Ionian 1331; luxury in 967; of Spartans, poorer Athenians etc. 881

dual forms 72 (*cr. n.*)

eagle symbol of sovereignty 1087

education 188

ellipse 50, 121, 318, 343, 520, 536 (*cr. n.*)

Eumenides' altar 1312

excommunication, form of 1288

farmer as hero in Aristophanes 41

foxes eaten by Greeks 1077

For EU product safety concerns, contact us at Calle de José Abascal, 56–1°,
28003 Madrid, Spain or eugpsr@cambridge.org.

www.ingramcontent.com/pod-product-compliance
Ingram Content Group UK Ltd.
Pitfield, Milton Keynes, MK11 3LW, UK
UKHW040619240426

470322UK00010B/220